AF761400

Using New Media for Citizen Engagement and Participation

Marco Adria
University of Alberta, Canada

IGI Global
DISSEMINATOR OF KNOWLEDGE

A volume in the Advances in Public Policy and Administration (APPA) Book Series

Published in the United States of America by
IGI Global
Information Science Reference (an imprint of IGI Global)
701 E. Chocolate Avenue
Hershey PA, USA 17033
Tel: 717-533-8845
Fax: 717-533-8661
E-mail: cust@igi-global.com
Web site: http://www.igi-global.com

Library of Congress Cataloging-in-Publication Data

Names: Adria, Marco L., 1959- editor.
Title: Using new media for citizen engagement and participation / Marco Adria, editor.
Description: Hershey, PA : Information Science Reference, [2020] | Includes bibliographical references and index. | Summary: "This book explores the theoretical and practical aspects of how social media should be added to public-involvement activities such as citizen juries, public deliberation, and citizen panels"-- Provided by publisher.
Identifiers: LCCN 2019034096 (print) | LCCN 2019034097 (ebook) | ISBN 9781799818281 (hardcover) | ISBN 9781799836568 (softcover) | ISBN 9781799818298 (ebook)
Subjects: LCSH: Social media--Political aspects. | Social participation. | Mass media--Social aspects. | Political participation.
Classification: LCC HM742 .H373 2020 (print) | LCC HM742 (ebook) | DDC 302.23/1--dc23
LC record available at https://lccn.loc.gov/2019034096
LC ebook record available at https://lccn.loc.gov/2019034097

This book is published in the IGI Global book series Advances in Public Policy and Administration (APPA) (ISSN: 2475-6644; eISSN: 2475-6652)

British Cataloguing in Publication Data
A Cataloguing in Publication record for this book is available from the British Library.

Advances in Public Policy and Administration (APPA) Book Series

ISSN:2475-6644
EISSN:2475-6652

Mission

Proper management of the public sphere is necessary in order to maintain order in modern society. Research developments in the field of public policy and administration can assist in uncovering the latest tools, practices, and methodologies for governing societies around the world.

The **Advances in Public Policy and Administration (APPA) Book Series** aims to publish scholarly publications focused on topics pertaining to the governance of the public domain. APPA's focus on timely topics relating to government, public funding, politics, public safety, policy, and law enforcement is particularly relevant to academicians, government officials, and upper-level students seeking the most up-to-date research in their field.

Coverage

- Government
- Law Enforcement
- Political Economy
- Politics
- Public Administration
- Public Funding
- Public Policy
- Resource Allocation
- Urban Planning

IGI Global is currently accepting manuscripts for publication within this series. To submit a proposal for a volume in this series, please contact our Acquisition Editors at Acquisitions@igi-global.com or visit: http://www.igi-global.com/publish/.

The Advances in Public Policy and Administration (APPA) Book Series (ISSN 2475-6644) is published by IGI Global, 701 E. Chocolate Avenue, Hershey, PA 17033-1240, USA, www.igi-global.com. This series is composed of titles available for purchase individually; each title is edited to be contextually exclusive from any other title within the series. For pricing and ordering information please visit http://www.igi-global.com/book-series/advances-public-policy-administration/97862. Postmaster: Send all address changes to above address.

Titles in this Series

For a list of additional titles in this series, please visit: https://www.igi-global.com/book-series/advances-public-policy-administration/97862

Financial Determinants in Local Re-Election Rates Emerging Research and Opportunities
Ana Maria Cunha (Polytechnic Institute of Cávado and Ave, Portugal) Augusta Ferreira (University of Aveiro, Portugal) Maria José Fernandes (Polytechnic Institute of Cávado and Ave, Portugal) and Patrícia Gomes (Polytechnic Institute of Cávado and Ave, Porugal)
Business Science Reference • © 2020 • 220pp • H/C (ISBN: 9781522578208) • US $185.00

Community Risk and Protective Factors for Probation and Parole Risk Assessment Tools Emerging Research and Opportunities
Edwina Louise Dorch (Texas A&M University, USA)
Information Science Reference • © 2020 • 192pp • H/C (ISBN: 9781799811473) • US $165.00

Political Propaganda, Advertising, and Public Relations Emerging Research and Opportunities
Samet Kavoğlu (Marmara University, Turkey) and Meryem Salar (Kastamonu University, Turkey)
Information Science Reference • © 2020 • 212pp • H/C (ISBN: 9781799817345) • US $195.00

Political, Economic, and Social Factors Affecting the Development of Russian Statehood Emerging Research and Opportunities
Bogdan Ershov (Voronezh State Technical University, Russia) Natalia Muhina (Voronezh State Technical University, Russia) and Igor Ashmarov (Voronezh State Institute of Arts, Russia)
Information Science Reference • © 2020 • 155pp • H/C (ISBN: 9781522599852) • US $155.00

Participation of Young People in Governance Processes in Africa
Jeffrey Kurebwa (Bindura University of Science Education, Zimbabwe) and Obadiah Dodo (Bindura University of Science Education, Zimbabwe)
Information Science Reference • © 2019 • 350pp • H/C (ISBN: 9781522593881) • US $195.00

Information Systems Strategic Planning for Public Service Delivery in the Digital Era
Emanuel Camilleri (University of Malta, Malta)
Information Science Reference • © 2019 • 372pp • H/C (ISBN: 9781522596479) • US $225.00

Impacts of Political Instability on Economics in the MENA Region
Philippe W. Zgheib (Lebanese American University, Lebanon)
Information Science Reference • © 2019 • 300pp • H/C (ISBN: 9781522582472) • US $195.00

IGI Global
DISSEMINATOR OF KNOWLEDGE

701 East Chocolate Avenue, Hershey, PA 17033, USA
Tel: 717-533-8845 x100 • Fax: 717-533-8661
E-Mail: cust@igi-global.com • www.igi-global.com

Table of Contents

Detailed Table of Contents

Platforms like Uber, Deliveroo, and Upwork have disrupted labor markets around the world. These platforms vary enormously in form and function, but generally contain three parts: digital platforms, which set the rules and intermediate communication and transactions between the other two parts, consumers and platform workers. Platform work is a diverse type of labor that developed around these platforms, and it has great potential to increase citizen participation. However, it is under intense scrutiny in light of widely publicized protests and court cases. This report attempts to disentangle the rhetoric surrounding platform work by discussing its emergence and conceptualization, key challenges, and how it may increase participation in the socio-economic sphere. The conclusion discusses how most policy proposals to regulate platform work fail to address the core issues, while potentially stifling innovative practices. Instead, the author suggests more tailored and proportionate regulatory responses.

The goal of this chapter is to draw attention to the interrelation of multiple mediatized relationships, including face-to-face interaction, in local civic engagement around biodiversity and the environment. The authors propose that civic engagement and participation transcend the type of media used, and that artificial distinctions between online and offline participation are unproductive. Their argument is supported by three examples of participatory projects in which social media-based and face-to-face interactions are closely interrelated. This contribution highlights local uses of social media and the web. It shows how engagement plays out across multiple channels and how resources can be found in a variety of media formats. In particular, online media significantly alter the visibility of both local actions and of the resulting data.

This chapter explores the opportunities, limitations, and risks of integrating multiple channels of citizen engagement within a democratic innovation. Using examples and case studies of recent face-to-face and online multichannel democratic innovations, the authors challenge the emerging consensus that redundancy and diversification of venues of participation are always positively correlated with the success of democratic innovations. Applying their concrete experience in areas of the world in which a systemic organization of different channels of citizen participation exists, the authors provide guidelines for achieving better integration of multiple channels of social dialogue.

North America has experienced a resurgence of measles outbreak due to unprecedentedly low Mumps-Measles and Rubella vaccination coverage rates facilitated by the anti-vaccination movement. The objective of this chapter is to explore the new online public space and public discourse using Web 2.0 in the public health arena to answer the question, 'What is driving public acceptance of or hesitancy towards the MMR vaccine?' More specifically, typologies of online public engagement will be examined using MMR vaccine hesitancy as a case study to illustrate the different approaches used by pro- and anti-vaccine groups to inform, consult with, and engage the public on a public health issue that has been the subject of long-standing public debate and confusion. This chapter provides an overview of the cyclical discourse of anti-vaccination movements. The authors hypothesize that anti-vaccination, vaccine hesitant, and pro-vaccination representations on the online public sphere are reflective of competing values (e.g., modernism, post-modernism) in contemporary society.

Contextualized within the popularity of new media, youth engagement is a very important concept in the practice of public involvement. Guided by the current literature on youth engagement and media studies, this chapter examines the key engagement-related notions involving youth and media usage. Being informed by a variety of case studies on youth engagement through the use of media within various contexts globally, the chapter discusses the opportunities and challenges of engaging youth through media involvement. The specific notions covered in this chapter include (1) the role of "hybrid" media in youth engagement, (2) "intersectionality" illustrating the diversity of youth populations and their media usage, (3) meaning-making through media involvement among youth, and (4) building global social relationships and social and cultural capital through youth's media usage. Importantly, the use of new media can be seen as a means of reclaiming and reshaping the ways in which youth are engaged, as key meaning-making processes, to address personal, social, and cultural issues.

The notion of news networks has changed from primarily one of print and broadcast networks to one of social networks and social media. This study examines the intersection of technological affordances, dialogic activity, and where traditional news gatekeepers are now situated in the contemporary multigated and networked media environment. Using genetically modified organisms (GMOs) as a topical issue, social data was collected from Twitter. The most connected (and connecting) users were algorithmically identified and then sorted into 'community' groups. The resultant graphs visually and statistically identify which users were important gatekeepers and how the flow of information on this topic was being structured around and by certain users that acted as 'hubs' of communication in the network. Results suggest that the ongoing evolution of networked gatekeeping has led to the virtual absence of journalists and news organizations from prominence in social media coverage on certain topics, in this instance GMOs. Normative implications are discussed.

This chapter investigates the link between young adults' attention to campaign information on offline and online media and their knowledge about political facts and candidate issues. The findings, based on a unique, three-wave panel survey conducted during the 2012 U.S. presidential election, show that attention to campaign information on offline sources, such as television, hard-copy newspapers, and radio, was not significantly related to political knowledge. Instead, young adults' attention to online sources played a more important role. Specifically, political knowledge levels were significantly and positively linked to attention to campaign information in online newspapers and television campaign websites. In contrast, attention to campaign information on social media, particularly Facebook and Google+, was negatively related to political knowledge levels during the fall campaign period. Therefore, this study suggests that certain forms of online media serve as a drain on political knowledge whereas attention to other digital outlets can serve as hubs of information.

The last decade has brought several advanced technologies for journalists. This in turn brought in a new era of revolutionary concepts of journalism. One among them is citizen journalism. Although the practice of citizen journalism existed centuries before, it is new media that has accelerated its pace in contemporary times. Citizen journalism is one of the most novel trends in journalism at present. Nowadays, several alternative news sources are available on the internet, such as blogs, social networking websites, etc. These offer a wide variety of news, thus giving a good competition to mainstream media. On many occasions, citizen journalists have reported breaking news faster than professional journalists. With the result, mainstream media no longer serves as the sole source of news. Many established television channels and newspapers are bringing in innovations in their operations to compete with what can be termed as new forms of journalism. The chapter underlines the significance and limitations of citizen journalism, which is only going to grow in the coming times.

Commercial social media (CSM) play a vital role in support of community outreach and engagement. Despite the apparent benefits of CSM, its widespread use raises important concerns about privacy and surveillance, limits on innovation, and data residency for the organizations that increasingly rely on them. This chapter will consider these concerns in relation to an international research collaboration involving technology stewardship training. Technology stewardship is an approach adapted from the communities of practice literature intended to promote effective use of digital ICTs for engagement. The program currently focuses on using commercial social media platforms for introductory capacity building, but this chapter will suggest important reasons to assist them in exploring non-commercial alternative social media (ASM) platforms. The chapter describes how the technology stewardship model offers a pathway for communities of practice interested in adopting ASM for outreach and engagement.

Social media has played important roles in social movements in many parts of the world. It has been used to raise people's awareness about the injustice they suffer as well as to mobilize them to challenge a repressive government. Social media enables people to define public interests by themselves, taking over the role previously taken by elites. It is all due to its simplicity which allows anyone to be both a producer and consumer of information. Citizens are no longer the spectators of political games played by the elites, but they can participate and even mobilize public opinions challenging those in power. The possibility of anonymous interactions allows anyone to express any view without the fear of disapproval and sanction, which leads to the plurality of discourse, which in turn increases the possibility of democratization. However, the impact of social media is not deterministic, and it is not always beneficial to public. Even those in power can use it to preserve the existing hierarchy of power.

In order to understand the contradiction of freedom versus control regarding the internet use in an authoritarian rule, this study is designed to explore a gradual political effect by investigating the agenda-setting effect of internet activism on government political agenda in China from 1994 to 2011. In total, 144 internet activism cases and 526 articles from official newspapers are collected for the analysis and discussion. The results suggest a bottom-up agenda-setting effect from online activism on political agenda, and this agenda-setting effect includes a potential transition from issue level to attribute level. This study also finds that the development of online activism itself obtained a stronger attention from official media, and the continuous growth of activism in forms and scopes generated constant pressure that finally gradually brought about the change of government behavior and strategy.

Participedia (participedia.net) is a wiki-based library of some 1,000 cases of democratic innovations in their historical and cultural contexts. Public-involvement (PI) practitioners can learn about changes in their field of practice. The relative strength of the five dialogic qualities available in Participedia is important because of the values of communicative understanding inherent in the domain of democratic innovations. The question addressed in the study is, How does a community of practice (COP) augment Participedia's capacity to provide a ground for dialogue about PI? A quasi-experiment was carried out among 13 PI practitioners. COP members met face-to-face over a period of four weeks to learn about, apply, and deliberate upon Participedia's online resources. A focus group was then carried out in which the PI practitioners reflected on the qualities of dialogue available in the COP-Participedia experience. Themes from the focus group support the argument that COP-Participedia can augment the dialogic qualities of mutuality, propinquity, and empathy.

Peruvian electoral campaigning, centered on the candidate and lacking a significant connection with contention politics occurring in years previous to the poll, is a very diverse exercise, trying to achieve success through a variety of actions while facing a common-sense interpretation of politics as unreliable and not trustworthy. This fixes an agenda from which candidates have to develop their campaigns, focused on convincing others of their commitment to specific groups and willingness to change whatever does not directly affect each specific constituency that is being appealed to for voting. This behavior is replicated even in Facebook, where candidates try to fix their own issues as salient, but usually failing to respond to the media-set agenda. The potential effectiveness of social media, particularly Facebook, would rest in using discursive opportunities emerging during the campaign to construct self-salience, countering the biases of conventional media.

Taiwan's Sunflower Student Movement on March 18, 2014 has been characterized as a social movement with its sophisticated integration of social and mobile media into mobilizing Taiwanese society through participant recruitment and resource mobilization domestically and globally. Ample research has contributed the roles of these emerging media platforms as one of the main reasons for its success. This study was based on resource mobilization theory (RMT) to examine the roles of new communication technologies

Preface

Citizen engagement and public participation have historical roots in the deliberations that unfolded in the public meeting space of the ancient Greek agora, beginning in the 10th century BC. The agora was designed to ensure that citizens would know where and when competing arguments would be subjected to rational and systematic consideration – and to offer those same citizens the opportunity to participate. The agora also became a marketplace where merchants, traders, and shoppers met. The agora therefore foretold something of our own time, in which social media are used for both political and commercial purposes.

The effective communicative power of the agora was limited by scale. Only one speaker could be heard by the citizenry at any one time. "[T]he ability of only one person to speak and be heard at a time," John Durham Peters (1999) reminds us, is "the hardest argument against democracy" (p. 261). Today, we would require a network of many thousands of agoras, organized and operated simultaneously, in order to "hear" from all citizens. To this general end, online media, beginning with computer discussion boards, have been used by organizations and governments for the purpose of delivering a flow of opinion from citizens to policymakers (Lee & Kan, 2009; Alvarez & Hall, 2008; Zhou & Moy, 2007). More recently, these same organizations and governments have been adopting social media for similar purposes (Bertot, Jaeger, & Grimes, 2010).

Social media, like all media, arrive in a social environment linked to a set of ideas about democratic change. Gouldner (1976) argued that prevailing ideas have become associated with the diffusion of a new communication medium in complex but discernible ways in history. On the one hand, a new medium provides a material demonstration of the benefits that certain ideas, when diffused, will deliver to individuals and groups. The agora, for example, offered the opportunity to hear and be heard. On the other hand, ideas can serve as a social code for interpreting the medium's ultimate purposes, which may otherwise remain unclear or hidden. The agora was not only a place for the expression of ideas (that is, a place representing a changing social environment) but also, when it became a marketplace, a site for displaying existing and continuing social relations. Gouldner argued that such mutually operating social functions – change and continuity – become especially critical when an explanation for unequal social relations is required.

Gouldner provided the example of the rise of the newspaper in Europe in the 18th century. The newspaper created a large literary audience, the largest in history to that time. Members of the audience in that golden age of the newspaper could read the political opinions of newspaper editors daily. In the coffee-houses of England, France, and Germany, they could also exchange these and other opinions about public life and policy. The newspaper audience constituted a new market for the circulation, consumption, and generation of political opinion. As a consequence, participation and engagement by citizens came to be accompanied by little risk, which had the social effect of separating political ideas from their consequences. In our contemporary terminology, political ideas could now be tested publicly through the use of "trial balloons." The response of citizens to proposed policies could for the first time be estimated with some precision before finalization. By linking the idea of a politically literate audience with the wide use of a new medium, Gouldner demonstrated how social and political conditions were established for expanding European power over two centuries. The newspaper represented change in offering citizens the change to receive and generate informed opinion; it represented continuity in offering elites an expanded capacity for managing public opinion.

Are there lessons for scholars and practitioners, or at least sensitizing questions, which can be harvested from the history of new media in relation to innovations in citizen engagement and public participation? Assessing the experience of the German citizenry after World War II, political scientist Elizabeth Noelle-Neumann (1993) theorized a public of listeners who were keenly sensitive to public opinion. If an opinion was outside the norm, it would tend to remain unexpressed. She argued that citizens relied on mass media – television and radio, but particularly for Germans in this period, the newspaper – in order to maintain the "quasi-statistical" sense required to compare their own opinions with those of the majority. Citizens gauged public opinion and then adjusted their opinions accordingly. We might ask whether something similar as regards public opinion could occur in the age of social media. In particular, we could ask, "Is the use of social media for citizen engagement and public participation likely to lead to a more homogeneous pool of opinion, even as it promises free expression to all?"

Section 1 of this book, entitled "Online Spaces for Citizen Engagement: Recent Developments," offers some emerging answers to this question. The chapters in Section 1 deal with, in sequence, the following dimensions of social-media use for citizen engagement and public participation: economic context (for example, platform work), social context (the need to connect "data and place"), practical methods (such as the management of multiple methods), citizen motivations (for instance, to become a social entrepreneur), and demography (in particular, youth).

The first chapter in Section 1, entitled, "Platform Work and Participation: Disentangling the Rhetoric," addresses the powerful development of the platform and of platform work. Platforms and platform working mean that engagement and participation are bounded for entire sectors of the economy. The most accessible platforms (for example, Uber and AirBnB) have a kind of monopoly on how the engagement and participation of its workers takes place because of the affordances of platform technologies and the algorithms on which they operate. The author of the chapter, Zachary Kilhoffer, describes and assesses the status and trajectory of citizen engagement for platform workers.

In their chapter, "Citizen Engagement in Local Environmental Issues: Reaping the Benefits of a Diverse Media Landscape," Lorna Heaton and Patrícia Días da Silva argue that for environmental issues for which citizens are invited to engage and participate, local contexts require more attention than they have been given previously. Social media, particularly in their mobile form, continue to reduce barriers of space for communication. Even so, there must remain the recognition that different spaces represent different social and natural contexts. The authors point out that although citizen-science projects are global in scale, it is at the local level that citizens are likely to connect "data and place," an important capability holding the promise of helping to maintain diverse opinions.

Section 1 also gives attention to the methods used for engagement and participation. The diverse methods used for citizen engagement and public participation are made possible in part by social media's ubiquity. In their chapter entitled, "When Democratic Innovations Integrate Multiple and Diverse Channels of Social Dialogue: Opportunities and Challenges," Paolo Spada and Giovanni Allegretti examine participatory-budgeting (PB) processes. The authors' objective is to highlight the consequences of using more than one method, or "channel," for engagement and participation. They argue that the consequences of multiple channels are significant. Where conflicts of purpose arise, the authors propose practical alleviating responses for use by planners and organizers. These responses have the capacity to maintain the diverse opinions that are generated from the use of multiple channels of engagement and participation.

Engagement and participation events and initiatives are often designed to ensure that citizens have the capacity to act independently, under the assumption that a kind of "independence deficit" may exist or could develop. The next chapter in Section 1 concerns itself with the question of the relative autonomy of citizens and citizen groups. In "Public Engagement and Policy Entrepreneurship on Social Media in the Time of Anti-Vaccination Movements," Melodie Yun-Ju Song and Julia Abelson demonstrate that citizen groups have varying motivations for adopting one position or another. Citizen concerns may include safety, misinformation that remains unaddressed, or a simple lack of two-way communication with public-health authorities. Social media, the authors point out, allow for entrepreneurial actions that would otherwise be more difficult to carry out. The authors devise a typology of citizen and citizen-group motivations, suggesting something of a counterweight to the hypothesis of an increasing homogeneity of opinion. Citizens have varying motivations for participating in public discussions, and these motivations must be considered in analyses of the use of social media.

The last chapter in Section 1 reminds us that social media do not erase or occlude the character and influence of existing demographic characteristics on processes of citizen engagement and public participation. In fact, these characteristics may well continue to contribute to an existing diversity of opinion. Yoshitaka Iwasaki, in his chapter entitled, "Centrality of Youth Engagement in Media Involvement," describes the "hybrid" use of media by youth for engagement and participation. He describes the meaning-making that youth accomplish through social media use, arguing that the creation of social and cultural capital must be considered if we are to understand youth engagement and participation.

With an understanding of the history of the advent of new media, examples of which are provided in the introductory comments for Section 1, we should expect a period of increased interest in ideas about democratic innovation as a consequence of the *occasion* of the rise of social media. Comparable historical waves of interest accompanied previous technological inventions. In the U.S. and Canada of the 1930s and 1940s, for example, the almost-universal diffusion of radio sets in the home stimulated the creation of political discussion groups in living rooms and kitchens of the rural west (Adria, 2010). In the rhetoric of the day, the new medium of radio heralded an era of unprecedented citizen education and involvement in public affairs (Faris, 1975).

Two decades later, television in the home had a similar result. Publicly funded television expanded its scope and reach. Broadcasts in the U.S., for example, allowed citizens to deliberate on public-policy issues such as healthcare and urban planning (Engelman, 1996). Radio and television are still with us, but the most dynamic ideas of citizen engagement and public participation have migrated to opportunities opened by the advent of social media.

Section 2 of this book, "Using New Media and Traditional Media for Citizen Engagement: New Connections, New Questions," considers some patterns in the use of social media, especially as these patterns may be compared with the concurrent use of mass media for citizen engagement and public participation. The first chapter in this section retrieves a theoretical concept from the age of television and the newspaper. *Gatekeeping* was a term coined in the 1950s to describe how news stories and images were chosen for publication or broadcast. In his chapter entitled, "Exploring a Methdological Model for

Social Media Gatekeeping on Contentious Topics: A Case Study of Twitter Interactions About GMOs," Jacob Groshek revisits the gatekeeping function in the age of social media. He finds that traditional mass media organizations and journalists do not generally participate actively in shaping news about genetically modified organisms (GMOs) on Twitter. Instead, gatekeepers are more likely to be ordinary but engaged users of social media who "rise to relative prominence by leveraging technical affordances."

Terri Towner provides evidence that online sources of information may not increase citizens' knowledge about substantive issues. Her article entitled, "Information Hubs or Drains? The Role of Online Sources in Campaign Learning," reports on research examining how young people use online sources for electoral information in the weeks leading up to a national election. The results are mixed. Some users increase their knowledge about issues and candidates by reading online newspapers and similar resources. Other users decrease their knowledge over the same period while using such social media as Facebook and Google+.

The chapter entitled "Citizen Journalism: New-Age Newsgathering," by Rabia Noor, provides a theoretical and practical discussion of the meaning and consequences of citizen journalism as part of the broader context of citizen engagement and public participation. By listing and explaining the characteristics of the citizen journalist, using examples from the national context of India, the author shows that citizen journalism exemplifies and extends the values of an engaged and participative citizenry.

While social media are widely adopted and growing in use, the newspaper has been in dramatic decline in North America since 2009, the year that the *Seattle Post-Intelligencer*, a major newspaper, went completely online (Rosenthal, 2009). Most newspapers' complement of reporters has become much smaller. Investigative reporting has migrated to such online venues as *propublica.com*. Newspaper publishers focus on online delivery and the sale of online advertising, rendering the daily delivery of the hardcopy version a much smaller enterprise than it once was.

The decline of the newspaper represents a transformation in how citizens receive and then use news in exchanges of political opinion, a transformation that has given rise to the chapters in this book. In recognition of this decline, Habermas (2006) has observed that the role of the expert is lost in public deliberation taking place online, when compared to public discussions occurring in mass media. Habermas states that, unlike the case of online news, the mass media:

Focuses the attention of an anonymous and dispersed public on select topics and information, allowing citizens to concentrate on the same critically filtered issues and journalistic pieces at any given time.

Citizens can tune into many issues at any time. This becomes a disadvantage when a single issue is developed intensively through public deliberation. Additionally, social media are bound to decrease the quality of public discussions, because of a reduction in the use of valid evidence and of the principles of deliberation. Habermas points out that we now have decentralized access to news stories and images, but these may not be edited. They may be misleading or inaccurate. Habermas is not referring, of course, to those contexts for citizen engagement and public participation, including many described in this book, in which methods of deliberation are used by, or at least recommended to, citizens. In these instances, citizens may use valid methods of deliberation, including the consideration of relevant evidence (Steiner, Bächtiger, Spörndli, & Steenbergen, 2004; Davies & Blackstock, 2005).

In recognition of these and similar weaknesses of social media, the authors in Section 3, which is entitled, "Citizen Engagement Using New Media as an Adjunct to Face-to-Face Communication," examine methods for citizen engagement and public participation that have been used to complement, extend, and enrich the use of social media. We can consider the example of the public issue of online voting. Estonia was the first country to adopt binding online elections (Madise & Martens 2006), but widespread acceptance has not taken hold in other countries. Much hope is held out for online voting, because it carries with it the promise of renewed democratic energy (Norris, 2005; Alvarez & Hall, 2008).

In Edmonton, Alberta, a major Canadian city, the City government worked with the Centre for Public Involvement at the University of Alberta to plan and carry out a citizen engagement and public participation project that asked citizens to make their best recommendation about whether online voting should be implemented. The Citizen Jury on Online Voting in Edmonton brought together 17 citizen participants who met for 20 hours on a weekend in the autumn of 2012 to consider and provide a verdict on the following question on behalf of all citizens in the city: "Should the City of Edmonton adopt online voting as an option for future general elections?" An advisory committee consisting of researchers, practitioners, and administrators met weekly during the project to give direction and suggestions as the Citizen Jury was formed and then carried out its work. Arrangements were made in advance to ensure that senior municipal administrators and elected representatives were committed to the idea of not only bringing the Citizen Jury together but also hearing and responding to the verdict and whatever recommendations the Jury saw fit to draft for City Council's consideration. Much attention was given to ensuring that the Citizen Jury "looked and sounded" like the population of Edmonton in terms of both demography and opinion. After learning about the advantages and disadvantages of online voting, hearing from expert witnesses, asking questions of the witnesses, and deliberating among themselves, the Citizen Jury voted to recommend the adoption of online voting as part of general elections, with 16 of the 17 jurors in favor of this option.

Social media were an adjunct to, rather than a focal channel for, the process of considering the merits of online voting in Edmonton. Non-jury citizens used social media to comment on the process as it unfolded and on the Jury's recommendation when it was announced. A full account of the Citizen Jury event in Edmonton, including detailed results and outcomes, is available in Kamenova and Goodman (2015).

Section 3 provides reports and analyses from jurisdictions from around the world in which social media have been a critical factor in citizen engagement and public participation, but in which auxiliary channels of communication were also used. In his chapter entitled "Alternative Social Media for Outreach and Engagement: Consideirng Technology Stewardship as a Pathway to Adoption," author Gordon Gow describes the principles and practices of what has become known as technology stewardship. He outlines a training program that forms part of an international action research project in community informatics. The program provides a well-developed example of systematic planning and management associated with social media use combined with interpersonal contact in social-development contexts.

The media channels described in Section 3 include the gathering of citizens in a common space either similar to the Citizen Jury in its emphasis on process and procedure, or in emergent forms such as the one described by Ikbal Maulana in the chapter entitled, "Social Media as Public Political Instrument." The author considers the use of social media as part of the movement towards more liberal democratic practices. In such situations, social media provide citizens with access to information and a platform for publishing opinion and reportage in real time. The author's account of citizen use of social media for political change is not unidimensional. He describes social media as not only giving "voice to the voiceless," but also enabling those in power to preserve their domination. "Giving voice to the voiceless" is therefore only the first stage of moving towards sustainable democratization. Yuan Yuan's "A Gradual Political Change? The Agenda Setting Effect of Online Activism in China 1994 - 2011" describes the use of online media by activists as leading to slow, but discernible outcomes for political discourse and change. The author uses "agenda setting," the idea that media can influence what issues elites are likely to address, to theorize that online activism in an authoritarian country can nudge certain policies and issues on to the list of government priorities.

The authors of "Participedia as a Ground for Dialogue" assess the capability of a wiki-based library of some 1,000 cases of democratic innovations in their historical and cultural contexts to offer a "ground for dialogue." This library, found at *participedia.net*, provides public-involvement practitioners – professionals, advocates, activists – with information about changes occurring in their field of practice. The question addressed in the chapter is, "How does a community of practice augment Participedia's capacity to provide a ground for dialogue about public involvement?" The authors find that Participedia can support dialogue among public-involvement practitioners in communities of practice and that such dialogue is seen by these practitioners as beneficial to their work.

Social media have had the immediate effect of "giving voice to the voiceless," to use the phrase of one of the authors in Section 3. They also have the capacity to help coordinate and manage the gathering of citizens in real time and space. Furthermore, they can be used as an adjunct medium when expert opinion and formal deliberation are chosen as part of a democratic process. And they can ultimately be used to raise questions, as do the authors of the last chapter in Section 3, about the legitimacy of democratic institutions and processes in the context of a particular nation-state.

The final part of this book, Section 4, entitled "Cases in Citizen Engagement: Integrating Social Media, Mass Media, and Personal Outreach," provides descriptions of social media use in engagement and participation events from around the world. The unit of analysis for most of the cases presented in the section, and indeed for many of the chapters of the book, is the national context. The nation-state remains an active site for debate about historical and contemporary meanings of citizenship (Kymlicka, 2001; Adria, 2010; Jayal, 2013).

The cases offer an opportunity for further analysis through comparison. The comparative dimension of national context can be used, or that of social media's relationship to mass media and face-to-face interaction. Social media in the cases function, variously, as a means by which an "alternative rhetoric" is established in public discourse, a mode in which entertainment as well as political deliberation co-exist on a media platform, a coordinating and mobilizing technology for face-to-face interaction, and evidence of an expansion of the public sphere.

In the first chapter of this section, entitled, "Salience, Self-Salience, and Discursive Opportunities: An Effective Media Presence Construction Through Social Media in the Peruvian Presidential Election," Eduardo Enrique Villanueva-Mansilla argues that salience, which is the relevance that a political campaigner establishes in relation to the priorities (often called the agenda) of mass media, can be strengthened and even created using Facebook. The author argues that political actors themselves can create issue salience. As the author demonstrates, creating salience, or achieving "self-salience," involves the three steps of (a) raising the visibility of an issue; (b) developing and disseminating (or "priming") a discourse that resonates among target audiences; and (c) establishing a legitimate claim over the issue through by interpreting it, so that it has a positive valence or effect on members of the audience, though the valence may be negative to some. By developing the salience of a Facebook message in this way, campaigners and their supporters can find an indirect pathway to the political discourse as shaped by mass media. Homogeneity in the public discourse would potentially be reduced. As a theoretical development, salience as discussed in the chapter has the potential to be tested in many local, regional, and national contexts.

But citizens are not, of course, exclusively concerned with public questions and issues such as national elections.

In “Political Mobilization Strategies in Taiwan’s Sunflower Student Movement on March 18, 2014: A Text Mining Analysis of Cross-National Media Corpus,” Kenneth C.C. Yang and Yowei Kang argue that social media were used in protest movements to challenge the mainstream media’s information and interpretations. Social media also supported the mobilization of resources across national movements. For example, a crowdfunding platform created to support a national protest movement could be used subsequently by citizens in a different national context.

The authors of “Social Media and the Public Sphere in China: A Case Study of Political Discussion on Weibo after the Wenzhou High-Speed Rail Scandal” use a critical lens when describing public discourse using social media. Zhou Shan and Lu Tang argue that blogs have become a significant part of the public sphere. By examining the role of blogs in a high-profile investigation of a train accident, they find evidence that blogs help to direct subsequent public and official discourses about accountability. This occurs, for example, through the sustained posing of questions about responsibility, establishing comparisons with similar accidents in other countries, and providing a site for the memorialization of grief and anguish through the publication of poems and the expression of condolences.

In both obvious and subtle ways, there is continuing value in the dictum of that old prophet of technology, Marshall McLuhan (2003), who observed that the invention and diffusion of a new medium is reliably followed by immediate and enduring changes in the social environment. The story of the arrival of social media as a successor in a series of democratic innovations in history is hardly complete and as yet unclear in its outcomes. However, we can already see that social media will contribute to changes in prevailing views of what democracy is and how it should develop. Some of these changes will remain beyond the control of individuals or groups. Some changes will not be completely out of the reach of citizens, as Chapter 6 concerning gatekeepers and GMOs helps to illustrate. As Chapter 2 about citizens and local environmental issues shows, cultural and social contexts will need to be taken into account when considering how citizens will understand, use, and be influenced by social media.

McLuhan often referred to the implications for culture and society of the transition from a print culture, which began with the invention of the printing press in 1440, to a culture of electricity, which he judged to have begun with the invention of the telegraph in the 19th century. While a print culture is individualistic and critical, reflected in the practice of private and silent reading, an electric culture is characterized by speed, and by many things happening at once. If McLuhan were still with us, he might well describe our own time as primarily that of a screen culture, in which social media are embraced and immediately incorporated into the social environment. He would not be surprised by the skillful, hybrid use of media by youth described in Chapter 5.

McLuhan looked ahead to the implications for democratic practices of a continually increasing abundancy of information but also, and in particular, its increasing velocity:

As the speed of information increases, the tendency is for politics to move away from representation and delegation of constituents toward immediate involvement of the entire community in the central acts of decision. (p. 275)

The increasing speed of information is allowing citizens to find patterns and devise alternatives long before elected representatives are able to do. Chapter 4, in its description of anti-vaccination policy entrepreneurs, provides an example of citizens anticipating policy decisions, well in advance of government.

Table 1. Changes in the social environment occasioned by the rise of social media

	Citizens	Media	Social Environment
Age of print	Individualistic, critical	One idea at a time, daily cycle of information, dominance of the word	Representation and delegation in political processes
Screen age	Collaborative, involved	Many ideas at once, continuous information, dominance of the image	Immediate involvement of the entire community

Chapters 7 and 15 demonstrate how social media are being used to, respectively, facilitate learning by citizens in other polities, and transform the public sphere.

The broad changes occasioned by the rise of social media for citizen engagement and public participation are summarized in Table 1.

As a means of weaving together the thematic strands of the book, we might consider McLuhan's love and extensive us of metaphors. Metaphors helped McLuhan to understand and express the ultimate meaning of a new medium, especially during the disorienting period of time in which the new medium is having its initial effects on the social environment. In this sense, the television screen can be understood using the metaphor of mirrors. The effect of mirrors was first experienced by the experience of looking into still water. McLuhan reminds us that the mirror effect is described in the story of the mythological figure of Narcissus. Narcissus sees his reflection in the water and believes it to be beautiful. He becomes enchanted and wants to possess this "other" person. So unsettling is the experience that he eventually commits suicide by plunging a dagger into his chest.

"Narcissus oil" is still made and sold. Narcotics constitute a category of chemical agents whose etymology may be traced to the name Narcissus. The myth of Narcissus carries the lesson that observing our image in the mirror, and therefore in our screens, can have a mesmerizing influence. The effects that follow their use can be psychological and neural. The mythological Narcissus has been smitten in both mind and body. McLuhan describes the "numbing" effects of media:

Narcissus mistook his own reflection in the water for another person. This extension of himself by a mirror numbed his perceptions until he became the servomechanism of his own extended or repeated image. The nymph Echo tried to win his love with fragments of his own speech, but in vain. He was numb. He had adapted to his extension of himself and had become a closed system. (p. 63)

For McLuhan, the use of a new communications medium constitutes an exchange. A medium grants the benefit of heightened perception, but at a cost. The cost is often the loss of broader understanding. The new medium changes the social environment in ways that are largely unobserved. As a medium, the mirror has extended human capacities. It has allowed us to see something we had never seen before – ourselves.

The use of social media as part of the process by which new democratic practices are enacted will show us what we have not seen before. Social media will help us to manage risk and generate innovations in much faster cycles. They may create closed feedback loops of information and images. These loop may make it difficult to, for example, draw on memory and experience rather than information, or provide time for contemplation in place of continuous analysis.

McLuhan might say that the metaphor of the mirror can contribute to a fuller understanding of the new social environment that we are creating. Use of the metaphor for undrstanding may also relieve some of the numbness that accompanies the wide use of social media. The chapters in this book are a hopeful contribution to efforts to understand the new democratic environment coming into view.

REFERENCES

Adria, M. (2010). *Technology and nationalism*. Montreal: McGill-Queen's University Press.

Alvarez, M., & Hall, T. (2008). *Electronic elections: The perils and promises of digital democracy*. Princeton University Press.

Bertot, J., Jaeger, J., & Grimes, J. (2010). Using ICTs to create a culture of transparency: E-government and social media as openness and anti-corruption tools for societies. *Government Information Quarterly*, *27*(3), 264–271. doi:10.1016/j.giq.2010.03.001

Davies, B., Blackstock, K., & Rauschmayer, F. (2005). "Recruitment," "composition," and "mandate" issues in deliberative processes: Should we focus on arguments rather than individuals? *Environment and Planning. C, Government & Policy*, *23*(4), 599–615. doi:10.1068/c04112s

Engelman, R. (1996). *Public radio and television in America: A political history*. Thousand Oaks, CA: Sage.

Evans, E. (1917). *A history of the Australian ballot in the United States*. Chicago: University of Chicago Press.

Faris, R. (1975). *The passionate educators: Voluntary associations and the struggle for control of adult educational broadcasting in Canada 1919-52*. Toronto: Peter Martin Associates.

Gouldner, A. (1976). *The dialectic of ideology and technology: The origins, grammar, and future of ideology*. London: Macmillan. doi:10.1007/978-1-349-15663-4

Habermas, J. (2006). Towards a United States of Europe. *signandsite.com*. Available at: http://www.signandsight.com/features/676.html

Jayal, N. (2013). *Citizenship and its discontents: An Indian history*. Cambridge, MA: Harvard University Press.

Kamenova, K., & Goodman, N. (2015). Public engagement with Internet voting in Edmonton: Design, outcomes, and challenges to deliberative models. *Journal of Public Deliberation*, *11*(2), 4. Available at http://www.publicdeliberation.net/jpd/vol11/iss2/art4

Kymlicka, W. (2001). *Politics in the vernacular: Nationalism, multiculturalism, and citizenship*. Oxford, UK: Oxford University Press. doi:10.1093/0199240981.001.0001

Madise, Ü., & Martens, T. (2006). E-voting in Estonia 2005: The first practice of country-wide binding Internet voting in the world. In R. Krimmer (Ed.), *Electronic Voting 2006, GI Lecture Notes in Informatics*. Bonn: Academic Press.

McLuhan, M. (2003). *Understanding media: The extensions of man*. Berkeley, CA: Gingko Press. (Original work published 1964)

Noelle-Neumann, E. (1993). *The spiral of silence: Public opinion – our social skin* (2nd ed.). Chicago: University of Chicago Press.

Norris, P. (2005). E-voting as the magic bullet for European parliamentary elections? In A. Trechsel & F. Mendez (Eds.), *The European Union and e-voting*. London: Routledge.

Peters, J. D. (1999). *Speaking into the air: A history of the idea of communication*. Chicago, IL: University of Chicago Press. doi:10.7208/chicago/9780226922638.001.0001

Rosenthal, P. (2009). *Seattle Post-Intelligencer to go online-only; Rocky Mountain News alumni seek to launch own Denver site*. Academic Press.

Steiner, J., Bächtiger, A., Spörndli, M., & Steenbergen, M. (2004). *Deliberative politics in action: Analyzing parliamentary discourse*. Cambridge, UK: Cambridge University Press.

Zhou, Y., & Moy, P. (2007). Parsing framing processes: The interplay between online public opinion and media coverage. *Journal of Communication*, *57*, 79–98.

Chapter 1
Platform Work and Participation:
Disentangling the Rhetoric

Zachary Kilhoffer
Centre for European Policy Studies, Belgium

ABSTRACT

Platforms like Uber, Deliveroo, and Upwork have disrupted labor markets around the world. These platforms vary enormously in form and function, but generally contain three parts: digital platforms, which set the rules and intermediate communication and transactions between the other two parts, consumers and platform workers. Platform work is a diverse type of labor that developed around these platforms, and it has great potential to increase citizen participation. However, it is under intense scrutiny in light of widely publicized protests and court cases. This report attempts to disentangle the rhetoric surrounding platform work by discussing its emergence and conceptualization, key challenges, and how it may increase participation in the socio-economic sphere. The conclusion discusses how most policy proposals to regulate platform work fail to address the core issues, while potentially stifling innovative practices. Instead, the author suggests more tailored and proportionate regulatory responses.

PLATFORM WORK AND PARTICIPATION: DISENTANGLING THE RHETORIC

From Uber to AirBnB, Deliveroo to Upwork, platforms have disrupted labor markets around the world. These platforms vary enormously in form and function, but essentially act as two-sided markets with three primary parts: digital platforms, which set the rules and intermediate communication and transactions between the other two parts, consumers, and platform workers. It is already clear that platforms are emerging and growing at an incredible rate. Uber best demonstrates this prolific growth, having surpassed the value of General Motors and Ford at the age of five and a half years in 2015.

The literature emphasizes the connection between participation and happiness (Barker and Martin, 2011). In this respect platforms have the potential to augment citizens' participation and engagement, allowing individuals to directly interact with one another and exchange goods and services in local and global marketplaces. This can serve to improve economic and overall well-being for both consumers and platform workers.

DOI: 10.4018/978-1-7998-1828-1.ch001

The benefits of platformization to consumers are rather straightforward: access to faster, cheaper, and better goods and services. Simultaneously, platform workers may benefit from the ability to be their own boss, set their own schedule, and make money on their terms. The structure of platform work does not require an intensive selection process, so it provides a means of labor market access with relatively low entry barriers. Without bosses in the traditional sense, platform workers can have more autonomy in selecting and carrying out their work.

Some evidence even suggests that platform work creates opportunities for people traditionally marginalized in the labor market, such as recent migrants, single mothers, and people with disabilities. Platforms promise workers flexibility and economic empowerment, which may increase their power over decisions affecting their lives, and facilitate greater participation in the family and work spheres.

However, platform work exists in a great variety of forms, and the narrative of empowerment requires careful scrutiny. Policy-makers, trade unions, and platform workers have emphasized risks including low earnings, a lack of access to social protection, undeclared work, and labor market polarization. Platform work can represent the ultimate dead-end job, where workers face social isolation and arbitrary sanctions from their de facto boss - the platform's algorithms. As platforms continue to grow, so too will the challenges of platform work.

This essay provides a brief overview of how the concept of platform work developed. It continues with a simplified model of platform work, and discusses a few of its most pressing challenges. Next, it discusses a few arguments concerning platforms as a tool to empower citizens. Finally, it argues that stakeholders should avoid overly simplistic understandings of platform work, instead recognizing it as a neutral tool that, managed properly, can benefit citizens of all stripes.

WHAT IS MEANT BY PLATFORM, PLATFORM ECONOMY, AND PLATFORM WORK?

The platform economy is new, fast-growing, and has great potential to change how citizens work and consume. Still, 'platform economy' and related terms remain poorly defined, and definitional clarity is the topic of considerable ongoing debate (Codagnone, Biagi and Abadie, 2016; Codagnone and Martens, 2016; Drahokoupil and Fabo, 2017; Maselli, Lenaerts and Beblavý, 2016; Riso, 2019). The background and underlying motivations for the platform economy are worth closer examination.

The related term 'collaborative economy', often used by authors and EU institutions, seems to have evolved from Rachel Botsman's 2010 Ted Talk, where she introduced the idea of collaborative consumption (Kilhoffer, Lenaerts and Beblavý, 2017). The idea behind collaborative consumption is that new communication tools allow us to change the way we consume, which means ownership is no longer imperative, and we can be more efficient and less wasteful. To illustrate the point, Botsman asked her audience how many of them own a power drill, and most of the audience raised their hands. Botsman quipped,

That power drill will be used around 12 to 15 minutes in its entire lifetime. It's kind of ridiculous, isn't it? Because what you need is the hole, not the drill. Why don't you rent the drill? Or rent out your own drill to other people and make some money from it?

Thus, the platform economy (or collaborative economy, sharing economy, or any of a hundred other names) concerns **distribution of excess**, yielding efficiency gains. Ride-sharing platforms like BlaBlaCar, Europe's first unicorn in the platform economy, cater to individuals who want to rent out an empty seat in their car while they make a trip, and platforms like RelayRides allow users to rent the car itself. Other platforms allow users to share many types of goods, with or without a profit motive.

Similarly to how a power drill or car sits motionless and unproductive for a large part of its life, and mostly empty cars make trips to and fro, people's idle time came to be a tradable commodity in the platform economy. Soon enough, platforms began intermediating transactions of services as well as goods. This platform work can be treated as side gig or full-time occupation.

Uber and similar commercial platforms often argue that they are a part of Botsman's collaborative mold, offering a means for people to use their extra time and resources to help one another. This somewhat muddied the waters, calling into question normatively-leading terms like 'sharing' and 'collaborative economy'.[1] The same reasons prompted some authors to develop and debate typologies for what constitutes a 'true' sharing economy platform, versus a digital tool used by companies for intermediating labor (Codagnone, Biagi and Abadie, 2016; Frenken et al., 2015). These debates were not merely academic exercises – in light of dozens of court cases, legislative proposals, and even violent protests challenging platform work, it became necessary to disentangle enormously different, yet related, platforms from one other. Of course, regulating giants like Uber alongside non-profit 'genuine sharing' platforms makes little sense.

In short, the broad term 'platform economy' can invoke both altruism and neo-liberalism. In the excellent essay 'The Passions and the Interests', Codagnone et al. argue that the heart of the platform economy is **digital tools that lower transaction costs** between individuals (and even businesses), and allow a means to **exchange excess capacity** (2016).

This chapter is primarily concerned with the neo-liberal or commercial subset of the platform economy called platform work. At its core, **platform work is a triangular work relationship involving the exchange of services for payment, with intermediation provided by a digital platform**.

Among the first instances of platform work derives from a 'crowdsourcing' proposal from IBM around 2010 (Kawalec and Menz, 2013). In this model, IBM managers would not delegate tasks to specific employees. Instead, managers would post tasks to an online platform, where one of the workers in the 'crowd' would accept the task. This practice is sometimes called 'internal crowdsourcing' or 'cloudworking' in the literature.

While novel, IBM's idea had more significant effects when applied externally, beyond a single organization. This 'external crowdsourcing' bears a close resemblance to outsourcing. Tasks traditionally performed by employees are instead delegated to independent contractors via algorithmic management. In some instances, this form of platform work closely resembles a boss and employees exchanging roles with AI and contractors.

The common banner of platform work refers to very different companies and practices. This further emphasizes the conceptual difficulty of platform work. Due to its diversity, it is extremely difficult to create a model that accurately describes all platforms in a satisfactory way. Still, such a model remains useful to present illustrate what qualifies as platform work.

A simple but robust model comes from De Groen et al (2016), separating forms of platform work by location and complexity. This model distinguishes higher- and lower-skilled services offered online. Higher-skilled tasks performed online can include programming (Topcoder) and designing marketing campaigns (Jovoto), to data entry, image recognition, and filling out surveys (Amazon Mechanical

Figure 1. Conceptualization of platform work
Source: author's own elaboration.

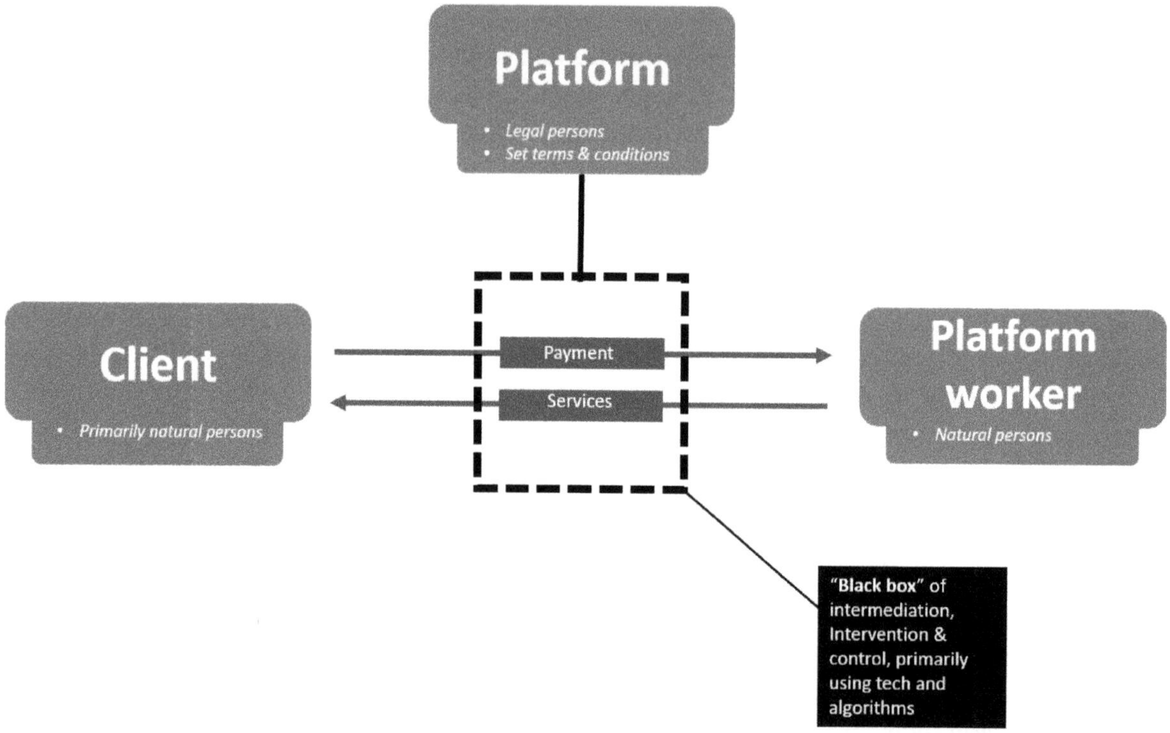

Turk, Clickworker). Higher-skilled services provided locally include the niche platforms emerging for workers in manual trades, such as electricians, plumbers, and roofers (Listminut, MyHammer, to some extent TaskRabbit). Lower-skilled services provided on-location include pet-sitting (PetSitter), cleaning (Helpling, Hilfr) and most prominently, personal transportation (Uber, Lyft, Didi Chuxing, Ola) and food delivery (Deliveroo, Foodora, UberEats).

Other typologies include more distinctions, such as how work is distributed (e.g. to an indeterminate crowd or an individual person) and the means of securing contract, such as via a contest system (99designs) or online marketplace (Upwork).[2]

One could ask, not without justification, how such disparate companies, platforms, and work forms can be lumped together under a single banner. Obviously these platforms within and between Types 1-4 are very different.

Even so, 'platform work' is distinguishable from other types of digital, independent, and atypical work forms. What unites platform workers of all stripes is performing labor, exchanged for payment, intermediated by the use of digital intermediation, with substantial input from algorithms. As will be discussed, the benefits and challenges in platform work merit close examination.

Figure 2. Four part typology of platform work
Source: Author's own elaboration based on De Groen et al. (2016).

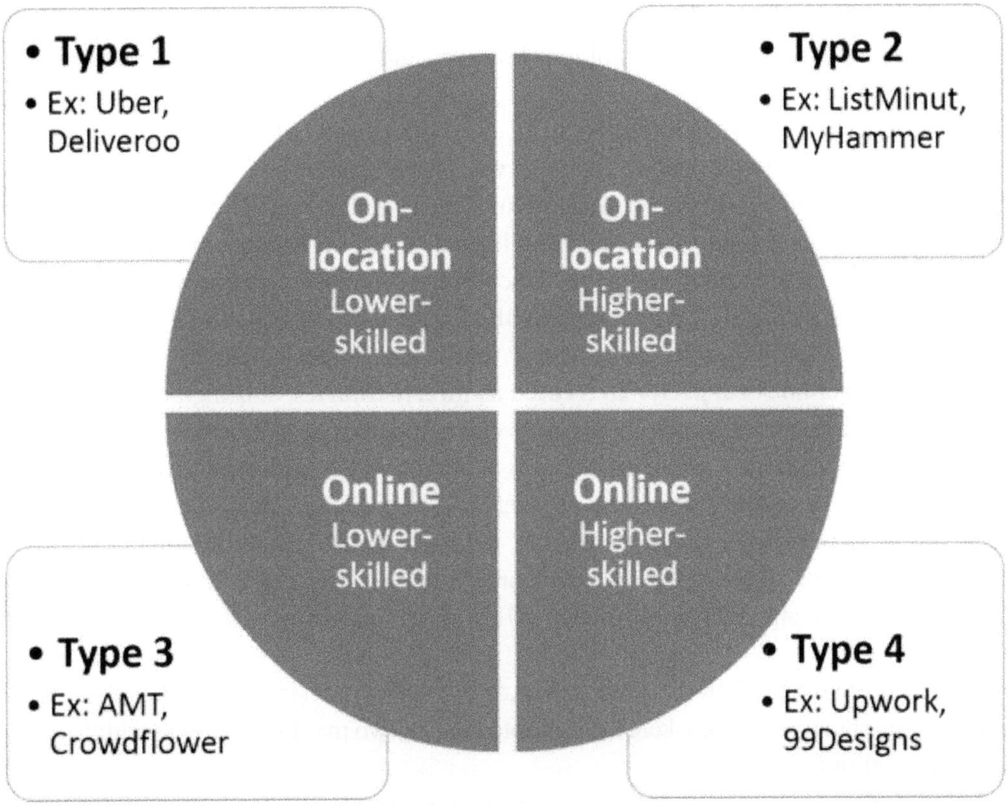

CHALLENGES, CLASHES AND SOLUTIONS

Platform work creates numerous challenges to legal regimes, competing industries, and platform workers themselves. In part this stems from platform work's similarities to both traditional employment and self-employment, which are regulated very differently. Platform work challenges clearly delineated working time and space, and so muddles the personal and professional lives of citizens. Platform workers often fit the profile of vulnerable workers. For example, they are disproportionately young people, recent migrants, or others who struggle to participate in the traditional labor market. Platform work also has questionable impacts on workers with regard to income security, job satisfaction, and overall well-being.

While far from exhaustive, this section aims to highlight a few of the important challenges associated with platform work.

Competition with Existing Industries

The platform economy has disrupted a number of industries – perhaps none so obviously as transportation and hospitality.

The taxi industry tends to be highly regulated, though regulations vary substantially at local and national levels. As such, taxi drivers face substantial costs and barriers to entry. For example, a number of large cities require taxi drivers to possess a medallion, certifying their right to operate. Only a finite number of medallions or operating permits are available at a given time, so costs can be extremely high – easily reaching hundreds of thousands of dollars annually. Many localities require taxi drivers to establish a business, with all the related obligations, costs and delays. Taxi fares and other elements of the service are often strictly controlled.

In short, the average citizen cannot decide to be a taxi driver and begin the next day – which is more or less the premise of Uber. In particular, Uber's service UberPop allows virtually anyone to begin working like a taxi driver, provided they pass a background check and have a valid driver's license.[3] For this reason, UberPop has been the subject of unending legal disputes in the US and Europe. In the majority of these cases, the taxi industry has challenged Uber on the grounds of competition law.

In a relevant and high-profile case decided by the European Court of Justice, the court considered whether Uber is a transportation company, rather than a mere intermediation service (Scott, 2017). Similarly, **platforms of all sorts prefer to treated as intermediaries**, shifting burdens like regulatory compliance and dispute resolution from employers and companies to platform workers.

Like taxi services, temporary accommodation is a rather tightly regulated sector. Hotels, motels, and hostels are required to meet stringent criteria on safety and cleanliness. Special taxes and occupancy fees also apply. When AirBnB first entered the market, the hotel industry took little notice. However, with residency rates and hotel revenues falling, and more consumers looking first to offerings on AirBnB, the hotel industry has changed its tune (Benner, 2017; Mody and Gomez, 2018; Zervas, Proserpio and Byers, 2014).

The typical pattern is that platforms enter a market, disrupt an industry, and ultimately face pushback. In response to complaints, policy-makers have adopted one of two main strategies to address competition of platforms to traditional industries.

Option one is to increase regulations on platforms – e.g. ensure existing, sector-specific regulations are applied to the new entrants. This strategy is seen across Europe, where UberPop has essentially been discontinued, and only UberX and UberBlack services remain active. Unlike the former, UberX and UberBlack require drivers to hold professional licenses for personal transportation. Similarly, many localities have passed ordinances requiring AirBnB to levy occupancy fees and report data to ensure tax compliance.

Option two is to reduce regulations across the board. For example, Estonia and Slovenia reduced the regulatory burden on the taxi industry in response to the entrance of ride-sharing platforms.[4] Christoph Juen, former CEO of the Swiss Hotel Association, remarked that "the emergence of online platforms such as Airbnb creates a chance to reduce regulation in the entire hotel and tourism industry" (Deloitte, 2015).

Both options one and two have the ultimate goal of creating a more level playing field for platforms competing in a given industry.

In other cases, established industries have recognized and seized on the potential of the platform economy. Crowd Companies is a business association representing giants including Nestlé, Johnson & Johnson, BMW and MasterCard.[5] This organization is dedicated to helping corporations capitalize on developments in the platform economy. Similarly, large auto manufacturers, notably those in Germany, rely heavily on platform work to train their safety software, and the necessary AI for self-driving cars (Schmidt, 2019).[6]

In short, platform work is behind a few different competition narratives. The more cynical view calls out a regulatory race to the bottom, where working conditions decline for both platform workers and employees in competing industries. A more optimistic view sees platform work as a driving force to modernize overly restrictive and antiquated regulatory regimes, opening up space for new growth and work opportunities.

Employment and Outsourcing

Among the most contentious debates in platform work concerns employment status. Employment status is a particularly important issue because only employees fall under most labor laws, and benefit from access to certain social protections, such as accident insurance, paid sick leave, and unemployment insurance. Employees can (usually) join a trade union and collectively bargain for better working conditions, whereas self-employed attempting the same run afoul of competition and cartel laws.[7]

The employment relationship, typically defined by an employee and employer bound by employment contract, creates a relationship of subordination. Subject to labor code restrictions, employers can require employees to continually show up at a given location and time, do a series of tasks as directed, and legally impose certain sanctions otherwise.

In order to prevent abuse and minimize harms of this power disparity, employees have a number of special legal protections and rights. Because of these additional rights (paid holidays and sick leave, unemployment insurance, etc.), employees represent additional costs to employers compared to using acquiring services in other ways. Typically, both employees and employers are responsible for apportion of statutory contributions. These additional costs are often necessary, however, because employers gain a substantial level of control over employees, which increases reliability of services.[8]

The traditional employment relationship is premised on an employer's need for similar services over a period of time – which made perfect sense when the majority of workers operated in factories or farms. In most cases, contracting labor was possible, but not feasible when consistency is required. A contractor cannot be ordered to work Monday through Friday, 9:00-5:00.

However, the trends of digitalization[9] and automation allows for the fragmentation of work into smaller chunks, while reducing the importance of location. Platforms reduce frictions in contracting labor, which has changed allowed employers to hire fewer employees and still acquire necessary services. Wired Magazine made first reference of this phenomenon, writing "It's not outsourcing; it's crowdsourcing" (Howe, 2006).

As noted in a Wallstreet Journal article aptly titled "The End of Employees", companies of all shapes and sizes are increasingly thinking "Can I automate it? If not, can I outsource it? If not, can I give it to an independent contractor or freelancer" (Weber, 2017)? Platforms have greatly empowered companies, and even individuals, to benefit from labor without employees or any lasting connection to a worker.

Platform work has made outsourcing tasks and hiring independent contractors faster, cheaper, easier, and more reliable than ever before. In their paper "The global gig economy: Towards a planetary labour market", Graham and Anwar discuss how platform work minimizes the importance of geographic location, increases the potential pool of laborers, and results in a massive oversupply of labor. In effect, this increases the bargaining power of companies, and reduces that of individual (platform) workers, creating downwards wage pressure (Graham and Anwar, 2019).

Outsourcing through platforms has proven highly attractive for companies, who are some of the biggest customers of platforms. For example, recent research highlights that large automakers rely on platform work to train and develop AI for safety features and self-driving capabilities (Schmidt, 2019). Companies large and small have taken to using platforms to develop advertising concepts (logos, artwork, campaign ideas) through platforms using 'contest' models (De Groen, Kilhoffer and Lenaerts, 2018).

Bogus Self-Employment

In virtually all circumstances, platform workers are self-employed. This may or may not be stated explicitly in the platform's terms and conditions. This has proven contentious and resulted in numerous court cases around the world – particularly for platform workers providing personal transport or food delivery services. The practice of 'bogus' or 'false self-employment' refers to a situation where somebody is registered as self-employed (or freelancer, independent contractor, etc.), while in fact carrying out professional activity under the subordination of another company. This circumvents labor legislation and reduces tax and social security contributions for the would-be employer.

Countries have varying legal definitions of employee, and thus handle bogus self-employment claims differently. In Germany for example, an employee is defined by economic and personal dependency on an employer (De Groen, Kilhoffer and Lenaerts, 2018). In the US, an employee is determined by evidence the degree of control and independence in three categories: behavioral, financial, and type of relationship.[10] In some legal contexts, intermediate statuses also exist between employee and self-employed. At times, platform workers have been classified under these 'third statuses'.

In many cases platform workers meet some but not all criteria for employment. Platform work can be very difficult in this respect, as it includes similarities to both self-employed/independent forms of work, as well as subordinated/employed work. With no employer in the platform work relationship, control over the platform worker can come from both platform and client. Furthermore, the exact amount of subordination is not always clear due to the 'black box' of intermediation. These uncertainties have led to court cases across many countries, aiming to reclassify certain platform workers as employees.

Most commonly, bogus self-employment claims concern personal transport or food delivery service platform workers. In one exemplary case, the TMB, a British trade union, filed a case against Uber alleging bogus self-employment. The TMB won the ruling, with the court concluding that Uber drivers are employees entitled to holiday pay and minimum wage. The judgement was very critical of Uber, stating (Osborne, 2016):

The notion that Uber in London is a mosaic of 30,000 small businesses linked by a common 'platform' is to our minds faintly ridiculous... Drivers do not and cannot negotiate with passengers ... They are offered and accept trips strictly on Uber's terms.

In a number of European countries, notably the UK and Spain, judges have considered similar complaints and ruled differently on the issue of employment status. Slightly different facts in the cases, as well as judicial discretion, are likely causes. Overall, however, the majority of cases have sided with platforms, determining platform workers to be self-employed, independent contractors.

Couriers represent a special subset of platform workers on platforms like Foodora, Deliveroo, and UberEats. These platform workers typically ride bikes or scooters to deliver food from restaurants to clients' homes. This form of platform work has come under particular scrutiny due in part to widespread worker protests highlighting low pay, dangerous working conditions, and a lack of collective worker voice.

In claiming bogus self-employment, couriers, and the trade unions backing them, can point to many practices indicating subordination. Many platforms require riders to wear uniforms and ubiquitous, cube shaped backpacks to store meals. Like Uber drivers, couriers cannot set their prices or determine for themselves how they provide their service. Unlike Uber drivers, couriers typically register for shifts and face sanctions if they fail to show up or find a replacement. Very few factual aspects of the couriers' work resembles self-employment, with the exception of some flexibility in shifts, and (usually) no requirement to pass a job interview to begin working. Interestingly, some courier platforms, such as Foodora in Vienna, use a mixture of employees and self-employed. A few practical differences separate the two, with employees being required to complete a minimum number of shifts per month, being paid hourly instead of per delivery, and participating in the works council organized by the trade union Vida (De Groen et al., 2018).

An additional issue is that couriers put themselves at risk on the job, particularly because they are paid per task and operate under time pressure. They may feel pressured to go faster or work when tired, increasing risks of accident. In most cases, platform workers are responsible for their own safety gear, though at times platforms have provided helmets, lights, and even winter tires. In most cases, these provisions were in response to platform worker or trade union complaints (EU-OSHA, 2019).

Because couriers operate in the same spaces in the same cities, they are more visible to one another than most platform workers, and they have more sense of a collective identity. This identity helps contribute to collective actions protesting what they see as harmful practices.

In a few court cases, platform workers have alleged bogus self-employment after being suspended by the platform. Account suspension can happen automatically, such as when Uber drivers have too low of a star rating for a period of time, or with inputs from humans. Part of the issue is that account suspension can happen arbitrarily or without clear reason, and platform workers rarely have a means to better understand or dispute the decision. Because account suspension closely resembles termination of an employment contract, and the rules are often opaque, it is a topic of much discussion in platform work literature.

Platforms as a Tool of Citizen Empowerment

Having discussed some of the more prominent challenges[11] of platform work, it is necessary to highlight its benefits. From many dozens of interviews with platform workers over a variety of projects,[12] I am fairly comfortable making a few generalizations.

First, most platform workers indicated they are overall satisfied with their platform work. The reasoning behind this is fairly clear; if they were not satisfied, little stops them from leaving.[13] Indeed, platform work is associated with very high turnover, which reinforces the second point; most treat platform work as a side activity. The majority of platform workers have full-time occupations, whether jobs, studies, or care-taking duties. These activities can restrict the possibility of more traditional employment, only leaving free sporadic and less predictable working times. The majority of platform workers report being happy to use their spare time to stay active and earn some money. Most consider it a way to top up their income, rather than a 'real job'.

Third, due to its low barriers to entry, platform work can disproportionately benefit vulnerable people. This includes young people, people with less education, recent migrants, and people with disabilities.

For example, some evidence suggests that platform work can be an equalizer for people with disabilities. Platform work creates more accessible forms of work that can be performed from home, which disproportionately benefits people with limited mobility. Some people with disabilities even indicated they view platform work as an *equalizing* tool; they feel judged on the merits of their work, rather than assumptions about their disability.[14]

One excellent example of platform work as a tool of empowerment is 'ava' - an Austrian platform from the company 'atempo'. ava is notable because it intermediates care-taking services for people with disabilities. Companies offering these services work on fixed schedules, whereas the need for care-taking services can be unpredictable. To illustrate the issue, we learned from interviews of one individual who required a caretaker to accompany them on a train ride to a job interview, so they scheduled someone through a local company. When the caretaker called in sick the day before, this individual called other local services hoping to find a replacement. However, no other care-takers were available, so they had no choice but to cancel the interview. In this regard, ava provides a much more efficient way to match supply and demand for care-taking services, which can allow people with disabilities greater ability to participate in the labor market and society generally (Kilhoffer et al., 2019).

In other cases, women disproportionately benefit from platforms. The marketplace Etsy is primarily about transfer of goods rather than services, so it is slightly beyond the focus of this essay. However, it is notable that over 85% of Etsy sellers are women. Etsy seems to have offered crafty and entrepreneurial women a chance to expand their customer base. This is particular beneficial for women with care-taking duties or other responsibilities that limit their ability to participate in the traditional labor market. It is also clear that prior to selling on Etsy, a sizable minority of sellers had no income-generating activities (Zarya, 2015).

CONCLUSION, REFLECTION, AND THE RIGHT KIND OF REGULATION

One key takeaway is that platform work carries benefits and risks for individual people, industries, and the future of labor. It is a digital tool - and like any other tool, it is inherently neutral, but makes certain processes easier or possible.

For a number of reasons, the traditional labor market is often rigid. However, the demand for more flexible forms of work is evident. Platforms can play an important role in satisfying that demand, allowing greater participation in the private (work) sphere.

However, discussions on platform work are often overly simplistic. Many authors treat labor platforms as the new face of capitalist exploitation, glossing over the benefits many platform workers enjoy. Such one-sided arguments fail to capture the diversity and nuance of platform worker experiences. Granted, platform work can isolate and stratify individuals, effectively trapping them in precarious vocations of low-quality and low pay. Just as easily, it can empower citizens, who otherwise would have been inactive, to participate in the socio-economic sphere.

Drivers and couriers on platforms like Uber and Deliveroo have organized demonstrations to improve their working conditions, wages, and bargaining power. Endless court cases concerning these platforms continue to be decided and appealed. The struggles of these platform workers are very important, but they have come to dominate the policy discussion. In many cases, policy-makers have proposed stringent regulatory frameworks that might make sense for the Uber driver - whose only real autonomy is their working hours - but overly stifle other forms of platform work.

In many cases, the most important problems of platform work have little to do with platform work in particular. For example, difficulty in accessing social protection is characteristic of self-employment, rather than platform work per se. Solving this problem involves reducing the disparity in social protection between employees and self-employed. This would have considerable benefits for many platform workers who lack statutory or affordable access to benefits, but require a much more ambitious rethinking of regulatory frameworks.

As with social protection, policy-makers intending to regulate platform work may be cognizant of broader labor market problems, but fail to address issues deriving from platform work itself.

Earlier in this essay, I argued that the most defining feature of platform work is the 'black box' of intermediation. I posit here that the challenges unique to platform workers usually derive from this intermediation, which results in a significant information and power disparity. One important example is that platforms can and do suspend workers arbitrarily. Platforms that control prices may unilaterally decide to cut wages, and platform workers have no recourse but to leave. Leaving itself can pose a considerable challenge, as platforms often dominate a given market and face no real competition. In the worst case, such actions can result in people losing their livelihoods, generally with little explanation and no potential for disputing a platform's decision. This represents an unacceptable situation, all the more so when platform work requires substantial investment.[15]

The most defining attribute of platform work - the black box - is simultaneously the most important aspect to regulate. However, it is somewhat more technical in nature than issues like social protection and employment status, which may make it more difficult to properly confront. In spite of this difficulty, we ought to think more about the transparency of platforms' operations, which would allow platform workers to make their own informed decisions.

An excellent case in point is Regulation (EU) 2019/1150, also known as the P2B Regulation.[16] The P2B Regulation, which passed in summer 2019 and goes into force in the EU in summer 2020, focuses heavily on the transparency of online intermediaries. While not specifically aimed at platform workers, the P2B Regulation is likely to have wide-reaching effects on e-commerce marketplaces (e.g. Amazon), social networks, and even labor platforms.

The P2B addresses the information disparity between platform users and the platform itself. It stipulates notifications when terms and conditions are changed, waiting periods for implementing certain changes, and requires platforms to provide neutral arbitration procedures to settle disputes such as non-payment or account suspension. It even allows a measure of collective bargaining for self-employed business users, subject to national law in EU Member States.

The P2B may well be a model regulation, but its actual applicability for platform workers remains to be seen. For starters, it applies to 'business users' of online intermediation platforms. This probably means it applies to at least some self-employed platform workers, but the correct application of employment status remains a thorny and unresolved issue. Other stipulations[17] may result in many platform workers being excluded from coverage.

Still, P2B represents a very important step towards preventing abusive practices and ensuring fairer platform work. The legislation is proportionate and sufficiently targeted, allowing platform work to remain an invaluable tool for citizen's participation in the socio-economic sphere.

REFERENCES

Barker, C., & Martin, B. (2011). Participation: The Happiness Connection. *Journal of Public Deliberation, 7*(1), 9.

Benner, K. (2017). Inside the Hotel Industry's Plan to Combat Airbnb. *The New York Times*. Retrieved from https://www.nytimes.com/2017/04/16/technology/inside-the-hotel-industrys-plan-to-combat-airbnb.html

Chen, A. (2019). *Desperate Venezuelans are making money by training AI for self-driving cars*. Retrieved from https://www.technologyreview.com/s/614194/venezuela-crisis-platform-work-trains-self-driving-car-ai-data/

Codagnone, C., Biagi, F., & Abadie, F. (2016). *The Passions and the Interests: Unpacking the 'Sharing Economy*. JRC Science for Policy Report.

Codagnone, C., & Martens, B. (2016). *Scoping the Sharing Economy: Origins, Definitions, Impact and Regulatory Issues*. JRC Technical Reports.

De Groen, Maselli, & Fabo. (2016). *The Digital Market for Local Services: A one-night stand for workers? An example from the on-demand economy*. Academic Press.

De Groen, W. P., Kilhoffer, Z., & Lenaerts, K. (2018). Digital Age - Employment and working conditions of selected types of platform work: National context analysis Germany. *Eurofound*. Retrieved from https://www.ceps.eu/publications/digital-age-employment-and-working-conditions-selected-types-platform-work-national

Deloitte. (2015). *The sharing economy: Share and make money. How does Switzerland compare?* Author.

Drahokoupil, J., & Fabo, B. (2017). *Outsourcing, offshoring and the deconstruction of employment: New and old challenges in the digital economy*. Retrieved from https://papers.ssrn.com/sol3/papers.cfm?abstract_id=2975363

Frenken, K. (2015). *Smarter regulation for the sharing economy*. Retrieved from https://www.theguardian.com/science/political-science/2015/may/20/smarter-regulation-for-the-sharing-economy

Graham, M., & Anwar, M. A. (2019). The global gig economy: Towards a planetary labour market? *First Monday, 24*(4). doi:10.5210/fm.v24i4.9913

Howe, J. (2006). The rise of crowdsourcing. *Wired*. Retrieved from https://www.wired.com/2006/06/crowds/

Kawalec & Menz. (2013). Die Verflüssigung von Arbeit | Crowdsourcing als unternehmerische Reorganisationsstrategie – das Beispiel IBM. *Arbeits- und Industriesoziologische Studien, 6*(2), 5–23.

Kilhoffer, Lenaerts, & Beblavý. (2017). *The Platform Economy and Industrial Relations: Applying the old framework to the new reality*. CEPS Research Report 2017/12.

Kilhoffer, Z., Baiocco, S., Beblavý, M., & Cirule, E. (2019). Final Report - The impact of digitalisation on labour market inclusion of people with disabilities. *Bundesministerium für Arbeit, Soziales, Gesundheit und Konsumentenschutz (BMASGK).* Retrieved from https://www.sozialministerium.at/cms/site/attachments/2/3/1/CH3839/CMS1563200794559/endbericht-en.pdf

Maselli, Lenaerts, & Beblavý. (2016). *Five things we need to know about the on-demand economy.* CEPS Essay 21.

Mody, M., & Gomez, M. (2018). Airbnb and the Hotel Industry: The Past, Present, and Future of Sales, Marketing, Branding, and Revenue Management. *Boston Hospitality Review, 6*(3). Retrieved from https://www.bu.edu/bhr/2018/10/31/airbnb-and-the-hotel-industry-the-past-present-and-future-of-sales-marketing-branding-and-revenue-management/

Osborne, H. (2016). Uber loses right to classify UK drivers as self-employed. *The Guardian.* Retrieved from https://www.theguardian.com/technology/2016/oct/28/uber-uk-tribunal-self-employed-status

Riso, S. (2019). *Mapping the contours of the platform economy.* Eurofound Working Paper, Eurofound. Retrieved from https://www.eurofound.europa.eu/sites/default/files/wpef19060.pdf

Schmidt, F.A. (2017). *Digital Labour Markets in the Platform Economy: Mapping the Political Challenges of Crowd Work and Gig Work.* Retrieved from

Schmidt, F. A. (2019). *Crowdsourced Production of AI Training Data: How Human Workers Teach Self-Driving Cars How to See.* Working Paper Forschungsförderung 155, Hans Böckler Stiftung. Retrieved from https://www.boeckler.de/pdf/p_fofoe_WP_155_2019.pdf

Scott, M. (2017). *Uber is a transportation company, Europe's highest court rules.* Retrieved from https://www.politico.eu/article/uber-ecj-ruling/

Simonovitz, B., Shvets, I., & Hannah, T. (2018). Discrimination in the sharing economy: Evidence from a Hungarian field experiment. *Corvinus Journal of Sociology and Social Policy, 9*(1), 55–79. doi:10.14267/CJSSP.2018.1.03

Weber, L. (2017). The End of Employees. *Wall Street Journal.* Retrieved from https://www.wsj.com/articles/the-end-of-employees-1486050443

Zarya, V. (2015). Meet the 86%: This is why most Etsy sellers are women. *Fortune.* Retrieved from https://fortune.com/2015/08/02/etsy-sellers-women-2/

Zervas, G., Proserpio, D., & Byers, J. W. (2014). The rise of the sharing economy: Estimating the impact of Airbnb on the hotel industry. *Journal of Marketing Research.* Retrieved from http://journals.ama.org/doi/abs/10.1509/jmr.15.0204

ENDNOTES

1 The European Parliament encouraged the use of the term 'platform economy' in 2016 as the most objective term, while suggesting more uniform and less normative terminology. See (Procedure 2017/2003(INI)).

2 A particularly though-provoking typology is attributed to Schmidt (2017), whose model incorporates additional elements of the wider platform economy, such as commercial platforms for crowdfunding (Indiegogo, GoFundMe), social media (Facebook), and entertainment (YouTube).

3 A few other requirements apply, such as holding a driver's license a certain number of years, being 21 years or older, and potentially more depending on local regulations and practices.

4 See the forthcoming report from DG EMPL on platform work, titled "Study to gather evidence on the working conditions of platform workers".

5 See http://www.catalystcompanies.co/, last accessed September 2, 2019.

6 As an interesting side note, some evidence highlights that many of these platform workers hail from Venezuela, which continues to suffer from its political and economic crisis. Chen writes, "Next time you hear about the wonderful future of self-driving cars, picture this: Venezuelans, living in crisis conditions after their economy collapsed, sitting at laptops and outlining pictures of trees and bikes so that the robotic vehicles don't crash (2019). According to Schmidt, who interviewed Venezuelan platform workers, they, "were aware that, on one level, it's exploitation and they have to do it because everything else failed them". Nevertheless, they were happy to have found work and a steady flow of income. This reinforces the narrative that platform workers may be particularly vulnerable.

7 Note that while generally true that self-employed have fewer protections and less access to social protection than employees, the actual gap varies in different countries and sectors.

8 This broad, simplified description of the employment relationship developed over time in different nations in the context of industrialization, in parallel to workers' rights movements and systems of industrial relations.

9 Broadly meaning the transformation of processes using digital technologies, and the integration of physical and digital systems.

10 See https://www.irs.gov/businesses/small-businesses-self-employed/independent-contractor-self-employed-or-employee, last accessed September 2, 2019.

11 Others include pay, discrimination, and health and safety. One good introduction to these topics is Eurofound's "Platform Work: Types and implications for work and employment", available here.

12 These interviews contributed to Eurofound's "Employment and working conditions of selected types of platform work" and related working papers, available here. The ILO's work on the topic is also excellent, focusing on 'micro-tasks', especially in developing countries. See here.

13 Some platform workers do describe feeling they have no other opportunities to earn money, but this seems to represent a fairly small minority.

[14] Platforms can show more or less information about platform workers to clients. This argument primarily refers to online forms of work where work history (e.g. average rating) is most important to consumers. However, platforms can also empower consumers to discriminate. See, for example, Simonovitz et al. (2018).

[15] A frequent example would be purchasing or leasing a car.

[16] Regulation (EU) 2019/1150 of the European Parliament and of the Council of 20 June 2019 on promoting fairness and transparency for business users of online intermediation services.

[17] For example, many platform workers provide services to businesses. P2B applies to 'business users' providing services to 'consumers', who are defined as natural persons. In discussing the matter with several legal experts, it remains unclear how many platform workers will be covered by P2B in its present form.

Chapter 2
Civic Engagement in Local Environmental Initiatives:
Reaping the Benefits of a Diverse Media Landscape

Lorna Heaton
Université de Montréal, Canada

Patrícia Días da Silva
International Union for Health Promotion and Education, Canada

ABSTRACT

The goal of this chapter is to draw attention to the interrelation of multiple mediatized relationships, including face-to-face interaction, in local civic engagement around biodiversity and the environment. The authors propose that civic engagement and participation transcend the type of media used, and that artificial distinctions between online and offline participation are unproductive. Their argument is supported by three examples of participatory projects in which social media-based and face-to-face interactions are closely interrelated. This contribution highlights local uses of social media and the web. It shows how engagement plays out across multiple channels and how resources can be found in a variety of media formats. In particular, online media significantly alter the visibility of both local actions and of the resulting data.

INTRODUCTION

When studying civic engagement and public participation, one policy area cannot be overlooked in international and national debate: the environment. Throughout the 20th century, concerns about pollution, conservation of biodiversity as well as about energy sources and their environmental implications gained in visibility. The 21st century has brought a push towards sustainable development as institutions, governments and citizens have started "going green." Despite growing awareness, the complexity of both environmental issues themselves and the interplay between diverse stakeholders have often limited public

DOI: 10.4018/978-1-7998-1828-1.ch002

participation. As scientific knowledge is often required to allow for a better grasp of key problems and prospective solutions, initiatives to improve public understanding of science and enlarge opportunities for participation in scientific projects to non-professionals have increased in the environmental sciences and related fields such as biology and zoology (Bonney, Cooper & Ballard, 2016; Nascimento, Pereira & Ghezzi, 2014; Science Communication Unit, 2013).

Networked information technologies are changing the way environmental knowledge is produced and communicated. On the one hand, the digitization and availability of research data on the Internet enables its circulation among increasingly diverse publics – across disciplines, with government actors, the public, and so on. On the other, social media and participatory platforms create spaces that facilitate communication and interactions between professionals and amateurs.

The goal of this chapter is to draw attention to the interrelation of multiple mediatized relationships, including face-to-face interaction, in sustaining and structuring communicative practices and local civic engagement around biodiversity and environmental issues. The rapidly evolving media landscape creates both challenges and opportunities for media management by environmental organizations. The chapter highlights the local uses of social media and the Web and argues that the relationship between public involvement and the media can be fruitfully theorized without focusing specifically on the type of media used.[1] The authors propose that civic engagement and participation transcend the type of media used, and that one interaction format nourishes the other in many cases. They support their argument with several examples of participatory projects, all connected with environmental issues, and in which social media-based and face-to-face interactions are closely interrelated. The examples come from different parts of the world, all are relatively local in scale and all rely on both personal outreach and social media. These cases challenge the established (social, scientific or political) order in different ways and open up spaces in which alternative sustainable futures may be shaped. These results have concrete implications for environmental NGOs using digital media to raise awareness, create spaces for exchange or increase visibility.

The chapter is organized in three sections. The background section contains a brief literature review and an outline of three cases studied by the authors in two research projects (see Acknowledgements). The discussion is organized thematically in two parts. First, the authors draw attention to the importance of place and local anchoring experienced by participants, and to how local actions and contributions can participate in knowledge creation and mobilization at larger scales. They then discuss the relationship between various media and mediatized relationships in this process. The cases illustrate multiple channels for exchange, and the use of resources in a variety of media formats, from books, local media and flyers to email, databases, interactive maps and social media. In particular, online media significantly alter the visibility of local actions and their results. The increased visibility afforded by the Internet and social media appears as both an advantage and a potential problem.

BACKGROUND

Civic Engagement and the Environment

The environmental science and policy literature recognizes the importance of civic engagement as a means of collecting data, advocating for social change and environmental justice, making science more inclusive, and enhancing social-ecological connections (Danielsen, Burgess, & Balmford, 2005; McKinley et al., 2017). Within the vast literature on "citizen science," certain researchers have focused on the ways in which the public becomes engaged in participatory scientific learning and environmental advocacy (Ellis & Waterton, 2004), as well as on outcomes, suggesting that participation in such projects can increase "ecological knowledge, inquiry, and place-based nature experiences" and that they may help channel environmental information within social networks (Dickinson, Crain, Reeve, & Schuldt, 2013; Overdevest, Orr, & Stepenuck, 2004).

The extension of traditional environmental monitoring and data collection activities to the Web radically changes their scope (Brofeldt et al., 2018; Cornwell & Campbell, 2012; Heaton et al., 2018). As a result, many citizen science projects are global in scale, such as eBird, Wildbook or Herbonauts. Data quality is a key concern in terms of the scientific validity of these projects (Kosmala et al., 2016), since they rely on minimal contributions from an anonymous mass of contributors called citizen scientists or volunteers. It is a lesser issue when contributors are known, they contribute more regularly and their expertise in local situations is recognized (Wynne, 1992). In contrast to that of scientists, citizens' knowledge on a particular topic is typically acquired outside of formal education settings and distinct from scientific knowledge. Although citizen scientists' participation takes place on the worldwide stage of the web, it can be anchored in "traditional ecological knowledge" (TEK) or local ecological knowledge (LEK), which "has been gained through lifetime observations and experience, often related to some professional activity" (Thiel et al., 2014, p.259). A number of projects, particularly those focused on participatory monitoring, harness local ecological knowledge (Brofeldt et al., 2018; Elbroch et al., 2011), however the integration of such knowledge into the design of participatory science research protocols and infrastructure has not reached its full potential, and little is known of how ecological knowledge of place is formed and interpreted among individuals local to an area (Haywood, 2014).

Sense of Place and Place Attachment

"Place" has become an important focus of research on the relationship between humans and their environment (Cantrill, 2016). The idea of a sense of place can be broadly described as "an experiential process created by the setting, combined with what a person brings to it" (Steele, 1981, p. 9). An important aspect of sense of place is attachment (Lewicka, 2011). Among geographers, place attachment encompasses aspects of identity, physical or social dependence, and emotional connection to specific aspects of the physical environment or other creatures that share such space (see Trentelman, 2009 for a review of scholarship on place). Several studies have identified a positive relation between sense of place and pro-environmental attitudes and behaviours (see examples in Brehm, Eisenhauer & Stedman, 2013). What is more, an increase in participants' awareness of and relationship to their local environments has been identified as an important outcome of some citizen science programs (Cornwell & Campbell, 2012; Haywood et al, 2016).

In the context of participatory environmental projects, Haywood (2014, p. 71) notes that "peoples' bonds with important sites will influence their engagement in those places… The degree to which one identifies with a place may have some bearing on the sense of responsibility felt for that place." He argues that this may in turn influence broader civic engagement or spur community-initiated efforts that enhance participants' feelings of empowerment or self-efficacy. What is more, place attachment also has a social dimension. The sense of belonging or community that develops as individuals interact with each other in specific places may become associated with a particular place. The setting thus becomes an integral part of that communal relationship and can lead to what Ramkissoon, Weiler and Smith (2012) refer to as "place social bonding." Haywood (2014) posits that communal place attachment is positively associated with confidence in collective action, as well as increased trust, access and sharing of scientific information. Still, place attachment may change over time and though it may contribute positively to environmental engagement at the local level, it is not necessarily an important factor at the national level, unless both have a close connection (Vorkinn & Riese, 2001).

Multiple Media in Human Interaction: Online and Offline

The extent to which physical proximity enables or constrains human interaction and collaboration has been explored in the communication literature for decades. Various telecommunications technologies, not least social media associated with the Internet, have made it possible to more easily communicate over distance. A rich body of literature explores how these technologies have altered communication behaviour, or the role of distance in facilitating social bonds and enriching communication in various fields.[2] Although social media and Web 2.0 platforms create new spaces for exchange and opportunities for participation, people have not become disconnected from their local interpersonal and physical contexts. Early discourse around how the global village would change our relations to our local surroundings and above all to the people around us has been tempered: we remain in place (Haywood, 2014; Meyrowitz, 2005). With experience, fears around people being more connected to their Internet friends to the detriment of face-to-face interaction have proven largely unfounded. What emerges is a more nuanced portrait in which individuals move fluidly between online and offline worlds. Communities became 'glocalised' (Hampton & Wellman, 2002; Mok, Wellman, & Carrasco, 2010), with extensive local contact alongside amplified long-distance connectivity. In addition, the online world may also be local or support goals at the local level.

Communication across multiple channels or media has been theorized in various ways in the literature, often to suggest that one media may be more appropriate than another in a given situation, theorizing the richness of various media (Trevino, Lengel, & Daft, 1987), media appropriateness or "fit" (Rice, 1993), channel effects (Walther, 1996), or affordances (Bucher & Helmond, 2017). In contrast, more recent literature has tended to focus on the interrelationships between different media and their ecologies, prioritizing what people are doing, and then examining the various media they employ (Bjur et al, 2014; Hasbrink & Hepp, 2017). For instance, Baym, Zhang and Lin's (2004) study of interpersonal communication among college students insists on the need to view relationships as maintained through multiple media, while Wajcman and Rose (2011) examine knowledge work practices anchored in multiple media, and Jung and Lyttinen (2014) provide an ecological account of media choice. In our highly mediatized world, it appears obvious that almost everyone is using multiple media in their daily lives, and in different ways according to the specifics of the situation. This chapter assumes that people routinely reinvent, hybridize, converge and bridge technologies from one platform to another.

MAIN FOCUS OF THE CHAPTER

Three Examples of Participatory Environmental Initiatives

The three examples presented here were studied as part of two consecutive research projects (see Acknowledgements) on local participation in biodiversity and how information technologies have affected this participation. They share the same approach, namely one that is based on qualitative methods and ethnographically informed. In all cases, the authors draw on multiple data sources: semi-structured interviews with key actors, observations, analysis of communication materials (such as flyers or books) and analysis of online activity (such as websites or social media presence).

Established in 2009, **Alerta Ambiental** encourages citizens of the Madre de Dios region of Peru to monitor activities in their environment. The non-profit association works with citizens to signal illegal deforestation and mining activities, document the extent of the problem by compiling a database and provide a reliable, anonymous channel for treating complaints and ensuring prompt follow-up. Its actions exert pressure on local and national authorities to take action and increase visibility of the damage done to the environment beyond the Madre de Dios region. In 2014, it added an online platform to its activities and greatly increased its media presence. The platform makes visible and public the extent and effects of deforestation or illegal mining activities in this remote region by sharing maps, photographs and associated information online. New allegations and weekly case updates on the platform are also posted on Facebook and Twitter, and sent to strategic allies and especially journalists, who can further publicize what is happening in Madre de Dios. The platform also aggregates information: working together, citizens can add information or comment on what is written and thus improve the content of the database.

Founded in 2004, the **Observatoire Naturaliste des Écosystèmes Méditerranéens (ONEM)** is a non-profit association whose mission is to increase naturalistic and environmental knowledge in the Mediterranean region, to serve as a point of reference for naturalists, researchers and managers of environmental services in the region, and to provide accessible scientific information to the general public. ONEM is thus strongly anchored in a territory, the Mediterranean region, but paradoxically it coordinates its activities exclusively over the Internet and has no physical location or paid staff. The web site is based on an open-source Wiki and integrates a cartography module. ONEM's principal activity is conducting species-specific "inquiries." Anyone can propose or participate in an inquiry on a Mediterranean species. Subjects are typically chosen with a view to enhancing the visibility of little known species and/or to increasing knowledge of poorly understood or poorly documented species. Participation is conceived of as a both an online and offline activity. Publishing advertisements in local newspapers and distributing paper flyers in local town halls and meeting places enable ONEM to reach a large, local public. Participants report their observations by completing an online form with details such as the date, exact location, number of specimens, as well as their names and contact information. Their observations and names then appear on an interactive map.

People remain most interested in their local environments – species distributions in their municipalities, or environmental changes near their homes. The example of **the protection of threatened and/or vulnerable plants in Quebe**c shows how surveying, photographing and georeferencing enhances understanding of local environmental issues, and leads to public engagement for some. In the pursuit of their interests, amateur botanists interact frequently with professionals and authorities in both face-to-face and technologically mediated settings. FloraQuebeca is a nonprofit association oriented toward the public, decision-makers and enterprises. It is active both offline – through outings, workshops and meetings, and online – through Facebook and their website, which has both a public and a member-reserved area. Many members of FloraQuebeca also belong to a Facebook group dedicated to the rare plants of Quebec. Posting photos is the main practice of this group, to entice other members to identify a plant, and/or to share their outings.

Local Engagement in Environmental Issues

A sense of place comes out strongly in all three of our examples. These findings are in line with previous research results that indicate that place attachment continues to be strong or may have even grown in recent years (Lewicka, 2011). In Madre de Dios, citizens file reports about abuses to their environmental rights. In some cases, the land has been in the family for generations. But this is not only an individual relationship. Although only the landowner can file an official complaint, members of local communities at large are also encouraged to participate in signalling and documenting abuses or illegal activities taking place around them. In this sense, Alerta Ambiental participates in environmental monitoring activities, beyond its legal actions. To this end, the platform distinguishes between "alerts," for which a legal process is underway, and "news," violations that are not piloted through the courts by their judicial partner, and enables all those in the region to voice their matters of concern.

Alerta Ambiental was founded and its orientation and strategy established in close collaboration with the region's citizens, and the Tambotapa Management committee. The region's legal aid office is staffed by people who have been in the area for nearly ten years, and who understand the realities of the local population. This shared history is extremely important in creating the climate of trust necessary to enable people to come forward (sometimes despite threats to their personal safety).

ONEM is also strongly anchored territorially, in the Mediterranean region generally and in people's local environments more specifically. ONEM inquiries are local/regional in scope. Participants are encouraged to explore the natural world around them and to post their observations on a dynamic map of the region. ONEM thus proposes an activity in which the "field" component is primordial, and for which the online platform is a complement. Species are chosen with a view to reaching the largest number of potentially interested people, so that over half of contributors are the general public, as opposed to more knowledgeable naturalists. This choice of easily identifiable species encourages not only participation but also appropriation and increased knowledge of the surrounding environment. What is more, being able to see one's own observation recorded on the map also incited people to revisit the site, either to confirm its presence or to compare with other observations.

The protection of rare plants in Quebec involves a variety of actors, at different levels, all of whose actions are anchored in or directed at this specific region. Among them are federal, provincial and municipal institutions, a university research center, and the general public, both individually and organised in associations. For instance, FloraQuebeca brings together professional and amateurs botanists as well as public authorities. This association often organises outings that may imply travel within Quebec; however, those interested in rare plants also take walks around their daily surroundings. The photos shared on the Facebook rare plants group result from this lived experience. They are not collected online from websites and do not represent the plant in general; rather, they are photos of rare plants actually growing in Quebec. Although Facebook posts tend to indicate the region or habitat, exact information on the location is not usually shared. In addition, even though collecting specimens is a key botanical practice and the only way to identify a plant beyond a shadow of a doubt, amateurs exercise prudence unless it is obviously a common plant.

Following Haywood (2014), the authors argue that place identification is visible in the way Quebecois feel responsible for the forests, bogs and fields they walk in, for the plants they photograph, and the ethical behaviour that is expected from all those attached to rare plants. In fact, concern with excessive harvesting for commercial purposes was behind the creation of FloraQuebeca. In Peru, communal place attachment allows for the building of trust and confidence in their joint effort (Haywood, 2014), both of which are necessary in order for people to contribute to a monitoring activity that may sometimes put them in danger. In the three cases analysed here, the understanding of individuals' attachment to their "places" requires attention to both social and physical factors (Lewicka, 2011), since their relation to nature itself seems to play a role in addition to the social ties each context fosters or is grounded upon (Overdevest et al., 2004).

In ONEM, for example, participants are accorded the status of "witnesses." In some parts of the site, observations are not referred to as data but as testimonials or evidence (*témoignages*). Using this term keeps a bond between the individual and the data collected. "Contributors are not considered simple observers, inventors, or anonymous data contributors, but as eyewitnesses to the history of our natural heritage" (Presentation of a book on the Saga pedo inquiry, ONEM, 2007).[3] This stance acknowledges all contributions as significant.

Both Alerta Ambiental and the rare plants initiatives in Quebec appear to illustrate Danielsen et al.'s (2005) observation that people are most likely to engage in locally based monitoring when the thing being monitored is either under threat or provides them with direct benefit. For FloraQuebeca's president, one of the services this association can provide is a more precise and localised knowledge of plant rarity in Quebec, while the members of the Facebook group often highlight that the plants are "theirs" and promote inventories that may inform conservation initiatives. In turn, Alerta Ambiental was born of the observation that people living outside the Madre de Dios region did not necessarily know the extent of illegal mining, and deforestation activities in that region. Even within Madre de Dios, inhabitants of one area might be aware of local problems, but unaware that the same thing was going on in the next valley. The site's map provides clear evidence of how widespread the problems are. Its process of applying pressure to following up on complaints will be discussed more fully in the section on visibility, but it is also a question of increasing awareness and enabling citizens to act locally to effect changes on a larger scale.

One of the important elements is the scientific interest and also to what extent the inquiry will lead the general public to better appropriate knowledge about nature in the Mediterranean region. ... Most of the inquiries are on species that are relatively easy to identify. On very, very specific things, we've tended to respond negatively because we think that the [specialists] who want to conduct such specific inquiries ... have other means to conduct their inquiry. We're using tools for the general public that aren't really adapted for ultra-specialized things. That's not where we've put our energy. (ONEM coordinator, personal communication, March 2, 2010)

ONEM's experience with the Saga pedo inquiry (also described in Heaton et al., 2016) is consistent with Brofeldt et al., (2018) in which local data collection methods enabled scaling up to determine large-scale changes in habitat area. On the other hand, the ONEM coordinator's statement above supports Danielson et al (2005)'s argument that local methods are not well suited to studies in which identification or census of species are difficult to perform with sufficient exactitude. However, in some cases, local knowledge can be an asset in the search for hard to find species, a fact that is recognised by Quebec's Ministère du Développement durable, de l'Environnement et de la Lutte contre les changements climatiques (Ministry of sustainable development, environment and fight against climate change - MDDELCC) as they reach out to associations like FloraQuebeca for observational data on endangered or vulnerable plants for official purposes. As Wynne (1992) observed with Cumbrian farmers, amateurs sometimes know their forests and fields better than professional botanists and play a key role in identifying the presence of rare plants close to home.

Since I went to the woods every day, I came across rare plants, one of which was very rare. And I talked to my sister-in-law and she said 'Call so and so, a local botanist... It isn't possible'... So I asked him to come and see. I had found wild leek, I had found ginseng... and right next to my house, a very rare orchid... So, I took him to see the ginseng, he couldn't believe it, it's the second most important in Quebec and there's almost none left. Afterwards, when he saw the wild leek, he couldn't believe it. And when he saw the orchid, he said 'It's the first time I find an amateur who shows me all this. You have to come with us to FloraQuebeca'. (FloraQuebeca member, personal communication, March 6, 2014)

Popular guides do not include information on many rare plants and, as a result, amateur botanists frequently create their own guides. One of the advantages of becoming a member of FloraQuebeca is access to identification keys for difficult genera that have been created by other members (FloraQuebeca, 2015). Although professional botanists are also involved in this association, it is important to note that such shared knowledge is strongly anchored on observations made locally. The unique sense of place of participants shapes and influences the scientific knowledge that is produced in participatory science programs and similar initiatives in which the public is asked for contributions. The federal government and municipalities, for instance, rely on FloraQuebeca members to help with flora inventories organised by biologists, namely by asking them to participate in intensive biological surveys carried out over a short period of time. Such bioblitz initiatives are also announced on the rare plants Facebook group. In the specific case of rare plant information collected by FloraQuebeca members and other Quebecois, this shared local ecological knowledge, is pivotal in helping scientists and authorities to better understand local experiences and priorities (Buytaert et al., 2014; Wynne, 1992). In France and in Quebec, biodiversity inquiries and observations aim to promote awareness of local issues while also benefiting from local expertise. In all of the cases discussed here, participants' locations define their possibility to contribute to existing knowledge on deforestation, rare plants and different animals. In addition, the participants build their own capacities by taking part in these activities.

ONEM's and FloraQuebeca's strategies closely follow Danielsen et al.'s (2005) recommendation to keep locally-based monitoring as simple and locally appropriate as possible for it to be sustainable. They further stress the importance of increasing participants' abilities in field techniques and species identification, as well as enlarging their understanding of potential data uses. Again, this is not neglected by FloraQuebeca whose mission statement includes raising awareness, educating and increasing knowledge on the indigenous flora of Quebec. They pursue this goal through publishing educational articles, organising workshops and outings, as well as with information made available through their website.

Crall et al. (2015) conclude from their study of invasive species' distribution that local initiatives are most useful when data synergies are in operation, that is, when they can be integrated with larger scale databases to help "fill in the gaps." Similarly, in Quebec local observations of rare plants feed governmental databases that provide an overview of the situation of those plants at the provincial level. The policy or scientific value of a dataset is related to its trustworthiness and credibility (Darch, 2014) and several methods to validate data and to control quality are used in online participatory initiatives

(Kosmala, et al. 2016). Although the quality of volunteer-generated data has often been questioned (Crall et al., 2015), simple protocols and adequate training have been shown to improve reliability (Danielsen et al., 2017). The Quebec ministry's Centre de données sur le patrimoine naturel (Natural Heritage Data Center), for instance, provided a template for registering observations of rare plants. FloraQuebeca, in turn, added additional information to the request posted on their website to avoid confusion on how to indicate geographical coordinates, therefore trying to pre-empt potential accuracy problems that could compromise the rare plants dataset.

Data quality is also a concern for ONEM inquiries, particularly given the simplicity of the online form. ONEM uses two types of data validation. Firstly, since participants see their contributions immediately and raw data are always available on the site, "if someone notices something that seems wrong, he can [bring it up]. So validity is ensured by a permanent collective monitoring" (Inquiry coordinator, personal communication, July 13, 2011). The accuracy of observational data identified as questionable can then be confirmed use a variety of measures, such as providing a photo of the species, personal knowledge of participant skills/expertise and direct contact with participants about unusual reports (Heaton et al., 2016).

Exactitude is of the utmost importance for Alerta Ambiental, given the judicial nature of the complaint process. An alert appears on Alerta Ambiental only after it has been carefully verified and validated. Local authorities, legal representative and the Management committee will visit the site with the complainant, take photos or video and geolocate it on a map. The process is well established and the fact that stakeholders physically visit the site together provides additional validity. Others may subsequently add photos or information to enrich the case documentation.

The three cases discussed here share many points in common with the benefits assessment made by Danielsen et al. (2005) regarding community-based monitoring schemes: from improving relations between stakeholders and government authorities, enhancing awareness on environmental issues and promoting changes in attitude, increasing law compliance concerning the protection of natural resources, to empowering local residents. Subsequent studies (Brammler et al., 2016; Brofeldt et al., 2018) have also found that community-based schemes facilitate community involvement in data analysis and interpretation as well as the implementation of management actions. Teaching members of FloraQuebeca and the general public to better identify plants, promoting community monitoring, like Alerta Ambiental, and fostering collective validation, as ONEM does, enables the public to contribute high quality information to surveys that then can be used by both scientists and authorities, hence informing decision and policy-making on environmental issues. These volunteers become more engaged with the protection of their environment, in a very direct and practical way. The fact that, through those activities, participants deepen their knowledge on conservation matters allows environmental issues to be made personal, "owned." In this sense, Hungerford (1996) argues that individuals take more of a citizen responsibility towards issues when they fully understand what is at stake. Civic engagement concerning the environment is hence connected with knowledge, much like citizen participation in general (Milner, 2002).

The Relation Between Online and Offline Modes of Communication

Although it is impossible to ignore the role of place and the locality of the engagement discussed in this chapter, offline communication channels and information resources are used together with online channels and resources, accessible worldwide. Online and offline modes work together, as all three cases use multiple channels for exchanging information and interaction.

For ONEM, participation is conceived of as both an online and offline activity. Observing nature is, by definition, a local activity. Publishing advertisements in local newspapers and distributing paper flyers in local town halls and meeting places enabled ONEM to reach a large, local public, many of whom were not constantly connected to the Internet. While ONEM does not use social media, it is integrated within a network of environmental associations in the region, some of which have a strong online presence. As in FloraQuebeca, participants and coordinators often belong to other groups, and people often learn of ONEM's activities by word-of-mouth. While actual field observations are a major part of participating in an ONEM inquiry, participants also use an online form to register their observations. What is more, their experience is enhanced by consulting various resources available on the Internet, such as discussion lists on their preferred species.

The other cases make more intensive use of digital media. Alerta Ambiental's "news" section serves to relay and amplify news originating outside the platform. News may originate in traditional media such as television reports, government documents (such as statistics on deforestation), or legal proceedings that have been initiated elsewhere. They may also concern violations in nature reserves whose public status makes a private judicial complaint impossible. Interested parties can also subscribe to an electronic newsletter sent by email, and the association sends regular press releases to selected journalists and other important stakeholders. The platform's father NGO is actively involved in technical and policy discussions and seeks to promote environmental and social responsibility of enterprises and other social actors. To this end, this civil sector association has an important Web presence, including an environmental news website, a YouTube channel, as well as Facebook and Twitter profiles. Similarly, Alerta Ambiental amplifies its online presence through Facebook and Twitter. Thus, alerts may be publicized through a variety of channels, meeting people where they are, instead of expecting them to visit their website. Yet, Alerta Ambiental draws its information and credibility largely from offline interactions. Citizens who want to file a complaint may do so on the platform or in person at the legal office. Once a complaint exists, it is documented offline by site visits. Without previous knowledge and trust of the association's staff gained through face-to-face interaction over an extended period of time, it is unlikely that Madre de Dios inhabitants would file complaints, given the potential dangers involved.

FloraQuebeca extends its website's reach through a Facebook page and offline interactions remain very important, especially in the outings it organises or associates with as well as in the conferences, training workshops and courses it sets up to improve public knowledge and awareness. There are also two long-standing events: an annual assembly (which includes morning conferences and an afternoon general assembly to discuss association matters) and an annual weekend botanical rendez-vous. FloraQuebeca holds its annual assembly simultaneously in Montreal and Quebec City – with a live feed between the two locations. In 2018, FloraQuebeca organised its first annual conference that included three sections: presentations by government representatives of the MDDELCC, academic research and workshops focused on increasing knowledge about the flora and plant families of a specific region. The following edition repeated this three-part model. In terms of online resources, members of FloraQuebeca as well as anyone interested in Quebec's flora can join a mailing list which allows them to exchange information. It is not just an announcements list, email is used in practical ways: "For instance, say someone finds a plant but he doesn't know its name. He needs help to identify it. He sends an email and everyone receives it. Anyone who wants to react to the message can do so. But it isn't an obligation" (FloraQuebeca member, personal communication, November 16, 2014).

Only members can publish and comment in the Facebook group on Quebec's endangered flora, but everyone can see the group's publications and discussions. Like FloraQuebeca, this group has a strong pedagogical mission. The rare plants Facebook group sharing practices and the activities and resources offered by FloraQuebeca are part of their members' "free-choice learning," defined as "the learning that individuals engage in throughout their lives when they have the opportunity to choose what, where, when and with whom, to learn" (Falk, Storksdieck, & Dierking, 2007, p. 456), and that plays a key role in enhancing public understanding of science. In this online group, correct plant identification is taken very seriously: quizzes based on members' photos are published regularly; the group managers validate the answers and often add resources to provide more information on rare plants. Such resources include the Database of Vascular Plants of Canada – VASCAN (on which the Facebook group founder collaborates) or Go Botany, an identification aid developed by the New England Wild Flower Society, university and government websites, scientific articles and Wikipedia (especially for information on explorers and collectors). Members also refer to this group for advice as part of their prudent approach to collecting. In addition, the group shares announcements from associations like FloraQuebeca or about recent flora publications as well as news articles and documentaries.

FloraQuebeca and Alerta Ambiental balance offline and online interactions: participants engage in what Büscher (2016) terms "Nature 2.0" in addition to their physical involvement. This intertwining is part of a large movement, as social media have become an important part of conservation organizations' communication and outreach strategies, including offering engagement possibilities to potential supporters. Büscher (2016, p. 728) argues that, beyond the "possibility of enabling conservation supporters to partly co-create the (information about) natures and conservation they want to 'consume'… [nature 2.0] also includes sharing, liking and linking these through social media, and indeed captures the full spectrum of possibilities for interactive online communication and action." However, the same value is not always assigned to online and offline activity. Despite many members expressing pleasure in sharing their photos and participating in online exchanges on Quebec's endangered flora, others believe that practices such as these do not constitute actual engagement in the protection of these plants.

What is more, individuals who are engaged in environmental activities tend to be engaged in more than one project (Hines, Hungerford, & Tomera, 1987). Some FloraQuebeca members are also volunteers at the Marie-Victorin Herbarium and have multiple involvements in nature activities and environmental protection, while ONEM contributors are active in other environmental associations, such as the Écologistes de l'Euzière. This multiple participation opens the door for multiple interactions and cross-fertilization across projects (Overdevest et al., 2004). For instance, the Marie-Victorin volunteers are extremely aware of the importance of their contribution for understanding larger trends and analyzing environmental issues. In a media-ecological perspective, engagement of this type follows a logic of connective (rather than collective) action and is greatly facilitated by the array of digitally mediated social networks that organize and coordinate. "In this connective logic, taking public action or contributing to a common good becomes an act of personal expression and recognition or self-validation achieved by sharing ideas and actions in trusted relationships" (Bennett & Segerberg, 2012, pp. 752–3).

Beyond the obvious individual benefits of integrating online and offline communication, the use of digital media by environmental organizations opens up new possibilities. Among them are the ability to act more effectively. As noted above, digital platforms and social media play an important role in coordinating and organizing action. Heaton, Millerand and Proulx (2011) have shown how their centralization and aggregation of content allows them to act as resources for subsequent action in some cases and to coordinate action more directly in others. ONEM's and Alerta Ambiental's databases clearly fall into the first category, while the calendar and list of upcoming events on FloraQuebeca's website is an example of the latter. Brofledt et al. (2018) and Brammler et al. (2016) both found that the use of digital technologies helped generate community interest in environmental monitoring. What is more, Brofeldt et al. (2018) also found evidence that, combined with ease of use, they helped maintain that interest, encouraging ongoing participation. Finally, the rapidity associated with digital formats allows data to be treated more rapidly, reducing delays in reporting results and allowing concrete management actions (Brofledt et al., 2018).

One of the most salient features of digital media use by environmental organizations is the change in the conditions for visibility of environmental politics (Cox & Schwartze, 2015). They have the potential to raise awareness and create spaces for exchange, thus helping increase visibility and distribute information independently, potentially changing the relationships with traditional mews media. Alerta Ambiental's *raison d'être* is visibility. It is described as a megaphone for environmental complaints. To this end, it also reaches out to traditional media, for instance national newspapers have sometimes picked up a story from the platform. In seeking to give wide visibility to environmental destruction and its human consequences, it follows the rationale that the citizens of Madre de Dios need the support of all Peruvians to pressure the relevant authorities to deal with complaints efficiently and rapidly. This public pressure is brought to bear in multiple ways.

It may seem paradoxical but perhaps, I don't know if we planned it to be like that, Alerta Ambiental is more useful outside Madre de Dios. Although it has Madre de Dios in mind, it's designed to raise awareness on things people have no idea are happening there and to lead to public pressure by the citizens, but also from public officials to public officials. In this sense, many of the public officials that can exert pressure are not there [...] Rather, it's intended for the ministry of the environment, the environment people to become aware of what is going on and lobby to increase the budget. [...] It isn't as important, to our mind, that a lot of people in Madre de Dios know about or follow Alerta Ambiental. (Alerta Ambiental member, personal communication, January 8, 2015)

Alerta Ambiental's efforts seem to have born fruit. The First International Conference on Environmental Justice took place in Madre de Dios in 2017. This event included the announcement of an historical decision: the creation in Madre de Dios of the first Peruvian court specialized in environmental issues. These actions are linked to the "Madre de Dios Pact for Environmental Justice," a document including ten commitments to improve environmental justice in Peru, and Madre de Dios in particular.

In contrast, for FloraQuebeca and the rare plants Facebook group, there is no expressed intent to widen visibility beyond Quebec. Sharing photographs, observation notes and accounts of the outings aims to make plants visible locally, ultimately to enhance the idea of responsibility for one's environment. Therefore, the goal is not to show the plants to the world, but to make Quebecois proud of their flora. As put by FloraQuebeca's coordinator, "The issue is always the protection of the habitats and our heritage" (personal communication, February 27, 2014). The Facebook group on rare plants has a wide variety of material available both offline (e.g. publications or workshops) and online (e.g. databases, articles, official websites). Although these resources are both local and global, they mainly aim to improve local knowledge on Quebec's rare plants, as a large majority of the members of this Facebook group are indeed from this region. The description of the group also points to a more local visibility being sought, even if it is on a global digital social network: "We discuss **our** finds/discoveries, things to help **us** identify **our** endangered or vulnerable species or those that might soon be designated as such" (emphasis added,

Facebook page, May 13, 2015). Yet, it does not mean that international collaborations are not desired. FloraQuebeca would like to have stronger ties with TelaBotanica, a francophone network of amateur and professional botanists. In addition, individuals try to extend their connections throughout the territory and even beyond Quebec's borders. FloraQuebeca members curate their own websites and interact with people from different countries, making them feel they are part of an "extraterritorial network" (FloraQuebeca member, personal communication, November 16, 2014).

Two points in particular concerning visibility are particularly important. First is the role of dynamic maps and the visualization of geographic location. In Madre de Dios, maps allow people both within and outside the region to visualize the extent of destruction and to localize problematic activities. Illegal activities are localized with one of three colored "pins" (mining, deforestation, change of land use) and superimposed upon an aerial photograph that can be zoomed. This, combined with photographs taken onsite, provides precise, eloquent evidence of the state of the jungle.

Of the three examples, FloraQuebeca's cartographic visualisation tool offers the least information. Its "online observation journal" makes it possible for the public to see the locations of past botanical outings and "rendez-vous," superimposed on a Google map. However, it only offers the name of the site and the date of the activity; it does not even indicate which activity it refers to. On the other hand, ONEM'S dynamic map lists the details of every participant's contributions on the inquiry's website. In addition to emphasizing the value of participation, this feature greatly enhances the visibility of individual contributions. Several coordinators affirm that the visibility of contributions on the interactive map reinforced participation.

That's what people tell us ... In ONEM feedback is immediate. You enter an observation on the map and the next second you see your point on the map. Your name and your observation are shown in a [popup] extension. And that's totally innovative, because in most participatory science programs, the general public contributes observations, but these observations aren't valued later. They're usually transformed [aggregated]. Whereas, in ONEM every contribution is put online and is accessible to everyone – as is. It's the result of someone's work and it is preserved on the site in the same way it was entered. (Co-founder of ONEM, personal communication, July 13, 2011)

This is consistent with eBird's experience that the number of individuals submitting data nearly tripled when its website was upgraded with new features that allowed personalized views of their own observations and comparison with those of others (Bonney et al., 2009).

Secondly, there is the question of selective visibility. While Alerta Ambiental seeks widespread media coverage and visibility outside the Madre de Dios regions, it downplays its presence within the region. To protect the security of citizens and Alerta employees within the region, the parent association's logo is not displayed on the platform, and the names of complainants are often withheld. This has not prevented complainants from receiving threats. Visibility can be a danger not only to the people involved, but to the natural environment they are in fact trying to protect. As mentioned above, participants take great care when sharing information on rare and endangered plants. Recommendations not to disclose exact information on Facebook are recurrent, and FloraQuebeca offers very limited information in its online observation journal.

CONCLUSION

This chapter has argued that civic engagement and participation in environmental advocacy transcend the type of media used, and that one interaction format nourishes the other in many cases. In this media-ecological view, social media are but one part of the picture, and it is the goal, not the availability or features of the media "tool," that drives action. This is consistent with what has been learned about the use of social media in social movements, such as the Arab Spring or the Occupy protests.

In the cases discussed here, online communication channels and resources facilitate engagement, in part by organizing information and providing tools for people to organize themselves. In a logic of connective action, social media and Web-based platforms can serve as powerful instruments for coordination. This may be important locally, as well as on a global scale. Digital media also significantly alter the visibility of both local actions and of the resulting data. They can be used to amplify or extend the reach of a message beyond its local context, thus increasing awareness and potentially enrolling other/more supporters. In fact, studies of social media tend to focus on the ever-widening web of connections and the global reach of such platforms and services.

Today's media landscape offers many opportunities for increased civic participation. In the specific context of environmental engagement, it is important not to lose sight of its local, concrete character, however. The environment is by definition a place-based phenomenon. It is difficult to conceive of significant environmental engagement in the abstract, dissociated from specific places. Local knowledge and local interactions, often face-to-face, play a vital role. The cases presented here illustrate how volunteers can become involved in protecting the environment in very direct, practical ways. This in turn may lead to enhanced awareness of environmental issues as participants deepen their knowledge on conservation matters and assume "ownership" of environmental issues. Civic engagement concerning the environment is thus intimately connected with knowledge, much like citizen participation in general. It may also improve relations between stakeholders and government authorities and produce a sense of collective empowerment. In terms of challenges, environmental organisations must strike a fine balance between online and offline, local and global, as well as in terms of sharing information. As we saw, given the sensitivity of these issues, too much visibility can be detrimental to conservation efforts.

Taken together, the cases described in this chapter suggest the possibility of challenging established ways of working in environmental communication and policy. Long before the advent of social media, Bucchi (1996) suggested that the communication of science at the popular level has this potential since it does not share the same constraints and conventions of scientific work and communication directed at experts. Using a variety of communication channels, including social media and online platforms, ONEM's inquiries, Alerta Ambiental's platform and rare plants initiatives in Quebec are fostering engagement and communicating science by encouraging participation in it.

ACKNOWLEDGMENT

The examples presented here were studied as part of two research projects: "La Co-évolution des outils et des expertises: le cas de l'organisation Outils-Réseaux" (R0017335) and "Reconfigurations of scientific work: contributions of amateurs and information technologies in biodiversity" (R-N303-02838). We would like to thank our colleagues, in particular our research assistants, Amel Gherbi and Alejandra Paniagua, the various organization members who spoke with us, as well as our funding source for these projects, the Social Sciences and Humanities Research Council of Canada.

REFERENCES

Baym, N. K., Zhang, Y. B., & Lin, M.-C. (2004). Social interactions across media interpersonal communication on the internet, telephone and face-to-face. *New Media & Society*, *6*(3), 299–318. doi:10.1177/1461444804041438

Bennett, W. L., & Segerberg, A. (2012). The logic of connective action: Digital media and the personalization of contentious politics. *Information Communication and Society*, *15*(5), 739–768. doi:10.1080/1369118X.2012.670661

Bjur, J., Schrøder, K., & Hasebrink, U. (2014). Cross-media use: Unfolding complexities in contemporary audiencehood. In N. Carpentier, K. C. Schrøder, & L. Hallet (Eds.), *Audience Transformations. Shifting Audience Positions in Late Modernity* (pp. 15–29). London: Routledge.

Bonney, R., Cooper, C. B., & Ballard, H. (2016). The Theory and Practice of Citizen Science: Launching a New Journal. *Citizen Science: Theory and Practice*, *1*(1), 1. doi:10.5334/cstp.65

Bonney, R., Cooper, C. B., Dickinson, J., Kelling, S., Phillips, T., Rosenberg, K. V., & Shirk, J. (2009). Citizen science: A developing tool for expanding science knowledge and scientific literacy. *Bioscience*, *59*(11), 977–984. doi:10.1525/bio.2009.59.11.9

Brammler, J. R., Brunet, N. D., Burton, A. C., Cuerrier, A., Danielsen, F., Dewan, K., & … . (2016). The role of digital data entry in participatory environmental monitoring. *Conservation Biology*, *30*(6), 1277–1287. doi:10.1111/cobi.12727 PMID:27032080

Brehm, J. M., Eisenhauer, B. W., & Stedman, R. C. (2013). Environmental Concern: Examining the Role of Place Meaning and Place Attachment. *Society & Natural Resources*, *26*(5), 522–538. doi:10.1080/08941920.2012.715726

Brofeldt, S., Argyriou, D., Turreira-García, N., Meilby, H., Danielsen, F., & Theilade, I. (2018). Community-Based Monitoring of Tropical Forest Crimes and Forest Resources Using Information and Communication Technology – Experiences from Prey Lang, Cambodia. *Citizen Science: Theory and Practice*, *3*(2), 4. doi:10.5334/cstp.129

Bucchi, M. (1996). When scientists turn to the public: Alternative routes in science communication. *Public Understanding of Science (Bristol, England)*, *5*(4), 375–394. doi:10.1088/0963-6625/5/4/005

Bucher, T., & Helmond, A. (2017). The affordances of social media platforms. In J. Burgess, T. Poell, & A. Marwick (Eds.), *The SAGE handbook of social media* (pp. 233–253). London: Sage.

Büscher, B. (2016). Nature 2.0: Exploring and theorizing the links between new media and nature conservation. *New Media & Society*, *18*(5), 726–743. doi:10.1177/1461444814545841

Buytaert, W., Zulkafli, Z., Grainger, S., Acosta, L., Alemie, T. C., Bastiaensen, J., ... Zhumanova, M. (2014). Citizen science in hydrology and water resources: Opportunities for knowledge generation, ecosystem service management, and sustainable development. *Frontiers of Earth Science*, *2*(26), 1–21. doi:10.3389/feart.2014.00026

Cantrill, J. G. (2016). On Seeing "Places" for What They Are, and Not What We Want Them to Be. *Environmental Communication*, *10*(4), 525–538. doi:10.1080/17524032.2015.1048268

Cornwell, M. L., & Campbell, L. M. (2012). Co-producing conservation and knowledge: Citizen-based sea turtle monitoring in North Carolina, USA. *Social Studies of Science*, *42*(1), 101–120. doi:10.1177/0306312711430440

Cox, R., & Schwarze, S. (2015). The Media/communication strategies of environmental pressure groups and NGOs. In A. Hansen & R. Cox (Eds.), *The Routledge Handbook of Environment and Communication* (pp. 73–85). London: Routledge.

Crall, A. W., Jarnevich, C. S., Young, N. E., Panke, B. J., Renz, M., & Stohlgren, T. J. (2015). Citizen science contributes to our knowledge of invasive plant species distributions. *Biological Invasions*, *17*(8), 2415–2427. doi:10.100710530-015-0885-4

Danielsen, F., Burgess, N. D., & Balmford, A. (2005). Monitoring Matters: Examining the Potential of Locally-based Approaches. *Biodiversity and Conservation*, *14*(11), 2507–2542. doi:10.100710531-005-8375-0

Danielsen, F., Enghoff, M., Magnussen, E., Mustonen, T., Degteva, A., Hansen, K. K., & Slettemark, Ø. (2017). Citizen Science Tools for Engaging Local Stakeholders and Promoting Local and Traditional Knowledge in Landscape Stewardship. In C. Bieling & T. Plieninger (Eds.), *The Science and Practice of Landscape Stewardship* (pp. 80–98). Cambridge, UK: Cambridge University Press. doi:10.1017/9781316499016.009

Dickinson, J. L., Crain, R. L., Reeve, H. K., & Schuldt, J. P. (2013). Can evolutionary design of social networks make it easier to be "green"? *Trends in Ecology & Evolution*, *28*(9), 561–569. doi:10.1016/j.tree.2013.05.011 PMID:23787089

Dimitrova, D., Mok, D., & Wellman, B. (2015). Changing Ties in a Far-Flung, Multidisciplinary Research Network The Case of GRAND. *The American Behavioral Scientist*, *59*(5), 599–616. doi:10.1177/0002764214556803

Elbroch, M., Mwampamba, T. H., Santos, M. J., Zylberberg, M., Liebenberg, L., Minye, J., ... Reddy, E. (2011). The Value, Limitations, and Challenges of Employing Local Experts in Conservation Research. *Conservation Biology*, *25*(6), 1195–1202. doi:10.1111/j.1523-1739.2011.01740.x PMID:21966985

Ellis, R., & Waterton, C. (2004). Environmental citizenship in the making: The participation of volunteer naturalists in UK biological recording and biodiversity policy. *Science & Public Policy, 31*(2), 95–105. doi:10.3152/147154304781780055

Falk, J. H., Storksdieck, M., & Dierking, L. D. (2007). Investigating public science interest and understanding: Evidence for the importance of free-choice learning. *Public Understanding of Science (Bristol, England), 16*(4), 455–469. doi:10.1177/0963662506064240

FloraQuebeca. (2015). Devenir membre ou renouveler votre adhésion. *FloraQuebeca.* Retrieved June 16, 2015, from http://www.floraquebeca.qc.ca/a-propos/devenir-membre/

Hampton, K., & Wellman, B. (2002). The not so global village of Netville. In B. Wellman & C. Haythornthwaite (Eds.), *The Internet in everyday life* (pp. 345–371). Oxford, UK: Blackwell. doi:10.1002/9780470774298.ch12

Hasebrink, U., & Hepp, A. (2017). How to research cross-media practices? Investigating media repertoires and media ensembles. *Convergence (London), 23*(4), 362–377. doi:10.1177/1354856517700384

Haywood, B. K. (2014). A "Sense of Place" in Public Participation in Scientific Research. *Science Education, 98*(1), 64–83. doi:10.1002ce.21087

Haywood, B. K., Parrish, J. K., & Dolliver, J. (2016). Place-based and data-rich citizen science as a precursor for conservation action. *Conservation Biology, 30*(3), 476–486. doi:10.1111/cobi.12702 PMID:27110934

Heaton, L., Millerand, F., Dias da Silva, P., & Proulx, S. (Eds.). (2018). *La reconfiguration du travail scientifique en biodiversité: pratiques amateurs et technologies numériques.* Montréal: Presses de l'Université de Montréal.

Heaton, L., Millerand, F., Liu, X., & Crespel, É. (2016). Participatory Science: Encouraging public engagement in ONEM. *International Journal of Science Education. Part B, 6*(1), 1–22. doi:10.1080/21548455.2014.942241

Heaton, L., Millerand, F., & Proulx, S. (2011). *The Role of Collaborative Tools in Making Coordination Sustainable : The Case of TelaBotanica.* Presented at the *International Communication Association Annual Conference*, Boston, MA.

Hines, J. M., Hungerford, H. R., & Tomera, A. N. (1987). Analysis and synthesis of research on responsible environmental behavior: A meta-analysis. *The Journal of Environmental Education, 18*(2), 1–8. doi:10.1080/00958964.1987.9943482

Hungerford, H. R. (1996). The Development of Responsible Environmental Citizenship: A Critical Challenge. *Journal of Interpretation Research, 1*(1), 25–37.

Jung, Y., & Lyytinen, K. (2014). Towards an ecological account of media choice: A case study on pluralistic reasoning while choosing email. *Information Systems Journal, 24*(3), 271–293. doi:10.1111/isj.12024

Kosmala, M., Wiggins, A., Swanson, A., & Simmons, B. (2016). Assessing data quality in citizen science. *Frontiers in Ecology and the Environment, 14*(10), 551–560. doi:10.1002/fee.1436

Kraut, R., Egido, C., & Galegher, J. (1988). Patterns of contact and communication in scientific research collaboration. In *Proceedings of the 1988 ACM conference on Computer-supported cooperative work* (pp. 1–12). New York: ACM. 10.1145/62266.62267

Lewicka, M. (2011). Place attachment: How far have we come in the last 40 years? *Journal of Environmental Psychology, 31*(3), 207–230. doi:10.1016/j.jenvp.2010.10.001

McKinley, D. C., Miller-Rushing, A. J., Ballard, H. L., Bonney, R., Brown, H., Cook-Patton, S. C., ... Ryan, S. F. (2017). Citizen science can improve conservation science, natural resource management, and environmental protection. *Biological Conservation, 208*, 15–28. doi:10.1016/j.biocon.2016.05.015

Meyrowitz, J. (2005). The Rise of Glocality: New senses of place and identity in the global village. In N. Kristóf (Ed.), *A Sense of Place: The global and the local in mobile communication* (pp. 21–30). Vienna: Passagen Verlag.

Milner, H. (2002). *Civic Literacy. How Informed Citizens Make Democracy Work*. Hanover: University Press of New England.

Mok, D., Wellman, B., & Carrasco, J. (2010). Does distance matter in the age of the Internet? *Urban Studies (Edinburgh, Scotland), 47*(13), 2747–2783. doi:10.1177/0042098010377363

Nascimento, S., Pereira, Â., & Ghezzi, A. (2014*). From Citizen Science to Do It Yourself Science. An annotated account of an on-going movement* (No. JRC93942). Luxembourg: Publications Office of the European Union. Retrieved April 7, 2015, from http://publications.jrc.ec.europa.eu/repository/handle/JRC93942

ONEM. (2007, December 9). *Un livre sur Saga pedo, pourquoi, quand, comment?* Retrieved June 26, 2015, from http://www.onem-france.org/saga/wakka.php?wiki=LivreArgumentaire

Overdevest, C., Orr, C. H., & Stepenuck, K. (2004). Volunteer stream monitoring and local participation in natural resource issues. *Human Ecology Review, 11*(2), 177–185.

Ramkissoon, H., Weiler, B., & Smith, L. D. G. (2012). Place attachment and pro-environmental behaviour in national parks: The development of a conceptual framework. *Journal of Sustainable Tourism, 20*(2), 257–276. doi:10.1080/09669582.2011.602194

Rice, R. E. (1993). Media appropriateness: Using social presence theory to compare traditional and new organizational media. *Human Communication Research, 19*(4), 451–484. doi:10.1111/j.1468-2958.1993.tb00309.x

Science Communication Unit, University of West of England. (2013*). Science for Environment Policy In-depth Report: Environmental Citizen Science*. European Commission DG Environment. Retrieved June 16, 2016, from http: //ec.europa.eu/science-environment-policy

Steele, F. (1981). *The sense of place*. Boston: CBI Publishing.

Thiel, M., Penna-Díaz, M. A., Luna-Jorquera, G., Salas, S., Sellanes, J., & Stotz, W. (2014). Citizen scientists and marine research: volunteer participants, their contributions, and projection for the future. In R. N. Hughes, D. J. Hughes, & I. P. Smith (Eds.), *Oceanography and Marine Biology: An Annual Review* (Vol. 52, pp. 257–314). London: CRC Press. doi:10.1201/b17143-6

Trentelman, C. K. (2009). Place Attachment and Community Attachment: A Primer Grounded in the Lived Experience of a Community Sociologist. *Society & Natural Resources*, *22*(3), 191–210. doi:10.1080/08941920802191712

Trevino, L. K., Lengel, R. H., & Daft, R. L. (1987). Media symbolism, media richness, and media choice in organizations: A symbolic interactionist perspective. *Communication Research*, *14*(5), 553–574. doi:10.1177/009365087014005006

Vorkinn, M., & Riese, H. (2001). Environmental Concern in a Local Context The Significance of Place Attachment. *Environment and Behavior*, *33*(2), 249–263. doi:10.1177/00139160121972972

Wajcman, J., & Rose, E. (2011). Constant connectivity: Rethinking interruptions at work. *Organization Studies*, *32*(7), 941–961. doi:10.1177/0170840611410829

Walther, J. B. (1996). Computer-mediated communication impersonal, interpersonal, and hyperpersonal interaction. *Communication Research*, *23*(1), 3–43. doi:10.1177/009365096023001001

Wynne, B. (1992). Misunderstood misunderstanding: Social identities and public uptake of science. *Public Understanding of Science (Bristol, England)*, *1*(3), 281–304. doi:10.1088/0963-6625/1/3/004

ENDNOTES

1 The chapter does not explore the vast literature on framing of environmental issues and strategies for diffusion in the mass media (see Cox & Schwarze, 2015 for a review).

2 See, for example, Kraut et al. (1988) and Dimitrova et al. (2015) for explorations of geographic distance in scientific collaboration; and Earl and Kimport, (2011) on new media in social movements and civic engagement.

3 All quotes have been translated, from French in the cases of ONEM and Quebec rare plants and from Spanish for Alerta Ambiental.

Chapter 3
When Democratic Innovations Integrate Multiple and Diverse Channels of Social Dialogue:
Opportunities and Challenges

Paolo Spada
University of Southampton, UK

Giovanni Allegretti
Coimbra University, Portugal

ABSTRACT

This chapter explores the opportunities, limitations, and risks of integrating multiple channels of citizen engagement within a democratic innovation. Using examples and case studies of recent face-to-face and online multichannel democratic innovations, the authors challenge the emerging consensus that redundancy and diversification of venues of participation are always positively correlated with the success of democratic innovations. Applying their concrete experience in areas of the world in which a systemic organization of different channels of citizen participation exists, the authors provide guidelines for achieving better integration of multiple channels of social dialogue.

INTRODUCTION

In June 2017, the annual edition of the general Conference of the International Observatory of Participatory Democracy (IOPD), held in Montreal, dedicated an important space to participatory and consultation experiences "using a number of different channels simultaneously"[1] (p. 14). The topic, which also became the Centre of a special working group of IODP members on a permanent basis, inspired a wide survey carried on among the IODP cities by the "*Empatia*" project group[2] at the University of Coimbra (Portugal). Answering to the survey on the connections created between different channels of citizens involvement in their territories, 104 cities displayed the existence of a more or less developed "system"

DOI: 10.4018/978-1-7998-1828-1.ch003

that tries to coordinate and make interact different Democratic Innovations happening simultaneously or in temporal sequences within their administrative borders.

What above-mentioned photographs an interesting transformation taking place at the same time in different continents, which is giving a growing space to conceptualize and shape "systems" of Democratic Innovations, that previously often co-existed but rarely were coordinated, and somehow also need to be related to other forms of citizens engagements that develop bottom-up not only in the form of "participatory practices by invitation", but also in the form of "*practices of irruption*" (Blas & Ibarra, 2006) through which citizens and social movements struggle to conquer spaces where their voice could be heard. In this perspective, it seems that a new awareness has been growing global in last decade, that genuine "democratic innovations" – i.e. those capable of developing "democratic common goods" in a creative way – must be read as part of larger ecosystems of patterns of civic engagement in polity matters. According to this new wide-spreading approach, the same definition of Democratic Innovation seems to be slightly evolving, so that today they can be defined as experiences related to facilitation and increase of the access and the substantive participation, both through "institutions specifically designed to increase citizens' participation" (Smith, 2009) and also "through bottom-up experiences able to connect with institutional practices in the processes of policy-making and political decision-making" (Sorice, 2019).

Under this perspective, Democratic Innovations could be seen both as a large family of participatory practices by "invitation", including different tools that must be tailored to diverse contexts, and also a series of tensions with other forms of expression of citizen engagement, which develop independently from (of even in reaction to) those more formalized and institutionalized experiments. A similar vision must still be further elaborated and accepted, being that is not so obvious – as demonstrated by many cases in which public institutions tend to deny legitimacy (or even criminalize, sometimes) to all forms of citizens mobilizations that do not happen in a controllable framework or space pre-accepted by those institutions themselves.

In view of such variated panorama of interpretations (which is still not uniquely accepting to enlarge the domain of Democratic Innovations to a coexistent mix of top-down and bottom-up practices of civic engagement), in the next paragraphs we will continue to use the concept of Democratic Innovations to depict those processes and institutions "designed specifically to increase and deepen citizen participation in the political decision-making" (Smith, 2009), which are become an increasingly common feature of policymaking and governance building. In doing so, we declaredly would like to preserve the vision well expressed by the founding team of "Participedia", a global network of scholars that maps democratic innovations using a variety of new crowdsourcing methods: i.e. the conviction that the fast diffusion of democratic innovations represents "a transformation of democracy—one possibly as revolutionary as the development of the representative, party-based form of democracy that evolved out of the universal franchise."[3]

It is worth to underline, here, that some democratic innovations are very simple and involve a single public in a set of tasks. Examples of single channel democratic innovations could be the Town hall meetings (Bryan, 2003), many mini-publics (Smith & Ryan, 2014), issue-reporting digital platforms (Sjoberg, Mellon, & Peixoto, 2015) or participatory monitoring processes (Bjorkman & Svensson, 2007). Other democratic innovations, instead, are more complex and can be better understood as a system that integrates multiple channels of engagement, i.e., multiple online and/or offline spaces designed to promote the participation of a specific segment of the population. The most complex of these systems engage more than a million people (Aggio, & Sampaio, 2013). It is also important to stress that - while the existing literature has mostly investigated the interactions between democratic innovations and other existing institutions, both theoretically (Mansbridge et al., 2012) and empirically (Wampler, 2007), very little is known about the interactions of channels of engagement *within* a Democratic Innovation, or within an environment of coordinated Democratic Innovations.

Nevertheless, the few existing case studies on multichannel innovations highlight the potential benefits of these institutional designs (Best, Ribeiro, Matheus, & Vaz, 2010; Peruzzotti, Magnelli, & Peixoto, 2011). While up to now the experimental literature has focused on exploring the effects of small organizational features of a democratic innovation[4] (what we can view and we will refer to as the smallest 'LEGO® blocks' of a democratic innovation architecture), no experiment to date has investigated different sequences and integration mechanisms of such LEGO blocks. In sum, the current literature offers many insights into the macro-level interactions, and the effect of micro-design choices, but provides very little insight into the meso-level interactions.

Using a vast collection of recent and not-so-recent examples, this chapter aims at presenting an overview of the advantages and disadvantages of integrating multiple channels of engagement. Under such a perspective, it begins by offering a definition of channels of engagement and multichannel democratic innovations systematizing concepts developed by practitioners in recent years. In doing so, the authors make reference to (and expand) ideas developed by the literature on marketing to include and reinterpret some concepts developed in the democratic innovations literature.

The paper draws the majority of examples from three main families of democratic innovations that employ multiple channels of engagement: participatory budgeting processes (PBs), citizens' assemblies (CAs) and participatory systems (PS or CRMPs - citizens' relations management platforms). The first allows the participation of non-elected citizens in the conception and/or selection of public projects (Sintomer et al., 2013) and is today experimented in more than 7,700 public authorities worldwide (Dias, 2018). The second allows the participation of non-elected citizens in the conception or reform of a complex legislation (Warner and Pearse, 2008), while the third - and most recent - allows citizens to interact with multiple democratic innovations and government services from a single website. While the first two are well known and well analyzed by a vast international literature, participatory systems – at least up to now - have attracted little attention from the literature on Democratic Innovations. That is why we consider that the literature on marketing could offer a useful framework for analyzing customer relations management that can be used to analyze these complex innovations (Buttle, & Maklan 2008). Nevertheless, this literature requires significant adaption, otherwise it risks to induce a commodification of the idea of "citizens", together with an extreme simplification of the concept of democratic innovation as a mere arena for exchange of information between a producer a nd a consumer of services, knowledge data, etc. (Dutil, Howard, Langford 2008).

In line with want mentioned above, the majority of the examples that will be referred in this chapter are participatory spaces designed by governments and other techno-political organizations to involve citizen in decision-making (so *"invited spaces"* or *"participatory spaces by invitation"*, as we called them before, using Blas & Ibarra definition*)*. In fact, an in-depth analysis of multiple channels of engagement that can be activated within *"invented spaces"* (i.e. participatory spaces claimed by social movements – see Miraftab, 2004), is beyond the page limitations of this chapter. For a similar reason - since this chapter focuses on innovations designed specifically to deepen democracy - it does not discuss cases in which social movements and organizations leverage social networks as Twitter, Istagram or Facebook (as well as many other digital technologies) to deepen the intensity of democracy in their territories. Lastly, the authors would like to stress that a detailed overview of the interdisciplinary literature that analyzes the diffusion, variety and impact of the three families of innovations under consideration (PBs, CAs, and

PSs) is also beyond the scope of this paper. In fact, its main objective is that of leveraging these three families of examples to analyze the advantages and disadvantages of multichannel democratic innovations and to present the most common integration mechanisms.

In order to do so, a specific language to describe the phenomena we are interested in is needed. Thus, the next section introduces a series of definitions, that do not aspire to become a standard, but are a disposable tool useful to jumpstart the discussion and reduce the level of confusion that currently characterizes the debate on multichannel democratic innovations .The next section also introduces the definition of *action*, the smallest building block of an engagement channel, and then discusses *phases* and *cycles*, clusters of actions frequently used by academics and practitioners to describe the inner workings of complex innovations.

Following, the authors discuss the challenges/opportunities of integrating multiple channels of engagement, and present three different integration models: competition, regulation and separation. These models are not exhaustive of the variety of possible integration mechanisms, but they are common to the family of innovations the chapter analyzes. Then, a discussion of the findings is offered, together with some recommendations for effective integration of participatory channels, and an insight on further possible research.

IMAGINING THE "LEGO © BLOCKS" OF DEMOCRACY

Preliminary conceptualization of multichannel customer relations emerged at the end of the '90s (Holmsen, Palter, Simon, & Weberg, 1998; Stone, Hobbs, & Khaleeli, 2002), when academics were beginning to employ experiments to optimize messages and select the best medium to promote voting in elections (Green, & Gerber; 2000). The main result of the getting-out-to-vote (GOTV) literature was, and still is, that authentic dialogue is the most important element that motivates people to vote or participate in a campaign. Building upon such concepts the Obama campaigns of 2008 and 2012 showed the high potential of multichannel engagement across a variety of media (Hendrick and Denton, 2010; Creiss, 2012; Stromer-Galley, 2013; Bimber 2014). Since then, these practices have spread to charity campaigns worldwide and have entered popular internet culture generating a large grey literature (Issemberg 2012, Kapin and Ward 2013). This chapter adapts this body of ideas to the field of democratic innovations, introducing *themes and normative goals that are absent in the marketing and GOTV literature*.

In marketing, a channel is "a set of interdependent organizations and practices that allows and promotes the sales of goods or services" (Kotler & Armstrong, 2012). Multichannel marketing integrates such organizational practices across multiple channels, including advertising and customer relations. Multichannel advertising and customer relations have the objective of creating more or less authentic dialogic interactions with the public that has been consistently shown to have the most persuasive effect on people. Micro-targeting in advertising is the norm, nowadays. Global players as Amazon, Google and Facebook track users' available information to maximize the probability of inducing a purchase by customizing the products shown in their platforms. These firms employ a combination of randomized controlled trials, large observational data analysis and qualitative studies of customers' opinions to optimize messages and platform interfaces.[5] Different versions of the website are shown to users in different locations, and across a variety of platforms. Engagement in customer relations is also becoming more frequent. More and more, firms rely on community forums, Facebook and Twitter, to engage customers in complex discussions about past, current and future products.

Multichannel engagement goes one step further, and micro-targets entire participatory processes in which a segment of the public can collaborate with the public organization which develop the participatory process, to achieve a goal. Some of these processes are two-way vertical relations between participants and the organizers; some others are multi-way interactions in which participants collaborate both horizontally among themselves and vertically with the organization to generate an output of interest. The videogame industry is a pioneer of these engagement practices. For example, videogame companies often allow the most active participants in their community to shape small features of games in development. In some engagement processes (as happens in several participatory budgeting especially in Brazil and Spain), participants can even affect elements of the rules that govern the architecture and agenda of the process itself.

Using these examples, we could define a *channel of engagement as a combination of messages and participatory processes designed to encourage a specific behavior in a target public.* The previous definition is very broad, and purely procedural. It applies to a variety of purposes such as: selling goods and services; campaigning; petitioning; gathering volunteers; and crowdsourcing information, ideas and money. In what follows the authors will focus on the subset of multichannel engagement processes designed to deepen democracy — multichannel democratic innovations – so to shrink the field to which the above-mentioned definition will be applied.

Adapting Smith (2009) to this field, with could eventually define multichannel democratic innovations as institutions that integrate messages and participatory spaces targeted to different segments of the population in a system specifically designed to increase and deepen citizen participation in the political decision-making process.

MULTICHANNEL BEYOND MERE HYBRIDITY

The most common multichannel democratic innovations are hybrid consultation processes integrating online and offline venues of discussion targeted to different types of participants (Bittle, Haller, & Kadlek, 2009; Andersson, Burall, & Fennel, 2010; Gupta, Gouvier, & Gordon, 2012). However, multichannel democratic innovations should not be reduced to hybrid innovations that combine online and offline media. In fact, on one hand, face-to-face innovations can be multichannel. For example, the participatory budgeting of Lisbon and Cascais (in Portugal) organize public "actor-based" meetings with different rules (and even languages) for children, university students, architects and designers, elderly persons or immigrants: so, they target different segments of the population in different meetings, beyond those spaces of discussion that are neighborhood-based and, thus, devoted to every citizens who reside or work in each specific area of the urban fabric. The 2004 British Columbia Citizens' Assembly (Canada) alternated meetings that were open only to a randomly selected group of participants, with public meetings open to all (Warren & Pearse, 2008).

On the other hand, hybrid democratic innovations can be single channel; hybridization does not automatically create a new channel. For example, the District Eight PB process in New York City employs digital technologies to map the implementation of the winning projects, but such hybridization is just a data visualization tool that supports the participants' monitoring activity and does not create a separate channel of engagement.[6]

ACTIONS, PHASES AND CYCLES: OTHER ADDITIONAL LEGO © BLOCKS?

It is important to distinguish between channels and the *actions that a user can perform within a participatory process*. For example: some typical actions in face-to-face participatory processes include listening, talking, creating proposals, reading, ranking, and voting. Some typical actions in digital citizens' relations management platforms (CRMPs) include reporting issues[7], accessing and rating services.[8] Recent CRMPs include e-consultation channels, such as Loomio,[9] Ideascale,[10] and Liquidfeedback.[11] Typical actions in such channels are generating, commenting and ranking ideas.

It is common knowledge that users tend to intervene and contribute differently to participatory processes. Studies on internet-based participation, for example, have shown that 1% of users will contribute content to a wiki, 9% will edit and refine it, while 90% will lurk.[12] According to the authors' definition, such users/actions clusters are not separate channels of engagement, unless the platform includes a dedicated participatory process targeted to them. For example, multichannel e-collaboration platforms integrate a channel for the general users and a channel with more privileges restricted to the more active users. This is the same strategy that face-to-face participatory processes use when restricting certain actions to representatives selected by the participants or by sortition (in participatory budgeting, for example, the so-called "councils of delegates" or "councils of spoke-persons"; while in citizens assemblies all spaces dedicated to random-selected citizens).

The new definition also allows to distinguish between phases and channels. *A democratic innovation* ***phase*** *is a set of actions aimed at achieving a goal in a specific amount of time*. Most deliberative mini-publics first involve a learning phase, followed by an experts' consultation phase and then a deliberation phase (Fishkin and Luskin 2005). These phases are significantly different in design, and allow participants to perform different sets of actions, but do not target different publics; hence, they are not different channels of engagement. All participants in a deliberative mini-public go through each of the phases.

A ***cycle*** *is a set of phases or actions that repeats itself.* For example, PB processes employ a yearly cycle that combines phases that last a specific number of months and restart every year. PBs usually integrate three phases: an initial brainstorming phase, in which participants propose potential public projects, a project selection phase[13] in which participants affect the selection of projects that will enter the budget, and a monitoring phase in which participants gather information on the implementation of projects (Wampler, 2015; Ganuza & Frances, 2012; Baiocchi, 2005; Avritzer & Navarro, 2003). However, in most PBs these three phases are designed for the same public and thus they do not constitute separate channels of engagement. Large cities' PBs are considered multichannel democratic innovations according to our definition, *not because they combine multiple phases, but because they integrate multiple district level participatory processes with specific rules, different amounts of resources and separate engagement campaigns*. For example, the PB in Porto Alegre, Brazil, integrates 17 slightly different district PB processes,[14] while the PB in New York City first integrated four different districts processes in 2011, and later 10 and 27[15], before been extended to all the city by a petition voted in November 2018[16].

Citizens' assemblies offer many examples of cycles of actions. For example, small group discussions and plenaries are often repeated multiple times during each of the three phases of the assembly (learning, consulting, deliberating) to transmit the information across groups. In most cases, small groups do not target different segments of the participants (e.g. youth vs adults), and thus, according to our definition, are not considerable as separate channels of engagement.

However, in consultations that allow the participants to self-select in different small group discussions focusing on different topics chosen by the participants themselves, the groups can become channels of engagement. The 2015 Citizens' Assembly on devolution in Southampton (UK) offers a recent example of an open space conference within a democratic innovation. In the second weekend of the assembly, the organizers introduced an open space conference that enabled the participants to discuss topics of their own choosing.[17] The participants divided themselves into five invented subgroups. This phase of the CA was designed by the organizers to re-introduce the freedom of *invented spaces* and to allow the participants to step out the choice architecture that had been carefully set up for them. These subgroups constitute multiple channels of engagement. The latter is an example that shows how concepts introduced by this chapter can be scaled-up or down; a phase can have multiple channels, and a channel can have multiple phases.

In sum, what distinguishes channels of engagement is not the medium (face-to-face vs text message vs web), nor the phase (learning vs deliberation), or the fact that citizens can participate in different ways (lurking vs creating), but the fact that each channel is designed for a specific segment of the population in a specific moment of the process. A channel can be as simple as an additional face-to-face meeting targeted to a specific minority within a phase, and as complex as an entire democratic innovation.

OPPORTUNITIES

A growing consensus is emerging among practitioners that the more channels of engagement a democratic innovation has, the better. Many consider the integration of multiple channels of engagement a method to *diversify* the risk that one single channel could be ineffective, and a way to *differentiate* channels of engagement to better accommodate the interests and goals of different types of people (Maia, & Marques, 2010; Bittle, Haller, & Kadlec, 2009). In that sense, creating a specific channel can potentiate and optimize an effort of outreach for involving a specific target group of persons.

Diversification

Going back to its origins, the concept of product diversification in management describes the strategy of offering different goods and services that experience different cycles and shocks so that the average profit is less volatile. In the realm of democratic innovations, diversification refers to the integration of different channels of engagement with different objectives, procedures and publics. Cities are now developing integrated citizens' relations management platforms (CRMPs) that combine long-term face-to-face consultation,[18] issue-reporting software, open data initiatives, engagement initiatives for youth, social marketing initiatives for sustainability, people panels for recurrent surveying[19] and classic e-government services just to name a few. Some of these channels are stand-alone democratic innovations with different goals and objectives targeting a different segment of the population.

Pioneers of this diversification strategy were the Gabinete Digital in the state of Rio Grande do Sul in Brazil, active between 2011 and 2014 (Spada, Mellon, Peixoto, & Sjoberg 2016), and the New Urban Mechanics offices in Boston and Philadelphia.[20] This trend is gaining ground due to the development of reusable digital participatory channels that cities can apply and modify to their needs with little effort. Poplus is a repository of such reusable software,[21] while Empatia is a new European project aimed at creating a free modular platform specifically designed for multichannel democratic innovations.[22]

The main practical advantage of diversification is the massive number of participants it can attract. The Gabinete Digital, for example (with is very different tools of social dialogue), engaged more than one million people every year. Another advantage that is often discussed by practitioners, particularly those in democratic innovations that support protest movements or campaign to change behavior, is the increased resilience. This concept is directly inspired by the idea of redundancy in engineering. If a campaign uses a variety of channels to try to achieve an objective, even if one channel fails, the others might succeed. To our knowledge, there are no studies documenting the increased resilience of multichannel innovations, and the supposed benefit is currently mostly theoretical or anecdotical. As the next section shows, there are instead very concrete examples of multichannel innovations that experienced a legitimacy crisis due to the failure of one channel or conflicts between two channels. Therefore, while the idea of risk diversification is theoretically appealing it probably applies only to a subset of democratic innovations and under a specific set of local conditions.

Differentiation

The concept of differentiation originates in marketing and refers to the construction of a brand and specific messages aimed at distinguishing a product or service from its competitors. In the realm of engagement, differentiation is mostly done by micro-targeting messages and spaces of participation. The Obama campaign was the first to show how to operationalize the process to increase the number, diversity and satisfaction of participants in a campaign (Kreiss, 2012).

E-petition platforms such as Avaaz and Change.org that routinely micro-target the possibility of participating in specific campaigns have globalized multichannel engagement campaigns. On its website Change.org claims to engage more than 140 million people in 196 countries and to win campaigns every day.[23] Change.org is a for-profit company and is a typical example of the emerging sector of a business in civic technology that enables democratic innovations. Change.org per se is not a democratic innovation, it is a company that makes money by accepting sponsored petitions by charities and by displaying advertising. However, some of the multichannel campaigns enabled by Change.org are designed to deepen democracy and are democratic innovations according to the definition of Graham Smith (Smith, 2009). The distinction might be subtle, but is an important one to make in order to navigate the field of civic technology.

One of the main advantages of differentiation for democratic innovation is to better engage some difficult-to-reach segments of the population. For example, the New York participatory budgeting organizes multiple district meetings that target linguistic and religious minorities offering a modified set of rules and services tailored to such groups. PB also offers a specific channel for formerly incarcerated people that lost their right to vote in the US. This is a differentiation strategy because the overall objective of these different meetings is the same — coming up with projects for the PB process during the brainstorming phase — but each meeting differs from the other for its location, the language used, and sometimes the rules of discussion employed. For example, meetings in Orthodox Jewish communities divide discussion groups by gender. The same happen in Senegal, Mozambique and other countries where the risk of keeping different typologies of people all in a general assembly is favoring "self-censorship" behaviors by some social groups: that is why women or youngsters are initially invited to join specific actor-based group, Where the homogeneity of participants seems to better favor the capacity of expressing themselves, feeling at easy with the others in the space for debating and decision-making.

Efficiency

Beyond the benefits in terms of efficacy and broader and more diverse participation, multichannel democratic innovations can gain efficiency due to the sharing of resources and information across channels. Canoas, a city in Southern Brazil, in 2012 gradually introduced a "Municipal Systems of Participation"[24], a citizens' relations management platform that integrates different channels of social dialogue to improve transparency, accountability and efficiency. The system combines 13 on-line as well as off-line participatory tools (collective arenas as PB or the Forum of Services, but also individual-based forms of dialogue between the mayor and commuter workers) targeted to different segments of the population (Martins, 2015). The key innovation introduced by Canoas consists of a complex system of public proceedings of all these different channels that allows the city officials, interested citizens and civil society organizations to track issues raised by individuals and groups in each of these different channels.

Increased Choice and Other Individual Level Benefits

There are also benefits for the participants, such as increased choice in the way they can interact with the participatory innovation and the ability to switch between channels or participate in multiple channels at the same time. The literature on democratic innovations has yet to analyze these benefits in detail, but the literature in marketing offer many examples of the benefits of increased choice.

Democratic Benefits

The emerging literature on multi-channel democratic innovations has mostly highlighted the benefit of these institutions on the quantity of participants, little is known about their impact on the democratic goods often discussed by the literature (Smith 2009, Mansbridge *et al.* 2012). Smith for example identifies five democratic goods, inclusiveness, popular control, considered judgement, transparency and the promotion of better institutional capacity.

The multiplication of channels of engagement can be used to promote inclusion and to strenghten popular control and oversight over policy making. Randomly selected assemblies in CAs are designed to represent the population and to prevent interest groups from hijacking the participatory decision-making process. Thus, the presence of this channel of engagement in CAs contributes both to better inclusion and better popular control.

The case of the Grandview-Woodland Citizens' Assembly implemented in 2015 offers a clear example of these benefits. [25] Between 2012 and 2013 the City of Vancouver (Canada) engaged in a participatory consultation process with the Grandview-Woodland community to define a 30 years neighborhood plan. The process involved many sessions and engaged a few thousand residents – mostly homeowners and representatives of homeowners' associations. The consultation generated a plan skewed toward conservation and had very few provisions for promoting housing densification. Vancouver will increase its population exponentially in the next ten years and the city hoped to use the Grandview-Woodland neighborhood as a main site for development. The ill-advised reaction of the city government was to overrule the crowd-sourced neighborhood plan releasing a document, called *Emerging Directions* that introduced significant urban densification. However, this document generated a huge outcry from the community. The backlash was such that a new umbrella organization representing citizens disillusioned with the planning process emerged, Our Community Our Plan (OCOP).[26] To overcome this impasse the city introduced a randomly selected assembly[27] that was designed specifically to reduce the power of homeowners by recruiting half of the assembly among renters. Initially, many perceived this democratic innovation as a way to undermine pre-existing civil society organizations, and a way to reduce conflict during an electoral year. In the first months of implementation, numerous critiques from homeowners and representatives of OCOP emerged in local newspapers and social media.[28] Some of such critiques described the process as a mechanism to manufacture consent.[29] However, after a few months, the legitimacy of the well-executed process eased the citizens' mistrust and criticism decreased significantly. The assembly effectively managed to convey the importance of hearing the voice of the previously excluded renters and countered the effect of vocal interest groups (Beauvais & Warren, 2015). The assembly has recently issued a new set of recommendations, and the residents are waiting to see if the city council will implement the new guidelines. If the procedure works, and the resulting document is an acceptable compromise between the needs of owners and renters, the case of Vancouver will be a groundbreaking example of troubleshooting an engagement process using multichannel integration.

Participatory Budgets often promote inclusion and better judgment by providing channels specifically targeted to women, youth and minorities, subgroups of the population that often have difficulties in making their voice heard in general assemblies. The recent experimental literature on male-dominated small group discussions and quality of deliberation (Karpowitz, Mendelberg, & Shaker, 2012) suggests that enclave deliberation promotes the capacity of women to make their voices heard. These spaces contribute to the inclusion of ideas and instances that would not emerge otherwise and arguably promote better decision-making (Landemore, 2013).

The current generation of Citizens' relations management platforms (CMRPs) focuses on generating high number of participants, reducing costs and promoting better institutional capacity. The latter results complement similar observations in the broader literature on e-government (Chadwick, May, 2003; Torres, Pina & Acerete, 2006).

WHICH OPEN CHALLENGES?

While reviewing existing case studies and interviewing practitioners the authors also found many interesting examples in which the introduction of additional channels of engagement within a democratic innovation backfired. In the following pages, five families that summarize the most common challenges will be listed.

Direct Negative Interactions Among Channels

First, channels of engagement might interact negatively; a new channel might divert users' attention and interests in unexpected ways. If one channel is particularly successful in attracting participants, others might suffer due to a loss of participants. Similarly, if a channel is particularly unsuccessful, others might suffer because they are part of a system that has a non-working component. This is particularly important when considering the fact that democratic innovations are often introduced in the midst of fierce opposition, and that opponents, to delegitimize the entire process, will exploits weaknesses.

The Grandview-Woodland CA, presents an example of one channel entering into direct conflict with another. As mentioned, in the first months of the assembly, participants in the meetings open to the public criticized the randomly selected assembly as a mechanism to bypass pre-existing local organizations (Beauvais & Warren 2015).

Channels can also compete over resources, and one channel might *cannibalize* the resources of another, ultimately weakening the entire architecture of a democratic innovation. For example, scholars interpret the introduction of the so-called Governança Solidária Local in Porto Alegre in 2005, a process parallel to PB, which was aimed at generating partnership with private contractors and CSOs, as the beginning of the decline of the Porto Alegre process (Baierle, 2007, Langelier, 2015). In 1989, the closure of similar privileged channels was one of the key mechanisms that empowered the PB process in Porto Alegre (Baiocchi & Ganuza 2014). The re-opening of such channels implied that interest groups did not have to pass through the more transparent and accountable PB process, but could directly engage the city government. This new channel *cannibalized* the amount of resources dedicated to the rest of PB and reduced its bargaining power vis-à-vis the city government.

Increased Chances for Free Riding

When multiple channels are available, participants might chose the one that generates the most rewards for the least cost. This form of soft *free-riding* reduces the legitimacy of a democratic innovation. The more channels are active, the more a participant can select the one that generates the most returns for the least effort. The latter was a particular problem in some experiments of face-to-face participatory budgeting that introduced the possibility of voting online in order to attract youth and the middle class. In some cases, participants perceived the new online voting channel as a mechanism that allowed *slacktivists*[30] to affect the PB outcomes. This loss of legitimacy becomes particularly problematic when intersected with issues of digital divide as in the case of Recife (Brazil) and Vignola (Italy). In Recife, middle-class e-participants overturned the results chosen by poor face-to-face participants creating significant protest (Ferreira, 2010). In Vignola, in Italy, youth participating online overturned the result of elderly people participating in person, generating a backlash which led to the suspension of participatory budgeting in 2005 (Cunha, Allegretti and Matias 2011).

Increased Complexity of the Integration Mechanism that Leads to Reduced Legitimacy, Transparency and Accountability

Third, the greater the number of channels that exists, the more complex the integration mechanism becomes. Complexity not only generates costs in terms of management, but also increases the difficulty of explaining and justifying the design of the participatory process to the participants. This reduces the overall transparency and accountability of the democratic innovation and, in some cases, its legitimacy. Complexity often reduces the ability of participants to truly own the process and affect its agenda.

A typical example of this problem concerns the multiplication of brainstorming channels aimed at collecting participants' proposals. What has happened in Lisbon's PB since 2009 is an example of this risk: to deal with the almost 1,000 proposals of investments generated by citizens every year in face-to-face and online meetings, the municipality had to organize an interdisciplinary working group of civil servants to merge and pre-select the proposals. The pared down list – 200 projects – sparked numerous complaints by citizens who saw their ideas disappearing or being distorted (Sintomer & Allegretti, 2016).

The history of citizens' assemblies shows how difficult it is to integrate the deliberative channel open only to a random sample of the population, with the public referendum. Historically the majority of citizens' assemblies referendums have failed to ratify the recommendations proposed by the citizens' assemblies because the public did not pay much attention to the activity of the mini-public (Fournier et al. 2011).

Another example of this problem is the proliferation of unaccountable messages in micro-targeted campaigns (Jamieson, 2013). This example has been studied primarily in U.S. political campaigns, but it has a natural extension to the micro-targeting of participatory processes. First, the proliferation of micro-targeted engagement channels can create expectations that cannot be met, second such proliferation divides the participants reducing their ability to make the platform accountable. While there are no studies yet that explicitly link the presence of multiple channels of engagement with the challenge of managing expectations and the issues of cooptation, contestation and bargaining power, the PB literature offers many examples of multichannel innovations suffering such problems (Wampler 2007, Sintomer & Allegretti, 2015).

Increased Probability that an Oligarchy of Participants Emerges

Fourth, complex democratic innovations that combine different channels of engagement with different privileges might facilitate the emergence of an oligarchy of super participants. The case of Porto Alegre is one of such example (Fedozzi, 2007; Langelier, 2015). Over time the members of the elected citywide assembly of district representatives (Conselho do Orçamento Participativo, or COP) that has the most control over the PB process have become an oligarchy with very little turnover (Figure 1). As we can see from the graph, the percentage of new participants in this key assembly decreases over time. During the 90s new participants composed 70% of this assembly. After 2000, the number of new members declines sharply. By 2011, new members composed only 30% of the assembly.

The COP is a channel that requires significantly more effort that any other channel in the PB systems. The meetings are more frequent and the discussions are more complex. At the same time, the COP has the most influence over the final allocation of projects. The combination of channels that require more effort and provide more privileges increases the probability that a selected group of people that has the time and the interest will monopolizes such channels. The example of Porto Alegre provides only anecdotal evidence, but it is helpful as a cautionary tale for complex democratic innovations that employ gamification mechanisms and other complex systems of rewards and incentives.

Increased Risk of Imposing a Constrictive Structure Over a Segment of the Participants

A fifth and final challenge resides in the risk of overdesigning the democratic innovation. If the organizers impose a new channel of engagement, participants might end up feeling like cattle in a chute, rather than valued partners. The introduction of thematic assemblies in some PBs provides the typical example of poorly designed channel. Returning to the case of Porto Alegre, during the mid-90s, the city government introduced a new set of citywide assemblies in an attempt to overcome the fact that projects proposed in district assemblies were limited in scope and concentrated on filling basic infrastructural deficits in informal neighborhoods. These thematic assemblies, attempted to tackle citywide problems such as transportation, education, employment and environmental pollution. But people rarely used the

Figure 1. Percentage of new participants in the COP of Porto Alegre
Source: Data collected by the ONG Cidade in Porto Alegre for the years 1990-2008; for the years 2008-2012 authors' calculations based on the list of members of COP published in the yearly issue of the Regimento Interno.

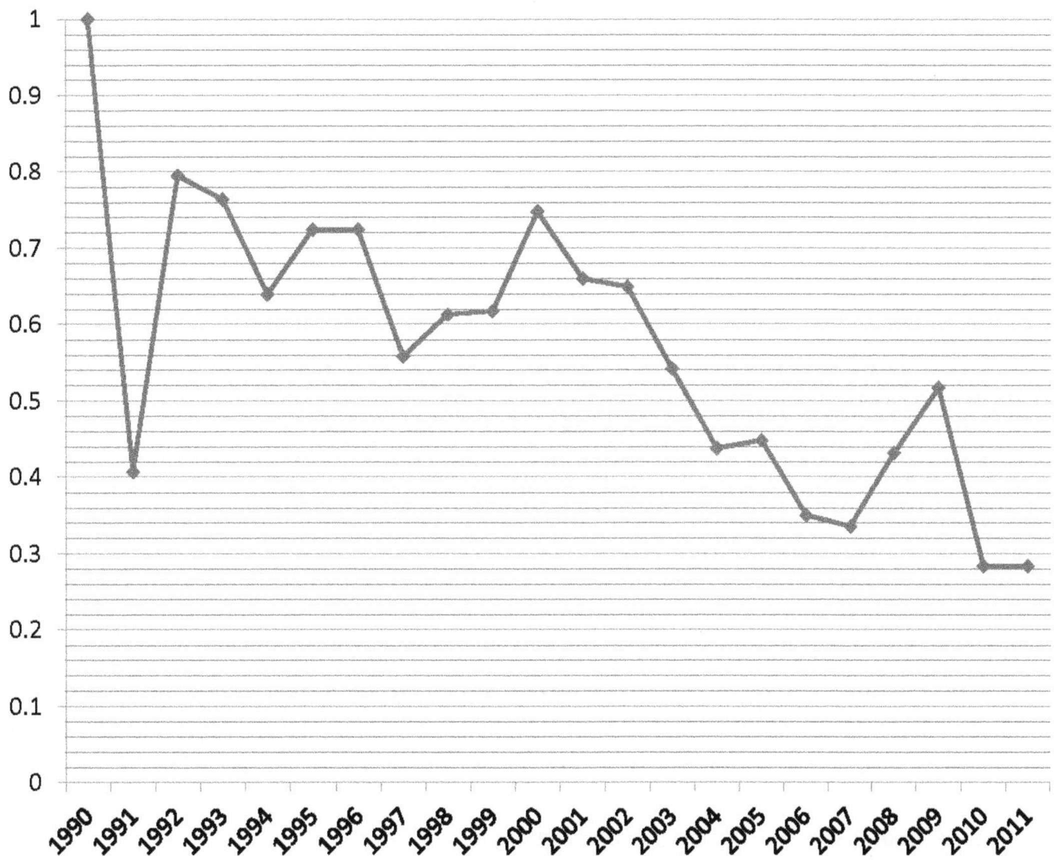

thematic assemblies as intended, instead they used them to re-propose projects that had not been selected in the district assemblies.

SOME COMMON MODELS OF INTEGRATION AMONG DIVERSIFIED TOOLS

After having introduced the concept of channels of engagement and having discussed the benefits and drawbacks of integrating multiple channels of engagement within a democratic innovation, this section describes the most common integration mechanisms the authors have encountered in their review of democratic innovation cases.

Analyzing how participatory budgets (PBs), citizens' assemblies (CAs) and citizens' relations management platforms (CRMPs) have managed multichannel integration to leverage benefits and minimize disadvantages, three main models of integration emerge: managed competition, regulation and isolation.

Managed Competition

One integration strategy is to allow the channels to compete for resources. In Porto Alegre, the district level assemblies compete for the engagement of participants. Citizens are asked to rank the policy priorities for their district and to present projects. The overall ranking of policy priorities, combined with the number of people that participates affects the allocation of resources to each neighborhood (Abers 2000).

The risk of this approach is that it can create disruptive competition, instead of promoting democracy enhancing agonism (Mouffe 1999). While disruptive competition might be a good strategy to optimize firms' marketing channels, the examples of Recife and Vignola show that in democratic innovations, it reduces legitimacy and creates citizens' frustration. This might have something to do with the fact that the relationship between a customer and a firm is different from the relationship between a participant and the organizers of engagement processes. The customer has no large stake in the failure of a marketing channel, but a citizen who has invested a significant amount of time and resources in a channel will be extremely disappointed if such channel fails. In many cases, a channel becomes a living community, and the failure of a channel implies the death of such community and the loss of a unique space to interact with fellow citizens and friends.

However, the disruptive competition model might be optimal in democratic innovations that are *invented spaces*. For example, in agile campaigns and social movement actions in which the cost of experimenting with channels directly initiated by participants is very low, disruptive competition might be an optimal strategy to promote fast innovation and adaptability. Such campaigns by jumpstarting many channels at the same time might quickly experiment which one attracts most participants, and which one has the most influence achieving the overall campaign goal. However, a detailed investigation of the advantages and disadvantages of competition in such *invented spaces* is beyond the scope of this chapter and these empirical questions are left to future research.

Integration Based on Rules and Procedures

The most common integration mechanism is to adopt a system of rules and procedures that manages the interactions among channels.

Citizens' assemblies require rules that allocate tasks between the closed randomly selected assembly and the meetings open to the public. In the Vancouver Grandview-Woodland CA the organizers established that the closed assembly would gather two rounds of feedback on the proposal for the neighborhood plan they were writing. Participants in the open assemblies wanted a third round of feedback, but the organizers gauged that the amount of work an additional round would have imposed on the members of the closed assembly would have been excessive.

Citizen relations management platforms often employ gamification strategies to govern the access to different channels of engagement. Participants might be required to complete capacity-building actions, social actions or reaching out actions (Gupta, Bouvier, & Gordon, 2012) before having access to a channel of engagement that has higher privileges or higher status. For example, the Repurpose project during the Obama campaign integrated a campaigning channel, with an e-collaboration channel. Volunteers earned points by canvassing and making phone calls in the campaign channel. They could then spend such points to reshape the campaign itself,[31] from buying certain ads in certain locations, to sending more organizers to some electoral districts, to support political actions beyond the election. Repurpose emerged as an evolution of previous incentives schemes based exclusively on badges and dinners. Nudges

are also another subtler approach that is widely used to optimize messages and choice architectures in engagement channels (Sunstein & Thaler 2008). While the growing literature that explores the advantages and disadvantages of nudges offers many insights for the design of democratic innovations (Hausman and Welch, 2010; Holler, 2015), few scholars have started investigating such issues (John *et al.,* 2013).

The system of rules governing a complex democratic innovation is, in some instances, open to discussion. For example, many participatory budgeting processes create a sort of constitution that describes the principles governing the process and establish a procedure to review it. At first glance, opening up the rules to discussion increases transparency and empower participants to adapt the process to their needs (Lerner, & Secondo 2012, Allegretti 2014). But, in Porto Alegre, this channel was exploited in a way that solidified the control of the oligarchy of participants over the process and reduced the possibility of spontaneity during open assemblies (Baierle 2007, Langelier 2015).

Everything we have presented thus far, describes integration mechanisms to improve the efficiency and internal legitimacy of multichannel democratic innovations. These mechanisms encourage the behavior that the innovation architects have identified as ideal. However, other interesting integration mechanisms of multichannel democratic innovations are designed to strengthen the sense of community across channels (De Cindio, Gentile, Grew, & Redolfi 2003) and promote overall playfulness (Sicart, 2014). These design choices allow the participants to redefine the meaning of their actions within the platform in new ways (Lerner 2014, Gordon & Walter 2016) beyond the goals of the project.

Some authors argue that the creation of a long-lasting community of engaged citizens is the most concrete benefits of democratic innovations and thus design innovations that strengthen the community via social and playful activities that have nothing to do with the primary task of the democratic innovation (Stortone & De Cindio 2015). Successful democratic innovations offer an array of examples of these *meaningful inefficiencies*. These elements bring back the energy of *invented spaces* within *invited spaces* and transform grey institutions in lively spaces. A catalogue of these reinventions of democratic innovations is beyond the page limitations of this chapter. PB district meetings in Brazilian Cities are often preceded/followed by parties that include a variety of artistic representation that showcase the energy of the community. The Youth Participatory Budgeting process in Boston is currently experimenting with social initiatives to promote friendship among participants after the first-year evaluation surveys highlighted 'making new friends' as the number one reason for participating in the process. Citizens' Assemblies include social nights, dinners and often games. For example, the Irish Citizens Assemblies employed a game during the first social dinner that had the participants explore different voting mechanisms to select the dessert. CRMPs often have a community channel, off-topic forums and playful contests.

Isolation

The complete isolation of two channels of engagement is a third form of integration strategy often adopted in PB processes. The case of Belo Horizonte is proto-typical. Belo Horizonte, Brazil, created an online e-PB channel that has its own budget and is effectively an entirely separate space with limited interaction with the face-to-face PB process. This strategy was designed to prevent the emergence of the conflict that had plagued Recife (Sampaio, Maia, & Marques, 2010; Allegretti, 2012). Isolation might also be particularly useful to prevent the tyranny of majority and dedicate specific spaces to youth or other minorities. PB and CRMPs processes sometimes activate a specific channel for women, or youth or LGBTQAI+ groups. It is difficult to find examples of isolated channels in citizens' assemblies because a key feature of these processes is the attempt to represent the population via a random sample.

However, part of the ratio of having a randomly selected assembly is to isolate such assembly from the effect of interest groups, thus in such respect Citizens assemblies offer an example of an isolated channel.

AN OPEN COMCLUSION

This chapter begun by noticing that the most successful democratic innovations, like – for example - participatory budgeting, often consist of a coherent system of overlapping channels of engagement and participation. But introducing multiple channels of engagement also introduces risks. The chapter describes five challenges that many democratic innovations that merge multiple parallel engagement processes face. First, different channels might enter in conflict and undermine each other. Second, the presences of different channels of participation that have different cost of participation, but generate the same return, runs the risk of generating '*soft free-riding*' behavior in the participants, and thus might undermine the legitimacy of the process. Third, the multiplication of engagement processes often leads to the creation of a large number of redundant of project ideas and participants' requests that need to be filtered with costly processes. In many cases, these filtering mechanisms are not sufficiently transparent and reduce legitimacy. Fourth, the more ideas are proposed, the more ideas will not be approved due to budget constraints, and thus the more expectations will be frustrated. Failing to manage the participants' expectations is without a doubt one of the most common problem experienced by democratic innovations. Fifth, the presence of different venues of participation with different privileges facilitates the creation of an oligarchy of participants that monopolize the channel(s) with the most net benefits.

In this chapter we tried to introduce some classificatory schemes that identify multichannel democratic innovations separating them from the concept of multichannel engagement and multichannel marketing. We also tried to review a number of advantages and disadvantages of such innovations using three main families of democratic innovations as a source of examples: participatory budgeting, citizens' assemblies and citizen relations management platforms.

Unlike previous research that investigated innovations and their interaction with existing institutions (macro-level), or analyzed experimentally the role of different organizational elements within one innovation (micro-level), we have examined clusters of *actions* that are designed specifically to engage a segment of the public – what this chapter calls channels of engagement. To our knowledge, this meso-level analysis has never been attempted before.

These comparisons have uncovered three models of integration: managed competition, regulation, and isolation. These three models are certainly not exhaustive of the variety of possible integration methods, but are first steps in the exploration of the sequence and integration of different combinations of the LEGO blocks that compose democratic innovations.

What has also emerged from this chapter's analysis of the most recent cases is that the examples integrating the largest number of channels appear to be more concerned with quantity, efficiency and satisfaction of participants, than effectively empowering citizens. Using the normative conceptualization introduce by Graham Smith (2009), these integration mechanisms focus more on improving institutional capacity than creating democratic goods. Therefore, we believe that the next step in the research agenda on multichannel democratic innovations should be to explore the impact of different integration models on the division of power between participants and organizers, in order to promote the development of a new generation of integrating platforms that include in their code stronger democratic principles.

Finalizing this reflection, we would like to underline that while there are no simple and *plug-and-play* designs that can magically find solutions to respond to these challenges, the examples reviewed in this chapter show some promising and concrete step forward. In this perspective, such examples are not meant to offer blueprints or recipes that should be copied, but to reveal an underpinning systemic approach that could be positively emulated. This systemic approach is based on:

1. A careful attention to the interaction between different channels of participation and the risks and challenges of their possible conflicts, overlapping, duplication or integrative complementarity of effects;
2. A user-centric design approach that collects data on the variety of users' needs and skills, and tailors new channels of participation to specific types of participants;
3. A recognition of the multiplicity of reasons behind the choice of participating in different ways to the process (e.g, a single working parent can only participate online late at night) that translates in a valorization of all forms of input, even those that require little or no effort;
4. A recognition of the centrality of including difficult to engage participants;
5. A recognition of the centrality of empowerment and capacity building of all different typologies of participants;
6. A meaningful gamification approach, that abandons superficial and tokenistic incentive schemes (e.g., badges) in favor of providing increasing control privileges within the democratic innovation as reward for sustained participation, completion of capacity building exercises or achievement of certain transparent objectives;
7. A careful attention to the overall architecture of the participatory process that needs to balance the internal justice of the system (assigning greater privileges to participants that exerts the most effort) with the promotion of inclusion of new participants and minorities;
8. A careful attention to the management of participants' expectations that is grounded in the ex-ante disclosures of the limits of each democratic innovation, in the increased transparency of idea-filtering procedures, and in the systematic answering of users' feedback;
9. A renovated emphasis on the oversight of public actions (including the functioning of the participatory arenas themselves), as a measure for increasing the legitimacy of the different spaces and channels of social dialogue;
10. A careful attention to the changes in the incentive structure that might emerge due to the evolution of the environment (e.g., changes in the political coalition governing the city implementing the democratic innovation) and the evolution of the process itself (e.g., the emergence of an oligarchy of participants).

These ten guidelines offer the initial basis of a systemic design approach that can support the creation of democratic innovations that combine more effectively multiple channels of engagement and can guide the decision to introduce or eliminate a specific channel of engagement. As all design recommendations, these guidelines are not meant to be blindly followed. So, we encourage practitioners to reinterpret them at the light of their specific local conditions and their specific objectives.

REFERENCES

Abers, R. (2000). *Inventing Local Democracy: Grassroots Politics in Brazil*. Boulder, CO: Lynne Rienner Publishers.

Aggio, C., & Sampaio, R. (2013). Democracia digital e participação: os modelos de consulta e os desafios do Gabinete Digital. Gabinete digital: análise de uma experiência. Porto Alegre: Companhia Rio-Grandense de Artes Gráficas (CORAG), 19-38.

Allegretti, G. (2005). *Porto Alegre:una biografia territoriale. Ricercando la qualità urbana a partire dal patrimonio sociale*. Florence: University Press. doi:10.26530/OAPEN_347516

Allegretti, G. (2012). From Skepticism to Mutual Support: Towards a Structural Change in the Relations between Participatory Budgeting and the Information and Communication Technologies? In *Legitimacy_2.0. E-Democracy and Public Opinion in the Digital Age*. Frankfurt am Main: Goethe University Press.

Allegretti, G. (2013). Os orçamentos participativos sabem escutar? Reflexões para reforçar a sustentabilidade dos orçamentos participativos. In Orçamento Participativo olhares e perpesctivas. Livraria Paulo Freire Ed.

Allegretti, G. (2014). Paying attention to the participants perceptions in order to trigger a virtuous circle. In Hope For Democracy. 25 Years Of Participatory Budgeting Worldwide. S. Brás de Alportel: In Loco.

Allegretti, G. (2017). When Citizen Participation Unexpectedly Grows in Quality and Quantity. In *Crisis, Austerity, and Transformation. How Disciplinary Neoliberalism is Changing Portugal* (pp. 157–178). London: Lexington Books.

Allegretti, G., & Copello, K. (2018). Winding around money issues. What's new in Participatory Budgeting and which windows of opportunity are being opened? In *Hope for Democracy - 30 Years of Participatory Budgeting Worldwide* (pp. 35–54). Faro, Cuba: Oficina/Epopeia.

Andersson, E., Burall, S., & Fennell, E. (2010). *Talking for a Change: a distributed dialogue approach to complex issues*. London: Involve. Available online at: http://www.involve.org.uk/wp-content/uploads/2011/03/Involve2010TalkingforaChange2.pdf

Avritzer, L., & Navarro, Z. (2003). A inovação democrática no Brasil: o Orçamento Participativo. Ed. Cortez.

Baierle, S. G. (2007). *Urban Struggles in Porto Alegre: Between Political Revolution and Transformism*. Document prepared for the Project MAPAS Active Monitoring of Public Policies under Lula's Government (2004-2005), coordinated by the Brazilian NGO IBASE. Available for download at www.ongcidade.org

Baiocchi, G. (2005). *Militants and citizens: the politics of participatory democracy in Porto Alegre*. Stanford, CA: Stanford University Press.

Baiocchi, G., & Ganuza, E. (2014). Participatory budgeting as if emancipation mattered. *Politics & Society*, *42*(1), 29–50. doi:10.1177/0032329213512978

Beauvais, E., & Warren, M. (2015). *Can Citizens' Assemblies Deepen Urban Democracy?* Paper presented at the American Political Science Association conference.

Besson, S., Marti, J. L., & Seiler, V. (2006). *Deliberative Democracy and Its Discontents.* Ashgate Publishing Company.

Best, N. J., Ribeiro, M. M., Matheus, R., & Vaz, J. C. (2010). Internet e a participação cidadã nas experiências de orçamento participativo digital no Brasil. Cadernos PPG-AU/UFBA, 9.

Bimber, B. (2014). Digital media in the Obama campaigns of 2008 and 2012: Adaptation to the personalized political communication environment. *Journal of Information Technology & Politics*, *11*(2), 130–150. doi:10.1080/19331681.2014.895691

Bittle, S., Haller, C., & Kadlec, A. (2009). *Promising Practices in Online Engagement.* Occasional Paper, n. 3, Center for Advancement of Public Engagement.

Bjorkman Nyqvist, M., & Svensson, J. (2007). *Power to the People: Evidence from a Randomized Field Experiment of a Community-Based Monitoring Project in Uganda.* Policy Research Working Paper Series 4268, The World Bank.

Blas, A., & Ibarra, P. (2006). La participación: Estado de la cuestión. *Cuadernos Hegoa*, *39*, 5–35.

Buttle, F., & Maklan, S. (2008). *Customer Relationship Management* (2nd ed.). Routledge. doi:10.4324/9780080949611

Chadwick, A., & May, C. (2003). Interaction between states and citizens in the age of the Internet: 'e-Government' in the United States, Britain, and the European Union. *Governance: Int. J. Policy Admin. Institutions*, *16*(2), 271–300. doi:10.1111/1468-0491.00216

Cunha, E. S., Allegretti, G., & Matias, M. (2011). Participatory Budgeting and the Use of Information and Communication Technologies: A Virtuous Cycle? *Revista Critica de Ciencias Sociais*, 3.

De Cindio, F., Gentile, O., Grew, P., & Redolfi, D. (2003). Community Networks: Rules of Behavior and Social Structure Special Issue: ICTs and Community Networking. *The Information Society*, *19*(5), 395–406. doi:10.1080/714044686

Dias, M. R. (2002). *Sob o signo da vontade popular: o orçamento participativo e o dilema da Câmara Municipal de Porto Alegre.* Rio de Janeiro: IUPERJ.

Dias, N. (2018). *Hope for Democracy - 30 Years of Participatory Budgeting Worldwide.* Faro, Cuba: Oficina/Epopeia.

Dutil, P. A., Howard, C., Langford, J., & Roy, J. (2008). Rethinking government-public relationships in a digital world: Customers, clients, or citizens? *Journal of Information Technology & Politics*, *4*(1), 77–90. doi:10.1300/J516v04n01_06

Falanga, R. (2018). *Como aumentar a escala dos orçamentos participativos? O Orçamento Participativo Portugal (OPP) e o Orçamento Participativo Jovem Portugal (OPJP).* ICS-Policy Brief.

Farrar, C., Fishkin, J. S., Green, D. P., List, C., Luskin, R. C., & Paluck, E. L. (2010). Disaggregating deliberation's effects: An experiment within a deliberative poll. *British Journal of Political Science*, *40*(02), 333–347. doi:10.1017/S0007123409990433

Farrar, C., Green, D. P., Green, J. E., Nickerson, D. W., & Shewfelt, S. (2009). Does discussion group composition affect policy preferences? Results from three randomized experiments. *Political Psychology*, *30*(4), 615–647. doi:10.1111/j.1467-9221.2009.00717.x

Fedozzi, L. (2000). *O poder da aldeia: gênese e história do orçamento participativo de Porto Alegre*. Porto Alegre: Tomo Editorial.

Fedozzi, L. (2007). *Observando o Orçamento Participativo de Porto Alegre. Análise histórica de dados: perfil social e associativo, avaliação e expectativas*. Porto Alegre: Tomo Editorial/Prefeitura de Porto Alegre/OBSERVAPOA.

Ferreira, D. E. S. (2010). *Inclusão, Participação, Associativismo e Qualidade da Deliberação Pública no Orçamento Participativo Digitalde Belo Horizonte*. Paper presented IV Congresso Latino Americano de Opinião Pública.

Fishkin, J. S., & Luskin, R. C. (2005). Experimenting with a democratic ideal: Deliberative polling and public opinion. *Acta Politica*, *40*(3), 284–298. doi:10.1057/palgrave.ap.5500121

Floridia, A. (2012). La legge toscana sulla partecipazione: una difficile scommessa. In F. Bortolotti & C. Corsi (Eds.), *La Partecipazione politica e sociale tra crisi e innovazione: il caso della Toscana* (pp. 331–362). Roma: Ediesse.

Fournier, P., van der Kolk, H., Kenneth Carty, R., Blais, A., & Rose, J. (2011). *When Citizens Decide: Lessons from the Citizen Assemblies on Electoral Reform*. Oxford, UK: Oxford University Press. doi:10.1093/acprof:oso/9780199567843.001.0001

Ganuza, E., & Frances, F. (2012). *El círculo virtuoso de la democracia: los presupuestos participativos a debate*. Madrid: Colección Monografías CIS.

Gerber, A. S., & Green, D. P. (2000). The effect of canvassing, direct mail, and telephone contact on turnout: A field experiment. *The American Political Science Review*, *94*, 653–663. doi:10.2307/2585837

Goldfrank, B. (2012). The world bank and the globalization of participatory budgeting. *Journal of Public Deliberation*, *8*(2).

Goldfrank, B., & Schneider, A. (2006). Competitive Institution Building: The PT and Participatory Budgeting in Rio Grande do Sul. *Latin American Politics and Society*, *48*(3), 1–31. doi:10.1111/j.1548-2456.2006.tb00354.x

Gordon, E., & Walter, S. (2016). *Meaningful Inefficiencies: Resisting the Logic of Technological Efficiency in the Design of Civic Systems*. MIT Press.

Gupta, J., Bouvier, J., & Gordon, E. (2012). *Exploring New Modalities of Public Engagement. An Evaluation of Digital Gaming Platforms on Civic Capacity and Collective Action in the Boston Public School District*. Engagement Lab Evaluation White Paper.

Hausman, D. M., & Welch, B. (2010). Debate: To Nudge or Not to Nudge. *Journal of Political Philosophy*, *18*(1), 123–136. doi:10.1111/j.1467-9760.2009.00351.x

Hendricks, J., & Denton, R. Jr. (2010). *Communicator-in-Chief: How Barack Obama use new media technology to win the White House*. New York: Lexington Books.

Holler, M. J. (2015). Paternalism, Gamification, or Art: An Introductory Note. *Homo Oeconomicus, 32*(2), 275.

Holmsen, C. A., Palter, R. N., Simon, P. R. & Weberg, P. K. (1998). Retail Banking: Managing Competition among Your Own Channels. *The McKinsey Quarterly*, (1).

Humphreys, M., Masters, W. A., & Sandbu, M. E. (2006). The role of leaders in democratic deliberations: Results from a field experiment in São Tomé and Príncipe. *World Politics, 58*(04), 583–622. doi:10.1353/wp.2007.0008

Hunter, W. (2009). *The Transformation of the Workers' Party in Brazil, 1989-2009*. Cambridge University Press.

Issemberg, S. (2012). *The Victory Lab: The Secret Science of Winning Campaigns*. New York: Crown Publishers.

John, P., Cotterill, S., Moseley, A., Moseley, A., Stoker, G., Wales, C., & Smith, G. (2011). *Nudge, Nudge, Think, Think: Experimenting with Ways to Change Civic Behaviour*. London: Bloomsbury Academic. doi:10.5040/9781849662284

Kapin, A., & Ward, A. S. (2013). *Social Change Anytime Everywhere: How to Implement Online Multichannel Strategies to Spark Advocacy, Raise Money, and Engage Your Community*. San Francisco: John Wiley and Sons.

Karpowitz, C. F., Mendelberg, T., & Shaker, L. (2012). Gender inequality in deliberative participation. *The American Political Science Review, 106*(03), 533–547. doi:10.1017/S0003055412000329

Kreiss, D. (2012). *Taking our country back: The crafting of networked politics from Howard Dean to Barack Obama*. New York, NY: Oxford University Press. doi:10.1093/acprof:oso/9780199782536.001.0001

Landemore, H. (2013). *Democratic Reason: Politics, Collective Intelligence, and the Rule of the Many*. Princeton, NJ: Princeton University Press.

Langelier, S. (2011). Que reste-t-il de l'expérience pionnière de Porto Alegre? Le Monde Diplomatique.

Langelier, S. (2015). *Le démantèlement du Budget Participatif de Porto Alegre? Démocratie participative et communauté politique*. l'Harmattan.

Lerner, J. (2014). *Making Democracy Fun: How Game Design Can Empower Citizens and Transform Politics*. Cambridge, MA: MIT Press. doi:10.7551/mitpress/9785.001.0001

Mansbridge, J. J., Bohman, J., Chambers, S., Christiano, T., Fung, A., Parkinson, J. R., ... Warren, M. (2012). A systemic approach to deliberative democracy. In J. R. Parkinson & J. J. Mansbridge (Eds.), *Deliberative systems: deliberative democracy at the large scale. Theories of Institutional Design*. Cambridge, UK: Cambridge University Press. doi:10.1017/CBO9781139178914.002

Mansuri, G., & Rao, R. (2013). *Localizing Development: Does Participation Work?* World Bank Policy Research Reports.

Martins, V. (2015). O Sistema de participação popular e cidadã de Canoas. Redes. Reflexões (in)oportunas, (2), 52-57.

Medaglia, R. (2007). The challenged identity of a field: The state of the art of eParticipation research. *Information Polity*, *12*(3), 169–181. doi:10.3233/IP-2007-0114

Miraftab, F. (2004). Invited and invented spaces of participation: Neoliberal citizenship and feminists' expanded notion of politics. *Wagadu*, *1*, 1–7.

Morrell, M. E. (1999). Citizen's evaluations of participatory democratic procedures: Normative theory meets empirical science. *Political Research Quarterly*, *52*(2), 293–322.

Mouffe, C. (1999). Deliberative Democracy or Agonistic Pluralism? *Social Research*, *66*(3).

Nitzsche, P., Pistoia, A., & Elsãber, M. (2012). *Development of an Evaluation Tool for Participative E-Government Services: A Case Study of Electronic Participatory Budgeting Projects in Germany*. Revista de Administratie si Management Public.

Parkinson, J. (2004). Why deliberate? The encounter between deliberation and new public man-agers. *Public Administration*, *82*(2), 377–395. doi:10.1111/j.0033-3298.2004.00399.x

Peruzzotti, E., Magnelli, M., & Peixoto, T. (2011). *Multichannel Participatory Budgeting*. Available online at: http://www.vitalizing-democracy.org/site/downloads/277_265_Case_Study_La_Plata.pdf

Sampaio, R. C., Maia, R. C. M., & Marques, F. P. J. A. (2010). Participação e deliberação na internet: Um estudo de caso do Orçamento Participativo Digital de Belo Horizonte. *Opinião Pública*, *16*(2), 446–477. doi:10.1590/S0104-62762010000200007

Sintomer, Y. (2010). Saberes dos cidadãos e saber político. Revista Crítica de Ciências Sociais, 91, 135-153. doi:10.4000/rccs.4185

Sintomer, Y., & Allegretti, G. (2016). *Os Orçamentos Participativos na Europa. Entre democracia participativa e modernização dos serviços públicos*. Coimbra: Almedina.

Sintomer, Y., Allegretti, G., Herzberg, C., & Röcke, A. (2013). *Learning from the South: Participatory Budgeting Worldwide –an Invitation to Global Cooperation*. Bonn: Service Agency for Communities.

Sintomer, Y., & Blondiaux, L. (2002). L'impératif délibératif. *Revue des sciences sociales du politique*, *57*, 17-35.

Sintomer, Y., Herzberg, C., & Röcke, A. (2008). Participatory Budgeting in Europe: Potentials and Challenges. International Journal of Urban and Regional Research, 32(1).

Sintomer, Y., Herzberg, C., Röcke, A., & Allegretti, G. (2012). *Transnational Models of Citizen*. Academic Press.

Sjoberg, F. M., Mellon, J., & Peixoto, T. (2015). *The Effect of Government Responsiveness on Future Political Participation*. Available at https://www.mysociety.org/research/government-responsiveness-political-participation/

Smith, G. (2009). *Democratic Innovations. Designing Institutions for Citizen Participation*. Cambridge, UK: Cambridge University Press. doi:10.1017/CBO9780511609848

Smith, G., & Ryan, M. (2014). Defining Mini-Publics: Making Senseof Existing Conceptions. In K. Grönlund, A. Bächtiger, & M. Setälä (Eds.), *Deliberative Mini-Publics: Involving Citizens in the Democratic Process*. Colchester, UK: ECPR Press.

Sorice, M. (2019). *Partecipazione democratica*. Milano: Mondadori.

Spada, P. (2012). *Political Competition in Deliberative and Participatory Institutions* (Dissertation). Yale University.

Spada, P. (2014). *Political Competition and the Diffusion of Policy Innovations in Local Government: The Case of Participatory Budgeting in Brazil*. Paper presented at the annual Meeting of the Latin American Studies Association. Available online at: http://www.spadap.com/app/download/8877410668/The%20 Diffusion%20of%20Democratic%20Innovations_2015.pdf?t=1434577381

Spada, P., Klein, M., Calabretta, R., Iandoli, L., & Quinto, I. (2015). *A First Step toward Scaling-up Deliberation: Optimizing Large Group E-Deliberation Using Argument Maps*. Paper presented at the annual conference of the American Political Science Association. Available online at: http://www.spadap.com/app/download/8877667268/scalingup_june2015.pdf?t=1434577381

Spada, P., & Vreeland, J. R. (2013). Who Moderates the Moderators? *Journal of Public Deliberation*, *9*(2).

Steenbergen, M. S., Bächtiger, A., Pedrini, S., & Gautschi, T. (2015). Information, Deliberation, and Direct Democracy. In Y. Peter Lang (Ed.), Deliberation and Democracy: Innovative Processes and Institutions (p. 187). Academic Press.

Stone, M., Hobbs, M., & Khaleeli, M. (2002). Multichannel Customer Management: the Benefits and Challenges. *Journal of Database Marketing & Customer Strategy Management*, *10*(1).

Stortone, S., & De Cindio, F. (2015). Hybrid Participatory Budgeting: Local Democratic Practices in the Digital Era. In Citizen's Right to the Digital City (pp. 177-197). Springer Singapore.

Stromer-Galley, J. (2013). *Presidential campaigning in the Internet age*. New York, NY: Oxford University Press.

Sunstein, C. R., & Thaler, R. (2008). Nudge. The politics of libertarian paternalism.

Torres, L., Pina, V., & Acerate, B. (2006). E-governance developments in European Union cities: Reshaping government's relationship with citizens. *Governance: Int. J. Policy Admin. Institutions*, *19*(2), 277–302. doi:10.1111/j.1468-0491.2006.00315.x

Trechsel, A., Kies, R., Mendez, F., & Schmitter, P. (2003). *Evaluation of the Use of New Technologies in order to Facilitate Democracy in Europe. E-democratizing the Parliaments and Parties of Europe*. Study on behalf of the European Parliament for Scientific Technology Options Assessment.

Wampler, B. (2007). *Participatory Budgeting in Brazil. Contestation, Cooperation, and Accountability*. Penn State Press.

Wampler, B. (2015). *Activating Democracy in Brazil. Popular Participation, Social Justice, and Interlocking Institutions*. University of Notre Dame Press.

Wampler, B., & Hartz-karp, J. (2012). Participatory Budgeting: Diffusion and Outcomes across the World. *Journal of Public Deliberation*, *8*(2), 13. Available online at http://www.publicdeliberation.net/jpd/vol8/iss2/art13

Warren, M. E., & Pearse, H. (2008). *Designing Deliberative Democracy*. The British Columbia Citizens' Assembly, Cambridge University Press. doi:10.1017/CBO9780511491177

Yildiz, M. (2007). E-government research: Reviewing the literature, limitations and ways forward. *Government Information Quarterly*, *24*(3), 646–665. doi:10.1016/j.giq.2007.01.002

ENDNOTES

1 See: http://oidp2017mtl.com/sites/oidp2017mtl.com/files/pdf/EN_actesOIDP_web.pdf

2 https://empatia-project.eu

3 See http://www.participedia.net/en/news/2015/10/01/global-research-partnership-awarded-significant-grant-support-participedia

4 Some examples are: experimental studies on facilitators (Humphreys, Masters, & Sandbu, 2006; Farrar et al., 2010; Spada & Vreeland, 2013), different online platforms for ideation (Spada, Klein, Calabretta, Iandoli & Quinto 2015), the role of group composition (Farrar et al., 2009; Karpowitz, Mendelberg, & Shaker, 2012), the role of different decision-making processes (Morrell 1999), and the role of information vs deliberation (Steenbergen, Bächtiger, Pedrini, & Gautschi, 2015).

5 View the following for a description of the Facebook algorithm http://www.slate.com/articles/technology/cover_story/2016/01/how_facebook_s_news_feed_algorithm_works.html

6 See http://backend.pbnyc.org/maps/?d=8&display_type=winners

7 See https://www.fixmystreet.com/

8 See https://assets.digital.cabinet-office.gov.uk/spotlight/documents/Policy-Housing-74ee84f-968933609e499c9dc3e3a158d.pdf

9 See https://www.loomio.org/

10 See https://ideascale.com/

11 See http://liquidfeedback.org/

12 See https://en.wikipedia.org/wiki/1%25_rule_%28Internet_culture%29

13 Some PB processes, particularly digital PB process (e-PB) in Germany employ an ideation software that combines the brainstorming phase with the selection phase. In Bonn e-PB participants employ a software similar to Ideascale and can propose ideas and then immediately rank them. Other PB processes, such as the ones employed in North America and designed by the Participatory Budgeting Project, instead divide the selection phase into a refining phase and a voting phase. During the refining phase volunteers take the projects generated in the brainstorming phase and together with the city staff refine them to generate a ballot. During the voting phase the entire city is invited to vote for the projects on the ballot.

14 See http://www2.portoalegre.rs.gov.br/op/

15 See http://labs.council.nyc/pb/participate/

16 https://citylimits.org/2018/11/02/cityviews-five-reasons-to-vote-yes-on-proposal-2/

17 See the report on the assembly http://citizensassembly.co.uk/assembly-south-overview-report/

18 In Brazil many cities every five years implement a participatory process called Plano Pluriennal Participativo (Multi-year Participatory Plan) to design the zoning plan and the guidelines for city public projects. Similar participatory planning processes are adopted by neighborhoods and cities around the world.

19 People's panels are a common practice of UK cities. The Southampton people panel is a typical example: https://www.southampton.gov.uk/council-democracy/have-your-say/peoples-panel.aspx

20 See http://newurbanmechanics.org/

21 See http://poplus.org/

22 See http://empatia-project.eu/

23 See https://www.change.org/impact

24 See: https://oidp.net/pt/experience.php?id=1149

25 For a detailed case study and background documentation see the Participedia case study: http://participedia.net/en/cases/grandview-woodland-citizens-assembly

26 See https://ourcommunityourplan.wordpress.com/about/

27 See http://www.grandview-woodland.ca/

28 See http://www.straight.com/news/676076/grandview-woodland-citizens-assembly-process-draws-criticism

29 See https://elizabethmurphyblog.wordpress.com/2015/01/08/citys-grandview-planning/

30 Wikipedia defines slacktivism as a portmanteau of the words slacker and activism. The word is usually considered a pejorative term that describes feel-good measures in support of a social cause that have little practical effects.

31 http://repurpose.workersvoice.org/how_it_works

Chapter 4
Public Engagement and Policy Entrepreneurship on Social Media in the Time of Anti-Vaccination Movements

Melodie Yunju Song
https://orcid.org/0000-0002-3492-6835
Ted Rogers School of Management, Ryerson University, Canada

ABSTRACT

North America has experienced a resurgence of measles outbreak due to unprecedentedly low Mumps-Measles and Rubella vaccination coverage rates facilitated by the anti-vaccination movement. The objective of this chapter is to explore the new online public space and public discourse using Web 2.0 in the public health arena to answer the question, 'What is driving public acceptance of or hesitancy towards the MMR vaccine?' More specifically, typologies of online public engagement will be examined using MMR vaccine hesitancy as a case study to illustrate the different approaches used by pro- and anti-vaccine groups to inform, consult with, and engage the public on a public health issue that has been the subject of long-standing public debate and confusion. This chapter provides an overview of the cyclical discourse of anti-vaccination movements. The authors hypothesize that anti-vaccination, vaccine hesitant, and pro-vaccination representations on the online public sphere are reflective of competing values (e.g., modernism, post-modernism) in contemporary society.

INTRODUCTION

A highly contagious disease, measles deaths claimed 110,000 lives in 2017, with children under the age of 5 taking the hardest toll (World Health Organization, 2019c). In most Organization for Economic Co-operation and Development (OECD) countries, MMR vaccine is highly accessible, provided for free by the state or provincial government. Despite so, the rate of unvaccinated children are rising (Larson, Jarrett, Eckersberg, Smith, & Patterson, 2014). According to the World Health Organization (WHO),

DOI: 10.4018/978-1-7998-1828-1.ch004

reported cases of measles in 2019 increase by 300% (n=112,163) compared to 2018 in the first three months alone (World Health Organization, 2019b). Since reported cases makes up 10% of the actual cases, and global MMR immunization coverage is currently at merely 67%, it is projected that measles outbreaks will continue an upwards trajectory if immunization rates remain below the targeted global coverage rate of 95% (ibid).

WHO has declared vaccine hesitancy as one of the top 10 threats to global health in 2019 (World Health Organization, 2019a). Research shows that decreased immunization coverage rates due to vaccine hesitancy leads to periodic and sustained vaccine-preventable outbreaks in the US (Bolton, Memory, & McMillan, 2015), France (Ward, 2016), Croatia (Repalust, Šević, Rihtar, & Štulhofer, 2016), China (Wagner et al., 2017), Japan (Okuhara, Ishikawa, Okada, Kato, & Kiuchi, 2017), Malaysia (Mohd, Kew, & Moy, 2017), Italy (Aquino et al., 2017), Ukraine (The Lancet Editorial, 2018), and Brasil (Sato, 2018).

One of the most common reasons for vaccine hesitancy relates to the concern that MMR vaccines cause autism, an erroneous claim that first appeared in a false publication in a reputable journal - The Lancet – in 1998 (Wakefield et al., 1998). Wakefield's fraudulent paper was the match that ignited the fiery skepticism to MMR vaccination. Powerful international and national advocacy groups such as the National Vaccine Information Center Advocacy Portal (NVICAC), the Californian Coalition for Vaccination Choice (CCVC) uses social media and websites to actively disseminate and sign petitions against all types of vaccines, calling for vaccine exemption for their children based on philosophical grounds (CCVC, 2015). Although the Lancet retracted the article in 2010, the damage was done. The paper was circulated for 12 years, the false results were reported by the media, discussed in press, and on the internet, and had been cited by thousands.

Researchers in medicine, public health, communication, mass media, computer science and informatics are boggled by the resistance to one of the safest medical interventions in humanity. These researchers ask the same question from various angles in hopes of finding out 'What drives some segments of society to accept the MMR vaccine while others are reject the vaccine?'

We use the case of vaccine hesitancy to explore public health discourse using online media to answer our question of interest. Typologies of online public engagement will be examined to illustrate the different approaches used by pro- and anti-vaccine groups to inform, consult with and engage with the public on public health issues that has been the subject of long-standing debate and confusion. The parallel narratives of two existing paradigms (modernism and post-modernism) are used to explain how different perceptions of vaccination have been shaped by vaccination proponents and opponents. In the first section, we provide a brief account of anti-vaccination movements in the West starting with resistance of the smallpox vaccine in the UK in the 19th century. In the second section, we propose that an ideological clash between practitioners of modernism and the postmodernists is the overarching reason for anti-vaccination movements to persist. The third section touches on the typologies of public engagement online and compare and contrast the different methods of online engagement tactics employed by pro- and anti-vaccine agencies. Finally, we draw on the psychological and political frameworks on issue framing to discuss the plausible reasons for the persistence of anti-vaccination movements on a micro-level.

BACKGROUND

The Cyclical Discourse of Anti-Vaccination Movements in the West

Since the first commercially available vaccination was developed in 1796 by Edward Jenner to create immunity to smallpox, vaccine hesitancy has been a prevailing conversation in the public sphere. Hesitancy towards new technology – in this case, a procedure that eliminates the possibility of getting deadly diseases such as the chicken pox, exists as long as technocultural strife in the public sphere continues to be regurgitated and discussed.

The First Wave: Late 1850's - 1900's

The first wave of anti-vaccination movements was targeted at mandatory vaccines such as smallpox vaccines and the polio vaccine. The first national anti-vaccination organization recorded in history was the National Anti-vaccination league (NAVL) (Durbach, 2004; The Cincinnati DailyGazette, 1879; Wolfe & Sharp, 2002). The NAVL impressively repealed the British Vaccination Acts of 1853, 1867, and 1871 in Britain due to the coalitions' claim that there was inconclusive evidence as to whether smallpox vaccine caused leprosy (Kakar, 1996; Porter & Porter, 1988). The Royal Commission conducted 11 enquiries from 1898-1907 on vaccine safety. The result was 'The Act of 1898', a law that allows parents to request exemption for their children under 'conscientious objection' in the UK (Salmon et al., 2006).

The NAVL excelled at communicating their agenda. They had their own monthly newspaper, regular town hall meetings, and they had enough donors to support holding the first International Congress of Anti-Vaccinators in 1883 (Sacramento Daily Union, 1983). NAVL also visited Canada and the US to help establish the Anti-Vaccination League of Canada in 1900 and the Anti-Vaccination Society of America in 1908 (Arnup, 1992; Poland & Jacobson, 2011). These movements were a by-product of resistance to the growing acceptance of mechanical and technological advancement in the late 19th century.

Around this time, public health first came into recognition in North America, representative of this was the Jacobson vs. Massachusetts law (1902) – the first landmark public health law that established a government's legal responsibility in protecting others' health by way of requesting mandatory vaccina- tion (Mariner, Annas, & Glantz, 2005; Parmet et al, 2005). The Jacobson vs. Massachusetts Law marked the end of the first anti-vaccination movement.

The Second Wave: Post World War II

Post-WWII marked the height of success in vaccination delivery with little anti-vaccination resistance from the public (Omer, Salmon, Orenstein, deHart, & Halsey, 2009). Opponents of universal vaccines came from within the scientific community. In the 1960's onwards, several groups of physicians published in medical journals questioning the rationality of the Diphtheria, Pertussis, and Tetanus (DPT) vaccine because of observed correlation between DPT vaccine inoculation and neurological complications, encephalitis, and its lack of efficacy (Baker, 2003, 2008; Gangarosa et al., 1998; Poland & Jacobson, 2001; Stewart, 1980; Stewart & Wilson, 1981; Strom, 1960), whooping coughs rarely kills (Gangarosa et al., 1998; Poland & Jacobson, 2011). Within this group of anti-DPT physicians, Professor Greg Stewart was considered the de facto spokesperson in the press and on the radio and television (Baker, 2003, 2008; Stewart, 1980; Stewart & Wilson, 1981).

Stewart's claim drew enough attention that the British Joint Committee on Vaccination and Immunization (JCVI) launched the National Childhood Encephalitis Study (NCES) based on cases submitted by the Association of Parents of Vaccine-Damaged Children, a UK-based, parent-led non-profit association (Baker, 2003). Subsequently, uptake of DPT decreased to 50% in 1980's compared to 91% in the early 70's, and pertussis endemic swept the UK, Sweden, Russia, Italy, and Australia (Baker, 2003). Where anti-vaccination movements were most vocal in printed press, many were highly educated and demanded justice for their children, they provided pamphlets and taught parents to write to local legislators to call for investigation (Fox, 2006). Although all cases pointed towards null correlation to neurological damage nor encephalitis with DPT vaccine, the public has lost its trust for DPT for a whole decade starting in the mid-70's (Baker, 2003).

The Third Wave: 1998 to Present

All medical interventions come with a risk, but the MMR vaccine is considered one of the safest and most cost-effective medical interventions in human history (Bloom, Marcuse, & Mnookin, 2014). In the 80's, vaccine production was thought to be a low return-rate, one-time only procedure that pharmaceutical companies had little interest in manufacturing; coupled with previous anti-vaccination safety concerns, willingness to produce vaccines was lukewarm (Offit, 2005).

The third wave of anti-vaccination movement began after a now-retracted fraudulent article on the linkage of autism and MMR vaccination was published on the Lancet (Wakefield et al., 1998). In the UK, media widely reported the study findings and English-speaking countries soon picked up on the report, attracting international attention from concerned parents, curious physicians, and skeptical immunologists and virologists. Amidst floating rumors that the vaccine's thiomersal content causes autism, some parties were more vocal than others, thus leading to the third wave of anti-vaccination movement and the most recent MMR outbreaks that are the focus of our case study.

In the wake of the Lancet article, a well-connected and tech-savvy Olmsted formed the Age of Autism (AoA) in 2007, posting daily content about mercury in vaccines and its causal link to autism, and the epidemic of autism in a pseudo-investigative manner (Age of Autism, 2015). Other anti-vaccination groups grew both in scale and in presence led by trailblazers such as The Canary, SafeMinds, Generation Rescue, and ThinkTwice who linked personal accounts of their children's autism to Wakefield's paper (Age of Autism, 2015; Callous Disregard.com, 2015).

As a counterbalance to these claims, the CDC, The American Academy of Pediatrics (AAP), the Institute of Medicine of the US National Academy of Sciences, the NHS in the UK, and the Cochrane Library conducted reviews that failed to replicate Wakefield's findings (CDC, 2014; Demicheli, Rivetti, Debalini, & Di Pietrantonj, 2012; Hornig et al., 2008; Jefferson, Price, Demicheli, & Bianco, 2003; NHS, 2013; Taylor, Swerdfeger, & Eslick, 2014). Nonetheless, these false claims led various states in the US to allow exemption from immunization for non-religious reasons (Fiebelkorn et al., 2010) due to strong resistance from the public and from concerned senators who have stood by this claim.

From 2000 – 2010, MMR vaccine coverage rates experienced alarming declines (Bloom et al., 2014). Many researchers have observed an increased frequency and severity of measles outbreaks correlated with areas with higher vaccine exemptions (Omer, Salmon, Orenstein, deHart, & Halsey, 2009). Regions with less than 90% of the population immunized against measles are expected to see an 'import effect' that leads to foreign measles carriers spreading the disease to measles-free countries with low vaccine coverage (Malani, 2015). In 2014 to 2015, the largest measles outbreak in the US and Canada occurred, extenuating the third wave of anti-vaccination movement to a scale larger than anticipated.

Anti-vaccination movements have caused sociopolitical turbulences as well as improvements of the regulation of vaccine safety in all regions around the world. In the first movement, seen in the Jacobson vs Massachusetts Law, the importance of public health held a higher regard over a person's right to choose. In the second wave of anti-vaccination movement, the adverse effects and safety concerns of DPT, polio, anddozensofothervaccinesdevelopedduringmid-90'sledtotheestablishmentof Vaccine Adverse Event Reporting System (VAERS) by the FDA and CDC in the US, and the National Advisory Committee on Immunization (NACI) under PHAC in Canada, and many compensatory programs for vaccine-related injuries in many high-income countries (Historyofvaccines.org, 2015). In the third wave of the anti- vaccination movement, as Web 2.0 has made interactive communication convenient, we have witnesseda plethora of online discussions from both proponents and opponents of MMR vaccines talking amongst themselves (Yaqub, Castle-Clarke, Sevdalis, & Chataway, 2014; Yom-Tov & Fernandez-Luque, 2014). The cyclical discourse illustrated above helps us understand that insofar as any type of vaccine is administered, vaccine hesitancy will persist. Table 1 is a compilation of various anti-vaccination move- ments against many types of vaccinations since the 1990's, and reasons for the resistance differs drasti- cally. In a sense, people who refuse to be vaccinated are refusing to accept not just the vaccine, but the ideology the vaccine stood for. By resisting the vaccine, one is openly resisting the idea the vaccine is trying to convey. The three waves of anti-vaccination movements are not all bad, if we consider that these initiatives started from the public by the public.

Publics, to be distinguished from formal organizations, transcend organizational group boundaries; publics can be mobilized despite organizational constraints (Umemoto, 1998). The fact that these movements were facilitated outside of formal organizations brings important meaning to contemporary practice of medicine – that all voices from the public (regardless of which public) deserve to be heard. We will draw on two distinct philosophical ideologies to support our observation that anti-vaccination groups is part of the reaction to the dominant format of decision-making in medicine that is evidence-based medicine (EBM).

A POSTMODERN UNDERSTANDING OF ONLINE ANTI-VACCINATION MOVEMENTS

Ana Kata from McMaster University observed the online tropes and rhetoric of anti-vaccinators from 2010-2013, she noted that it is we, those who are certain that vaccines are 'good', who need to understand what captures the curiosity and imaginations that concerned publics are discovering on the internet, or, as she calls it, 'the post-modern Pandora's box' (Kata, 2010, p.1).

To speak about post-modernism, we would first need to turn to modernism. Modernism is the 'belief in the existence of truth, objectivity, determinacy, causality, and impartial observation', it seeks to 'capture, define, understand, and control knowledge' (Rosenau, 1992, cited in Chan & Chan, 2000, p.1). Modernism is practiced through representations in forms of artistic expression, aesthetics in architecture, compositions in music and poetry, and in line with our chapter – applications of medical practice known as evidence-based medicine (EBM).

Table 1. Anti-vaccination movements around the world since the 1990's

Year	Country	Type of Vaccine	Reasons for resistance	Impact on public acceptability of vaccine
1984 - 97	US, UK, Russia, Sweden, Ukraine	DPT (Pertussis)	Scare of neurological damage, lead FDA-USA to inspect thimerosal level in DPT	Safety scares, low public trust in pertussis vaccines
1994-97	Mexico, the Philippines, Tanzania, and Nicaragua	Tetanus	Religious (Catholic Human Life International), vaccine rumored to cause sterilization	coverage dropped by 45%
1999	France	HiB	French government suspended recommendations for HiB in suspicion of vaccine efficacy	Coverage dropped by 70%
2003 - 09	Afghanistan, Nigeria, Pakistan	Polio	Militant religious groups claimed that vaccine is against the Quran and is a symbol of 'Westernism'	Polio pandemic in 18 polio-free countries
2010	India	HiB	Too expensive, hostility towards pharmaceutical companies	Anti-HiB campaigns and drop of coverage
2011	Japan	HiB	Suspected deaths investigation	Coverage dropped by 50%
2010- 13	The Netherlands	MMR	Religious	Sporadic outbreaks that lead unvaccinated foreigners to contract measles to carry to other countries
2013- 15	Canada, US	MMR	Religious, fear of autism (since 1998)	Worst Measles outbreak in the 21st century in USA and Canada.

All data extracted from Gangarosa et al., 1998; Omer, Salmon, Orenstein, deHart, & Halsey, 2009; Poland & Jacobson, 2001, 2011; Wolfe & Sharp, 2002

The modernist philosophy that perpetuated society in Western Europe and the US. EBM can be seen as an heir to the modernist philosophy developing in the 1990's as 'conscientious, explicit, and judicious use of current best evidence in making decisions about the care of individual patients' (Sackett, Rosenberg, Gray, Haynes, & Richardson, 1996, p.71). To Sackett and colleagues, practice becomes risk when physicians are not keeping up-to-date with the newest evidence. The authors encouraged practitioners and medical schools to welcome the idea of EBM for the benefit of the patients and for its unique bottom-up approach to treatment and care.

Contrary to the modernist paradigms, postmodern scholars acknowledge that reality is a multiple construct subject to scrutiny through text and relativism - its interpretations depend heavily on contextual, linguistic, and cultural factors of its time. 'Everything is a text' says Derrida, deconstructing thoughts and behaviors to text helps us think of an 'organization as a text – or, to shift to a slightly different parallel metaphor, to think of organization as a storytelling system' (Boje, 1995, cited in Tyler, 2005, p.2). Interpreted this way, we can see that dialogues occurring on the Web are, indeed, text; above all, these texts are organizations of self-contained 'storytelling systems' that breathes a life of its own and cannot be ignored or dismissed. It is under these conditions that concerned parents and vaccine hesitant publics have created their own narrative to the experience of risk in a technocultural society. For a concerned anti-vaxxer, browsing vaccine safety information online is meant for the individual to confront and disrupt preexisting discourse of medical paternalism – by acknowledging the dialogical processes involved in the continuous shaping of the meaning of anything that is 'current', we are allowing the development of alternative discourses in *petits récits* of vaccination (Chan & Chan, 2000).

To a modernist scholar, post-modernism is an amorphous concept that encompasses too many aspects to define or capture. The straightforward modernism, embodied in EBM, values hierarchy of research evidence, up from systematic reviews and meta-analysis, randomized control trials, cohort studies, down the ladder to case-control studies and so on. However, taking Beck's observation that today's society is preoccupied with risk over benefit, the EBM model that looks at exclusively 'effectiveness' and 'cost-benefit' tends to overlook the publics' increasing need to understand risks (Gray, 1999).

Sackett'scolleague Graywhoco-wrotethehighlycirculated British Medical Journalarticle 'Evidence-based medicine – what it is and what it is not' in 1996, curiously published an article in the Lancet three years later, titled "postmodern medicine" (Gray, 1999). In this article, he reflects on modern medicine's need to prepare for the tidal-wave of challenges that will come with technological and sociocultural changes. He identifies 5 postmodernist responsibilities that need to be tied to the EBM movementas follows: health services that are 'values-based', acknowledgement of a 'risk-preoccupied society', 'patient experience' interpreted subjectively by the patient, integrating bringing back healing to treatment processes, and finally, 'a shift in sapiential authority from clinician to patient' that encourages the breakdown barriers for the public to access to medical information (Gray, 1999, p.3). Gray's reflection illustrate that EBM alone is not enough to bring the public proper care in a rapidly changing society that demands to understand risk. Quoting David Eddy, 'Having opened the first black box- evidence- the second black box – preferences – will need to be opened in public (Gray, 1999, p.2).' Gray's observation confirms that the postmodernism interpretation of medicine by the public is alive and well, and it is not just misinformation about the false claim of linkage between autism and MMR vaccine that gives anti-vaccination the fuel for fire. In fact, parents who are well-educated and seek out information tend to delay or refuse vaccination for their children (Eisenstein, 2014; Yang, Delamater, Leslie, & Mello, 2016). In the first two sections of this chapter, we have shown that there is an overarching paradigm propel- ling the anti-vaccination movement. In the post-modernist medical paradigm of knowledge acquisition, anti-vaccination claims appeal to the 'self-taught' man, the notion that 'there are no objective facts but rather multiple meaning and ways of knowing' (Gray, 1999; cited in Kata, 2012, p.2). The public's behavior and trust are no longer influenced by public service announcements or carrot-and-stick poli- cies. Instead, a relative interpretation pertaining to personal experience acquired from Google triumphs hard science. In this case, at least. Discrepancies between the institutional perspective of information retrieval and information processing (i.e. modernist, paternalist) to that of the public on social media (i.e. post-modernist) are obvious. Understanding the strengths and weaknesses of these two co-existing paradigms may enable public health practitioners to replace the old-fashioned 'Public Service Announcement' approach.

A Case Study of Anti-and Pro-Vaccine Websites During the 2013-2014 Measles Outbreak

In July of 2013, the Public Health Agency of Canada (PHAC) issued a public health notice on their webpage and to traditional press that an unusual number of measles cases were reported in Alberta, British Columbia, Ontario, and Manitoba (Government of Canada, 2013). Previously, the province of Quebec alone reported 705 cases in 2011. These two outbreaks preceded the largest Canadian measles outbreak (2014-2015) since the 90's.

In Canada, over 65% of internet users are hooked into at least one form of social media (CIRA, 2015), and the numbers are growing each year. This not only creates opportunities for public participation in vaccination dialogues but an online *'agora'* in which openly accessible aggregates of population data on health behaviors and adoption of health beliefs can be traced and measured by readily available and 'rapidly expanding repertoire of social technologies'(Centola, 2013, p. 2135).

The Internet responded to the return of measles outbreaks with fervor and a search for 'where it all began' started. News media focused on Jenny McCarthy, an American talk show host who acted as the spokesperson for Autismspeaks.com, and an avid anti-vaxxer, to be the culprit in the outbreak. A plethora of academic articles were published to refute Wakefield's 1998 paper, pointing to him and his retracted paper as the culprit of the anti-vaccination movement and subsequent outbreaks (Offit, 2005). Health practitioners would also point to the lack of engagement of pediatricians and nurses and health educators in educating parents in clinics and hospitals (Omer et al., 2009). On the other hand, anti-vaxxers online have stood by Jenny McCarthy, including Wakefield, who described 'Jenny [a]s a decent individual trying hard to do the right thing' (AgeofAutism.com, 2013). Anti-vaxxers demanded an investigation into safer MMR vaccines and maintained that it is a parent's job to protect their child.

This parallel discourse between the EBM (modernism) and the anti-vaccination movement (postmodernism) suggests it maybe be time to change how medical professionals and authorities communicate information to the public regarding vaccination safety. What are the available typologies for engaging the online public, given that physicians, public health professionals, and health practitioners have been slow to perceive social media as a safe or effective platform for public engagement (Hanson et al., 2011; Keller, Labrique, Jain, Pekosz, & Levine, 2014)? Outbreaks are rarely caused by the ripple effect of one published paper, or celebrities, or health professionals who are unable to persuade parents to vaccinate their child. Looking at how vaccine information is being communicated in the online public space allows us to observe opportunities for pro-vaccination agencies to converse with the vaccine-hesitant and the anti-vaxxers more effectively, thus reducing the possibility of vaccine-refusal induced measles cases. To examine the current array of online public engagement methods being used and improved to promote two-way communication during the 2013-2014 measles outbreak in North America, we draw on Rowe and Frewer's typology of public engagement as our framework for this case study (Rowe & Frewer, 2005). The internet has experienced dynamic changes in functionality that can be categorized into two parts: Web 1.0 and Web 2.0. Web 1.0 depicts the web's static and unidirectional functionality popular in the 90's (e.g., static pages full of words, images, videos, and hyperlinking to other websites for more information, emailing).

Web 2.0, on the other hand, is 'all about harnessing collective intelligence' (O'Reilly & Battelle, 2009, p.1). According to proliferators of Web 2.0, it is a virtual *agora (Stone, 2008)* – a public open space used for assemblies and markets where ideas are tossed around and snatched or dismissed (Stone, 2008). In this sense, the web can be especially advantageous to engaging in effective vaccine information communication. According to Witteman and colleagues, there are three advantages of Web2.0 to harness for vaccine communication:

Table 2. Mechanisms of public engagement

Engagement Type	Examples	Directionality
Public Communication	Cable TV, Information broadcasts on the radio, Static internet information (webpages)	Uni-directional, one-way
Public Consultation	Citizen panel, Interactive websites, telepolling, survey	Bi-directional (information is pre-prepared, specific, and minimal.
Public Participation	User experience (UX) panel, deliberative opinion poll, Citizen's jury	Bi-directional, dialogical

Adopted from Rowe, G., & Frewer, L. J. (2005). A typology of public engagement mechanisms.

1. **Real-Time User Participation:** Anyone with an internet connection can find information and participate in dialogues to inform themselves of the newest information on vaccination.
2. **Openness:** Anyone can easily contribute, build, and retrieve information regardless of age, gender, race, or socioeconomic status.
3. **Network Effects:** Internet enhances our capacity to make connections with connect with likeminded people and 'enhance and enrich others' participation' (Witteman & Zikmund-Fisher, 2012, p.3735).

Our case is focused on examining how, amidst the Measles outbreak, anti-and pro-vaccine groups use Web 1.0 and Web 2.0 as a platform for engaging the public to understand the risks and benefits of vaccination. We draw on the typology of public engagement mechanisms developed by Rowe and Frewer which depicts public engagement as being enacted through a variety of structured mechanisms. First, one way *public communication* describes a process where information is initiated by those who wish to contact or spread information to the public. Examples on the web include using Web 1.0 for static information retrieval by internet users from pro-vaccination agencies, anti-vaccination agencies, and government agencies, information broadcasts TV, news, radio) and drop-in clinics for information retrieval. Second, one-way *public consultation* during which information is requested from an agency that is interested in hearing from other parties, for instance, using Web 2.0 to establish contact with pro-, anti-, and governmental agencies concerning vaccination information, and reaching out to the public by the forms of surveys, opinion polls, focus groups and citizen panels. Finally, *public participation* in which information is *exchanged* between the public and agencies in the form of deliberative opinion polls, action-planning workshops, and consensus conferences. Public participation is the most complex and complete mechanism of public engagement because it is characterized by an element of problem-solving by both the public and the agencies who wish to influence the public (see Table 2). We use this typology to describe the existing types of public engagement online used by pro-, anti-, and governmental agencies to communicate about vaccine information with the public.

Pro-Vaccine Agencies Promotes Vaccines through Web 1.0, Anti-Vaccine Agencies Engage the Public Using Web 2.0

We manually searched for pro-vaccine and anti-vaccine websites and social media platforms on the Canadian Google search engine in March of 2014. Search terms included "vaccination", "vaccine safety", "vaccine good", "vaccine bad", and "immunization OR immunization". Inclusion criteria included: English website, active websites that are represented by an organization that has made explicit their position on vaccination. Exclusion criteria included: a website containing only adult vaccination information (e.g. HPV vaccine, flu vaccine), new sources, and websites specializing in news in science. Only results shown in the top 10 pages on Google web search were included in our review. Of the 37 websites identified as pro- and anti-vaccination websites, we categorized the engagement according to the Rowe and Frewer typology. Public communication embedded in the Web 1.0 approach was the most popular form of engagement, all 37 websites exhibited one-way communication. The researcher further categorized the specific types of public engagement within the 3 mechanisms. Six forms of Web 1.0 engagement included:

1. Websites that allowed viewers to email agencies for inquiry and feedback,
2. Websites with downloadable brochures,
3. Informational websites with FAQs,
4. Blogs with information provided by a health authority or healthcare professional,
5. Websites containing vaccine information with a recognizable spokesperson, and
6. Scheduled immunization recommendations.

These forms of engagement are unilateral and provide no opportunity for direct feedback or bilateral engagement.

We also identified 8 forms of Web 2.0 engagement methods which included:

1. Real-time interactions on Twitter, Facebook, and blogs where authors respond to the questions directly to messages from their personal or official accounts,
2. Websites with direct phone number for informational inquiry,
3. Discussion forums,
4. Webpages allowing comments on webpage content and user experience (UX) feedback,
5. Applications on portable devices with personalized immunization plans and live newsfeed,
6. Interactive video sessions (e.g., sessions on Google Hangout or Skype) designated for Q&A for interested subscribers,
7. Official YouTube or Facebook and Twitter accounts that posts videos, Tweets under which viewers to post comments and contribute to content, and
8. The presence of recognizable spokespersons engaging in the above forms of social media.

In Table 3, we show that anti-vaccination agencies use both Web 1.0 and Web 2.0 approaches, but Web 2.0 engagement methods are more commonly used. The organizations that created the websites are gaining traction by engaging in dialogues via social media (i.e. Twitter, Facebook, YouTube, forums, and blogs). Anti-vaccine websites are 'repositories of vaccine information and vaccine-related resources' (Grant et al., 2015, p.1) that includes discussions, open forums and private forums to build a sense of inclusivity and protectiveness for anti-vaccination online participants.

Pro-vaccination websites have prescribed a traditional health communications approach, one that promotes three foci: awareness, education and accessibility to vaccine-related knowledge (Lee & Van-Dyke, 2016). Methods of Web 1.0 to announce services to the public are common in pro-vaccination websites except for non-profit parent-found websites like VoicesForVaccines.org. Although government websites like the Centers for Disease Control (CDC), PHAC (Public Health Agency of Canada), and provincial/regional health divisions like the Ministry of Health (MoH) of British Columbia have modi-

Table 3. Use of Web 1.0 and Web 2.0 for public engagement of pro- and anti-vaccine websites

			Number of Pro-Vaccine Groups (19)	Number of Anti-Vaccine Websites (18)
Web 1.0	1	Websites that allows viewers to email for inquiry and feedback	19	17
	2	Downloadable brochures, publications, and books	15	16
	3	Informational websites with FAQs	15	10
	4	Information provided by a health authority or healthcare professional,	19	0*
	5	Containing vaccine information with a recognizable spokesperson	1	6
	6	Scheduled immunization recommendations	11	7
Web 2.0	1	Twitter, Facebook, and Facebook pages where authors or organizational representatives respond to messages (from their personal or official accounts)	4	18
	2	Direct phone number for informational inquiry	8	13
	3	Interactive discussion forums, comment sections, and blogs affiliated to the organization	1	13
	4	Allowing comments on webpage content and user experience (UX) feedback	4	11
	5	Scheduled interactive video sessions (e.g., sessions on Google Hangout or Skype) designated for Q&A for interested subscribers	0	5
	6	Official YouTube accounts that posts videos under which viewers to post comments and contribute to content	1	10
	7	The presence of recognizable spokespersons engaging in social media.	1**	4

*Eleven anti-vaccine websites analyzed in this study have quoted Andrew Wakefield as their source of scientific evidence. All anti-vaccination websites have links to publications on autism and/or vaccination that does not appear on pro-vaccination websites or refuted by the WHO.

**All data retrieved in January, 2016

fied their webpages to accommodate the latest morbidity and mortality reports, vaccination information, and educational materials for the public to retrieve, these prescriptive one-way communication from the institutional perspective focusing on 'accurate transmissions of evidence-based scientific research' and 'government-endorsed vaccine-related practices.' are hinged on Web 1.0 approaches that are less salient for the average public. (Grant et al., 2015, p.1).

In this pilot study, we have also witnessed journalists and medical professionals resorting to quasi-two-way communications like blogging and Tweeting - in Rowe and Frewer's typology this can be typified as both public communication and public consultation. Science-Based Medicine is an influential blog curated and contributed by physicians in virology and pediatrics to refute claims of MMR's relation with Autism (Gorski, 2015), it has now grown to encompass a wide array of myth-busting content that is informational. Traces of pro-vaccination presence on social media are mostly represented by Tweeters and medical journalists (e.g., Andre Picard from the Globe and Mail, and Julia Belluz for Vox.com), this spectrum of content was left out of our categorization due to the lack of authority (and organization) behind medical journalism's investigative nature.

To understand vaccine hesitancy, pro-vaccination agencies and government authorities are lagging behind to engage the public in communication. Heath care professionals and government agencies in the modern era could approach the issue of anti-vaccine with the mindset of a communications specialist instead of a 'set it and forget it' paternal utilitarian modernism approach to address vaccine hesitancy

List of anti-vaccination websites analyzed (18):

www.ThinkTwice.com,
www.vaccinetruth.com,
www.Justthevaxx.blogspot.com,
www.thevaccinereaction.org,
www.vaccines.mercola.com,
www.Ageofautism.com,
www.Vactruth.com,
http://www.vaccinationinformationnetwork.com/,
www.Safeminds.org,
www.canaryparty.org,
www.thehealthyhomeeconomist.com,
www.vaccinationcouncil.org,
www.Autismspeaks.org,
www.Healthimpactnews.com,
http://www.fourteenstudies.org/,
http://vaccinechoicecanada.com/health-risks/autism/,
http://www.generationrescue.org/resources/vaccination/
http://www.globalresearch.ca/are-vaccines-safe/15669

List of pro-vaccination websites analyzed (19):

https://www.ontario.ca/page/vaccines (showed up as Ad on Google),
www.HistoryofVaccines.org,
www.cdc.gov/vaccines,
www.voicesforvaccines.org,
www.sciencebasedmedicine.org,
www.Immunize.ca,
http://www.phac-aspc.gc.ca/im/vs-sv/vs-faq03-eng.php,
http://www.centerforvaccinology.ca/,
http://www.immunize.org,
www.vaccinateyourbaby.org,
www.vaccines.gov,
www.healthychildren.org,
www.caringforkids.cps.ca,
www.whyichoose.org,
http://www.ovg.ox.ac.uk/mmr-vaccine,
http://kidshealth.org/parent/general/body/mmr-vaccine.html,
http://www.healthlinkbc.ca/healthfiles/hfile50c.stm,

http://www.nhs.uk/conditions/vaccinations/pages/mmr-vaccine.aspx,
http://www.vaccinesafety.edu/cc-mmr.htm

(Lee & VanDyke, 2016; Yaqub et al., 2014).

Dubé and colleagues reviewed the effectiveness of assuaging vaccine hesitancy using methods of public consultation or public communication and shows that is has little to no effect on influencing vaccine hesitancy, in some cases, it might exaggerate a vaccine-hesitant person to become anti-vaccine (Dubé, Gagnon, & MacDonald, 2015). In the same study, they concluded that 'there is no strong evidence on which to recommend any specific intervention to address vaccine hesitancy/refusal, suspecting that most interventions do not adequately address the 'underlying causes' of vaccine refusal (Dubé, Gagnon, & MacDonald, 2015, p.10).In this section, we applied Rowe and Frewer's typologies of public engagement to identify what types are used by pro- and anti-vaccine agencies. We provided a brief review which demonstrates that pro- vaccine agencies mainly use social media a portal for one-way communication (i.e. public consultation) and anti-vaccination agencies engage in various forms of two-way, dialogical communication, harness- ing the functions of Web 2.0 on social media to gain traction and support. If we hope for the public to understand and accept vaccination information, there is no easier way than using social media, after all, harnessing collective intelligence is what Web 2.0 does best.

SOLUTIONS AND RECOMMENDATIONS: ENGAGING WITH THE VACCINE HESITANT ON WEB 2.0

Web 2.0 is increasingly being valued as a source of public engagement for health promotion and behavioral change. Researchers generally acknowledge that the gap between the publics' uptake of social media and public health professionals' use of social media to engage the public is too big to ignore (Keller et al., 2014). Some current approaches to using Web 2.0 to tackle vaccine hesitancy on an interpersonal, programmatic, and organizational level are illustrated below.

On an interpersonal level, researchers have identified the 'Four C Model' of vaccine hesitancy – complacency, lack of confidence, calculation, and convenience, and proposed that public health campaigns debunk myths, changes risk perceptions, foster vaccine acceptance by framing information that are relatable, personable and focuses on gains versus losses are likely to be most successful (Betsch, Bohm, & Chapman, 2015; Betsch et al., 2012). On a programmatic level, Chou and colleagues reviewed 514 publications for evidence of Web 2.0's usefulness for health promotion. Results showed that social media interventions have the potential to effect behavioral change in health if a study design harnesses the participatory nature of social media when designing communication plans, the validates the ac- curacy and source of information on existing social media, and takes into consideration that the digital divide (Chou, Prestin, Lyons, & Wen, 2013). On an organizational level, recommendations for assuaging hesitancy include: focusing on understanding the determinants of hesitancy in a rapidly changing technocultural landscape, strengthening organizational capacity to address hesitancy through two-way communication and real-time feedback loops, and focusing on sharing lessons of successful development, validation and implementation of vaccine awareness across countries and disciplines. Starting in 2013, the European Advisory Group of Experts on Immunization (ETAGE) have pushed a program called TIP (Tailoring Immunization Programs) to WHO in which the program is designed to identify vaccine hesitant subgroups, diagnose their demand- and supply-side barriers and enablers, and design evidence-informed responses to hesitancy pertaining to the subgroup, context, and vaccine. (Butler & MacDonald, 2015; Eskola, Duclos, Schuster, & MacDonald, 2015).

CONCLUSION

In this chapter, we described the cyclical discourse of anti-vaccination movements and zoomed in on the third wave of anti-vaccination movement using three levels of analysis. First, at a macro-level, we looked at the parallel narratives of two existing paradigms (e.g. modernism versus postmodernism) and how it shapes our perception of vaccination. For the modernists, evidence-based medicine's adherence to 'know the facts' and accumulate best evidence for and during practice (Sackett et al, 1996) to support physicians' decision-making process is welcomed and accepted (Chan & Chan, 2000). For the postmodernists, Mannheim's notion that 'all knowledge must start with the assumption that there are spheres of thought in which it is impossible to conceive of absolute truth existing independently of the values and position of the subject and unrelated to the social context (Mannheim, 1971, p.79)' has never been more relevant. The online anti-vaccination movements accentuate that postmodern interpretations of risk in an increasingly risk-averse society creates strong tendencies for the public to seek health information pertaining to their own beliefs and notions of safety.

On a meso-level, we presented an array of public engagement mechanisms that proponents and opponents of vaccination are currently using on the Internet. Not only have institutions such as PHAC been emphasizing unidirectional means of public engagement (public communication and public consultation, according to Rowe and Frewer's typology of public engagement), they have not been using social media's functionality to its full potential. In the first section of our chapter, we witnessed three waves of anti-vaccine movements -- the trajectory of pro-vaccine agencies and its use of social media to public engagement are mostly paternalistic and have endured the test of time through different forms of media, the latest of which is social media. In response, anti-vaccination movements persevere.

Despite an increasing interest in academia to explicate anti-vaccination movements' growth and the means to overcome misinformation, it is not without limitations that at the time of this writing, it is unknown to what extent government agencies, research institutions, medical professionals, and academics are skeptical of the value of social media; it is also unclear to us to what degree would authorities appreciate dialogical forms of communication in the new online public sphere. Whether institutions perceive social media as a valid platform for public engagement needs greater examination. In other words, the ideological clashes and the various shades of grey between perceiving social media as a mechanism of truth propeller or myth-making machine serve as an important reminder that we need to understand the 'causes of causes' of measles outbreak, one that recognizes anti-vaccination movement not just as a general diagnosis of uninformed gullibility but as a reaction to the paternalistic one-way communication that exists in modernism and its subsidiaries (e.g., evidence-based medicine). To understand how public health discourses take shape in the online public space, the government must not underestimate the dialogical nature of social media and the real-life network it resembles, and we ought to encourage more interdisciplinary collaborations to explicate the mechanisms of public participation in this uniquely self-organized virtual agora. 'The medium is the message', as Marshall MacLuhan (1967) urged us to take note 30 years before our time – anti-vaccination movements are reactions to the risk and uncertainty involved in paternalistic immunization programs, and predictably so.

REFERENCES

Adamic, L. A., & Adar, E. (2003). Friends and neighbors on the web. *Social Networks, 25*(3), 211–230. doi:10.1016/S0378-8733(03)00009-1

Aquino, F., Donzelli, G., De Franco, E., Privitera, G., Lopalco, P. L., & Carducci, A. (2017). The web and public confidence in MMR vaccination in Italy. *Vaccine, 35*(35), 4494–4498. doi:10.1016/j.vaccine.2017.07.029 PMID:28736200

Arnup, K. (1992). Victims of vaccination? Opposition to Compulsory immunization in Ontario, 1900-90. *Canadian Bulletin of Medical History, 9*(1), 159–176. doi:10.3138/cbmh.9.2.159 PMID:11616229

Baker, J. P. (2003). The pertussis vaccine controversy in Great Britain, 1974–1986. *Vaccine, 21*(25), 4003–4010. doi:10.1016/S0264-410X(03)00302-5 PMID:12922137

Baker, J. P. (2008). Mercury, vaccines, and autism: One controversy, three histories. *American Journal of Public Health, 98*(2), 244–253. doi:10.2105/AJPH.2007.113159 PMID:18172138

Baxter, D. (2014). Opposition to vaccination and immunisation: The UK experience - from Smallpox to MMR. *Journal of Vaccines & Vaccination, 5*(6). doi:10.4172/2157-7560.1000254

Betsch, C., Bohm, R., & Chapman, G. B. (2015). Using behavioral insights to increase vaccina- tion policy effectiveness. *Policy Insights from the Behavioral and Brain Sciences, 2*(1), 61–73. doi:10.1177/2372732215600716

Betsch, C., Brewer, N. T., Brocard, P., Davies, P., Gaissmaier, W., Haase, N., & Stryk, M. (2012). Oppor- tunities and challenges of Web 2.0 for vaccination decisions. *Vaccine, 30*(25), 3727–3733. doi:.vaccine.2012.02.025 doi:10.1016/j

Bloom, B. R., Marcuse, E., & Mnookin, S. (2014). Addressing vaccine hesitancy. *Science, 344*(6182), 339–339. doi:10.1126cience.1254834 PMID:24763557

Bochner, E. (2015). *We support Dr. Andrew Wakefield.* Retrieved August 5th, 2015, from http://www.wesupportandywakefield.com/

Bolton, K., Memory, K., & McMillan, C. (2015). Herd immunity: Does social media affect adherence to the CDC childhood vaccination schedule? *The Journal of Undergraduate Research at the University of Tennessee, 6*(1), 5.

Butler, R., & MacDonald, N. E. (2015). Diagnosing the determinants of vaccine hesitancy in specific subgroups: The guide to Tailoring Immunization Programmes (TIP). *Vaccine, 33*(34), 4176–4179. doi:10.1016/j.vaccine.2015.04.038 PMID:25896376

California Coalition for Vaccine Choice. (2015). *No Shot. No school. California sb277 mandated vaccination every child every vaccine.* Retrieved July 29, 2015, from http://www.sb277.org/

Capurro, D., Cole, K., Echavarría, M. I., Joe, J., Neogi, T., & Turner, A. M. (2014). The use of social networking sites for public health practice and research: A systematic review. *Journal of Medical Internet Research, 16*(3), e79. doi:10.2196/jmir.2679 PMID:24642014

Centers for Disease Control. (2014). *Vaccines and autism: a summary of CDC conducted or sponsored studies*. Retrieved July 29, 2015, from http://www.cdc.gov/vaccinesafety/00_pdf/CDCStudiesonVaccinesandAutism.pdf

Centers for Disease Control. (2015). *Measles, cases and outbreaks*. Retrieved from http://www.cdc.gov/measles/cases-outbreaks.html

Centola, D. (2013). Social media and the science of health behavior. *Circulation*, *127*(21), 2135–2144. doi:10.1161/CIRCULATIONAHA.112.101816 PMID:23716382

Chan, J. J., & Chan, J. E. (2000). Medicine for the millennium: The challenge of postmodernism. *The Medical Journal of Australia*, *172*(7), 332–334. doi:10.5694/j.1326-5377.2000.tb123981.x PMID:10844921

Chou, W. S., Prestin, A., Lyons, C., & Wen, K. (2013). Web 2.0 for health promotion: Reviewing the current evidence. *American Journal of Public Health*, *103*(1), e9–e18. doi:10.2105/AJPH.2012.301071 PMID:23153164

Demicheli, V., Rivetti, A., Debalini, M. G., & Di Pietrantonj, C. (2012). Vaccines for measles, mumps and rubella in children. In The Cochrane Collaboration (Ed.), *Cochrane Database of Systematic Reviews*. Chichester, UK: John Wiley & Sons, Ltd. Retrieved December 21, 2015, from http://doi.wiley.com/10.1002/14651858.CD004407.pub3

Dubé, E., Gagnon, D., & MacDonald, N. E. (2015). Strategies intended to address vaccine hesitancy: Review of published reviews. *Vaccine*, *33*(34), 4191–4203. doi:10.1016/j.vaccine.2015.04.041 PMID:25896385

Durbach, N. (2004). *Bodily matters: the anti-vaccination movement in England, 1853–1907*. Durham, NC: Duke University Press; doi:10.1215/9780822386506

Eisenstein, M. (2014). Public health: An injection of trust. *Nature*, *507*(7490), S17–S19. doi:10.1038/507S17a PMID:24611174

Eskola, J., Duclos, P., Schuster, M., & MacDonald, N. E. (2015). How to deal with vaccine hesitancy? *Vaccine*, *33*(34), 4215–4217. doi:10.1016/j.vaccine.2015.04.043 PMID:25896378

Eysenbach, G. (2008). Medicine 2.0: Social networking, collaboration, participation, apomediation, and openness. *Journal of Medical Internet Research*, *10*(3), e22. doi:10.2196/jmir.1030 PMID:18725354

Fiebelkorn, A. P., Redd, S. B., Gallagher, K., Rota, P. A., Rota, J., Bellini, W., & Seward, J. (2010). Measles in the United States during the post elimination era. *The Journal of Infectious Diseases*, *202*(10), 1520–1528. doi:10.1086/656914 PMID:20929352

Fox, R. (2006). *Helen's story: a routine vaccination ruined my daughter's life forever. This is the inspiring story of how I took on the government... and won*. London: John Blake Publishing.

Gangarosa, E. J., Galazka, A. M., Wolfe, C. R., Phillips, L. M., Miller, E., Chen, R. T., & Gangarosa, R. E. (1998). Impact of anti-vaccine movements on pertussis control: The untold story. *Lancet*, *351*(9099), 356–361. doi:10.1016/S0140-6736(97)04334-1 PMID:9652634

Gorski, D. (2015, May 21). *The measles vaccine protects against more than just the measles.* Retrieved August 14, 2015, from https://www.sciencebasedmedicine.org/the-measles-vaccine-protects-against-more-than-just-the-measles/

Grant, L., Hausman, B. L., Cashion, M., Lucchesi, N., Patel, K., & Roberts, J. (2015). Vaccination persuasion online: A qualitative study of two provaccine and two vaccine-skeptical websites. *Journal of Medical Internet Research, 17*(5), e133. doi:10.2196/jmir.4153 PMID:26024907

Gray, J. M. (1999). Postmodern medicine. *Lancet, 354*(9189), 1550–1553. doi:10.1016/S0140-6736(98)08482-7 PMID:10551517

Hanson, C., West, J., Neiger, B., Thackeray, R., Barnes, M., & McIntyre, E. (2011). Use and acceptance of social media among health educators. *American Journal of Health Education, 42*(4), 197–204. doi:10.1080/19325037.2011.10599188

History of Vaccines. (n.d.). *Vaccine Injury Compensation Programs.* Retrieved July 23, 2015 from http://www.historyofvaccines.org/content/articles/vaccine-injury-compensation-programs

Hornig, M., Briese, T., Buie, T., Bauman, M. L., Lauwers, G., Siemetzki, U., & Lipkin, W. I. (2008). Lack of association between measles virus vaccine and autism with enteropathy: A case-control study. *PLoS One, 3*(9), e3140. doi:10.1371/journal.pone.0003140 PMID:18769550

Jefferson, T., Price, D., Demicheli, V., & Bianco, E. (2003). Unintended events following immunization with MMR: A systematic review. *Vaccine, 21*(25–26), 3954–3960. doi:10.1016/S0264-410X(03)00271-8 PMID:12922131

Kakar, S. (1996). Leprosy in British India, 1860–1940: Colonial politics and missionary medicine. *Medical History, 40*(02), 215–230. doi:10.1017/S0025727300061019 PMID:8936062

Kata, A. (2010). A postmodern Pandora's box: Anti-vaccination misinformation on the Internet. *Vaccine, 28*(7), 1709–1716. doi:10.1016/j.vaccine.2009.12.022 PMID:20045099

Kata, A. (2012). Anti-vaccine activists, Web 2.0, and the postmodern paradigm – An overview of tactics and tropes used online by the anti-vaccination movement. *Vaccine, 30*(25), 3778–3789. doi:. vaccine.2011.11.112 doi:10.1016/j

Katz, S. L., King, K., Varughese, P., Serres, G. D., Tipples, G., & Waters, J. (2004). Measles elimination in Canada. *The Journal of Infectious Diseases, 189*(s1), S236–S242. doi:10.1086/378499 PMID:15106117

Keller, B., Labrique, A., Jain, K. M., Pekosz, A., & Levine, O. (2014). Mind the Gap: Social media engagement by public health researchers. *Journal of Medical Internet Research, 16*(1), 8–15. doi:10.2196/jmir.2982 PMID:24425670

Larson, H. J., Eckersberg, E., Smith, D., & Patterson, P. (2014). Understanding vaccine hesitancy around vaccines and vaccination from a global perspective: A systematic review of global literature, 2007-2012. *Vaccine, 32*(19), 2150–2159. doi:10.1016/j.vaccine.2014.01.081 PMID:24598724

Lee, N., & VanDyke, M. (2016). Set it and forget it: The one way communication of social media by government agencies communicating science. *Science Communication, 37*(4), 533–541. doi:10.1177/1075547015588600

Malani, P. (2015). *Vaccination rates for us children remain generally high, but measles outbreaks underscore shortfalls in some regions.* Retrieved June 7, 2015, from http://newsatjama.jama.com/2013/09/16/vaccination-rates-for-us-children-remain-generally-high-but-measles-outbreaks-underscore-shortfalls-in-some-regions

Mannheim, K. (1971). *Ideology and Utopia. An Introduction to the Sociology of Knowledge.* New York: Harcourt Brace and World - Harvard Books.

Mariner, W. K., Annas, G. J., & Glantz, L. H. (2005). Jacobson v Massachusetts: It's not your great-great-grandfather's public health law. *American Journal of Public Health, 95*(4), 581–590. doi:10.2105/AJPH.2004.055160 PMID:15798113

McLuhan, M., Fiore, Q., & Agel, J. (1967). *The medium is the massage.* New York: Bantam Books.

Mohd, A. F. S., Kew, Y., & Moy, F. M. (2017). Vaccine hesitancy among parents in a multi-ethnic country, Malaysia. *Vaccine, 35*(22), 2955–2961. doi:10.1016/j.vaccine.2017.04.010 PMID:28434687

National Health Service. (2013, November 21). *MMR vaccine does not cause autism - NHS Choices.* Retrieved August 11, 2015, from http://www.nhs.uk/news/2007/January08/Pages/MMRvaccinedoesnotcauseautism.aspx

Norris, P. (2001). *Digital divide: civic engagement, information poverty, and the internet worldwide.* Cambridge, UK: Cambridge University Press. doi:10.1017/CBO9781139164887

O'Reilly, T., & Battelle, J. (2009). *Web squared: Web 2.0 five years on.* Retrieved from http://blsciblogs.baruch.cuny.edu/art3057fall2010/files/2010/08/OReilly-Battelle-websquared-whitepaper.pdf

Offit, P. A. (2005). *The Cutter incident: how America's first polio vaccine led to the growing vaccine crisis.* New Haven, CT: Yale University Press.

Okuhara, T., Ishikawa, H., Okada, M., Kato, M., & Kiuchi, T. (2017). Readability comparison of pro- and anti-HPV vaccination online messages in Japan. *Patient Education and Counseling, 100*(10), 1859–1866. doi:10.1016/j.pec.2017.04.013 PMID:28532860

Omer, S. B., Salmon, D. A., Orenstein, W. A., deHart, M. P., & Halsey, N. (2009). Vaccine refusal, mandatory immunization, and the risks of vaccine-preventable diseases. *The New England Journal of Medicine, 360*(19), 1981–1988. doi:10.1056/NEJMsa0806477 PMID:19420367

Parmet, W. E., Goodman, R. A., & Farber, A. (2005). Individual rights versus the public's health—100 years after Jacobson v. Massachusetts. *The New England Journal of Medicine, 352*(7), 652–654. doi:10.1056/NEJMp048209 PMID:15716558

Poland, G. A., & Jacobson, R. M. (2001). Understanding those who do not understand: A brief review of the anti-vaccine movement. *Vaccine, 19*(17), 2440–2445. doi:10.1016/S0264-410X(00)00469-2 PMID:11257375

Poland, G. A., & Jacobson, R. M. (2011). The age-old struggle against the antivaccinationists. *The New England Journal of Medicine, 364*(2), 97–99. doi:10.1056/NEJMp1010594 PMID:21226573

Porter, D., & Porter, R. (1988). The politics of prevention: Anti-vaccinationism and public health in nineteenth-century England. *Medical History*, *32*(03), 231–252. doi:10.1017/S0025727300048225 PMID:3063903

Public Health Agency Canada. (2015). *Measles and Rubella Weekly Monitoring Report - Public Health Agency of Canada*. Retrieved July 29, 2015, from http://www.phac-aspc.gc.ca/mrwr-rhrr/index-eng.php

Repalust, A., Šević, S., Rihtar, S., & Štulhofer, A. (2016). Childhood vaccine refusal and hesitancy intentions in Croatia: Insights from a population-based study. *Psychology Health and Medicine*, *0*(0), 1–11. doi:10.1080/13548506.2016.1263756 PMID:27899030

Rowe, G., & Frewer, L. (2005). A typology of public engagement mechanisms. *Science, Technology & Human Values*, *30*(2), 251–290. doi:10.1177/0162243904271724

Sackett, D. L., Rosenberg, W. M., Gray, J. A., Haynes, R. B., & Richardson, W. S. (1996). Evidence based medicine: What it is and what it isn't. *British Medical Journal*, *312*(7023), 71–72. doi:10.1136/bmj.312.7023.71 PMID:8555924

Sacramento Daily Union. (1983, October 31). *An International Congress of Anti-vacinators*. Retrieved on March 23, 2015, from http://cdnc.ucr.edu/cgi-bin/cdnc?a=d&d=SDU18831031.2.16

Salmon, D. A., Teret, S. P., MacIntyre, C. R., Salisbury, D., Burgess, M. A., & Halsey, N. A. (2006). Compulsoryvaccination and conscientious or philosophicalexemptions: Past, present, and future. *Lancet*, *367*(9508), 436–442. doi:10.1016/S0140-6736(06)68144-0 PMID:16458770

Sato, A. P. S. (2018). What is the importance of vaccine hesitancy in the drop of vaccination coverage in Brazil? *Revista de Saude Publica*, 52. PMID:30517523

Stagliano, K. (2013). *Parents speak out on behalf of Jenny McCarthy*. Retrieved August 9, 2015, from http://www.ageofautism.com/2013/07/parents-speak-out-on-behalf-of-jenny-mccarthy.html

Stewart, G. T. (1980). Benefits and risks of pertussis vaccine. *The New England Journal of Medicine*, *303*(17), 1004. doi:10.1056/NEJM198010233031718 PMID:7412844

Stewart, G. T., & Wilson, J. (1981). Pertussis vaccine and serious acute neurological illness in children. *British Medical Journal (Clinical Research Ed.)*, *282*(6280), 1968–1969. doi:10.1136/bmj.282.6280.1968 PMID:6786689

Stone, D. (2008). Global public policy, transnational policy communities, and their networks. *Policy Studies Journal: the Journal of the Policy Studies Organization*, *36*(1), 19–38. doi:10.1111/j.1541-0072.2007.00251.x

Strom, J. (1960). Is universal vaccination against pertussis always justified? *British Medical Journal*, *2*(5207), 1184–1186. doi:10.1136/bmj.2.5207.1184 PMID:20788967

Taylor, L. E., Swerdfeger, A. L., & Eslick, G. D. (2014). Vaccines are not associated with autism: An evidence-based meta-analysis of case-control and cohort studies. *Vaccine*, *32*(29), 3623–3629. doi:10.1016/j.vaccine.2014.04.085 PMID:24814559

The Cincinnati Daily Gazette. (1879). *Mr. William Tebb, the englishman, renews his war against vaccination in New York*. Retrieved from August 5, 2015, from http://www.genealogybank.com/gbnk/newspapers/?lname=Tebb&sort=_rank_%3AD

The Lancet Editorial. (2018). Measles, war, and health-care reforms in Ukraine. *Lancet*, *392*(10149), 711. doi:10.1016/S0140-6736(18)31984-6 PMID:30191812

Tyler, L. (2005). Towards a postmodern understanding of crisis communication. *Public Relations Review*, *31*(4), 566–571. doi:10.1016/j.pubrev.2005.08.017

Umemoto, K. N. (1998). *You don't see what I see: multiple publics and public policy in a Los Angeles gang war*. Cambridge, MA: Massachusetts Institute of Technology. Retrieved from http://dspace.mit.edu/handle/1721.1/9639

US Department of Health and Human Services. (n.d.). *Safety*. Retrieved on June 5th, 2015, from www.vaccines.gov

Wagner, A. L., Boulton, M. L., Sun, X., Huang, Z., Harmsen, I. A., Ren, J., & Zikmund-Fisher, B. J. (2017). Parents' concerns about vaccine scheduling in Shanghai, China. *Vaccine*, *35*(34), 4362–4367. doi:10.1016/j.vaccine.2017.06.077 PMID:28687407

Wakefield, A. J., Murch, S. H., Anthony, A., Linnell, J., Casson, D. M., Malik, M., ... Walker-Smith, J. A. (1998). RETRACTED: Ileal-lymphoid-nodular hyperplasia, non-specific colitis, and pervasive developmental disorder in children. *Lancet*, *351*(9103), 637–641. doi:10.1016/S0140-6736(97)11096-0 PMID:9500320

Ward, J. K. (2016). Rethinking the antivaccine movement concept: A case study of public criticism of the swine flu vaccine's safety in France. *Social Science & Medicine*, *159*, 48–57. doi:10.1016/j.socscimed.2016.05.003 PMID:27173740

Witteman, H. O., & Zikmund-Fisher, B. J. (2012). The defining characteristics of Web 2.0 and their potential influence in the online vaccination debate. *Vaccine*, *30*(25), 3734–3740. doi:10.1016/j.vaccine.2011.12.039 PMID:22178516

Wolfe, R. M., & Sharp, L. K. (2002). Anti-vaccinationists past and present. *British Medical Journal*, *325*(7361), 430–432. doi:10.1136/bmj.325.7361.430 PMID:12193361

World Health Organization. (2014). *Measles*. Retrieved July 10, 2015, from http://www.who.int/mediacentre/factsheets/fs286/en/

World Health Organization. (2019a). *Ten threats to global health in 2019*. Retrieved March 28, 2019, from https://www.who.int/emergencies/ten-threats-to-global-health-in-2019

World Health Organization. (2019b). *WHO | New measles surveillance data for 2019*. Retrieved July 8, 2019, from https://www.who.int/immunization/newsroom/measles-data-2019/en/

World Health Organization. (2019c, May 9). *Measles*. Retrieved July 9, 2019, from https://www.who.int/news-room/fact-sheets/detail/measles

Yang, Y. T., Delamater, P. L., Leslie, T. F., & Mello, M. M. (2016). Sociodemographic Predictors of Vac- cination Exemptions on the Basis of Personal Belief in California. *American Journal of Public Health, 106*(1), 172–177. doi:10.2105/AJPH.2015.302926 PMID:26562114

Yaqub, O., Castle-Clarke, S., Sevdalis, N., & Chataway, J. (2014). Attitudes to vaccination: A critical review. *Social Science & Medicine, 112*, 1–11. doi:10.1016/j.socscimed.2014.04.018 PMID:24788111

Yom-Tov, E., & Fernandez-Luque, L. (2014). Information is in the eye of the beholder: Seeking information on the MMR vaccine through an internet search engine. In *AMIA Annual Symposium Proceedings* (p. 1238). American Medical Informatics Association. Retrieved from http://www.ncbi.nlm.nih.gov/pmc/articles/PMC4419998/

KEY TERM AND DEFINITIONS

Evidence-Based Medicine (EBM): The practice of gathering evidence from published journal articles of well-designed epidemiological studies coupled with clinical expertise and patient values to inform practice in a clinical setting.

Misinformation: Information that is false and deceitful, not malicious by nature.

Modernism: A philosophical ideology that believes in the pursuit of truth in knowledge, certainty, objectivity, and logic that has contributed to shaping Western civilization from the late 19th century till early 20th century.

Postmodernism: A reaction to Modernism, the philosophy of questioning and abject truth and a shift of focus on interpretation, that is facts are meaningless until humans attach meaning and make judgements accordingly.

Sentiment Analysis: A form of semantics analysis to understand opinions, large sets of data can be collected from social media to understand user sentiment/opinion on a given subject.

Small-World Phenomenon: An empirically tested hypothesis that all people are connected by short chains to our acquaintance and beyond proposed by Stanley Milgram, it is now coined 'six degrees of separation'.

Social Media: Online platforms and applications that enables real-time interaction between users on user-generated content through text, imagery, and videos.

Technoculturalism: The study of cultural discourse shaped by human interactions with technology.

Vaccine Hesitant: People who are unsure about vaccines who are most vulnerable to misinformation. This is the target population for interventions and campaigns for both pro-vaccine and anti-vaccine groups.

Web 2.0: Proliferated by Tim O'Reilly, it describes new applications and technology on the web that harnesses collective intelligence such as Wikipedia, YouTube, Facebook, Twitter, and Torrent sites.

Chapter 5
Centrality of Youth Engagement in Media Involvement

Yoshitaka Iwasaki
San Jose State University, USA

ABSTRACT

Contextualized within the popularity of new media, youth engagement is a very important concept in the practice of public involvement. Guided by the current literature on youth engagement and media studies, this chapter examines the key engagement-related notions involving youth and media usage. Being informed by a variety of case studies on youth engagement through the use of media within various contexts globally, the chapter discusses the opportunities and challenges of engaging youth through media involvement. The specific notions covered in this chapter include (1) the role of "hybrid" media in youth engagement, (2) "intersectionality" illustrating the diversity of youth populations and their media usage, (3) meaning-making through media involvement among youth, and (4) building global social relationships and social and cultural capital through youth's media usage. Importantly, the use of new media can be seen as a means of reclaiming and reshaping the ways in which youth are engaged, as key meaning-making processes, to address personal, social, and cultural issues.

INTRODUCTION

Occasioned by the rise of new media, engaging youth in the practice of public involvement presents both opportunities and challenges in our increasingly global society. Guided by the current literature on youth engagement and media studies, this chapter will examine the key engagement-related concepts involving youth and media usage. By combining practice-based accounts with theoretical insights, the chapter will provide critical analyses and interpretations of empirical data from local/regional, national, and international case studies on youth engagement through the use of media. Specifically, attention will be given to how new and traditional media is being applied to youth engagement in international socio-political contexts. Broadly, the chapter will discuss the opportunities and challenges of engaging youth through media usage.

DOI: 10.4018/978-1-7998-1828-1.ch005

A key argument emphasized in this chapter is that hybrid forms of communications through digital and social media, face-to-face interactions, and traditional media can promote youth engagement, in which relationship-building (both within youth and between youth and adults) is a critical concept. Another main argument is that appreciation of the diversity of youth populations and their media usage from an intersectional perspective is essential to better understand the ways in which youth are engaged via media that can provide meaning-making, for example, on identity and cultural issues. Briefly, an intersectional framework addresses the complex ways in which the *key axes of power* in society (e.g., gender, race/ethnicity, class, ability, sexual orientation) intersect with each other (Crenshaw, 1995; Garnets, 2002; Iglesias & Cormier, 2002). In addition, the chapter suggests that youth engagement through media usage can help build global social relationships and social capital and can facilitate a youth-led transformation of our society to address social justice issues. Importantly, such multi-media usage can provide youth with creative outlets for civic engagement, community connections, and meaning-making within their lives.

In particular, this chapter posits that meaningful youth engagement is a key concept for both positive youth development (PYD; Alicea et al., 2012; Delgado, 2002; Lind, 2008) and social justice youth development (SJYD; Cammarota, 2011; Gharabaghi & Anderson-Nathe, 2012; Ross, 2011) and facilitates social/system change to more effectively support youth (Blanchet-Cohen & Salazar, 2009; Davidson et al., 2010; Yohalem & Martin, 2007; Wexler et al., 2009). Indeed, the integration of PYD and SJYD is proposed applicable to the use of hybrid forms of communications to promote youth engagement and development by appreciating the diversity of youth populations and their media usage (from an intersectional perspective), and by promoting meaning-making and social capital, and to facilitate a youth-led/guided transformation of our society to address social justice issues. Importantly, the power of youth in social change should not be underestimated, and this role can be effectively promoted by the use of hybrid forms of communications for youth engagement.

Accordingly, the chapter will address such concepts as "intersectionality," "meaning-making," and "global social relationships and social and cultural capital" to appreciate the diversity in the types and forms of youth engagement through media usage. Before describing each of these key concepts, the chapter will begin with summarizing a framework of PYD and SJYD and then providing insights into the role of various forms of media in youth engagement broadly.

Positive Youth Development (PYD) and Social Justice Youth Development (SJYD)

Youth's media usage is seen as a key youth-engagement activity, which has significant implications for youth development (Conner & Slattery, 2014; Dedman, 2011; Garcia et al., 2015; Kahne et al., 2012). Two of the most popular concepts concerning youth development include positive youth development (PYD; Alicea et al., 2012; Delgado, 2002; Lind, 2008) and social justice youth development (SJYD; Cammarota, 2011; Gharabaghi & Anderson-Nathe, 2012; Ross, 2011). First, PYD seeks to promote a variety of developmental competencies that young people need at individual, social, and system levels to become productive, contributing members of society (Alicea et al., 2012; Ersing, 2009; Lind, 2008; Yohalem & Martin, 2007). Rather than a pathological focus, PYD adopts a holistic view of development, giving attention to youth's physical, personal, social, emotional, intellectual, and spiritual development, and emphasizes the strengths, resources, and potentials of youth (Alicea et al., 2012; Ersing, 2009; Lind, 2008; Yohalem & Martin, 2007).

Second, SJYD involves youth's awareness of their personal potential, community responsibility, and broader humanity, and the engagement in social justice activities that counter oppressive conditions (Cammarota, 2011; Gharabaghi & Anderson-Nathe, 2012; Ginwright & James, 2002; Ross, 2011). Specifically, SJYD involves a critical analysis of social, economic, and political factors including race, gender, class, and culture, and addresses the systemic root causes of community problems (Suleiman, Soleimanpour, & London, 2006; Wilson et al., 2006). Importantly, the integration of PYD and SJYD conceptually supports the vital role of youth as a proactive agent for changes at personal (e.g., self-identity; constructive behaviours), social (e.g., advocacy for social change), and community (e.g., policy and practice change from social justice perspectives) levels (Ross, 2011). Accordingly, these two concepts will be considered as a key framework throughout the chapter.

The Role of "Hybrid" Media in Youth Engagement

Research has shown that the optimal use of digital and social media can complement and strengthen face-to-face interactions and traditional media, supporting the role of hybrid forms of communications in promoting youth engagement. Specifically, hybrid communication methods including various forms of politically driven, nonpolitical interest-driven, and friendship-driven online participation have been shown to promote youth engagement and youth activism (e.g., Chan & Guo, 2013; Kahne et al., 2011; Xenos et al., 2014). For example, Conner and Slattery (2014) reported the efforts of the Philadelphia Student Union, using the youth-led hybridization principle of social movements that combine online/new/informal and real-world/traditional/formal activism. In particular, their study showed how "youth organizing" through the use of new media offers a bridge across the three divines (the academic achievement gap, the digital participation gap, and the civic engagement gap) and facilitates the digital literacy, civic engagement, and academic achievement of low-income youth of color who might otherwise experience limited opportunities in these domains. Youth organizing refers to "a strategy that trains young people to engage in collective action to improve the institutions in their communities that directly affect them" (Conner & Slattery, 2014; p. 18). Youth organizing has implications for youth engagement and public involvement through hybrid forms of communications and activism.

The importance of hybrid media systems and public spaces is further demonstrated through the use of different media platforms and online and offline spaces that reinforce one another and promote youth engagement and youth-led social and political movements. Sloam's (2014) paper reported such importance using four case studies to examine the role that the Internet and new media have played in the political mobilization of young Europeans. Specifically, four case studies (in Germany, Italy, Portugal, and Spain) highlighted the stories of young, highly educated 'stand-by citizens' who have become activated by crises of youth unemployment, frustration with politics and public policy, and anger with corporate greed into 'digitally networked action' utilizing new technology platforms. The new media also provided a central tool to directly appeal to citizens (particularly, the young and highly educated) and facilitate youth-oriented movements in the digital age without having to play by the rules of the old media or channel their energies through established political institutions (Sloam, 2014).

Also, the use of digital media has been shown to mobilize young people into more active engagement with civic and political life through deliberative activities in schools, democratic peer norms, news consumption, and citizen communication. For example, Lee et al.'s (2013) examination of the national panel survey of parent-child pairs — the Future Voters Study — emphasized the centrality of communication, whether at schools, among peers, or through the media, to youth engagement in civic and political life.

Results indicate that information consumption through hybrid forms of traditional and digital media works through citizen communication to encourage civic engagement, including influences stemming from peers and schools onto civic engagement. Specifically, the results show strong online pathways to youth participation and engagement especially through news consumption and political expression via digital media technologies (Lee et al., 2013).

Using data from Dutch grade-eight students, van Kruistum et al. (2014) examined youth media lifestyles that encompass new media, traditional print-based media, and face-to-face (offline) interaction as "hybrid" forms. This examination was completed by exploring both interest-driven media engagement (e.g., for entertainment, to gain knowledge) and friendship-driven media engagement. They found four distinct media lifestyles defined in terms of: (a) the medium through which a particular media activity took place, (b) the social distance involved between sender and receiver, and (c) the function of the particular activity. These youth-media lifestyles were named as: (1) *omnivores* (appropriating all media for multiple functions in diverse social contexts), (2) *networkers* (staying connected with known others across offline and online), (3) *gamers* (specializing in a medium of entertainment within a distant social context), and (4) *low-frequency users* (not bringing offline interests and relationship online) (van Kruistum et al., 2014). Such study is useful to better understand the diversity in youth media lifestyles.

Drawing on international survey data from mentoring program staff and volunteer mentors primarily in US and Canada, Schwartz et al. (2014) examined the use of digital and social media in youth mentoring relationships. Their findings show that this media use does not seem to detract from the closeness and quality of face-to-face mentoring relationships, but may actually supplement and strengthen them. The findings also highlight the importance of creating an environment of reciprocity and mutuality, and reducing the chance of shaming and patronizing youth. Relationship-building (both within youth and between youth and adults) is a critical concept in youth engagement, which can be facilitated by the optimal use of new media that can complement face-to-face interactions and traditional media, again, supporting the effective use of hybrid forms of communications (Schwartz et al., 2014).

Also focusing on the use of hybrid forms of media, Skoric and Poor's (2013) study with young people in Singapore examined how youth navigate between the traditional and new media for civic and political participation. They found that social media use is positively related to traditional political participation (because new media are a means for political mobilization and organization of citizens due to their low barriers to entry and quick diffusion of information), while also providing evidence of the continued importance of traditional media for political engagement. Keipi and Oksanen (2014) explored youth narratives of the interaction of both opportunities and risks in the use of social media by youth in Finland. Their findings illuminated the role of new media in youth need-fulfillment toward self-exploration/expression, self-determination, identity development, and relationship-building, as well as the social risks that youth's new media use involves (e.g., cyberbullying, harassment).

Not surprisingly, the rapid dispersion of digital communication technologies in the last decade has spurred interest in how changes in communication technology might be reshaping and possibly reinvigorating youth's opportunities and inclinations for engagement. Research has been particularly focused on the engagement of young citizens, a population historically under-engaged and among the most active users of digital media. Existing literature suggests that recently created, online organizations will be most likely to embrace a newer, more youth-friendly communication style; those organizations working within the formal political realm may be most reticent (Bimber et al., 2012; Castells, 2009; Karpf, 2012). Wells' (2014) study of 60 organizations' (including government, interest groups, and community groups) communications through Facebook mainly confirms these expectations, but low levels of youth-friendly communications across the sample raise doubts about the likelihood of a civil society resurgence through social media.

In summary, research supports the role of hybrid forms of communications in promoting youth engagement by showing that the optimal use of digital/online and social media can complement face-to-face interactions and traditional media. Specifically, hybrid communication methods including various forms of politically driven, nonpolitical interest-driven, and friendship-driven online participation have been shown to promote youth engagement and youth activism. In particular, the youth-led hybridization principle of social movements combine online/new/informal and real-world/traditional/formal activism. The use of digital media has been shown to mobilize young people into more active engagement with civic and political life through activities in schools, democratic peer norms, news consumption, and citizen communication for the development of active citizens. Importantly, relationship-building (both within youth and between youth and adults) is a critical concept in youth engagement, which can be effectively facilitated by hybrid forms of communications. Furthermore, it is important to recognize the role of new media in youth need-fulfillment toward self-exploration/expression, self-determination, identity development, and relationship-building, as well as the social risks that youth's new media use involves (e.g., cyberbullying, harassment).

INTERSECTIONALITY: DIVERSITY OF YOUTH POPULATIONS AND THEIR MEDIA USAGE

Apparently, youth populations are diverse based on socio-demographic factors including: gender, race/ethnicity, age, social class, disability/ability, and sexual orientation. The framework of intersectionality is helpful to better understand influences of these diverse human characteristics on youth engagement via media. In particular, an intersectional framework addresses the complex ways in which the *key axes of power* in society (e.g., gender, race/ethnicity, class, ability, sexual orientation) intersect with each other (Crenshaw, 1995; Garnets, 2002; Iglesias & Cormier, 2002). Indeed, most people in our society have more than one identity in terms of gender roles, racial or ethnic identities, and identities related to social class, age, ability, and sexual orientation. These identities are linked to different experiences of social power, privilege, and oppression as related to the dominant culture. Intersectionality is a framework being used in various different disciplines (e.g., women's studies, cultural studies) to help recognize and analyze the multiple nature of identities and the interlocking systems of privilege and oppression in a non-additive sense within specific life contexts (Iwasaki et al., 2006; Razack, 1998; Ristock, 2002).

In addition to looking at such human characteristics separately, this section of the chapter will explore how young women and men with different races/ethnicities are engaged through various types of media. Besides the intersection of gender with race/ethnicity, I will give attention to the other dimensions of human diversity including sexual orientation, disability/ability, and social class. Through the lens of intersectionality, I will address in what ways and how the diversity among youth populations should be acknowledged to better understand opportunities and challenges of youth engagement through media.

One such community group characterizing the diversity of youth populations represents sexual minority youth. Research has shown that their engagement with online technology is a critical feature of their daily lives and development because this offers them with significantly safer spaces and vital community support and connectedness (e.g., Craig et al., 2014). For example, using a feminist, intersectional framework, Singh's (2013) qualitative study found a key theme for the use of social media to affirm one's identity as a transgendered youth of color and promote sense of connectedness. Also, Asakura and Craig (2014) explored resilience development in the accounts of lesbian, gay, bisexual, transgender, and queer (LGBTQ) youth, by analyzing videos posted for the *It Gets Better* social media campaign. The findings offer a nuanced look at the pathways to resilience development, which are described by four major themes emerged from the data: (1) leaving hostile social environments, (2) experiencing "coming out" in meaningful ways, (3) re-membering the social environment, and (4) turning challenges into opportunities and strengths. For instance, "by re-membering, many participants have developed their own clubs of life with selective members who have supported them through difficult times and valued their beings" (p. 261), whereas "the difficulties they experienced as youths also prepared them well to manage their adult lives" (p. 262).

Another instance of the diversity in youth populations and their media usage involves everyday use of digital technology and online social media by adolescents and young adults with physical disabilities and complex communication needs. To exemplify this notion, those youths in Hynan et al.'s (2014) study showed a desire to use the Internet and online social media as it is perceived to increase opportunities for self-determination and self-representation, while enriching friendships. The wide diversity of literacy and communication skills among youth with disabilities, as well as accessibility challenges, mean that the use of a collaborative approach is vital, for example, through receiving technical and social support from educational settings, families, and friends (Hynan et al., 2014).

Along with the growth of research on young women, we have seen the emergence of research on ethnic youth, implying the intersection of gender with ethnicity contextualized within the notion of youth subculture (e.g., Clark, 2012; Dedman, 2011; Gunter, 2010). Originally, Blackman (1995) advanced the idea of "youth cultural forms" and Thornton (1995) adapted Bourdieu's theory of cultural capital to speak about "subcultural capital." As emphasized by Blackman (2014), subcultures attract attention in culture, society, and the media because these have been theorized as not merely distinct from, but also in opposition to, the dominant culture. The new forms of subcultural communication through social media are considered as a key domain to promote knowledge, flexibility, participation, and collectivity transmitted through a subcultural network (Hodkinson & Lincoln, 2008; Williams, 2011). Blackman (2014) argues that youth cultural identities based on consumption, in which communications through social media play a key role, are structured by both material and social conditions of inequality (e.g., various forms of "isms"), while engagement with youth subcultures at a social and political level is critical by looking at, for example, deviant behaviour, connectedness, and social change to address social justice issues.

Importantly, the intersection of gender with ethnicity contextualized within the notion of youth subculture has implications for the broad topics of culture, society, and the media. Specifically, communications through social media play a key role in developing youth cultural identities. In this way, the use of media provides a key cultural sphere to create youth activist subcultures, which seek to contest a range of global injustices through collective means consistent with a SJYD framework described earlier.

For example, youth activist involvement includes the use of media, contextualized within the raced, classed, and gendered challenges of youth activist cultures from an intersectional perspective. To illustrate this notion, Kennelly's (2011) book, entitled "Citizen Youth: Culture, Activism, and Agency in a Neoliberal Era" explores youth activist subcultures undertaken as part of a year-long multi-sited ethnography in Canada's three largest urban centres: Toronto, Montreal and Vancouver. Specifically, the book examines the dilemmas and cultural dynamics of being young and politically engaged, including the use of media as a key cultural sphere. The book interrogates both macro-structural forces such as education, media, and politics, and micro-sociological factors shaping youth activists' lived realities, resulting in a portrayal of the day-to-day experiences of young people who seek to contest a range of global injustices through collective means. The major issues shaping youth activist engagement described include the use of media as a key resource to sustain activist involvement, and the development of raced, classed, and gendered activist cultures from an interactional perspective (Kennelly, 2011).

Contextualizing mobile media in teens' lives, Vickey's (2015) paper examines how ethnically diverse low-income, non-dominant teens mitigate reduced privacy levels in and through mobile technologies and social media, and with what consequences. Teens in the study utilized a variety of social media platforms (e.g., Facebook, Twitter, Tumblr, Instagram, YouTube) to reach different audiences, explore different identities, and form different communities. They deliberately used these multiple platforms as a way to cope with evolving privacy settings, social norms, and technological affordances — this was a deliberate strategy intended to resist social convergence (Vickey, 2015). As such, the boundaries of sharing and privacy are constantly renegotiated at the intersection of localized social norms, economic and social capital, and the technical affordances of particular platforms and devices. As shown in Vickey's study, mobile media provide youth with a sense of autonomy, independence, and privacy from adults (Ling, 2010) and facilitate more personalized forms of communication (Campbell & Park, 2008).

As an emerging form of culture, digital culture can be broadly defined as the multiple ways in which people engage with digital media and technologies in their daily lives (Livingstone, 2009). As a unique domain of digital culture, non-urban areas of a developing country would generate a distinct set of experiences. As shown by Pathak-Shelat and DeShano (2014), youth digital cultures in rural and small town India are influenced by and negotiate local, regional, national, and global discourses, for example, through homes, peers, schools, and official public messages. Youth in their study treat new media and technologies as one limited component of otherwise rich lives and social experiences. For example, financial interests that drive commercial aspects of digital culture obscure its layered power differentials through contradictory media experiences and end results (Pathak-Shelat & DeShano, 2014). Obviously, power dynamics play a role in the construction of digital culture among youth, which is contextualized both locally and globally.

As exemplified in this section, an intersectional perspective addresses the complex ways in which the *key axes of power* in society (e.g., gender, race/ethnicity, class, ability, sexual orientation) intersect with each other (Crenshaw, 1995; Garnets, 2002; Iglesias & Cormier, 2002). A variety of media forms, through which youth are engaged, address these power issues such as the intersection of various identities including gender roles, racial or ethnic identities, and identities related to social class, disability/ability, and sexual orientation. Indeed, these identities represent key factors for personal and collective experiences within the systems of social power, privilege, and oppression (Iwasaki et al., 2006; Razack, 1998; Ristock, 2002). In particular, the new forms of subcultural communication through new media promote knowledge, flexibility, participation, and collectivity transmitted through a subcultural network. Specifically, communications through new media play a major role in developing youth's cultural identities. Accordingly, the use of media provides a key cultural milieu to create youth activist subcultures, as a collective space to address social justice issues, in line with a SJYD framework. For example, youth activism includes the use of media, contextualized within the raced, classed, and gendered youth activist cultures from an intersectional perspective. Importantly, the use of new media can be seen as a means of reclaiming and reshaping the ways in which youth are engaged to address these power issues.

Meaning-Making Through Media Usage Among Youth

Another important idea is that the use of media in youth engagement is considered as an effective means of promoting *meaning-making* that can provide a variety of personal and collective benefits for youth. Meaning-making refers to the ways in which and how people gain meanings within life that are important for personal, social, cultural, spiritual, and community reasons (Markman, Proulx, & Lindberg, 2013; Park, 2010). Relevant to this chapter, the use of new media is seen as a key meaning-making process or activity to address identity, social/cultural, and power-related issues. For example, Halverson (2010) explored youth film-making as a medium for meaning-making, by seeing youth as producers of digital media. Her analysis demonstrated how films such as *Rules of Engagement* display the construction of a viable social identity where youth actively insert their understanding of: (a) how to represent complex portraits of how they see themselves, (b) how others see them, and (c) how they fit into their communities. The study showed how youth (in particular, youth living within marginalized conditions) engage with and make sense of identity issues as a critical meaning-making process through the media they create (Halverson, 2010).

Mutere et al. (2014) examined the roles of popular culture, media, and the arts in the health-seeking concerns and behaviours of 54 homeless youth in California, USA, with a focus on what they saw as barriers and aids. Their findings highlighted the importance of a creative arts-media intervention (e.g., graffiti as a multi-media platform) for homeless youth to promote a sense of life-meaning, civic engagement, and positive community connections and health outcomes in an age-appropriate and culturally-sensitive way. Specifically, multi-media usage (e.g., poetry, screenplays, stories, and web-logs) provided homeless youth with creative outlets for civic engagement, community connections, and meaning-making within their lives (Mutere et al., 2014). In particular, a peer-to-peer mentorship has been found to be beneficial for "marginalized" youth to meet their desire for a sense of meaning as demonstrated through a quote from a street-involved youth in Mutere et al.'s (2014) study:

I like to write raps. I like to draw. I'm really talented at it. Marijuana doesn't stop me from that. Those are things that I know I have a gift in. It's like everyone else... electronics, computers, whatever the case may be... A mentor can help them get past that problem and help them go somewhere in life... 'Cause that's what most people feel like they don't have... no life-meaning. You can't just directly say "no". You have to explain to them and encourage them to do better now. (p. 282)

By focusing on the construction of meaning and identity, Zemmels' (2012) study with American teens (13-17 years of age) in New Orleans documented those participants' engagement with new media in networked spaces and the everyday practices that surround their participation. The findings showed a complex pattern of relationships between interpersonal communication channels, the relative immediacy and intimacy of the channel, and the social relationship between participants. This pattern appeared to have a structuring influence on everyday communication practices of youth in networked publics, as they negotiate and construct meaning (e.g., aesthetic and social meaning through visual media) and identity in these networked publics (Zemmels, 2012).

In addition, it is useful to consider the digital media creation, distribution, and consumption process as "storytelling" in a shared space, in which a variety of perspectives and meanings are presented (Lambert et al, 2007). Accordingly, the space in which stories are shared and collaborated on becomes an entity with a life of its own. As mobile communication media and the internet become more pervasive, young people from different cultures and communities are afforded more opportunities for sharing and collaboration across previously unbridgeable distances (Botha et al., 2009). Botha et al.'s (2009) study with five teenagers from USA and five teenagers from South Africa demonstrated the role of mobile phones and the web as mediating technologies in the development of intercultural competencies and communication skills. Specifically, their study has shown that mobile phones have a place in the creation of meaningful user-generated content for improved cross-cultural awareness and communication — as communication devices, they have progressed "from text to context" (Botha et al., 2009). Increasingly, technology facilitates the ways in which the youth around the world communicate, consume content, and create meaning (e.g., South African teens mindful of explaining local slang and the meaning of Afrikaans words to American teens) across diverse cultural contexts.

For another example, with 35 young people in Philippine between the ages of thirteen and twenty-six in four focus groups, Portus (2008) explored how the urban poor acquire, use, and ascribe meaning to the mobile phone. This study found that the mobile phone allows the urban poor to pursue their gender-defined functions more effectively, being a source of desire and envy, most apparently among the women, as a highly sought-after and increasingly vital, meaningful part of their lives (e.g., social role fulfillment), despite grinding poverty (Portus, 2008).

A recent special issue of *Educational Studies* on "Youth, New Media, and Education" featured several papers that examined youth as both consumers and producers of popular culture, which lies at the intersections of traditional media and new digital media. As the issue editors, Luschen and Bogad (2010) commented that "youth representations of themselves have the capacity to shape the cultural landscape, interrupt and collude with existing discourses of youth, and teach what it means to be a youth in all its complexity, within and across difference... Reaching across boundaries between conventional and new media, these texts illustrate the complexities that a newly constituted popular culture provides" (p. 454-455). Through the process of youth's negotiations using various media forms, they produce, consume, and learn about popular culture as ways of meaning-making in their daily lives. Importantly, the use of new media can be seen as a means of reclaiming and reshaping the ways in which youth are engaged, as key meaning-making processes, to address significant social and cultural issues.

Building Global Social Relationships and Social and Cultural Capital Through Youth's Media Usage

Given the resurgence of digital and social media, youth engagement has become more globalized across cultural boundaries. One obvious outcome from this global process represents building cross-border social relationships and social and cultural capital facilitated by youth engagement through the use of media. For example, drawing from a comparative case study of the digital literacy practices of immigrant youth of Chinese descent, Lam (2014) examined the cross-border social relationships that are fostered between the youth and their peers in China. She showed how these cross-border relationships create unique social, linguistic, and cultural capital. The findings suggest that youth's online literacy practices need to be understood within the particular social fields/networks in which they are situated and how they allow the youth to navigate and take up a position within social fields across national boundaries. Importantly, media usage is considered as one of the significant and meaningful daily human activities within structured social spaces. Consequently, relationships built from using communication technologies can promote social capital (e.g., affiliations and networks) and cultural capital (e.g., cultural knowledge, skills such as bilingual or multilingual skills, and cultural dispositions/customs) (Bourdieu 1991). Specifically described in Lam's study include "bridging capital" to connect with the monolingual majority population in society, and "bonding capital" to connect with the minority population, as well as transnational engagement and resource development in digital art.

For another example, de Haan et al. (2014) examined the networked configurations for learning of migrant youth in the Netherlands, in relation to particular offline and online connections, their historical geographies, the development of learning 'places,' and particular learning affinities. Specifically, they described three ethnically different groups: (a) Dutch youth as 'unrooted' learners (who are networked according to individually expressed interests for exploration), (b) Moroccan-Dutch youth as 'routed' learners (who form collective affinities and interests within same generation ethnically informed spaces), and (c) Turkish-Dutch youth as 'rooted' learners (defined by more collectively formed interests embedded in family and ethnically based networks). This grouping shows examples of the diversity in globally dispersed, highly individualized yet collective networks within migrant youth to pursue tailored knowledge. Even within a single country at a local level, the development of global social relationships and social and cultural capital is a reality as increasingly facilitated by the use of media within youth populations internationally.

Furthermore, Garcia et al.'s (2015) study focused on civic engagement enacted through digital media participation by exploring the relationships between critical literacy practice, digital media production, and civic agency in the Council of Youth Research, a youth participatory action research program in Los Angeles, USA. In particular, their study articulates a vision of literacy that is tied to societal power structures as a way of building personal and social capital for the purpose of personal and social transformation. Specifically, the study highlights the ways in which student digital literacy production manifested powerful civic agency. The authors argue, "Academic and critical literacy development are crucial to beginning the process of empowerment for students to become critical consumers of information. When youth are empowered with the ability to make sense of the unjust conditions in their community and the skills to act, they become powerful agents of transformation" (p. 165). Importantly, meaning-making and mobilization of actions to address social justice issues are key empowerment and transformation processes, again, consistent with a SJYD framework described earlier.

Attractive to young people, modern music festivals have become sites of mediated brand management where commodified hyper-experiences are considered as new forms of contested cultural capital. As described by Flinna and Frewb (2014), the realm of music festivity has grown into a global circuit that responds to the demand for emotive experiential products and taps into postmodern themes that celebrate a lifestyle attitude of extended youth. Their study explored the phenomenon of festival culture through a case study of Glastonbury Festival of Contemporary Performing Arts in England. The study presented an innovative interpretation of festivity through multi and social media, showing that identity is a hybrid construct where the localised ephemeral and embodied experiences of festivity demand a simultaneously mediated and socially globalised reflection. The study portrayed that festivity is moving beyond management as it is increasingly dependent on the co-creative social media activity of consumers to perpetuate the fantasy and capital of festivity. This study depicted how festivity works in an age of ubiquitous social media where lifestyles are increasingly digitised and networked. Undoubtedly, the power of technology is a driving, transformational force in festivity as a form of building cultural capital.

As shown in this section of the chapter, youth engagement has become a more hybrid concept ranging from localized to globalized experiences across cultural boundaries prompted by the resurgence of digital and social media. Indeed, one key consequence of this emerging process includes building cross-border social relationships and social and cultural capital facilitated by meaningful youth engagement through the use of media.

SUMMARY AND CONCLUSION

Contextualized within the popularity of new media, youth engagement is a very important concept in the practice of public involvement. Guided by the current literature on youth engagement and media studies, this chapter examined the key engagement-related notions involving youth and media usage. Being informed by a variety of case studies on youth engagement through the use of media within various contexts globally, the chapter discussed the opportunities and challenges of engaging youth through media usage. Better understanding the ways in which youth use media for their engagement has significant implications for practice and policy on youth and public involvement at all system levels globally. The specific notions covered in this chapter include: (a) the role of "hybrid" media in youth engagement; (b) "intersectionality" illustrating the diversity of youth populations and their media usage; (c) meaning-making through media usage among youth; and (d) building global social relationships and social and cultural capital through youth's media usage.

In summary, hybrid forms of communications through digital and social media, face-to-face interactions, and traditional media can promote meaningful youth engagement and youth activism, in which relationship-building (both within youth and between youth and adults) is a critical concept. Appreciation of the diversity of youth populations and their media usage from an intersectional perspective is helpful to better understand the ways of youth engagement and activism via media that can promote meaning-making, for example, on identity and cultural issues. In addition, youth engagement through media usage can help build global social relationships and social, linguistic, and cultural capital and can facilitate a youth-led transformation of our society to address social justice issues. Importantly, multimedia usage provides youth with creative outlets for civic engagement, community connections, and meaning-making within their lives.

As described earlier, meaningful youth engagement is a key concept for both positive youth development (PYD; Alicea et al., 2012; Delgado, 2002; Lind, 2008) and social justice youth development (SJYD; Cammarota, 2011; Gharabaghi & Anderson-Nathe, 2012; Ross, 2011) and facilitates social/system change to more effectively support youth and their families (Blanchet-Cohen & Salazar, 2009; Davidson et al., 2010; Yohalem & Martin, 2007; Wexler et al., 2009). Importantly, the integration of PYD and SJYD conceptually supports the vital role of youth as a proactive agent for changes at personal (e.g., self-identity, constructive behaviours), social (e.g., collective identity, advocacy for social change), and community (e.g., policy and practice change from social justice perspectives) levels (Ross, 2011).

Indeed, this notion (i.e., the integration of PYD and SJYD) is highly applicable to the use of hybrid forms of communications to promote youth engagement and development by appreciating the diversity of youth populations and their media usage (from an intersectional perspective), and by promoting meaning-making and social and cultural capital, as well as to facilitate a youth-led/guided transformation of our society to address social justice issues. The power of youth in leading/guiding social change should not be underestimated, and this role can be effectively promoted by the use of hybrid forms of communications for youth engagement. Importantly, the use of new media provides youth with opportunities to re-define and re-create the ways in which youth are engaged, as key meaning-making processes, to address identity, social, and cultural issues.

REFERENCES

Alicea, S., Pardo, G., Conover, K., Gopalan, G., & McKay, M. (2012). Step-up: Promoting youth mental health and development in inner-city high schools. *Clinical Social Work Journal, 40*(2), 175–186. doi:10.100710615-011-0344-3 PMID:23564983

Asakura, K., & Craig, S. L. (2014). "It Gets Better" … but How? Exploring Resilience Development in the Accounts of LGBTQ Adults. *Journal of Human Behavior in the Social Environment, 24*(3), 253–266. doi:10.1080/10911359.2013.808971

Bimber, B., Flanagin, A., & Stohl, C. (2012). *Collective Action in Organizations: Interaction and Engagement in an Era of Technological Change*. Cambridge, UK: Cambridge University Press. doi:10.1017/CBO9780511978777

Blackman, S. (1995). *Youth: Positions and Oppositions—Style, Sexuality and Schooling*. Aldershot, UK: Avebury Press.

Blackman, S. (2014). Subculture theory: An historical and contemporary assessment of the concept for understanding deviance. *Deviant Behavior, 35*(6), 496–512. doi:10.1080/01639625.2013.859049

Blanchet-Cohen, N., & Salazar, J. (2009). Empowering practices for working with marginalized youth. *Relational Child & Youth Care Practice, 22*, 5–15.

Botha, A., Vosloo, S., Kuner, J., & van den Berg, M. (2009). Improving cross-cultural awareness and communication through mobile technologies. *International Journal of Mobile and Blended Learning, 1*(2), 39–53. doi:10.4018/jmbl.2009040103

Bourdieu, P. (1991). *Language and Symbolic Power*. Cambridge, MA: Harvard University Press.

Cammarota, J. (2011). From Hopelessness to Hope: Social Justice Pedagogy in Urban Education and Youth Development. *Urban Education, 46*(4), 828–844. doi:10.1177/0042085911399931

Campbell, S. W., & Park, Y. S. (2008). Social implications of mobile telephony: The rise of personal communication society. *Sociology Compass, 2*(2), 371–387. doi:10.1111/j.1751-9020.2007.00080.x

Castells, M. (2009). *Communication Power*. Oxford, UK: Oxford University Press.

Chan, M., & Guo, J. (2013). The role of political efficacy on the relationship between Facebook use and participatory behaviors: A comparative study of young American and Chinese adults. *Cyberpsychology, Behavior, and Social Networking, 16*(6), 460–463. doi:10.1089/cyber.2012.0468 PMID:23505970

Clark, P. (2012). *Youth Culture in China: From Red Guards to Netizens*. Cambridge, UK: Cambridge University Press. doi:10.1017/CBO9781139061162

Conner, J., & Slattery, A. (2014). New media and the power of youth organizing: Minding the gaps. *Equity & Excellence in Education*, *47*(1), 14–30. doi:10.1080/10665684.2014.866868

Craig, S. L., McInroy, L. B., McCready, L. T., Di Cesare, D. M., & Pettaway, L. D. (2014). Connecting without fear: Clinical implications of the consumption of information and communication technologies by sexual minority youth and young adults. *Clinical Social Work Journal*, *43*(2), 159–168. doi:10.100710615-014-0505-2

Crenshaw, K. (1995). Mapping the margins: Intersectionality, identity politics, and violence against women of color. In K. Crenshaw, N. Gotanda, G. Peller, & K. Thomas (Eds.), *Critical race theory: The key writings that formed the movement* (pp. 357–383). New York, NY: The New Press.

Davidson, J., Wien, S., & Anderson, K. (2010). Creating a Provincial Family Council to Engage Youth and Families in Child & Youth Mental Health Systems. *Journal of the Canadian Academy of Child and Adolescent Psychiatry*, *19*(3), 169–175. PMID:20842271

de Haana, M., Leanderb, K., Ünlüsoya, A., & Prinsenc, F. (2014). Challenging ideals of connected learning: The networked configurations for learning of migrant youth in the Netherlands. *Learning, Media and Technology*, *39*(4), 507–535. doi:10.1080/17439884.2014.964256

Dedman, T. (2011). Agency in UK Hip-Hop and Grime Youth Subcultures—Peripherals and Purists. *Journal of Youth Studies*, *14*(5), 507–522. doi:10.1080/13676261.2010.549820

Delgado, M. (2002). *New frontiers for youth development in the twenty-first century: Revitalizing and broadening youth development*. New York, NY: Columbia University Press.

Ersing, R. L. (2009). Building the Capacity of Youths through Community Cultural Arts: A Positive Youth Development Perspective. *Best Practices in Mental Health*, *5*(1), 26–43.

Flinn, J., & Frew, M. (2014). Glastonbury: Managing the mystification of Festivity. *Leisure Studies*, *33*(4), 418–433. doi:10.1080/02614367.2012.751121

Garcia, A., Mirra, N., Morrell, E., Martinez, A., & Scorza, D. (2015). The Council of Youth Research: Critical literacy and civic agency in the digital age. *Reading & Writing Quarterly*, *31*(2), 151–167. doi:10.1080/10573569.2014.962203

Garnets, L. D. (2002). Sexual orientations in perspective. *Cultural Diversity & Ethnic Minority Psychology*, *8*(2), 115–129. doi:10.1037/1099-9809.8.2.115 PMID:11987589

Gharabaghi, K., & Anderson-Nathe, B. (2012). In Search of New Ideas. *Child and Youth Services*, *33*(1), 1–4. doi:10.1080/0145935X.2012.665317

Ginwright, S., & James, T. (2002). From assets to agents of change: Social justice, organizing, and youth development. *New Directions for Youth Development*, *96*(96), 27–46. doi:10.1002/yd.25 PMID:12630272

Gunter, A. (2010). *Growing Up Bad*. London, UK: Tufnell Press.

Halverson, E. R. (2010). Film as Identity Exploration: A Multimodal Analysis of Youth-Produced Films. *Teachers College Record*, *112*(9), 2352–2378.

Hodkinson, P., & Lincoln, S. (2008). Online Journals as Virtual Bedrooms? Young People, Identity and Personal Space. *Young*, *16*(1), 27–46. doi:10.1177/110330880701600103

Hynan, A., Murray, J., & Goldbart, J. (2014). 'Happy and excited': Perceptions of using digital technology and social media by young people who use augmentative and alternative communication. *Child Language Teaching and Therapy*, *30*(2), 175–186. doi:10.1177/0265659013519258

Iglesias, E., & Cormier, S. (2002). The transformation of girls to women: Finding voice and developing strategies for liberation. *Journal of Multicultural Counseling and Development*, *30*, 259–271. doi:10.1002/j.2161-1912.2002.tb00523.x

Iwasaki, Y., MacKay, K., Mactavish, J., Ristock, J., & Bartlett, J. (2006). Voices from the margins: Stress, active living, and leisure as a contributor to coping with stress. *Leisure Sciences: An Interdisciplinary Journal*, *28*(2), 163–180. doi:10.1080/01490400500484065

Kahne, J., Middaugh, E., Lee, N. J., & Feezell, J. T. (2012). Youth online activity and exposure to diverse perspectives. *New Media & Society*, *14*(3), 492–512. doi:10.1177/1461444811420271

Karpf, D. (2012). *The MoveOn Effect: The Unexpected Transformation of American Political Advocacy*. New York, NY: Oxford University Press. doi:10.1093/acprof:oso/9780199898367.001.0001

Keipi, T., & Oksanen, A. (2014). Self-exploration, anonymity and risks in the online setting: Analysis of narratives by 14–18-year olds. *Journal of Youth Studies*, *17*(8), 1097–1113. doi:10.1080/13676261.2014.881988

Kennelly, J. (2011). *Citizen youth: Culture, activism, and agency in a neoliberal era*. London, UK: Palgrave Macmillan. doi:10.1057/9780230119611

Lam, W. S. E. (2014). Literacy and capital in immigrant youths' online networks across countries. *Learning, Media and Technology*, *39*(4), 488–506. doi:10.1080/17439884.2014.942665

Lambert, J., Mullen, N., Paull, C., Paulos, E., Soundararajan, T., Spagat, A., & … . (2007). *Digital storytelling cookbook and travelling companion*. Digital Diner Press.

Leander, K., & de Haan, M. (2014). Editorial. *Learning, Media and Technology*, *39*(4), 405–408. doi:10.1080/17439884.2014.964257

Lee, N. J., Shah, D. V., & McLeod, J. M. (2013). Processes of political socialization: A communication mediation approach to youth civic engagement. *Communication Research*, *40*(5), 669–697. doi:10.1177/0093650212436712

Lind, C. (2008). Knowledge development with adolescents in a PAR process. *Educational Action Research*, *16*(2), 221–233. doi:10.1080/09650790802011874

Ling, R. (2010). *New tech, new ties: How mobile communication reshapes social cohesion*. Cambridge, MA: The MIT Press.

Livingstone, S. (2009). *Children and the Internet: Great Expectations, Challenging Realities*. Cambridge, UK: Polity Press.

Luschen, K., & Bogad, L. (2010). Youth, new media and education: An introduction. *Educational Studies: Journal of the American Educational Studies Association, 46*(5), 450–456. doi:10.1080/00131946.2010.510402

Markman, K. D., Proulx, T., & Lindberg, M. J. (Eds.). (2013). *The psychology of meaning*. Washington, DC: American Psychological Association. doi:10.1037/14040-000

Mutere, M., Nyamathi, A., Christiani, A., Sweat, J., Avila, G., & Hobaica, L. Jr. (2014). Homeless Youth Seeking Health and Life-Meaning Through Popular Culture and the Arts. *Child and Youth Services, 35*(3), 273–287. doi:10.1080/0145935X.2014.950416

Park, C. L. (2010). Making sense of the meaning literature: An integrative review of meaning making and its effects on adjustment to stressful life events. *Psychological Bulletin, 136*(2), 257–301. doi:10.1037/a0018301 PMID:20192563

Pathak-Shelat, M., & DeShano, C. (2014). Digital youth cultures in small town and rural Gujarat, India. *New Media & Society, 16*(6), 983–1001. doi:10.1177/1461444813496611

Portus, L. M. (2008). How the urban poor acquire and give meaning to the mobile phone. In J. Katz (Ed.), *Handbook of mobile communication studies* (pp. 105–118). Cambridge, MA: MIT Press. doi:10.7551/mitpress/9780262113120.003.0009

Razack, S. (1998). *Looking White people in the eye*. Toronto, Canada: University of Toronto Press.

Ristock, J. (2002). Responding to lesbian relationship violence: An ethical challenge. In L. Tutty & C. Goard (Eds.), *Reclaiming self: Issues and resources for women abused by intimate partners* (pp. 98–116). Halifax, Canada: Fernwood Press.

Ross, L. (2011). Sustaining Youth Participation in a Long-term Tobacco Control Initiative: Consideration of a Social Justice Perspective. *Youth & Society, 43*(2), 681–704. doi:10.1177/0044118X10366672

Schwartz, S. E. O., Rhodes, J. E., Liang, B., Sánchez, B., Spencer, R., Kremer, S., & Kanchewa, S. (2014). Mentoring in the digital age: Social media use in adult–youth relationships. *Children and Youth Services Review, 47*, 205–213. doi:10.1016/j.childyouth.2014.09.004

Singh, A. A. (2013). Transgender Youth of Color and Resilience: Negotiating Oppression and Finding Support. *Sex Roles, 68*(11-12), 690–702. doi:10.100711199-012-0149-z

Skoric, M. M., & Poor, N. (2013). Youth Engagement in Singapore: The Interplay of Social and Traditional Media. *Journal of Broadcasting & Electronic Media, 57*(2), 187–204. doi:10.1080/08838151.2013.787076

Sloam, J. (2014). 'The outraged young': Young Europeans, civic engagement and the new media in a time of crisis. *Information Communication and Society, 17*(2), 217–231. doi:10.1080/1369118X.2013.868019

Suleiman, A., Soleimanpour, S., & London, J. (2006). Youth action for health through youth-led research. *Journal of Community Practice, 14*(1-2), 125–145. doi:10.1300/J125v14n01_08

Thornton, S. (1995). *Club Culture: Music, Media and Subcultural Capital*. Cambridge, UK: Polity Press.

van Kruistum, C., Leseman, P. M., & de Haan, M. (2014). Youth Media Lifestyles. *Human Communication Research, 40*(4), 508–529. doi:10.1111/hcre.12033

Vickery, J. R. (2015). 'I don't have anything to hide, but…': The challenges and negotiations of social and mobile media privacy for non-dominant youth. *Information Communication and Society, 18*(3), 281–294. doi:10.1080/1369118X.2014.989251

Wells, C. (2014). Two eras of civic information and the evolving relationship between civil society organizations and young citizens. *New Media & Society, 16*(4), 615–636. doi:10.1177/1461444813487962

Wexler, L. M., DiFluvio, G., & Burke, T. K. (2009). Resilience and marginalized youth: Making a case for personal and collective meaning-making as part of resilience research in public health. *Social Science & Medicine, 69*(4), 565–570. doi:10.1016/j.socscimed.2009.06.022 PMID:19596503

Williams, J. P. (2011). *Subcultural Theory*. Cambridge, UK: Polity Press.

Wilson, N., Minkler, M., Dasho, S., Carrillo, R., Wallerstein, N., & Garcia, D. (2006). Training students as facilitators in the Youth Empowerment Strategies (YES!) Project. *Journal of Community Practice, 14*(1-2), 201–217. doi:10.1300/J125v14n01_12

Xenos, M., Vromen, A., & Loader, B. D. (2014). The great equalizer? Patterns of social media use and youth political engagement in three advanced democracies. *Information Communication and Society, 17*(2), 151–167. doi:10.1080/1369118X.2013.871318

Yohalem, N., & Martin, S. (2007). Building the evidence base for youth engagement: Reflections on youth and democracy. *Journal of Community Psychology, 35*(6), 807–810. doi:10.1002/jcop.20180

Zemmels, D. R. (2012). Youth and new media: Constructing meaning and identity in networked spaces. *Dissertation Abstracts International. A, The Humanities and Social Sciences, 72*(10-A), 3570.

Chapter 6
Exploring a Methodological Model for Social Media Gatekeeping on Contentious Topics:
A Case Study of Twitter Interactions About GMOs

Jacob Groshek
Kansas State University, USA

ABSTRACT

The notion of news networks has changed from primarily one of print and broadcast networks to one of social networks and social media. This study examines the intersection of technological affordances, dialogic activity, and where traditional news gatekeepers are now situated in the contemporary multigated and networked media environment. Using genetically modified organisms (GMOs) as a topical issue, social data was collected from Twitter. The most connected (and connecting) users were algorithmically identified and then sorted into 'community' groups. The resultant graphs visually and statistically identify which users were important gatekeepers and how the flow of information on this topic was being structured around and by certain users that acted as 'hubs' of communication in the network. Results suggest that the ongoing evolution of networked gatekeeping has led to the virtual absence of journalists and news organizations from prominence in social media coverage on certain topics, in this instance GMOs. Normative implications are discussed.

DOI: 10.4018/978-1-7998-1828-1.ch006

INTRODUCTION

The concept of media gatekeeping is one that dates back generations and generally has come to be accepted as part and parcel of the activities journalists and editors carry out as they construct the news (Gitlin, 1980). To some extent, the activity of gatekeeping was observed to be an essential byproduct of traditional media outlets such as newspapers, televisions and radio programs having a *finite* amount of space and time to cover news (Shoemaker & Vos, 2009). Put simply, in the course of a given news cycle, media reports could not cover all events or topics that occurred, so journalists and editors adapted professional strategies and routines in the performance of news gathering and the selection of news stories (Gans, 1979) such that, at least historically speaking, "the news aims to tell us what we want to know, need to know, and should know" (Tuchman, 1978, p. 1).

In one of the first formalizations of gatekeeping as a theoretical framework in the journalism and communication field, White (1950) examined how a "gatekeeper" in the complex channels of media organizations managed the news gate. In that study the editorial decision-making process and resultant information flow in two American newspapers was modeled through analyses of the criteria that editors used to make judgments about whether a story was newsworthy or not. Since the White study—where he researched why particular wire editors selected or rejected the news stories that were filed based on their perceived importance, available space and timeliness—there has been an ongoing stream of research that has considered how gatekeeping has been transformed in response to technological developments and shifts in sociocultural norms. Indeed, based explicitly on White's original formulation (1950), Ali and Fahmy wrote that gatekeeping as a theory "is defined as the selection process of choosing stories and/or visuals that follow the organization's' news routines and narratives" (2013, p. 65).

Yet since White's seminal work that identified "gatekeeping as a selection process where 'gatekeepers' pick and choose which news articles and/or visual images to run in the media" (as cited in Ali & Fahmy, 2013, p. 55), the conceptualization of gatekeeping has come to take on finer and more nuanced perspectives. Specifically, in looking at network gatekeeping (Barzilai-Nahon, 2008), it is clear that gatekeeping has morphed into an increasingly dynamic and situation-specific activity taken on by an increasingly wider scope of individuals. In short, as online and social media technology has democratized the capacity for individuals to create and share media, the notion of gatekeeping has conceptually remained intact but has expanded as a practice far beyond White's original conceptualization of who gatekeepers are.

Just as communication technologies have opened up vast opportunities for the re-orientation of information flows around non-hierarchical users as gatekeepers, technological advances have also facilitated the increased production of genetically modified organisms (GMOs), which have emerged into the food stream since at least the late 1980s as a commercially available product (Chassy, 2007). While the historical roots of humans genetically altering plants date at least to Mendel and his hybridization of peas in the early 1800's (Henig, 2000), GMOs have taken on a contentious position socially and politically in many countries in the last several decades (Stephan, 2014). As examples, there were anti-GMO demonstrations that took place in approximately 400 cities around the globe on May 23, 2015 (Guardian, 2015) yet exactly two months later, on July 23, 2015, the U.S. House of Representatives approved a pro-GMO ban on states requiring GMO labeling on food (House Committee on Agriculture, 2015).

Altogether, this study is thus positioned to offer insights into not only the ongoing renegotiation of traditional news organizations and journalists as gatekeepers in the contemporary emergent and multi-gated media environment but also how this transformation of the public sphere continues to take shape (Galata, Karantinisis & Hess, 2014) on social media in coverage of GMOs.

Theorizing Models of Gatekeeping in an Emergent Media Environment

Writing in 2003, Bowman and Willis foreshadowed the rapid changes that were looming large on the horizon of the news industry as the Internet was not only rapidly diffusing but also evolving into a media platform where users were becoming more active in creating and sharing media content through decentralized and non-hierarchical linkages. They wrote, "The venerable profession of journalism finds itself at a rare moment in history where, for the first time, its hegemony as *gatekeeper* [emphasis added] of the news is threatened by not just new technology and competitors but, potentially, by the *audience* [emphasis added] it serves" (Bowman & Willis, 2003, p. 7).

To some extent, the re-organizaiton of gatekeeping has been welcomed, particularly along the lines of citizen journalism, which has highlighted the ways in which technological affordances like user creation and sharing have made it possible for "media production and information dissemination outside the confines of established journalism, and thus for bypassing the gatekeepers of the traditional media business" (Hintz, 2012, p. 128). Considering the critiques that have been leveled at mainstream mass media (Gitlin, 1980; McChesney, 1999) it was broadly accepted by scholars, activists, and (alternative) media producers that a more egalitarian and decentralized system of media production and sharing would be normatively preferable in the pursuit of truth and related democratic ideals (Groshek & Han, 2011).

One of the most important features of gatekeeping, either in historical or contemporary accounts is that it is a series of decision-making processes at the individual level, which were typically articulated in a larger journalistic environment. In other words, gatekeeping is, at its core, a judgment about newsworthiness (Shoemaker & Vos, 2009) and the product of the professionalization of gatekeeping resulted in observable features and patterns that operationalized news production (Gans, 1979; Tuchman, 1978; Soroka, 2012). Laidlaw (2015) further expanded that network gatekeepers are required to be active in making a series of choices that shape content in much the same manner as White (1950) observed decades ago, but—importantly—the requirements set forth by Laidlaw are not professionalized routines, nor are they enforced through socialization or other quality checks as in a media organization.

Put briefly, Laidlaw outlined that an act of gatekeeping is simply the movement of information as selected by a gatekeeper through a given gatekeeping process and mechanism. More specifically, she wrote, "A gatekeeping process involves doing some level of selecting, channeling, shaping, manipulating and deleting information" (2015, p. 45). Though these are broad parameters, network gatekeeping is useful as a framework for identifying processes and mechanisms, such as hyperlinks or mentioning others that signify gatekeeping as an action, if not a component of a professional occupation. As informed greatly by Barzilai-Nahon's (2008) network gatekeeping model, which identifies thirteen 'gatekeeping bases' that are unique but not mutually exclusive, it is clear that the practice of gatekeeping is still relevant and ongoing but adapted to a media environment that has been and continues to be reshaped and reordered through sequences of technological and social change.

Clearly, the traditional one-to-many unidirectional flow of mass media gatekeeping has been redefined by emerging media technologies and practices (Groshek & Tandoc, 2016; Lewis, Holton, & Coddington, 2013). Indeed, as outlined by the network gatekeeping model, there is a "multidirectional flow by which all actors [in a network] have the potential to influence one another and the flow of information, effectively connecting everyday individuals to organizations by primarily channeling through the mediation of the hub consisting of networked individuals and professional communicators" (Chin-Fook & Simmonds, 2011, p. 30). Users that act as 'hubs' of information sharing are identified by mutual processes of selecting and reinforcing topical authority within the network of communicators, and thus serve a reconstituted information function by gatekeeping for an audience that is "exposed to various information options such as news articles processed by media professionals, social reporting by citizen journalists, and raw sources directly accessible from the respective online databases" (Kwon, Oh, Agrawal, & Rao, 2012, p. 215).

Given that there is now a wealth of media content and information of all types readily available in what can be considered the digital news era, Bruns (2003) has identified the concept of 'gatewatchers' rather than gatekeepers. Bruns' rationale rests principally upon the premise that the terminology of gatewatching reflects the user-centric "practice of *publicizing* rather than controlling information under conditions of information abundance" (Goode, 2012, p. 1295). In short, there is an ongoing debate of what constitutes contemporary gatekeeping in a networked, multi-gated media environment. However, Goode further and contrarily suggests that the term gatekeeper ought to be retained, primarily because:

...visibility and attention, if not information, remain scarce resources in the online news sphere: whether or not a particular story reaches the front page of a popular online news site or remains buried several pages deep has consequences akin to 'traditional' gatekeeping processes even if the underlying process differs significantly. (2012, p. 1295).

Research by Shoemaker and Vos (2009) has advanced that the online audience itself represents another gatekeeper in media systems. Moreover, gatekeeping as an activity remains a central mechanism in digital news networks, though that function may well be carried out by individualized synthesizing and filtering—in some cases algorithmically or in combination with human editors (Thielman, 2016)—a multitude of potential senders and receivers. To this point, additional research has suggested that gatekeeping "in traditional media was performed by individual editors, in digital networks it embodies nodes taking part in the story and redesigning the process through which ideas and information are filtered for publication" (Bastos, Raimundo, & Travitzki, 2013, p. 3).

Still, it would be remiss to ignore the larger issue raised by Shoemaker and Vos (2009) that to some degree, journalists in digital media environments are more regularly exercising their selection of stories around audience interests. It has been reported by Vu (2013) that professionalized gatekeeping in the contemporary media environment is heavily audience-centric, with editors noting that their gatekeeping decisions have been directly affected by audience-related factors. These editorial decisions are also related to economic considerations and the more advanced technological means of audience analytics and popularity of stories relative to advertising revenues (Vu, 2013), but are of course a part of long history of ad-supported journalistic endeavors and the implications therein (Bennett, 2012; Underwood, 1995).

As related to one of key points in Bennett's work is the how users (and followers) on Twitter (and other social networking sites) can readily formulate their own criteria for what they determine to be newsworthy and thus important to share with their followers (Diakopoulos & Zubiaga, 2014). In acting as gatekeepers, Twitter users not only consume incoming information from within their own Twitter network and/or outside of the system, but also broadcast the consumed information to their own networks of followers (Kwon et al., 2012). An especially important contribution to this topic is that of Meraz and Papacharissi (2013), where they identified that in the instance of the 2011 Egyptian uprisings,

Prominent gatekeepers arose from elite and nonelite [emphases added] media institutions, with activist or journalistic agendas, or both, contributing to the labeling of this movement as a revolution, and thus, in some way, prefacing its destiny through expressive gestures that were affective, premediated, and anticipatory. (2013, p. 21).

Following from this conclusion—and in some manner being most relevant to the study described here—Bastos, Raimundo and Travitzki (2013) studied the gatekeeping structures of Twitter when looking at political hashtags. In their analyses, Bastos and colleagues noted that that "traditional gatekeepers such as newspaper and media corporations are well represented in Twitter and their coverage is widely distributed throughout the environment" (p. 10). However, their results further demonstrated that a relatively small portion of tweets received by ordinary users actually originates from traditional media outlets and that network gatekeeping is shaped by additional factors including message fitness.

In conceptualizing message fitness of GMOs and their media coverage, there is seemingly no end to truth claims both in favor of and opposed to GMOs (Katiraee, 2015; Saletan, 2015). Thus, given this now longstanding debate, the goal of the study presented here is therefore to examine these socio-technological factors to better understand both the affordances of social media and the role of traditional gatekeepers in covering the GMO debate online.

As a case study of contemporary gatekeeping, this research fill a gap insofar as there is relatively little literature to date that has explicitly examined GMOs in news reporting (Galata, Karantinisis & Hess, 2014; Marks et al., 2003). Moreover, almost no scholarly attention has been paid to the role of social media in framing the GMO debate. This contribution is especially important considering that recent research (Pew, 2015) has found social media platforms such as Facebook and Twitter to be important, if not primary, sources of news for several (age-based) sectors of the American population.

Considering all of these factors and the overarching goals of this study, the following research question and hypothesis are posed:

RQ1: In the intersection of news networks and social networks, where are the once-exclusive traditional media gatekeepers now situated in the contemporary multi-gated media environment?

H1: Other, non-journalistic actors will emerge as influential informational hubs by more actively engaging the social affordances made technologically available on Twitter.

METHODS

Data for this study comprised tweets that used at least one of the following key words or phrases: "biotech foods, genetically altered food, genetically engineered crops, genetically engineered foods, genetically modified crops, genetically modified foods, GMO, GMO crops, or GMO foods" during the period 1 May 2015 through 15 July 2015. These parameters resulted in the collection of 327,235 tweets from the Boston University Twitter Content and Analysis Toolkit (BU-TCAT), which utilizes the public Twitter application programming interface (API). As it relates to this study, the BU-TCAT is an installation of open source software originally developed by Borra and Rieder (2014) to capture a generalizable sample of public tweets (Gerlitz & Reider, 2013; Groshek, 2014). In short, the data analyzed here does not claim to have captured every tweet posted using the identified key words or phrases outlined above, but it does constitute a sample of Twitter that has been shown to be representative of the broader spectrum of communication in that arena.

To test the research question and hypothesis advanced in this study, the BU-TCAT system created a series of network files in order to algorithmically sort and visualize the most central 'hub' users in the (also open-source) software program Gephi. These analyses further allow the processing of calculated network statistics into sortable spreadsheet format, and model various spatializations of underlying network structures that emphasize the importance of certain nodes and linkages in the data. In addition, nodes are sized and colored to follow the contours of certain algorithms found in parsing the data into measures of influence and community.

The analysis as applied here situates users active in discussing the topic of GMOs into a broader narrative surrounding networked gatekeeping and social media analysis. Importantly, while Meraz (2009) noted that many scholars who study gatekeeping online "have used the hyperlink as a symbolic representation of a single gatekeeping act" (2009, p. 685) this study instead engages @username mentions on Twitter as reference points that signal a form of dialogic interaction by users (Groshek & Al-Rawi, 2015; Tandoc, 2015).

FINDINGS

This study began by examining users (RQ1) that tweeted about GMO-related topics in keywords and phrases. Here, several algorithmic sorting techniques were brought to bear with the software program Gephi. These analyses contributed to the creation of a visual and statistical representation of users in this dataset. Specifically, algorithms available to deploy in Gephi were calculated to determine measures of influence and community in this specific network of users as well as spatialize those users into an interactive graph.

Here, the HITS (Hyperlink-Induced Topic Search) algorithm was applied to determine the size of the nodes and model influential users in this analysis. As noted by McSweeny (2009, p. 2) HITS computes the value of individual nodes as 'hubs' in the network, where the hub score "estimates the value of the links outgoing from the page (node)." In other words, this output weights the size of a given node based on how frequently it links to other nodes that have shown some authority on a subject (Chien, Hoong, & Ho, 2014), in this case GMOs on Twitter. Influential users, or "nodes," in this analysis and related graphs are thus best understood as active hubs that point to many other users that are likewise important to the flow of information in the network (Brin & Page, 1998; Smith, Rainie, Shneiderman, & Himelboim, 2014).

In this analysis, color was applied to nodes in this network of users with the modularity algorithm, which was developed for the purpose of detecting communities of users that have frequent interactions with one another within the network (Newman, 2006). At this juncture it is worthwhile to note that the graph under consideration here is directional, which means that the links between users are not necessarily reciprocal. In other words, users on Twitter can mention another user publicly in a tweet by using the @username reference marker as a way to initiate or sustain conversation or to invoke a certain user as a point of reference but that user, at his or her discretion may choose to respond or ignore the mention.

When examining this sample of users and their measurable connectedness and influence, there were 148,371 users who composed 327,235 tweets that mentioned GMO-related keywords or phrases. For purposes of this study, these users were summarized into 1,500 most-mentioned (user) nodes and 11,773 directed (co-mentioned) edges. As noted earlier, this analysis and subsequent model does not include every user that tweeted or that was mentioned during this timeframe, but instead is a general map of users that acted as informational hubs in this topical communicative network.

One additional parameter of this analysis is the spatialization of this visualization, which was interpreted using the OpenOrd algorithm. Also available through Gephi, OpenOrd is designed to separate nodes into more distinct visual clusters. Once spatialized with OpenOrd, the Noverlap algorithm was also applied to make visual interpretation clearer by preventing nodes from overlapping one another. These steps converge in Figure 1. In addition to the static image found there, an interactive version has been made available here so that readers can zoom, center, and otherwise more effectively explore nodes and edges in better detail.

This figure is further interpreted by sorting users on the basis of their agency as hubs in the network. Here, it can be observed that there is a wide ideological (including both pro- and anti-GMO) range of active users that are important hubs of sharing information about GMOs and connecting authoritative users on Twitter. As rank-ordered by the HITS computation of user hub scores, the 25 most important users in this topical Twitter network are as follows here with a brief description: (1) gmwatch – activist group, (2) 8extremes – citizen (3) gmofreeusa – activist group, (4) thegopjesus – citizen, (5) virginiaincal – citizen, (6) rosevine3 – citizen, (7) rachelsnews – activist / journalist, (8) genengnetwork – activist group, (9) food_democracy – activist group, (10) kevinfolta – food scientist / professor, (11) pgoeltz – activist / anonymous, (12) organicconsumer – activist group, (13) monsantoco – GMO manufacturer, (14) fuller_derek – citizen, (15) marchagainstm – activist group, (16) elizabethzen – writer / editor / biologist, (17) gmoinside – activist group, (18) justlabelit – activist group, (19) notogmos – activist group, (20) geneticliteracy – activist / journalist, (21) truefoodnow – activist group, (22) positivelyjoan – citizen, (23) mem_somerville – scientist, (24) naturalsociety – activist group, (25) 2sense2 – citizen.

In terms of answering RQ1 and identifying gatekeepers in this intersection of news networks and social networks, it is abundantly clear that legacy media news organizations and journalists have ceded their once-exclusive position and now function in tandem with a host of other actors. In this multi-gated media environment, activists from both sides of this debate are largely dominant in constructing and shaping the flow of social media coverage of GMOs, and a proportion of self-identified scientists and researchers regularly enter the fold in engaging dialogic activities and contesting truth claims. There is also a noticeable contribution of users that could be considered 'ordinary' citizens based on their somewhat nondescript profiles.

In addition to understanding the profiles of these users, who were the most active hubs in receiving and sharing GMO content with authoritative users, it is notable that 806 of the top 1,500 users considered in this dataset had a hub score greater than zero. This finding—combined with the observation of 11,773 co-mentions among the users that were tweeting about GMOs—identifies this communicative network as one that is not only active but also densely interconnected across distinct community clusters of users where those co-mentions were even more pronounced, even as frequency of interactions did not fully align with modularity. This outcome signals that users were active in mentioning and communicating with one another even if they did not share similar ideological viewpoints on the topic of the safety and utility of genetically modified organisms.

In examining RQ1 further, and exploring more precisely the aspect of where *geographically* are those users and gatekeepers situated, this study also included a geospatial map of Twitter users who were posting about GMOs. Here, Figure 2 identifies that the majority of GMO tweets in this subsample originated from the United States, though there were tweets represented from every populated continent.

Figure 1.

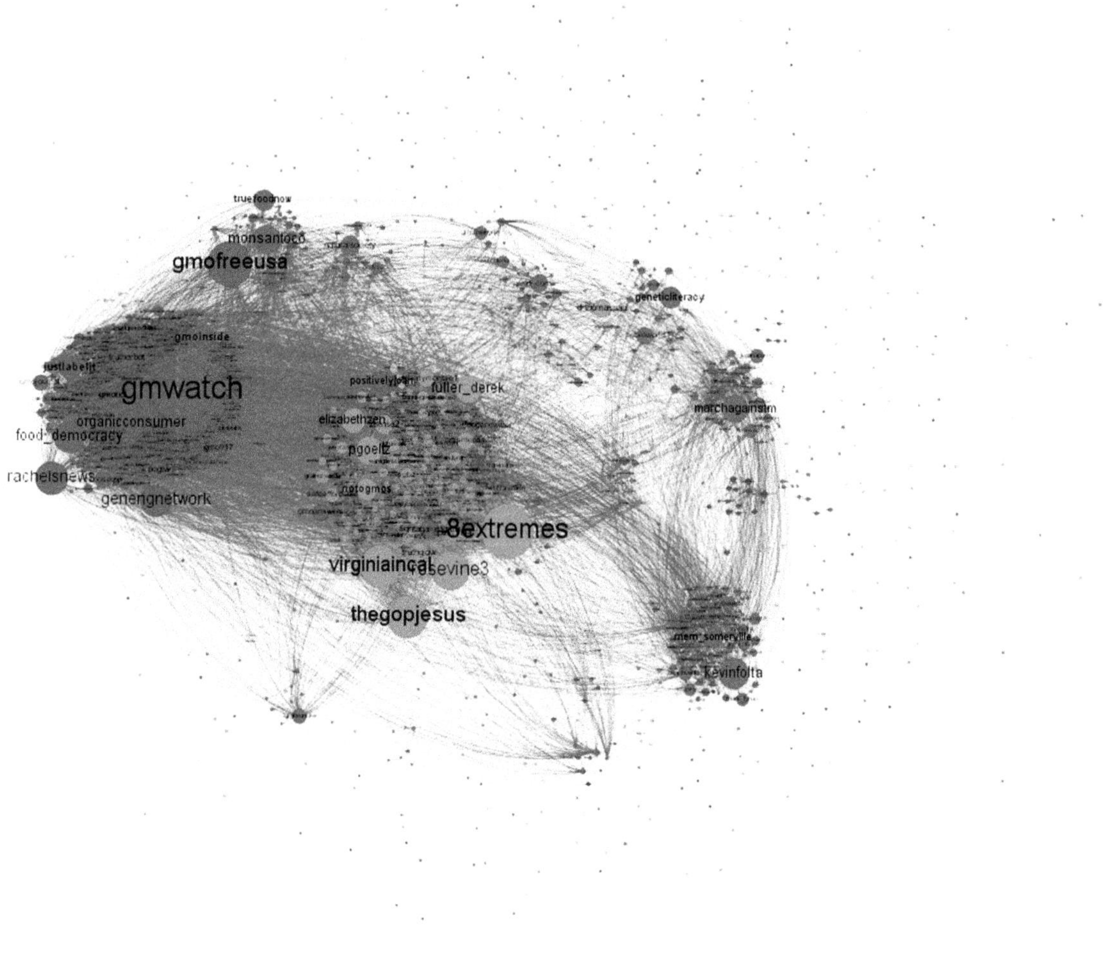

Perhaps somewhat unsurprisingly considering this geographical distribution, the majority (68.44 percent) of geolocative GMO tweets were from users that self-identified their language as English, which was followed by Spanish (7.11 percent), Japanese (6.70 percent), Indonesian (3.76 percent), and Norwegian (2.70 percent).

Of course, it is worthwhile to note that currently geolocation is an opt-in feature of Twitter, and generally speaking, most estimates place between only one or two percent of all Twitter users actively selecting to make their exact coordinates readily available (Groshek, 2015). Though this renders geolocative data essentially non-generalizable to Twitter users as a population—and certainly to the public more broadly (Jurgens et al., 2015)—it is informative to observe 1,223 tweets in this dataset had geolocation enabled during this time period. This figure is 0.37 percent of the 327,235 tweets collected here. In this small

Figure 2.

subsample, it is nonetheless clear that GMOs are often most tweeted about from the United States (and in English) but that this topic is an issue that connects Twitter users from around the globe.

DISCUSSION AND CONCLUSION

This study sought to examine where traditional media gatekeepers are contemporarily situated in the prevalent multi-gated media environment by modeling the contentious and visible topic of genetically modified organisms. Analyses of over 325,000 tweets about GMO-related topics were analyzed and users were sorted algorithmically on the basis of their mentioning activity within this network. The results observed here build on and contribute to a body of scholarship in the interrelated fields of media and environmental communication. As Galata, Karantinisis, and Hess (2014, p. 307) identified the current time period (2000 – now) as being the third round of mediating responses of GMOs in the public sphere, the insights offered here advance the combined theoretical and practical understanding of gatekeeping in these arenas.

With these analyses considered together, the answer to the first research question is that traditional media news organizations and journalists are all but absent in the intersection of GMO news and social networks. Gatekeepers in this environment are largely activists that are either strongly opposed to or strongly in favor of GMOs, with an intermingling of what could be considered pro-GMO food scientists and researchers along with smaller groups of users that are most efficiently categorized as ordinary citizens, many of which frequently express their opposition to GMOs as well. Here, these findings identify that the flow of information about GMOs on Twitter was decidedly not hierarchical or exclusionary. Rather, there were regular interactions among a wide variety of actors, which on the surface suggests the formation of a certain kind of public sphere. Yet not explicitly studied here was the tone of these interactions and the content circulated by users to and within one another, which could shape not only the information exchange itself but also the attitudes and beliefs of users to the content being circulated. Future work into additional scalable and machine-learning content analyses is part of a larger project on this topic and thus important to connect what is being said with the users advancing or debating truth claims.

Still, the findings reported here, where ordinary users rise to relative prominence by leveraging technical affordances (namely @mentions) align with previous work that has shown the network topology of Twitter is not necessarily correlated with message diffusion and that "gatekeeping might actually emerge as a function of the message frequency instead of the network structure, thus contradicting the description of gatekeepers as a bottleneck of interconnections that determines information flow" (Bastos, Raimundo, & Travitzki, 2013, p. 4). Likewise, as pointed out by Kwon, Oh, Agrawal, and Rao (2012) the 'status' of users that can be considered ordinary audience members in covering GMOs on Twitter are noticeably more influential gatekeepers within that network than are news organizations or journalists.

Considering the findings for RQ1, it is almost a non-starter to test the proposition of H1 that other, non-journalistic actors will emerge as influential informational hubs by more actively engaging the social affordances made technologically available on Twitter. Without question, other actors and not journalists or news organizations were more influential informational hubs when examining GMOs on Twitter. In fact, when all users were sorted from most to least connected by their HITS hub score, the most connected traditional media user on Twitter was @nprfood, which was ranked 477th and is where National Public Radio personality James Beard has tweets about items related to his food blog. Other notable legacy media accounts in this dataset all had a hub score of zero, and a non-exhaustive list includes @ cnn, @natgeo, @latimes, @motherjones, @foxnews, @msnbc, and @bbc. While it is vital to note that none of these accounts tweeted even once into this dataset, each account was mentioned by other users at least dozens of times.

In other words, these news organizations in particular were explicitly and repeatedly mentioned, they effectively declined in all instances to weigh in on this topic and fulfill their longstanding role as cullers, sorters, and sharers of information. Apart from clearly supporting the expectations of the first hypothesis, this finding also signals an important departure of journalists and mainstream, traditional media organizations from their previously identified function as filters and leading agenda-setters on controversial topics, at least in social media coverage of GMOs on Twitter.

Ultimately, the sum of these analyses indicates a need for objective journalism that is more engaged with its audience. Previous studies have shown that advances in technology have made it increasingly possible for news organizations to record audience metrics and reactions to stories for the purpose of gauging their preferences (Vu, 2013). The call here, though, is for news organization and journalists to begin to re-invoke their role as active gatekeepers, not merely observers in the construction of facts as they exist around a given topic, as was the case in the analyses reported in this study. For news organizations and journalists to re-realize this function, there must be a greater effort made in dialogic affordances, particularly on Twitter (but more broadly across social media platforms). Rather than ignoring mentions and choosing not to engage at all on certain issues, news organizations and journalists can choose to reciprocate with mentions and more actively following users of diverse ideologies, particularly those that are more influential to have a better sense of issues they may be covering. In other words, news organizations and journalists ought to become gatekeeping hubs themselves through adopting practices instead of observing from a distance as quasi-impartial but relatively disinterested figures separate from the discourse.

The results of this study make it is quite clear that, consistent with previous work (Bastos, Raimundo, & Travitzki, 2013; Wu, Hofman, Mason, & Watts, 2011), users on Twitter are apt to both receive and share information without the necessity of mediation by news organizations. Still, while legacy media organizations and professional mainstream journalists all but ignored the topic of GMOs on Twitter, there were a number of users that could be considered journalists or fulfilling those roles explicitly as citizen journalists online. Specifically, @rachelsnews, @elizabethzen, and @geneticliteracy were among the top 25 users as sorted by hub scores. As such, the conversation that can be broadly conceived on Twitter was shaped not by a relatively small and homogenous set of self-segregating users but rather engaged a more balanced set of sub-communities and ideological viewpoints.

Thus, while professional journalism all but abdicated in its social responsibility functions in covering GMOs, a discursive communicative space coalesced through the nonhierarchical and seemingly organic emergence of gatekeepers that constructed parameters and information flows around topics and events. The observed relationships in this data therefore depart somewhat from the typical finding that gatekeepers, particularly on Twitter, have become more and more atomized and fragmented (Bastos, Raimundo, & Travitzki, 2013) and instead suggest the possibility of initiating and maintaining dialogic activity across parties – even if those interactions can range in terms of civility and politeness.

Important as these findings can be in terms of evidencing potentially productive forms of discussion among ideologically disparate individuals, it is also important to point out that in a charged online environment such as this it is possible for communication to turn uncivil. Among the tweets collected here, even the activity of mentioning could be considered harassing, particularly in the event of tweets themselves being hostile and personal. Though content markers are not explicitly modeled in this study, the repeated and unreciprocated @username mentions may also signal interactions that on the surface are dialogic markers to the network but as received by individual users could be interpreted as shouting rather than reasoning and attempting to overwhelm the parameters of discussion and silence rather than to persuade others. Again, this activity or any sort of trolling presents more areas where network gatekeeping would benefit from journalists as de facto (if not active) moderators of truth claims through engaging in verification, attribution, and actively targeted sharing.

There are, of course, limitations to what has been reported here. Most importantly, as a case study of GMOs on Twitter, the findings cannot be generalized more broadly to other topics on Twitter or even to the communication patterns about GMOs on other social media platforms. Also, without processing the content of what was being tweeted and how sentiment was emergent in this space among these users, it is difficult to model with certainty the nature of key issues that were being discussed and how they were being debated. Nonetheless, even given these limitations, this study sets a series of systematic and normative markers than can be applied in future research efforts to construct comparative analyses on diverse timelines and topics. Additional steps that would benefit future research in the areas of both network gatekeeping and communicating GMOs would be to add layers of qualitative work through communicating directly with prominent users in the corpus. In fact, some of that work is already underway as part of a later stage of this research project.

Gatekeeping has become somewhat simplified by judging it as only the practice of choosing certain media content over others. While that activity has been made available to increasingly broad numbers of actors—indeed, it is possible that "every user on Twitter is a gatekeeper, with the discretion to share or not share a news item with their audience" (Diakopoulos & Zubiaga, 2014, p. 587)—such de-professionalization may ultimately diminish the quality of gatekeeping and its function in the flow of information. In other words, there are better gatekeepers than others and it has been shown that users on

Twitter often filter content on the basis of their own personal preferences (Jürgens, Jungherr, & Schoen, 2011), a gatekeeping method with a different set of criteria and implications than those identified by editors and news professionals (White, 1950; Tuchman, 1978).

Along these lines, Jiang wrote that "the requirements on news gatekeepers' judgment ability on news value become higher" (2014, p. 850) and that gatekeepers "should learn to optimize the structure of the news, discover the intrinsic link between the different news and information, and arrange the structures of the news through certain transition and correlation to enhance the transmission effect of the news and enhance the expressive force of the news information" (2014, p. 852). Among other points, this study has identified that not only have traditional media gatekeepers been overtaken by other, non-journalistic actors in the multi-gated media environment of GMOs on Twitter, but also it is precisely because those traditional media agents are failing to actively engaging the social affordances that are technologically available.

While the sea change in media production and sharing toward users has had the benefit of opening up communicative spaces, it has also, at least on topics such as GMOs, left a void where professional journalism stands to make a vital and necessary contribution. As the findings of this study align with others in a larger body of scholarship on gatekeeping in network media, the continued decline or virtual absence of news organizations and journalists as gatekeepers within the public sphere may prove quite perilous, particularly on contentious issues that would benefit considerably from journalistic focusing and vetting.

REFERENCES

Ali, S. R., & Fahmy, S. (2013). Gatekeeping and citizen journalism: The use of social media during the recent uprisings in Iran, Egypt, and Libya. *Media War Conflict, 6*(1950), 55–69. doi:10.1177/1750635212469906

Barzilai-Nahon, K. (2008). Toward a Theory of Network Gatekeeping: A Framework for Exploring Information Control. *Journal of the American Society for Information Science and Technology, 59*(9), 1493–1512. doi:10.1002/asi.20857

Bastos, M. T., Raimundo, R. L. G., & Travitzki, R. (2013). Gatekeeping Twitter: Message diffusion in political hashtags. *Media Culture & Society, 35*(2), 260–270. doi:10.1177/0163443712467594

Bennett, W. L. (2012). *News: The Politics of Illusion* (9th ed.). Chicago, IL: University of Chicago Press.

Borra, E., & Rieder, B. (2014). Programmed method: Developing a toolset for capturing and analyzing tweets. *Asian Journal of Information Management, 66*(3), 262–278. doi:10.1108/AJIM-09-2013-0094

Bowman, S., & Willis, C. (2003). We Media: How Audiences Are Shaping the Future of News and Information. *New Directions for News and the Media Center, American Press Institute*. Retrieved March 21, 2015 from http://www.hypergene.net/wemedia/download/we_media.pdf

Brin, S., & Page, L. (1998). The anatomy of a large-scale hypertextual Web search engine. *Computer Networks and ISDN Systems, 33*(1-7), 107–117. doi:10.1016/S0169-7552(98)00110-X

Chassy, B. M. (2007). The History and Future of GMOs in Food and Agriculture. *Cereal Foods World, 52*(4), 169–172.

Chien, O. K., Hoong, P. K., & Ho, C. C. (2014). *A Comparative Study of HITS vs PageRank algorithms for Twitter users analysis*. Presented to *International Conference on Computational Science and Technology*, Kota Kinablu, Malaysia.

Chin-Fook, L., & Simmonds, H. (2011). Redefining Gatekeeping Theory for a Digital Generation. *McMaster Journal of Communication*, *8*, 7–34.

Diakopoulos, N., & Zubiaga, A. (2014). Newsworthiness and Network Gatekeeping on Twitter: The Role of Social Deviance. *International Conference on Weblogs and Social Media.*

Galata, L., Karantininis, K., & Hess, S. (2014). Cross-Atlantic Differences in Biotechnology and GMOs: A Media Content Analysis. In *Agricultural Cooperative Management and Policy* (pp. 299–314). doi:10.1007/978-3-319-06635-6_16

Gans, H. (1979). *Deciding What's News*. New York, NY: Pantheon Books.

Gerlitz, C., & Rieder, B. (2013). Mining one percent of Twitter: Collections, baselines, sampling. *M/C Journal, 16*(2). Retrieved from http://journal.media-culture.org.au/index.php/mcjournal/article/view/620

Gitlin, T. (1980). *The Whole World Is Watching: Mass Media in the Making & Unmaking of the New Left*. Berkeley, CA: University of California Press.

Goode, L. (2012). News as conversation citizens as gatekeepers : Where is digital news taking us? *Ethical Space: The International Journal of Communication Ethics*, *9*(1), 32–40.

Groshek, J. (2014). *Twitter Collection and Analysis Toolkit (TCAT) at Boston University*. Retrieved July 14, 2015 from http://www.bu.edu/com/bu-tcat/

Groshek, J. (2015). *Geolocation in Gephi with Twitter Data Tutorial*. Retrieved July 21, 2015 from http://www.jgroshek.org/blog/2015/5/5/geolocation-in-gephi-with-twitter-data-tutorial

Groshek, J., & Al-Rawi, A. (2015). Anti-Austerity in the Euro crisis: Modeling Protest Movements through Online-Mobile-Social Media Use and Content. *International Journal of Communication*, *9*, 3280–3303.

Groshek, J., & Han, Y. (2011). Negotiated Hegemony and Reconstructed Boundaries in Alternative Media Coverage of Globalization. *International Journal of Communication*, *5*, 1523–1544.

Groshek, J., & Tandoc, E. T. (2016). *The Affordance Effect: Gatekeeping and (Non)reciprocal Journalism on Twitter*. Paper presented at the Social Media and Society Conference, London, UK.

Guardian. (2015, May 24). *Tens of thousands march worldwide against Monsanto and GM crops*. Retrieved July 24, 2015 from http://www.theguardian.com/environment/2015/may/24/tens-of-thousands-march-worldwide-against-monsanto-and-gm-crops

Henig, R. M. (2000). *The Monk in the Garden: The Lost and Found Genius of Gregor Mendel, the Father of Genetics*. New York, NY: Houghton Mifflin.

Hintz, A. (2012). Challenging the Digital Gatekeepers : International policy initiatives for free expression. *Journal of Information Policy*, *2*, 128–150. doi:10.5325/jinfopoli.2.2012.0128

House Committee on Agriculture. (2015, July 23). *House Passes H.R. 1599, the Safe and Accurate Food Labeling Act.* Retrieved July 24, 2015 from http://agriculture.house.gov/press-release/house-passes-hr-1599-safe-and-accurate-food-labeling-act

Jiang, H. (2014). Thoughts on Standard Orientation of News Gatekeeper in the Context of Modern Media. *Proceedings from the 3rd International Conference on Science and Social Research*, 849–853. 10.2991/icssr-14.2014.186

Jurgens, D., Finnethy, T., McCorriston, J., Xu, Y. T., & Ruths, D. (2015). Geolocation Prediction in Twitter Using Social Networks: A Critical Analysis and Review of Current Practice. *Association for the Advancement of Artificial Intelligence.* Retrieved July 21, 2015 from http://cs.mcgill.ca/~jurgens/docs/jurgens-et-al_icwsm-2015.pdf

Jürgens, P., Jungherr, A., & Schoen, H. (2011). Small Worlds with a Difference : New Gatekeepers and the Filtering of Political Information on Twitter. *Websci*, *11*, 1–5. doi:10.1145/2527031.2527034

Katiraee, L. (2015, January 26). 10 studies proving GMOs are harmful? Not if science matters. *Genetic Literacy Project.* Retrieved July 25, 2015 from http://www.geneticliteracyproject.org/2015/01/26/10-studies-proving-gmos-are-harmful-not-if-science-matters/

Kwon, K. H., Oh, O., Agrawal, M., & Rao, H. R. (2012). Audience Gatekeeping in the Twitter Service: An investigation of tweets about the 2009 Gaza Conflict. *Transactions on Human-Computer Interaction*, *4*(4), 212–229. doi:10.17705/1thci.00047

Laidlaw, E. B. (2015). *Regulating Speech in Cyberspace: Gatekeepers, Human Rights and Corporate Responsibility*. Cambridge, UK: Cambridge University Press. doi:10.1017/CBO9781107278721

Lewis, S. C., Holton, A. E., & Coddington, M. (2013). Reciprocal journalism: A concept of mutual exchange between journalists and audiences. *Journalism Practice*, *8*(2), 229–241. doi:10.1080/17512786.2013.859840

Marks, L. A., Kalaitzandonakes, N., Allison, K., & Zakharova, L. (2003). Media Coverage of Agrobiotechnology: Did the Butterfly Have an Effect? *Journal of Agribusiness*, *21*(1), 1–20.

McChesney, R. (1999). *Rich Media, Poor Democracy: Communication Politics in Dubious Times*. Chicago, IL: University of Illinois Press.

McSweeney, P. J. (2009). *Gephi Network Statistics*. Google Summer of Code 2009 Project Proposal. Retrieved July 15, 2015 from http://web.ecs.syr.edu/~pjmcswee/gephi.pdf

Meraz, S. (2009). Is there an elite hold? Traditional media to social media agenda setting influence in blog networks. *Journal of Computer-Mediated Communication*, *14*(3), 682–707. doi:10.1111/j.1083-6101.2009.01458.x

Meraz, S., & Papacharissi, Z. (2013). Networked gatekeeping and networked framing on #egypt. *The International Journal of Press/Politics*, *18*(2), 138–166. doi:10.1177/1940161212474472

Newman, M. E. J. (2006). Modularity and community structure in networks. *Proceedings of the National Academy of Sciences of the United States of America*, *103*(23), 8577–8582. doi:10.1073/pnas.0601602103 PMID:16723398

Pew. (2015, July 14). *The Evolving Role of News on Twitter and Facebook*. Retrieved July 21, 2015 from http://www.journalism.org/2015/07/14/the-evolving-role-of-news-on-twitter-and-facebook/

Saletan, W. (2015, July 15). Unhealthy Fixation: The war against genetically modified organisms is full of fearmongering, errors, and fraud. Labeling them will not make you safer. *Slate*. Retrieved July 22, 2015 from http://www.slate.com/articles/health_and_science/science/2015/07/are_gmos_safe_yes_the_case_against_them_is_full_of_fraud_lies_and_errors.html

Shoemaker, P. J., & Vos, T. P. (2009). *Gatekeeping Theory*. New York, NY: Taylor & Francis. doi:10.4324/9780203931653

Smith, M. A., Rainie, L., Shneiderman, B., & Himelboim, I. (2014). *Mapping Twitter Topic Networks: From Polarized Crowds to Community Clusters*. Retrieved July 5, 2015 from http://www.pewinternet.org/2014/02/20/mapping-twitter-topic-networks-from-polarized-crowds-to-community-clusters/

Soroka, S. N. (2012). The Gatekeeping Function: Distributions of Information in Media and the Real World. *The Journal of Politics*, *74*(2), 514–528. doi:10.1017/S002238161100171X

Stephan, H. R. (2014). *Cultural Politics and the Transatlantic Divide over GMOs*. London, UK: Palgrave Macmillan.

Tandoc, E. (2015, May). *Conventional and Dialogical Uses of Social Media in the Newsroom: How Journalists Use Facebook and Twitter, and Why*. Paper presented at the International Communication Association annual convention, San Juan, Puerto Rico.

Thielman, S. (2016). Facebook news selection is in hands of editors not algorithms, documents show. *The Guardian*. Retrieved May 23, 2016 from https://www.theguardian.com/technology/2016/may/12/facebook-trending-news-leaked-documents-editor-guidelines

Tuchman, G. (1978). *Making News: A Study in the Construction of Reality*. New York, NY: The Free Press.

Underwood, D. (1995). *When MBA's Rule the Newsroom*. New York, NY: Columbia University Press.

Vu, H. T. (2013). The online audience as gatekeeper: The influence of reader metrics on news editorial selection. *Journalism*, *15*(8), 1094–1110. doi:10.1177/1464884913504259

White, D. M. (1950). The Gate-keeper. A case study in the selection of news. *The Journalism Quarterly*, *27*(4), 383–396. doi:10.1177/107769905002700403

Wu, S., Hofman, J. M., Mason, W. A., & Watts, D. J. (2011). Who says what to whom on Twitter? Presented to the *International World Wide Web Conference Committee*, Hyderabad, India. 10.1145/1963405.1963504

Chapter 7
Information Hubs or Drains?
The Role of Online Sources in Campaign Learning

Terri Towner
Oakland University, USA

ABSTRACT

This chapter investigates the link between young adults' attention to campaign information on offline and online media and their knowledge about political facts and candidate issues. The findings, based on a unique, three-wave panel survey conducted during the 2012 U.S. presidential election, show that attention to campaign information on offline sources, such as television, hard-copy newspapers, and radio, was not significantly related to political knowledge. Instead, young adults' attention to online sources played a more important role. Specifically, political knowledge levels were significantly and positively linked to attention to campaign information in online newspapers and television campaign websites. In contrast, attention to campaign information on social media, particularly Facebook and Google+, was negatively related to political knowledge levels during the fall campaign period. Therefore, this study suggests that certain forms of online media serve as a drain on political knowledge whereas attention to other digital outlets can serve as hubs of information.

INTRODUCTION

Many political pundits and observers dubbed the 2008 U.S. presidential election as "the Facebook" election or "the social media election", as Barack Obama's campaign employed online outlets, such as Facebook, Twitter, Flickr, YouTube, and blogs, to reach voters, raise money, build a grassroots network, and ultimately win the White House. Few would dispute, however, that the 2008 campaign was just the beginning, as the 2012 presidential elections truly saw the expansion of online tools in political campaigns. Along with traditional media, the Obama and Romney campaigns used microblogs, wikis, social networks, photo-sharing websites, mobile apps, and video-sharing websites to reach the electorate. According to the Pew Research Center (2012a), both campaigns strongly embraced social media

DOI: 10.4018/978-1-7998-1828-1.ch007

tools and the Internet, indicating that online tools are now necessary to reach voters as well as mobilize and inform them. Given the latter, the 2012 presidential election offers the best opportunity to examine the influence of attention to campaign information in traditional and online media on political attitudes.

This research's goal is to examine the influence of attention to campaign information in various online media sources on political knowledge, specifically factual political information (or differentiated knowledge) and candidate issue stances (or integrated knowledge). Presently, it is unclear if online sources serve as information hubs during a political campaign, aiding in knowledge about issues and candidates, or drains, providing little to no information about the political arena. Previous research examining traditional media's role in informing the electorate have generally confirmed some positive associations between television and hard-copy newspapers and political knowledge (e.g., Drew & Weaver, 2006; Druckman, 2005; Robinson & Levy, 1986; Sotirovic & McLeod, 2004; Weaver & Drew, 2001; Zhao & Chaffee, 1995). More recently, scholarly attention has shifted to the effects of online sources on political attitudes. Surprisingly, however, evidence regarding online sources' contribution in creating a more informed electorate remains elusive. On one hand, recent studies suggest that the influence of certain online sources, particularly social networks such as Facebook and Twitter, in creating an informed citizenry is minimal (Baumgartner & Morris, 2010; Dimitrova, Shehata, Stromback, & Nord, 2014; Groshek & Dimitrova, 2011; Kaufhold, Valenzuela, & Gil de Zuniga, 2010; Pasek, More, & Romer, 2009; Towner & Dulio, 2011a) whereas as others find evidence that attention to some online outlets, principally online newspapers, can increase political knowledge levels (Dalrymple & Scheufele, 2007). Clearly, then, the influence of attention to campaign information in various online sources on political learning requires further examination.

This research examines attention to campaign information in online and offline media using a three-wave panel survey of college students during the 2012 presidential campaign. The survey focuses on measuring young adults' attention to campaign information on various online sources, particularly online newspapers, television network websites, presidential candidate websites, Facebook, Google+, YouTube, Twitter, Tumblr, and political blogs. In addition, respondents' level of political knowledge is measured, such as knowledge of political facts and candidate issues. The goal is to determine if there is significant relationship between attention paid to campaign information on different media outlets and political knowledge throughout the 2012 campaign period.

For many reasons, the relationship between young adults' media consumption and their political knowledge levels is important to examine. One such reason is that young adults are the most information starved age cohort and are the least likely to engage politically (Wattenberg, 2012). In addition, young adults are more likely to use online news sources for political news than older adults (Kaid, McKinney, & Tedesco, 2007). Today, young adults (18-24 year olds) employ the Internet, social media, and mobile technology to engage and learn about the world around them more than any other age cohort (Pew Research Center, 2014). The latter was apparent during both the 2008 and 2012 presidential campaigns (Fernandes, Giurcanu, Bowers, & Neely, 2010; Haridakis & Hanson, 2011; Pew Research Center, 2012a; Smith, 2013; Vitak, Zube, Smock, Carr, Ellison, & Lampe, 2011). Are online sources the "cure" for the lack of political information and understanding among youths? Will attention to Facebook, YouTube, and Twitter act as hubs of information, enlightening young adults about candidates, issues, and the general political arena?

MASS MEDIA AND POLITICAL KNOWLEDGE

The mass media play a central role in informing its citizens in a democracy, acting as a liaison between citizens and government. During presidential elections, the media's information function becomes more important as voters rely on the press to provide information about the candidates, parties, and issues. A labyrinth of research has examined the contributions of various offline sources, especially television and hard-copy newspapers, on political knowledge. Empirical findings, however, are relatively mixed, many with contradictory claims. Some studies suggest that hard-copy newspaper readers are more knowledgeable about politics than non-hard-copy newspaper readers (Robinson & Levy, 1986; Weaver & Drew, 1993) and television viewers (Sotirovic & McLeod, 2004). Hard-copy newspaper reading is often linked to more factual knowledge (Becker & Dunwoody, 1982; Dalrymple & Scheufele, 2007; Pettey, 1988) and candidate/party issue knowledge (Chaffee, Zhao, & Leshner, 1994; Druckman, 2005; Eveland & Scheufele, 2000; Patterson & McClure, 1976; Weaver & Drew, 1993; see also Moy & Pfau, 2000). In contrast, other scholars are more skeptical, finding that newspaper reading is weakly linked to information levels (e.g., Mondak, 1995; Neuman, Just, & Crigler., 1992; Price & Zaller, 1993). Other scholars find that newspaper reading is not associated with candidate likeability and ideological knowledge (Dalrymple & Scheufele, 2007; Eveland & Scheufele, 2000). Similarly, research examining the influence of television on information levels also varies. On one hand, some scholars find that television viewing boosts an individual's knowledge of candidates and issues (Becker & Dunwoody, 1982; Chaffee, Zhao, & Leshner, 1994; Lowden, Anderson, Dozier, & Lauzen, 1994; Weaver & Drew, 1993; Zhao & Chaffee, 1995). On the other hand, other research finds evidence that television news viewing is not associated with information levels (e.g., Dalrymple & Scheufele, 2007; Druckman, 2005). In sum, the above findings indicate that traditional media – both television and print newspapers – can sometimes play an important role in political information levels.

Recently, the rise of digital technology has led to a dramatic change in the mass media landscape. As a result, the Internet's effects on knowledge and information levels have been examined, also with varying conclusions. Some studies have found that the Internet is an important information source and its use is positively related to political knowledge (Dimitrova et al., 2014; Drew & Weaver, 2006; Kenski & Stroud, 2006; Norris, 2000; Shah, McLeod, & Yoon, 2001; Sotirovic & McLeod, 2004; Xenos & Moy, 2007). Other studies indicate that Internet usage and attention do not contribute to political knowledge (DiMaggio, Hargittai, Neuman, & Robinson, 2001; Jennings & Zeitner, 2003; Johnson, Briama, & Sothirajah, 1999; Wei & Ven-hwei, 2008). One study found that searching the Internet for entertainment purposes significantly *lowers* knowledge levels (Scheufele & Nisbet, 2002).

Indeed, the above findings regarding Internet effects on knowledge vary, but there are several reasons that may explain this: First, perhaps the Internet is simply not conducive for learning, particularly for the computer novice or those who are not Internet savvy. For example, Eveland and Dunwoody (2000) demonstrate that nonlinear or hypermedia systems may inhibit learning because their content and structure demand more cognitive skills. Linear formats, such as hard-copy newspapers and television, require less effort, allowing effective information processing to occur (see also Eveland & Dunwoody, 2001, 2002). Interestingly, Tewksbury and Althaus (2000) find that online readers of *The New York Times* are less likely to recall and describe news topics than hard-copy readers.

Second, previous research linking media attention and knowledge examines the effects of the "Internet", one online source, or lumps many online sources together into one latent variable. Given the varying features and designs of online newspapers, television network websites, presidential candidate websites,

Facebook, Google+, YouTube, Twitter, Tumblr, and political blogs, this research argues that each online source contributes differently to various knowledge structures. As explained in more detail below, it is argued that "Facebooking" is qualitatively different from watching a political video on YouTube. Each of these online sources has different features, functions, and purposes, but their comparative effects are rarely empirically examined (for exceptions, see Towner, 2013; Towner & Dulio, 2011a, 2011b).

Third, studies of Internet effects often do not distinguish among different types of knowledge, which are often divided into categories: differentiated and integrated knowledge. Differentiated knowledge is linked to the factual recall of names, issues and events, whereas integrated knowledge is the individual's ability to link the differentiated items together (Neuman, 1981). As noted above, attention to offline and online sources can have different effects on different types of knowledge. Eveland and his colleagues, for instance, found that nonlinear formats do not improve factual or differentiated knowledge, yet hypermedia can increase knowledge structure and organization (Eveland, Marton, & Seo, 2004; Eveland, Seo, & Marton, 2002; Eveland, Cortese, Park, & Dunwoody, 2004). The latter scholars assert that online and print sources influence knowledge structures differently due to the varying structure and organization of offline and online media. Furthermore, many studies conclude that various Internet uses, such as searching for general, political, and entertainment information, have disparate effects on knowledge levels (Prior, 2005; Scheufele & Nisbet, 2002; Shah, Kwak, & Holbert, 2001). In this research, both differentiated and integrated political knowledge are examined by measuring young adults' ability to recall factual political information (differentiated) and the 2012 presidential candidate issue stances (integrated).

DIFFERENTIAL EFFECTS OF ONLINE SOURCES

Building on Foot and Schneider's (2006) framework, this research first distinguishes between the four functions of online campaigning: (1) informing voters; (2) involving supporters; (3) connecting online users with political actors; and (4) mobilization. Clearly, this work focuses on the information function of online campaigning. According to Foot and Schneider (2006), the practice of informing voters during a campaign involves providing information, such as the candidate's personal biography and the campaign message, to users via an online structure. These online structures offer information in the form of online news articles, newsletters, press releases, streaming audio, and video. Foot and Schneider (2006) argue that informing voters is a primary goal of an online campaign and that almost all web campaigns engage in a form of informing citizens politically.

As Towner and Dulio (2011a) have shown, attention to specific online media sources have differential effects on young adults' political knowledge because online media sources differ in content, form, and function. Moreover, young adults themselves use these online sources for different reasons and goals. For example, Facebook is a social networking site that allows users to build online profiles and connect and communicate with other people whereas YouTube is a video-sharing service permitting users to upload, view, and share video clips. During political campaigns, these various forms of online media offer different levels of information, interaction, and mobilization, which may have different effects on levels of knowledge. The latter argument is not unlike those made about differences between television and hard-copy newspapers regarding quality and quantity of election coverage. In general, compared to television, print newspapers contain more election coverage, which often focuses more on substantive political issues. Television offers less coverage of political issues and tends to focus more on candidate personal characteristics as well as the "horse race" (e.g., Cappella & Jamieson, 1997; Druckman, 2005;

Patterson, 1993; Project for Excellence in Journalism, 2012). Due to these differences in election coverage, these traditional outlets influence political knowledge in different ways – often with print newspapers rather than television news – playing a significant role in informing the electorate (e.g., Dalrymple & Scheufele, 2007; Druckman, 2005).

Online Newspapers

Online newspapers are often viewed as an extension of hard-copy newspapers produced by the traditional, professional media (see Kaufhold et al., 2010). Unlike social networks and micro-blogs, which provide opportunities for connections, involvement, or mobilization, online newspapers focus on disseminating substantive political information in textual format. Users likely read and watch these sources because they want to learn about the upcoming elections, candidates, and the latest polling. That is, readers are seeking relevant and substantial political content.

Regarding the effects of online newspaper reading on knowledge, prior research findings are mixed. Dalrymple and Scheufele (2007) found that online newspaper attention during the 2004 presidential campaign significantly increased factual knowledge, candidate issue knowledge, and candidate likeability among a national sample of adults – even when controlling for attention to television and print newspapers. During the 2008 presidential campaign, Towner and Dulio (2011a), however, found that online newspaper attention among young adults had no influence on different types of knowledge. However, much has changed in the world of digital newspapers since the 2008 presidential campaign. Online newspapers have increased in numbers as well as popularity (Edmonds, Guskin, Rosenstiel, & Mitchell, 2012). With the advent of the iPad (in 2010) and the increasing use of smart phones and other mobile devices, many citizens, particularly young adults, are finding it easy and cost-effective to read newspaper e-editions. Most important, online newspapers offer not only general information about politics in textual format, but also hyperlinks – either in text or in a sidebar – to related content. These links may provide the reader with additional context, background or historical information, or similar or related topics – all informing readers about the topic's interconnected nature. Therefore, this research anticipates that attention to 2012 campaign information on online newspapers will positively influence both factual (H1a) and candidate issue-stance knowledge (H1b).

Television Websites

Similar to online newspapers, television websites are also considered an arm of television, seeking to inform the public on the top news items of the day. Although major television networks are embracing Internet technology and placing many broadcasts online for viewing, there is relatively little research on the effects of television websites on political attitudes. Towner and Dulio (2011a) found that attention to television websites did not politically inform young adults in the 2008 presidential campaign. Again, considering the changing digital landscape since the 2008 election, particularly the increase in cable cord cutting, streaming and downloading video viewing, and usage of non-network sites (e.g, Hulu), television websites may have more influence on political attitudes in the 2012 campaign. Indeed, a Pew Research Center (2012b) study reports that many Americans learn about the campaign from television websites, particularly CNN, Fox News, and MSNBC. It is anticipated that young adults' attention to television websites for campaign information will positively influence both factual (H2a) and candidate issue-stance knowledge (H2b).

Candidate Websites

In the 2012 presidential campaigns, candidate websites were considered the "central hub of digital political messaging", as many citizens used these websites to donate money, join a community, and volunteer (Pew Research Center, 2012a). Candidate websites offer the one place where candidates can tout their views and policy positions without the filter of the mainstream media. For example, Bimber and Davis (2003) reported that subjects using a presidential campaign website did learn something new about the presidential candidate's issue positions and about the candidate as a person. Yet, subjects viewing these sites were more likely to learn about issue positions than the candidate as a person. Bimber and Davis (2003) also found that exposure to candidate websites did not influence candidate likeability. Other experimental research, however, observed that interactivity with candidate websites during the 2000 presidential primary increased candidate likeability and learning (Ahem, Stomer-Galley, & Neuman, 2000). More recently, Towner and Dulio (2011a) found that more attention to candidate websites resulted in higher candidate issue stance knowledge, but candidate websites had no influence on factual knowledge or candidate likeability. The latter should not be surprising, as candidate websites focus predominately on the candidate's issue positions and platform rather than general political facts. Therefore, it is expected that presidential candidate websites will have no influence on factual knowledge (H3a), but will significantly increase candidate issue stance knowledge (H3b).

Facebook and Google+

During a political campaign, it is well known that the primary functions of social networking sites, particularly Facebook and Google+, are to connect users, increase political involvement, and encourage political mobilization. Users can join political groups or fan pages, "fan" or "like" candidates, and share weblinks and videos with friends. Their purpose is not to politically inform, but to connect users with other users. Thus, on Facebook and Google+, much of the political information is in the form of personal political expressions, such as comments or sharing videos or photos. Studies reveal that young people who obtain news and information from social networks learn very little information about politics and candidates (Baumgartner & Morris, 2010; Groshek & Dimitrova, 2011; Pasek, More, & Romer, 2009; Towner & Dulio, 2011a). Simply put, individuals are not employing Facebook and Google+ to become more knowledgeable about the presidential campaign (e.g., Pew Research Center, 2012b). Instead, they are using these platforms to connect with friends, family, or people in their community rather than political information-seeking (Anderson & Caumont, 2014; Cornfield, 2010; Dimitrova et al., 2014). Based on this, it is anticipated that attention to campaign information on Facebook will have a negative influence on factual (H4a) and issue stance knowledge (H4b). Similarly, attention to campaign information on Google+ will have a negative impact on both forms of knowledge (H5a and H5b).

YouTube

YouTube features videos about the presidential campaign created by the campaign, candidates themselves, the public, and trained journalists. Therefore, all types of political information can be accessed on YouTube – from a campaign's latest television ad to political satire. That is, online videos did not always contain substantive political information. Smith and Duggan (2012) reported that registered voters are actively watching a variety of online video with 48% of Internet-using registered voters watched online video news reports about the election or politics, 37% watched humorous or parody videos about politics, and 36% watching political advertisements. In most cases, users watched online videos that are recommended or shared by others, suggesting that political video watching is highly social. Haridakis and Hanson (2011) confirm the latter, finding that people watched YouTube for convenient entertainment, information-seeking, co-viewing and social interaction (see also Wallsten, 2010). While citizens are watching YouTube videos for campaign information (Pew Research Center, 2012b), recent studies conducted during the 2008 presidential campaign found that respondents who got news and information from video-sharing websites learned very little information about politics and the candidates (Baumgartner & Morris, 2010; Groshek & Dimitrova, 2011; Towner & Dulio, 2011a). These prior works suggest that YouTube is mainly used for entertainment or infotainment purposes with little consumption of substantive political information. Considering previous findings, it is expected that attention to 2012 campaign information on YouTube will have no influence on both factual (H6a) and candidate issue stance knowledge (H6b).

Twitter and Tumblr

Twitter and Tumblr are often defined as microblogging networks of real-time "tweets" or posts. To compare, Twitter has become a collective discussion of top trending topics and events whereas Tumblr is regarded as a topic-based image blog. During campaigns, candidates employ Twitter to connect followers, heighten involvement in the campaign, and mobilize the politically inactive (for example, see Bekafigo & Pingley, 2014; Parmelee & Bichard, 2012). Compared to Facebook and Google+, Twitter is considered primarily a digital megaphone for campaigns, offering multiple, short bursts of information to followers. In 2012, President Obama used Twitter largely to ask users to volunteer, vote on Election Day, and share campaign information with others whereas Mitt Romney employed Twitter to solicit donations, ask for votes, and share campaign information (Pew Research Center, 2012a; Svensson, Kiousis, & Stromback, 2014). In an experimental study conducted during the 2014 midterms, Towner (2016) exposed subjects to specific gubernatorial and senatorial candidate Twitter messages or "tweets" about calls to action, policy information, and general campaign information. Exposure to these tweet frames during the campaign period were found to significantly influence subject's vote choice and candidate credibility, providing some evidence that Twitter can impact political attitudes. Given that Twitter largely focuses on the daily hot, trending topics rather than general political facts, it is expected that attention to campaign information on Twitter will have no influence on factual political knowledge (H7a). Nonetheless, some Twitter users employ the platform to discover different points of view on politics, access live, spontaneous information, or just to make sense of the election (see Smith, 2011). Considering the latter, young adults' attention to campaign information on Twitter will positively influence issue-stance knowledge (H7b).

On Tumblr, political dialogue mostly consists of photos, videos, memes, and GIFs. Candidates and campaigns largely use pictures and images shared on Tumblr to drive traffic to their campaign websites and other digital platforms. During the 2012 presidential campaign, Obama's Tumblr feed contained funny photos, GIF images, videos, quotes, and pop culture references. For example, Obama's campaign team reminded Tumblr users about the first presidential debate by posting a clip of Lindsay Lohan saying "It's October 3" from the comedy move "Mean Girls". Similarly, Romney posted photos and gimmicky slogans on Tumblr (Unionmetrics, 2012). Overall, substantive political information, particularly textual information, was largely lacking on Tumblr. Therefore, it is expected that attention to campaign information on Tumblr will have no significant influence on both factual (H8a) and issue-stance knowledge (H8b).

Political Blogs

Much of the relevant blog research focuses on blog use and its influence on political participation (Lawrence, Sides, & Farrell, 2010). There is little research examining attention to blogs and its impact on political information levels. Unlike the balanced and neutral mainstream media, non-journalists write political blogs, usually with a specific ideological lens. Thus, blog content often includes ideological commentary, negative remarks about candidates, blatant mockery of government, and partisan debates (see Fung, Vraga, & Thorson, 2010). Despite the latter, political blogs are sometimes considered viable "checks" on the mainstream media, often viewed as more credible sources (Johnson & Kaye, 2004). Alternatively, other scholars consider blogs riddled with misinformation and inaccuracies due to lack of fact checking and official sources by citizen journalists (Davis, 2009). Due to the partisan nature of political blogs as well as the lack of general political information, it is anticipated that attention to campaign information on blogs will have no significant influence on factual (H9a) and issue-stance knowledge (H9b).

This analysis also examines the empirical effects of attention campaign information in traditional media sources, particularly television, hard-copy newspapers, and radio, alongside the above online sources. Formal hypotheses regarding the effects of these traditional sources on knowledge levels are not offered, however, as previous literature has thoroughly explored their influence (e.g., Chaffee & Frank, 1996; Druckman, 2005; Neuman, Just, & Crigler, 1992; Tewksbury & Althaus, 2000; Zhao & Chaffee, 1995). Instead, the following research question is proposed: How does attention to television, hard-copy newspapers, and radio for presidential campaign information influence factual political knowledge (RQa) and candidate issue-stance knowledge (RQb)?

DATA AND METHODS

These data come from a three-wave, panel survey of college students at a medium-sized, Midwestern university conducted in the fall of 2012. A panel survey allows a better examination of the causal links between a respondent's attention to presidential campaign information in online sources and various knowledge structures, allowing for an analysis of how the variables changed over time rather than a snapshot at a single point in time. Specifically, the design's purpose is to detect changes in young adult's attention to campaign information in the media and their political knowledge levels throughout the campaign. Therefore, a panel study is more likely to suggest cause-and-effect relationships than a cross-sectional study.

From September 26, 2012, to October 7, 2012, the first wave of the online survey was advertised via email to over 1,000 students enrolled in introductory-level political science, sociology, and psychology courses. This recruitment method elicited 595 responses, a response rate of 52 percent. The survey's second wave was in the field from October 29, 2012, to November 5, 2012. Eighty percent (N = 476) of the respondents from the first wave were re-interviewed in the second wave. The survey's third wave was in the field from November 18, 2012, to November 28, 2012. Four hundred and five respondents (68 percent of the initial sample) completed all three waves.

The respondents interviewed in all three waves were relatively representative of the typical college student. The average age was 20.91 years (SD = 5.10). Thirty-six percent were first-year college students. Seventy percent were women, and 78% identified themselves as Caucasian. The sample's disciplinary background represented a broad range of majors from the liberal arts and sciences: political science (8%), social work (9%), psychology (13%), and various other fields. Thirty-eight percent identified themselves as either a strong Democrat or a Democrat and 26 percent self-identified as a strong Republican or Republican. When comparing the sample's demographics to the typical young adult in the U.S., this sample is representative with a few exceptions: Caucasians and females were slightly overrepresented (U.S. Census Bureau, 2013).

Dependent Variables

Two measures of political knowledge were examined, representing both differentiated and integrated knowledge. The first dependent variable was political factual recall knowledge (differentiated). Factual knowledge was measured with a battery of six true or false statements, ranging from who is the current Vice President and if the Republican Party was more conservative. These items were subsequently recoded into an additive factual knowledge scale (α=.58), ranging from 0 (all incorrect answers) to 6 (all correct answers). See Table 2 for question wording.

The second dependent variable was candidate issue stance knowledge (integrated). Six items measured candidate issue stance knowledge, asking respondents to identify which of the two presidential candidates (Obama or Romney) promised proposals, such as repealing the Affordable Health Care Act and withdrawing troops from Iraq. The latter issues were selected because they were central to the 2012 presidential campaign, as shown by media coverage. These items were recoded into an additive candidate issue stance knowledge scale (α=.74), ranging from 0 (all incorrect answers) to 6 (all correct answers). See Table 2 for question wording.

Independent Variables

To measure media attention, respondents were asked to gauge how much attention they paid to campaign information in traditional and online outlets. A measure of "attention" was employed to obtain a more reliable and valid measure of attention and exposure to information on online or digital sources. In a today's digital world, young adults are exposed to much more various types of media, which can occur anywhere at any time, and most important, even at the same time (Valkenburg & Peter, 2013). For traditional media, attention to television, hard-copy newspapers, and radio was assessed. Regarding online media, attention to nine Internet sources was evaluated. In each survey wave, respondents were asked the following question: "How much attention did you pay to information on [television] about the campaign for President?" (1=none, 2=very little, 3=some, 4=quite a bit, 5=a great deal). In subsequent questions, the phrase "television" was replaced with the words "hard-copy newspapers," "radio," "online newspapers," "Facebook," "Google+," "Twitter," "Tumblr," "YouTube," "political blog," "television network websites," and "presidential candidate websites." To measure the change in media attention variables during the panel period, first-wave measures were subtracted from the third-wave measures for each.

Control Variables

In analyses of information acquisition, it is important to control for individual factors as well as political predispositions, as these variables may influence knowledge levels. Two categories of control measures were included in first wave of the panel survey. First, demographic variables, such as age (in years), gender (1=male, 0=female), year in school (1=freshmen, 2=sophomore, 3=junior, 4=senior) and race (1=White, 0=non-White), were asked of respondents. Second, political predispositional variables, particularly political interest and party identification, were also included. For political interest, respondents were asked "Some people don't pay much attention to political campaigns. How about you? Would you say that you have been very much interested, somewhat interested or not much interested in the political campaigns so far this year?" (1=not interested at all, 3=moderately interested, 5=extremely interested). To measure partisan attachment, two questions were used: (1) "Generally speaking, do you usually think of yourself as a Republican, a Democrat, an Independent, or something else?" and (2) "[If respondent indicated Republican or Democrat]: Would you call yourself a strong Democrat/Republican or a not-very-strong Democrat/Republican?" Answers to both questions were combined into a five-point scale (1=strong Democrat, 2=Democrat, 3= Independent, Don't know, No preference, 4=Republican, 5=strong Republican). Descriptive statistics for all variables in survey waves one and three are noted in Table 1.

RESULTS

Did young adults experience any changes in their political knowledge levels from September 2012 to November 2012? Table 2 shows the trends for the two knowledge measures among panel respondents. For the factual political knowledge questions, increases were modest, with an 8 to 11 percentage point increase for only two out of the six measures. The other four factual knowledge questions reveal little knowledge gains over the campaign period. Regarding candidate issue stance knowledge, increases were more prominent among four out of the six measures. Given these increases in political knowledge during the 2012 presidential campaign, an examination of the effects of offline and online media outlets on knowledge levels is warranted.

Wave 1: September 2012

Factual Political Knowledge

This research begins by examining the predictors of factual and candidate issue stance knowledge in the months preceding Election Day. The regression models include first-wave measures of attention to traditional and online media as well as demographic and political predispositional variables that may influence each dependent variable. Table 3 presents the results among the full first-wave sample conducted in September 2012. In column 1, the first notable finding is that attention to traditional media sources – television, hard-copy newspapers, and radio – had no statistically significant influence on factual political knowledge (RQa). Young people who paid attention to traditional media sources are not more knowledgeable about political facts than those who did not pay attention to these sources. The latter result confirms previous work on the influence of traditional media on political knowledge that finds little to no relationship, especially among the young.

Table 1. Descriptive statistics

Measure	Wave 1		Wave 3	
	Mean	SD	Mean	SD
Political Factual Recall Knowledge	3.77	1.46	4.04	1.53
Candidate Issue Stance Knowledge	3.39	1.89	3.83	1.76
Television	3.31	1.18	3.27	1.17
Hard-copy newspaper	2.17	1.17	2.03	1.09
Radio	2.58	1.20	2.35	1.19
Online newspaper	2.28	1.25	2.07	1.18
Television websites	2.21	1.26	2.07	1.25
Presidential websites	1.81	1.13	1.66	1.05
Facebook	2.37	1.24	2.32	1.19
Google+	1.75	1.14	1.47	.923
YouTube	2.04	1.19	1.88	1.14
Twitter	1.89	1.25	1.81	1.21
Tumblr	1.43	.953	1.40	.956
Political blogs	1.69	1.05	1.58	.987
Age	20.92	5.00	20.91	5.10
Gender	.30	.457	.30	.461
Race	.78	.417	.78	.416
Year in school	2.14	1.07	2.14	1.06
Party Identification	2.89	1.23	2.88	1.29
Political Interest	2.67	1.15	2.79	1.06
N	595		405	

Turning to online sources in Table 3, the findings in column 1 show that attention to campaign information in online newspapers was strongly related to factual knowledge, ultimately confirming expectations (H1a) as well as some prior research (Dalrymple & Scheufele, 2007; but see Towner & Dulio, 2011a). That is, young adults who paid more attention to information about the presidential campaign in online newspapers were significantly more knowledgeable about political facts; or conversely, higher factual knowledge leads to increased attention to online newspapers. Unlike online newspapers, attention to other online sources, particularly social media and blogs, did not positively influence factual knowledge at this point in the fall campaign. Confirming some expectations, attention to presidential candidate websites (H3a), Facebook (H4a), and Google+ (H5a) significantly decreased factual political information among young adults. The latter results are consistent with studies suggesting that online social networks, such as Facebook and Google+, are more for socializing, connecting, and mobilizing rather than actually informing users about politics (Baumgartner & Morris, 2010; Cornfield, 2010; Towner & Dulio, 2011a). The significant negative impact of attention to candidate websites was unexpected, however, as "no influence" on factual knowledge was hypothesized (H3a). Although, perhaps this effect is not startling. Candidate websites are a hub of campaign information, such as how to register to vote and how to volunteer for the campaign; however, these sites offer little general information about the political arena (Bimber &

Table 2. Political knowledge among panel respondents

	Wave 1	Wave 2	Wave 3
Factual Political Knowledge			
Joe Biden is the current vice president of the U.S.	90%	92%	93%
It is Congress' responsibility to determine if a law is constitutional or not.	45	44	45
A two-thirds vote is required in the U.S. Senate and House to override a presidential veto.	88	87	87
The Democratic Party had the most members in the House of Representatives in Washington last month.	43	43	51
The Republican Party is more conservative than the Democratic Party at the national level.	78	80	80
John Roberts is chief justice of the U.S. Supreme Court.	40	45	51
Candidate Issue Stance Knowledge			
To repeal the Affordable Care Act, or health care reform.	67	76	67
To raise taxes on the highest income (over $250,000) Americans.	68	75	76
To allow illegal immigrants who were brought to the U.S. as children to remain in the country.	65	69	74
To reform Medicare, creating a program that provides future retirees with a fixed payment for purchasing private coverage or traditional Medicare.	35	48	45
To withdraw troops from Afghanistan by 2014.	70	74	77
To raise the retirement age and create personal retirement investment account for younger workers.	42	47	45

Note: N = 405. The numbers represent the percentages of those who correctly responded

Davis, 2003). Candidate websites focus on the candidate, particularly personal background and policy platforms. In line with expectations, attention to presidential campaign information on YouTube (H6a), Twitter (H7a), Tumblr (H8a), and blogs (H9a) was unrelated to factual political knowledge.

Candidate Issue Stance Knowledge

Similar to factual knowledge, the results in column 2 in Table 3 show that attention to traditional media sources did not significantly influence candidate issue knowledge (RQb). The latter is likely anticipated, as most traditional media focuses on candidate personalities, images, and the "horse race" during the campaign period rather than candidate issue stands. As expected, an important finding here in column 2 is that attention to traditional media's digital counterparts – online newspapers (H1b) and television websites (H2b) – was positively and significantly related to issue stance knowledge. Specifically, early in the fall 2012 campaign, young adults who paid more attention to presidential campaign information in online newspapers and television websites had significantly more understanding of candidate issues; or vice versa – higher candidate issue knowledge lead to increased attention to online newspapers and television websites.

Table 3. Factual political knowledge and candidate issue stance knowledge by media attention from September 26 to October 7, 2012 (Wave 1)

	Factual Political Knowledge		Issue Stance Knowledge	
Television	.018	(.067)	.001	(.090)
Hard-copy newspaper	.078	(.064)	.055	(.085)
Radio	.010	(.062)	-.010	(.083)
Online newspaper	.266	(.064)***	.255	(.085)***
Television websites	-.028	(.065)	.155	(.086)*
Presidential websites	-.122	(.074)*	-.109	(.098)
Facebook	-.110	(.063)*	-.117	(.083)*
Google+	-.126	(.064)**	-.082	(.085)
YouTube	.043	(.068)	.043	(.089)
Twitter	.057	(.059)	.022	(.079)
Tumblr	.045	(.072)	-.120	(.094)*
Blogs	.018	(.078)	.069	(.102)
Male	.650	(.141)**	.479	(.186)
Race	-.124	(.166)	.185	(.217)
Year in School	.120	(.059)**	.218	(.077)***
Republican	.078	(.053)	.028	(.069)
Interest	.305	(.063)***	.423	(.083)***
Constant	2.04	(.330)***	.756	(.756)*
R^2 Adjusted R^2	24.2 21.1		22.8 19.7	
N	530		533	

Note. All estimates are unstandardized ordinary least squares coefficients, with standard errors in parentheses. *$p < .10$. **$p < .05$. ***$p < .01$.

The positive impact of attention to online newspapers and television websites contrasts with the negative effects of attention to social media, particularly Facebook (H4b) and Tumblr (H8b), on issue stance knowledge (column 2). Young adults using social media during campaigns may be driven primarily by the motivation to connect and communicate rather than to obtain political information. This rationale extends to the lack of association between knowledge of candidate issues and young adults' attention to Google+, YouTube, Twitter, and blogs (column 2). For instance, in contrast with expectations (H7b), attention to Twitter for campaign information was not significantly linked to candidate issue stance knowledge. At this point in the 2012 campaign, there was no relationship between social media and micro blogs and political information levels. Unexpectedly, attention to presidential candidate websites had no significant influence on candidate issue stance knowledge (H3b), although prior research suggests that usage of candidate websites boosts issue knowledge (see Bimber & Davis, 2003; Towner & Dulio, 2011a). The interpretation of this unanticipated result is that young adults who paid attention to candidate websites for political purposes in the few months before Election Day used these sites to get involved and mobilize rather than to obtain information about the candidate. By September 2012, users who turn to campaign websites already know about the candidate and are previously informed of their policy stance. Simply put, the candidate website likely ranks higher as a hub for political involvement and mobilizing rather than an information hub.

Wave Three: November 2012.

As the campaign continued, factual and candidate issue stance knowledge increased among panel respondents (see Table 2). What shaped individual-level change in knowledge levels? To address this question, a series of static-score models for each third-wave dependent variable were estimated. In each model, the third-wave media attention measures, change in media attention measures, demographics, predispositions, and a lagged dependent variable were included. The lagged dependent variable, which is the first-wave value of the dependent variable, is included in the static-score models because previous levels of political knowledge are likely related to political knowledge levels in the following period. This allows for an examination of the causal effects of the independent variables on political knowledge variables while controlling for the respondent's original level of knowledge (see Finkel, 1995).

Factual Political Knowledge

As column 1 in Table 4 shows, all of the coefficients for attention to traditional and online media sources fell short of statistical significance. Controlling for prior levels of factual knowledge, there were no significant effects of media attention on changes in factual knowledge. In other words, it cannot be concluded that young adults who paid attention to offline and online media during the campaign period were any more or less likely than those not paying attention to exhibit increases in factual knowledge, controlling for initial levels of factual knowledge; nor can it be reported that young people who changed their media attention were any more or less likely than those who did not to exhibit such increases. The one exception to the latter is the significant influence of change in attention to Google+ on factual knowledge. This finding suggests that young people who changed their attention to Google+ were more likely than those who did not change their attention to exhibit increases in factual knowledge. Overall, these results imply that young adult's attention to traditional and online media sources did not influence their factual knowledge late in this campaign period.

Candidate Issue Stance Knowledge

Column 2 in Table 5 shows that attention to traditional media had no statistically significant influence on changes in candidate issue stance knowledge. This finding confirms that traditional media has no influence on issue knowledge throughout the fall campaign period (see Tables 3 and 4). Some online sources, however, did influence issue knowledge. By November 2012, attention to television network websites no longer increased candidate issue stance knowledge, as hypothesized in wave 1 (H2b). Instead, young adults who paid more attention to campaign information on television websites were significantly less likely to be informed on candidate issues. As proposed (H1b), attention to online newspapers appeared as a significant, positive variable in September 2012 (Table 3, column 2), but was no longer significant later in the campaign. A link between attention to Twitter campaign content and issue knowledge was not present in September (Table 3, column 2), but emerged later in the election period as a positive – but

Table 4. Factual political knowledge and candidate issue stance knowledge by media attention from November 18-28, 2012 (Wave 3)

	Factual Political Knowledge		Issue Stance Knowledge	
Lagged Dep. Variable	.625	(.043)***	.445	(.048)***
Television	.090	(.077)	.155	(.108)
Hard-copy newspaper	-.019	(.071)	.000	(.101)
Radio	-.031	(.073)	-.106	(.103)
Online newspaper	-.030	(.075)	.037	(.104)
Television websites	.003	(.083)	-.237	(.116)**
Presidential websites	-.129	(.097)	.128	(.139)
Facebook	.035	(.068)	.103	(.094)
Google+	-.086	(.090)	-.032	(.127)
YouTube	-.041	(.075)	-.060	(.106)
Twitter	.004	(.063)	.147	(.088)*
Tumblr	-.007	(.075)	-.033	(.105)
Blogs	.121	(.096)	.010	(.134)
Change in TV attention	-.063	(.070)	-.163	(.096)*
Change in hard-copy newspaper attention	-.087	(.072)	-.140	(.098)
Change in radio attention	.073	(.058)	.071	(.083)
Change in online newspaper attention	.037	(.071)	.120	(.098)
Change in TV network website attention	.088	(.062)	.161	(.088)*
Change in Presidential website attention	.058	(.079)	-.061	(.108)
Change in Facebook attention	-.053	(.067)	-.080	(.094)
Change in Google+ attention	.168	(.071)**	.165	(.098)*
Change in YouTube attention	-.099	(.074)	.089	(.102)
Change in Twitter attention	.068	(.072)	-.117	(.102)
Change in Tumblr attention	.067	(.090)	-.109	(.127)
Change in Blog attention	-.050	(.074)	-.148	(.104)
Age	-.026	(.014)*	-.051	(.020)***
Male	.436	(.136)***	.469	(.188)***
White	.318	(.157)**	-.064	(.222)
Year in School	-.038	(.061)	-.039	(.085)
Republican	.016	(.046)	.044	(.065)
Interest	.183	(.070)***	.205	(.099)**
Constant	51.9	(27.8)*	102.9	(39.4)***
R^2	61.4		44.3	
Adjusted R^2	57.0		38.0	
N	401		405	

Note. All estimates are unstandardized ordinary least squares coefficients, with standard errors in parentheses. Results were similar when estimated using ordered probit. $^{*}p < .10$. $^{**}p < .05$. $^{***}p < .01$

modest – predictor. The latter finding offers some support for the proposed hypothesis, asserting that attention to Twitter is positively linked to issue-stance knowledge (H7b).

The change in media attention variables produced some notable findings. Examining the change variables in column 2 in Table 4, it can be concluded that respondents who changed their attention to television were less likely than those who did not change their attention to exhibit increases in issue knowledge. In addition, young adults who changed their attention to television network websites and blogs were more likely than those who did not change their attention to exhibit increases in issue knowledge.

DISCUSSION AND CONCLUSION

Previous research provides mixed findings about the relationships between online media outlets and political knowledge, leaving important questions unanswered. Does the array of media offerings – both traditional and online - widen or reduce the relative gap in knowledge levels among young citizens? Based on this analysis, the evidence is again mixed. When considering the political implications of online media during the 2012 presidential campaign period, it is apparent that scholars can both applaud some online sources for serving as knowledge hubs as well as condemn others for acting as drains. Attention to online newspapers during the early fall campaign boosted both factual and issue stance knowledge among young people. This finding may suggest that the online versions of hard-copy newspapers offer users something different – and maybe better. Online newspapers provide more background and in-depth information about the candidates or campaign, rapidly disseminating news via mobile alerts, news feeds, and social media. Readers can interact with the news by searching content, clicking on related hyperlinks, watching online video, and reading in-depth analyses, editorials, and blogs (Dalrymple & Scheufele, 2007). Due to infinite digital space, online newspapers offer more information than their print counterparts; thus, resulting in more factual political knowledge. Similarly, it should be highlighted that young adults' attention to television websites modestly increased their candidate issue stance knowledge early in the campaign period.

It is important to note that the relationship between online newspapers and television websites changed during the fall election period. For instance, attention to online newspapers was positively associated with factual and issue stance knowledge in September 2012 but these sources were not positively linked to individual-level change in knowledge levels in the following months. In fact, those who paid attention to campaign information on television websites were significantly less likely to be informed on candidate issues by November 2012. In other words, online newspaper and television network website no longer served as hubs late in the campaign.

Online newspapers and television network websites are indeed online extensions of the traditional press. These digital sources offer up-to-the minute campaign coverage from trained journalists and broadcasters that is considered balanced, neutral, and credible. There is no need to buy a print newspaper or wait for the evening news on television. These online sources are at young adults' fingertips – most likely via their smart phone or iPad. As print newspaper circulations decline (see Edmonds et al., 2012) and television news becomes more ideological, particularly on cable channels, more and more citizens may turn to these digital components of the traditional press.

Alternatively, one might point to Facebook and Google+, noting that attention to campaign information on Facebook is negatively associated to factual and issue-stance knowledge early in the campaign period. In addition, Google+ is negatively linked to factual knowledge. These latter digital sources do not politically inform, but focus more on mobilizing, connecting, and involving users. It is likely that any political information that is gleaned from these sites is likely incidental and indirect rather than actively gathered and absorbed. Moreover, it can be argued that young adults are not using social networks as a source or hub for political information. Instead, these sites are more for interpersonal connections and expressions with family and friends. Considering this, it is likely that those paying attention to Facebook and Google + for politics are consuming homogenous discussion or one-sided arguments rather than a diversity of political information, which is detrimental to knowledge gains. That is, the information on social networks is likely reinforcing rather than educational.

The analysis presented here shows that some online sources – online newspapers and television network websites – are hubs of campaign information whereas other digital outlets – Facebook and Google+ – are drains on information levels. Based on this evidence, are online newspapers and network websites "the answer" to low knowledge levels among young people today? Probably not. To increase political information levels, can one simply tout online newspapers and discourage Facebook use? Maybe. Young people must be interested in politics and the campaign beforehand as well as motivated to use online newspaper as a source of political information. Indeed, this research confirms that young adult's media choices during a presidential campaign are one key to understanding their political knowledge levels.

It is important to briefly conclude with research limitations as well as groundwork for future scholarship. First, the survey sample draws on college students, which clearly limits the sample frame and generalizability. Therefore, conclusions here should be viewed with some caution, as a national sample of adults may produce different findings. Moreover, citizens' attention to media sources may have different effects on their political knowledge levels during midterm elections and non-campaign periods. Furthermore, this study employs survey data that cannot determine the cause-and-effect relationship between media attention and knowledge. Indeed, attention to some media sources may directly influence political knowledge, but it is also likely that the more knowledgeable pay more attention to certain media sources. Despite this, these findings contribute to the political communication research by offering evidence that attention to online sources and political knowledge are empirically linked.

Last, online media sources in campaigning are rapidly changing and evolving. For instance, Twitter was barely used in the 2008 presidential campaigns and then burst on the scene in 2012. Thus, one cannot expect the effects of online sources to remain the same election after election. Moreover, there are virtually no studies on the role of Instagram, Snapchat, Flickr, Pinterest, and Reddit, in political campaigning. It is critical that future research examine the content, use, and influence of these online sources. In addition, future research should push beyond examining knowledge of national political facts and presidential candidate issue stances to include knowledge of local issues and candidates as well as knowledge of international affairs. In sum, this study signals some interesting patterns among young adults that may help scholars and pundits understand our rapidly changing media landscape.

REFERENCES

Ahem, R. K., Stomer-Galley, J., & Neuman, W. R. (2000). *When voters can interact and compare candidates online: Experimentally investigating political web effects*. Paper presented at the meeting of the International Communications Associations Annual Conference, Acapulco, Mexico.

Anderson, M., & Caumont, A. (2014). How social media is reshaping news. *Pew Research Center*. Retrieved on June 1, 2015, from http://www.pewresearch.org/fact-tank/2014/09/24/how-social-media-is-reshaping-news/

Baumgartner, J. C., & Morris, J. S. (2010). MyFaceTube politics: Social networking websites and political engagement of young adults. *Social Science Computer Review*, *28*(1), 24–44. doi:10.1177/0894439309334325

Becker, L. B., & Dunwoody, S. (1982). Media use, public affairs knowledge and voting in a local election. *The Journalism Quarterly*, *59*(2), 212–218. doi:10.1177/107769908205900203

Bekafigo, M. A., & Pingley, A. (2014). *Tweeting negative: Determinants of negative campaigning in the 2011 gubernatorial elections*. Presented at the Annual Meeting of the Midwest Political Science Association, Chicago, IL.

Bimber, B., & Davis, R. (2003). *Campaigning online*. New York: Oxford University Press.

Cappella, J., & Jamieson, K. (1997). *Spiral of cynicism*. New York: Oxford University Press.

Chaffee, S. H., & Frank, S. (1996). How Americans get political information: Print versus broadcast news. *The Annals of the American Academy of Political and Social Science*, *546*(1), 48–58. doi:10.1177/0002716296546001005

Chaffee, S. H., Zhao, X., & Leshner, G. (1994). Political knowledge and the campaign media of 1992. *Communication Research*, *21*(3), 305–324. doi:10.1177/009365094021003004

Cornfield, M. (2010). Game-changers: New technology and the 2008 presidential elections. In L. J. Sabato (Ed.), *The year of Obama* (pp. 205–230). New York: Longman.

Dalrymple, K., & Scheufele, D. (2007). Finally informing the electorate? How the Internet got people thinking about presidential politics in 2004. *The Harvard International Journal of Press/Politics*, *12*(3), 96–111. doi:10.1177/1081180X07302881

Davis, R. (2009). *Typing politics*. New York: Oxford University Press.

DiMaggio, P., Hargittai, F., Neuman, W. R., & Robinson, J. P. (2001). Social implications of the Internet. *Annual Review of Sociology*, *27*(1), 307–336. doi:10.1146/annurev.soc.27.1.307

Dimitrova, D. V., Shehata, A., Stromback, J., & Nord, L. W. (2014). The effects of digital media on political knowledge and participation in election campaigns: Evidence from panel data. *Communication Research*, *41*(1), 95–118. doi:10.1177/0093650211426004

Drew, D., & Weaver, D. (2006). Voter learning in the 2004 presidential election: Did the media matter? *Journalism & Mass Communication Quarterly*, *83*(1), 25–42. doi:10.1177/107769900608300103

Druckman, J. N. (2005). Media matter: How newspapers and television news cover campaignsand influence voters. *Political Communication*, *22*(4), 463–481. doi:10.1080/10584600500311394

Edmonds, R., Guskin, E., Rosenstiel, T., & Mitchell, A. (2012). Newspapers: Building digital revenues proves painfully slow. *The State of the News Media 2012*. Retrieved on January 1, 2015, from http://www.stateofthemedia.org/2012/newspapers-building-digital-revenues-proves-painfully-slow/

Eveland, W. P., Cortese, E., Park, H., & Dunwoody, S. (2004). How Web site organization influences free recall, factual knowledge, and knowledge structure density. *Human Communication Research*, *30*(2), 208–233. doi:10.1111/j.1468-2958.2004.tb00731.x

Eveland, W. P. Jr, & Dunwoody, S. (2000). Examining information processing on the World Wide Web using think aloud protocols. *Media Psychology*, *2*(3), 219–244. doi:10.1207/S1532785XMEP0203_2

Eveland, W. P. Jr, & Dunwoody, S. (2001). User control and structural isomorphism or disorientation and cognitive load? Learning from the Web versus print. *Communication Research*, *28*(1), 48–78. doi:10.1177/009365001028001002

Eveland, W. P. Jr, & Dunwoody, S. (2002). An investigation of elaboration and selective scanning as mediators of learning from the Web versus print. *Journal of Broadcasting & Electronic Media*, *46*(1), 34–53. doi:10.120715506878jobem4601_3

Eveland, W. P. Jr, Marton, K., & Seo, M. (2004). Moving beyond "just the facts": The influence of online news on the content and structure of public affairs knowledge. *Communication Research*, *31*(1), 82–108. doi:10.1177/0093650203260203

Eveland, W. P. Jr, & Scheufele, D. A. (2000). Connecting news media use with gaps in knowledge. *Political Communication*, *17*(3), 215–237. doi:10.1080/105846000414250

Eveland, W. P. Jr, Seo, M., & Marton, K. (2002). Learning from the news in campaign 2000: An experimental comparison of TV news, newspapers, and online news. *Media Psychology*, *4*(4), 355–380. doi:10.1207/S1532785XMEP0404_03

Fernandes, J., Giurcanu, M., Bowers, K. W., & Neely, J. C. (2010). The writing on the wall: A content analysis of college students' Facebook groups for the 2008 presidential election. *Mass Communication & Society*, *13*(5), 653–675. doi:10.1080/15205436.2010.516865

Finkel, S. (1995). *Causal analysis with panel data*. Thousand Oaks, CA: Sage. doi:10.4135/9781412983594

Foot, K., & Schneider, S. M. (2006). *Web campaigning*. Cambridge, MA: MIT Press. doi:10.7551/mitpress/7186.001.0001

Fung, T. K. F., Vraga, E., & Thorson, K. (2011). When bloggers attack: Examining the effect of negative citizen-initiated campaigning in the 2008 presidential election. In J. A. Hendricks & L. L. Kaid (Eds.), *Techno politics in presidential campaigning* (pp. 83–101). New York: Routledge.

Groshek, J., & Dimitrova, D. (2011). A Cross-section of voter learning, campaign interest and intention to vote in the 2008 American election: Did Web 2.0 matter? *Studies in Communications*, *9*, 355–375.

Haridakis, P., & Hanson, G. (2011). Campaign 2008: Comparing YouTube, social networking, and other media use among younger and older voters. In J. A. Hendricks & L. L. Kaid (Eds.), *Techno-politics in presidential campaigning* (pp. 61-82). New York: Routledge.

Jennings, M. K., & Zeitner, B. (2003). Internet use and civic engagement: A longitudinal analysis. *Public Opinion Quarterly*, *67*(3), 311–334. doi:10.1086/376947

Johnson, T. J., Briama, M. A., & Sothirajah, J. (1999). Doing the traditional media sidestep: Comparing the effects of the Internet and other nontraditional media with traditional media in the 1996 presidential campaign. *Journalism & Mass Communication Quarterly*, *76*(1), 99–123. doi:10.1177/107769909907600108

Johnson, T. J., & Kaye, B. K. (2004). Wag the blog: How reliance on traditional media and the Internet influence perceptions of credibility of weblogs among blog users. *Journalism & Mass Communication Quarterly*, *81*(3), 622–642. doi:10.1177/107769900408100310

Kaid, L. L., McKinney, M. S., & Tedesco, J. C. (2007). Political information efficacy and young voters. *The American Behavioral Scientist*, *50*, 1093–1111. doi:10.1177/0002764207300040

Kaufhold, K., Valenzuela, S., & Gil de Zuniga, H. (2010). Citizen journalism and democracy: How user-generated news use relates to political knowledge. *Journalism & Mass Communication Quarterly*, *87*(3-4), 515–529. doi:10.1177/107769901008700305

Kenski, K., & Stroud, N. J. (2006). Connections between Internet use and political efficacy, knowledge, and political participation. *Journal of Broadcasting & Electronic Media*, *50*(2), 173–192. doi:10.120715506878jobem5002_1

Lawrence, E., Sides, J., & Farrell, H. (2010). Self-segregation or deliberation? Blog readership, participation, and polarization in American politics. *PS: Persepctives on Politics*, *8*(1), 141–157.

Lowden, N. B., Anderson, P. A., Dozier, D. M., & Lauzen, M. M. (1994). Media use in the primary election: A secondary medium model. *Communication Research*, *21*(3), 293–304. doi:10.1177/009365094021003003

Mondak, J. (1995). *Nothing to read*. Ann Arbor, MI: University of Michigan Press. doi:10.3998/mpub.10442

Moy, P., & Pfau, M. (2000). *With malice toward all?* Westport, CT: Praeger.

Neuman, W. R. (1981). Differentiation and integration: Two dimensions of political thinking. *American Journal of Sociology*, *86*(6), 1236–1268. doi:10.1086/227384

Neuman, W. R., Just, M. R., & Crigler, A. N. (1992). *Common knowledge*. Chicago: University of Chicago Press.

Norris, P. (2000). *A virtuous circle*. Cambridge, UK: Cambridge University Press; doi:10.7208/chicago/9780226161174.001.0001.

Parmelee, J., & Bichard, S. (2012). *Politics and the Twitter revolution*. Lanham, MD: Lexington Books.

Pasek, J., More, E., & Romer, D. (2009). Realizing the social Internet? Online social networking meets offline social capital. *Journal of Information Technology & Politics*, *6*(3-4), 197–215. doi:10.1080/19331680902996403

Patterson, T. E. (1993). *Out of order*. New York: Knopf.

Patterson, T. E., & McClure, R. D. (1976). *The unseeing eye*. New York: Putnam.

Pettey, G. R. (1988). The interaction of the individual's social environment, attention and interest, and public affairs media use on political knowledge holding. *Communication Research, 15*(3), 265–281. doi:10.1177/009365088015003003

Pew Research Center. (2012a). *How the presidential candidates use the web and social media*. Retrieved January 1, 2015, from http://www.journalism.org/files/legacy/DIRECT%20ACCESS%20FINAL.pdf

Pew Research Center. (2012b). *Cable leads the pack as campaign news source*. Retrieved June 1, 2015, from http://www.people-press.org/files/legacy- pdf/2012%20Communicating%20Release.pdf

Pew Research Center. (2014). *Millennials in adulthood: Detached from institutions, networked with friends*. Retrieved January 1, 2015, from http://www.pewsocialtrends.org/files/2014/03/2014-03-07_generations-report-version-for-web.pdf

Price, V., & Zaller, J. (1993). Who gets the news? Alternative measures of new reception and their implications for research. *Public Opinion Quarterly, 57*(2), 133–164. doi:10.1086/269363

Prior, M. (2005). News vs. entertainment: How increasing media choice widens gaps in political knowledge and turnout. *American Journal of Political Science, 49*(3), 577–592. doi:10.1111/j.1540-5907.2005.00143.x

Project for Excellence in Journalism. (2012). *Winning the media campaign 2012*. Retrieved January 1, 2015, from http://www.journalism.org/files/legacy/Winningthemediacampaign2012.pdf

Robinson, J. P., & Levy, M. K. (1986). *The main source*. Beverly Hills, CA: Sage.

Scheufele, D. A., & Nisbet, M. C. (2002). Being a citizen online: New opportunities and dead ends. *The Harvard International Journal of Press/Politics, 7*(3), 55–75.

Shah, D., McLeod, D., & Yoon, S. (2001). Communication, context, and community: An exploration of print, broadcast, and Internet influences. *Communication Research, 28*(4), 464–506. doi:10.1177/009365001028004005

Shah, D. V., Kwak, N., & Holbert, R. L. (2001). Connecting" and "disconnecting" with civic life: Patterns of Internet use and the production of social capital. *Political Communication, 18*, 141–162. doi:10.1080/105846001750322952

Smith, A. (2011). *22% of online Americans used social networking or Twitter for politics in 2010 campaign*. Pew Research Center. Retrieved on June 1, 2015, from, http://www.pewinternet.org/files/old-media//Files/Reports/2011/PIP-Social-Media-and-2010-Election.pdf

Smith, A., & Duggan, M. (2012). *Online political videos and campaign 2012*. Pew Research Center's Internet & American Life Project. Retrieved on January 1, 2015, from http://pewinternet.org/Reports/2012/Election-2012-Video.aspx

Smith, A. (2013). *Civic engagement in the digital age*. Pew Research Center.

Sotirovic, M., & McLeod, J. (2004). Knowledge as understanding: The information processing approach to political learning. In L. Kaid (Ed.), *Handbook of Political Communication Research* (pp. 357–394). Hillsdale, NJ: Lawrence Erlbaum Associates.

Svensson, E., Kiousis, S., & Stromback, J. (2014). Creating a win-win situation? Relationship cultivation and the use of social media in the 2012 campaigns. In J. A. Hendricks & L. L. Kaid (Eds.), *Presidential Campaigning and Social Media* (pp. 28–43). New York: Oxford University Press.

Tewksbury, D., & Althaus, S. L. (2000). Differences in knowledge acquisition among readers of the paper and online versions of a national newspaper. *Journalism & Mass Communication Quarterly*, *77*(3), 457–479. doi:10.1177/107769900007700301

Towner, T. L. (2013). All political participation is socially networked?: New media and the 2012 election. *Social Science Computer Review*, *31*(5), 527–541. doi:10.1177/0894439313489656

Towner, T. L. (2016). The influence of Twitter posts on candidate perceptions: The 2014 Michigan midterms. In J. A. Hendricks & D. Schill (Eds.), *Media, message, and mobilization*. New York: Palgrave.

Towner, T. L., & Dulio, D. A. (2011a). The Web 2.0 election: Voter learning in the 2008 presidential campaign. In J. A. Hendricks & L. L. Kaid (Eds.), *Techno-politics in presidential campaigning* (pp. 22–43). New York: Routledge.

Towner, T. L., & Dulio, D. A. (2011b). The Web 2.0 election: Does the online medium matter? *Journal of Political Marketing*, *10*(1-2), 165–188. doi:10.1080/15377857.2011.540220

Unionmetrics. (2012). *Comparing Tumblr analytics for Mitt Romney and Barack Obama*. Retrieved on January 1, 2015, from http://unionmetrics.tumblr.com/post/34660150228/comparing-tumblr-analytics-for-mitt-romney-and

U.S. Census Bureau. (2013). *U.S. Census Current Population Survey's estimate of the 18-29 citizen population.* Retrieved on January 1, 2015, from http://www.census.gov/

Valkenburg, P., & Peter, J. (2013). The differential susceptibility to media effects model. *Journal of Communication*, *63*(2), 221–243. doi:10.1111/jcom.12024

Vitak, J., Zube, P., Smock, A., Carr, C. T., Ellison, N., & Lampe, C. (2011). It's complicated: Facebook users' political participation in the 2008 election. *Cyberpsychology, Behavior, and Social Networking*, *14*(3), 107–114. doi:10.1089/cyber.2009.0226 PMID:20649449

Wallsten, K. (2010). "Yes we can": How online viewership, blog discussion, campaign statements, and mainstream media coverage produced a viral video phenomenon. *Journal of Information Technology & Politics*, *7*(2), 163–181. doi:10.1080/19331681003749030

Wattenberg, M. (2012). *Is voting for young people?* New York: Pearson Longman.

Weaver, D., & Drew, D. (1993). Voter learning in the 1990 off-year election: Did the media matter? *The Journalism Quarterly*, *70*(2), 356–368. doi:10.1177/107769909307000211

Weaver, D., & Drew, D. (2001). Voter learning and interest in the 2000 presidential election: Did the media matter? *Journalism & Mass Communication Quarterly*, *78*(4), 787–798. doi:10.1177/107769900107800411

Wei, R., & Ven-hwei, L. (2008). News media use and knowledge about the 2006 U.S. midterm elections: Why exposure matters in voter learning. *International Journal of Public Opinion Research, 20*(3), 347–362. doi:10.1093/ijpor/edn032

Xenos, M., & Moy, P. (2007). Direct and differential effects of the Internet on political and civic engagement. *Journal of Communication, 57*(4), 704–718. doi:10.1111/j.1460-2466.2007.00364.x

Zhao, X., & Chaffee, S. H. (1995). Campaign advertisements versus television news as sources of political issue information. *Public Opinion Quarterly, 59*(1), 41–65. doi:10.1086/269457

Chapter 8
Citizen Journalism: New-Age Newsgathering

Rabia Noor
Islamic University of Science and Technology, India

ABSTRACT

The last decade has brought several advanced technologies for journalists. This in turn brought in a new era of revolutionary concepts of journalism. One among them is citizen journalism. Although the practice of citizen journalism existed centuries before, it is new media that has accelerated its pace in contemporary times. Citizen journalism is one of the most novel trends in journalism at present. Nowadays, several alternative news sources are available on the internet, such as blogs, social networking websites, etc. These offer a wide variety of news, thus giving a good competition to mainstream media. On many occasions, citizen journalists have reported breaking news faster than professional journalists. With the result, mainstream media no longer serves as the sole source of news. Many established television channels and newspapers are bringing in innovations in their operations to compete with what can be termed as new forms of journalism. The chapter underlines the significance and limitations of citizen journalism, which is only going to grow in the coming times.

CONCEPT

Citizen journalism is a concept in media that refers to journalistic activities of ordinary people. It means citizens themselves report the issues confronting them. Citizen journalism has enabled people to raise their voice on what they feel need attention. These people are, thus, termed as citizen journalists. Citizen journalists or amateur reporters are none but the general audience, that is, viewers, readers and listeners of mainstream media.

Duffy, Thorson and Jahng (2010) have defined citizen journalist as "an individual, who is not a trained professional, but who nonetheless may report on his or her neighbourhood or community." Referring to citizen journalists as "people formerly known as the audience", *PressThink* blogger Jay Rosen (2006) mentions that "earlier they would be on the receiving end of a media system that ran one way, in a broadcasting pattern, with high entry fees and a few firms competing to speak very loudly, while the rest of the

DOI: 10.4018/978-1-7998-1828-1.ch008

population listened in isolation from one another." He, however, argues that presently they are no more in a situation like that. The founder of the *Centre for Citizen Media,* Dan Gillmor (2004) defines citizen reporter as "any person, who participates in such a conversation that is helpful, and who is not patently a 'fake' citizen, that is, someone representing a corporate interest" (as cited in Tilley & Cokley, 2008).

The key to practice of citizen journalism lies in the proactive nature of citizens. It sits well with what Coleman (2001) has rightly stated that "to be an active citizen is to be a communicative agent" and that "there can be no community without communication". This implies that a citizen journalist is an active citizen, for citizen journalism derives its significance from communicative acts of citizens. Wilson (1993) discusses that "the term 'citizen' has three current standard meanings: (i) someone born in a particular place or nation; (ii) a voting member of a republican city, nation, or state, who has various rights and responsibilities because of that status; and (iii) a civilian, as contrasted with a soldier or other official." However, Tilley and Cokley (2008) observe that none of these translates directly into the application of the term 'citizen journalist'. They assert that "a citizen journalist may be a 'netizen' (Internet user) rather than being identified with a particular nation-state; a citizen journalist may not be a voter; and a military official can also be posting to news sites as a citizen journalist."

Citizen journalism is also known as participatory and democratic journalism (Baase, 2008). There are various other synonyms used for citizen journalism—'public journalism', 'civic journalism', 'stand-alone journalism', 'networked journalism', 'open source journalism', 'crowd-sourced journalism', 'collaborative journalism', 'grassroots journalism', 'community journalism', 'bridge media' and so on. Cohn (2007) argues that all these terms refer to different acts. "These forms of journalism are related to 'citizen journalism', but each is a unique species that has evolved out of a larger family of social media."

One of the most accepted and inclusive definitions of citizen journalism has been put forward by Bowman and Willis (2003) in *New Media.* They define citizen journalism as "the act of non-professionals, playing an active role in the process of collecting, reporting, analysing and disseminating news and information." This definition covers all the possible activities of citizen journalists in existence. The authors further write, "The intent of this participation is to provide independent, reliable, accurate, wide-ranging and relevant information that a democracy requires."

Ross and Cormier (2010) have defined citizen journalism "as a rapidly evolving form of journalism", where ordinary citizens "take the initiative to report news or express views about happenings within their community".

News reported by citizens is of the people, by the people and for the people. Citizen journalists are independent and freelancing reporters. They are not constrained by conventional journalistic processes or methodologies, and they usually function without editorial oversight. Citizen journalists gather, process, research, report, analyse and publish news and information, most often utilising a variety of technologies made possible by the Internet.

Radsch (2013) defines citizen journalism "as an alternative and activist form of newsgathering and reporting that functions outside mainstream media institutions, often as repose to shortcoming in the professional journalistic field." Quinn and Lamble (2008) provide a more formal definition of citizen journalism. According to them, citizen journalism occurs in two forms:

The first is when members of the public, who are not professional journalists, contribute content that is published on traditional media. The second form of citizen journalism occurs when members of the public produce blogs or community websites or publications for a specific purpose. In other words, citizens assume the role of journalists.

It remains uncertain as to where did the term 'citizen journalism' come from (Gillmor, 2008). However, it is certain that the term did not exist before the advent of the Internet. Citizen journalism is believed to have grown in tandem with the growth of the Internet. As per some research work, the term 'citizen journalism' has been in use since 1999 (Corthesy, 2012). Tilley and Cokley (2008) mention that the terms 'citizen journalist' and 'citizen journalism' arose when people who were not journalists by profession began to "collect, edit and provide publishers with (or publish directly) news material that was out of publishers' reach. Typically, this material reported sudden events, such as fires, crashes, floods and other disasters, which desk-bound reporters could not attend due to time constraints, or odd on-the-spot items." The term 'citizen media' has been coined by Clemencia Rodriguez, who defines this concept as 'the transformative processes they bring about within participants and their communities'.

Citizens' media implies first that a collectivity is enacting its citizenship by actively intervening and transforming the established mediascape; second, that these media are contesting social codes, legitimised identities, and institutionalised social relations; and third, that these communication practices are empowering the community involved, to the point where these transformations and changes are possible. (as cited in Graham, 2004).

This focus on social processes leads Rodriguez to a view of citizens' media as belonging to the ordinary, impermanent and transitory realm of the everyday (Coyer, Dowmunt & Fountain, 2007). However, as Gillmor (2008) points out, not all citizen media is citizen journalism. It can be, therefore, concluded that citizen media refers to the content produced by ordinary citizens, who are not professional journalists. Citizen journalism, on the other hand, is a broader term that includes everything from content to activities of citizen journalists.

Citizen journalism derives its legitimacy from Article 19(i)(a) of the Indian Constitution, which guarantees freedom of expression for every citizen, which includes right to publish news and comment on public affairs; and right to receive information. The British journalist, Ian Hargreaves (1999) argues that everyone is a journalist in a democracy. This is because in a democracy, everyone has the right to communicate a fact or a point of view, even if it is trivial or hideous. Tilley and Cokley (2008) note that the ontology of 'citizen journalist' includes positive as well as negative terms:

The positive terms include the views that citizen journalism tends to:

i. democratise journalism, so that gatekeeping and agenda-setting tasks of deciding 'what's news' are spread wider than those complicit in selling audiences to advertisers; ii. pluralise voices in the public sphere by providing more ways for dissenting voices and views to be heard; and iii. enable deployment of new in situ technologies to drive change among pre-existing traditional media. The negative terms include the views that citizen journalism tends to: a) devalue the ethical and commercial worth of the term 'journalist' and with it the specialised information processing skills—coping and crafting; b) erode the overall quality of available information by promoting a 'mirror ball effect', in which a daz-

zling cacophony of competing raw sources overwhelms less colourful output from skilled information gatherers and disseminators; and c. undermine society by enabling unchallenged and unchecked access by false 'citizen' voices, such as malignant commercial interests or criminals, who use fraud and 'spin' to manufacture false consent by posing as 'citizens'.

To become a citizen journalist, all one needs is a story to tell and a means to make it public. One of such means is to type a story on computer and submit it to some organisation inviting citizen journalism content. Stories can range from a few paragraphs to many pages in length. Another means available with citizens is to capture a situation in the form of photographs and videos. This is an easier way to gather news than writing news stories. The proliferation of the camera phones has made it possible for ordinary citizens to document the newsworthy situations around them. Nowadays they have all the facilities available to gather and circulate news like never before. The phenomenon of citizen journalism has been spurred on by the rise in the availability of the new media platforms of desk-top publishing. The advanced new media technologies have lent a new life to the movement of citizen journalists globally. With the advent of cellular phones, digital cameras, tablet computers and Internet, many people nowadays are contributing their bit to journalism by capturing news and circulating it globally. The digital platform has led everyone, irrespective of their age group, class, qualification or experience, to write or capture news for the general masses.

Gillmor (2004) cites what he terms as "the explosion in ownership of an array of citizen journalism tools such as digital cameras, camera mobile phones, computers and iPods" as the one of the major reasons for the growth of citizen journalism. The author states, "With these tools affordable and broadband penetrating more homes than ever, citizen journalism makes inroads into communities once dominated by a single newspaper or television station." Rutigliano (2008) notes that citizen journalism is a product of the network society, and argues, "It relies on the digital technology that drives many of the processes behind the simultaneous fragmentation and coordination occurring on a global level." Some of the technologies that have come to characterise citizen journalism are catalogued by Gillmor (2006) as follows:

- *Mail lists and forums, made of diverse communities of interest;*
- *Weblogs, a 'many to many, few to few' medium whose 'ecosystem' is expanding into the space between email and the web, and could well be the missing link in the communications chain;*
- *Wikis, server programmes that allow users to collaborate in forming the content of a website;*
- *SMSs, a service offered by network providers, which allows customers to send text messages over the cell phones;*
- *Mobile-connected cameras, which include the every-day digital cameras that allow users to download, store, edit, and transmit pictures anytime, anywhere;*
- *Internet 'broadcasting', whereby ordinary people can record and upload anything on the Internet, as well as distribute it;*
- *Peer-to-peer or P2P sharing of files (P2P describes applications, in which people can use the Internet to communicate or share and distribute digital files with each other directly or through a mediating web server); and*
- *RSS (Really Simple Syndication), which allows readers of blogs and other kinds of sites to have their computers and other devices automatically retrieve the content they care about.*

Similarly, Ganesh (2006) describes various forms of citizen journalism, such as online discussion groups, collaborative publishing communities, weblogs (web-pages made up of short, frequently updated text blocks or entries arranged in reverse chronological order), Peer-to-Peer (P2P) and so on. Ganesh further states that since its inception, participation has been a fundamental component of the Internet. "Newsgroups, mailing lists and bulletin boards were the early cousins to the forums, weblogs and collaborative communities flourishing today. Those early forms are still thriving, a testament to the need of the man to stay connected to the social networks."

Bentley et al. (2005) observe that citizen journalism is partly built on the personal nature of blog writing. It, however, has been noticed that citizen journalism sites are usually designed like a news site, not a blog, and thus there are layered pages, in which there is a main front page and several topic categories. Still, the gatekeeper role is greatly diminished from what it would be at a typical news site, because at a typical mainstream news publication the editor would determine both what makes the front page and what stories make it onto the site. Unless the stories violate standards for submission, citizen journalism sites tend to publish anything submitted. These standards depend on the site, but they do tend to be less restrictive than typical news sites (Bentley et al., 2005; Bentley, 2004). Thus, the editor's true gatekeeping power comes in story placement more than story selection.

Editor of the blog *Media Shift* and contributor to the *Online Journalism Review*, Mark Glaser (2006) states that the idea behind citizen journalism is that people without professional journalism training can use the tools of modern technology and the global distribution of the Internet to create, augment or fact-check media on their own or in collaboration with others.

For example, one might write about a city council meeting on his or her blog or in an online forum. Or one could fact-check a newspaper article from the mainstream media and point out factual errors or bias on the blog. Or one might snap a digital photo of a newsworthy event happening in their town and post it online. Or one might videotape a similar event and post it on a site such as YouTube.

According to Glaser, one of the main concepts behind citizen journalism is that "mainstream media reporters and producers are not the exclusive center of knowledge on a subject—the audience knows more collectively than the reporter alone." Kovach and Rosenstiel (2001) make a compelling argument that the news business is undergoing a momentous transition. As per them, each time there has been a period of significant, social, economic and technological change, a transformation in news occurred.

This happened in the 1830-40s with the advent of the telegraph; the 1880s with a drop in paper prices and a wave of immigration; the 1920s with radio and the rise of gossip and celebrity culture; the 1950s at the onset of the Cold War and television... New technology, along with globalisation and the conglomeration of media, is causing a shift away from journalism that is connected to citizen building and one that supports a healthy democracy.

Kellett (2008) notes that citizen journalism has brought about significant change in the fourth estate, content and treatment of news, and participatory role of people. "The ability of the press to frame political discourse or advocate a limited agenda has been altered fundamentally. The very nature of the anonymity of the Internet has allowed previously unheard voices to contribute meaningfully to the national and international dialog of news stories throughout the world." Robert Huesca, an Associate Professor of Communication at Trinity University at San Antonio, Texas, deems that "doing citizen journalism right means crafting a crew of correspondents, who are typically excluded from or misrepresented by local television news: demographic and lifestyle groups, who have little access to the media and that advertisers don't want" (as cited in Nandi, 2006).

At present various user-generated websites, including news portals and blog sites, are operating across the globe that offer common masses a platform to be citizen journalists and share their stories with rest of the world. Some notable citizen journalism websites of the world include *Cable News Network's (CNN) iReport feature* that was launched in 2006, *Al-Jazeera's Sharek Portal* (which means "share") launched in late 2007 (Dreier, 2012), Germany's *myHeimat.de,* launched in 2005, which has been structured as an aggregated hyperlocal news site (Bruns, 2009) and South Korea's popular and commercially successful online news website *OhMyNews*, which was founded on February 22, 2000 by Oh Yeon Ho with the motto, *"Every Citizen is a Reporter."* The open source business model of *OhMyNews* is to accept, edit and publish articles from its readers. Whilst the *OhMyNews* model is doing well in South Korea, it failed in Japan to take off and was forced to close down in 2007 (The Open News Room, 2011). About 80 per cent of its content comes from freelance contributors, who are mostly ordinary citizens, while the rest is generated by its staff comprising of traditional reporters and editors. The site has been credited with transforming South Korea's conservative political environment (Nandi, 2006). Zhang (2011) reports that "*CNN's* citizen journalism initiative, *iReport,* has proved to be valuable as a source of imagery during disasters and protests." However, it has also received criticism for not paying for submitted photographs, including those that are subsequently broadcast worldwide. Another noted citizen journalism website is *Malaysiakini.com,* which was established in 1999 by two young journalists, Steven Gan and Premesh Chandran, who had become disaffected with the degree of state control over and self-censorship within Malaysia's print and broadcast media, and saw an opportunity to use the Internet to provide free and fair news to the Malaysian public and to support the development of freedom of speech, social justice and democracy in Malaysia. In Britain, the *British Broadcasting Corporation (BBC)* is promoting a citizen journalism model linked to community activism from within its own portal, through its *Action Network* initiative (www.bbc.co.uk/dna/actionnetwork/), while *The Guardian* promotes user interaction through its *Comment is Free* pages. In Australia sites such as *Crikey, New Matilda* and *On Line Opinion* seek both to promote new stories, and to generate alternative means of gathering and aggregating news and opinion online. Internationally, the *Indymedia* network, founded in the United States in the context of the 1999 *'Battle of Seattle'* protests against the inaugural meeting of the World Trade Organisation, is a global, activist-based network of print, satellite television, video and radio that is all user-generated (Flew, 2007).

Over past some years, various exclusive citizen journalism news portals have emerged in India as well that are trying their best in inviting and highlighting the unheard voices of citizens. The number of citizen journalism sites is constantly increasing as the number of Internet users and new media writers continues to rise. Although the cost of starting and maintaining a website is low, such activities are not free. Mensing (2007) identifies four basic financial models for online profits: "advertising, subscriptions, transactional and the 'bundled model'."

Advertising has proven to be the most successful source of revenue for online publications. The subscription model has been found to be much harder to implement online than in print. Transactional model involves small charges for connecting people to services or products and earning a small percentage of the resulting income to the link. Bundled sites often use a variety of strategies for financial support, including memberships, advertising, grants and donors. Citizen journalism sites may use any of these models for generating revenue as per their convenience.

Based on the given concept of citizen journalism, following parameters of citizen journalism can be framed:

1. Citizen journalism is the act of non-professionals. People from different walks of life, who are not journalists by profession, contribute towards news gathering and dissemination process.
2. Citizen journalism is participatory in nature. It has enabled citizens participate in journalism, which they do by way of covering newsworthy situations around them and disseminate them among others.
3. Citizen journalism is interactive. Earlier citizens used to be at the receiving end of mainstream media that would run one way. But now they not only send their feedback to mainstream news organisations regarding news coverage, but also share their own stories with fellow citizens.
4. Citizen journalism is technology-dependent. In fact, modern citizen journalism owes its birth to new media technologies. Citizen journalists rely highly on digital technologies, like Internet, camera phones and data sharing devices for covering and sharing their stories.
5. Citizen journalism is a platform for ordinary people to highlight the issues concerning them. It provides an opportunity to citizens to raise their voice like never before.
6. Citizen journalism can act as a source of news for mainstream journalism. It, thus, supplements the job of mainstream journalists and plays a supportive role in the news-gathering process.

EVOLUTION OF CITIZEN JOURNALISM

The history of 'citizen journalism' is vast and needs to be thoroughly understood. Citizen journalism is generally seen as a new trend in journalism. However, some media researchers argue that citizen journalism has a history older than professional journalism. What makes it appear new could be the late assignment of the term 'citizen journalism' formally to journalistic activities of ordinary people. The term is believed to have come to be used following the democratisation of media in the digital era.

The world's first journalism school was established in 1908 (Hughes, 2010), whereas world's earliest newspapers in print were started as early as 1605 ("Happy 400th Birthday for Newspapers," 2005), when there was no concept of professional journalism. In other words, the practice of journalism existed even centuries before journalism schools were thrown open for the first time. This means, by the time professional journalism came into existence, journalism was practised by ordinary people with no professional journalism training. Hughes (2010) points out that the most common misconception about citizen journalism held by people today is that "it is a new phenomenon that emerged with the technological innovations of the late twentieth and early twenty-first centuries."

This is far from the truth. In reality, citizen journalism has been around longer than even the profession of journalism itself. In 1908, the University of Missouri opened the doors of the world's first journalism school, but newspapers had been around for centuries before that. As a matter of fact, early colonial newspapers in the United States had such an impact on the country that founders included a clause in the First Amendment protecting freedom of the press. But if the country had no professional journalists (since the profession had not been created, yet), then what were the framers of the Constitution protect-

ing? The answer is citizen journalists – those with different backgrounds who practiced journalism on the side, despite having no "formal" journalistic background.

Hughes argues that the idea of citizens reporting the news is not new, but "it existed well before professional journalists came about." McCracken (2011) makes a similar argument that there is nothing new about the concept of citizen journalism. He states that citizen journalism has been around since the beginning of print media. "The newfound opportunity for an individual to create and distribute news content via Internet to a mass audience has further fuelled the process of citizen journalism." Armoogum (2013) asserts that citizen journalism has existed for centuries in Europe and Asia.

When a King was to announce an event, his herald would blow a trumpet while riding a horse. The communication was made instantly to an assembly of people. It was quite customary that these people in turn would transmit the news to others through word of mouth. Finally the communication reached the whole society. This way, citizens have contributed significantly to the dissemination of information in ancient times. Some scholars trace the origins of citizen journalism back to seventeenth and eighteenth century pamphleteering.

Fiedler (2009) mentions that "since the invention of the printing press, non-professional writers have shared information and highlighted perceived injustices through pamphlets and brochures." As per a study conducted by Educause Learning Initiative (2007), "over the years, citizen journalism has benefited from the development of various technologies, including the printing press, the telegraph and tape recorders, each of which offered new opportunities for people to participate in sharing news and commentary." However, Fiedler (2009) notes, these early forms of citizen journalism had their restrictions:

Information could only be shared with a limited number of people, and only after a lengthy, and often costly, production process. However, with the onset of the age of Web 2.0 and advent of digital technologies, sharing information with millions of netizens around the world within seconds has become a reality for anyone, who can access the Internet.

Citizen journalism is believed to have a long history in the United States as well. Hughes (2010) observes that "the early American press laid the foundation for modern citizen journalists practicing in the United States. Citizen journalism in the United States dates back to the time of the original 13 colonies." Hughes divulges some interesting facts about how citizen journalism was practised centuries ago, even though the term did not exist at that time.

Boston proved to be the epicentre of the development of colonial newspapers, producing the colonies' first three newspapers. The first (multi-page) newspaper in America, Publick Occurrences Both Forreign and Domestick, was published by what today's standards would classify as a citizen journalist. Its creator was Benjamin Harris...Publick Occurrences was printed on September 25, 1690, and was meant to be a monthly publication. The last page was intentionally left blank so that Bostonians could add news items and notes by hand when forwarding the paper to friends. Unfortunately for Harris, his newspaper was shut down four days after its publication for not operating with a license. Although the first colonial newspaper was unsuccessful, it still laid the framework for news reporting done by the public.

That was a kind of citizen journalism practiced centuries ago. In 2007, Bill Densmore discussed that prior to the Industrial Revolution, things moved at a slower pace and citizens themselves would communicate civic affairs to each other, thus there wasn't much need for a journalist.

But as the world population grew, globalisation occurred, and business and communication took place at a faster pace, citizens were less able to personally experience everything that was going on around them; so the civic sphere began to depend upon proxies of the public to gather critical news—journalists. Stephen Wilmarth, in 2007, stated that the concept of citizen journalism has been constantly changing and evolving every day. He further observed that citizen journalism is redefining the concept of community on the Internet. (as cited in Goh, 2007).

Therefore, citizen journalism can be broadly classified into old citizen journalism and modern citizen journalism. Modern citizen journalism refers to journalistic activities of non-professionals in the post-Internet era, whereas pre-Internet citizen journalism can be termed as old citizen journalism. Internet was first made available for public access in 1992.

The modern citizen journalism emerged towards the end of the twentieth century. Even though freedom of speech had received the recognition as an important human right in the twentieth century, only a small percentage of population could easily share their ideas with many people simultaneously. As Rettberg (2008) points out, listener and reader contributions to mainstream media, such as television, radio and newspapers existed, but were always positioned in carefully boundaried spaces.

In twentieth-century democratic societies, people wishing to have their words and ideas published or broadcast had to contend with editorial policies that were generally based on ideology or on what advertisers would support or the public would buy. In such a media landscape, many stories would never be deemed 'newsworthy' enough to be heard. In non-democratic societies, censorship and ideological suppression by the state stopped other kinds of stories from reaching an audience. In either case, those who did own a press were not able to spread their ideas.

Rettberg opines that "the Internet changed one of the greatest obstacles to true freedom of the press by eliminating or greatly reducing the cost of production and distribution. By the end of the twentieth century, bloggers could, in effect, own a press—'modem'—a modern and lightweight version of the press. This new freedom to publish at will has caused journalists and editors to re-evaluate the role of mainstream and professional media."

Meyer (1995) points out that "the modern citizen journalist movement took place after journalists themselves began to question the predictability of their coverage of such events as the 1988 U.S. presidential elections. Those journalists became part of the public, or civic, journalism movement, a countermeasure against the eroding trust in the news media and widespread public disillusionment with politics and civic affairs."

Jay Rosen, notable blogger and a Journalism Professor at New York University, was one of the earliest proponents of public journalism movement. Nandi (2006) mentions that from 1993 to 1997, he directed the Project on *Public Life and the Press,* funded by the Knight Foundation and housed at New York University.

Former Wichita Eagle editor Davis "Buzz" Merit steered his newspapers in a public journalism direction and wrote 'Public Journalism and Public Life', published in 1995. Academics and others, who had written about the topic include Ted Glaser, Philip Meyer and his students, Arthur Charity, Lewis Friedland, Jeff Dvorkin, Leonard Witt, Herbert Gans, and Jan Schaffer. Initially, discussions of public journalism focused on promoting journalism that was 'for the people' by changing the way professional reporters did their work.

As per a report of Pew Center for Civic Journalism (2002), at least 20 percent of the 1,500 daily U.S. newspapers practiced some form of civic journalism between 1994 and 2001. Nearly all, said it, had a positive effect on the community. Miller and Kurpius (2008) state that "one of the goals of civic journalism is to more accurately portray the views of people in their communities dealing with the issues that are the central focus of the news coverage. Thus, citizen sources are given a consistent voice on the issues and are not simply used as storytelling devices to open or close news stories, as is often seen in media coverage nowadays."

According to Leonard Witt, however, early public journalism efforts were often part of 'special projects' that were expensive, time-consuming and episodic.

Too often these projects dealt with an issue and moved on. Journalists were driving the discussion. They would say, 'Let's do a story on welfare-to-work (or the environment, or traffic problems or the economy)', and then they would recruit a cross-section of citizen and chronicle their points of view. Since not all reporters and editors bought into public journalism, and some outright opposed it, reaching out to the people from the newsroom was never an easy task. By 2003, in fact, the movement seemed to be petering out, with the Pew Center for Civic Journalism closing its doors. Simultaneously, however, journalism that was 'by the people' began to flourish, enabled in part by emerging Internet and networking technologies, such as weblogs, chat rooms, message boards, wikis and mobile computing (Nandi, 2006).

This 'by the people' journalism came to be termed as citizen journalism. Stephens (2012) argue that "although civic journalism did not succeed in traditional news to the extent that media researchers would have liked, that does not mean all hope is lost for citizen voice in the news production and information distribution process. As the Internet's presence increases within traditional news structures, new forms for citizen participation present themselves."

According to the Pew Internet and American Life Project (*One Year Later: September 11 and the Internet*), the terrorist attacks of September 11, 2001, generated the most traffic to traditional news sites in the history of the web. Many large news sites buckled under the immense demand and people turned to e-mail, weblogs and forums "as conduits for information, commentary, and action related to 9/11 events." The response on the Internet gave rise to a new proliferation of "do-it-yourself journalism." Everything from eyewitness accounts and photo galleries to commentary and personal storytelling emerged to help people collectively grasp the confusion, anger and loss felt in the wake of the tragedy. Before the Iraq war, which erupted in 2003, the *British Broadcasting Corporation (BBC)* knew that it could not possibly deploy enough photojournalists to cover the millions of people worldwide who marched in anti-war demonstrations. Reaching out to its audience, the *BBC News* asked readers to send in images taken with digital cameras and cell phones with built-in cameras, and it published the best ones on its website. During the first few days of the war in Iraq, Pew Internet and American Life Project *(The Internet and the Iraq War: How Online Americans Have Used the Internet to Learn War News, Understand*

Events, and Promote their Views) found that 17 percent of online Americans used the Internet as their principal source of information about the Iraq war, a level more than five times greater than those who got their news online immediately after the September 11 terrorist attacks (3 percent). The report also noted that "weblogs (were) gaining some following among a small number of Internet users (4 percent)" (as cited in Bowman & Willis, 2003). Kellett (2008) discusses that during the Iraq war, weblogs such as *'Where is Raed?'* allowed the world to see the invasion of Iraq from a *Sunni* perspective. *Where is Raed* is maintained from Baghdad by a citizen Salam Pax, reporting on the situation in the city. In other words, an individual not representative of any government contributed meaningfully to the coverage of the news story.

Immediately after the Columbia Space Shuttle Disaster, which occurred on February 1, 2003, news and government organisations, in particular *The Dallas Morning News* and NASA, called upon the public to submit eyewitness accounts and photographs that might lead to clues to the cause of the spacecraft's disintegration. In another instance, presidential candidate Howard Dean guest-blogged on Larry Lessig's weblog for a week in July 2003. A future president of the United States might be chosen not only on his or her merits, charisma, experience or voting record, but on the basis of how well he or she blogs. *ABCNews.com's 'The Note'* covered 2004 political candidates and gave each an individual weblog to comment back on what was reported (as cited in Bowman & Willis, 2003). During the 2004 U.S. presidential elections, both the Democratic and Republican parties issued press credentials to citizen bloggers covering the convention, making a new level of influence and credibility of nontraditional journalists. Some bloggers also began to watchdog the work of conventional journalists, monitoring their work for biases and inaccuracy. A recent trend in citizen journalism has been the emergence of what New York academic and blogger Jeff Jarvis terms 'hyperlocal journalism', as online news sites invite contributions from local residents of their subscription areas, who often report on topics that conventional newspapers tend to ignore (Nandi, 2006). Hyperlocal websites are online repositories of news and information unique to a specific town or neighbourhood, with content largely provided by unpaid contributors. These websites may be created by existing news companies, entrepreneurs or activists (Kelly, 2009).

Kovach and Rosenstiel (2007) argue that technology has enabled citizens to be players in the news and become partners of traditional media in times of crisis. On the morning of July 7, 2005, three bombs exploded in the London subway, followed shortly by an explosion on a double-decker bus. The suicide bombings killed fifty-two people in an attack evocative of the 2004 train explosions in Madrid. The *BBC* threw its staff at this important story, trying to get the information. Meanwhile, on the same day, the *BBC* received unprecedented help from London residents. Six hours after the attack, the organisation counted more than 1,000 photographs, twenty video clips, 4,000 text messages, and 20,000 emails—all sent in by citizens. Despite the surprise response, the *BBC* made good use of the material, going as far as to open a newscast with video footage received from citizens. The *BBC* had always encouraged citizen involvement in the news, but this level of participation was new. Director of the news division of *BBC,* Richard Sambrook (2005) writes that the quantity and quality of the public's contributions moved them beyond novelty, tokenism or the exceptional and raised major implications that they are still working through. The *BBC* holds a license from the government that enables it to experiment with citizen journalism and social networks. The *BBC* model of interacting with citizens proves that dramatic events are not the only time when citizen journalists can or should be used. For instance, a participatory media project called *Island Blogging* was started by local authorities on the islands off the coast of Scotland with the help of the *BBC Scotland.* Islanders were issued a personal computer and a narrowband web connection, which they put to use posting pictures and stories, and sparking debates on numerous community issues. They even broke news, such as the beaching of a whale, later picked up by mainstream Scottish media.

On many occasions citizen journalists have reported breaking news stories mostly through social media. The social networking and micro-blogging website, *Twitter,* is one of the main platforms available to people, which they can use to upload content. Famous examples include militant group *Al-Qaeda's* founder Osama bin Laden's raid and death, one of the biggest news stories of 2011, which was reported unwittingly in tweets by a local Information Technology consultant a day before President Barack Obama announced it to the world (Horton, 2013). Sohaib Athar, a 33-year-old blogger living in Abbottabad, Pakistan, live-tweeted Osama bin Laden's death on May 2, 2011. *"Helicopter hovering above Abbottabad at 1 AM (is a rare event),"* he wrote on *Twitter* through his account *ReallyVirtual.* Later Barack Obama called a rare evening press conference to announce the news (Gross, 2012). Similarly American recording artist, singer and actress Whitney Houston's death in 2012 was reported on *Twitter* over an hour before any mainstream press picked up on it. Additionally, the live chase for the men guilty of the Boston Marathon bombings in April 2013 saw news channels relying heavily upon the updates of citizens living in the area to establish what was happening. This was captured through videos, photographs, tweets, *Skype* calls, blogs and many more mediums (Horton, 2013).

Citizen Journalism has played a vital role in the reporting of major global events and provides on-the-street accounts of events unfolding around the world, such as the 2009 Iranian elections, Arab Spring, 2013 protests in Turkey, Japanese Earthquake and Occupy movement (National Digital Stewardship Alliance, 2013). In all such events, citizen journalists have broken news stories even before professional journalists by presenting the first-hand account of the impact of the events. The dramatic street protests following the Iranian elections of June 2009 provided one of the best examples of how the new Internet tools like *YouTube, Facebook* and *Twitter* began to change the way media content is produced, distributed and consumed. The role of participatory and social media in Iran and earlier examples such as the 26/11 Mumbai attacks caused blogger Jeff Jarvis (2008) to argue that 'the witnesses are taking over the news' that is contemporary times are witnessing a historic shift of control from traditional news organisations to the audience themselves.

The Arab Spring is a media term for demonstrations and protests, riots, and civil wars in the Arab world that began on December 18, 2010. Salama (2012) outlines that "the Arab Spring has been a defining term for media, both Arab and foreign, forcing journalists to grapple with unconventional and extremely challenging circumstances, from the interruption of Egypt's Internet and mobile phone services during protests, to captivity and detention in Libya, to the virtual blackout of ground reporting by mainstream international media outlets in Syria."

"The obstacle for news organisations throughout the pan-Arab revolt has been to continue finding ways to tell the story while maintaining the objectivity. It has been in this backdrop that citizens of Arab nations resorted to covering themselves the situations in their respective places. The Arab Spring uprisings are believed to have been proliferated by citizen journalism."

IFEX (2013) reports that "citizen journalists have been at the forefront of documenting the Arab Spring uprisings – often in response to shortcomings in the mainstream and government-controlled media." Knight (2012) illustrates that "during the Arab Spring, citizen journalists, using *Facebook, Twitter,* emails and iPhones, undermined state censorship and contributed to the success of massive pro-democracy demonstrations in places like Cairo and Tunisia. In Iran, many of the activists were arrested, while in case of the Iranian ally, Syria, the government attacked them with tanks." Corthesy (2012) discusses that "social media in the Arab world gained credibility as effective tools that could be used to help rebels fight repressive regimes."

With the flourishing growth of social networking technologies, such as blogs and chat rooms, the Arab Spring proved to be one of the biggest events, in which social media became the primary tool for spreading the word, uniting the people, and providing journalists and reporters with sources. Protesters risked their lives daily in the hopes of making a change in their societies.

The news agency *Al-Jazeera* that began experimenting with its *Sharek Portal* in 2007 was well-positioned to capture striking first-person views during the Arab Spring uprisings of 2010 and 2011. The portal allowed *Al-Jazeera* to cover a variety of stories in places where reporters were neither safe nor welcome. *Al-Jazeera's* work in citizen journalism started as mobile devices with video cameras began taking off. The organisation has now taken its citizen journalism portal a little farther, with a re-designed *Sharek Portal.* Citizens can submit videos to *Al-Jazeera* through email or the smartphone apps the agency has created. For those with lesser advanced phones, *Al-Jazeera* also accepts reports through SMS (Dreier, 2012). Simon (2012) divulges how citizen journalism helped people in Egypt highlight atrocities meted out to them by authorities when the latter enforced information blackout in the country:

The most important battles of the Arab Spring were fought on the streets, but there was also a fierce battle over control of information. In Egypt, the government unplugged the Internet, shut down satellite channels, and orchestrated attacks on foreign correspondents. None of it worked. Protesters were able to keep channels of communication open to win sympathy and support for their cause, highlight the Egyptian government's record of abuse and corruption, and ensure there would be witnesses to any violence against them. The global visibility of the protests raised the cost of government repression to the point where it became unsustainable. The new information platforms such as Twitter and Facebook helped journalists and other citizens break (former Egyptian President) Hosni Mubarak's information blockade has been the source of legitimate excitement.

Salama (2012) observes that "Syrian activists (citizen journalists) have been defying government blocks and censorship by uploading videos online, often supplying foreign media organisations with what little footage they are able to access. The desperate hope is that their message will be heard and the plight of the Syrian people will not go ignored by the international community." Salama further notes that "a new set of challenges have emerged in Syria as part of the effort to report the Arab Spring, as domestic and foreign journalists are increasingly deemed targets by President Bashar al-Assad's regime. Foreign journalists have been forced to take one of the three approaches to tell the story in Syria: enter through official channels in Damascus at the mercy of government minders; enter clandestinely through Lebanon or Turkey and thus subjecting themselves to serious danger; or report remotely and have citizen journalists inside Syria relay the news."

The *Voice of America's* David Arnold (2012) mentions that "in response to media gag enforced by the government of President Bashar al-Assad, hundreds of Syrian activists picked up smart phones to visually document events and report in 140 characters or less about the conflict." Terming citizen journalists as "army of self-anointed reporters", Arnold says that they have uploaded thousands upon thousands of *YouTube* videos, and used *Twitter, Facebook,* and *Skype* in heretofore almost unimagined ways to show the world that their government was committing unspoken atrocities against its own people. "Few of Syria's new breed of citizen-journalists reveal their real names. Many have fled their homes to avoid being uncovered by Syrian authorities in a country, which journalist advocacy organisations are now calling the most dangerous place in the world for reporters."

The consequences of citizen journalists covering Arab Spring uprisings have been severe many a time. Many citizen journalists have been detained, tortured and even killed while trying to reveal the ground situations in the Arab world, especially in Syria. Many of them armed with a camera lens or mobile phone to bring the world images from Syria, Libya, Egypt, Tunisia and elsewhere lost their lives during the process. In May 2012, Abdul Ghani Kaakeh, a 19-year-old citizen journalist, died after he was allegedly targeted by security forces while filming a demonstration in Aleppo, Syria's biggest city. Kaakeh was shot in the neck while filming a demonstration. He was believed to have been targeted because of his activities. Earlier Kaakeh was reported to have been arrested several times for posting footage of demonstrations on the Internet (UNESCO, 2012). In another incident in May 2012, Bassel Shahade, a 28-year-old film student at Syracuse University, was killed in the city of Homs as he filmed clashes between protestors and security forces and aftermath of attacks by government security forces (Raftery, 2012). A citizen journalist, namely Mohammad Abdelmawla al-Hariri, was issued a death sentence in May 2012 for "high treason and contacts with foreign parties. He was arrested in connection with an interview he had given to the news organisation *Al-Jazeera* about unrest in his hometown of Dara'a (Reporters Without Borders, 2012a). Another citizen journalist, Wael Omar Bard, was shot at the heart on June 20, 2012, when he was filming the conflict. Bard, a native of Syria, lived in Saudi Arabia before the uprising. When the conflict broke out, he decided to return to Syria, and was armed with just a video camera (Global Journalist, 2012). Citizen journalist Omar Al-Ghantawi, 19, was killed by a sniper while filming the shelling of the districts of Jobar and Al-Sultaniyeh in Homs on June 21, 2012. He had given up his job as a mobile phone technician in order to cover the revolution and had shot hundreds of photos and videos documenting the Assad regime's atrocities. Ghias Khaled Al-Hmouria was shot dead while filming an operation by the rebel Free Syrian Army in the Damascus suburb of Douma on June 25, 2012. Citizen journalist Suhaib Dib, a secondary school student, was killed by the security forces in the Damascus suburb of Al-Meliha on July 4, 2012. He had been circulating news reports and content about the uprising and the government crackdown (Reporters Without Borders, 2012b). Later on May 21, 2013, a 14-year-old citizen journalist, Omar Qatifaan, was killed while covering clashes between the Syrian Army and the rebel Free Army in the southern Daraa al-Ballad area of Syria near the border with Jordan (Alhames, 2013). The death toll continues to rise.

A study of women cyber-activists in several Arab countries, titled *'Unveiling the Revolutionaries: Cyberactivism and Women's Role in the Arab Uprisings'*, found that 'a significant proportion of cyberactivism revolves around influencing the mainstream media agenda, as an increasingly symbiotic relationship between citizen and professional journalism has developed throughout the Arab Spring' (Radsch, 2012). Crouch (2012) mentions that "a rise in citizen-generated video during the Arab revolutions created space for mainstream media in these countries to report the uprisings and amplify the protesters' message. Citizen journalism gave established and official media outlets a 'political cover' to address topics long kept under wraps, says a report by the Committee to Protect Journalists, an independent watchdog based in New York." The Arab Spring has lead mainstream photojournalists use camera phones for covering some major events on the lines of citizen journalists.

David Batty (2011) notes that photographs and videos from the public have been increasingly used in media coverage. The camera phones entered the mainstream of photojournalism in 2011 due to a combination of the Arab uprisings, the Occupy protests and improved technology. *The Guardian,* wire agencies and major broadcasters use many more camera phone and video images than ever before. Batty, while quoting Michele McNally, Assistant Managing Editor for photography at the *New York Times,* writes, the use of mobile phones in news coverage by professional photojournalists has increased a hundredfold, and that's largely because of the Arab spring. Citizen media was an "instant document" of an event rather than a replacement for skilled photojournalism, Michele McNally was quoted as saying.

Mishra and Krishnaswami (2015) conclude that citizen journalism did not have much effect on the media or the citizens a few years ago, but with the advancement in technology and access to Internet and mobile phones applications, "citizens began actively participating in events and reporting news as their came across and sharing on common platform. Looking at the potential and speed at which news and information were shared media started to use their contents, videos and Photographs as a result more and more came forward and began to act as Citizen journalist. Now, with the growing trend of Citizen Journalism, citizens are making a serious effort to bring in whatever they think is important in the forefront, which has been neglected by the media."

SIGNIFICANCE OF CITIZEN JOURNALISM

Citizen journalism has proved significant wherever mainstream media has failed to make it owing to time constraints, inaccessibility, organisational policy issues or personal biases. It has drawn attention to issues that are otherwise skipped by professional journalists. Paul (2011) argues that most of the media audiences are usually disappointed by not finding many stories of their interest. The author further writes, "by allowing multiple voices to be heard from all points of view, everyone has the chance to become contributors, provided that the editor shows no bias toward a specific ideology. As a result, open-minded readers have access to a more nuanced and rounded assessment of an issue. Topics that may not have even made it into the local print publications have unlimited space to be published, something unheard of in traditional print models. Personal stories, little stories, quips, ramblings, pictures, videos, news, gossip, are all given a place in this emerging redefinition of what news is, and can be."

Media researchers observe that citizen journalism assumes great significance at the time of accidents and natural disasters, when it becomes difficult for professional journalists to reach the spot on time and cover the newsworthy situations. As per a study conducted by The Open News Room (2011), given the sheer magnitude and the impact of a number of natural disasters (such as *the 2004 Boxing Day tsunamis in Southeast Asia*) that occurred in the last few years, "it would have been very challenging for any media organisation to cover, no matter how deep their pockets are."

Journalist Steve Outing (2005), shares on *Poynter.org* that the earthquakes and tsunamis in South Asia and their aftermath "represented a tipping point in citizen journalism, a fact, which is now common knowledge and alluded to by many in the media and in communication research." Similarly, Educause Learning Initiative (2007) writes that citizen journalism epitomises the belief that "the experiences of people personally involved with an issue present a different—and often more complete—picture of events than can be derived from the perspective of an outsider."

LIMITATIONS OF CITIZEN JOURNALISM

No doubt potential benefits of citizen journalism as a source of up-to-date news have been widely acknowledged by media professionals and researchers. However, as per some debates, the risks and disadvantages of citizen journalism outweigh its benefits and advantages. The ability to hide behind the anonymity of Internet and potentially share false information is believed to be the biggest risk of citizen journalism. Media researchers fear that given the instantaneous nature of the Internet and its global reach, people with hidden agenda while concealing their identity can post fake stories and spread them globally within no time. Since they have no ethics and media laws to worry about unlike in mainstream media, citizen journalists can invite an anonymous debate based on bogus or unverified information.

So far thousands of stories have been uploaded by citizen journalists on the Internet. Some of these stories have risen to prominence for the wrong reasons. Such stories serve as a reminder of the dangers of publishing stories from anonymous, untrained sources or without verifying the information. One of the instances that illustrates dangers of citizen journalism is a hoax story posted on *CNN's* citizen journalism site *iReport* on October 3, 2008, which headlined *'Steve Jobs rushed to ER following severe heart attack'.* Since (late) Steve Jobs was the Chief Operating Officer of the multinational corporation, *Apple,* the story affected the company's share price, according to a story done by *San Francisco Chronicle* journalist, Reyhan Harmanci (2008).

There are numerous other instances, wherein unverified reports have been posted on Internet only to turn out to be false or manipulated. Such incidents raise a question over the authenticity of citizen journalism. Potential false news reports are just one of the many possible ramifications of sourcing news from anonymous sources. The Open News Room (2011) presumes that the news could be factually correct, but have flaws like "blatant disregard of ethics, lack of objectivity, impartiality and balance." In this context, noted columnist and a Professor of Journalism Ethics, Stephen J. A. Ward (2012) raises various ethical questions and concerns over unregulated nature of citizen journalism and what he terms as 'new news media'. One of the issues raised is manipulation of images. Ward has raised some questions in this regard: "Can newsrooms trust the easily obtained images of citizens and citizen journalists? Who is the sender and how do we know that this image is really of the event in question?" Another issue is whether a citizen used technology to alter the photograph, say, to add an object to the picture or to take an object out. Ward argues that "democratisation of media – technology that allows citizens to engage in journalism and publication of many kinds – blurs the identity of journalists and the idea of what constitutes journalism. In the previous century, journalists were a clearly defined group. For the most part, they were professionals who wrote for major mainstream newspapers and broadcasters. The public had no great difficulty in identifying members of the 'press'. Today, however, citizens without journalistic training and who do not work for mainstream media calls themselves journalists, or write in ways that fall under the general description of a journalist as someone who regularly writes on public issues for the public or audience."

The unregulated nature of citizen journalism has drawn criticism from media researchers and professional journalists for being too subjective, amateurish and haphazard in quality and coverage. In May 2013, in an address to the students of the *Express Institute of Media Studies (EXIMS),* Shekhar Gupta, Editor-in-Chief of the *Express Group,* mentioned today everybody who has a mobile phone or a laptop and an opinion thinks he is a journalist. He argued that journalism needs training and skills, whereas hidden cameras and spy-cams can only be tools, and not shortcuts to journalism. "You give me citizen doctors and citizen lawyers and I will give you citizen journalists" ("Technology has changed way we work," 2013). Many research works have found that the citizen journalism articles lack quality and content. Tom Grubisich (2005) reviews ten new citizen journalism sites and finds many of them lacking in quality and content. He concludes that "the sites with the weakest editorial content are able to aggressively expand because they have stronger financial resources." An academic paper by Vincent Maher (2005), the head of the New Media Lab at Rhodes University, outlines several weaknesses in the claims made by citizen journalists in terms of the "three deadly E's", referring to ethics, economics and epistemology. Staff writer of *Washington Post* Jennifer Harper (2008) writes that the "prospects for user-created content appear limited and less valuable" and that "the much-ballyhooed world of citizen blogs, meanwhile, may have limitations." Former Chicago Tribune publisher Jack Fuller (1996), in his book *News Values*, sums it up well: "The new interactive medium both threatens the status quo and promises an exciting new way of learning about the world." This deftly describes both camps of opinion concerning participation by the audience in journalism.

George (2005) examines *Backfence,* a citizen journalism site, which attracted limited citizen contributions. He mentions, "clicking through *Backfence's* pages feels like frontier land– remote, often lonely, zoned for people but not home to any. The site recently launched for Arlington, Virginia. However, without more settlers, *Backfence* may wind up creating more ghost towns." An editorial published by The Digital Journalist web magazine (2005) expresses a similar position, advocating to abolish the term "citizen journalist", and replacing it with "citizen news gatherer". Educause Learning Initiative (2007) too mentions that the quality of any citizen journalism project reflects "the contributions of those, who choose to participate, and such projects can be havens for triviality or unreliable content."

CITIZEN JOURNALISM VS. MAINSTREAM JOURNALISM

As citizen journalism is growing, more and more people are looking at its relationship with mainstream journalism. At the onset of the current millennium, media researchers predicted the demise of mainstream journalism at the hands of citizen journalism. They feared that mainstream journalism shall lose its audience to citizen journalism, since the latter was the creation of the audience itself. However, on the other hand, many scholars dismissed the argument, saying citizen journalism does not have potential to replace professional journalism. The news content produced by professional journalists still holds more credibility and authenticity in the eyes of the audiences as compared to citizen journalism content. The former argument has been supported by Bowman and Willis (2003), who state that the hegemony of professional journalism as gatekeeper of the news content is threatened as much by the audience it serves as by new technology and competitors:

Armed with easy-to-use web publishing tools, always-on connections and increasingly powerful mobile devices, the online audience has the means to become an active participant in the creation and dissemination of news and information. And it's doing just that on the Internet.

A similar conclusion has been drawn by the Project for Excellence in Journalism (2008) in their annual report. It has concluded that while a lot of communications researchers and scholars have been "scripting the demise of the profession at the hands of citizen journalists or the contributors", some research suggests that "citizen journalism is an overrated phenomenon. The prospects for user-created content once thought possibly central to the next era of journalism, now appear more limited. News people report that the most promising parts of citizen input are new ideas, sources, comments, pictures, and videos. But citizens posting news content has proved less valuable, with too little that is new or verifiable."

Many scholars, however, have put forward entirely opposite views. Bentley (2008) affirms that citizen journalism can never replace professional journalism. He argues that citizen journalists want people hear them just because professional journalists are "too busy with the big stories to see the little items that mean so much to people." Former Baltimore *Sun* reporter and writer/producer of the popular TV series, *'The Wire'*, David Simon (2005) criticises the concept of citizen journalism—claiming that unpaid bloggers can never replace trained, professional and seasoned journalists:

I am offended to think that anyone, anywhere believes American institutions as insulated, self-preserving and self-justifying as police departments, school systems, legislatures and chief executives can be held to gathered facts by amateurs pursuing the task without compensation, training or, for that matter, sufficient standing to make public officials even care to whom it is they are lying to.

While citizen journalism content is generally seen as haphazard and incredible, mainstream journalists also misreport facts occasionally that are correctly reported by citizen journalists. In this context, many researchers have highlighted citizen journalists' role in supplementing the work of mainstream journalists. They conclude that citizen journalism plays a supportive role in the news-gathering process, thus complementing rather than replacing professional journalism. Deuze, Bruns and Neuberger (2007) investigate the emergence of citizen journalism in Australia, Germany, the Netherlands and the United States to find out how mainstream media is using citizen journalism content:

For all its success, citizen journalism remains dependent to a significant extent on mainstream news organisations, whose output it debates, critiques, recombines and debunks by harnessing large and distributed communities of users. At the same time, increasingly mainstream news is taking note of what the citizen journalists are saying, and uses content generated by users as an alternative to vox-pops, opinion polls, or in some cases indeed as a partial replacement of editorial work.

According to a study published in the *Newspaper Research Journal,* citizen journalism sites, including both news sites and blogs, complement rather than substitute commercial news sites. The study conducted by Lacy, Duffy, Riffe, Thorson and Fleming (2010) evaluated which sites publish content on a daily basis, and how similar the content is between citizen and mainstream sources. The researchers at Michigan State University, the University of Missouri, and the University of North Carolina examined content from 86 citizen blog sites, 53 citizen news sites and 63 daily newspaper sites in June and July 2009. The researchers noted that like weeklies, citizen news and blog sites can serve as complements to daily newspapers.

Nel, Ward and Rawlinson (2007) state that unless citizens improve upon their contributions in the form of news photographs and videos, their content shall struggle for time and attention. Kellet (2008) makes a mention of the process of consolidation started by traditional media in 1990s that resulted "in previously independent news voices being absorbed into ever larger corporations." The author further writes that initially these voices were widely ignored. However, "as the voices became louder, traditional media began to evaluate the contribution that the citizen journalist could bring to its coverage of the news. Traditional media began to include web-based content in their respective mediums and the blossoming of citizen journalism continued."

Figure 1. Direct citizen journalism model

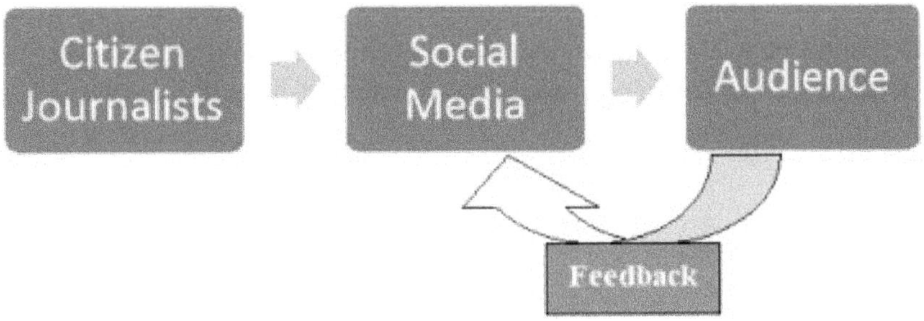

Figure 2. Ideal citizen journalism model

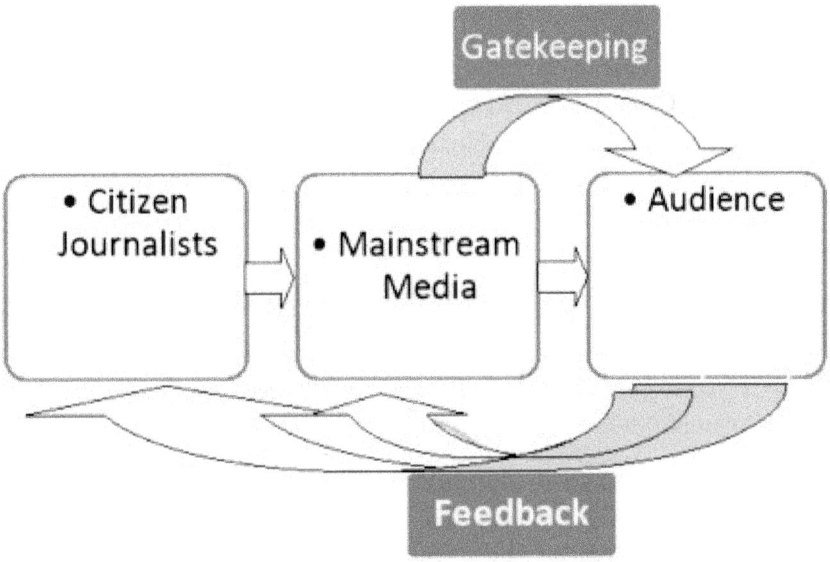

CITIZEN JOURNALISM MODELS

The author proposes two models of citizen journalism, viz., *Direct Citizen Journalism Model* that deals with citizen journalism through social media **(Figure 1),** and *Ideal Citizen Journalism Model,* which stresses on implementation of gatekeeping by mainstream media for citizen journalism content **(Figure 2).** In *Direct Citizen Journalism Model,* citizens post their submissions directly on social media like blogs and social networking sites, and make them public without the intervention of the mainstream media. They also receive direct feedback from the audience.

In *Ideal Citizen Journalism Model,* citizens approach mainstream media with their stories, while the later verifies their authenticity, before making them public, through the process of gatekeeping. In mainstream media, gatekeeping is done by experienced and trained journalists and editors, using their tools and skills, and in-house or commercial stylebooks, such as the *Associated Press Stylebook.* These trained journalists are ideal to filter citizen journalism content as well. This way, citizen journalists can disseminate their stories among the audience in a professional manner. The audiences can send their feedback either to the citizen journalists since their byline is given in the story (provided their contact information is available) or to the mainstream news organisation publishing citizens' contents, or to both. The *Ideal Citizen Journalism Model* can work wonders in revealing the facts that often skip the attention of professional journalists. It is citizen journalists' prerogative to choose any of these models for publicising their content.

REFERENCES

Alhames, R. (2013, May 22). *14-year-old Citizen Journalist Killed Covering Clashes in Syria.* Retrieved from http://globalvoicesonline.org/2013/05/22/teen-citizen-journalist-killed-in-syria/

Armoogum, N. (2013). *Can Citizen Journalists produce Professional Journalism?* Center for International Media Ethics. Retrieved from http://www.cimethics.org/home/newsletter/jun2013/Nanda%20 Armoogum_EDITED.pdf

Arnold, D. (2012, June 30). *Syrian-Armenians Seek A New Life Far From Fighting.* Retrieved from http://www.rferl.org/content/syria-war-reported-by-citizen-journalists-social-media/24630841.html

Baase, S. (2008). *A Gift of Fire* (3rd ed.). Lebanon: Prentice Hall.

Batty, D. (2011, December 29). Arab Spring Leads Surge in Events Captured on Cameraphones. *The Guardian.* Retrieved from http://www.theguardian.com/world/2011/dec/29/arab-spring-captured-on-cameraphones

Bentley, C. H. (2004). *Wanted: Your Ideas, Your Prose, Your Photos.* Retrieved from http://groups.yahoo.com/group/freecycleColumbiaMO/

Bentley, C. H. (2008, June 20-21). *Citizen Journalism: Back to the Future.* Discussion paper presented at the Carnegie Knight Conference on the Future of Journalism, Cambridge, MA. Retrieved from http://blogimg.ohmynews.com/attach/752/1098233647.pdf

Bentley, C. H., Hamman, B., Littau, J., Meyer, H., Watson, H., & Welsh, B. (2005). *The Citizen Journalism Movement: MyMissourian as a Case Study.* Presented at AEJMC Annual Convention San Antonio, Texas. Retrieved from http://citizenjournalism.missouri.edu/researchpapers/casestudy.doc

Bowman, S., & Willis, C. (2003). *We Media: How Audiences are Shaping the Future of News and Information.* Reston, VA: The Media Center at the American Press Institute. Retrieved from http://www.hypergene.net/wemedia/weblog.php?id=P36#5

Bruns, A. (2009, September 9-10). *Citizen Journalism and Everyday Life: A Case Study of Germany's myHeimat.de.* Paper presented at Future of Journalism Conference, Cardiff, UK. Retrieved from http://snurb.info/files/2010/Citizen%20Journalism%20and%20Everyday%20Life.pdf

Cohn, D. (2007, November 15). *Time Citizen Journalism Pulled Its Acts Together.* Retrieved from http://www.pressgazette.co.uk/node/39443

Coleman, S. (2001). The Transformation of Citizenship? In B. Axford & R. Huggins (Eds.), *New Media and Politics* (p. 111). London: SAGE Publications. doi:10.4135/9781446218846.n5

Computer Hope. (n.d.). *Who Invented the Internet?* Retrieved from http://www.computerhope.com/issues/ch001016.htm

Corthesy, J. (2012). *The Frayed Edges of Citizen Journalism: An Analysis of Al Jazeera's Relationship with Citizen Journalism*. Geneva: Webster University. Retrieved from www.webster.ch/sites/www.webster.ch/files/Cortesy.pdf

Coyer, K., Dowmunt, T., & Fountain, A. (2007). *The Alternative Media Handbook*. London: Routledge Taylor and Francis Group.

Crouch, D. (2012, February 21). *Arab Media Make Most of Citizen Journalism*. Retrieved from http://www.ft.com/cms/s/0/6e224b6a-5bb2-11e1-a447-00144feabdc0.html#axzz2az4ozSTE

Deuze, M., Bruns, A., & Neuberger, C. (2007, September 19). Preparing for an Age of Participatory News. *Journalism Practice*, *1*(3), 322–338. doi:10.1080/17512780701504864

Dreier, T. (2012, August-September). Al-Jazeera Enables Citizen Journalism With Online Video. *Streaming Media Magazine*. Retrieved from http://www.streamingmedia.com/Articles/Editorial/Featured-Articles/Al-Jazeera-Enables-Citizen-Journalism-With-Online-Video-84268.aspx

Duffy, M., Thorson, E., & Jahng, M. (2010, June 22). *Comparing Legacy News Sites with Citizen News and Blog Sites: Where is the Best Journalism?* Paper presented at the Annual Meeting of the International Communication Association, Suntec Singapore International Convention and Exhibition Centre, Suntec City, Singapore.

Educause Learning Initiative. (2007, November). *7 Things You Should Know About Citizen Journalism*. Retrieved from http://net.educause.edu/ir/library/pdf/ELI7031.pdf

Fiedler, T. (2009). Crisis Alert: Barack Obama Meets a Citizen Journalist. In S. Allan & E. Thorson (Eds.), *Citizen Journalism: Global Perspectives* (p. 211). New York: Peter Lang Publishing.

Flew, T. (2007). *A Citizen Journalism Primer.* Presented to Communications Policy Research Forum, University of Technology, Sydney, Australia. Retrieved from http://eprints.qut.edu.au/10232/1/10232.pdf

Fuller, J. (1996). *News Values: Ideas for an Information Age*. University of Chicago Press.

Ganesh, T. K. (2006). *Digital Media: Building the Global Audience*. Delhi: GNOSIS Publishers of Educational Books.

George, E. (2005, November 30). *Guest Writer Liz George of Baristanet Reviews Backfence.com Seven Months After Launch.* Pressthink. Retrieved from http://archive.pressthink.org/2005/11/30/lz_bcfc.html

Gillmor, D. (2004). *We the Media: Grassroots Journalism by the People, for the People*. Sebastopol, CA: O'Reilly Media. doi:10.1145/1012807.1012808

Gillmor, D. (2006). We the Media: Grassroots Journalism by the People, For the People. Beijing: O'Reilly.

Gillmor, D. (2008, July 14). *Where Did "Citizen Journalist" Come From?* Retrieved from http://citmedia.org/blog/2008/07/14/where-did-citizen-journalist-come-from/

Glaser, M. (2006, September 27). *Digging Deeper: Your Guide to Citizen Journalism.* Retrieved from http://www.pbs.org/mediashift/2006/09/your-guide-to-citizen-journalism270.html

Global Journalist. (2012, July 26). *Citizen and Professional Journalists Killed While Covering Conflicts in Syria.* Retrieved from http://www.globaljournalist.org/freepresswatch/2012/07/syria/citizen-and-professional-journalists-killed-while-covering-conflicts-in-syria/

Goh, R. (2007, April 20). *Mainstream Media Meets Citizen Journalism: In Search of a New Model* (CMS Senior Thesis). Retrieved from http://www.mediagiraffe.org/tufts-thesis/tufts-thesis.pdf

Graham, M. (2004). Networks of Influence: Internet Activism in Australia and Beyond. In G. Goggin (Ed.), *Virtual Nation: The Internet in Australia* (pp. 76–83). Sydney: University of New South Wales Press.

Gross, D. (2012, March 12). *Tweeting Osama's Death: The Accidental Citizen Journalist.* Retrieved from http://edition.cnn.com/2012/03/10/tech/social-media/twitter-osama-death/

Grubisich, T. (2005, October 5). Grassroots Journalism: Actual Content Vs. Shining Ideal. *Online Journalism Review.* Retrieved from http://www.ojr.org/p051006/

Happy 400th Birthday for Newspapers: Gutenberg Museum Says Birth Certificate of First Newspaper Dated 1605, And Not 1609. (2005, March 3). *The Times of India,* p. 13.

Hargreaves, I. (1999). The Ethical Boundaries of Reporting. In M. Ungersma (Ed.), *Reporters and the Reported* (p. 4). Cardiff, UK: Centre for Journalism Studies.

Harmanci, R. (2008, October 5). Citizen Journalism Carries Unique Pitfalls. *San Francisco Chronicle.* Retrieved from http://www.sfgate.com/cgibin/article.cgi?f=/c/a/2008/10/05/MNIV13B9E4.DTL

Harper, J. (2008, March 17). *Journalism Troubled, Not Lost.* Retrieved from http://www.washingtontimes.com/news/2008/mar/17/journalism-troubled-not-lost-reportsuggests/print/

Horton, G. (2013, September 13). *What Is Citizen Journalism and How Does It Influence News?* Retrieved from http://www.brandwatch.com/2013/09/what-is-citizen-journalism-and-how-does-it-influence-news/

Hughes, W. (2010). *Citizen Journalism: Historical Roots and Contemporary Challenges* (Honors College Capstone Experience/ Thesis Projects. Paper 305, Western Kentucky University, Kentucky, USA). Retrieved from http://digitalcommons.wku.edu/stu_hon_theses/305

IFEX. (2013, February 6). *Gallery: The Arab Spring Uprisings through the Eyes of Citizen Journalists.* Retrieved from http://www.ifex.org/middle_east_north_africa/2013/02/06/gallery_arab_spring_citizen_journalists/

Jarvis, J. (2008, December 1). Mumbai Terror-digital Media. *Guardian.* Retrieved from http://www.guardian.co.uk/media/2008/dec/01/mumbai-terrordigital-media

Kellett, T. (2008, March 5). *The Origins of Citizen Journalism.* Retrieved from http://www.helium.com/items/909409-the-origins-of-citizen-journalism

Kelly, J. (2009). *Red Kayaks and Hidden Gold: The Rise, Challenges and Value of Citizen Journalism.* Reuters Institute for the Study of Journalism Challenges, University of Oxford. Retrieved from https://reutersinstitute.politics.ox.ac.uk/fileadmin/documents/Publications/Red_Kayaks___Hidden_Gold.pdf

Knight, A. (2012, April 26). *The Limits of Citizen Journalism.* Retrieved from http://alanknight.wordpress.com/2012/04/26/the-limits-of-citizen-journalism/

Kovach, B., & Rosensteil, T. (2001). *The Elements of Journalism: What Newspeople Should Know and The Public Should Expect*. New York: Three Rivers Press.

Kovach, B., & Rosensteil, T. (2007). *The Elements of Journalism: What Newspeople Should Know and The Public Should Expect*. New York: Three Rivers Press.

Lacy, S., Duffy, M., Riffe, D., Thorson, E., & Fleming, K. (2010, Spring). Citizen Journalism Web Sites Complement Newspapers. *Newspaper Research Journal, 31*(2), 34–46. doi:10.1177/073953291003100204

Maher, V. (2005). *Citizen Journalism is Dead. New Media Lab.* School of Journalism and Media Studies, Rhodes University.

McCracken, B. J. (2011, May 11). *Are New Media Credible? A Multidimensional Approach to Measuring News Consumers' Credibility and Bias Perceptions and the Frequency of News Consumption* (Master's thesis). The Rochester Institute of Technology, Department of Communication, College of Liberal Arts. Rochester, NY. Retrieved from https://ritdml.rit.edu/bitstream/handle/1850/13729/BMcCrackenThesis5-11-2011.pdf?sequence=1

Mensing, D. (2007, Spring). Online Revenue Business Model Has Changed Little Since 1996. *Newspaper Research Journal, 28*(2), 22–37. doi:10.1177/073953290702800202

Meyer, E. P. (1995, September). *Public Journalism and the Problem of Objectivity.* Speech Given at Investigative Reporters and Editors Conference on Computer Assisted Reporting in Cleveland. Retrieved from http://www.unc.edu/~pmeyer/ire95pj.htm

Miller, A., & Kurpius, D. (2008, August 6). *A Citizen-Eye View of Television News Source Credibility.* Paper presented at the Annual Meeting of the Association for Education in Journalism and Mass Communication, Marriott Downtown, Chicago, IL.

Mishra, K. D., & Krishnaswami, K. (2015, June). A New Genre of Journalism - Citizen Journalism. *International Journal of English Language, Literature and Humanities, 3*(4), 65. Retrieved from http://ijellh.com/papers/2015/June/06-52-67-June-2015.pdf

Nandi, C. (2006). *Print Media and Photojournalism.* New Delhi: Media Offset Press.

National Digital Stewardship Alliance. (2013, February 15). *Case Study: Citizen Journalism.* Retrieved from http://www.digitalpreservation.gov/ndsa/working_groups/documents/NDSA_CaseStudy_CitizenJournalism.pdf

Nel, F., Ward, M., & Rawlinson, A. (2007). Online Journalism. In P. J. Anderson & G. Ward (Eds.), *The Future of Journalism in the Advanced Democracies* (pp. 121–122). Aldershot, UK: Ashgate.

Outing, S. (2005, January 6). *Taking Tsunami Coverage into Their Own Hands.* Retrieved from http://www.poynter.org/content/content_view.asp?id=76520

Paul, H. (2011, March 2). *Why is Citizen Journalism Important?* Retrieved from http://sierrabear.com/home/index.php?option=com_content&task=view&id=133\

Paul. (2010, February 21). *CNN IBN Recognizes Muzaffar Bhat's Work with Citizen Journalist Award.* Retrieved from http://www.jkrtimovement.com/cnn-ibn-recognizes-muzaffar-bhats-work-with-citizen-journalist-award-20-feb-2010/

Pew Center for Civic Journalism. (2002, November 4). *Community Impact, Journalism Shifts Cited in New Civic Journalism Study.* Retrieved from http://www.pewcenter.org/doingcj/spotlight/index.php

Project for Excellence in Journalism. (2008). *The State of The News Media: An Annual Report on American Journalism.* Retrieved from http://stateofthemedia.org/2008/overview/major-trends/

Quinn, S., & Lamble, S. (2008). *Online Newsgathering: Research and Reporting for Journalism.* Amsterdam: Focal Press. doi:10.1016/B978-0-240-80851-2.50006-0

Radsch, C. C. (2012, May). *Unveiling the Revolutionaries: Cyberactivism and the Role of Women in the Arab Uprisings.* James A. Baker III Institute for Public Policy, Rice University. Retrieved from http://bakerinstitute.org/media/files/news/130a8d9a/ITP-pub-CyberactivismAndWomen-051712.pdf

Radsch, C. C. (2013). *The Revolutions will be Blogged: Cyberactivism and the 4th Estate in Egypt* (Doctoral Dissertation). American University.

Raftery, I. (2012, May 30). *US Student Killed While Filming Violence in Syria.* Retrieved from http://worldnews.nbcnews.com/_news/2012/05/29/11943194-us-student-killed-while-filming-violence-in-syria

Reporters Without Borders. (2012a, May 18). *Citizen Journalist Sentenced to Death for Al-Jazeera Interview.* Retrieved from http://en.rsf.org/syria-citizen-journalist-sentenced-to-18-05-2012,42641.html

Reporters Without Borders. (2012b, July 12). *Targeted Murders of Citizen Journalists.* Retrieved from http://en.rsf.org/syria-number-of-citizen-journalists-01-06-2012,42715.html

Rettberg, J. L. (2008). *Blogging.* Cambridge, UK: Polity Press.

Rosen, J. (2006, June 27). The People Formerly Known as the Audience. *PressThink.* Retrieved from http://archive.pressthink.org/2006/06/27/ppl_frmr.html

Ross, R., & Cormier, S. C. (2010). Handbook for Citizen Journalists. Denver, CO: National Association of Citizen Journalists (NACJ).

Rutigliano, L. W. (2008, August). *Covering the Unknown City: Citizen Journalism and Marginalized Communities* (Ph.D thesis). Faculty of the Graduate School, The University of Texas, Austin, TX. Retrieved from http://repositories.lib.utexas.edu/bitstream/handle/2152/17904/rutiglianol.pdf?sequence=2

Salama, V. (2012, October). Covering Syria. *The International Journal of Press/Politics, 17*(4), 516–517. doi:10.1177/1940161212456774

Sambrook, R. (2005, Winter). Citizen Journalism and the BBC. *Nieman Reports, 59*(4), 13-16. Retrieved from http://www.encoreleaders.org/wp-content/uploads/2013/06/Nieman-Reports-_-Citizen-Journalism-and-the-BBC.pdf

Simon, D. (2005). *Wire Creator David Simon Testifies on the Future of Journalism.* Retrieved from http://www.reclaimthemedia.org/journalistic_practice/wire_creator_david_simon_testi0719

Simon, J. (2012). The Next Information Revolution: Abolishing Censorship. In *Committee to Protect Journalists. Attacks on the Press in 2011: A Worldwide Survey by the Committee to Protect Journalists* (p. 3). New York: United Book Press.

Stephens, M. (2012, May 24). *A New Site for Participatory Democracy?: Journalists' Perceptions of Online Comment Sections.* Paper presented at the Annual Meeting of the International Communication Association, Sheraton Phoenix Downtown, Phoenix, AZ.

Technology has changed way we work, need multi-skilling: Shobhana Bhartia. (2013, May 30). *The Indian Express.* Retrieved from http://m.indianexpress.com/news/technology-has-changed-way-we-work-need-multiskilling-shobhana-bhartia/1122468/

The Digital Journalist. (2009, December). *Let's abolish the term 'Citizen Journalists'.* Retrieved from http://digitaljournalist.org/issue0912/lets-abolish-citizen-journalists.html

The Open News Room. (2011). *Citizen Journalism: A Primer on the Definition, Risks and Benefits, and Main Debates in Media Communications Research.* Retrieved from http://www.theopennewsroom.com/documents/Citizen_%20journalism_phenomenon.pdf

Tilley, E., & Cokley, J. (2008). Deconstructing the Discourse of Citizens Journalism: Who Says What and Why It Matters. *Pacific Journalism Review, 14*(1). Retrieved from http://www.massey.ac.nz/massey/fms/Colleges/College%20of%20Business/Communication%20and%20Journalism/Staff/Staff%20research%20files/ETilley/Deconstructing%20the%20discourse%20of%20citizens%20journalism_Who%20says%20what%20and%20why%20it%20matters.pdf

UNESCO. (2012, May 15). *Director General Condemns Targeting of Syrian Citizen Journalist Abdul Ghani Kaakeh.* Retrieved from http://www.unesco.org/new/en/media-services/single-view/news/director_general_condemns_targeting_of_syrian_citizen_journalist_abdul_ghani_kaakeh/

Ward, S. J. A. (2012). *Digital Media Ethics.* Centre for Journalism Ethics, School of Journalism and Mass Communication, University of Wisconsin-Madison. Retrieved from http://ethics.journalism.wisc.edu/resources/digital-media-ethics/

Wilson, K. G. (1993). *The Columbia Guide to Standard American English.* Columbia University Press.

Zhang, M. (2011, November 29). *CNN Lays Off Photojournalists, Citing the Accessibility of Quality Cameras.* Retrieved from http://petapixel.com/2011/11/29/cnn-lays-off-photojournalists-citing-the-accessibility-of-quality-cameras/

Chapter 9
Alternative Social Media for Outreach and Engagement:
Considering Technology Stewardship as a Pathway to Adoption

Gordon A. Gow
https://orcid.org/0000-0002-4811-4651
University of Alberta, Canada

ABSTRACT

Commercial social media (CSM) play a vital role in support of community outreach and engagement. Despite the apparent benefits of CSM, its widespread use raises important concerns about privacy and surveillance, limits on innovation, and data residency for the organizations that increasingly rely on them. This chapter will consider these concerns in relation to an international research collaboration involving technology stewardship training. Technology stewardship is an approach adapted from the communities of practice literature intended to promote effective use of digital ICTs for engagement. The program currently focuses on using commercial social media platforms for introductory capacity building, but this chapter will suggest important reasons to assist them in exploring non-commercial alternative social media (ASM) platforms. The chapter describes how the technology stewardship model offers a pathway for communities of practice interested in adopting ASM for outreach and engagement.

INTRODUCTION

The platforms that host and inform our networked public sphere are unelected, unaccountable, and often impossible to audit or oversee. (Barabas, Narula & Zuckerman, 2017)

For many organizations, commercial social media (CSM) serves an important role as a communications channel for outreach and engagement (Young, 2018). The widespread availability of mobile devices, the advanced features and affordances, and the low cost of using CSM makes it an irresistible choice,

DOI: 10.4018/978-1-7998-1828-1.ch009

particularly in resource-constrained settings. Moreover, it has provided real and tangible benefits to those organizations and their constituents that can be difficult to dispute.

Recent revelations around privacy and surveillance with CSM, not to mention ongoing challenges with mis/disinformation campaigns, and politically-motivated shutdowns of Facebook and other popular services, have raised awareness, if not grave concerns, about the trade-offs that we all make when deciding to use CSM. Free, of course, is never "free" in the sense that our digital labour and personal data becomes part of a commercial ecosystem with significant implications for organizations that use these channels for outreach and engagement. Some of the hidden costs of CSM includes accounts being banned or suspended due to posts that may include content that violates (or is misinterpreted as such) ever-changing rules and policies; limited control over data residency and lack of cross-platform interoperability; conformity to CSM-imposed standards for profiles and exchanges; lack of control over (or understanding of) algorithmic filtering and AI operations, as well as other privacy-related practices of CSM providers (see, for example, Barrett, 2018).

WHAT IS ALTERNATIVE SOCIAL MEDIA?

Gehl (2018) has summarized several concerns with CSM pertaining to technology infrastructure, political economy, and cultural practices. From a technological standpoint, the tendency with CSM is toward the centralization of data flows, proprietary code and closed databases, as well as secretive algorithms that influence how and when content is displayed to users. In terms of political economy, CSMs have established their business models on monetizing the free labour provided by users within a digital ecosystem dominated mainly by Silicon Valley firms (at least in much of the world, although Chinese based CSM represent increasing competition). CSM have also fostered cultural practices that position users as willing data-driven and surveilled subjects with limited ability to influence how identity is portrayed and sociality is conducted in the online world.

Alternative social media (ASM) describes both a movement and a collection of platforms that respond to the concerns raised by CSM. In many cases, ASM are established as a mirror image of an existing CSM. For example, Diaspora and Friendica are self-hosted social networking services that provide an open-source alternative to Facebook. Twister is described as a peer-to-peer microblogging service similar to Twitter but with a decentralized architecture based on a blockchain-like protocol. Signal is a nonprofit foundation that provides an open-source alternative to WhatsApp for one-to-one or group messaging that supports cross-platform encryption.

On the one hand, these ASM projects are reminiscent of the early Internet pioneers in emphasizing end-to-end architecture and "permissionless innovation." Early efforts by activities in first-generation community networks (e.g., makingthenetwork.org, archived on the Wayback Machine), and by researchers in the community informatics field, struggled to achieve widespread uptake of local ICT initiatives, even while the popularity of commercial social media began to skyrocket (Gurstein, 2005). However, with growing anxieties around CSM, it seems timely to revisit and reconsider a role for non-commercial alternatives. For instance, Poell & van Dijck (2015) suggest that CSM are in fact, "antithetical to community formation" because of the shift in power to emphasize data collection for advertising and the use of proprietary algorithms in moderating content. As such, the interest in ASM represents a movement that resists much of what CSM today stands for, promoting a forward-looking vision of an Internet-based public sphere perhaps best expressed by the Internet Society's guiding principles (Internet Society, 2017):

All Internet users, regardless of where they live, should have the ability to connect to any other point on the Internet, without technical or other impediments.

All Internet users should have the means to communicate and collaborate without restriction.

Any individual or organization should have the ability to develop and distribute new applications and services, free of governmental or private sector restrictions for anyone to use.

An Internet access environment characterized by choice and transparency allows users to remain in control of their Internet experience.

Everyone's ability to connect, speak, innovate, share and choose hinges on trust. The security, reliability and stability of the network, applications and services are critical to building online trust.

These principles correspond with the fundamental properties of ASM initiatives (Gehl, 2015). The design of ASM platforms usually supports decentralization through federated or distributed network topologies, with open source code and accessible databases. Where algorithms are used, they tend to operate at the edge of the network and are user-created and configurable. The political economy of ASM is rooted in a refusal of advertising on most platforms, with greater attention paid to social equity in exchange for digital labour, and with a growing base of support in countries outside the United States and Europe. Culturally, ASM embraces a form of "democratic surveillance" that emphasizes shared control over administrative decisions on platforms, local control over one's data and personal information, freedom in choosing online identities in support of free speech, and the search for new metaphors for online sociality that are multi-dimensional and more nuanced than those used by CSM.

It should be noted, however, that ASM skeptics have presented essential points of critique in each of these areas as well. Some have suggested that network effects remain the most significant barrier to ASM adoption, as it is challenging to get sufficient numbers of users to migrate away from CSM and to these platforms. Related challenges include the development of sustainable business models, especially when it is difficult to achieve economies of scale with server infrastructure and purchasing bandwidth in bulk. Security also remains a significant concern for users, potentially undermining online trust with users. (Barabas, Narula & Zuckerman, 2017).

Gehl (2018) suggests that "techno-elitism" can play a role when novice users are treated with contempt by more established members of ASM communities. The strong emphasis on freedom of speech, personal choice in online identity (or anonymity) also presents a governance problem for ASM platforms that inevitably face instances of misinformation, online abuse, or hate speech.

There are many barriers to the widespread adoption of ASM, with network effects being among the foremost when it comes to using these platforms for community outreach and engagement. However, it is essential to ask if the standard against which to measure ASM should be as direct competitors to CSM, or whether we should see them as complementary platforms that may well serve specific communities of practice rather than, for example, the wider public? Indeed, the network effects nut may be easier to crack if we are working with more clearly defined and delineated user groups that can be transitioned into ASM through a program of training and experimentation. As the user base grows, there will be additional incentives and resources available to reduce technical barriers and improve the usability and security of ASM platforms through design improvements on both server and client sides. This would form a virtuous circle of innovation made possible by the open source licensing as a *sine qua non* of ASM.

TECHNOLOGY STEWARDSHIP

So how could we encourage organizations to consider adopting ASM for outreach and engagement? We could begin with the assumption that ASM need not be viewed as a direct competitor of CSM, and that it may be well suited to the needs and interests of specific communities of practice rather than the general public. Communities of practice are groups of individuals that share a common interest through informal and formal ties expressed through forms of mutual engagement. The term is used widely in numerous fields, such as health, education, business, and any domain where social learning through group interaction is valued:

Communities of practice are groups of people who share a concern, a set of problems, or a passion about a topic, and who deepen their knowledge and expertise in this area by interacting on an ongoing basis. (Wenger, McDermott & Snyder 2002, p.4)

In a 2009 publication titled *Digital Habitats*, Wenger, White & Smith (2009) introduced the term "technology stewardship" to describe a role for individuals within communities of practice who wished to encourage and support the adoption and use of digital technologies among community members. The technology steward is characterized as a leadership role that cultivates the digital habitat of a community of practice. The habitat metaphor describes the collection of digital tools and resources available to the community to carry out its various communications, outreach, and engagement activities. The steward pays attention to the digital life of the community members and encourages innovation through experimentation:

Technology stewards are people with enough experience of the working of a community to understand its technology needs, and enough experience with or interest in technology to take leadership in addressing those needs. Stewarding typically includes selecting and configuring the technology, as well as supporting its use in the practice of the community. (Wenger, White & Smith, 2009, p. 25)

Technology stewardship should not be viewed narrowly as IT support, but instead as a multifaceted role that requires intimate knowledge of the technology-related social practices of community members, the ability to engage with community members to create visions for the future in alignment with community aspirations, to be aware of developments and opportunities in the technology landscape, and to encourage and support innovative technology practices in fulfillment of community choice. "Choice" is an important consideration to the extent that a technology steward should not dictate solutions to the members but instead, following Kleine's (2013) "Choice Framework" for development, should aim to serve four key responsibilities:

- Make the community *aware* of the existence of choice (i.e., that other ways of doing things are possible).
- Help the community to develop *a clear sense* of choice (i.e., how they might take advantage of choices available to them)
- Facilitate and support the *effective use* of choice (i.e., assist with trying a new technology practice or deploying unfamiliar digital tools)
- Recognize and sustain the *achievement* of choice (i.e., report on the outcome of new deployments, analyze and understand points of failure, and acquire resources to build on success)

Technology stewardship is a role that may be taken up *ad hoc*, usually as a response to an immediate need in a community of practice. However, the role is also one that can be assigned to individuals and even professionalized through a process of formal training and recognition. Formal training provides an opportunity to establish a strategic connection between the goals of a community of practice and the deliberate cultivation of a digital habitat to help meet those goals. For organizations involved in outreach and engagement, the presence of a trained technology steward could expand the range of choices available for communications, including the deployment of ASM.

The Joint Education and Training Initiative (JETI)

Since 2012, the author has been leading a collaborative action research project with the primary goal of better understanding how to build capacity for effective use of ICT in resource-constrained settings (Gow, 2018). Those settings range from local community-based groups based in Edmonton, Canada, to private, public, and non-governmental organizations located in Asia and the Caribbean. This work has coalesced around a Joint Education and Training Initiative (JETI) that launched an introductory course in technology stewardship in 2016 through a partnership between the University of Alberta, the University of Guelph, the University of Peradeniya (Sri Lanka), and the University of the West Indies. This classroom-based course has run successfully twice in Sri Lanka and twice in Trinidad (Gow, Chowdhury, Ganpat & Ramjattan, 2018), with elements of it also being introduced in several Edmonton-based projects. A total of 80 participants have completed the course so far, and new offerings are being planned for the future.

The current version of the course is based on a model described in Wenger, White & Smith (2009) with adaptations made for a sector-specific audience; in this case, agricultural extension officers and advisors in Sri Lanka and Trinidad who are the primary focus of the JETI at this time. This version includes sector-relevant language and examples from an agricultural setting while adding activities in the areas of community engagement and evaluation of ICT in use (Gow *et al.*, 2018).

The course is conducted over two-days covering four sessions. Each session includes a mix of short lectures, hands-on activities, and group discussion:

Session 1: Principles and practices of technology stewardship
Session 2: Engaging the community and creating a campaign
Session 3: Choosing an ICT platform and rapid prototyping
Session 4: Planning and managing a campaign

The first session provides an opportunity for peer sharing of experiences with ICTs, with an emphasis on stories of both successes and failures. Course facilitators weave key concepts and practices in technology stewardship into this discussion using a case study. In the second session, participants working in small groups are asked to consider and choose a community of practice as a point of focus for the remaining activities. Participants are then directed through a set of activities using a course workbook to conduct an analysis of the community of practice and its challenges and to identify a priority concern for immediate action. This is followed by a set of procedures described in the workbook that results in a structured goal statement to be used to inform and evaluate an ICT-based pilot study ("campaign") with the community of practice. While these activities are introduced to participants in a classroom setting, the method is intended to be carried into the field setting and conducted with community members as a form of participatory action research.

Once participants have articulated a campaign goal, they are then taken through a series of steps leading to the identification, comparison, and provisional selection of an ICT tool or platform suitable for the campaign. Following the model in Wenger, White & Smith (2009), the course differentiates between ICT "tools" as discrete functional components (e.g., text messaging, photo sharing, video conferencing) and ICT "platforms" as a set of interoperable tools bundled together in a software application or service (e.g., WhatsApp, Google G Suite).

The course workbook includes a procedure for conducting "rapid prototyping" of the ICT platform to test functionality and suitability with the community. This step follows principles similar to those used in agile project management (Dearden and Rizvi, 2015), with an emphasis on developing and testing in small incremental steps. From a change leadership perspective (Kotter, 2007), rapid and provisional deployment of the ICT platform also creates an opportunity for a "short term win" by involving the community in the experience of experimentation with a new practice. In other words, rapid prototyping offers community members an opportunity to test and to provide comments on a new ICT application without having to make a long-term commitment to it at the outset.

The final classroom session leads participants through a three-phase campaign planning exercise that includes provision for collecting data at various stages that will contribute evidence to an evaluation. Evaluation is critically important to assess both formative and summative outcomes of the campaign and to be able to report results back to the community and organizational sponsors that may be vital to providing support going forward. Campaign evaluation is, therefore, an essential competency for the technology steward to be able to recognize and further encourage effective ICT use among community members.

The overall course design draws upon and references Kotter's (2007) change leadership model, as well as Kleine's "Choice Framework" (Kleine, 2013), to provide a normative framework for characterizing the overall contribution of a technology steward to community development (see Figure 1).

Participants complete the final classroom session by drafting an individual action plan (IAP) in which they select an activity to be completed with a community of practice outside the classroom as an optional capping project. The IAP provides a number of choices for participants based on the four training sessions, ranging from conducting a community engagement activity, completing a rapid prototyping exercise, to designing a campaign and evaluation plan. This final step in the course is where participants have an opportunity to apply the principles and practices of technology stewardship with their communities and provide the research team with valuable insights about how this role can foster innovative and effective ICT use. Table 1 summarizes the campaign ideas developed by participants in the most recent Trinidad and Sri Lanka cohorts.

Figure 1. Comparison of change leadership models

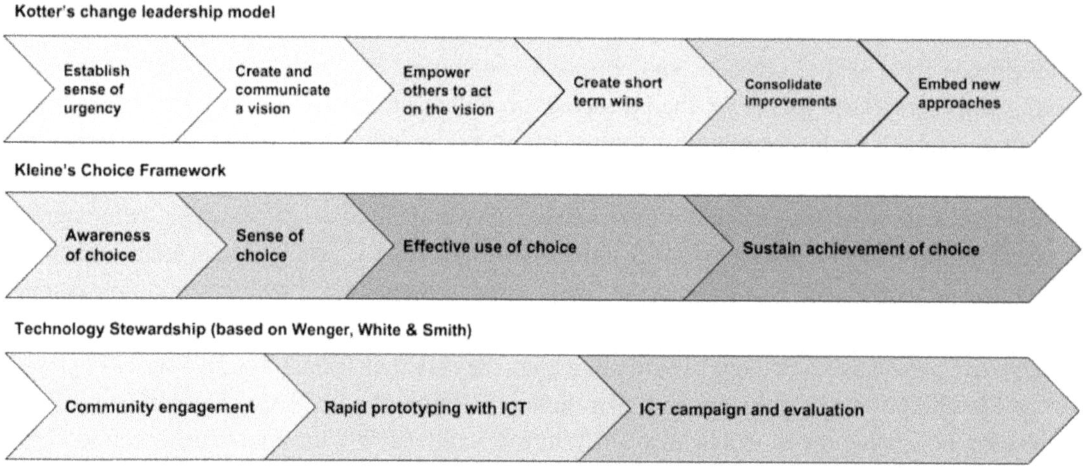

Table 1. Outcome of campaign planning activities carried out in the classroom

Community of Practice	Priority Action	Campaign Objective	Identified ICT needs
Beekeepers in Kandy District Sri Lanka	Instructional project	Introduce new beehive box	Group messaging; video tutorials
"Para Team" members of Hatton (tea) Plantations Sri Lanka	Organize and schedule meeting among members	Improve awareness of and attendance at training events	Individual/group messaging; photo sharing
Small scale coconut growers in Dankotuwa (Sri Lanka)	Access to expertise (Q&A)	Reduce cost and improve timeliness of responses to questions from growers	Individual/group messaging; photo sharing
Organic vegetable farmers in Ipalogama (Sri Lanka)	Attendance at meetings; access to expertise and information	Improve awareness of gov't employment opportunities; increase attendance at training programs;	Microblogging
Fishers in North East Trinidad	Access to expertise	Improve timeliness of weather bulletins and life safety information for fishers	Group text and photo messaging
Farmers in Tabaquite region (Trinidad)	Access to expertise	Reduce costs and improve timeliness of community notifications on pest management	Individual and group text messaging; photo sharing
Agricultural Society of Trinidad & Tobago	Organizing and scheduling meetings among members	Improve attendance at monthly meetings	Event scheduling (shared); text message reminders
Food Crop Farmers Association (Trinidad)	Farmer education and information updates	Improve awareness of topical issues and current events	Microblogging; group messaging

Table 2. Comparison of CSM and ASM choices for various ICT needs

ICT needs	CSM choices	ASM choices
Messaging	Facebook Messenger, WhatsApp, Telegram, Viber, Hangouts, etc.	Signal, MeWe, Jitsi, Friendica
Photo sharing	Google Photos, Flickr, Instagram, etc.	MeWe, Diaspora, Cluster, Friendica
Microblogging	Twitter, Facebook, Tumblr, LiveJournal	Ello, MeWe, Diaspora, Mastodon, Twister, GNU social
Shared calendar	Google Calendar, Facebook, Any.do	Kune, Thunderbird Lightning Calendar
Video sharing	YouTube, Facebook, Vimeo, Twitch, Dailymotion, etc.	MeWe, Bitchute, PeerTube, Kaltura

As indicated in Table 1, each of the groups of participants was able to identify and agree upon a community of practice for the classroom activities. The "priority actions" are generated from a set of categories of "community orientations" detailed in Wenger, White & Smith (2009, p. 70) that each group identifies as part of a campaign goal-setting activity.

While this was intended as a tabletop exercise for the course, each of the groups indicated that these priorities represented real and pressing concerns in those communities. If applied outside of the classroom, this activity would involve the technology steward facilitating direct community engagement with members to identify and validate priorities.

In keeping with the stewardship principle "keep it simple," all of the groups opted for a "use what you have" technology acquisition strategy, identifying ICT requirements and platforms suitable for their first campaign. Other possible technology acquisition strategies are presented in the course, including free/commercial platforms, patching pieces together through API integration, and building custom applications. It should be emphasized that the course material focuses on low cost and other "use what you have" choices as a preferred starting point for technology stewardship efforts. By default, this typically results in groups choosing a CSM platform for their ICT campaign plan. From the perspective of building capacity, a CSM platform like Google or WhatsApp (Facebook) usually offers some immediate benefits, such as low cost and high familiarity with most community members. Indeed, the groups in these cohorts opted for Facebook Messenger, Gmail, WhatsApp, or Twitter as the platform of choice in their campaign planning.

However, this choice comes bundled with the concerns mentioned above about CSM, particularly with organizations that wish to retain control over user-profiles and the data that moves across the platform. In these cases, CSM can serve a short-term goal by enabling a technology steward to lead a series of low-cost trials with the community of practice to understand new ICT-related practices better and to identify and validate other functional requirements for a platform. Over the longer term, the technology steward might be encouraged to explore and perhaps migrate the community of practice to an ASM platform that would provide a higher degree of control and autonomy while serving the essential purpose. A set of ASM choices (not exhaustive) matched to the cohort groups from Sri Lanka, and Trinidad is presented in Table 2.

As the table indicates, there are numerous ASM choices to fulfill the ICT needs specific in the campaign plans generated by the cohort. Based on the four responsibilities set out in the Choice Framework described above, a technology steward can take the first step by merely making members of the community of practice *aware* that ASM choices exist. This could then be followed by giving members *a sense of choice* by showing them how they might take advantage of ASM, perhaps by presenting a use case scenario, either hypothetical or based on a real example.

The next step of *facilitating choice* could be done by piloting an ASM platform with the community. This, however, is where the technical level of difficulty can rise quickly and, arguably, it is the uncertainty entailed in this step that may discourage many potential users at the outset. ASM platforms may require that the technology steward download and install software code, build and maintain a server, and provide cyber-security and do other support functions that can be somewhat sophisticated from a technical standpoint.

Resources remain another critical consideration, with access to server space and bandwidth is perhaps the most obvious. Some ASM platforms provide options for less technically intensive implementations. However, these come at some risk insofar as the stability of the platform from a technical and business standpoint may be precarious. The technology steward, in other words, will face several significant obstacles if they are to attempt an ASM choice with their community of practice.

A PATHWAY TO ADOPTION

Technology stewardship is a form of leadership practice that involves five primary streams of activity (Wenger, White & Smith, 2009, p. 26). These activities are integrated into our training course as three sequential modules of engagement, prototyping, and campaigning (see Figure 1), but they should be conceived as a complex set with certain activities taking precedence at certain times:

- Community understanding
- Technology awareness
- Selection and installation
- Adoption and transition
- Everyday use

The five activity streams present the basic framework of technology stewardship and provide a pathway for communities of practice to explore ASM in a way that emphasizes both social and technical implications that such a transition would entail. It is no guarantee that ASM will be accepted by members and integrated into the digital habitat of the community of practice. However, it does provide the basis for a plan of action that will support a systematic assessment of ASM, including its suitability from both a technical and social practice standpoint.

Community Understanding: Create Awareness of Choice

Understanding the constitution and social practices of the community is a fundamental requirement of technology stewardship. For technology use to be effective, it must not only serve the needs of the members but also be well integrated into the social practices of the community. The stewardship training program emphasizes this point with the first fundamental principle of *vision before technology*. Vision begins with understanding the community of practice from several perspectives, and the course introduces participants to an assessment tool that accounts for a range of baseline factors:

- Lifecycle
  - stage of maturity of the community of practice
- Constitution
  - diversity in location, language, demographics, integration with other communities or organizations
- Aspirations
  - Level of ICT interest and related skills among community members
- Access
  - Device ownership, internet access, cost and other financial considerations

The community assessment is carried out as a table-top exercise in the classroom, but ultimately should be validated with data f the community itself. The course provides a set of questions that result in a score for each of the four factors. The scores are primarily intended to inform decisions around the selection of appropriate ICT tools and platforms that align with the community context.

Understanding community context is essential for technology stewardship and applies when considering any technology acquisition strategy. In the context of an ASM strategy, however, the "Aspirations" score will be particularly important to consider. The technology steward will need to gather insights on several key questions:

- How interested are your community members in using or trying ICT tools and platforms?
- What is their capacity for learning new ICT tools and practices?
- What is the average current level of ICT-related skills among community members?
- Is there a probability of conflict in the community when introducing new ICT practices?
- How many ICT barriers are members willing to cross in order to use a new ICT platform (e.g., need to create new accounts and passwords, need to download new apps, metc.)

The course material provides a Likert scale ranking for each of these questions, which are then combined into an overall "Aspirations Score" for the community of practice A higher score suggests that community members may be willing to experiment with new ICT choices, but with this enthusiasm may also come strong opinions that could lead to potential conflict. This type of community might be open to the idea of ASM, but the technology steward will want to provide lots of opportunities for constructive feedback from community members during the prototyping and testing phase to identify concerns and diffuse points of conflict.

On the other hand, an Aspirations Score at the other end of the scale suggests a low level of tolerance for experimentation with ICT choices. Any changes the technology steward might wish to attempt should be simple and with relatively modest ambitions. The community context, in this case, would suggest that there are significant barriers to the adoption of ASM. However, a technology steward would be wise to focus on making community members aware of this choice and suggest possible ways that ASM might be used as an alternative without necessarily attempting an implementation. Over time, the community members may become more interested and willing to experiment with a simple ASM implementation and the technology steward could then move to facilitate that choice with a modest campaign.

Technology Awareness: Develop a Sense of Choice

The second fundamental principle of technology stewardship is to *keep it simple*, which means choosing ICT platforms that serve a clearly defined need concerning the goals of the community of practice. In practice, this principle establishes a logic that will often lead to choosing one of many CSM platforms because these usually offer the most obvious solutions to commonly identified ICT needs, as suggested in Table 2 above. However, the technology stewardship course emphasizes the difference between ICT *platforms* and ICT *tools*, following Wenger, White & Smith (2009, p. 154) on this point. ICT tools represent discrete functional components or services such as messaging, photo sharing, tagging, commenting, chat, and so forth. ICT platforms are defined as a *bundle of tools*, with many CSM offering similar collections even if these are not interoperable across platforms. For example, a comprehensive platform like Facebook includes a messaging tool (Messenger), as does Google's G-Suite (Messages), but these are not interoperable at this time. More specialized platforms such as WhatsApp (owned by Facebook) are primarily defined around a specific tool (messaging) but include other tools such as photo sharing, voice calling, and file sharing. The ASM space offers similar sets of tools and platforms in parallel with CSM, as indicated in Table 2.

For analytical purposes, ICT tools can be situated on a "tools landscape" diagram to assist the technology steward in understanding and conveying to members "how certain tools tend to influence community life in one direction or another" (Wenger, White & Smith, 2009, p. 60). The various affordances designed into specific ICT tools lend them to placement in relation to three polarities of social interaction (2009, p. 56), on the tools landscape diagram—although it is sometimes difficult to make clear distinctions: (1) tools that support synchronous versus asynchronous communications; (2) tools that support direct engagement (participation) versus reflective engagement (reification, documentation), and (3) tools that support individual versus group participation. Figure 2 depicts a rudimentary tools landscape diagram used in the course. Participants then build on this diagram by placing other types of ICT tools on the graph and discussing their decisions.

It is important to stress that this diagram is not intended to be definitive or exhaustive. The course material does include a more comprehensive reference for the technology stewards. However, the creation and validation of a tools landscape diagram should be viewed as an interpretive activity that forms part of the community engagement process facilitated by the technology steward.

The training course emphasizes that the technology steward should focus initially on defining the functional ICT needs in relation to the social practices of the community without committing to a specific provider or platform. The tools landscape diagram in conjunction with the community assessment tool is intended to produce a good fit between the technology choice with the social life of the community, whether that is to preserve existing dynamics or, in some cases, to foster new social practices.

Recognizing, of course, that community dynamics are complex, it is usually possible to identify "a typical pattern of activities and connections through which members experience being a community" (Wenger, White & Smith, 2009, p. 69). This typical pattern can be further categorized into a set of community orientations that characterize a set of social interactions that are then be matched with appropriate ICT tools. The course material presents six community orientations, which are referred to as "priorities" in relation to needs and goals:

Figure 2. A rudimentary tools landscape diagram

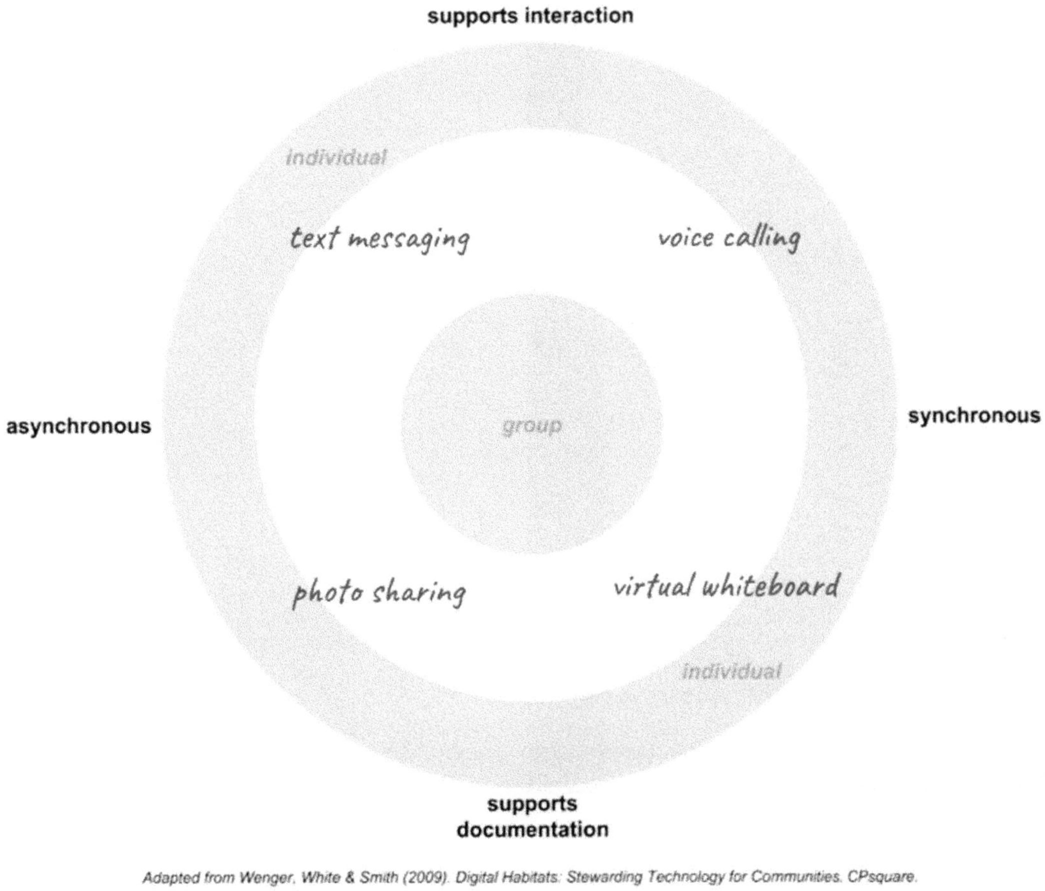

- Meetings
- Conversations
- Curated content
- Project management
- Access to expertise
- Social networking

Participants in the course are guided through a community assessment process using a problem/opportunity tree exercise, which then leads to a prioritization activity in which they rank the orientations in order of urgency or importance to the community (Figure 3).

This prioritization activity contributes to the *keep it simple* principle by providing a method by which the technology steward can narrow the focus to essential ICT tools in alignment with the needs and goals of the community. For example, Table 1 showed several communities of practice that have identified "Access to expertise" as a priority orientation. Access to expertise refers to "a focus on answering questions, fulfilling requests for advice, or engaging in collaborative, just-in-time problem solving" (Wenger, White & Smith, 2009, p. 84). Table 3 illustrates several activities under "Access to Expertise," along

Figure 3. Technology steward trainees use an opportunity tree exercise to prioritize community needs

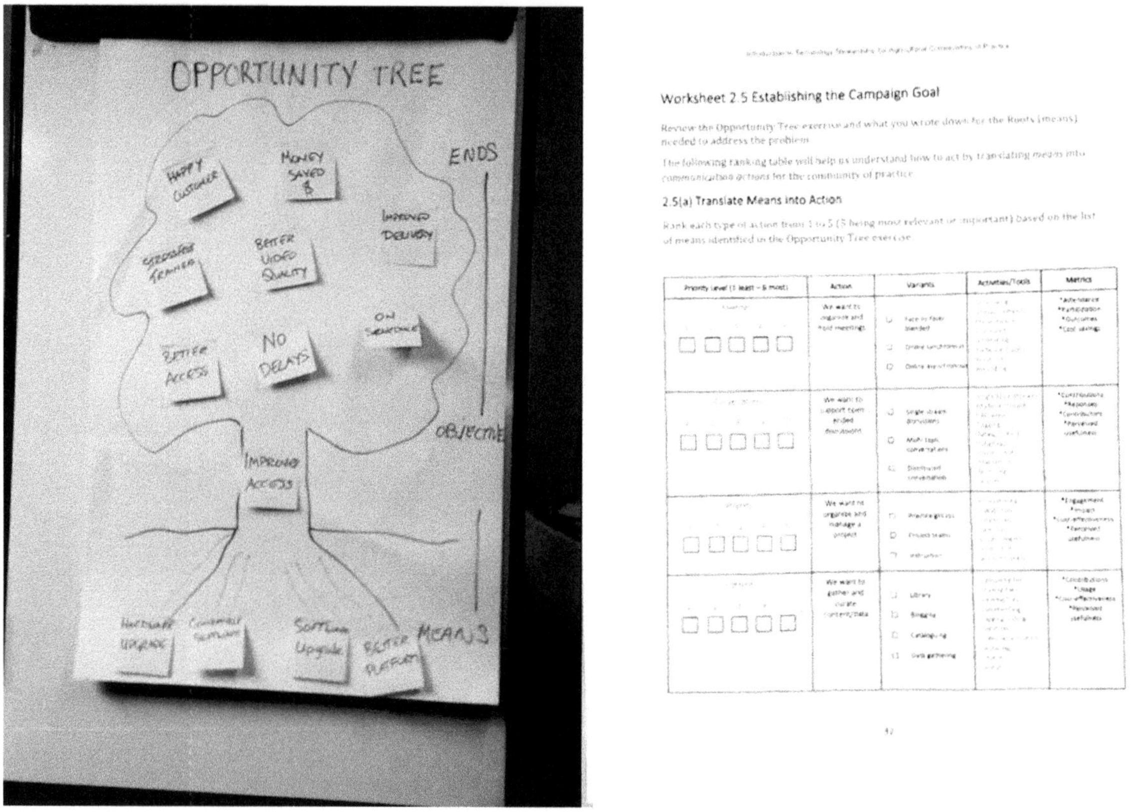

Table 3. Activities, practices, and ICT tools for the access to expertise orientation

Activity	Practice Notes	ICT tools
Questions and answers	Individual and/or group interactions; synchronous or asynchronous exchanges; documentation of responses (to create FAQs)	Text messaging; voice messaging; multimedia messaging; microblogging; chatbots;
Expertise locating	Finding the right person at the right time; managing accessibility; social norms around duty to contribute and share;	Member directories; profile page; ranking/ rating tool; visibility tool (offline/online);
Response rating	Categorizing responses to create FAQs; rating responses for quality; corrections and additions;	Rating tool; tagging tool; commenting tool; polling; wiki for documentation;

with a corresponding list of ICT tools, similar to something that a technology steward trainee might create during the course.

The next step, after having established the priority orientation for the community and listing key activities and associated ICT tools using the tools landscape diagram, is to identify the platform configurations in which these ICT tools are available. An extensive list of CSM is available on Wikipedia in the "List of Social Networking Sites" article and similar lists are relatively easy to locate elsewhere. A systematic

Figure 4. A Technology steward trainee evaluates three ICT platforms for her campaign

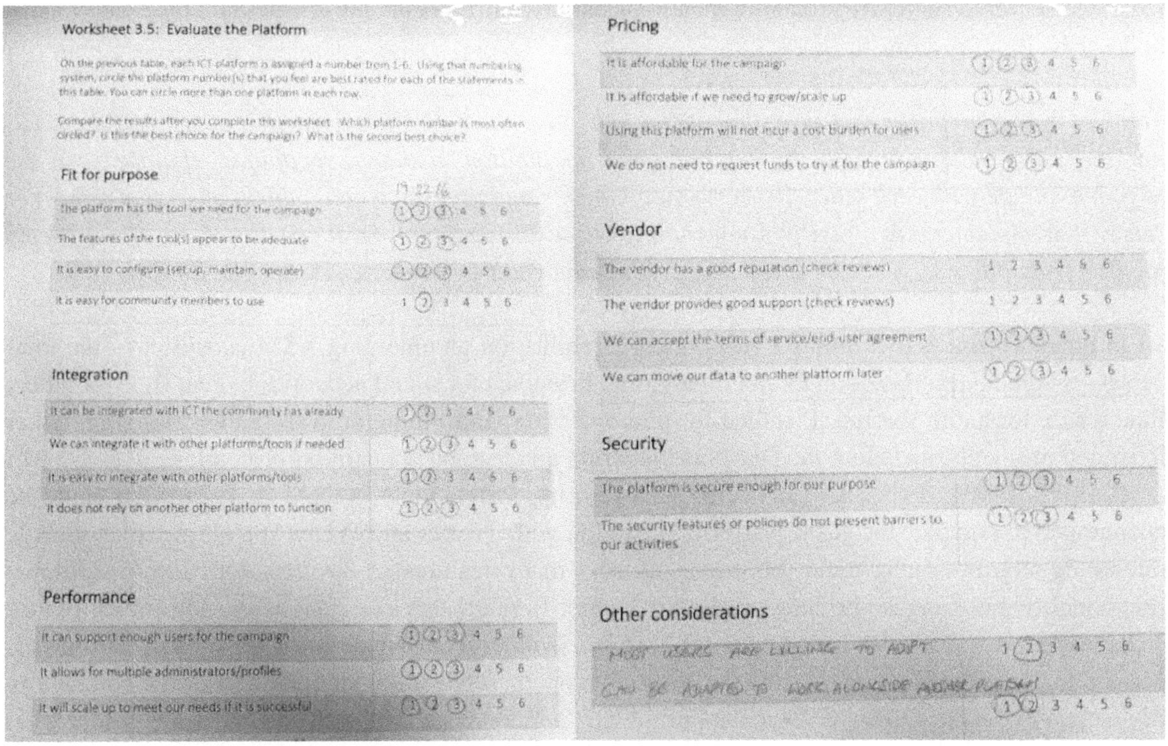

Worksheet 3.5: Evaluate the Platform

On the previous table, each ICT platform is assigned a number from 1-6. Using that numbering system, circle the platform number(s) that you feel are best rated for each of the statements in this table. You can circle more than one platform in each row.

Compare the results after you complete this worksheet. Which platform number is most often circled? Is this the best choice for the campaign? What is the second best choice?

Fit for purpose

The platform has the tool we need for the campaign	1 2 3 4 5 6
The features of the tool(s) appear to be adequate	1 2 3 4 5 6
It is easy to configure (set up, maintain, operate)	1 2 3 4 5 6
It is easy for community members to use	1 2 3 4 5 6

Integration

It can be integrated with ICT the community has already	1 2 3 4 5 6
We can integrate it with other platforms/tools if needed	1 2 3 4 5 6
It is easy to integrate with other platforms/tools	1 2 3 4 5 6
It does not rely on another other platform to function	1 2 3 4 5 6

Performance

It can support enough users for the campaign	1 2 3 4 5 6
It allows for multiple administrators/profiles	1 2 3 4 5 6
It will scale up to meet our needs if it is successful	1 2 3 4 5 6

Pricing

It is affordable for the campaign	1 2 3 4 5 6
It is affordable if we need to grow/scale up	1 2 3 4 5 6
Using this platform will not incur a cost burden for users	1 2 3 4 5 6
We do not need to request funds to try it for the campaign	1 2 3 4 5 6

Vendor

The vendor has a good reputation (check reviews)	1 2 3 4 5 6
The vendor provides good support (check reviews)	1 2 3 4 5 6
We can accept the terms of service/end-user agreement	1 2 3 4 5 6
We can move our data to another platform later	1 2 3 4 5 6

Security

The platform is secure enough for our purpose	1 2 3 4 5 6
The security features or policies do not present barriers to our activities	1 2 3 4 5 6

Other considerations

	1 2 3 4 5 6
	1 2 3 4 5 6

inventory of ASM is harder to locate, although The Social Media Alternatives Project (S-MAP, 2019) is an effort to compile an inventory under its "Omeka Archive." The Wikipedia page "Comparison of software and protocols for distributed social networking" maintains what is perhaps the most detailed list of both active as well as "dead or stalled" ASM projects.

Selection and Installation: Facilitate Effective Use of Choice

The technology stewardship training course includes a rating activity for comparing ICT platforms that encompasses several dimensions, each with a subset of ranking questions: goodness of fit, interoperability, scalability, pricing, vendor/developer support, and security. Tech steward trainees are encouraged to identify and compare at least three platforms as part of the rating activity before making a final choice for the campaign with their community of practice (see Figure 4).

During this step, trainees can be introduced to ASM platform options and asked to compare them with their CSM counterparts. Based on the outcome of the ranking exercise, the steward may elect to stick with a CSM, but there are opportunities at this point to consider piloting an ASM platform for the community of practice, particularly if privacy and data residency are identified as important considerations.

Recognizing that there are a number of ASM platform choices currently available, some key considerations are interoperability among platforms, independence, support, and scalability. One possible pathway into ASM is to explore the ecosystem of platforms connected through the ActivityPub protocol, otherwise known as the "fediverse" (Holloway, 2018). ActivityPub is a decentralized social networking protocol that "provides a client to server API for creating, updating and deleting content, as well as a federated server to server API for delivering notifications and content" (W3C, 2018). This excerpt helps to describe it in lay terms further:

Think of it as a language that describes social networks: the nouns are users and posts, and the verbs are like, follow, share, create... ActivityPub gives applications a shared vocabulary that they can use to communicate with each other. If a server implements ActivityPub, it can publish posts that any other server that implements ActivityPub knows how to share, like and reply to. It can also share, like, or reply to posts from other servers that speak ActivityPub on behalf of its users. (Dormitzer, 2018)

In other words, ActivityPub provides interoperability for an emerging ASM ecosystem—the fediverse—that includes Mastodon for microblogging, Friendica for social networking, PeerTube for video, Funkwhale for audio sharing, PixelFed for photo sharing, and Plume or Write.as for blogging. Other federated protocols, including the Diaspora Network, are designed on similar principles.

With "Access to Expertise" identified as a priority, for example, a technology steward could be encouraged to compare the ASM platform Mastodon with Twitter and WhatsApp all of which include microblogging/messaging tools. Mastodon mirrors many features of Twitter, with some additional functionality, but can also be integrated with Twitter through services such as the Mastodon Twitter crossposter (https://crossposter.masto.donte.com.br). In other words, experimenting with a platform like Mastodon can provide a gateway into the ASM ecosystem, while allowing members of the community of practice to continue using CSM to support of existing practices. The next section will consider what a transition campaign might entail using Mastodon as an example.

Adoption and Transition: Support Effective Use of Choice

Mastodon provides a pathway into the ASM ecosystem in part because it is linked to the Fediverse through its use of the ActivityPub protocol. While it is primarily a microblogging platform, it is possible to integrate with platforms that include other ICT tools such as video, audio, photo sharing, and social networking. In this sense, it can provide an entry point for a more ambitious ASM strategy, should a community of practice wish to explore this choice.

A federated system is designed to be decentralized, with each server (or, "instance" in Mastodon's terms) operating independently but with options for sharing data with other instances as determined by users and local administrators. The most straightforward implementation of Mastodon for an individual is to join an existing instance, such as the general-purpose mastodon.social, currently with about 331,000 users. As with most online communities, instances of Mastodon tend to form around themes or subjects, often unique or perhaps obscure, such as witches.live ("Are you a witch? Do you like spells, and spell accessories?") or eldritch.cafe ("For queer people, feminists, anarchists and their sympathizers"). Other instances are based on geography, such as aus.social ("A Mastodon instance for Australia"), toot.wales ("... the free and open microblog for Wales and the Welsh, at home and abroad").

A cursory examination of the current range of Mastodon instances confirms that network effects remain a barrier to ASM adoption, with many servers have only a few hundred members (or less). So, for many users, the existing Mastodon instances may have little appeal, and this option may not provide much of a pathway forward. As such, technology stewards could be encouraged to host their own instance of Mastodon for the community of practice. The ActivityPub protocol enables interoperability across

Figure 5. Screenshot of the author's Mastodon account

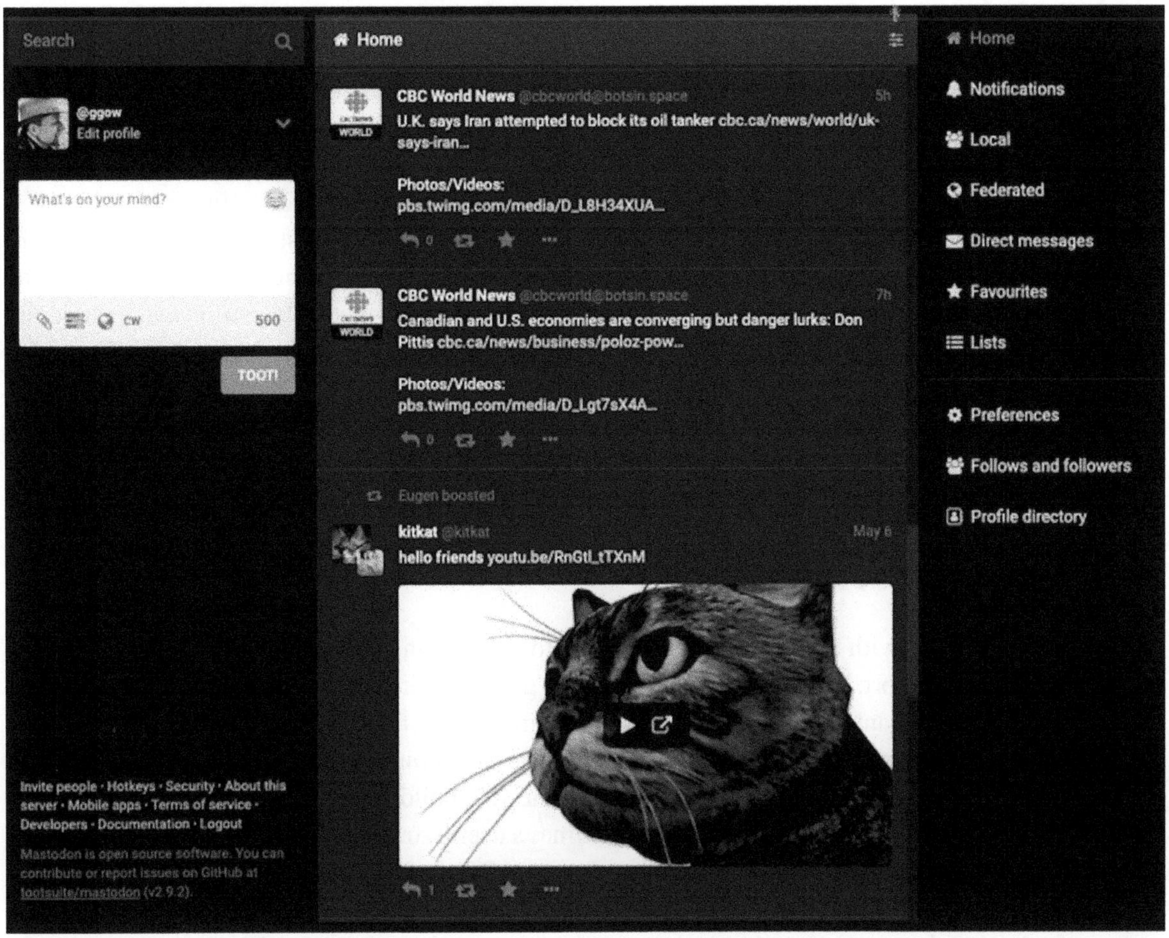

servers, so any community of practice can choose to operate entirely independently or integrate with other Mastodon instances to create a federation of communities. The challenge with this path forward includes the technical skills and resources needed to set up and operate a server. There is the option of fully-managed Mastodon hosting (https://masto.host/) for those not interested in taking on the full responsibility of running a server themselves.

In planning a campaign to explore Mastodon for microblogging with their community of practice, a technology steward will need to consider several steps. The first step is to decide on a Mastodon instance: create new or join existing? If creating a new instance, the steward will need to decide whether to host it themselves or to use a managed hosting service. This pathway provides the most autonomy for the community of practice but will depend on the organizational context, the technical skills of the technology steward, as well as the availability of resources and time for self-hosting, including day-to-day administration and oversight of the server. Purchasing a fully managed hosting service will still require some technical skill, and will entail a monthly cost, but maybe more feasible for communities of practice that are not yet committed to this pathway.

The technology steward will also need to introduce members of the community of practice to one or more Mastodon clients. The native web client works well, but others are available, including other web-based clients like Pinafore or Halcyon, desktop clients such as Whalebird or TheDesk, and mobile apps, including Amaroq (iOS) and Tusky (Android). In certain respects, these clients will be familiar to many users because of the similarities to the layout with Twitter. The client will include a local timeline showing posts from members of your instance, as well as a federated timeline that includes local posts plus those from other instances, which are followed by members of your instance (Figure 5).

The technology steward may need to assist members with creating a Mastodon account on the instance, although it will be familiar to those who have used Twitter. There are some differences with the Mastodon profile, the most notable being that users are provided with a metadata section that includes up to four labels and associated content, which is a design feature that eschews the imposition of platform defined categories typical of CSM.

The technology steward might also consider a transition plan that includes automated cross-posting with Twitter as a way to generate content and bootstrap discussion on the Mastodon instance timeline. This can be done by pointing members to a website like the Mastodon Twitter Crossposter, as noted above.

Everyday Use: Recognize and Sustain Achievement of Choice

Launching a campaign with a community of practice to explore an ASM platform like Mastodon can require considerable effort, and there is, of course, no guarantee it will succeed in changing existing practices in any significant way. The training course emphasizes two other principles of technology stewardship that are essential for campaign planning: *use the knowledge around you* and *understand failure and build on success*. Technology stewards will need to build a coalition of support from among members of the community of practice, so it is sometimes a useful strategy to invite a subset of interested individuals to participate in an exploratory trial of the new ICT platform. For example, several members might be invited to join an existing Mastodon instance to gain some initial experience before deciding to move forward with a more extensive scale campaign.

A technology steward might also need assistance from members with a deeper pool of IT-related knowledge, mainly if there is a desire to run a Mastodon instance or other self-hosted ASM platform. The JETI program also aims to foster a community of practice among technology stewards that could eventually serve as a global network of support for ASM-related efforts:

Stewarding technology should be treated as a team sport for two reasons. First, it helps to have a group within a community to share the work—or at least share in the understanding of the role. Second, it helps to connect with other stewards (from whatever community) who can provide a broader context, offer support, share ideas, tips, and innovation, and help in pressuring a tool developer to address community needs. Still, many technology stewards struggle alone. (Wenger, White & Smith, 2009, p. 25)

The concept of the campaign share features with an action research strategy (Stringer, 2013) insofar as it represents an intervention stage within an overall iterative framework that flows from and back into a community engagement and assessment stage carried out under the leadership of the technology steward. Campaign planning, therefore, begins with a community engagement leading to a clearly stated campaign goal that sets a specific objective for an identified priority action (or "orientation"). For example, a goal statement for a campaign oriented to improving access to expertise for an agricultural community of practice might be stated as follows:

We need to find a way to improve the timeliness and reduce the cost of exchanging messages between the extension officer and community members when scheduling meetings and responding to inquiries about crop management for vegetable farmers in St. George County.

This is a well-defined goal insofar as it contains three key details:

- it sets a specific target (improve the timeliness and reduce costs);
- for a specific priority action (exchanging messages for scheduling meetings and responding to inquiries);
- with a clearly defined community of practice (vegetable farmers in St. George County);

It is important to note that the goal statement does not mention a specific ICT tool or platform. The choice of an ICT platform is contingent and context-dependent. One strength of this approach is that it separates the goal from a specific ICT choice, reinforcing the "vision before technology" principle.

Having formulated the goal and *then* selecting an ICT platform for the campaign, the technology steward must consider several essential planning elements: timing and timeline (when is the best time to start? how long to run it?), implementation requirements (who should form a coalition of support? any formal approvals needed? Any ICT training required?), promotional and other costs, mitigation of potential security and privacy concerns, planning for evaluation, and wrapping up the campaign.

Both the campaign goal and the evaluation plan are critically important to the stewardship principle of *"understand failure and build on success."* On the one hand, without a clear goal in mind, it will be challenging to plan and implement a focussed campaign and manage members' expectations. On the other hand, without an evaluation plan, it will be difficult to assess the outcome of the campaign. Generally, campaigns will have one of four outcomes,

- Campaign goal achieved as anticipated
- Campaign goal partially achieved
- Campaign goal not achieved
- Campaign abandoned by the community

A good evaluation plan ensures that the right questions are being asked pre-, mid-, and post-campaign and that the right kinds of data are being collected to assess success or failure. The course introduces trainees to four critical metrics for the evaluation plan:

Interaction: the amount of activity on the ICT platform during the campaign. How many people joined the group? How many people posted messages? How many messages were posted? What time of day/day of the week was the activity most frequent? Are there any significant patterns in the activity?

Engagement: the type of activity on the ICT platform during the campaign. This is a more qualitative measure looking at the content of the interactions, such as the types of messages posted and types of content shared, uploaded, rated, commented on, and so forth;

Influence: the impact of the campaign relative to other methods of interaction and engagement. How many people are aware of the campaign? How many are participating (actively or passively) in the campaign? Has the campaign changed perceptions of ICT use? Has the campaign changed attitudes or perceptions of community members in relation to its intended outcome?

Behaviour change: the impact of the campaign on observable practices in relation to the intended outcome. Are community members doing things differently? Have they changed their communication practices? Has the campaign led to observable changes in professional or business practices of the community members in relation to its intended outcome?

Trainees are reminded in the course that, even in the worst-case scenario of campaign abandonment, there is no such thing as "failure" if you can understand what happened during the campaign attempt. Because learning from experience is integral to the action research process, an effective evaluation plan provides a foundation for understanding and adjusting plans. For instance, a campaign to introduce ASM for microblogging might not be successful with a community of practice, but a good evaluation plan should provide the technology steward with evidence to explain why that might be so, while also generating insight as to what might be attempted next in relation to the community's goals and priorities.

In the case of a successful campaign, technology stewarding can move into the background as the transition takes place. This involves the fourth responsibility of the technology steward in *recognizing and sustaining the achievement of choice* with community members. Background stewarding includes supporting new members in their use of the community's technology, identifying and spreading good practices, identifying and supporting innovative practices of members, and attending to evolving community dynamics concerning ICT use.

A successful introduction of an ASM platform into a community of practice involves both the foreground work leading up to and including the campaign, as well as these various aspects of "stewarding in the background" as a day to day role for the technology steward. Even as new members of the community of practice become more comfortable in the choice to use a new platform, the technology steward's role continues, particularly insofar as they are recognizing success and highlighting innovative practices of members. In the case of a Mastodon campaign presented as an example in this chapter, the technology might need to manage both an existing CSM (i.e., Twitter) and the ASM platform during a transition phase, or possibly ongoing as a blended set that makes up the community's overall digital habitat. Successful migration to Mastodon might also lead to further campaigns to integrate other ActivityPub-based ASM platforms featuring different ICT tools, such as photo or video sharing, and social networking.

CONCLUSION

There is no *prima facie* reason that a community of practice could not include both CSM and ASM platforms within its digital habitat. On the one hand, CSM will continue to be attractive for community engagement from the standpoint of affordances, cost, and reach. On the other hand, ASM promise similar toolsets with higher degrees of privacy, autonomy, and flexibility. While ASM may be limited in scope from a practical standpoint by technical barriers, trust issues, and network effects, they may very well serve an essential complement to CSM as part of a community's digital habitat.

Technology stewardship offers a pathway to the adoption of ASM through an action research approach that includes community engagement and ICT piloting using a campaign model. The goal is to provide members of a community of practice a more comprehensive range of choice in how they wish to communicate using digital technologies. Technology stewardship training can provide a foundation by which a community of practice can be made aware of the existence of ASM as a choice, shown how that choice might contribute to the digital habit, and supported in the effective use of ASM, should it be a choice that community members wish to exercise.

Looking ahead, ASM can play an essential role in the digital habitat of communities of practice that wish to retain a higher degree of control and autonomy with their communication practices and the data that flows from them. CSM will most likely continue to dominate, but the complementarity ASM offers worthy of further exploration under the right conditions. The technology stewardship model presented in this paper offers one possible pathway forward, but others are, of course, possible. Limited success in using ASM for community engagement will likely be achieved through other types of targeted initiatives with support from community development workers and research teams. An important step going forward will be to connect these initiatives through a global community of practice that can build on lessons learned and provide mutual support and encouragement for this choice.

ACKNOWLEDGMENT

This research was supported by the Social Sciences and Humanities Research Council of Canada (SSHRC). The author wishes to acknowledge additional and ongoing support from the Kule Institute for Advanced Study and the Faculty of Extension at the University of Alberta, the University of Guelph, the Postgraduate Institute of Agriculture at the University of Peradeniya, and the Faculty of Food and Agriculture at the University of the West Indies.

REFERENCES

Barabas, C., Narula, N., & Zuckerman, E. (2017, Sept. 8). Decentralized social networks sound great. Too bad they'll never work. Wired. Retrieved from https://www.wired.com/story/decentralized-social-networks-sound-great-too-bad-theyll-never-work/

Barrett, B. (2018, March 19). Facebook owes you more than this. Wired. Retrieved from https://www.wired.com/story/facebook-privacy-transparency-cambridge-analytica/

Dearden, A., & Rizvi, S. M. H. (2015). ICT4D and Participatory Design. In R. Mansell & P. H. Ang (Eds.), *The International Encyclopedia of Digital Communication and Society*. John Wiley & Sons; doi:10.1002/9781118767771.wbiedcs131.

Dormitzer, J. (2018). What is ActivityPub, and how will it change the internet? Retrieved from https://jeremydormitzer.com/blog/what-is-activitypub-and-how-will-it-change-the-internet/

Gehl, R. (2018). Alternative Social Media: From Critique to Code. In SAGE Handbook of Social Media (pp. 330–350). SAGE. doi:10.4135/9781473984066.n19

Gehl, R. W. (2015, July). The Case for Alternative Social Media. Social Media + Society, 1-12. doi:10.1177/2056305115604338

Gow, G. (2018). Introducing a Technology Stewardship Model to Encourage ICT Adoption in Agricultural Communities of Practice: Reflections on a Canada/Sri Lanka Partnership Project. In R. Duncombe (Ed.), *Digital Technologies for Agricultural and Rural Development in the Global South* (pp. 43–53). Boston: CABI; doi:10.1079/9781786393364.0043.

Gow, G., Chowdhury, A., Ganpat, W., & Ramjattan, J. (2018). Enhancing ICT adoption and use through change leadership approach: Technology Stewardship Training for Caribbean Agricultural Communities of Practice. *Journal of Learning for Development*, *5*(3).

Gow, G., Jayathilake, C., Hambly Odame, H., Dissanayeke, U., McMahon, R., Jayasinghe-Mudalige, U. K., & Waidyanatha, N. (2018). An Introduction to Technology Stewardship for Agricultural Communities of Practice: Course Workbook (2nd ed.). doi:10.7939/R3QV3CK28

Gurstein, M. (2005). Sustainability of Community ICTs and its Future. *Journal of Community Informatics*, *1*(2), 2–3.

Holloway, J. (2018). What on earth is the fediverse and why does it matter? Retrieved from https://newatlas.com/what-is-the-fediverse/56385/

Internet Society. (2017). Internet Society Global Internet Report: Paths to Our Digital Future. Retrieved from https://future.internetsociety.org/2017/

Kleine, D. (2013). *Technologies of Choice? ICTs, Development, and the Capabilities Approach.* Cambridge, MA: MIT Press; doi:10.7551/mitpress/9061.001.0001.

Kotter, J. P. (2007, January). Leading Change: Why Transformation Efforts Fail. *Harvard Business Review*, ▪▪▪, 96–103.

Poell, T., & Dijck, J. v. (2015). Social Media and Activist Communication. In C. Atton (Ed.), *The Routledge Companion to Alternative and Community Media* (pp. 527–537). London: Routledge.

S-MAP. (2019). Social Media Alternatives Project (S-MAP). Retrieved from https://www.socialmediaalternatives.org

W3C. (2018, 23 January). ActivityPub W3C Recommendations. Retrieved from https://www.w3.org/TR/activitypub/

Wenger, E., McDermott, R., & Snyder, W. (2002). *Cultivating Communities of Practice.* Boston: Harvard Business School Press.

Wenger, E., White, N., & Smith, J. D. (2009). Digital Habitats: Stewarding Technology for Communities. Portland, OR: CPSquare.

Young, J. A. (2017). Facebook, Twitter, and Blogs: The Adoption and Utilization of Social Media in Nonprofit Human Service Organizations. *Human Service Organizations, Management, Leadership & Governance*, *41*(1), 44–57. doi:10.1080/23303131.2016.1192574

Chapter 10
Social Media as Public Political Instrument

Ikbal Maulana
https://orcid.org/0000-0002-3727-3809
Indonesian Institute of Sciences, Indonesia

ABSTRACT

Social media has played important roles in social movements in many parts of the world. It has been used to raise people's awareness about the injustice they suffer as well as to mobilize them to challenge a repressive government. Social media enables people to define public interests by themselves, taking over the role previously taken by elites. It is all due to its simplicity which allows anyone to be both a producer and consumer of information. Citizens are no longer the spectators of political games played by the elites, but they can participate and even mobilize public opinions challenging those in power. The possibility of anonymous interactions allows anyone to express any view without the fear of disapproval and sanction, which leads to the plurality of discourse, which in turn increases the possibility of democratization. However, the impact of social media is not deterministic, and it is not always beneficial to public. Even those in power can use it to preserve the existing hierarchy of power.

INTRODUCTION

The recent intensive uses of social media in social and political activisms indicate that it has a great potential to reshape modern democracy by giving people their voice back which previously must be delegated to their political representatives. Social media might take the practice of democracy back to its original form as in Ancient Athens in which it was practiced directly by citizens without any representative mediation (Ober, 1996). Theoretically practicing democracy on social media would be more inclusive than that in the Ancient Athens which excluded women and slaves, because social media allows everyone to speak out her opinion without the limitation of gender, social status and, even, space and time.

The optimism regarding the positive impact of social media on democracy is supported by the recent social movements, from Occupy Wall Street to Arab Spring. Just as in the pre-social media era, in order to have a real political impact a social movement needs to manifest itself in public urban spaces, such

DOI: 10.4018/978-1-7998-1828-1.ch010

as streets or squares. Prior to the mobilization of the masses, activists need to do various efforts, from having coordination among themselves to raising issues to public. Most of these activities are conducted through the networks of acquaintances and contacts, and social media can best facilitate such activities by enhancing the speed of information exchanges and broadening the participation of people. Howard *et al.* (2011) found out that (i) social media played a central role in shaping political debates in the Arab Spring, (ii) a spike in online revolutionary conversations often preceded major events on the ground, and (iii) social media helped spread democratic ideas across international borders.

The Arab Spring has been hailed as a political change forced by people who organized themselves using social media. It has increased the rhetoric of the impact of social media on democratization. However, after years of turmoil, the expectation of democratization has steadily faded away as the old political players get back to the center of power, disappointing those who want a radical change in politics. While social media still facilitates people to express any political view, it cannot prevent the return of the unwanted political power despite the many refutations against them can always be expressed freely on social media. The impact of technology, including social media, on democratization is not deterministic. There is no unique correlation between technological progress and distribution of power (Feenberg, 1999, p. 76). Social media gives the opportunity to advance democracy, but, it is also possible, that this technology is used to preserve the existing hierarchy of power.

This chapter will discuss the extent to which social media can be used by citizens to promote and advance their political interests. It will also discuss if its extensive and intensive use will lead to democratization.

THE POLITICAL CONSTRUCTION OF PUBLIC

Politicians often speak on behalf of public as if it is a single concrete entity. But, is public really out there? If yes, then why it needs others to speak on its behalf? Can public not speak by itself? Even Habermas asserts that the main character of public is the existence of interactive speaking among its members, "A portion of the public sphere comes into being in every conversation in which private individuals assemble to form a public body" (Habermas, 1964, p. 49). Public, as well as society, consists of individuals who interact with each other. While society, by definition, can emerge in any condition, free or oppressed, under totalitarian or democratic regime, whereas "Citizens behave as a public body when they confer in an unrestricted fashion - that is, with the guarantee of freedom of assembly and association and the freedom to express and publish their opinions - about matters of general interest" (Habermas, 1964, p. 49).

It is hardly imaginable that populations of a town, moreover of a country, mostly strangers to each other, through conversations could converge into a single entity called public. The notion of public is abstracted from a society by reducing its complexity and variety that makes public to have only specific attributes and aspirations in accord with the interests of power holders which determine it. Therefore, public can be perceived as a political construction having weak correspondence with the reality, however "those, who do possess power can only claim legitimacy by speaking in its name and acting in its interests" (Coleman & Ross, 2010, p. 8). Even strong dictators need to claim everything they do is on behalf of the public.

Most often people inhabiting a vast area may have fragmented and sometimes conflicting interests. Without a leader or a spokesperson, it is hard for them to come up with a single voice. Democratic mechanisms have been developed to make the "public" claimed by the spokesperson correspond with the people having flesh and blood. Democracy is supposed to ensure that representatives well represent the voters who have elected them. Indeed, democratic system does not guarantee that people's aspirations will be fulfilled, but, so far the system has provided a fair procedure to select representatives then "the people can have no complaint because their rights have been safeguarded.... If the properly chosen representatives create policies not of their liking, it is the fault of the people. And the remedy is also at hand: at the next election, the people can choose other representatives" (Markovitz, 1999, p. 49).

Representation in modern democracy is the solution as well as the source of problems. In any country it is impossible to involve all adult people in every political decision making process, therefore a political representative system is needed. Public is then represented by the representatives who are selected in an election. Even though the representative mechanism is considered as the most fair solution but it cannot eliminate the following problems. First, there is no guarantee that each voice of the representatives represents the interest of their constituents, because when they were still the representative candidates they did not inquire people about all their interests. They just proposed a political position which they considered might attract people. There is unlikely a negotiation between the candidate and the people about the appropriateness of the former's political positions and the latter's interests. People only select a candidate who is most acceptable to them. Second, election is held once every four or five years, while, over time, politics most likely will be changing for various reasons, and politicians often resolve their differences by compromising their opinions, which in turn diverting them from their constituents.

The diversion of representatives from their constituents is often unavoidable, and the former compensate it by redefining new public interests which are in accord with their new political orientation. People who do not know each other are transformed by their representatives into a new public. They cannot prevent it, because "Never meeting in one place or speaking with one voice, the public is unable to represent itself. It is doomed to be represented" (Coleman & Rose, 2010, p. 8 – 9). Therefore, "the public is always a product of representation. There is no a priori public that is "captured" or "recorded" by the media. The public is invoked through processes of mediation that are dominated by political, institutional, economic, and cultural forces" (p.3).

As a political construction, "public" has always been the target of determination by competing political forces each of which has its own ideas of what public is, what its interests are, and to whom it refers. So, public is not a fixed defined entity, but "a space to be filled in" (Coleman & Rose, 2010, p. 2). Since there are competing interests, it becomes a space of contention around which innumerable institutional devices and discursive strategies have been deployed. Media have always been important instruments to influence and shape public. By transmitting messages through media elites persuade ordinary people to identify themselves with the public which has been defined by the former.

Those in power of course do not like the statement that public is a mere political construction, because it questions the legitimacy of their position. Democratic institutions and mechanisms have been developed to make public as close as possible to real people so that it can be claimed as the source of legitimacy. If an ideal democratic system cannot be realized, then the working system should be considered as the most fair of all possible systems by all parties, especially those to be represented. Since 'the public is doomed to be represented', the controversy emerging from the representative system should be prevented or minimized. One important way to do this is by measuring the degree of representation, that is by counting the number of those being represented. Numbers are important to legitimize political system, "... numbers determine who holds power, and whose claim to power is justified... Numbers, here, are part of the mechanism of conferring legitimacy on political leaders, authorities and institutions" (Rose,

2004, p. 197). Indeed, numbers trim the complexity of the people's aspirations, but they are the best solution that we can have right now.

People participating in current democratic systems are divided into two mutually exclusive categories: the representatives and the represented. While the former play active role in political debates and decision making, the latter can only judge the former and select them in an election. However, the election occurs every certain period of time, and in between the latter have no formal influences on politics, because the election has legitimately transferred the right of political decision making to the former.

Innovations have been developed to let the voice of people be heard outside an election period. For example, opinion polls are run to calibrate and quantify public feelings on political matters and social surveys are conducted "to transform the lives and views of individuals into numerical scales and percentages" (Rose, 2004, p. 197). However, the above political innovations only reveal public voice on questions raised by the opinion polls or surveys, while unquestioned issues will remain silent. And these kinds of questions only collect simplified answers and avoid the complexity of public problems.

Complex questions and answers are better accommodated by conventional media which can present complex narratives of people's stories and problems. However, most conventional media whose contents are created or selected by a group of organized people who have a collective interest tend to have certain discursive characteristics, which in turn simplify the picture of public as a single entity, with clear and non-conflicting attributes. Therefore, when they have to make public correspond to real people, they refer it to the groups which fit their created picture. And those that do not fit will be excluded. This inclusion and exclusion of people into politically defined public is conducted through the selection and exclusion of issues from political discourses. It is achieved by

... crucial reporting omissions or over-emphases on a systematic basis and so contribute to a subtle, long-term 'mobilisation of bias' in media reporting. This excludes certain groups in society. More significantly, it also ensures that chronic, long-term problems, many of which contribute to power imbalances, remain a minor part of public sphere discussions until they reach crisis point. Such tendencies have become all the more exacerbated by rising competition. Thus, the very discursive practices that are supposed to reveal the world as it is also, unwittingly, serve to leave crucial causal elements of inequality and crisis uncovered. (Davis, 2007, p. 36).

FIGHTING FOR PUBLIC EXISTENCE THROUGH CITIZENSHIP

Public is more often an object of definition and is manipulated to legitimize those who define it. It is claimed to be abstracted from the largest majority of real people, but is given specific attributes determined by particular interest. So, when its needs are satisfied, it will be the needs who define it which are satisfied.

Public does not have to be the object of definition of elites. Citizens, even though they are strangers to each other, still have an opportunity to constitute public by themselves. It can be achieved if they can be "regularly thrown into contact with one another and there had to be newspapers and pamphlets to provide a common focus of discussion and conversation. The public, then, was a society of conversationalists, or disputants if you prefer a more aggressive term, dependent upon printing" (Carey, 1995, p.381). Press or media in general provide focus on public conversation as well as preserve the conversation to be part of public memory.

Conventional media, especially printing media which has had a long history, is a constituting factor of public, because normatively "it exists to inform the public, to serve as the extended eyes and ears of the public. The press protects the public's interest and justifies itself in its name" (Carey, 1995, p. 381). The press does not just facilitate public conversation but also enriches the conversation by, for example, providing experts' opinions and investigative reporting. However, the power behind the press can also influence or dictate public discourse. Opinions of public or experts and investigative reporting are selected to frame public discourse in accord with the interests of power holders. This condition may result in journalism which "justifies itself in the public's name but in which the public plays no role, except as an audience" (Carey, 1995, p. 391).

On conventional media people do have the choice, not to determine the content of media, but to choose the media itself, such as which newspaper to read or which radio station to listen. As they choose the media, they have to accept the whole packages given by it. They may have impact on content, their preferences will be accommodated by the media, but more due to marketing considerations rather than democratic reasons of media owners. Media tends to become the stage of propaganda of which public is only the spectators and ratifier of decision made elsewhere (Carey, 1995). During the rise of broadcasting in the early twentieth century, the public was conceived as something to be molded and tamed. The media was given the task "to provide the public with what it needs, and indeed to reshape its needs so that it wants what is normatively better for it" (Coleman & Ross, 2010, p. 29). The public was seen as less intelligent than people of the media and therefore should be educated by the latter.

The Internet, especially its social media, has brought radical change to the constitution of public. It is partly due to the global operation of social media of which the owners are not interested in local politics. What they want are merely the maximum number of users and user generated contents which can be sold to advertisers. This profit motivated purpose has led to the development of increasingly user-friendly and widely accessible social media which provides users easy access to voice their concerns and ideas. Public can express their political opinions without conflicting with the interest of social media owners.

The practice of citizenship, which consists of making political judgment about public matter in relation to and with others (Barney, 2007), can be easily carried out on social media by anyone. Citizenship should be practiced in public sphere so that it can be watched by and affects others, and on social media a user's informational act is instantly visible to others who are online at the same time. Therefore social media has a great potential to achieve the ultimate end of citizenship, which is to make individual cause shared by public and trigger the intended change.

The level of democracy is closely related to the level of citizenship which "depends upon a series of rights of entry, ranging from the polling station to town squares to cyberspace where much contemporary interaction now occurs. In the absence of these rights of public access, democratic citizenship becomes a pious aspiration rather than a practicable commitment" (Coleman & Ross, 2010, p. 24). Ideally legitimate political decision requires a rational agreement among all citizens, which may only be achieved if all of them exercise active citizenship. "Thus the rationality proper to the communicative practice of everyday life points to the practice of argumentation as a court of appeal that makes it possible to continue communicative action with other means when disagreements can no longer be repaired with everyday routines and yet are not to be settled by the direct or strategic use of force" (Habermas, 1984, p. 17-8).

The above ideal has never been realized in practice, because involving all citizens in decision making is very costly, impractical and, most often, impossible. Only in a few rare cases all citizens are asked to make a direct political decision, such as in a secessionist referendum or a referendum for the adoption of a new constitution. In these cases they are only asked a very important but simple question that has been formulated by parliament and requires only yes or no answer. It is politically impractical to ask people with an open question. It would even be impossible to engage all people to seriously discuss political matters and make a political decision. Members of parliament, whose number is limited but legitimately represent people, can much more effectively achieve political consensus.

Democracy is developed by imperfect humans to collectively deal with their imperfection. The problems caused by the imperfection can never be removed, but it gives legitimation which can overcome dangerous conflicts. Measures are implemented to overcome particular imperfection lasting too long. For example, periodical election is held to prevent representatives from ignoring their constituents for too long. They have to keep paying attention to the people's interest if they want to keep their position in the next term. However, even the period between two consecutive elections is considered too long when people can no longer tolerate the representatives ignoring their voices and concerns on an important issue. In this case, they are prepared to engage in extra-parliamentary activity to force their representatives to listen to their voice. But this case rarely happens because this kind of citizenship requires a lot of cost and time to mobilize a sufficient number of people to represent public interest.

As democracy does not emerge instantly just because people choose to adopt it, people also do not practice active citizenship just because they are not satisfied with the politics. Citizenship is something which develops and needs to be developed. It is "a habit motivated by circumstance and obligation, cultivated through education and experience, consistently performed" (Barney, 2007, p. 39). While its effectiveness "rests not only on equality before and under the law but also upon relatively equal access to the social and material resources that allow people to act on these entitlements" (p.39).

Not everyone can readily practice citizenship if we regard that "The practice of citizenship is, at its core, the practice of political judgment" (Barney, 2007, p. 40). The views of some scholars which emphasize the important of argumentation also imply that not all people can involve in political decision making. Habermass (1984) suggests that only through the force of better argument we can make a cooperative search for the truth. Beiner also emphasizes the use of speech in politics. "Political experience as a specific mode of being in the world, is constituted by speech, by the capacity of human beings to humanize their world through communication, discourse and talk about what is shared and thus available for intersubjective judgment" (Beiner, 1983, p. xiv). Since the practice of citizenship relies on the practice of political judgment and the judgment should rely on and be expressed in rational argumentation, then elites have better skill than average people to make political judgment.

The views of Habermas or Beiner are too optimistic to be found in real politics in which people do not alway want to win the truth or to humanize the world. It is often the winning itself that matters the most. Relying citizenship only on rational argumentation will exclude and subordinate people who are not capable to make a good argumentation. Anyone can make a political judgment, and anyone is the best person to express a judgment which is related to her own problem. Therefore, to be just to all citizens it is necessary to acknowledge "the multiplicity of modes in which citizens might make political judgments, and the contribution made to the struggle for justice by these modes of expression and the people who use them" (Barney, 2007, p. 43). Peaceful political protest do not have to be expressed in speech, and people participating in a political rally are not to engage in a political debate.

TECHNOLOGICAL EMPOWERMENT OF PUBLIC

In contrast to instrumentalist view, which believes in the neutrality of technology, a small but growing number of scholars regard technology as having political quality (e.g. Mumford, 1964; Ellul, 1980; Feenberg, 2002; and Winner, 1986). The latter argue that technology has a political impact, that is influencing power relations in society in which the technology is used, and the design and use of technology are also influenced by the power relation. Mumford, for example, suggests that technology is not politically neutral,

> *... from late neolithic times in the Near East, right down to our own day, two technologies have recurrently existed side by side: one authoritarian, the other democratic, the first system-centered, immensely powerful, but inherently unstable, the other man-centered, relatively weak, but resourceful and durable. If I am right, we are now rapidly approaching a point at which, unless we radically alter our present course, our surviving democratic technics will be completely suppressed or supplanted, so that every residual autonomy will be wiped out, or will be permitted only as a playful device of government, like national ballotting for already chosen leaders in totalitarian countries (Mumford, 1964, p. 2).*

Following Mumford's division of technology, broadcasting technology, such as radio and television, can be regarded more as an authoritarian technology, whereas the Internet is a more democratic one. On the Internet users can be both receivers and senders of information, while radio listeners can only receive what is broadcasted by a radio station. It does not mean that democracy cannot grow out of a society whose mainstream media is radio technology. As long as there is no one who controls public information, and people have enough choices of media to select from, then people can avoid being dictated by a single media.

Regardless of the used technology, "Communication, whether through speech, manuscript, print, broadcast, or digital media has always been a crucial resource for political resistance, influencing cultural norms in the process" (Waite, 2013, p. 18). The more people get the opportunity to communicate, the more they can exercise power, and the more difficult for elites to dominate them. It does not imply that the development of communication technology will deterministically advance democracy. It depends on who can better utilize technology for their own benefits. Today, communication technologies, including the Internet, have been widely used in either democratic or undemocratic countries. However, there is a reasonable optimism regarding the potential of social media to empower people, because it gives the opportunity to anyone to express and share her views with others.

The relationship between the representative and the represented and the power relation between the ruler and the ruled have been challenged by Internet technologies which have given voice to those who are usually voiceless. While most technologies are "reducing individuals to mere appendages of the machine, computerization can provide a role for communicative skills and collective intelligence" (Feenberg, 2002, p.89). In the past, if there was a controversial government's policy or a controversial opinion raised by a politician, only public figures could participate in the polemics on conventional media. The majority of the people could only watch or discuss it in coffee shop without any influence on the politics. Social media has now given average people the opportunity to discuss it even at the national level. It proves that "evolving communication technologies have always altered who can say what to whom" (Waite, 2013, p. 18). Today politics is not only fought out in parliamentary building or on conventional media, social media has increasingly become political battlefield and instrument of the people to achieve their political goals. Even many people in developing countries, such as Indonesia (Lim, 2004) and some Arab countries (Howard *et al.,* 2011), have benefited from the empowerment of social media. There have been some cases that people were able to exert political pressure on parliamentary members or governments through raising issues on social media.

The political impacts of social media is not deterministic. Different countries having different local contexts experience the technology differently. "Consequently, what surfaces as a serious challenge for one country may not be the most important challenge for a country with different social norms" (Waite, 2013, p. 18). However, no country will remain unaffected by the transformative power of social media. Elites and general public will increasingly take advantages from the different kinds of use of social media. Some people may try to make others well-informed, while some other people may misinform and mislead others. The cooperative search for the truth as suggested by Habermas (1984) is not guaranteed, because even untruth can benefit some people and be the source of power.

The relatively easy access of social media makes it an inexpensive but effective instrument either to mobilize bias or organize social movement. The interactivity on social media can involve much more people than that in actual life using the combination face-to-face communication and conventional communication technologies. An important characteristics of social media is the use of number as the indication of the strength of information. The technology of social media can easily count the number of people who click "Likes" or share a message. This number may indicate the strength of a message, and it cannot be given by conventional media.

SIMPLICITY IS THE POWER

It seems counter-intuitive that complex social movements, such as Arab Springs, are supported by a very simple-to-use technology. Practically no significant technical and writing skills are required to be an active user of social media. The essential feature of social media is its simplicity which makes it more suitable for making social contact rather than sophisticated dialogues. The limited number of characters for each message makes trivial messages look normal. While the difference between a dumb and a smart blog is clear and impress readers differently, the difference between a dumb and a smart message on social media is much less clear. On social media users normally do not need to think a lot before posting a message. There are much higher number of simple messages circulating on social media than sophisticated ones which require a lot of thought to digest. Therefore social media attracts a much broader range of people, and link them to unprecedented social network.

The large number of social media users, most of whom exchange only unimportant messages to each other, has attracted those who want to benefit from that great number. Business people, social activists, intellectuals and politicians develop the skills to repackage a complex message into many small simple ones to be sent to the mass of social media users. Through a series of short messages a marketing campaign can be conducted, a social cause can gain massive support, and even people can be mobilized to take action on street. The user-friendliness of social media has eased and enhanced human contact and "...any technology that enhances human contact has democratic potentialities" (Feenberg, 2002, p. 92).

Social media has eased people's participation in a political discourse which was previously only the domain of elites. Technological development increasingly gives public what they most need, from products to information, and, ultimately to voice which in turn allows freedom to flourish (Grant, 1974). Does this development indicate that technology will take us to the future which will be better, wealthier, and, especially, more democratic? Will the development of the technology confirm the expectation of the utopianists like Negroponte (1995, p. 230) that "Digital technology can be a natural force drawing people into greater world harmony"?

Some thinkers - e.g. Marx, Marcuse (1964), and Feenberg (1999, 2002) - have explored the relationships between technology, public and power. The history of technology often shows that not all people benefit from technology equally. There are those who gain initial control and appropriate it to their interest. Those in power can take advantage of the development of technology, and secure the already existing social hierarchy. But, sometimes the development of technology challenges existing power, "new technology can also be used to undermine the existing social hierarchy or to force it to meet needs it has ignored" (Feenberg, 1999, p. 76). The impact of technology cannot always be anticipated, "there is no unique correlation between technological advance and the distribution of social power" (p.76). This is what Feenberg calls the ambivalence of technology: it might be used to support the conservation of hierarchy, but it could also push for the democratic rationalization of society.

COMPETING INTERESTS IN MEDIA

According to an optimistic view, affordable media technology which allows for easy access to information opens the door for "an educated and participatory democracy" (William, 2003, p. 156). Indeed, widely available information may improve the quality of public participation, but it does not necessarily make a society more democratic. People in many undemocratic countries also have access to various media technologies, from radio to television to the Internet, but "quite a lot of discursive energy is required to get from computers to data to information to democracy" (Saco, 2002, p. xiii). Media can be used for good or evil, either for democratic engagement or for indoctrination of people. People may not be aware of the undemocratic practices of media, that they cannot really distinguish between the mass media as instruments of information and entertainment, and as agents of manipulation and indoctrination (Marcuse, 1964).

There might be support as well as resistance coming from media owners whose interest is not ideological but financial profit. Democracy is not in their agenda. If making public well-informed is profitable, they will do it, if not, they will do something else. If the exploitation of public sentiment gives them more profit, then they will do it as well. They have been increasingly stronger in influencing our lives, that they "could reach farther into our lives, at every level from news to psychodrama, until individual and collective response to many different kinds of experience and problem became almost limited to choice between their programmed possibilities" (William, 2003, p. 157).

The industrialization of media does not necessarily deter democratization. If the source of profit can only be maximally exploited by satisfying the information need of the majority of people rather than the much smaller number of elites, then the industry will serve the people even though it does not have democratic agenda. History shows that "the demise of the bourgeois public sphere relates to the commercially transformative dynamic of the capitalist political economy" (Coleman & Ross, 2010, p. 31). The growth of media industry since the early of nineteenth century has enabled media institutions to become large-scale businesses "delivering news as a commodity with a view to profit" whereas "Ownership of the press was consolidated into the hands of business tycoons with little interest in the cultivation of bourgeois chatter" (p. 31).

Commercialization of media has put profit over public interest, which leads to change the social function of journalism. Conventional media no longer serves public to gain empowering information and reach social consensus, "but to produce entertainment and information that can be sold to individual consumers. And it clearly contributes to homogenization, undercutting the plurality of media systems rooted in particular political and cultural systems of individual nation states that characterized Europe through most of the twentieth century, and encouraging its replacement by a common global set of media practices" (Hallin & Mancini, 2004, p. 277).

The more subtle domination of media over public is through the mobilization of bias. People may not be aware that the discourse in which they engage has been directed to particular direction. Media has become one of the sophisticated instruments of exercising power which prevent the raising of issues which are detrimental to the power holder's set of preferences (Bachrach & Baratz, 1970). Through the creation and reinforcement of social and political values and institutional practices, which are partly best facilitated by media, potential conflicts are prevented even before they arise. It is natural for people or political organization to favor some issues over others to be discussed openly, as Schattschneider (1960: 71) states that "All forms of political organization have a bias in favour of the exploitation of some kinds of conflict and the suppression of others, because organization is the mobilization of bias. Some issues are organized into politics while others are organized out." By mobilization of bias, not only leaders can control what issues can be raised, but also shape others' desires. Political leaders "do not merely respond to the preferences of constituents; leaders also shape preferences" (Dahl, 1961, p. 164). And "... is it not the supreme exercise of power to get another or others to have the desires you want them to have - that is, to secure their compliance by controlling their thoughts and desires? .... thought control takes many less total and more mundane forms, through the control of information, through the mass media and through the processes of socialization" (Lukes, 2005, p. 27).

Conventional media is a powerful instrument to mobilize bias because it can pretend to report the world objectively. It can dictate political discourse by letting others to speak freely. But not all speeches will be published, only those which are in accord with their political agenda. "If we accept the existence of even the most benign form of agenda-setting on the part of the press, then who is allowed to speak in the news is just as important as which stories are selected for inclusion. Who speaks matters because access to the media is access to persuasive influence" (Coleman & Ross, 2010, p. 50).

Social media is not immune from the influence of business and political interests as well. Politicians and businesses can mobilize an army of social media users to mobilize bias, for example, by raising particular issues or directing attention of public to more acceptable problems. However, social media is much harder to control than conventional media because everyone is also an information provider even though anyone has different capability to influence others.

SOCIAL MEDIA AS A SOCIAL SPHERE

On social media anyone is simultaneously a producer, consumer, and distributor of information. Social media is even no longer media in traditional sense. It has become a social sphere, the world of its own, in which the exchanges of information can be conducted instantly as if people meet face-to-face with each other. Social media is even more 'social' in the sense that the interaction can involve more people each of whom has the opportunity to speak freely. One of the main differences between virtual world constructed on social media and the actual world is that the former will record everything that happens inside it. Every interaction in virtual world is automatically preserved and can be examined by anyone anytime later, while any event in the actual world needs media to record and report it.

Social media is more than just a world containing virtual versions of anything in the actual world. There are differences between what happen in both world. The social interactions on social media have their own characteristics and dynamics.

First, on social media all users have equal access to its technological services. There is no such thing as 'the rich has better access than the poor'. What makes users different from each other is the social network which they have built by themselves. Having different social networks, people may have access to different information, or participate in different types of interactions. But, it is the activeness, not the material wealth of users, which determine the extent of their social networks.

In the actual world, whether in democratic or undemocratic countries, political inequality can always be found. The main difference is that in democratic countries the inequality is not institutionalized but resulted from a political game which is not against the laws or constitution of the countries. For example, the concerns of the majority of people tend to dominate public discourses, because they have more people who raise their concerns. It can be claimed as the consequence of liberal democratic systems in which equal access of individuals to public sphere is given as the foundational principle and is secured by their constitutions (Peleg, 2007). In undemocratic countries the inequality is institutionalized to give privilege to dominant groups.

Conventional media may preserve inequality in a society, since it does not attempt to serve every individual or group of people equally. It is even impossible or, at least, impractical to serve every social group equally. Due to its limited space it is only targeted to particular market segment. The inequality is also influenced by unequal position between journalists and audiences of media. The former can control the content of media, whereas the latter can only select the media which best represent their interest.

On social media each user is both the producer and consumer of information. And the owners of social media mostly do not have interest in dictating discourses circulated on their platform. Their main business is to increase the number and activities of users in generating content, and then to sell them to advertisers.

Second, you do not have to be smart to be an active social media user. The limited length of information that you can send in a single message forces you to post only simple messages which do not require much thought. You can send any message spontaneously about anything serious, funny, or totally unimportant. It is not the content, but the contact you make, which is important. Social media equalizes everyone by lowering the technical and writing skill barriers to create its content. It is different from earlier Internet technologies, such as Webs or blogs which discriminate average users from those who have technical and/or writing skills. In the early history of the Web, people were required to have the knowledge of HTML to create a Web page. With the availability of blog services, technical skills have no longer been prerequisite to write a Web page, but users must have writing skills and commitment, because a blog post is normally written as a long essay. Therefore average or busy people had to wait until social media being invented to be active information producers on the Internet.

Third, the possibility of anonymous interaction on social media has enabled a more equal position among its users. In a country where the minority is under-represented or their interests do not have opportunity to be voiced, social media which allows fake identity has become the only public sphere in which anyone can voice any opinion without fearing of the judging eyes of others or, even, physical threats. However, there is the negative side of anonymity too: it allows irresponsibility which can make a virtual space become a battlefield of hatred rather than a place of practicing rational argumentation. In this case, virtual sphere is no longer a public sphere in which social consensus can be developed through communicative rationality.

Fourth, a virtual society can be different from an actual one due to the elimination of actual identity and space and time barriers to social interaction. With social media the same-minded people who are geographically dispersed or socially hidden can be easy to find one another and form a social group. The accessibility of social media through mobile technologies also allows geographically dispersed people to keep in touch with each other anytime and anywhere. In the physical world in order to make conversation with other people you firstly have to match your place and time with theirs, and ask their permission too. On social media you can send a message or respond to others' message anytime without the worry of bothering others.

Fifth, social media may cause the weakening of power distance. Hofstede *et al.* (2010, p. 61) defines power distance "as the extent to which the less powerful members of institutions and organizations within a country expect and accept that power is distributed unequally." A low-power distance society tend to be democratic in which they have leaders, but they elect them and can contradict them, and their leader have consultative style of decision-making. In high-power distance, submission to someone who has an authority is expected not only from those under her authority, but also from other people whose position in social or organizational hierarchy is similar to her subordinates. This submission becomes a social norm to which every member of a society has to comply. In high-power distance society, people tend to mingle only with those of the same social class. In real life overcoming power distance is no less difficult than overcoming geographical distance. But, on social media this power distance has been weakened. In the actual life the place where you work and socialize will determine the people who will become your friends, while on social media you are given the keys to the doors to any social group including those whom you do not have the chance to meet in actual life. This possibility is open because it is difficult to determine the social class to which an unknown person you meet online belongs. But, since it will not do any harm, you can expand your social network beyond your immediate friends or contacts.

Sixth, the equal access and the elimination of space and time barriers will in turn open the opportunity for any social media user, not just elites, to participate in the mobilization of political participation or the mobilization of bias. Users do not have to be aware that they engage in the mobilization. On social media something unplanned can develop into something surprising anyone, a simple message can develop and mutate into a complex set of ideas as it diffuses across many social media users (Shifman, 2014). A simple message responding to an event can trigger chains of responses which develop into a set of political opinions and even a mobilization of the masses. Therefore it is often difficult to trace who firstly triggers the raising of political issues. Most people do not need to know that, since on social media public does not need to appoint a spokesperson, because it can easily represent itself.

Seventh, just as in the actual world, on social media the formation of the opinion of a citizen is influenced to some extent by her social network. The difference is that on social media a user can create her own social network deliberately. She can select anyone she likes and deselects and blocks the one she does not. Theoretically, on social media anyone can create the social network whose opinions are in accord with hers. It leads to the development of a virtual world consisting many very diverse social groups each of which is much more homogeneous than an actual one. So, social media allows the plurality of public.

PRACTICING CITIZENSHIP THROUGH SOCIAL MEDIA

Democracy is supposed to provide citizens, not only elites, with the opportunity to influence the decision making processes that affect their life. The ideal of democracy, according to Habermas (1996), is that it enables a political problem – the problem concerning the organization of society in common – to be resolved through the force of better argument. He has been optimistic that, despite their different interest, people are able to find the best way to resolve their disputes through communicative reasons: the critical reflexive dialogues to find the most reasonable consensus to solve political problems. The question to be explored here is how social media can be used to practice collective communicative reasons.

A collective problem, either social or environmental, will be perceived differently by individuals from different positions. Victims and unaffected individuals will have different attitudes toward the problem due to different experiences with the problem. Individuals who suffer and bound together by a shared problem, such as a threat of pollution to their neighborhood or unintended result of policy implementation, develop a situated knowledge as they confront the problem (Feenberg, 1999). Such situated knowledge normally cannot be obtained unless you have real experience with the problem. All possible problems resulted from a development project cannot be anticipated in advance, therefore experts, bureaucrats, and politicians cannot have foreknowledge about them. With the emergence of social media, all ignored situated knowledge can easily be raised by the victims themselves.

Another important concern is Habermas' emphasis on the force of better argument in practicing citizenship. This kind of practice of citizenship will exclude people who have their own political preferences and judgments but cannot express them in reasoned speeches (Barney, 2007). That the best political solution can be found through political debate is only possible if the participants have no other interest than finding the truth. In practice, it is rarely the case. If better argument becomes the only mode of democratic decision making practice, then lay people can never compete against professional politicians. People who participate in political rally do not want to have arguments with the government, but just want to protest or to show their disappointment to them. They do not want to argue, but they support their statement with the showing up of the many people who participate in the rally. On social media, citizenship is expressed in information, either in text or picture or video. You can create the information by yourself, or you can do the least effort by clicking just a single button of "Share", "Retweet" or "Like".

Social media has facilitated the practice of citizenship by easing the making of political judgments in a public sphere. In actual life, when an average citizen without access to conventional media wants others to know about her opinion, then she must personally come to them and tell her opinion. And she will face the risk of being rejected or even socially sanctioned if her opinion contradicts theirs. On social media she does not have to face such risk. She can write anything on her virtual wall and her virtual friends who are online will read it without being asked to do so, and even they can share her message to other people. Her message is communicated automatically without specifically being addressed to them.

When social media was first invented no one expected that it could be used to topple a dictator. The constraints to have a long and deep argumentation in a single message seems to make it only suitable for trivial communications. At first sight its short message seems to be its limitation. But the simplicity of social media is the very reason that makes it attractive to many people, including those who have neither the technical knowledge of the Internet nor the capability nor time to write a long essay such as that on a blog service. Social media appears to be intended to facilitate to build a social network rather than to exchange serious content (Maulana, 2014). However, no social group can be developed without contents, without shared meanings and interests. Therefore, some users also develop the capability to decompose a complex idea into several simpler ones which enables any idea, social or political cause to be communicated to the virtual masses.

CRITIQUES AGAINST SOCIAL MEDIA

According to Hefner (1999, p. 158), "prospects of democratization increase with the development of multiple centers and power and a plurality of public discourses in society" because "a multiplicity of ideas and authorities makes it difficult for any single group to win a clear monopoly of power," therefore the competing parties come to agree to some kind of power sharing compromise. So democracy can also be perceived as a pragmatical solution when no one nor group can dominate or convince other political actors or groups, even though there are well people who pursue democracy due to ideological reasons.

On social media there is no monopoly of power. It can also accommodate unlimited plurality of public discourses, because anyone, especially if she has anonymous identity, can express anything without the fear of social or physical sanctions. If she is expelled from a particular virtual community, she can switch to another one or even finds other same-minded people to form a new one. On social media people can easily avoid discursive confrontation by isolating themselves in their own virtual community. Under this condition people may take no effort to develop a healthy democracy, because they can easily avoid engaging in rational argumentation or making consensus with others. Social media may lead to the fragmentation of society in which anyone only interacts with other same-minded people.

Social media has been hailed to be an important instrument behind the success of some social activisms (Howard *et al.,* 2011; Lim, 2004). We need to critically check our optimism about the potential of social media. To mobilize people virtually is much easier than to do it in real life. We may be able to gain support for a cause from thousands of people if what we ask them to do is only to click "like" or "yes" button. But, would this kind of click activism lead to real social change which often requires strong commitment, including willingness to face the risk? Gladwell argues that social network that we have on social media is built around weak ties.

This is in many ways a wonderful thing. There is strength in weak ties, as the sociologist Mark Granovetter has observed. Our acquaintances—not our friends—are our greatest source of new ideas and information. The Internet lets us exploit the power of these kinds of distant connections with marvellous efficiency. It's terrific at the diffusion of innovation, interdisciplinary collaboration, seamlessly matching up buyers and sellers, and the logistical functions of the dating world. But weak ties seldom lead to high-risk activism. (Gladwell, 2010).

Social media can be a world of its own, but if we expect it to have a real impact to change the actual world, then we need people who are willing to translate what happen virtually into real activities. Real social activisms often demand people to spend their money, time, and even willingness to risk their life which not everyone is ready to do. Without the fulfillment of the demands, the practice of citizenship on social media is just a discursive game.

CONCLUSION

Social media has given voice to the public which has been most of the time voiceless. The technology, which was initially developed to help people to make contact rather than content, has evolved to be a powerful public political instrument. Its simplicity and ubiquitousness have enabled lay people without technical and writing skills to develop extensive social networks without the limitation of geographical distance and social class distinction. Social media eases the development of the network of people having the same concerns and the mobilization of bias to support their concerns. Public which was previously doomed to be represented ultimately can, to some extent, to represent itself on social media. There have been cases of how social media is being used to mobilize social movement that can even topple powerful dictators. However, it requires a lot of energy to translate what have been achieved virtually into a real impact in the actual world.

In the current democratic system there is inevitable separation between the representative and the represented. Normatively the former should always represent the latter. In practice, those who claim to represent their constituents in an election may change their opinions later. The dynamics of parliamentary politics may cause politicians to compromise with one another, which in turn may change their political stances over time. Therefore it is not easy for them to stick to the promises they made to their constituents during the election. Even though it may disappoint the latter, most often they cannot do anything but wait until the next election, because within the current democratic system it often takes too much efforts for the represented to correct the changing opinions of the representatives.

Social media may change the above situation. Any social media user is both a producer and consumer of information. While conventional media make public the target of indoctrination and mobilization of bias, social media allows public not only to counter but also to participate in its own mobilization of bias. Even though not belonging to any political organization a user has the opportunity to raise an issue to the public and strengthen the issues raised by others. A political disappointment, if it is felt by many people, can easily be shared and blown up own social media. Through chains of simple messages people can confirm one another's disappointment.

There is also reason to be critical of the impact of social media on democratization. Social media stimulates the plurality of public which is good and necessary for maintaining a healthy democracy. But, democracy is an attempt at coexistence which requires people to resolve their conflicting interests and views. On the contrary, social media eases people to avoid confronting each other and interact only with the same-minded others, and therefore constraining them to make consensus with others who have conflicting interests. Even worse, the abundance of information does not prevent them to have prejudice toward others. On social media many people send and resend messages of hateful prejudice without checking their accuracy. Overcoming information overload, they select only information that suits their prejudice and ignore the other. Since social media can readily facilitate the formation of a virtual community among geographically dispersed people, consequently it may lead to social fragmentation of people within a particular geographical area. A virtual community may also gives an illusion that they are as real as an actual community, while they are indeed built around weak ties without real commitment other than sending information to each other.

REFERENCES

Bachrach, P., & Baratz, M. S. (1970). *Power and Poverty: Theory and Practice*. New York: Oxford University Press.

Barney, D. (2007). Radical Citizenship in the Republic of Technology: A Sketch. In L. Dahlberg & E. Siapera (Eds.), *Radical Democracy and the Internet*. New York, NY: Palgrave Macmillan. doi:10.1057/9780230592469_3

Beiner, R. (1983). *Political Judgment*. Chicago, IL: University of Chicago Press.

Carey, J. (1995). The press, public opinion, and public discourse. In T. Glasser & C. Salmon (Eds.), *Public Opinion and the Communication of Consent*. Guilford.

Coleman, S., & Ross, K. (2010). *The media and the public: "them" and "us" in media discourse*. Oxford, UK: Wiley-Blackwell. doi:10.1002/9781444318173

Dahl, R. A. (1961). *Who Governs? Democracy and Power in an American City*. New Haven, CT: Yale University Press.

Davis, A. (2007). *The Mediation of Power: A Critical Introduction*. London: Routledge. doi:10.4324/9780203945827

Ellul, J. (1980). *The Technological System* (J. Neugroschel, Trans.). New York, NY: The Continuum Publishing Corporation.

Feenberg, A. (2002). *Transforming Technology: A Critical Theory Revisited* (2nd ed.). Oxford: Oxford University Press.

Gladwell, M. (2010). *Small Change: Why the revolution will not be tweeted*. Retrieved June 20, 2014, from http://www.newyorker.com/reporting/2010/10/04/101004fa_fact_gladwell?currentPage=all

Grant, G. (1974). *English-Speaking Justice*. Toronto: Anansi.

Habermas, J. (1984). *The Theory of Communicative Action – Reason and the Rationalisation of Society* (Vol. I; T. McCarthy, Trans.). Boston, MA: Beacon Press.

Hallin, D. C., & Mancini, P. (2004). *Comparing Media Systems: Three Models of Media and Politics*. Cambridge, UK: Cambridge University Press. doi:10.1017/CBO9780511790867

Hefner, R. W. (1999). Civic Pluralism Denied? The New Media and *Jihadi* Violence in Indonesia. In D. F. Eickelman & J. W. Anderson (Eds.), *New Media in the Muslim World: The Emerging Public Sphere*. Bloomington, IN: Indiana University Press.

Hofstede, G., Hofstede, G. J., & Minkov, M. (2010). *Cultures and Organizations: Software of the Mind* (3rd ed.). New York: McGraw-Hill.

Howard, P. N., Duffy, A., Freelon, D., Hussain, M., Mari, W., & Mazaid, M. (2011). Opening Closed Regimes: What Was the Role of Social Media During the Arab Spring? *Project on Information Technology & Political Islam*. Retrieved from: http://pitpi.org/wp-content/uploads/2013/02/2011_Howard-Duffy-Freelon-Hussain-Mari-Mazaid_pITPI.pdf

Lim, M. (2014). Seeing spatially: people, networks and movements in digital and urban spaces. *IDPR, 36*(1).

Markovitz, I. L. (1999). Constitutions, The Federalist Papers, and the Transition to Democracy. In L. Anderson (Ed.), *Transitions to Democracy*. New York: Columbia University Press. doi:10.7312/ande11590-005

Negroponte, N. (1995). *Being Digital*. London: Hodder and Stoughton.

Ober, J. (1996). *The Athenian Revolution: Essays on Ancient Creek Democracy and Political Theory*. Princeton, NJ: Princeton University Press.

Peleg, I. (2007). *Democratizing the Hegemonic State: Political Transformation in the Age of Identity*. Cambridge, UK: Cambridge University Press. doi:10.1017/CBO9780511611254

Rose, N. (2004). *Powers of Freedom: Reframing Political Thought*. Cambridge, UK: Cambridge University Press.

Saco, D. (2002). *Cybering democracy: public space and the Internet*. Minneapolis, MN: University of Minnesota Press.

Schattschneider, E. E. (1960). *The Semi-Sovereign People: A Realist's View of Democracy in America*. New York, NY: Holt, Rhinehart & Winston.

Shifman, L. (2014). *Memes in Digital Culture*. Cambridge, MA: The MIT Press.

Waite, C. (2013). *The Digital Evolution of an American Identity*. New York, NY: Routledge. doi:10.4324/9780203066409

William, R. (2003). *Television: Technology and cultural form* (2nd ed.). London: Routledge Classics. doi:10.4324/9780203450277

Chapter 11
A Gradual Political Change?
The Agenda-Setting Effect of Online Activism in China 1994-2011

Yuan Yuan
https://orcid.org/0000-0003-1196-0288
Rutgers University, USA

ABSTRACT

In order to understand the contradiction of freedom versus control regarding the internet use in an authoritarian rule, this study is designed to explore a gradual political effect by investigating the agenda-setting effect of internet activism on government political agenda in China from 1994 to 2011. In total, 144 internet activism cases and 526 articles from official newspapers are collected for the analysis and discussion. The results suggest a bottom-up agenda-setting effect from online activism on political agenda, and this agenda-setting effect includes a potential transition from issue level to attribute level. This study also finds that the development of online activism itself obtained a stronger attention from official media, and the continuous growth of activism in forms and scopes generated constant pressure that finally gradually brought about the change of government behavior and strategy.

INTRODUCTION

Early studies on Internet believe that the technological advantages provided by the Internet can help the dissemination of information, accelerate the political participation and provide effective tools for collective actions. The Internet, therefore, could ultimately strengthen democracy in a society. However, with the fast diffusion of the Internet from developed countries to developing countries and from educated urban professionals to broader user groups, accumulated empirical studies have been conducted to examine the different dimensions of the Internet uses in different regions, and the results suggest that the role of the Internet in a society has been largely influenced and shaped by its political system. The usage of the Internet by ordinary citizens is actually restricted by many political, cultural and social factors.

DOI: 10.4018/978-1-7998-1828-1.ch011

Among them, government surveillance and censorship is the recognized obstacle to digital democracy particularly in authoritarian countries.

Internet activism research, as one of the fields in Internet and democracy studies, is usually conducted from two major perspectives. One of the perspectives is to focus on the capability of the Internet in promoting activism and focus predominantly on the analysis of individual incidents particularly the success stories. The other group of scholars puts the context first and argues that the use of Internet does not necessarily lead to a more democratic society. Particularly in the studies focusing on authoritarian regimes, the state usually plays a crucial role in supervising the development of the Internet, which makes the digital democracy still an optimistic hypothesis in these countries (Kalathil & Boas, 2003). Besides abundant case studies conducted from these two major perspectives, a few researchers also mentioned a "gradual change" view of point, which assume that the Internet use may set a process of gradual change to facilitate the democracy transition within a authoritarian rule (Kalathil & Boas, 2003; Yang, 2011). Inspired by this assumption, the current study is designed to explore whether Internet activism in China over a long period of time, regardless of success or failure, may bring about changes in to the government behavior with implications for the political culture and environment. This study analyzes the official newspaper reports on activism cases to explore whether there is a bottom-up agenda-setting effect of the activism agenda on official agenda, what is government's attitude towards and treatment of these reported Internet activism cases, and most importantly, whether government's strategies changed over time. These changes may disclose a gradual political transition driven by grassroots political pressure based on or enhanced by the Internet.

LITERATURE REVIEW

Internet Activism and Democracy

Activism is the practice of using intentional actions to support one side of a controversial issue. It usually relies on a network of individuals, groups, or organizations that share collective identity and attempt to bring about social, political, economic, cultural, or environmental changes (van de Donk, Loader, Nixon, & Rucht, 2004). Activism can take a wide rage of forms of action, from personal blogging to large-scale anti-globalization movement, or dispersive individual protest including cultural jamming. Internet activism, as the name suggests, refers to the activism enhanced by or based on new media technology[1]. The new media technology here includes mobile devices, Internet and a variety of digital contents and networking programs such as online videos, forums, blogs and social networking sites. Scholars focusing on Internet activism usually apply theories from two fields: contemporary social movement studies and new media studies. Social movement theorists regard the Internet as a new communication tool that can facilitate the progress, expand the influence, and mobilize the resources to repackage the traditional movement (Castells, 1997; Chadwick, 2005; Garrett, 2006). Media and Internet theorists, on the other hand, believe that the Internet has formed a public sphere that can promote political debate, political deliberation and then political activism (Dahlberg, 2001; Kahn & Kellner, 2005; Papacharissi, 2002). Thus a potential threat to the current regime can be posed. These different views are generated because of emphases on different types and dimensions of social protests. While in fact, in today's highly penetrated digital environment, the traditional movement and new media activism, or in other words, the offline protest and the online action always interweave with each other. The movement tool function and the public sphere function of the Internet are usually convergent, representing a comprehensive role of Internet activism in political change. Either from the social movement perspective or from the new media perspective, a common question addressed from the academic discussion is whether the use of the Internet can positively assist protests so as to increase the chance of progress toward democracy in a society.

There is always a controversy as to the technical development of the media and the consequence of political change. On one side, scholars celebrate the convenience, speed, interactivity and flexibility of new media, suggesting that it offers more freedom than traditional media by creating unlimited forms of interaction and resource sharing (Kedzie, 1997; Steele & Stein, 2002). The Internet can provide individuals with information and knowledge that was difficult to obtain or access before. It also offers a virtual space within which citizens can discuss, organize, and take actions. These new actors particularly refer to groups that are marginalized by mainstream political relationships (Bimber, 1998). On the other hand, scholars from "the dystopian school of technological determinists" (Garnham, 1993) argue that the future of any "new" technology will inevitably see more surveillance and control. While the new communication technologies provide more choices to the public, they give "ever-greater powers of surveillance and manipulation to power elites " simultaneously (Garnham, 1993, p.254). Apart from this, democracy associated with the Internet is also threatened from other aspects, such as the problem of digital divide and the increasing involvement of corporation powers (Pickard, 2008; Wright, 2004). While the authoritarian rule was considered as the context in this contention, the contradiction of freedom versus control is obvious.

Internet Activism in Authoritarian Countries

Internet activism is believed to be able to bring political change to authoritarian regimes because the nature of the Internet technology promises a decentralized political system and thus can empower the grassroots by forming potential political deliberation and generating political pressure. For instance, in Arab uprisings, scholars (Cohen, 2011; Webster, 2011; Zhou, Wellman, & Yu, 2011) believed that social media played important roles in the revolution by transforming organized groups and informal networks, establishing external linkages, developing a sense of modernity and community, and drawing global attention.

On the other hand, the authoritarian regime's approach toward Internet management is still state-centered, putting the party interests first, and following the propaganda model. Using China as an example, the government regards Internet as another mass media channel that can be used to sway public opinion. Its approach to control the Internet includes using a multilevel monitoring system, shutting down publications or websites, and jailing dissident journalists and activists (Zhao, 2007). A research conducted on Chinese censorship reveals that the postings related to potential collective actions are more likely to be deleted as compared to other oppositional opinions, while the quick deleting speed shows a very efficient "self-censorship" carried out by the corporations in Chinese cyberspace (King, Pan, & Robert, 2012; Zhu, Phipps, Pridgen, Crandall, & Wallach, 2013). In the context of an authoritarian government, the motivation to participate in political activities has been largely eliminated by the perceived political risks rather than the political opportunities offered by new technology. In China, the college students' lack of willingness to engage in online opinion expression is largely because of their worries about negative political impact on their personal and social life (Mou, Atkin, & Fu, 2011). In Azerbaijan, after the "donkey blogger "[2] affair, the arrest of two activists prevented the participation in further political protests and also demoralized the frequent Internet use by Azerbaijan netizens (Pearce & Kendzior, 2012).

In these authoritarian countries, as the mass media is usually controlled and operated as the propaganda tool of the government, whether Internet sphere could surpass the public sphere built by mass media to eventually reach the broader public and generate political pressure is also a problem. Hamdy and Gomaa's (2012) comparative study of news framing of the Egyptian uprising by state-run newspapers and social media discovers distinguishing frames of the same issue in different types of media. While social media are more likely to define the protests as "a revolution for freedom and social justice", the government newspaper frames the event negatively as "a conspiracy on the Egyptian state" with the warning of economic and political consequences. This could explain the popularity of social media and mainstream media's loss of the public's trust during the February 2011 uprisings. This also implies that new media as an alternative to mass media promotes the dissemination of uncensored information among grassroots users and weakens the dominant role of mass media in political crisis.

In countries like China where collective actions are usually not allowed, Chinese netizens are struggling to use the public sphere created in cyberspace to challenge and influence the political decision-making. In their studies of the Chinese blogosphere, Esarey & Xiao (2008, 2011) examine political blog contents in terms of political satires, critiques, and the level of criticism compared to traditional media. The result suggests a trend of the rise of online political discourse after 2003. The researchers believe that these online discourses empower Chinese netizens by enhancing their capability to set the public agenda and shape the political preferences. Hassid (2012) conducted a research on intermedia agenda-setting effect between Chinese mainstream newspaper and blogs. He found that when the issue is exposed by blogs first, the subsequent online debate is more likely to generate social tension that is usually not tolerated by the government. In contrast, when mainstream media sets the issue agenda, the debate on blogs can be the "safety valve" to relieve the possible social pressure generated by the issue.

In order to better understand the relationship between Internet activism and its political effect, Lynch (2011) suggests emphasize the long-term effect of activism online that may or may not lead to immediate political outcomes. Lim (2012) examines activism that took place in Egypt from 2004 to 2011. She explains that, for activists during this period, social media offered space and tools that activists could use to connect with each other and expand their networks. Although the government controlled the development and the result of a single protest, they were unable to prevent the expansion of such networks. These networks played a significant role in the Egyptian revolution later. By the same token, the long-term development of political attitudes, the building of shared repertoires of contention, and the skill of building effective framing are all necessary for a sustainable political change. In the case of China, Internet activism became more frequent in recent years, while the government also invests heavily in controlling online contents and the potential political oppositions. Considering this parallel in the growth of both online activism and state Internet control, conducting a longitudinal study as Lynch suggested can help us better understand this complicated process.

Center/Periphery Public Sphere

Democracy depends heavily on interactions between citizens and a shared voice that is generated as a result of this interaction. Creating a space where this deliberation can take place is essential for a civil society. Habermas formulated the term "public sphere" as a space of practices "between the private interests of everyday life in civil society and the realm of state power", in which "the circulation of information, the exchange of opinions and the formation of public opinion will be located" (Bentivegna, 2006; Kellner, 2000). The emergence of the Internet is immediately regarded as a new means of public sphere by many scholars because this Internet-based communication environment has the potential to be a public forum, and so-called cyberspace has the characteristics to be a "new public space" (Jones, 1997).

To distinguish the new media sphere and new media-based activism from the traditional mass media sphere, some scholars propose a multiplicity structure in regard to a public sphere. Among them, Downey and Fenton (2003) present two domains of public sphere, one of which is a "common domain" consisting of dominant media and the other is a "counter-public sphere" that is the public sphere of the dominated (p.188). Media in the common domain, such as cable television, dominate the information source for the society, while media in the counter-public sphere, such as alternative media, are used for activists and interest groups to promote their messages. This multiple public sphere echoes Habermas's center/periphery dichotomy in his later work as the revisiting of the structure of the public sphere. In this system, the center is the "complexes of administration" that has the capacity to act and the periphery is "those non-governmental and non-economic connections and voluntary associations" that enable conflicts in the private space to become a public topic (Salter, 2003, p.124). The link between these two is communicative actions that produce and maintain a public sphere. The role of media, in this sense, is their communicative ability to bring problems from the periphery to the center, to generate critical debate in a wider public, and ultimately to put problems on the action agenda.

This multiplicity structure of the public sphere is particularly useful for understanding the political impact of Internet activism in authoritarian countries. The Internet first contributes to the generation of a "microsphere" linking the private life and a deliberative space for people (Dahlgren, 2001). In this space, people exchange ideas, look for affiliations, form "diasporic communities" (Pavlik, 1994), and discuss solutions. Those linked groups across different geographic regions then use the Internet to make their ideas or problems known to a macrosphere, in which the mainstream media and administrative system can be reached. Before the emergence of the Internet, it was difficult for the public sphere built among activists to surpass the public sphere built by mass media (Gitlin, 1980). With the help of this digital technology, groups and individuals that "have been traditionally excluded or marginalized in the mass-media public sphere" have the capacity to deliver their opinions to a larger public and reach the mainstream media more effectively (Downey & Fenton, 2003).

In short, from current academic discussions, whether the Internet can promote democracy is still a controversy particularly in authoritarian countries. Many studies on Internet's political effect in authoritarian regimes are conducted from the perspective of the Internet users and therefore emphasize its positive effect in empowering the grassroots activists. But in reality, the surveillance and regulation made by the government and the government campaign against online political contentions make the Internet users in these countries perceive much more political risks than political opportunities. Meanwhile, it is also difficult for the online activism in these countries to break through the well-established mainstream media public sphere to eventually affect the political decision-making, which usually results in more failed cases than success stories. Current study is designed to understand this contradiction by studying the Internet activism from a longitudinal perspective as Lynch (2011) and Lim (2012) suggested. Based on Downey and Fenton's (2003) theory on center/periphery public sphere, the main purpose of this study is to explore whether the issue generated from the periphery public sphere by the Internet activists in China in a 20-year period can reach the center public sphere and further become the topics discussed in this dominant space.

METHODOLOGY AND DATA COLLECTION

Mass Media Agenda and the Internet Agenda in China

First developed by McCombs and Shaw in 1972 in their studies of the presidential election, agenda-setting theory describes the phenomenon that mass media can select certain issues/stories in a broad topic, make it important through the frequency and highlighting, and as a result influence what the audience should think about. The examination of the agenda-setting functions of the mass media does not only refer to the hypothesis about the influence of the news agenda on the public agenda, but also includes the study of the sources that can shape the media's agenda. There are many potential factors that can influence mass media's agenda, ranging from external sources in government, the political position of the news corporation, and the idiosyncrasies of individual journalists (McCombs, Einsiedel, & Weaver, 1991). In the case of China, the State Administration of Radio, Film, and Television (SARFTF) directly supervise the mainstream mass media. SARFTF determines the leadership of national level media enterprises such as China Central Television (CCTV) and has the responsibility to censor any materials in media that may touch sensitive areas of concern for the Chinese government, which means that the mass media agenda in China is usually highly consistent with the government agenda. In other words, the mass media are used as instruments through which the Party can propagate its ideologies and government policies (Pan, 2000).

The agenda from different media can also influence each other, which is called intermedia agenda-setting. The early research of intermedia influence focused on the relationship between traditional media, such as daily newspapers and national news agencies (McCombs & Shaw, 1976; Reese & Danielian, 1989). Most recently, the concept of intermedia agenda-setting is expanded to the intermedia influence between the Internet and other media, though most of them are focusing on online newspaper and campaign websites (Lee, Lancendorfer, & Lee, 2005; Roberts, Wanta, & Dzwo, 2002). Although in many activism studies the Internet has been confirmed as an important tool for activists to generate public attention and set the public agenda, in the current agenda-setting literature, very few studies put specific focus on Internet activism and its relationship to mass media agenda.

Although the importance of Internet activities in China has attracted increasing scholarly attention, the study on its agenda-setting effect is still limited and unsystematic. Some studies show that in China the agenda of discussion online is quite different from the agendas provided by Chinese official media particularly in political incidents (Li & Qin, 2001; Zhou & Moy, 2007). While the other studies found that these online opinion also cannot have an agenda-setting effect on the government. Instead, for some occasions, the government can lead the topic of online discussion (Luo, 2014). Current study fills both the gap of Internet activism agenda-setting studies and the Chinese Internet agenda-setting studies by investigating whether and how online agenda set by activists influences the official media agenda and the government at the national level in China. Since this study explores the agenda-setting effect of a series of activism cases over time, instead of emphasizing the individual cases, it will mainly investigate whether the activism issue generated online by the public has been covered by official media, and then in what way.

Data Collection

Data collection in this study includes two steps. The first step is to build the Chinese Internet activism index. This index will include the major Internet activism cases from 1994 to 2011. The Internet activism cases, in this study, refer to a series of actions, including online actions and offline protests, generated in a certain period to show netizens' support/opposition to a specific topic/issue/incident. Cases in this index are collected from both Chinese sources and English sources. The Chinese sources include the year-end summary and rankings provided by major Chinese language news portals and bulletin boards (*Tianya.net*), the *Annual Report on Internet Public Opinion* by people.com.cn (2009-2011) and research books on Internet incidents and public opinion (including *New Media Events Research* by Qiu and Chan (2011), *The Annual Report on Public Opinion in China* by Yu (2010, 2011, 2012), *Boiling Ice-cold* by Du (2009), *Study on Internet Event in China* by Deng (2012). All of these books contain a list of activism cases the scholars collected based on their own sources.

Meanwhile, considering that the domestic media in China including the Internet have been censored, which means the Internet record may exclude some valuable cases, we reference the English sources as supplement. The key words "Chinese" + "Internet" was used to search on The New York Times and The International New York Times online archive. Among the 502 news articles retrieved, 75 activism cases were collected, including cases that are not mentioned in Chinese sources. In addition, this index also references several independent online archives, including China Digital Times, which is an independent, bilingual media organization aiming to "bring uncensored news and online voices from China to the world," and Danwei, an online media intelligence publication which keeps tracking companies, brands, investments, topics and people on the Chinese Internet and in the Chinese media. The activism index based on above sources will be relatively integral and reliable as it covers data from Chinese Internet records, Chinese official documents, the credible international media from foreign countries, university affiliated organization, and independent organizations. As the result, in total 145 Internet activism cases from 1994 to 2011 are collected for current study.

The second step is to retrieve the official news reports on each activism cases from 1994 to 2011. We select *Renmin Ribao* (*People's Daily*) as the official news sources as it is directly affiliated with the Central Propaganda Department of Chinese Communist Party and is the official newspaper of the Central Committee of Chinese Communist Party. It is usually regarded as an authoritative source of the government policy agenda and accepted as the voice of the Communist Party (Li, Qin, & Kluver, 2003). In order to include all relevant articles, we prepared three keywords from each case, including "name of the key person," "location the incident took place," and "the incident name used by mass media." After examining the pilot data, we set six months as the time frame to count the total responses for each case, and finally, 526 articles were retrieved from *People's Daily*. Three questions are proposed for the analysis: RQ1. What activism cases have been reported or discussed by the official newspaper *People's Daily*? RQ2. How did the official newspaper *People's Daily* cover or discuss these cases? RQ3. Is there a trend of change regarding the government's strategy and treatment towards the Internet activism over time?

Table 1. The total number of activism cases per year and the number of activism cases reported by People's Daily per year

Year	No. of case	No. of case been reported	% of case been reported
1994	0	0	0%
1995	1	n/a	0%
1996	1	n/a	0%
1997	0	0	0%
1998	1	n/a	0%
1999	2	n/a	0%
2000	2	0	0%
2001	3	1	33%
2002	2	0	0%
2003	9	4	44%
2004	9	2	22%
2005	11	4	36%
2006	14	6	43%
2007	7	5	71%
2008	20	11	55%
2009	20	15	75%
2010	18	12	67%
2011	25	13	52%
Total	145	73	50%

RESULTS

Among the 145 Internet activism cases from 1994 to 2011 collected in this study, about half of them (50%) have been reported or discussed in official newspaper *People's Daily*. If we count by the year, the percentage of the activism cases that have relevant articles in official newspaper jumped from 0 to 33% in 2001, and reached its peak 75% in 2009. The number then gradually dropped to 52% in 2011, and by contrast at the same time the total number of Internet activism cases continued to grow.

Most of the activism cases before 2000 are online discussions and actions generated after intense political conflicts between China and other countries, such as Senkaku/Diaoyu Island dispute, United States bombing of the Chinese embassy in Belgrade, and riots in Indonesia. In these cases, the government's political goals converge with the activists' nationalist sentiment, These official coverage are entirely based on these issues' political significance as related to China's international policies. None of these articles are the responses to the online activities, and also the purpose of the Internet actions is not to set a new political agenda. Based on above reasons, we excluded these cases in Table 1.

The activism case-related articles in *People's Daily* present three types of content. The first group of articles simply responds to the issue/incident that triggered the activism, describing the occurrence of the incident, the process of the investigation if it has and the outcome. We define this kind of articles as "issue-centered" in this study. The articles will be categorized in a second group if it mainly discusses

Figure 1. Percentage of activism cases reported by People's Daily from 2000 to 2011

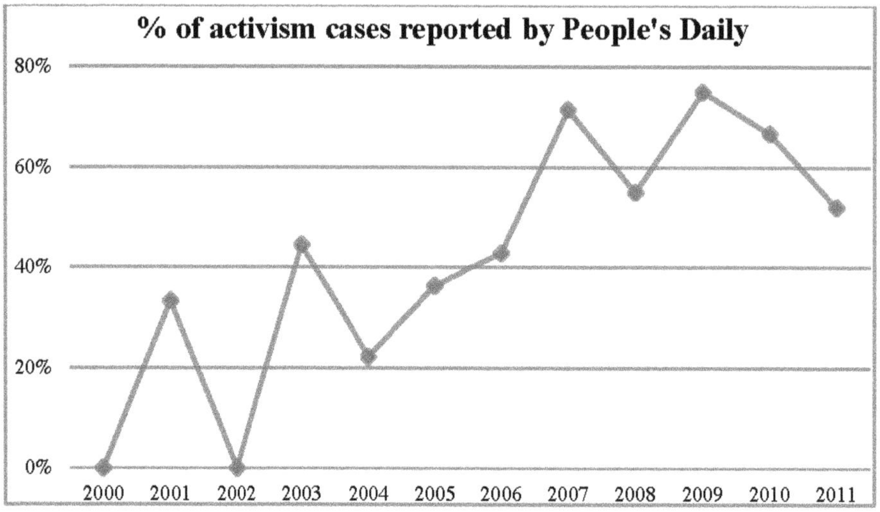

the underlying causes of the incident, the problem of the political environment, or the potential impact on relevant policies/regulations making. These "discussion-centered" articles show the importance attached by the government towards these issues/incidents. It may also indicate the success of setting government policy agenda by the Internet activism. The third group of articles focuses specifically on the role of Internet and the activism strategy by netizens, which is defined as "Internet-centered" responses in this study. This group of articles reflects the official media's framing of the Internet's role in these activism, which, to some extent, actually reveals the government's attitude and strategy to deal with this new contention format emerging from bottom-up.

DISCUSSIONS

Early Activism and "Issue-centered" Articles

Chinese online activism emerged as early as 1995, and before 2000 it largely referred to limited information dissemination, small-scale online debate and the forming of a collective hacking group "Honker Union." In August 1996, in response to the planting of a lighthouse and a Japanese National flag on the disputed Senkaku/Diaoyu Island by a Japanese right-wing group, Chinese civilians including activists from Hong Kong and Taiwan struggled to land on the island to protect and advocate Chinese sovereignty over the Islands (Pan, 2009, p.152). As the earliest Internet users in China, college students generated heated discussions on campus BBS (bulletin board system) from early September. The unusual gathering under such a sensitive topic resulted in the forum's temporary closure for maintenance and the removal of relevant discussion threads[3]. In comparison, the official newspaper only published one piece of report on this issue on October 1st about the death of Chan Yuk-cheung, a prominent leader of the protecting Island movement from Hong Kong. The content of the official report and the online activities do not show any agenda-setting effect from each other.

Table 2. The number of different types of official articles on activism per year

Year	Issue-centered	Discussion-centered	Internet-centered
2000	0	0	0
2001	30	0	0
2002	0	0	0
2003	10	3	0
2004	5	4	0
2005	13	5	0
2006	4	13	10
2007	26	20	4
2008	33	18	10
2009	25	31	10
2010	28	22	16
2011	29	41	14

Figure 2. Comparison of the three types of articles

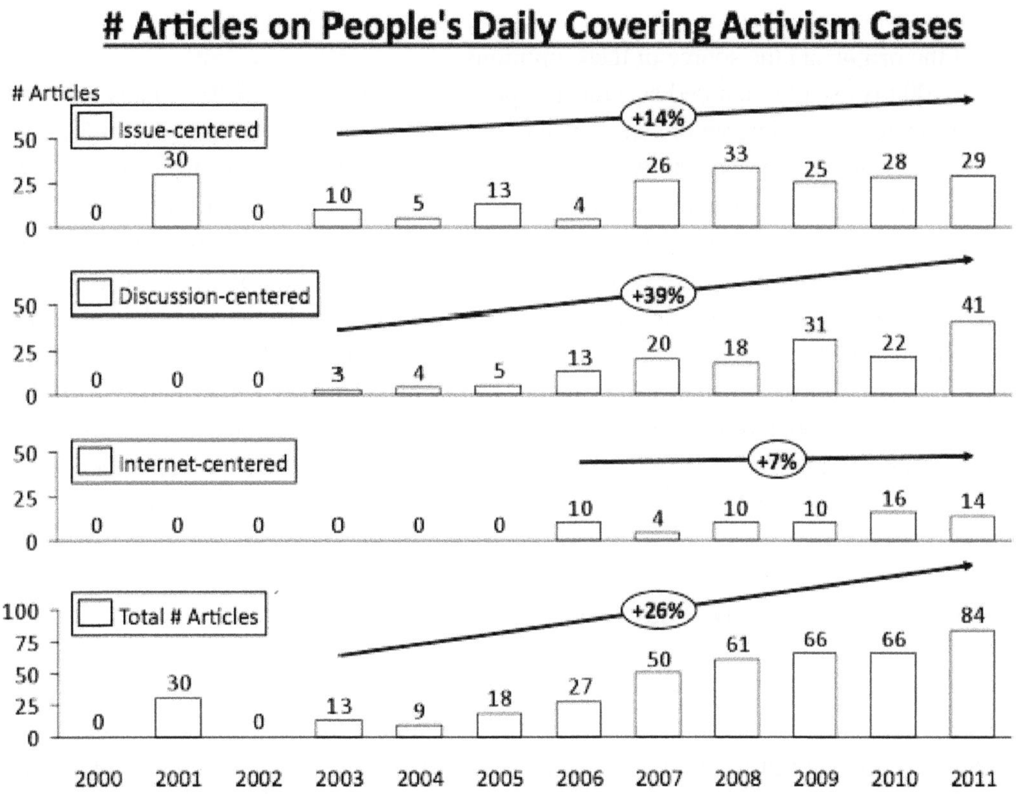

Then, the Honker Union[4], as an informal group of Chinese young hackers, formed later in 1996. Its Chinese name "red hacker," with red being the color of the communist party, suggested its connection to patriotism and nationalism. They launched a series of attacks on government-related websites in Indonesia, Taiwan, United States and Japan from 1996 to 2001. The group became inactive after 2001's "Hainan Island incident"[5] and finally announced the dissolution in 2004. As an important component and an extremely active group of online activism in the early stage of Chinese Internet, these activists and their hacktivism didn't get any attention from official newspaper. Despite the ignorance of hacking actions, the netizens' strong reactions that led to heated discussions did get mentioned in 2001 in the case of US – China aircraft crash. Under the subtitle "fully reflect public opinion: let the netizens speak," the article described that "the number of postings about 'aircraft crash' in Qiangguo (Strong Nation) forum of *People's Daily Online* is more than hundred thousand…the netizens sent a large number of e-mails to *People's Daily* to strongly condemned the hegemonic act of the US government and to express their patriotism."(Liao, 2001)[6] This first-time positive description of online activities was actually used to support the advocacy of the critical role of *People's Daily Online* in major national events as a channel for the public to speak out.

"Nandan Mine Accident" in 2001 is the first activism case that the journalists and netizens used online exposure and discussion to disclose a corruption-caused disaster, in which the local officials attempted to cover up the death of 81 workers in a mine accident. All of the 12 relevant articles in *People's Daily* are issue-centered, emphasizing the effort of central government to supervise the investigations and the severe punishment on mine owner and officials deemed responsible for this accidents. Only one of the articles ambiguously mentioned the role of public opinion in this case in urging the investigation without pointing out the origin and the source of these opinions.

The year 2003 is usually regarded as a turning point of Chinese online activism, as since this year, the online activism cases grew rapidly and diversified in forms and scopes. The case of Sun Zhigang[7], one of the most influential online activism cases in 2003, obviously attracted strong attention from official media. However, among its five relevant articles in *People's Daily*, none of them mentioned about the outrage and the discussion online, not to mention Internet activists' effort in gaining the public and political attention on the injustice in this case and their query on the rationale of Custody and Repatriation system. Later in the same year, the Huang Jing case[8], which also generated a sustained online activism, combined with media attention and legal activism as the Sun Zhigang case did, does not get any reports from the official newspaper. The analysis of these issue-centered official reports shows that cases promoted by Internet activism have started to obtain the official newspaper's attention as early as 2001 but only in the issue-level. The official reports still followed their own political agenda instead of reflecting the concerns generated from the online discussions. The role of the Internet in these activism cases was also largely neglected in the official reports.

From "Issue-Centered" to "Discussion-Centered"

The official newspaper's first response to netizens' discussions online is in the BMW case in early 2004. In this case, in response to the online criticism, the government formed a judicial panel to look into the possibility of improper prevention to justice. The two relevant articles in *People's Daily* discus the reinvestigation that was taken under public pressure and point out the lack of information transparency in law enforcement in this case.

Internet-enhanced environmental demonstration started and quickly became a major activism category from 2005. The official report on this category is very selective though. Among the three environmental cases in 2005[9], two have been reported by official newspaper. These articles include both "issue-centered" and "discussion-centered" responses and reflect opinions from environmental activists and netizens. The larger-scale environmental activism including Xiamen protest against the building of a paraxylene (PX) plant in 2007[10] and a nationwide PM 2.5 campaign in 2011 are also reported in detail by official newspaper with the emphasis on discussing relevant policies and environmental problems. However, the smaller-scale environmental protests, such as anti-maglev campaign in 2008, Zhoushan protest against the building of a chemical plant in 2008, and Haimen protest against expanding a power plant in 2011 are less likely to get any attention from official newspaper.

When cultural activism and social moral topics outbroke in 2006, Internet-based actions, including cultural jamming, blog debates, and human flesh search engine have been widely used by netizens, which immediately caught media's attention. The official newspaper responded to most of these cases and drew a lot of space to criticize the negative effect of Internet-based actions instead of the issue it-self. These criticisms increase the visibility of netizens and their online activities in the public agenda. Cited paragraphs from bulletin boards, blogs and weibo[11] became common in these official reports, though most times citations were still used to support the official's point of view. In 2006, the number of discussion-centered responses first time exceeded the number of issue-centered responses, suggesting that the influence of online activism to government agenda have turned from issue level to attribute level.

Two new categories of online activism emerged in 2008, which generated more interactions between netizens and the government. The first one is a series of activism asking for the investigations on food safety problems including the Sanlu milk scandal[12]. In this case, not only does the official newspaper cite online discussions to show the public opinion, but it also inviteds the officials in charge to answer the netizens' questions regarding the investigation results in a virtual interview set by *People's Daily online*. The second emerging category of activism refers to a series of online exposure of corruption cases started late 2008, including Zhou Jiugeng scandal[13], the government delegation scandal[14] and official sexual harassment scandal[15]. The human flesh search engine and cultural jamming have been effectively used in these cases, but this time the netizens' activities in anti-corruption have been highly praised by official media.

There is an obvious trend that the issue-centered articles are gradually replaced by discussion-centered and Internet-centered articles after 2009. In Qian Yunhui case[16] in 2010, instead of criticizing the netizens' guesses as rumor as in other previous cases, the official reports responded to each major assumptions raised by netizens by providing the detail report of the investigation. In the articles responding Zhou Senfeng case[17], the official media pointed out that the online activism, instead of targeting individuals, actually pointing out the problem of information disclosure mechanism and public opinion feedback mechanism of local government. The official media also first time positively discussed the emotional expressions by netizens in activism cases, describing them a form of "respect to the life, persistence to kindness" in Wang Yue case[18]. From these cases, we could see the effort of official media to arrange their discussions in consistent with the Internet agenda, though only on the cases selected for reports.

"Internet-Centered": Framing of Internet Activism in Official Newspaper

From 2006 to 2011, although there is little change of the number of Internet-centered activism relevant articles in official newspaper, the content, or in other words, the framing of Internet and Internet activism in these articles changes over time.

In year 2006, among the total 10 Internet-centered articles, 9 of them focus on the downsides of Internet activism. It criticized Egao – a form of cultural jamming – as a form of Internet infringement, a negative cultural value and the spokesperson of marginalized culture. The marginalized culture was further defined as a problematic culture in a society (Chen, 2006)[19], which shows the strong denial by the elite and mainstream cultural circle to this Internet activism culture. Blog, which has been introduced to Chinese netizens around 2002, was first time appeared in official reports because of "uncouth" blogger behavior. The official articles also censured the Internet actions taken by grassroots netizens in some cases, calling these "online arrest warrant" and "human flesh search engine" Internet violence. Underlying these severe criticism is the forming of a potential government agenda - considering the negative effect of netizens' activities, the Internet need supervision.

The 4 Internet-centered articles in 2007 show a transition in official newspaper's framing of Internet. Two of the articles are in accordance with the tune of criticism in 2006, while the other two start to look into the relationship between the activism cases and the misconduct of officials. In Brick Slave scandal, the governor in Shanxi province where the scandal happened summarized the lesson from this incident that "the ignorance of online opinion by the local officials resulted in the delay of investigation and government reaction." (Ji, 2007)[20] The Internet then was commented as the "direct channel to collect public opinion" (Ji, 2007)[21] in one of the Internet-centered articles, which also suggested that the party and government officials at all level need to learn knowledge of Internet in order to better guide the public opinion.

The positive role of Internet activism in solving public issues was highlighted in 2008's internet-centered articles. The netizens' activity online was given a new name "citizen participation," and because of the Internet, "citizen, the unfamiliar word for Chinese people is now getting closer to our life."(Shi & Bai, 2008)[22] Netizens were also praised for the "effectives in promoting the socialism democratic construction."(Li, 2008)[23] From 2006 to 2008, this is a huge change of framing regarding Internet activism in official newspaper. In 2008, Internet activism was described as an important component of political life for citizens, having the potential to influence the political environment in China (Li & Zhang, 2008; He, 2008)[24]. This change from derogatory to praise can be understood as a response to the report of seventeenth National Congress of the Communist Party held in October 2007,which asked for strengthening citizen's political participation in a well-organized manner. The framing of a positive Internet also reflected this guiding principle. All Internet-centered articles in 2008 emphasized that the participation of Internet or new technology users in political life should be in order and in control, which is "the fundamental of Chinese socialism democratic ecology."(Li, 2008)[25] With this guidance, three articles also started to discuss the necessary to establish Internet regulation and build up the netizens' self-constraint.

The rise of anti-corruption activism in late 2008 led the framing of activism articles in 2009, and the official newspaper started to frame the Internet as the helper, collaborator and supervising tools for the government. According to these internet-centered articles, netizens' participation in political decision-makings has been initially formed, and therefore, building a healthy interaction between netizens and the government was the core work of officials. In this sense, the official newspaper provided further directions that include "(under the supervision of the Internet), the government needs to reply timely, increase information transparency, and seek for active interactions with netizens;" "provide a faster and sincere reply to the public, ... use the public supervision as the chance to tackle social problems" and called this the "technique of governing" in an Internet era (Lu, 2009; Chen, 2009)[26]. The official newspaper also changed its attitude to activism culture. In the article "The social culture ecology of hot words is worth paying attention to," after a detailed account of the backgrounds and the origins of several Egao cases, the article made a rare comment calling this phenomenon the prelude of "stars shining of Chinese thinking and academic circle." (Lv & Zhao, 2009)[27]

In 2010, while the internet-centered articles continued to affirm the essential of citizen participation in political decision-makings, building the "Internet governing techniques" has become the focus of framing. Through analyzing several activism cases, the government found that Internet actually can "resolve possible conflicts between cadres and the masses."[28] It then provided more detailed guidelines to improve the skills of coping with the Internet activism such as "golden four hours rule"(Li, 2010)[29], which suggested an effective response time frame for officials and relevant government departments in unexpected activism cases. Furthermore, the official newspaper also made requests, asking the government officials to take a more initiative role in Internet politics, which included the strategies to build up the reputation of official forum, let mainstream discourse get into the cyberspace, and institutionalize the Internet opinion into government system. The once criticized activism culture was also re-analyzed and was finally considered as a kind of expression of public opinion. (Fang, 2010)[30]

With a more sophisticated treatment to the Internet, the official articles started to underline that the Internet opinion only reflect partial of the public opinion and has many limitations including the authenticity of online speech. Among the 14 Internet-centered articles in 2011, 10 discussed the Internet management, including strengthening the discourse power of government in cyberspace, encouraging the opening of official's social media accounts, and advocating Internet real-name system. Regarding the problem of government itself such as the lack of government's credibility that was reflected from the Internet discussion, these official articles also responded positively, calling for the improvement of transparency and the change of governance approach, as well as the mediator role of traditional media and the discipline of Internet users themselves. The well-controlled interaction between the Internet political discourse and government reactions was also described as "the valve of social grievance and the lubricants between the public and officials."(Shan, 2011)[31] These responses from the official newspaper showed a more active and confident role of the government in dealing with the rapidly development of Internet activism. Their strategy and treatment to these Internet struggles is clear and firm as mentioned by one of the articles "the right choice (of strategy) is to combine supervision and use, and to reach the effective control of the Internet through making use of it."(Wang & Zhang, 2011)[32]

CONCLUSION

Through analyzing the relevant articles in *People's Daily* on activism cases from 1994 to 2011, we did find a bottom-up agenda-setting effect from online activism on political agenda. And there is a trend that an increasing number of activism cases were brought to the mainstream public sphere gradually over time. The agenda-setting effect also includes a potential transition from issue level to attribute level. While many studies are focusing on individual case effect, we found that the development of online activism itself obtained a stronger attention from official media, and the continuous growth of activism in forms and scopes generated constant pressure that finally gradually brought about the change of government behavior and strategy. The most obvious change is that the government's attitude to the Internet activism changed from ignorance to selective attention, which indicates that some of the topics generated by the periphery public sphere successfully reach the center public sphere. The expanding discussions on specific cases also made the issues generated by the activism become the political agenda.

Highly selective is the main limitation of this bottom-up agenda-setting. Many factors may affect the chances of an online activism case being selected by official media, such as the scale of the demonstration, the timing and location of the activism, the person or groups involved, and the tactic used by netizens. Since each activism case has its specific characteristic and dynamic surrounding political environment, the protests with the similar causes and strategies can embrace distinguish treatments from the government. From the current data, we found that the general category of the activism case does not determine whether or not a case will be reported by government media. Some categories, such as anti-corruption related activism cases, increased the chance to be reported particularly after 2008. However, to the contrary, the category can be a determining factor that tells the chance of not being reported by official media. There is a category in our index that never get any reply from official newspaper, which is the call to release dissidents in detention and the activism asking for immediate democratic revolution. One direction of the further studies could focus on this area and investigates the factors of case characteristics that may increase the chance of a case to enter the center public sphere.

Regarding the activism cases that have been selected, it also took several years for the official newspaper from picking only the issue to report to discussing the features of the case that was concerned by the netizens. In a few of cases, the online "rumors" also got responses from the official channel. Being reported by official newspaper usually means that the case has gotten the attention from the central government and has been properly settled down. In addition, through analyzing these official articles, we found that, besides solving the case itself, this bottom-up agenda-setting have also brought changes to the government behavior, or at least boosted the process for changing. These changes include but not limited to: the official articles repeatedly emphasized on improving information transparency to meet public's right to know; made the anti-corruption a lasting and recognized Internet campaign; in some cases, the netizens' opinion successfully pushed back the government's initiatives to tighten the Internet management; and the government has significantly improved the communication channel between officials and the public.

There is a significant turning point during 2008 when the official media started to acknowledge the legitimacy of Internet activism by framing them as beneficial activities to national stability by assisting the party to solve the conflicts between the political elites and the public. This shift, on one hand, eased the nearly uncontrolled situation that the public is more likely to turn to the Internet to look for justice and ask for collective actions. While on the other hand, it reclaims the party's leadership through making this activism form as a component of the "public opinion supervision system" that is defined by and serve the ruling party. Despite its political intention, the change of the rhetoric by this most authoritative newspaper on Internet activism sill gives the positive signals to the public to make them feel that their voices can be heard and believe that there is a channel connecting the periphery public sphere and the center public sphere, which can create more political opportunities for grassroots activists.

However, the existence of the bottom-up agenda-setting effect does not guarantee the open door of the center public sphere, as the Chinese government also actively reshaped and redefined the boundaries of political discourse. According to the Internet-centered articles in *People's Daily* after 2009, while it asserted the positive role of the Internet in uncovering social problems and collecting public opinions, the agenda asking for a better monitoring and participating role of the government in Internet activities has been highlighted as well. In fact, the agenda on building more effective management and regulation of Internet use emerged on official newspaper as early as 2006, and after that, the government never gave up the effort on seeking for approaches to tighten up the Internet activities to bring them back to the controllable track, which they called "well-organized political participation" or "healthy interaction between the netizens and the government." Among the many strategies and treatments, bringing thousands of official accounts to the social media platforms and expanding the government agencies' influence on the Internet did achieve beneficial results.

This study examines the possible bottom-up agenda-setting effect to explore the gradual process that the Internet activism affected the government behavior over time. During these repeated confrontations with the government, Chinese netizens indeed opened up some extra space for political discourse and the opportunities to enter the mainstream public sphere. While on the other hand, their struggles also resulted in a possible tightened management of the Internet. This strategic "management", instead of the rigorous censorship or mandatory control, can better describe the status quo of Chinese government's Internet policy that is the "combination of supervision and use." Although the official newspaper showed the result of this bottom-up agenda-setting, it provided very limited information on how it happened. The process of transferring the Internet agenda to the center public sphere and to finally generate a political or policy change is much more complicated than the current data can present. It usually involves various agents or agencies that will define the issue, translate the message, organize the online gathering, and lead the emotional mobilization in the different stages of the activism. These agencies, combining with the political opportunities appear at the right time, are the real components of the "channel" connecting the periphery public sphere and the center public sphere. The future studies can further investigate the mechanism of this channel to build a better understanding and model to explain Internet's political effect.

REFERENCES

Bentivegna, S. (2006). Rethinking politics in the world of ICTs. *European Journal of Communication, 21*(3), 331–343. doi:10.1177/0267323106066638

Bimber, B. (1998). The Internet and political transformation: Populism, community, and accelerated pluralism. *Polity, 31*(1), 133–160. doi:10.2307/3235370

Castells, M. (1997). The Information Age: Economy, Society and Culture: Vol. I. *The power of identity*. Oxford, UK: Blackwell.

Chadwick, A. (2005). *The Internet, political mobilization and organizational hybridity: 'Deanspace', MoveOn.org and the 2004 US Presidential campaign*. Retrieved on Feb 10, 2016 from http://www.rhul.ac.uk/politics-and-ir/About-Us/Chadwick/pdf/A_Chadwick_Internet_Mobilization_and_Organizational_Hybridity_PSA_2005.pdf

Cohen, R. (2011). Facebook and Arab dignity. *New York Times,* Retrieved on Feb 10, 2016 from http://www.nytimes.com/2011/01/25iht-edcohen25.html

Dahlgren, P. (2001). The public sphere and the net: Structure, space, and communication. *Mediated politics: Communication in the future of democracy*, 33-55.

Downey, J., & Fenton, N. (2003). New media, counter publicity and the public sphere. *New Media & Society*, *5*(2), 185–202. doi:10.1177/1461444803005002003

Esarey, A., & Xiao, Q. (2008). Below the Radar: Political Expression in the Chinese Blogosphere. *Asian Survey*, *48*(5), 752–772. doi:10.1525/AS.2008.48.5.752

Esarey, A., & Xiao, X. (2011). Digital communication and political communication in China. *International Journal of Communication*, *5*, 298–319.

Garnham, N. (1993). The mass media, cultural identity, and the public sphere in the modern world. *Public Culture*, *5*(2), 251–265. doi:10.1215/08992363-5-2-251

Garrett, R. K. (2006). Protest in an information society: A review of literature on social movements and new ICTs. *Information Communication and Society*, *9*(2), 202–224. doi:10.1080/13691180600630773

Gitlin, T. (1980). *The whole world is watching: Mass media in the making & unmaking of the new left*. University of California Press.

Hamdy, N., & Gomaa, E. (2012). Framing the Egyptian uprising in Arabic language newspapers and social media. *Journal of Communication*, *62*(2), 195–211. doi:10.1111/j.1460-2466.2012.01637.x

Hassid, J. (2012). Safety valve or pressure cooker? Blogs in Chinese political life. *Journal of Communication*, *62*(2), 212–230. doi:10.1111/j.1460-2466.2012.01634.x

Jones, S. G. (1997). The Internet and its social landscape. In S. G. Jones (Eds.), Virtual Culture: Identity and Communication in Cybersociety (pp. 7-35). Thousand Oaks, CA: Sage.

Kahn, R., & Kellner, D. M. (2005) Oppositional politics and the Internet: A critical /reconstructive approach. In M.G. Durham & D. M. Kellner (Eds.), Media and cultural studies. Revisited (2nd ed.; pp. 703-725). Malden, MA: Blackwell Publishing Ltd.

Kalathil, S., & Boas, T. C. (2003). *Open Networks, Closed Regimes*. Carnegie Endowment for International Peace.

Kedzie, C. R. (1997). *Communication and democracy: Coincident revolutions and the emergent dictator's dilemma*. Retrieved on Feb 10, 2016 from http://www.rand.org/pubs/rgs_dissertations/RGSD127.html

Kellner, D. (2000). Habermas, the public sphere, and democracy: A critical intervention. *Perspectives on Habermas*, 259-288.

King, G., Pan, J., & Robert, M. (2012). How censorship in china allows government criticism but silences collective expression. *The American Political Science Review*, *107*(2), 1–18.

Lee, B., Lancendorfer, K., & Lee, J. (2005). Agenda-setting and the Internet: The intermedia influence of Internet bulletin boards on newspaper coverage of the 2000 general election in South Korea. *Asian Journal of Communication*, *15*(1), 57–71. doi:10.1080/0129298042000329793

Li, X., & Qin, X. (2001). Who is setting the Chinese agenda? The impact of BBS forums on the agenda of party press in prominent news events. *Journal of Communication*, *3*, 55–62.

Li, X., Qin, X., & Kluver, R. (2003). Who is setting the Chinese agenda? The impact of online chatrooms on Party press. In K. C. Ho, R. Klwer, & C. C. Yang (Eds.), *Asian.Com: Asian encounters the Internet* (pp. 143–158). London, UK: Routledge.

Lim, M. (2012). Clicks, cabs, and coffee houses: Social media and oppositional movements in Egypt, 2004-2011. *Journal of Communication, 62*(2), 363–248. doi:10.1111/j.1460-2466.2012.01628.x

Luo, Y. (2014). The Internet and Agenda-setting in China: The Influence of Online Public Opinion on Media Coverage and Government Policy. *International Journal of Communication, 8*(204), 1289–1312.

Lynch, M. (2011). After Egypt: The limits and promise of online challenges to the authoritarian Arab state. *Perspectives on Politics, 9*(2), 301–310. doi:10.1017/S1537592711000910

McCombs, M., Einsiedel, E., & Weaver, D. (1991). *Contemporary public opinion*. Hillsdale, NJ: Erlbaum.

McCombs, M., & Shaw, D. (1976). Structuring the "unseen environment.". *Journal of Communication, 2*(2), 18–22. doi:10.1111/j.1460-2466.1976.tb01374.x

Mou, Y., Atkin, D., & Fu, H. (2011). Predicting political discussion in a censored virtual environment. *Political Communication, 28*(3), 341–356. doi:10.1080/10584609.2011.572466

Paltemaa, L., & Vuori, J. (2009). Regime transition and the Chinese politics of technology: From mass science to the controlled Internet. *Asian Journal of Political Science, 17*(1), 1–23. doi:10.1080/02185370902767557

Pan, J. W. (2009). *Toward a New Framework for Peaceful Settlement of China's Territorial and Boundary Disputes*. Brill: Nijhoff.

Pan, Z. (2000). Improving reform activities: The changing reality of journalistic practice in China. In C. C. Lee (Ed.), *Power, money, and media: Communication patterns and bureaucratic control in cultural China* (pp. 68–111). Evanston, IL: Northwestern University Press.

Papacharissi, Z. (2002). The virtual space: The Internet as a public sphere. *New Media & Society, 4*(1), 9–27. doi:10.1177/14614440222226244

Pavlik, J. V. (1994). Citizen access, involvement, and freedom of expression in an electronic environment. In F. Williams & J. V. Pavlik (Eds.), *The People's Right to Know: Media, Democracy, and the Information Highway, (pp. 139-62)*. Hillsdale, NJ: Erlbaum.

Pearce, E. K., & Kendzior, S. (2012). Networked authoritarianism and social media in Azerbaijan. *Journal of Communication, 62*(2), 283–289. doi:10.1111/j.1460-2466.2012.01633.x

Pickard, V. W. (2008). Cooptation and cooperation: Institutional exemplars of democratic Internet technology. *New Media & Society, 10*(4), 625–645. doi:10.1177/1461444808093734

Qiu, L., & Chan, M. (Eds.). (2011). *New Media Events Research*. Beijing: Renmin University Press.

Reese, S. D., & Danielian, L. H. (1989). Intermedia influence and the drug issue: converging on co- caine. In P. Shoemaker (Ed.), *Communication campaigns about drugs: Government, media and the public* (pp. 47–66). Hillside, NJ: Lawrence Erlbaum Associates.

Roberts, M., Wanta, W., & Dzwo, T. (2002). Agenda-setting and issue salience online. *Communication Research, 29*(4), 452–465. doi:10.1177/0093650202029004004

Salter, L. (2003). Democracy, new social movements, and the Internet. *Cyberactivism: Online activism in theory and practice*, 117-144.

Steele, C., & Stein, A. (2002). Communications revolutions and international politics. In J. E. Allison (Ed.), *Technology, development, and democracy* (pp. 25–54). Albany, NY: State University of New York Press.

Tarrow, S. (1998). Fishnets, Internets, and Catnets: Globalization and transnational collective action. *Challenging authority: The historical study of contentious politics*, 228-244.

Tilly, C., & Tarrow, S. (2007). *Contentious Politics*. Paradigm Publishers.

van de Donk, W., Loader, D. B., Nixon, P., & Rucht, D. (Eds.). (2004). Cyberprotest: New Media, Citizens and Social Movements. New York: Routledge.

Vegh, S. (2003). Classifying forms of online activism: The case of cyberprotests against the World Bank. In M. McCaughey & M. D. Ayers (Eds.), Cyberactivism: Online Activism in Theory and Practice. New York: Routledge.

Webster, G. R. (2011). Guard your revolution": Comments on the" Arab Spring" Essays. *Arab World Geographer, 14*(2), 160–165.

Wright, S. (2004). Informing, communicating and ICTs in contemporary anti-capitalist movements. In W., van de Donk, D. B., Loader, P., Nixon, & D, Rucht (Eds.), Cyberprotest: New Media, Citizens and Social Movements (pp. 69-83). New York: Routledge.

Yang, G. (2009). *The Power of the Internet in China: Citizen Activism Online*. Columbia University Press.

Yang, G. (2011). China's Gradual Revolution. *New York Times*. Retrieved on Feb 10, 2016 from http://www.nytimes.com/2011/03/14/opinion/14Yang.html?_r=0

Zhao, Y. Z. (2007). After Mobile Phones, What? Re-embedding the Social in China's "Digital Revolution.". *International Journal of Communication, 1*, 92–120.

Zhou, X., Wellman, B. & Yu, J. (2011, July). Egypt: The first Internet revolt? *Peace Magazine*, 6-10.

Zhou, Y., & Moy, P. (2007). Parsing framing processes: The Interplay between online public opinion and media coverage. *Journal of Communication, 57*, 79–98.

Zhu, T., Phipps, D., Pridgen, A., Crandall, J., & Wallach, D. (2013). *The Velocity of Censorship: High-Fidelity Detection of Microblog Post Deletions*. Retrieved from http://arxiv.org/abs/1303.0597

ENDNOTES

1 Internet-enhanced refers to the use of websites, email lists, or alternative media as the additional tool to communicate and to mobilize physical movements. Internet-based, by contrast, is used to describe the action that can only take place online as a new form of activism, such as hacktivism or email bombing (Vegh, 2003).

2 "Donkey blogger" refers to a satirical video posted on YouTube, mocking the Azerbaijan government for wasting oil revenues to import two donkeys for $41,000 each. The two activists and bloggers responsible for the video were arrested later.

3 Recorded in the online article "The Chronicle of the Events on SMTH BBS" retrieved from https://bbs.sjtu.edu.cn

4 Also known as "Red Hacker Alliance"

5 Hainan Island incident refers to an aircraft collision between U.S. and China in 2001.

6 Liao, H. (2001, April 14). People's Daily Online: With the Major Events, *People's Daily*, p.5.

7 Sun Zhigang is a graphic designer working in Guangzhou. He was found dead of a hemorrhage and heart attack while in police custody. This incident generated thousands of discussion online and the questions to Custody and Repatriation policy. As the result of this incident, the government announced the abolishment of the abusive Custody and Repatriation system during late 2003.

8 Huang Jing is a primary school teacher who was found dead in her dormitory and her boyfriend, Jiang Junwu, an official with the local taxation administration, admitted to attempting to have sex with Huang, but denied raping or murdering her. This case was considered to facilitate the reform of the forensic expertise system starting in 2005.

9 These three cases include the controversy on the building of Nujiang Dam, the contamination of Songhua River after the explosion of a chemical plant, and the Dong Zhou protest against building a new power plant by infilling the bay.

10 An environmental protest by local residents in Xiamen against the building of a PX plant. After the street demonstration organized by cell phone, the government was forced to relocate the plant to Zhangzhou.

11 Also called microblogging. It is Chinese version twitter.

12 In July 2008, after sixteen infants in Gansu Province were diagnosed with kidney stones, the milk products from 21 companies, including Sanlu Group was found to be adulterated with melamine. The issue raised concerns about food safety and political corruption in China.

13 Zhou Jiugeng was the director of Nanjing's property bureau. He was put in prison after the exposure of his luxury lifestyle by netizens.

14 A group of officials from Wenzhou and Xinyu were punished after that a set of lavish travel expenses for their trip to Las Vegas was posted on the internet.

15 A Shenzhen's marine affairs bureau official was fired after a video of him molesting an 11-year-old girl appeared on the internet.

16 Qian Yunhui is a village head, who died in a controversial traffic accident. In this case, the Chinese Internet activist organized their own investigation to the crime scene.

17 Zhou Senfeng was promoted to be the youngest mayor in China in 2011, which drew many skeptics from netizens who doubted his qualifications and questioned the covert procedures involved in his appointment.

18 A two years girl who was run over by two vehicles and ignored by 18 passers-by. She was eventually helped by a female rubbish scavenger and died eight days later.

19 Chen, Q. (2006, July 23). Internet created "hot topic." *People's Daily*, p. 8.

20 Ji, Y. (2007, August 14). Party and government officials need to face the Internet era. *People's Daily*, p. 10.

21 Ji, Y. (2007, August 14). Party and government officials need to face the Internet era. *People's Daily*, p.10.

22 Shi, G, & Bai, L. (2008, January 2). 2008: feel the power of citizen participation. *People's Daily*, p. 13.

23 Li, H. (2008). (2008, January 4), 2007: listen to Chinese netizens. *People's Daily*, p. 5.

24 Li, F, & Zhang, J. (2008, November 27). Chinese Internet: Internet renovates life. *People's Daily*, p. 16.; He, Z. (2008, June 25). Using the power of Internet to push China. *People's Daily*, p. 4.

25 Li, H. (2008, January 4), 2007: listen to Chinese netizens. *People's Daily*, p. 5

26 Lu, X. (2009, June 24). How does government respond to microphone era? *People's Daily*, p.5 ; Chen, K. (2009, October 27) The Shanghai example of "power" respect "right" *People's Daily*, p.6.

27 Lv, S. & Zhao, Z. (2009, October 13). The social culture ecology of hot words is worth paying attention to. *People's Daily*, p.11.

28 Internet dialogue, witness the political civilization. (2010, January 7). *People's Daily*, p.6.

29 Li, H. (2010, February 2). New media era: Four hours rule of handling unexpected events. *People's Daily*, p.19.

30 Fang, K. (2010, June 1). Rethink Internet culture. *People's Daily*, p. 15.

31 Shan, X. (2011, June 30). How does the power of microblogging leverage the reality. *People's Daily*, p.5.

32 Wang, S. & Zhang, Y. (2011, August 30). Microblogging governing" promotes government behavior change. *People's Daily*, p. 5.

Chapter 12
Participedia as a Ground for Dialogue

Marco Adria
https://orcid.org/0000-0001-6622-5884
University of Alberta, Canada

Paul Richard Messinger
University of Alberta, Canada

Edrick A. Andrews
University of Alberta, Canada

Chelsey Ehresman
Medicine Hat College, Canada

ABSTRACT

Participedia (participedia.net) is a wiki-based library of some 1,000 cases of democratic innovations in their historical and cultural contexts. Public-involvement (PI) practitioners can learn about changes in their field of practice. The relative strength of the five dialogic qualities available in Participedia is important because of the values of communicative understanding inherent in the domain of democratic innovations. The question addressed in the study is, How does a community of practice (COP) augment Participedia's capacity to provide a ground for dialogue about PI? A quasi-experiment was carried out among 13 PI practitioners. COP members met face-to-face over a period of four weeks to learn about, apply, and deliberate upon Participedia's online resources. A focus group was then carried out in which the PI practitioners reflected on the qualities of dialogue available in the COP-Participedia experience. Themes from the focus group support the argument that COP-Participedia can augment the dialogic qualities of mutuality, propinquity, and empathy.

DOI: 10.4018/978-1-7998-1828-1.ch012

INTRODUCTION

Participedia, the Domain of Democratic Innovations, and Its Practitioners

Fung and Warren (2011) observe that most democratic institutions have failed to keep pace with the demands of citizens for involvement in important policy decisions that affect them. This is in spite of the fact that public involvement (PI) is more likely to lend legitimacy to policy decisions and to build public support for them (Mao & Adria, 2013). A significant factor for explaining the lag between citizen expectations and institutional responses is the change and variation characteristic of the domain of democratic innovations:

Our knowledge of this rapidly expanding universe is shallow, especially when we compare our knowledge of these emerging institutions to those we have been studying for many decades: representative legislatures, executive offices and bureaucracies, municipal councils, and various forms of authoritarianism. What kinds of processes are appropriate for what kinds of issues? What kinds of processes are likely to generate better rather than worse outcomes—more legitimacy, justice, or effectiveness, say—given the characteristics of the issues and the constraints of time and money (Fung & Warren, p. 342)?

Participedia (participedia.net) is a website and research platform that collects crowdsourced data about democratic innovations from around the world. Since its establishment in 2009, Participedia has generated some 1,000 cases, along with other resources about methods and organizations associated with democratic innovations. Openly licensed with Creative Commons, Participedia's origins were shaped in significant part by the purposes of researchers. Participedia allows researchers systematically to compare data about democratic innovations (Gastil, Richards, Ryan, & Smith, 2017). Participedia is also used by PI practitioners. These practitioners work as advocates, activists, and professional staff in NGOs and government, seeking to identify, apply, and improve methods that are fit for the purpose of involving citizens in decisions that affect them.

The challenge of change and variation in the field for PI practitioners can be illustrated using the example of public transportation. Grossardt, Bailey, and Brum (2003) describe the history since the early 1980s of involving the public in important policy decisions related to how public transportation is planned and designed by a given urban or metropolitan government authority. While research continues to identify PI as critical to the success of major transportation-planning initiatives (Khisty, 1996; Reinke & Malarkey, 1996), input from non-practitioners "sometimes fails to include detailed consideration of [public involvement] while describing thoroughly all other phases of the planning effort" (Grossardt et al., 2003, p. 95). Even when PI efforts are made, significant disagreements may arise among members of the public. These disagreements may eventually be "reproduced" in an advisory committee, whose input may not be as specific and as targeted to an appropriate stage of planning as it would have been. The continuing question for PI in major transportation projects is to determine the level or quality of engagement with the public that allows input to be directed to best effect.

To answer this question, a current and comprehensive map of change and variation in the field of PI, described in various cultural and economic contexts, is required. Participedia provides resources that help create such a map, a "landscape of new participatory institutions," as Fung and Warren (2011) call it. Participedia's use extends beyond transportation planning to all major areas of decision-making in which PI has a key function in improving the quality of decisions and strengthening the accountability and responsiveness of democratic institutions.

The Dialogic Affordances of Participedia

As a well-developed website, Participedia offers a dialogic experience through the online affordances that it offers. These affordances are:

- Dialogic loops
- Useful information
- Generation of return visits
- Intuitive interfaces, and
- Conservation of visitors (Kent & Taylor 1998).

Not all of the five affordances contribute equally to a dialogic experience for users. Instead, the affordances of useful information, intuitive interfaces, and conservation of visitors form a "technical and design cluster," upon which the "dialogic cluster" can be developed (Taylor et al., 2001). These affordances constituting the technical and design cluster are necessary but not sufficient for the creation of a dialogic website. The dialogic cluster, which is formed by dialogic loops and generation of return visitors, is dependent on the technical and design cluster.

An example of how the dialogic affordances of Participedia are formed may be considered in relation to the affordance of dialogic loops. A dialogic loop is the opportunity offered to users to respond to information and to receive feedback or a response in return. Participedia accomplishes this in several ways, including through the provision of contact information, by which users receive a response from a staff member, a FAQs section, and a presence on social media. A dialogic loop may also be provided in the form of email updates for users, or requests for opinion and input from users. Participedia sends out such updates to users and also circulates a newsletter.

A second example would be in relation to the affordance of useful information. The usefulness of information in the case of Participedia must be determined in relation to two audiences: PI practitioners, and the academic audience of students and researchers. Usefulness of information is accomplished through such methods as posting a mission statement and philosophy. It is also established through the provision of clear directions for joining the Participedia network and the prominent display of the Participedia logo. Additionally, the member base is identified and described on Participedia. Cases and other information are downloadable, and the capacity for audio and visual content is available. Usefulness is augmented because members themselves post new material.

A third example would be the affordance of the generation of return visits. Participedia directly invites users to return to the site. Such an invitation signals to users that the site is dynamic and that the return visits may be valuable. Users are given the opportunity to comment on and engage in online discussions about the cases. Timely news stories are provided on the splash page, which is updated frequently to ensure that up-to-date news is always available.

Fourth, the affordance of intuitive interfaces is offered to users through such features as a site map, the provision of a search box within the site, and the sparing use of graphics. Links are available throughout the site, offering users the opportunity to move easily and effectively throughout the site.

Table 1. Participedia as Ground for Dialogue

Dialogical Quality	
Mutuality	Low
Propinquity	Low
Empathy	Potentially high
Risk	Low
Commitment	medium

Finally, the conservation of visitors in Participedia is accomplished through such methods as displaying important information, as well as time-sensitive announcements, on the splash page. The time and date of postings allow users to return to the site in order to find updates and new content. The loading time of the site has been optimized thereby reducing waiting time for users.

Participedia as a Ground for Dialogue

Although Participedia offers dialogic affordances as described in the previous section, the question remains how and under what conditions it offers a fully formed ground for dialogue.

Dialogue is a social process, a form of information exchange involving at least two people, in which meaning is created. Bohm (2003) argues that dialogue can be used as a means of engaging people to understand others' positions more clearly and in the process to reduce conflict and eliminate false claims. Describing the dialogic process as he observed it, Bohm stated that people could move from fixed positions to more informed and tolerant positions. In the process, friendship could develop:

A new kind of mind thus begins to come into being which is based on the development of a common meaning that is constantly transforming in the process of the dialogue. People are no longer primarily in opposition, nor can they be said to be interacting, rather they are participating in this pool of common meaning which is capable of constant development and change. In this development the group has no pre-established purpose, though at each moment a purpose that is free to change may reveal itself. The group thus begins to engage in a new dynamic relationship in which no speaker is excluded, and in which no particular content is excluded (Bohm 2003, p. 175).

Dialogue in this sense is a type of conversation whose purpose is mainly to enhance collective thinking (Barge & Little 2002, p. 385). It occurs only in specific moments and under certain conditions. Furthermore, dialogic practices can be prescribed before a dialogic session.

Kent and Taylor (2002) identify the following qualities as constituting dialogue: mutuality, propinquity, empathy, risk, and commitment.

Mutuality refers to the shared nature of dialogue. Partners in dialogue establish a relationship in which actions and feelings are jointly held and expressed. As shown in Table 1, the quality of mutuality offered by Participedia is considered to be low. Partners are separated by both time and space. They generally communicate asynchronously and are not assumed to be collocated.

Propinquity is the quality of dialogue by which partners communicate in proximity to one another. Dialogic partners seek closeness for the purpose of enhancing or improving their relationship. Propinquity can increase the extent to which dialogic partners may act or feel together. It is low for Participedia users because they are not collocated and they communicate asynchronously. As with the quality of mutuality, partners in communication are separated by distance and by time.

Empathy is the felt and expressed quality of understanding the feelings of others. It suggests going beyond only jointly held feelings to commonly held knowledge of others' contexts and histories. Empathy, like commitment, may be low or high. A PI practitioner who is new to the area may have relatively low empathy. An experienced, senior professional or researcher might have high empathy.

Risk suggests that partners in dialogue do not avoid situations in which some form of personal loss may occur, as might be the case, for example, in which someone feels embarrassed or ashamed. The risk of using the network is low. Responses to existing material are carried out in a context in which negative feedback is likely to be relatively rare. Moderation and oversight of discussions are carried out by Participedia staff, thereby reducing the possibility that intense negative interactions will take place.

Commitment is the condition under which partners agree to remain in a dialogic relationship for some period of time and in spite of adverse conditions. Like empathy, commitment may be high or low, depending on factors such as the length of time someone has been interested in the area. However, it may be regarded between the poles of high and low, as medium, because some level of commitment must be present before someone joins the network or uses the website.

The COP-Participedia Experience

A COP is a social group comprising the three elements of domain, community, and practice (Cummings & van Zee, 2005). A COP's *domain* is an area of interest and shared competence, and these imply a commitment to the domain. Members participate because they have an affinity for and sense of mission related to the domain. A COP's *community* is the set of members engaged in activities and discussion together. The community is not necessarily collocated continuously. Members may meet from time to time and then return to separate places of work. A COP's *practice*, Cummings and van Zee note, is what distinguishes the community from functioning only as an interest group. Members of a COP practice professionally and possess commitment to, and a sense of mission for, their chosen area. Such dedication allows members to "develop a shared repertoire of resources: experiences, stories, tools, ways of addressing recurring problems, namely a shared practice" (p. 10).

Members of a COP seek to add value to their practice. In fact, this goal is a defining characteristic of a COP, since it is a primary means by which commitment and a sense of mission in relation to the area of practice are expressed and developed. The value generated in a COP leads to the production and reproduction of the knowledge, skills, and information required to respond to varied citizen audiences, and to the practice's changing circumstances and contexts.

Members of a shared professional practice seek value in various ways. Wenger, Trayner, and de Laat (2011) distinguish between the value generated by networks versus that generated by communities. A network allows for information exchange and meaningful accruals of value. It differs from a community mainly in terms of the sense of identity offered by a community:

The network aspect refers to the set of relationships, personal interactions, and connections among participants who have personal reasons to connect. . . a set of nodes and links with affordances for learning, such as information flows, helpful linkages, joint problem solving, and knowledge creation. The community aspect refers to the development of a shared identity around a topic or set of challenges. It represents a collective intention – however tacit and distributed – to steward a domain of knowledge and to sustain learning about it (p. 19).

Using this distinction, Participedia represents a set of resources used by a *network*. Participedia is a network characterized by openness. No requirements or restrictions are in place for users of the network or for contributors of content. Participedia as a network comprises the paid staff managing and developing "affordances for learning," that is, those who have taken on the responsibility for ensuring that Participedia continues to be available for use. The network also includes the "volunteers," the researchers and practitioners who contribute cases and other materials. By viewing, reading, and using the website's resources, a user becomes part of a network of like-minded citizens and thereby becomes linked with the purpose of the network. To contribute material, or to revise or comment on existing resources, the user must register, thereby formalizing the relationship with the network.

In this study, the COP developed a nascent shared identity and therefore had the purpose and outcome of establishing a *community*. Participants shared both a commitment to an area of practice and an intent to generate and accrue value through participation in the community. The group's shared identity was that of like-minded practitioners seeking to learn more about PI through co-present exchanges that were built up in richness over a period of weeks. The study documents the views and insights of members of the COP using Participedia resources, to which we refer as the *COP-Participedia experience*, or simply *COP-Participedia.*

METHOD

Sample

Thirteen people participated in the COP: seven women and six men. Most participants were mid-career professionals, aged 30 to 60, with two participants older than 60. All had studied public and professional communication at the graduate level, either by completing a master's degree in the area or taking an elective course as part of a related graduate program. See Appendix 1 for a complete list of participants and their occupations. Most participants did not know one another before they were invited by the researchers to the first COP meeting.

In the initial phase, participants met in order to select themes of public involvement that were timely and significant for the professional practice of public involvement. These themes in turn were used by the researchers to select Participedia cases for discussion in the COP. Suggestions were solicited from participants, from which an initial list of 10 potential themes was created. The three themes receiving the most votes from the group were then adopted as the themes to be discussed in the subsequent COP-Participedia sessions. The themes, along with the Participedia cases and other resources used in each COP session, are listed in Appendix 2.

Table 2. Schedule for study participants

Week	Activity
1	Rank and choose COP-Participedia session topics
2	No activity
3	COP-Participedia Session 1
4	COP-Participedia Session 2
5	COP-Participedia Session 3
6	No activity
7	Focus Group

The second phase of the study involved attending three COP sessions. At each COP-Participedia session, Participedia resources were provided to participants to inform and stimulate the discussion. Participedia resources were presented to participants twice. They were presented first in advance of each session via weblink circulated by email. Participants could examine the materials before the COP-Participedia session. Participants then received the materials a second time via a summary and introduction by the moderator, which occurred at the beginning of each COP-Participedia session.

The third phase of the project involved attending a focus group in which participants contributed to a moderated discussion about how views and values associated with the practice of public involvement had changed during the COP-Participedia sessions. The schedule for participants is provided in Table 2.

COP-Participedia sessions were 90 minutes in length and were facilitated by researchers. The direction and development of topics and ideas within the discussions were shaped by participants.

Focus-Group Design and Data Analysis

The focus group was broadly based in its origins and synergistic in operation. For example, a COP-Participedia meeting might have influenced a participant to talk to a decision-maker in the workplace on an issue related to public involvement. Similarly, after a session a participant might now think about public involvement differently, using a different conceptual framework. Such value would be relatively enduring, rather than transactional. Wenger et al. refers to such value as *reframing value*, the final and deepest cycle of value when considering the qualities of dialogue. It requires participants to consider how the COP-Participedia experience changed, and perhaps transformed, how they regarded success in the context of public involvement. Such value may eventually result in "renegotiation with the powers-that-be who have the legitimacy to define success" (Wenger et al., 2011, p. 21). An example of realized value would be influencing a decision-maker in the professional workplace. The focus group allowed participants to compare perspectives about reframing value and to range more broadly in their discussions about the value that COP-Participedia offered to their professional practice.

The focus group allowed participants to consider value-creation in COP-Participedia more deeply and in a reflective way, in collaboration with colleagues. The cycles of immediate, potential, and applied value could be identified and discussed in the focus group, but participants would be asked to consider these cycles of value in connection to whether they had led to changes in how participants viewed their professional work more fundamentally, that is, in terms of the cycle of reframing value.

Table 3. Most frequently coded units and their frequency identified during open coding

Coded Unit	Frequency
Community/communities	52
(diverse) group(s)	45
Tool(s)	31
Decision(s)	26
Process	25
Technology	25
Conversation	17
Understand(ing)	17
Influence	15
Opinion	10
Experience	9
Solution(s)	9
Discussion	8
Diversity	8
Other people	6
Approach	6
Complexity	5

Eleven of the 13 study participants attended the focus group. The discussion was 90 minutes in length and was transcribed for analysis. The questions posed to participants addressed the following areas as they related to the research question:

1. general questions about whether and how participants had changed either their view of public involvement as a field of practice or their status as practitioners;
2. the experience of learning about and using the network and resources of Participedia;
3. the experience of participating in a community of practice with colleagues.

The complete focus-group guide is provided in Appendix 2.

RESULTS

The focus-group transcript was analyzed by the researchers using a form of constant-comparison analysis (Onwuegbuzie, Dickinson, Leech, & Zoran, 2005), which is a qualitative technique first developed and applied by Glaser and Strauss (1967). The technique follows three stages of analysis (Strauss & Corbin, 1998). The transcript data is first reduced using *open coding*. Coded units in the transcript were either single words or short phrases of 10 words or less.

Table 3 lists the most frequently coded words and the frequency of their occurrence.

Table 4. Categories with corresponding codes and frequencies, developed during axial coding

LFC (X 135)	SCX (X 47)	SSD (X46)	BTT (X 192)	STO (X 32)
Learning from COP colleagues and from Participedia	Appreciating the complexity of PI processes	Understanding the diversity of PI audiences	PI tools and techniques	Seeing the outcomes of PI

In the second stage of analysis using this technique, codes are grouped into categories of like units, using what is called *axial coding*, to allow the emergence of like meanings. At this stage, five categories in the transcript were established. The coded units were assigned throughout the focus-group transcript.

The five categories and their codes are provided in Table 4.

While each category provides a means of creating like meanings, it is not a complete statement or assertion. Therefore, during the third and final stage of analysis, that of *selective coding*, a complete theme is developed for each of the categories. Each theme provides the basis for a conclusion drawn from the data. The themes are discussed in the *Results* and *Discussion* sections of the study.

Two steps were taken to determine an end point for sampling and coding. These steps correspond, respectively, to sample saturation and theoretical saturation (Glaser & Strauss, 1967). Sample saturation can be considered to occur when all significant words or phrases have been coded. This is the point at which further coding does not generate further data. The proportion of the transcript that was coded was measured. The transcript was 9,895 words in length (48 double-spaced pages). During open coding, an average of 10.42 coded words or phrases were created for each page of the transcript for a total of approximately 500 coded words and phrases for the entire transcript. The transcript contained 859 sentences, meaning that about 60 per cent of the sentences in the transcript featured at least one coded word or phrase. All nouns that were mentioned five or more times in the discussion were coded.

In terms of theoretical saturation, the five categories were tested for conceptual integrity. As shown in Figure 1, the categories developed during axial coding represent an ecosystem of the professional practice of public involvement in the context of the COP-Participedia experience. Category 1 (code LFC) refers to new skills and knowledge, as well as reinforcement of existing skills and knowledge. The category represents participants as they describe *learning about public involvement*, either through exchanges within COP-Participedia or by gathering information directly from Participedia. Participants in COP-Participedia used the opportunities for discussion with colleagues in the COP, informed by Participedia cases and resources, to "co-create knowledge." The co-creation of knowledge suggests that participants acted together to reinforce existing knowledge and identify new knowledge. Such co-creation can be associated with synergies (more effective and efficient knowledge generation), and it may result in richer forms of knowledge than would otherwise be possible (Rowley, Kupiec-Teahan, & Leeming, 2013).

Category 2 (code SCX) refers to new and renewed appreciation of the complexity of public-involvement processes. The category includes participant descriptions of how they learn from observing and assessing the practice of public involvement. This is *learning from public involvement.*

Categories 3 and 4 (codes, respectively SSD and BTT) represent *public-involvement inputs*. These inputs are, first, a strengthened understanding of the diverse character of public-involvement audience, and second, the tools and techniques used by public-involvement practitioners.

Figure 1. Conceptual framework of public involvement as an ecosystem of professional practice, incorporating the five categories of coded focus-group data

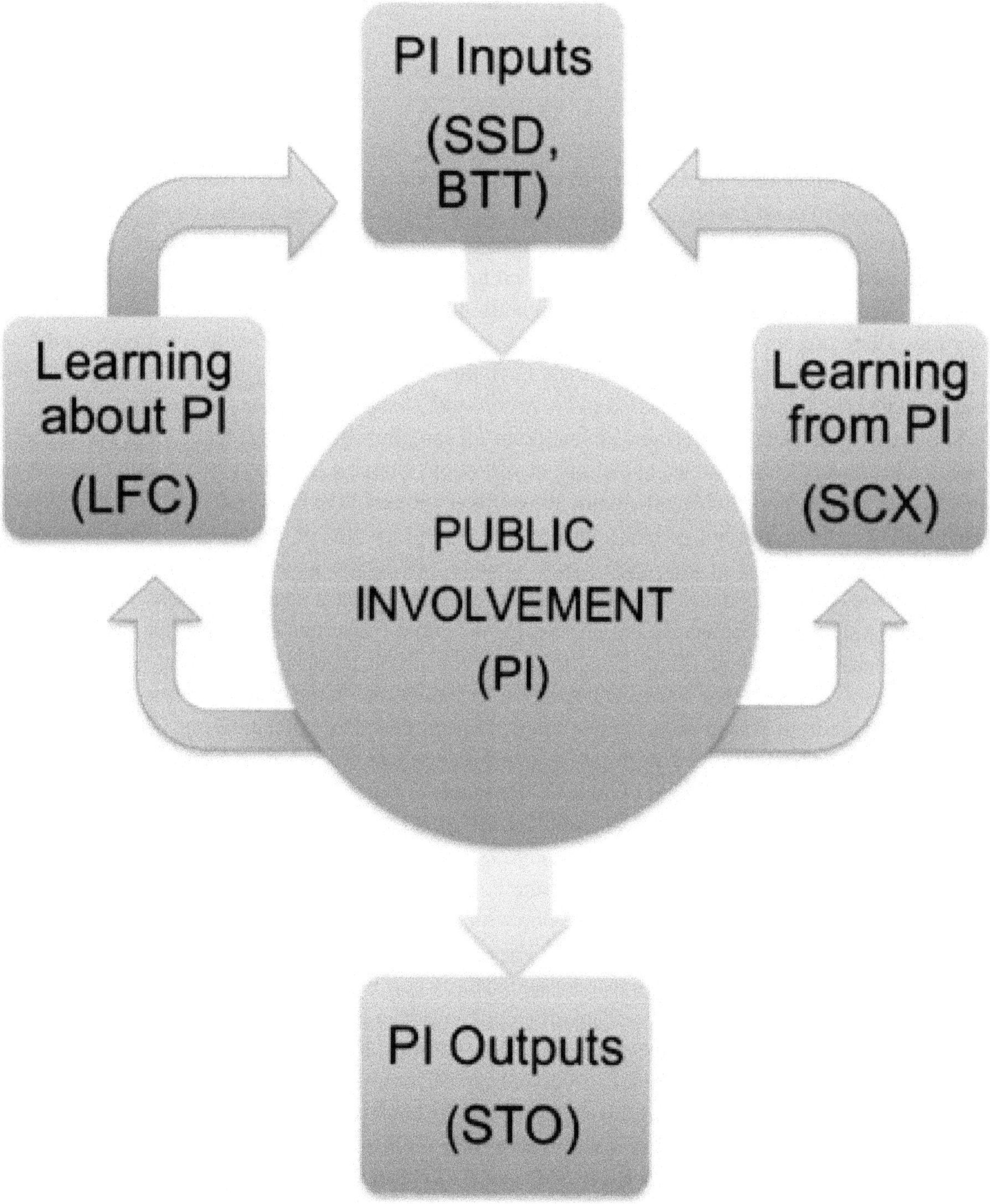

Finally, Category 5 (code STO) describes new ways of seeing and describing the outcomes of public involvement for stakeholders. These are the *public-involvement outputs*, which refer to the ultimate effects, in society and in social systems, of public involvement as a field of practice.

The conceptual framework provided a marker indicating that theoretical saturation had been reached. The key components of public involvement as a field of professional practice, along with the basic elements of the COP-Participedia experience, were identified within the five categories.

DISCUSSION

The objective of the quasi-experiment was to explore the COP-Participedia's potential for strengthening the capacity of Participedia to offer a ground for dialogue. The two categories discussed most intensively by the focus-group participants were *Learning from COP colleagues and from Participedia* (LFC) and *Appreciating the complexity of PI processes* (SCX). These categories are discussed below and applied to the five dialogical qualities. The qualities of mutuality, propinquity, and commitment are increased in their capacity to form a ground for dialogue.

Learning from Colleagues and from Participedia (LFC)

COP-Participedia Participants commented on the personal and professional influence of one another within COP-Participedia. They stated that they had learned from one another and that such learning had a quality that separated it from other kinds of learning, because it was carried out within the welcoming climate of a professional community. Collette, an educational activist and doctoral student, for example, said,

I found that [COP-Participedia] gave me confidence to speak about my own [public-involvement] project. It gave me a frame to speak about it. It also leveraged the language that I would be able to use, and people could relate to it.

A change in the language that participants were capable of using as a result of COP-Participedia is a transformative change, because language use is fundamental to conceptualization of a body of knowledge.

Sally, a senior public-involvement specialist in government, referred to a deepening of her commitment and her capacity to advocate and express herself as a public-involvement practitioner: "[COP-Participedia] allowed me exposure . . . to all the other perspectives in the room, to actually start to 'beam out' that there's such a broad perspective to what public involvement means." For her, COP-Participedia carried the same style and effect of learning that had taken place in her master's degree studies:

I would feel energized when I left. Like I had fresh air for my brain, I would call it. And then when I went back and went online and continued those discussions, I felt like I was in the room with everybody. I could see [a former fellow student] talking and his mannerisms when he explained something. I understood the context from which he came, his background, in his online presence.

Horn (2010) points out that conversations among participants in a COP can have a latent influence on colleagues who are not co-present. Effects move beyond the COP and therefore "act back" on it. Participants referred to this influence. Knut stated, "[COP-Participedia] allows me to talk on a . . . better basis of understanding with other people." Collette referred in a similar way to the value of the mutual influence of the members of a COP but also of the influence that extended beyond COP-Participedia:

Having a variety of professionals meeting and discussing different topics pushes me to the next level. It helps to spark creativity and innovation in the conversation I'm having with decision-makers about how we're going to pull a project together.

Focus-group participants also commented on the value of face-to-face communication in relation to other modes of communication. They expressed the vibrancy and immediacy of meeting face-to-face. Will, a university instructor and arts activist, described this influence in terms of the symmetry of conversation:

You can have an exchange instead of just a one-sided presentation. . . . I valued just generally getting around the table and having everyone have a voice.

Another value of COP-Participedia discussed by participants was a kind of reversal of the face-to-face mode of COP-Participedia. Participedia is an information repository, to which access is provided online. However, its cases are based on the observation of mainly face-to-face encounters, as mentioned by Knut, a retired engineer:

Participedia is the outcome of the in-person thing. This is the richest way we're ever going to communicate. The moment you go to a Participedia or any other way of communicating, there's the intermediary aspect of the technology. You can only see so many people on the screen. You can only have so many people working on it. If you have different time zones, you are now asynchronic in terms of communicating. Although doesn't mean that they're not useful tools.

Participants expressed the sentiment that coming together with colleagues to discuss matters of mutual interest in COP-Participedia provided a time away from distractions, as well as a welcome pause from the routine of the workplace. Tod, a senior public relations professional in government, expressed a sense of being refreshed within his practitioner context:

[COP-Participedia] was fun . . . and engaging with professionals and colleagues again was good. I was looking forward to coming every week. For me, that was exciting. I've missed a lot of that. You get saddled with your job and you don't explore, expand. So, I really enjoyed this.

Participants suggested that the "time away" of COP-Participedia allowed for reconsidering perspectives but that it also qualified as a "place set apart" allowing for renewed vision. Sally stated:

One of the things I find, no matter what work you're doing, you get close to it. And sometimes you can't see the forest for the trees. And sometimes backing up or having a conversation with other people about what you're doing will help you see more clearly what your own path needs to be when you're developing your engagement strategy.

Table 5. Participedia and COP-Participedia as grounds for dialogue

Dialogic quality	Participedia as a ground for dialogue	COP-Participedia as a ground for dialogue
Mutuality	Low	High
Propinquity	Low	High
Empathy	Potentially High	High
Risk	Low	Low
Commitment	Medium	Medium

Godfrey, a college communications instructor, summarized the particular character of face-to-face discussion, on which other participants had commented, in his observation of COP-Participedia: "You're never going to beat a dozen people sitting around the table with a common goal."

Summarizing the cycle of immediate value, participants responded to each of the questionnaire items by reporting an increase in value. The focus group revealed the emergent influence of COP-Participedia discussions both within and beyond the group, and the value of face-to-face communication as compared to other modes of communication.

Appreciating the Complexity of PI Processes (SCX)

Participants stated that COP-Participedia had served to emphasize for them the complexity of public-involvement processes. This occurred in three ways. It occurred in the depiction of the balance of power among participants and groups in public involvement. It was also introduced by the demand that public-involvement initiatives lead to substantive change and not to a situation in which a problem has been displaced to another part of society. And it became evident in the demands for a comprehensive planning process, which COP-Participedia had clarified.

Complexity was identified by some participants as a distinctive and perhaps overarching value of COP-Participedia. Mary stated this sentiment in relation to the case-based character of Participedia:

The thing that resonated the most was complexity. I appreciated that the cases selected had a level of complexity to them that allowed us to take a good dive into the content and knowledge. And then the level of complexity served us in deliberation around the case studies.

The dialogical qualities of COP-Participedia, in comparison with the qualities of Participedia, are shown in Table 5. The qualities of mutuality and propinquity are strengthened, based on the analysis of focus-group responses. The dialogical quality of commitment, which is also strengthened in COP-Participedia does not change because it is high without the use of the COP.

Implications for PI Practitioners

The results of the study support the benefits of COP-Participedia for practitioners in two ways. First, they point to the advantage of viewing Participedia as a "ground for dialogue." Viewed this way, COP-Participedia leverages face-to-face communication to offer a mode in which a deeper form of understanding about public-involvement practice can be achieved. Second, the study reveals the benefits of a COP as a practical opportunity for practitioners. The opportunity is likely to be of special interest to practitioners requiring or seeking a deeper form of understanding of the field.

Dialogue may be distinguished from other ways of "talking together" by its characteristics of "confronting one's own and others' assumptions, revealing feelings, and building common ground" (Schein, 1993, p. 46). Such dialogue is not simply a useful addition to public involvement as a form of social action. Instead, as Schein notes, dialogue in organizations and in professional work is a *condition* for action:

[D]ialogue is a necessary condition for effective group action, because only with a period of dialogue is it possible to determine whether or not the communication that is going on is valid. If it is not valid, in the sense that different members are using words differently or have different mental models without realizing it, the possibilities of solving problems or making effective decisions are markedly reduced (p. 42).

Participedia provided a ground for dialogue, that is, a common space and idiom within which knowledge could be co-created and understanding strengthened, through the conversations, interactions, and information exchange that are characteristic of deliberation. Viewing and responding to Participedia as a ground for dialogue generated value for the study's participants. Such a view of Participedia may be quite different than that held by researchers using Participedia. While a researcher's view gives priority to Participedia's capacity to offer reliable and valid data or evidence, a practitioner seeks opportunities to generate, frame, and pose questions about how data can be mobilized and used in practice.

The words of one of the study participants, Collette, offer a means of expressing the potential of COP-Participedia as a ground for dialogue for practitioners as they seek to develop their skills, knowledge, techniques, and theories of practice. COP-Participedia provided an opportunity to increase, rapidly and effectively, the sense of an identity within a community of practice. To exploit the potential of this opportunity, public-involvement practitioners can use a community of practice to stimulate and nurture the latent value of Participedia:

A community of practice . . . creates a vision of community and people collaborating and solving problems, making options for decisions to be made, and envisioning pathways. . . . So you can predict and create solutions for scenarios that arise.

Such an approach will have particular relevance for public-involvement practitioners who work in independent practice and do not regularly compare approaches with other practitioners. In these situations, practitioners will benefit by the opportunity of engaging in dialogue with other practitioners in contexts similar to COP-Participedia. COP-Participedia might also be useful in organizations or spheres of practice that do no support and enhance a sense of identity for public-involvement practitioners. The community identity developed within a COP can support discussions and exchanges that go deeper into the challenges in practice in the field of public involvement than would otherwise occur.

CONCLUDING COMMENTS

At this early stage of Participedia's development it is appropriate to explore the question of whether further innovation may lead to new forms of value for users. In this sense, the COP - which is a well-tested and validated method for mobilizing knowledge (Wenger, 1998) - functioned in the study as an "informal coordination mechanism" of the kind that Jansen, Van Den Bosch, and Volberda (2006) argue, "not only contribute[s] to pursuing exploratory and exploitative innovations, but [is] also more important than formal coordination mechanisms for developing either exploratory or exploitative innovation" (p. 1670). A recent, parallel approach to public deliberation has combined shared political documentary viewing with focus-group discussion (Pitts, Kenski, Smith, & Pavlich, 2017).

Participants mentioned the value in COP-Participedia of seeing more clearly the power dynamics among individuals and groups participating in public-involvement initiatives. This theme was developed as participants compared the rational basis of public-involvement practice with what Seth called a "reductionist" public sphere, using the public debate about Brexit as an example:

[I]t doesn't matter how many seminars, how many newspapers, how much effort is made that goes into the detail about what the European Union is, right? It's still a citizenry that believes, "I don't have time. I don't have to read that. I don't have to go.

Caitlyn, a community activist, also referred to a polarized public sphere and the complexity this introduced into public-involvement work. Furthermore, as Collette noted, COP-Participedia provided a context within which a differential in literacy or rationality could be considered:

It was interesting that Lil brought up the "inside and outside" thing. . . . The boundaries of our work are tied into the propaganda or rhetoric around our work. And so when we escape that and come to a broader circle of open ideas, then we can take that back and spark some new ways of thinking.

In a similar vein, COP-Participedia, according to Collette, had helped her to see more clearly and to appreciate more deeply the diversity of public-involvement audiences:

The challenge . . . that has been brought forward from [COP-Participedia], once again, is that it's provoking me to figure out how am I to reach diverse groups of people and bring them in?

Similarly, Caitlyn formulated a rhetorical question to make the point that COP-Participedia offered the distinct benefit of conceptually linking planning, process, and outcomes: "So, think about planning and the importance of looking at the whole process. . . . If we do this, what are the potential outcomes?"

The study had two limitations. First, the COP was an emergent community, rather than a fully developed community with an identity discernible by members. Focus-group participants mentioned that the COP had an intentionally superficial purpose in that it had been organized for the particular purpose of the study. On the other hand, participants commented on the value of exchanging insights with colleagues who had similar, if not identical, professional interests and experiences. Second, the study was carried out in one social context with a limited number of participants. It could be replicated in multiple social contexts with a larger number of participants as part of an effort to increase the reliability of its findings.

REFERENCES

Anderson, R., Baxter, L. A., & Cissna, K. N. (Eds.). (2004b). *Dialogue. Theorizing Difference in Communication Studies*. Thousand Oaks, CA: Sage Publications. doi:10.4135/9781483328683

Anderson, R., & Cissna, K. N. (2008). Fresh perspectives in dialogue theory. *Communication Theory*, *18*(1), 1–4. doi:10.1111/j.1468-2885.2007.00310.x

Barge, J. K. (2002). Enlarging the meaning of group deliberation. In L. R. Frey (Ed.), *New directions in group communication* (pp. 159–177). Thousand Oaks, CA: Sage Publications.

Barge, J. K., & Little, M. (2002). Dialogical Wisdom, Communicative Practice, and Organizational Life. *Communication Theory*, *12*(4), 375–397. doi:10.1111/j.1468-2885.2002.tb00275.x

Bohm, D. (2003). *On dialogue, E-library*. Taylor and Francis.

Bokeno, R., & Gantt, V. W. (2000). Dialogic mentoring. Core relationships for organizacional learning. *Management Communication Quarterly*, *14*(2), 237–270. doi:10.1177/0893318900142002

Botan, C. (1992). International public relations critique and reformulation. *Public Relations Review*, *18*(2), 149–159. doi:10.1016/0363-8111(92)90006-K

Buber, M. (1970). *I and Thou* (W. Kaufmann, Trans.). New York: Charles Scribner's Sons.

Cummings, S., & van Zee, A. (2005). Communities of practice and networks: Reviewing two perspectives on social learning. *Knowledge Management for Development*, *1*(1), 8–22.

Fung, A., & Warren, M. (2011). The Participedia project: An introduction. *International Public Management Journal*, *14*(3), 341–362. doi:10.1080/10967494.2011.618309

Gastil, J., Richards, R. Jr, Ryan, M., & Smith, G. (2017). Testing assumptions in deliberative democratic design: A preliminary assessment of the efficacy of the Participedia data archive as an analytic tool. *Journal of Public Deliberation*, *13*(2), 1. Available at https://www.publicdeliberation.net/jpd/vol13/iss2/art1

Glaser, B., & Strauss, A. (1967). *The discovery of grounded theory: Strategies of qualitative research*. Chicago, IL: Aldine.

Grossardt, T., Bailey, K., & Brum, J. (2003). Structured public involvement: Problems and prospects for improvement. *Transportation Research Record: Journal of the Transportation Research Board*, (1858): 95–102.

Horn, I. (2010). Teaching replays, teaching rehearsals, and re-visions of practice: Learning from colleagues in a mathematics teacher community. *Teachers College Record*, *112*(1), 225–259.

Jansen, J., Van Den Bosch, F., & Volberda, H. (2006). Exploratory innovation, exploitative innovation, and performance: Effects of organizational antecedents and environmental moderators. *Management Science*, *52*(11), 1661–1674. doi:10.1287/mnsc.1060.0576

Kent, M., & Taylor, M. (1998). Building dialogic relationship through the World Wide Web. *Public Relations Review*, *24*(3), 321–334. doi:10.1016/S0363-8111(99)80143-X

Kent, M., & Taylor, M. (2002). Toward a dialogic theory of public relations. *Public Relations Review*, *28*(1), 21–37. doi:10.1016/S0363-8111(02)00108-X

Khisty, C. (1996). Education and training of transportation engineers and planners vis-a-vis public involvement. *Transportation Research Record: Journal of the Transportation Research Board*, *1552*(1), 171–176. doi:10.1177/0361198196155200123

Mao, Y., & Adria, M. (2013). Deciding who will decide: Assessing random selection for participants in Edmonton's Citizen Panel on budget priorities. *Canadian Public Administration/Administration publique du Canada*, *56*(4), 610-37.

Onwuegbuzie, A., Dickinson, W., Leech, N., & Zoran, A. (2009). A qualitative framework for collecting and analyzing data in focus group research. *International Journal of Qualitative Methods*, *8*(3), 1–21. doi:10.1177/160940690900800301

Peters, J. (2000). *Speaking into the air: A history of the idea of communication*. Chicago: University of Chicago Press.

Pitts, M., Kenski, K., Smith, S., & Pavlich, C. (2017). Focus group discussions as sites for public deliberation and sensemaking following shared political documentary viewing. *Journal of Public Deliberation*, *13*(2), 6. Available at https://www.publicdeliberation.net/jpd/vol13/iss2/art6

Reinke, D., & Malarkey, D. (1996). Implementing integrated transportation planning in metropolitan planning organizations: Procedural and analytical issues. *Transportation Research Record: Journal of the Transportation Research Board*, *1552*(1), 71–78. doi:10.1177/0361198196155200110

Rogers, C. (1994). The necessary and sufficient conditions of therapeutic personality change. In R. Anderson, K. Cissna, & R. Arnett (Eds.), *The Reach of Dialogue: Confirmation, Voice, and Community* (pp. 126–140). Cresskill, NJ: Hampton Press.

Rowley, J., Kupiec-Teahan, B., & Leeming, E. (2013). Customer community and co-creation: A case study. *Marketing Intelligence & Planning*, *25*(2), 136–146. doi:10.1108/02634500710737924

Schein, E. (1993). On dialogue, culture, and organizational learning. *Organizational Dynamics*, *22*.

Strauss, A., & Corbin, J. (1998). *Basics of qualitative research: Techniques and procedures for developing grounded theory*. Thousand Oaks, CA: Sage.

Taylor, M., Kent, M., & White, W. (2001). How activist organizations are using the Internet to build relationships. *Public Relations Review*, *27*(3), 263–284. doi:10.1016/S0363-8111(01)00086-8

Wenger, E. (1998). *Communities of practice: learning, meaning and identity*. New York, NY: Cambridge University Press. doi:10.1017/CBO9780511803932

Wenger, E., Trayner, B., & de Laat, M. (2011). *Promoting and assessing value creation in communities and networks: A conceptual framework*. Rapport 18, Ruud de Moore Centrum, Open University of the Netherlands. Available at: http://wenger-trayner.com/wp-content/uploads/2011/12/1104Wenger_Trayner_DeLaat_Value_creation.pdf

APPENDIX 1

Table 6. Participants and Occupations

CODED NAME	OCCUPATION
Tod	Senior public-relations professional in government
Godfrey	College instructor in communications
Sally	Senior public-involvement specialist in government
Knut	Retired engineer
Barb	University associate dean
Caitlyn	Community activist
Mary	Senior public-involvement consultant
Will	University instructor in arts
Collette	Educational activist and doctoral student
Seth	Architect and community activist
Lil	University professional in community-service learning
Not in attendance at the focus group:	
Deb	Senior public-relations professional in government
Israel	Citizen activist and former broadcaster

APPENDIX 2

COP-Participedia Themes and Resources

Session 1: Innovations for stimulating dialogue across varying stakeholder values and opinions
CASE: Deliberative Poll on Education Policy in Northern Ireland
https://participedia.net/en/cases/deliberative-poll-education-policy-northern-ireland
METHOD: ConsiderIt
https://participedia.net/en/methods/considerit-0
http://www.consider.it
ORGANIZATION: National Coalition for Dialogue and Deliberation
https://participedia.net/en/organizations/national-coalition-dialogue-deliberation
http://ncdd.org/rc/item/tag/ncdd-publications
Session 2: New approaches to understanding and responding to power differentials among stakeholders or citizens
CASE: Reclaim November Ohio!
https://participedia.net/en/cases/reclaim-november-ohio
METHOD: Focus Group
https://participedia.net/en/methods/focus-group
ORGANIZATION: CitizenLab

https://participedia.net/en/organizations/citizenlab
Session 3: New ideas for achieving deep, reflective, and critical thinking in public-involvement initiatives
CASE: The Citizen's Archive of Pakistan
https://participedia.net/en/cases/citizens-archive-pakistan-oral-history-project
METHOD: Montreal's Right of Initative to Public Consultations
https://participedia.net/en/methods/right-initiative-public-consultations
ORGANIZATION: Australian Study Circles Network
https://participedia.net/en/organizations/australian-study-circles-network

Focus-Group Guide

Welcome

Thank you for joining us.

Overview of the Topic

Today we will be asking you to comment and discuss characteristics of the community of practice (COP) experience using Participedia. We're interested in your views about both the COP as a method, and Participedia as a source of information or knowledge – *and about using the two together, as we have done in the last several weeks.*

Today we are especially interested in talking about how the COP experience with Participedia changed, perhaps transformed, how you think about things. In other words we are asking you today how the COP sessions may influence and shape how you practice public involvement from now on.

Chelsey and Edrick will be making notes about who is speaking.

Ground Rules

1. Try to remember to mention your first name before speaking.
2. You may say whatever you like during our 60 minutes of discussion – your responses will be anonymous in the final report.
3. I will pose questions but it is up to you to shape the conversation.
4. Respond to one another, rather than to me.
5. Mind the microphones – try not to cover them up or rustle paper near them.
6. Respect and care for one another.

Questions

GENERAL (15 minutes)

First, I want to ask generally about your experience.

1. How did our meetings together lead you to change your thinking about what matters most in public involvement? Any examples that come to mind?

2. How are you considering using new ways to measure success in public involvement (through evaluations, for example)?
3. Would anyone like to share a story that illustrates something about your experience over the last several weeks?
4. In what ways did you influence a senior decision maker in some way because of your experience with Participedia and the community of practice?
   OPTIONAL:

How has your workplace changed, if at all, as a result of our COP meetings together?

PARTICIPEDIA (20 minutes)

Now let's think about Participedia as a source of information and knowledge.

5. How has Participedia been most relevant and useful to you as a PI practitioner? Can you give examples?
6. Tell us a story about your experience with Participedia.
7. How will you measure things differently or use new criteria for public involvement as a result of using Participedia?
   OPTIONAL:

How did Participedia help or hinder you in your experience of discussing matters related to the practice of PI?

How would you continue to use Participedia? If not, why not?

COMMUNITY OF PRACTICE (20 minutes)

Now we turn to the series of three meetings in which we discussed topics related to public involvement.

8. How important was the community of practice (meeting with other people with a common interest) for you as you understood and used Participedia?
9. Tell us a story about your experience with the community of practice.
10. How did you influence someone who has power in your organization or practice because of your experience in the COP?
    OPTIONAL:

How did the COP help or hinder you as you explored topics related to PI?

How would you continue to participate in a community of practice – not necessarily this one. If not, why not?

SUMMARY AND CONCLUSION (5 minutes)

11. Tell us a story that illustrates your experience with Participedia and the COP.
12. Thinking about everything we have talked about in the last several weeks, including today, how would you describe what resonated with you the most or perhaps stimulated your thinking the most?
13. Anything we missed in our discussion today?

Thank you, all!

Chapter 13
Salience, Self-Salience, and Discursive Opportunities:
An Effective Media Presence Construction Through Social Media in the Peruvian Presidential Election

Eduardo Villanueva-Mansilla
https://orcid.org/0000-0003-1312-4873
Department of Communications, Pontificia Universidad Católica del Perú, Peru

ABSTRACT

Peruvian electoral campaigning, centered on the candidate and lacking a significant connection with contention politics occurring in years previous to the poll, is a very diverse exercise, trying to achieve success through a variety of actions while facing a common-sense interpretation of politics as unreliable and not trustworthy. This fixes an agenda from which candidates have to develop their campaigns, focused on convincing others of their commitment to specific groups and willingness to change whatever does not directly affect each specific constituency that is being appealed to for voting. This behavior is replicated even in Facebook, where candidates try to fix their own issues as salient, but usually failing to respond to the media-set agenda. The potential effectiveness of social media, particularly Facebook, would rest in using discursive opportunities emerging during the campaign to construct self-salience, countering the biases of conventional media.

EMPOWERED POLITICAL ACTORS AND THE PRESS

With digital media transforming the access and understanding of news, all aspects of social life are being affected, as is the case with elections. This is valid even for countries where penetration of the Internet is not as deep as in the developed world (Bennett & Pfetsch, 2018; Walsham, 2017); also, this transformation requires considering that both political and press systems in emerging economies work in a very different way than on established, old democracies (Harlow & Salaverria, 2016).

DOI: 10.4018/978-1-7998-1828-1.ch013

One particularly relevant aspect is the relationship between the press and political parties during elections. While both are ideally independent actors, their mutual need is evident: political parties require the press to disseminate their actions and proposals, and the press needs access to provide the best possible coverage of electoral and political processes. This coming and going is fraught with issues, but even considering the different kinds of relations that are developed in different polities, in the end the benefit for both set of actors is clear.

The manifestation of such relationship is how issue salience is developed by the press. The way coverage displays the issues promoted by political candidates in electoral processes results in some issue becoming salient, while other languish without attention. Political actors can promote and try to nudge press actors to promote some issues under specific conditions, highlighting some aspects while diminishing attention to others; but in the end it is the press actor the one traditionally in charge of defining what is salient. The physical manifestation of such issue salience is shown in the news media products: a front page, above the fold news item, against no coverage at all.

However, as the Internet and social media has radically changed the news environment around the world, the relationship described above has also changed. Press coverage has lost importance against the tools of direct, personalized campaigning that targeted media provides; the media has also grown significantly, with a wide variety of outlets making difficult to identify exactly who is consuming what and when. It is not possible to discard the importance of the media during elections, but it is also true that in such changed environment the reality of political engagement and dissemination has been transformed, and that political actors have to considered alternative strategies.

Issue salience is still relevant, though: many political actors, especially in the wide variety of electoral conditions occurring beyond established democracies, the mere fact of getting the electorate to know about what a candidate is a challenge in itself. But the tools available to political actors allow for different approaches that may provide a better outcome. Using an specific case, this paper proposes that political actors have now the ability of produce self-salience: complementing or replacing the role of the press of making some issues salient in an electoral process through their use of social media, thus gaining control and increasing their chances of being heard in a crowded political environment.

USING FACEBOOK IN ELECTORAL CAMPAIGNS

Though it is not the only tool available, the fact remains that Facebook is the most popular social media service worldwide, making it a fundamental component of any electoral strategy since at least the late noughties.

This development has modified the usual sequence of political communication: dissemination of messages among specific audience should produce mobilization, for instance attendance of public gatherings and similar events, and then participation, as in voting, but also as in leaflet distribution, or polling station monitoring: from attention to being part of public events to making oneself available to the candidate for whatever is needed (Downing & Brooten, 2009). In social media terms, this becomes a series of digital actions: attention is demonstrated by "liking", mobilization is sharing, and participation is actively disseminating or even creating new content as requested by the campaign.

Attention, in the context of a digital campaign on Facebook, would be happen each time an official campaign page gets a "like", indicating that a Facebook user, for whatever reason, is interested in whatever has been displayed in that particular page. Automatically, Facebook will offer updates of such page in the user's feed, unless the user actively denies that choice. Mobilization means acting as a multiplier: sharing mostly, although commenting in a positive way is also valid. Finally: participation would mean creating content for the campaign under the personal terms that each user finds relevant.

It is understood that the success of certain messages may motivate digital mobilization, but that only through precise information on the likes and dislikes of the voters is possible to obtain precision useful to multiply the impact, with the goal of participation (Bimber, 2014; Williamson, 2010). The voter must feel that their actions contribute to the success of the candidate, and that more than just simple "liking" is necessary.

The absence of inputs to make this happen has been part of the limitations of Peru's political candidacies. Due to mediocre organization, lack of financial resources and the rather occasional nature of political action in the country (Tanaka, 2009), there are no examples of data collection that allow a better, finer approach to communication, beyond responding to voters interests —which is expressed in an increase of attention— in specific circumstances.

Therefore, digital strategies were rather an exercise of messaging offers than a proper analysis of voter demands, towards achieving a better connection with a candidacy. Strategies, as they were manifest in the acting of the candidates, did not show significant capacities to widen or cousins the electoral narratives, nor of searching for salience in media; without these elements, priming a candidacy in the public sphere appears unlikely, or at least beyond the control of political actors.

This transformation originates on two dimensions of Facebook's influence on political messaging: a narrative aspect, and an analytical one.

From a narrative point of view, Facebook allows for immediate, direct contact between candidates and voters, without conventional mass media filters, with a wide variety of communicational resources; as the interface is familiar to users, it is not required to invest in design and maintenance of websites. While the actual audience reached may not be completely under the candidate's control, nor the reach meaning necessary convincing a voter —as a "like" does not beget a vote— even the significant opaqueness of the algorithms defining how posts disseminate can be used and gamed as necessary.

Analytically, it is possible to identify many different strands of expression and groups of interest that can be reached and groomed through very diverse messaging, providing voice to many sectors of the electorate in the process, or at least demonstrating interest through the attention the candidate shows. As voters express themselves in a candidate's page, a careful approach that consider grooming voters while priming issues according to positions held by the candidate —or advantageous to vote-capturing strategies—, such issues can allow a powerful diversity of messaging that would not function through a broader, conventional-media based approach; thanks to the analytical tools that Facebook and other firms have developed, patterns and groups of users are easily determined, and mobilization towards both digital and conventional activism appears as a good possibility.

The combination of narrative and analytical approaches can be presented as a linear course of action for political actors, in which each step increases engagement but with diminished numbers of participants, as engagement can be understood as a form of connective action (Bennett & Segerberg, 2012) that brings increased returns to its participants but requires increased dedication. This can be understood under a simple model: attention —digital mobilization — participation — actual mobilization. Active participation in a campaign is the end result of a process that starts by requesting attention through specific messaging, mobilize in the specific context of digital engagement (promoting liking, commenting and sharing), participating in messaging and finally, acting in the "real" world; though it has to be considered that such course of action demands significant dedication of resources by the political actors.

Expanding this notions, at the narrative level it is possible to propose that there is an specific connection with issue salience development, as a process that starts by controlling a candidate's narrative as expressed through the actor's social media outlet, and then producing salience in those outlets.

As Facebook provides far more control of what is said, how it is said and when it is said —without the costs of catching the attention of media organizations— constructing a narrative is a way to offer voters a world and politics outlook that they can identify with, even though there is no full coincidence with policy proposal or ideological positions. For instance, a popular conceit is a candidate presenting him or herself as committed to "mano dura" (strong hand, or emphatic application of law and order principles without much consideration of human rights and due process: something very common in Latin America): this is not to mean something explicit but rather a narrative of being tough and decisive, of a candidate that, when in power, will have no doubts to act when it is expected. Any potential considerations to due process or human rights issues can be simply ignored, while it may be inevitable that those considerations may arise on the press, affecting the intended narrative.

Salience Development

Issue salience, one of the components of agenda setting analysis (Roberts, Wanna & Dzwo, 2002), is created through the treatment that a given issue receives from the press and similar actors; or by the political actor itself, when social media is involved, of course under the limits that each individual medium entail (Kluknavska, 2014).

Following Kiousis (2004: 73-76), salience is determined by observing intrinsic and extrinsic characteristics of a media object. Intrinsic characteristics come from the specific attention given by media objects to specific issues, through the amount and diversity of mentions, the voice given to actors expressing positions about an issue, or through the prominence that a given issue receive against other issues in a given media object. The main extrinsic attribute is valence: positive or negative treatment of an issue augments valence, while neutral treatment reduces it. Positive presentation is not inherent to the subject being discussed, but rather reflects the biases of the medium, through the frames used to draw attention to those valuations. Most models rely just on the intrinsic aspects (Lim, 2010), but Kiousis extension of the model is particularly useful to understand the process taking place in this particular case.

Electoral actors develop salience by choosing certain issues, bringing attention to and priming them, and adding valence, as part of the process of developing and controlling the political narrative being looked for. Specifically, *value-driven salience* would be the kind of salience produced through valence, something more complex and favorable than the mere intrinsic achievement of larger attention or prominence. This would be because valence implies that something is set up positively for some actors and negatively for others, in a way that provides, potentially, an advantage in discursive terms agains other electoral contenders. As such, while being extrinsic to the object makes it dependent of the way it is assess by readers, a value-driven salient object would reflect the impact on the electorate of a discursive item, that is, a campaign object that has been drafted to promote a discursive position by a political o media actor.

In its relationship with press actors, a political actor will provide as much issue salience with positive valence as possible, but in most circumstances a press actor will have final say on the level of similarity that a media object would share with the news release or political activity conducted by the political actor. The significant difference that social media brings is the possibility of constructing media items that reflect and perfect the salience proposed during political activities, under the complete control of the political actor.

Of course, the downside of such strategy is that in electoral conditions, only a subset of voters will be exposed to the now-salient issues; if the narrative constructed through this approach only "talks" to those already convinced the results should not be significant in terms of increased attention and potentially increased poll numbers. Therein, the need to consider these issues as relevant to sections of the electorate that are not part of the "convinced", using the newly gained attention to widen the scope of appeal.

Discursive Opportunities Model and Facebook

When creating issue salience on social media, a political actor proposes a narrative that attempts to take control of public discussion, at least among its followers, and that may reverberate beyond them towards the general electorate. Thus, the most valuable approach should try to increase the effect of this self-developed salience among those not yet convinced, by using events that may offer an opportunity to shift the political discussion into issues and positions about these issues, that are advantageous to the political actor.

This may be better discussed from the perspective of Discursive Opportunities, and specifically the Discursive Opportunities Structure model, (DOS) as defined by Molaei (2014) —following Koopmans (2004; also Koopmans & Olzak, 2004)— as an structured set of discourses that allow involving the voters in a political dialog, in an specific moment in time and specific political conditions that prime a contested political position.

Such collection of discourses should help to shape public responses to events, and to mobilize the citizens / voters, promoting political participation. The actual elaboration of discourses is determined by the actions of a candidate, if electoral process are the end point; or political leaders if contested conditions are occurring in a given time. The DOS model include the institutional elements, the formal political actors in the public sphere, and the media structure, both at the mass media and social media arenas.

Although most of the literature on DOS analyzes social movement and contested politics cases, it is not inadequate to transport the concept into an electoral campaign, especially when considering the specifics of Peru's presidential elections campaigning, the case in point. Political parties in Peru are created around and about political figures, exists mostly for one election, and have no articulation at the regional and local level; the few political parties with a existence measured beyond one campaign are not the largest political players, and submit themselves to specific candidates when the times arrive. Thus, they act around the agenda of the candidate, and have the sustainability of many social movements. This connects perfectly with the DOS model, as it allows for opportunistic usage of specific issues at campaign moments. DOS is made around the positioning on issues that emerge at any given time, and the political impact that can be developed thanks to them.

Koopman & Olzak (2004: 204-206), propose three concurring dimensions that create opportunities: the visibility of an issue, its resonance, and its legitimacy. For instance, in Peru's case, an issue like marriage equality has become visible in the past years, mostly due to the international context and its coverage in the media and popular entertainment; its resonance is high, as it presents a moral dilemma that clearly evokes contradictory valuations; but its legitimacy is low, at least among most of the population, since it is opposed by the Catholic Church as well as by many evangelical congregations. This opens a opportunity for a discursive approach that promotes action around the impending coming of marriage equality, that may poach on its lack of legitimacy if addressing most of the population, or allows for becoming a champion of the minority that defends and claims for marriage equality. (Corrales, 2019).

Either on electoral or contested political conditions, an actor will not shun the press, but rather will try to find a way to take its message from the medium they control into the media they do not control. This means developing discursive approaches to take control of issues, priming these issues to their immediate audience, and expecting issue salience in the media, as they are then left for the press to be presented to the larger public, perhaps not necessary under the best possible light. This means that as a strategy, issue salience requires a welcoming press willing to hear and then discuss the issues that political candidates wish to become salient. Those discursive opportunities get lost in the press, but can be release quite powerfully through social media, and even become more salient in the press through the repercussions of social media salience.

Thus, while issue salience has been traditionally a feature of press coverage, under this new political environment it is possible to produce what could be called self-salience: the developing of issue salience by the political actor itself. The Peruvian election of 2016 offers a case to explore this approach and to find its limitations.

CASE STUDY: PERUVIAN PRESIDENTIAL POLL OF 2016 AND FACEBOOK

Following what is called by Dahlgren & Alvares (2014) as a micro portrait of political agency, the usage of Facebook by a number of candidates in the Peruvian presidential poll of 2016 is used to present the limitations and possibilities that Peruvian citizens were afforded through social media to influence the political process, within the boundaries of local political culture, the political system and the realities of political practice. Specifically, and as an example of such approach, the discursive opportunities structure model allows to appreciate value-driven self-salience achievement.

Peru is a country that has experienced a long period of relative economic and political stability (Loayza & Jauregui, 2015), with a press sector that is clearly aligned with the political interests of the larger economic actors (Castilla, Castro & Yañez, 2016); opposite to it, there are weak political parties that are always looking for opportunities to win an election with little if any party militants or traditional commitments to specific sectors of the population.

The press, including radio and television news, is also aligned with larger economic actors and does not have a traditional of fair, neutral reporting (Mendoza, 2015). While in 2016, when the last presidential took place, only 28,4% of homes had access to the Internet, 45,5% of the population over 6 years old reported accessing the Internet regularly; this means that a large part of the electorate in a country were voting is mandatory from 18 to 70 years of age, had access to the Internet[1]. Informal reporting from print media accepts that readership is down significantly, although actual data is not made available to the public; neither are data about radio or television news coverage.

Peruvian political actors have been always aware of the reception they will get from news media: most of the outlets will welcome messaging from right and center right actors, while ignoring if not criticizing actively any left wing like position (Fowks, 2017). At the same time, the increased relevance of the Internet makes possible for political actors to engage directly with the electorate, thus appearing as an alternative to gain attention and obtaining a fair share of the electorate engaged. Electing a president and two vice-presidents (through ballotage) and the whole one-chamber congress of 130 members, Peru's 2016 polls were the eighth consecutive elections since the last military dictatorship ended in

1980. Since 2006, the participation of the daughter of past president Alberto Fujimori, Keiko, has been a feature at every election, with the country facing a continual debate between the Fujimoristas and the rest of the body politic. Alberto was president from 1990 to 2000, but after significant accusations of human rights abuses and corruption, he fled the country, and on his return, was prosecuted, sentenced and jailed (Crabtree, 2001; Laplante & Fenicie, 2010).

While the period prior to the election was characterized by social conflict and mobilization by a number of social and labour actors, the actual election came to be a direct choice between Fuerza Popular, Keiko Fujimori's party, and the rest of candidates, who presented a varied gamut of positions to the electorate. From the conventional left of the Broad Front (Frente Amplio), with Veronika Mendoza, a young woman from Cuzco with a French mother; to the conventional right wing of Peruanos Por el Kambio (a pun of the name of the candidate) represented by Pedro Pablo Kuzcynski, a 78-old politician and businessman running for the second consecutive time; the electorate had plenty of choice but a real two-way race: for Fujimori or against her.

The first round took place on April 10th, 2016; though the process started with 19 candidacies, in the end only 10 got to the poll itself: two were disqualified and seven decide to retire their candidacies. All the candidacies had a presence in Facebook, although with a wide range of content and dedication: some published almost any content imaginable every day, while others (mostly those that ended leaving the process) had minimal activity.

In Peru, with some mandatory programming on TV and radio for presidential candidacies —but only in the state's broadcaster— any further presence had to be paid for as advertising. Press coverage was clearly concentrated in the candidacies seen as most viable or on well-known public figures, like previous presidents; many candidacies, including the three ones self-identified as left wing, had minimal coverage by the national media, and then mostly oppositional. While some candidacies maintained its original trajectories and ended up where they were expected to end (or left the process to avoid such outcome), a couple of candidacies managed to grow their expected share of votes, becoming the center of attention for short periods.

Analyzing the process as it took place, it was evident that the different candidates had not developed a clear social media strategy, but rather used Facebook mostly as an ersatz press office, publishing campaign materials and press releases; Twitter had a similar usage, with most candidates trying to avoid getting into fights; and some experiments were just left as that.

But as the campaign developed, it became evident that a few of the candidacies detected discursive opportunities that were used to shift the conversation into their preferred subjects; this can be understood as an exercise in creating value-driven issue salience but directly through a medium controlled by the political actor, instead of using whatever salient subjects the media presented as the basis for the debate. The relative success that can be attached to such exercises is explained and discussed below.

Traditional Media vs. Social Media

Political communication, mobilization and participation will depend on the characteristics of a given political system. In Peru's case, voting is mandatory, so the emphasis lies not on convincing people to actually vote, but on choosing a given candidate, and not to vote blank or spoil the ballot.

This leads to the question about media influence on electorate behavior: as explained by Lang & Lang (2009:1020), it is usually assumed that there are three conditions that predispose to media influences on a voter: weak partisan preferences at the beginning of the process; issues arising during the campaign; and family and peers pressure. As already stated, the first condition is almost constant in Peru; the second one would vary according with the behavior of different candidates; and the pressures coming from social networks are noticeable in social media, though there is scant data available, from public opinion polls, to determine its actual importance.

It is also possible to state that traditional media firms have their own agenda, considering their financial interests as much as any perception of a public role; and that salience would be at least partly the outcome of the press's own interests than the result of public interest reporting.

Before the appearance of social media, "the street" was the main conduit of such an alternative: that is how Alberto Fujimori was elected in 1990, when he started as a complete unknown and one week before the election was considered "an unknown factor" by the national press, only to end up as runner-up and, in the *ballotage*, being elected. Fujimori's strategy —basically walkabouts in markets and poor areas of different cities, depending on word of mouth and only at the end of the campaign on media coverage— brought some level of attention, mostly focused on his utter uniqueness as a "non-political" candidate and his Japanese ancestry, but almost no coverage on the issues, because he had no position about them: his candidacy was mostly improvised and caught by surprise by its success as much as the rest of the country (Rousseau, 2006; Weyland, 2000).

Nowadays, his impact would have noticeable on social media way earlier than it was reflected on the national press in 1990. The issues at stake were simple and non-issue like, but still fit into the pattern of DOS: using his Japanese ancestry was visible (he is the son of two Japanese immigrants), resonant (culturally there are a number of virtues associated with Nikkei people in Peru, and he could bring those virtues into play as he incarnated them as a modestly successful college professor with a solid middle class lifestyle) and certainly legitimate: in the midst of a terrible economic crisis, a plain spoken person of Japanese origins was seen as a good bet against all the standard political types offering much of the same that had brought the country to the sorry condition were it was lying. The media only noticed the impact he was having by the end of the campaign, and could not recover in time to de-legitimize his candidacy at all; famously some news magazines ignored his possible success even a week from the poll.

Taking into account the changed reality of campaigning, it is possible to think that a social media-based campaign for someone like Fujimori would have, in 2016, would have significant potential. Facebook appeared as the main conduit for making the soft, personal virtues of a candidate salient.

Considering the Full Facebook Campaign

Using data collected from January 18th to April 8th 2016, not including some of the candidates —as they were expected to fail to connect with the electorate— the main variable, attention, is reflected in the eight cases for which we have complete coverage.

In terms of promoting attention, the most successful candidacy was the most passive. Keiko Fujimori started the process with a high level of attention, as reflection of the her years of working towards achieving recognition by the electorate through small, dedicated campaigning; the growth of digital attention was slow but constant, without any significant digital activity beyond very simple posts sharing political gatherings in a very straightforward manner. It was evident that organizational build-up and connection with the population were already in the conditions that the candidate wished to have, and the campaign itself was more about not making mistakes than saying or doing anything to increase support. Impacting the media was the result of her primacy in the opinion polls, rather than a reflection of any specific actions or proposals during the campaign (Ayala & Patriau, 2017). Her success, shown by winning the first round by a very large margin that almost meant winning straight away, indicated both a well design strategy but a structural limitation: the need to innovate during the second part of the campaign, before the final round, left her exposed and showing absence of reflexes and resources, finally producing a reversal in the nick of time.

The eventual winner, Pedro Pablo Kuczysnki (or PPK, as he was known), had a singular trajectory: starting from a very commercial-style campaign, based on gimmicks likes mascots getting married or endorsing the visit of the Rolling Stones as a demonstration that "there is no age limitation to be the best", no gain in attention nor voting intent was achieved. During the final days of campaigning it was evident from opinion polling that there was a significant possibility that PPK would lose second place to the left wing candidacy of Veronika Mendoza, so one final attempt was made, based on a sensationalist video called "48 horas para salvar al Perú" (48 hours to save Peru) (https://www.youtube.com/watch?v=ywSYHpnqfA8), presenting a group of middle class people sharing a meal and discussing the risks of a left wing victory, and asking for voters to send PPK to the second round. A rough, emotional appeal shown only online and rapidly viralized by many followers, the video sought to sow fear among not just middle income but mostly "emerging" middle class (those that have benefited from the economic expansion of the past decades), mobilized a significant number of people and was the single most commented item of the whole campaign. It can be alleged that it achieved its objective: PPK won second place by a slight margin.

Dealing with Discursive Opportunities

While there were political and policy issues that were critical during the election, for the purposes of this article the relevant material has to do more with communicative performance rather than policy discussions. Thus, three cases demand analysis, for diverging reasons.

First of all, Mendoza, the left wing candidate of the Broad Front, compensated a rather diffuse strategy without specific routes towards capturing attention, with two specific instances during the campaign that were used to develop attention through discursive opportunities. The first one happened during a hostile interview by a right-wing commentator, who opted to start by mocking Mendoza's French heritage from her mother's side, speaking to her in (an atrocious) French; Mendoza opted to return the mockery by asking him why he could not speak Quechua, the most importante Andean aboriginal language of Peru. The contrast between "white liberals" from Lima against a young woman from Cuzco was quite clear, and was used by her and her campaign as the source of a sustained discourse about her authenticity and how that authenticity reflected a real potential for listening to the needs of the people. The impact of this performance was significant, both in attention and in poll responses. The salience of the "indigenous question" has been quite low in Peru, even though the issue has been critical for as long as the country has existed; her actions brought attention not just to her performance and her heritage, but to a whole set of issues that normally are ignored by the media.

About three weeks later Mendoza caught on with a new opportunity: her candidacy has stressed "green" issues, and a leak in the Amazon rain forest's main oil duct offered her the chance not only of saying something quickly, but to skip planned events and travel to the area, where her pictures showing her hands covered in oil were attention grabbers, and showed her credentials on ecological issues. This self-made opportunity reinforced her narrative as a different kind of left-wing politician, as well as brought attention to her, as a champion of green issues.

From one percent vote intention to her final 19% in third position, Mendoza built national support from her strengths and her ability to use discursive opportunities. There is little doubt that other factors, that cannot be explained thoroughly here, were also determinant of her success, but the decisions taken contributed, and the digital coverage of her actions helped to make the two issues arising from the described situations as salient beyond her Facebook page and into the wider media.

What is more important is that the conversation she started through posts on Facebook was useful in shifting attention towards her take on the issues, and even more so, to present a perspective on such issues that starting to seep into the conversation. She overcome the fact of being a leftist to become an authentic green candidate, concerned with expanding rights and discussing issues that were different to the traditional economic success stories. She promoted through Facebook a favorable, specific approach, with highly positive valence, about those issues: she gave positive salience to her take on issues of interest.

By contrast, Alfredo Barnechea, from the middle-class Popular Action party, was a candidate with a middle class, technocratic approach, with a cosmopolitan slant that did not ignore his roots as the son of mid-level landowners. Undeniably, he managed to catch attention from a slice of the electorate thanks to his presentation skills and his calm, knowledgeable approach to the issues. This brought attention from the press at the same that the demand to grow his appeal beyond his small base (about 7% of the potential vote) became urgent for his backers. The digital growth was impressive: well over 1000% growth of his fan page in less than two months; and the two most shared posts of all the digital campaign, calling for his supporters to search for potential voters and to promote his candidacy.

This made it possible to consider that perhaps he could find a way to leap above the second tier candidates to get through to ballotage. As this possibility became evident, a new approach to campaigning began, with walkabouts in markets and streets, meaning direct exposure to the electorate. But, beyond his comfort zone, Barnechea was ill prepared for campaign traditions: one episode in particular caught the public's attention, when he refused the offer of a morsel of food from a market vendor. This episode had huge salience on the press, almost totally with negative valence, and marked the beginning of his downfall: no contrasting discurse was provided, and even the most radical attempts to shift attention from his apparent loftiness and cultural disconnect with the rest of the country was a failure. Tagged off as a "white people's candidate", he eventually finished fourth, far from Mendoza.

It is quite clear that most of these campaign rituals are negative discursive opportunities: if done wrong, they get all the negative attention possible, while done right only mean that you checked a box. The whole press coverage and the collective perception happening thereof creates an opportunity to fail, and fail he did. All the other candidates went on market walkabouts, but no one expected more than cursory coverage. And the complete lack of preparedness to counter balance these failures at the digital level meant losing the one advantage that he had, the attention gained on a committed but small slice of the electorate. His complete absence of alternative takes on the issues that drew negative attention left his candidacy out of the running.

Finally, the curious case of the PPKuy, the mascot from the eventual winner's campaign. The cuy, or guinea pig, is a common animal in Peru, used mostly as a source of meat in the Andes. A pun on the candidate's more accesible nickname, the PPKuy was used as a mascot both in the failed attempt in 2011 and in this occasion. However, it was used really as a mascot, promoting it independently of the candidacy with little connection with any specific issues or positions: attention for attention's sake, constructing salience that led nowhere in terms of political narrative or credibility. This led to a particularly absurd situation when an invitation to the "marriage" of the PPKuy with his suddenly-invented girlfriend, the PPUkuya (the "a" as a female ending in Spanish) was disseminated through social media. The event took place on a Sunday at noon, in a very concurred square in downtown Lima, with the attendance of a number of candidates to Congress but without the candidate himself; besides assorted hangers-on cheering, the reception was mostly amused bewilderment by the passers-by. That very night an opinion poll was released showing that PPK's candidacy was laying stiff at fourth place, thus burying any mention of the marriage and leading to the abandonment of the mascot without any explanation. This search for empty attention did not even deserve mockery on social media, and PPK's campaign realigned its messaging towards policy proposals, and in the end, to scaremongering, as the "48 hours…" video did.

Electoral Outcomes

While not deciding elections by themselves, digital strategies are a significant element in the electoral process, as a mechanism to create, reinforce or simply compound a communication strategy. Evidence shows that it is not about the amount of content but the way it is used to mobilize, through specific messaging, groups or collective voices towards a larger outcome.

Social media provides a captive audience, where the attention gained is organic but at the same time not as relevant as that coming from traditional media: it is not a route to convince the undecided, but to get the already convinced to become committed and to make them dedicate themselves to the convincing of others. This is a simple way to describe what the concept of connective action purports to explain.

While traditional issue salience has the value of coming from a independent actor, the definition of independence varies when the press actor does not pretend to act neutrally —in the political sense—, but rather as a partisan proposer of specific policies. Within a large gamut, there is no actual press neutrality, but less or more noisy, in-your-face partisanship; if we accept this premise, then any salience offered to an issue will be a function of political interests, and the obtaining of salience a reflection of a coincidence (organic or tactical) between a political candidate and a press outlet.

In a way, salience is transactional: the credibility of such results would come from the closeness of a given member of the public to the political positions expressed by the political actor, reflected in a given press outlet. The valence of each specific salient feature will reflect the coincidence between this triad of actors, but would be irrelevant to someone who is far from convinced of the positions of a political candidate or a press outlet.

But when the middleman is not available, or when a transaction is too expensive in political capital or credibility for a candidate, social media offers the chance of promoting *self-salience*. As Facebook provides for tools to differentiate a range of potential audiences, and to address hem separately, each situation can be used to create specific discursive approaches; of course, this makes sense as a whole strategy combining each messaging instance with a clear, encompassing narrative; as the valence of an issue starts moving towards zero after some time in the spotlight, especially under the stressful conditions of an presidential campaign, the demand for capturing attention grows and the need to promote new issues become overwhelming.

In other words, the costs of maintaining positive issue salience could be considered higher, but the results more beneficial, when the campaign promote them through the media they control, i.e., social media; this is inversely proportional for issue salience based on traditional media, as shown in the cases already explained for the Peruvian election of 2016.

CONCEPTUALIZING NEW FORMS OF SALIENCE

While media analysis shows salience as a measure of outcomes from a diversity of media and news actors, the argument thus far purports that for social media, issue salience would be a construction by the political actors themselves, rather than a secondary outcome of political activity. This construction of self-salience would be the outcome of using discursive opportunities emerging during political action, through specific action on social media, and would be reflected in secondary salience in traditional media

It is proposed that creating salience in social media —self-salience— means conducting a three step process: raising visibility of an issue, thus drawing attention to it; disseminating a discourse that resonates among specific groups or audiences, which could be seen as a form of priming; and finally, establishing a legitimate claim over such issue through the discurse created to interpret it, with positive valence among the members of the group, though it may mean negative valence to other people. The outcome would be digital participation: to get people to move and promote the discurse as the right way to address the original issue. In this way, it is possible to fulfill the expectation of using social media as a tool to achieve connective action.

More specifically: visibility means developing the presence of an issue on social media as to draw attention. If a political actor has a captive audience, making an issue visible is not particularly hard, but to sustain visibility is necessary to present it under a variety of positions, as to maintain attention along a defined period. This continuous presentation would have to provide a bias adequate to the kind of valence being looked for: positive or negative, never neutral. Resonance will require to make the issue go beyond the immediate audience through a varied connection to larger issues or discussions, re-defining the original issue in a way that turns it into an urgent affair, rather than just confort food for the original audience; for instance, adjusting the discurse towards a wider audience, as well as developing a variety of resources, worked for Mendoza at the time when the issue of linguistic authenticity was drawing attention. The issue was primed and the media started to present it, at least for a few days; in particular, the issue was set upon the terms that the discursive approach that Mendoza had defined —should politicians speak Quechua. This in itself was a discursive victory.

Finally, to achieve participation, some specific campaign arrangements are necessary. These arrangements are not the focus of this research but that we can state were not in place in any of the Peruvian campaigns of 2016. The arrangements would have been necessary to promote and conduct digital participation in a manner that may benefit the campaigns, but none of them had the resources or the disposition to attempt such route.

But legitimacy is required before the managerial and communication arrangements start to work. Social acceptance and buy-in of a given discursive presentation, coming from a understanding that a position may come from a political actor but that it represents interests beyond the actor itself. This also creates legitimacy for the political actor, something quite important in a country like Peru, where there is no tradition of actor's continuity and very low approval ratings for almost any politician and political organization. This does not preclude confrontation: in fact, the press may attack a political discursive interpretation of an issue, coming from a newly legitimized political actor, thus valuing it very negatively; but the presence of the combination actor / issue is in itself an indicator of success, and the attacks may further legitimize the actor.

This requires consistency between the discurse promoted and the issue selected, and the narrative being offered. If you are attempting to convince the electorate that your candidacy is a serious, technocratic one, to spend resources in promoting a mascot is due to bring failure: not even if you try to augment visibility this particular issue will be resonant to anyone. Similarly, if you decide to offer yourself as a serious person with a wider understanding of society, some alternative discurse regarding your lack of connection with common people's cultural practices has to be ready to counterbalance any situation where your distance to the common people is put in evidence. But if your roots are a powerful componente of your narrative, to make those roots visible, resonant and to legitimize them by appropriating them into your discurse, reinforces the narrative.

However, self-salience faces the limits of attention that social media suffers. At some point, your discourse has to break through your controlled environment and be shared by other media actors. The oil leakage is a good example: while it helped to define Mendoza's candidacy as the only one concerned with environmental issues, the fact is that most of the media ignored her attempt, perhaps because it could not be spun in a way that put her under a bad light. Whatever positive valence was promoted by responses to Mendoza's social media outlets, to sustain such valence both adversaries and the media have to take it into consideration and express an opinion about it, even if it tries to shift the discurse towards negative valence. No matter how much legitimacy the issue had under the discurse created by Mendoza: its absence from the media sphere meant it did not matter much.

Achieving self-salience, then, is an exercise on controlling variables composing the construction of discursive opportunities; this is valid for traditional and self-salience. However, as it has been discussed, the limitations of self-salience do not compensate properly if there is a strong negative valence resulting from it, especially if that allow for a new negative perspective to be carried to traditional media; of course, this is predicated on traditional media paying attention to postings, something that may not happen for a variety of reasons.

Here emerges the need for controlling valence, as the most critical aspect of issue self-salience. By definition, political actors have less influence over the valuation of issues that traditional media, as the former speak to their constituents while the latter speak to society as a whole, even when doing so from a partisan position. Thus, the reporting of an issue may come with negative valence attached and there is little a candidacy can do about it. If a candidacy decides to offer a highly positive presentation of an issue, only those media outlets completely in agreement with it would be interested in disseminating such presentation, which is sort of useless; or they may choose to bring a completely negative discussion, which is quite contrary to the interests of the campaign.

Following this, it can be postulated that for self-salience, the valence of an issue is defined by the reactions expressed by the readers through the Facebook sequence of participation: liking, commenting and sharing. An item without comments or shares will have no valence; the number of positive comments, for instance, is a measure of positive valence. Of course, participation of partisan users with the intent to spoil the discussion (or trolls, as they are known) will unbalanced valence; but for Mendoza's case, most of the comments were positive, thus indicating positive valence. However, as the ultimate achievement will depend on converting self-salient issues into conventionally salient issue on the media, the highest risk is provoking an extreme reaction on the press that shifts valence, and thus public opinion, into a negative valuation of the issue.

Of course further research should be conducted to really establish the conceptual basis for self-salience as a feature of political communication analysis. In most cases, the particularities of each political system would create specific demands for incorporating such a concept; but the information presented regarding this particular case shows the potential for self-salience to provide a new path for explaining the influence of social media in political campaigning,

REFERENCES

Anduiza, E., Gallego, A., & Cantijoch, M. (2010). Online Political Participation in Spain: The Impact of Traditional and Internet Resources. *Journal of Information Technology & Politics*, *7*(4), 356–368. doi:10.1080/19331681003791891

Ayala, V., & Patriau, E. (2017). Equipos en campaña. In F. Tuesta (Ed.), Perú Elecciones 2016: un país dividido y un resultado inesperado (pp. 155-177). Lima: PUCP.

Bennett, W. L., & Pfetsch, B. (2018). Rethinking political communication in a time of disrupted public spheres. *Journal of Communication*, *68*(2), 243–253. doi:10.1093/joc/jqx017

Bennett, W. L., & Segerberg, A. (2012). The Logic of connective action. *Information Communication and Society*, *15*(5), 739–768. doi:10.1080/1369118X.2012.670661

Bimber, B. (2014). Digital Media in the Obama Campaigns of 2008 and 2012: Adaptation to the Personalized Political Communication Environment. *Journal of Information Technology & Politics*, *11*(2), 130–150. doi:10.1080/19331681.2014.895691

Campbell, S. W., & Kwak, N. (2011). Political Involvement in 'Mobilized' Society: The Interactive Relationships Among Mobile Communication, Network Characteristics, and Political Participation. *Journal of Communication*, *61*(6), 1005–1024. doi:10.1111/j.1460-2466.2011.01601.x

Castilla, O., Castro, J., & Yañez, L. (2016). *Dueños de la Noticia*. Retrieved from https://duenosdelanoticia.ojo-publico.com/articulo/los-duenos-de-la-noticia/

Corrales, J. (2019). *The Expansion of LGBT Rights in Latin America and the Backlash. In The Oxford Handbook of Global LGBT and Sexual Diversity Politics*. doi:10.1093/oxfordhb/9780190673741.013.14

Dahlgren, P. (2005). The Internet, Public Spheres, and Political Communication: Dispersion and Deliberation. *Political Communication*, *22*(2), 147–162. doi:10.1080/10584600590933160

Downing, J. D. H., & Brooten, L. (2009). ICTs and political movements. In The Oxford handbook of information and communication technologies (pp. 537-544). Oxford University Press. doi:10.1093/oxfordhb/9780199548798.003.0023

Gibson, R., Römmele, A., & Williamson, A. (2014). Chasing the Digital Wave: International Perspectives on the Growth of Online Campaigning. *Journal of Information Technology & Politics*, *11*(2), 123–129. doi:10.1080/19331681.2014.903064

Harlow, S., & Salaverría, R. (2016). *Regenerating Journalism*. Digital Journalism. doi:10.1080/21670811.2015.1135752

Howard, P. N., & Parks, M. R. (2012). Social Media and Political Change: Capacity, Constraint, and Consequence. *Journal of Communication*, *62*(2), 359–362. doi:10.1111/j.1460-2466.2012.01626.x

Kalsnes, B. (2016). The Social Media Paradox Explained: Comparing Political Parties' Facebook Strategy Versus Practice. *Social Media and Society*, *2*(2), 1–11. doi:10.1177/2056305116644616

Kiousis, S. (2000). Explicating Media Salience: A Factor Analysis of New York Times Issue Coverage During the 2000 U.S. Presidential Election. *Journal of Communication, 54*(1), 71-87, doi:10.1111/j.1460-2466.2004.tb02614.x

Kluknavska, A. (2014). A Right-wing Extremist or People's Protector?? Media Coverage of Extreme Right Leader Marian Kotleba in 2013 Regional Elections in Slovakia. *Intersections, 1*(1), 147–165. doi:10.17356/ieejsp.vlil.35

Kreisi, H. (2004). Political context and opportunity. In The Blackwell Companion to Social Movements (pp. 68-90). Blackwell. doi:10.1002/9780470999103.ch4

Lang, K., Lang, G.E. (2009). Mass Society, Mass Culture, and Mass Communication: The Meaning of Mass. *International Journal of Communication, 3*, 998-1024.

Loiaza, R., & Jauregui, S. (2015). Evolución del Mercado de Telecomunicaciones Móviles en el Perú. Gerencia de Políticas Regulatorias y Competencia Subgerencia de Evaluación y Políticas de Competencia I OSIPTEL, Lima.

Mendoza, M. (2015). Gestión de las empresas periodísticas regionales: El Sol, de Cusco; El Tiempo, de Piura e ímpetu, de Ucayali. *Revista de Comunicación, 14*, 70–99.

Molaei, H. (2014). Discursive opportunity structure and the contribution of social media to the success of social movements in Indonesia. *Information Communication and Society, 18*(1), 94–108. doi:10.1080/1369118X.2014.934388

Motta, R. (2015). Transnational Discursive Opportunities and Social Movement Risk Frames Opposing GMOs. *Social Movement Studies, 14*(5), 576–595. doi:10.1080/14742837.2014.947253

Postmes, T., & Brunsting, S. (2002). Collective Action in the Age of the Internet: Mass Communication and Online Mobilization. *Social Science Computer Review, 20*(3), 290–301. doi:10.1177/089443930202000306

Roberts, M., Wanta, W., & Dzwo, D. (2002). Agenda Setting and Issue Salience Online. *Communication Research, 29*(4), 452–465. doi:10.1177/0093650202029004004

Rousseau, S. (2006). Women's Citizenship and Neopopulism: Peru Under the Fujimori Regime. *Latin American Politics and Society, 48*(1), 117–141. doi:10.1111/j.1548-2456.2006.tb00340.x

Tanaka, M. (2009). El sistema de partidos 'realmente existente' en el Perú, desafíos de la construcción de una representación política nacional y cómo encumbra la reforma política. *Economía y Sociedad*, 79.

Vissers, S., & Stolle, D. (2014). Spill-Over Effects Between Facebook and On/Offline Political Participation? Evidence from a Two-Wave Panel Study. *Journal of Information Technology & Politics, 11*(3), 259–275. doi:10.1080/19331681.2014.888383

Walsham, G. (2017). ICT4D research: Reflections on history and future agenda. *Information Technology for Development, 23*(1), 18–41. doi:10.1080/02681102.2016.1246406

Weyland, K. (2000). A Paradox of Success? Determinants of Political Support for President Fujimori. *International Studies Quarterly, 44*(3), 481–502. doi:10.1111/0020-8833.00168

Williamson, A. (2010). Inside the digital campaign. In The internet and the 2010 election: Putting the small 'p' back in politics? (pp. 17-26). Londres: Hansard.

KEY TERMS AND DEFINITIONS

Ballotage: An electoral mechanism in which the two most voted candidate for an executive or legislative position participate in a second round of elections, where the most voted will have at least 51% + 1 of the votes, thus allowing a clear majority of the electorate to support him or her. In Peru it has been used exclusively for presidential elections, but in countries such as France is used for both presidential and congressional elections.

Electoral Campaign: A political campaign designed to promote a candidate for public office, set around and happening before a public poll; such a campaign looks to achieve the mobilization of citizens to make them vote for a given candidate against others, or to choose a political position against another in plebiscite elections.

Narrative: It is understood as the coherent, partisan interpretation of complex events that is used as a mechanism to achieve consensus and political gain, regarding matters of public interest that are contested in the public sphere.

Salience: In communication studies, salience occurs when any news or media item captures and holds attention from a group of public, and becomes a significant element of public discussion. A salient item is one that features such properties as to gain salience. Salience is usually understood as the result of news media work, as these organizations decide how and when to promote and feature a given news or media item.

Self-Salience: It is proposed that self-salience happens when a political, social or commercial organizations uses its social media outlet to promote an issue of interest, thus making it salient among its users/consumers. Through this process, these organizations are able to by-pass the usual control exerted by news media of public sphere discussion.

Social Media: Media designed to allow the production of content by all its users, and to disseminate it to the members of one user's group of connections, i.e., his or her social network.

Traditional Media: For the purposes of this contribution, this refers to organizations and practices usually called "mass media," addressing the general public or specific segments of it through electronic means, a coordinated, schedule-based programming, and perfunctory public participation. Though it may be accessed through computers or computational devices, traditional media is designed around specific-medium devices like television sets and radio receivers.

ENDNOTE

1 All data about internet penetration in Peru comes from the official statistics agency of Peru, and it is available here: https://www.inei.gob.pe/estadisticas/indice-tematico/tecnologias-de-la-informacion-y-telecomunicaciones/

Chapter 14
Political Mobilization Strategies in Taiwan's Sunflower Student Movement on March 18, 2014:
A Text-Mining Analysis of Cross-National Media Corpus

Kenneth C. C. Yang
https://orcid.org/0000-0002-4176-6219
The University of Texas at El Paso, USA

Yowei Kang
https://orcid.org/0000-0002-7060-194X
National Taiwan Ocean University, Taiwan

ABSTRACT

Taiwan's Sunflower Student Movement on March 18, 2014 has been characterized as a social movement with its sophisticated integration of social and mobile media into mobilizing Taiwanese society through participant recruitment and resource mobilization domestically and globally. Ample research has contributed the roles of these emerging media platforms as one of the main reasons for its success. This study was based on resource mobilization theory (RMT) to examine the roles of new communication technologies on mobilizing resources. This chapter focuses on the resource mobilization strategies by activists and organizations of the 318 Sunflower Student Movement. A large-scale text mining study was developed to examine how cross-national English media have described this social movement in Taiwan. Results and implications were discussed.

DOI: 10.4018/978-1-7998-1828-1.ch014

INTRODUCTION

Taiwan's *318 Sunflower Student Movement* in 2014 has impacted and restructured the island country's political landscape (Chiou, 2014). As predicted in an earlier study by Yang and Kang (2017), its repercussions have been widely felt in Taiwan's subsequent presidential and legislature elections in 2016, which results in then ruling KMT's collapse in terms of controlling central government and its majority to the opposition party, DPP. Dr. Ing-Wen Tsai ultimately became the first female president after replacing the unpopular China-friendly President Yi-Jeou Ma (Bardenhagen, 2014; Rahaula, 2015) and defeated the KMT's Presidential candidate, Eric Chu (Bush, 2016). Dr. Tsai has won 56.1% of the popular vote, compared with 30.1% of KMT's Eric Chu and 12.8% of PFP's James Soong (Bush, 2016). DPP also won the dominant majority in the Legislative Yuan, achieving 68 out of 113 seats (Bush, 2016; Kuo, 2019). The sweeping victory of DPP in 2016 has given Dr. Tsai sufficient political capital for her social and political agendas (Bush, 2016). With her full control of the Legislative Yuan, DPP also finalized its pension reforms in 2017 to reduce the privileged benefits of civil servants, teachers, and military personnel (Schubert, 2017). In May, 2019, Taiwan also became the first Asia country to legalize same sex marriage (Kuo, 2019).

On March 12, 1930, Mohandas Gandhi began his march to the sea to protest British monopoly on salt in India (The History Channel, 2010), civil disobedience movement, or civil resistance movement similar to Gandhi's, has swept most parts of the world because of many social issues related to the corporate power, unemployment (particularly among the youth and less skilled workers), income inequality, wealth distribution, etc (Penney & Dadas, 2014). The *Yellow Jacket Protest* in France was also triggered by French's president's tax reforms, but has its root in the country's high cost of living and people' sense of being left out by the political elites (Smith, 2018). In Hong Kong, the month-long *Anti-Extradition Law Protest* is also deep-rooted in the special administrative region's rising property price and lack of opportunities for its youths (Associated Press, 2019; Chan, 2019; Pao, 2019). Like other social movements and protests, they serve as an important function in a robust democracy (Jha, 2008) when the pressure in the society needs to released, metaphorically speaking.

In Taiwan, increasing numbers of social and civil disobedience movements have also been attributed to government tax and real estate policies, frictions due to closer economic ties with China, strategies and tactics when dealings with China, etc (Cole, 2014). The depressing job prospect and stagnant salary for many Taiwanese youths has continued to affect every aspect of Taiwanese society (Smith, 2017). For example, a total of 720,000 highly trained Taiwanese have moved to China to seek better job opportunities and higher salaries (Smith, 2017). Small social movement groups (such as *Citizen 1985* and *the Black Island Nation Youth Alliance*) have risen as a result of these increasing tensions (Cole, 2014). Compounding with the worsened social situations in Taiwan are the threats from China's rising hegemony (Kelly, 2014) and intentionally meddling with Taiwan's identity and affairs (Smith, 2017). China intends to expand her sphere of influence to cover a wide area of Asia and to replace the U.S. as the region's dominant player (Lind, 2018). From a geo-political perspective, China's grand strategy is "prioritize land power and aim to become preponderant on the continent before it can challenge US' command of the global commons and kick it out from its natural zone of influence" (The Policy Tensor, 2013, para 35). The hegemony of China has increasingly impacted on Taiwan's ways of lives. China has long made its intention clear to use economic integration as the strategy to dilute Taiwan's local national identity and ultimately subdue to its own "One China" principle (Smith, 2017) to recognize Taiwan as part of China.

Taiwan, a de factor independent island country near China's eastern coastline, has been claimed by China to be its province (Kan & Morrison, 2011), her sovereign territory, and to be her "core interests" (Campbell, Meick, Hsu, & Murra, 2013). Despite international diplomatic recognition by 23 countries (including Vatican), China's sovereign claim over Taiwan has led to the exclusion of Taiwan from many international organizations (such as the United Nations) and the establishment of diplomatic ties with other countries (including the U.S.) (Herrington & Lee, 2014; Winkler, 2012). Under President Xi's "Chinese Dream" grandiose rhetoric and tough words, China has strengthened its pressure on Taiwan in recent years (Horton, 2019; Wong, 2018). For example, President Xi has threatened on multiple occasions that Taiwan "must be and will be" united with China and warned that independence efforts could be met by armed force" (Horton, 2019, n.p.). Other tactics by China include forcing airlines, foreign companies, and international organizations to refer to Taiwan, as part of China (Palmer & Allen-Ebrahimian, 2018).

The close economic relationship with China is a double-edge sword for Taiwan's burgeoning democracy. Taiwan's economic recovery from the global economic crisis in 2009 particularly relied on China to boost its export-oriented economy (Kan & Morrison, 2011). China's economy has increased Taiwan's imports and exports by 44.3% and 35.1% respectively in Taiwan (Kan & Morrison, 2011). China has replaced the U.S. as the most important trading partner with Taiwan (Kan & Morrison, 2011). China continues to the largest trading partner of China and accounts for 30% of the country's total trade (Albert, 2019). Trade between Taiwan and China has reached USD$150.5 billion in 2018, while, in 1999, cross-strait trade is only less than USD$30 billion (Albert, 2019). The 2010 Economic Cooperation Framework Agreement (ECFA), signed between pro-China President Ma and China, only worsens the negative effect of close economic ties between Taiwan and China, including the "hollowing-out" of small- to medium-sized businesses in Taiwan (Morris, 2018). Big corporations benefit most from the close economic relationship (Albert, 2019), while depressing local salaries and employment opportunities.

In this chapter, the authors examine technology-enabled mobilization strategies in this successful civil disobedience movement in Taiwan. Situated within a larger trend of social media's role in political communication in *Arab Spring*, China's defunct *Jasmine Revolution*, and North America's *Occupy Wall Street Movement*, the authors aim to examine how the English language mass media have described these technology-enabled resource mobilization strategies that help *the 318 Sunflower Student Movement* through the theoretical lens of Resource Management Theory (Eltantawy & Wiest, 2011) to examine the role of social media in organizing a variety of resources (such as temporal, monetary, psychological, and social) that contribute to the success of this social movement.

On the basis of the above discussion, this book chapter aims to answer the following questions:

Research Question 1: How are data mining and text mining methods relevant to the study of political mobilization strategies in Taiwan's *Sunflower Student Movement* on March 18, 2014?

Research Question 2: What are the recurrent keywords, phrases, and topics as found in the collected media corpus on Taiwan's *Sunflower Student Movement* on March 18, 2014?

Research Question 3: What will be cross-country variations in terms of the media representations of Taiwan's *Sunflower Student Movement* on March 18, 2014?

BACKGROUND

The *318 Sunflower Student Movement* in Taiwan

On March 18, 2014, a group of student protestors raided and occupied the Legislative Yuan and later the Executive Yuan in Taiwan. Such an activity is said to the first time in history (Li, 2014; Pesek, 2014). At the height of this student movement, there were 500,000 Taiwanese congregating at the central government district in downtown Taipei (Morris, 2018). The student-led social movement lasted for about 3 weeks after then Taiwan's President Ma made significant concessions to change his non-transparent practices when signing *the Cross-Strait Service Trade Agreement* (henceforth, CSSTA) with People's Republic of China (Spangler, 2014; Taiwanese Central News Agency, 2014 May 19). Critics have questioned President Ma's handling of the signing process of CCSTA despite opposition party's multiple attempts to demand the concerns of civil society, labor group, and opposition party should be considered (Spangler, 2014). As a result, mostly labelled as a movement of civil disobedience against an authoritarian government and her dealings with China, *the 318 Sunflower Student Movement* is viewed as "a further democratization of Taiwan, with additional safeguards to let the people, not any political party, decide the fate of Taiwan." according to BBC (Sui, 2014). The movement has accumulated a large number of international supporters among Taiwanese communities who reside overseas. Repercussions include later events that occurred in Hong-Kong (2014, June) and Macao (2014, May) that demonstrate similar civil disobedience movements.

Local politicians in Taiwan have viewed this student-led movement from different perspectives. For example, Joseph Wu, secretary general of Taiwan's Democratic Progressive Party (a major opposition party) described *the 318 Sunflower Student Movement* as "an awakening movement among the young in Taiwan" (Jennings, 2014, p. 2). *The Sunflower Movement* has been claimed to change the political narratives in Taiwan (Morris, 1998) and carries noteworthy characteristics of generational politics (Liu, 2014). Participants of *the Sunflower Student Movement* have been found to be mainly composed of 6th generation Taiwanese who are confident of saying no to China, but "not in the functionality of Taiwan's democracy in terms of solving their concerns about Taiwan's political future and bringing them economic hope" (Liu, 2014, n.p.). Therefore, some political scientists have predicted that this issue-based social movement is less likely to sustain over the long period of time (Liu, 2014).

On the other hand, foreign media have depicted this student-led movement as a referendum on Ma's pro-China policy. As Pesek (2014) observed, *the Sunflower Student Movement* suggests "the calm across the Taiwan Strait that Beijing and Washington took for granted may officially be over" (para 4). Some scholars have viewed *the Sunflower Student Movement* as a continuation of Taiwan's growing anti-Sinoism and brewing civic nationalism (Au, 2017). Au (2017) made a daring claim that a series of social protests since 2004 are defined as opposition to Taiwan's economic and political ties with China. These protests include the followings: *228 Hand-in-Hand Rally* (2004), *the 1025 Demonstration* (2008), *the Wild Strawberries Movement* (2008), and *the 517 Protest* (2009) (Au, 2017)—all of which have impacts on Taiwan's political and social backdrop. Subsequent social movements to fight against China's omnipresence in Taiwan include *Anti-Red Media* in Taiwan on June 23, 2019 to protest again the creation and spread of fake news by media outlets controlled by pro-China business-turned media tycoon (Hsu, 2019).

It has been generally observed by many foreign media and experts that the student-led *318 Sunflower Movement* has halted the further economic integration between Taiwan and China as well as other cross-strait ties (Ching, 2014) by replacing KMT's president, legislative majority, and several key county and city majors in 2014 and 2016 domestic and national elections (Hioe, 2016). Such a consequence is likely to lead to what China most fears—Taiwan's continuing progression to independence with its rising national identity. As Professor Zhu Weidon, deputy direction of the Taiwan Institute, the Chinese Academy of Social Sciences (a top think tank in China) concluded pessimistically that "We spent the last six years just stopping Taiwan from veering towards independence, we had not succeeded in changing its course toward unification. Now we have to start all over again" (Ching, 2014, para 24). To respond to *the Sunflower Student Movement*, China immediately launched several new policies to attract the angry young protestors (Keck, 2014).

The repercussions of *the 318 Sunflower Student Movement* has been felt throughout Taiwan. One of the subsequent movements is to question the status quo. In August, 2014, high-school students in Taiwan began their protest of the statutes of Chiang Kai-Shek on school campuses (Jennings, 2014). The late President Chiang, a dictator who had ruled Taiwan for over 30 years under the martial law, has been tied to *the 228 Massacre*, *White Terror*, and political persecution of many political activists (Jennings, 2014). As Joseph Wu, secretary general of Taiwan's leading opposition party, observed "The newest move by the high school students represents an awakening to question the existence of Chiang's statues when Taiwan is supposed to be democratized" (Jennings, 2014, p. 4). New political forces have also emerged after *the Sunflower Student Movement* that has profoundly changed how Taiwanese perceive politics, especially among younger generation (Liu, 2016). Two student leaders, Lin Fei-fan and Chen Wei-ting has organized a brand new political group to push the reform of Taiwan's tight-fisted referendum law (Taiwanese Central News Agency, 2014, May 19). The culmination of these movements and the formation of new political groups or parties have changed Taiwan's political landscape. Au (2017) also observed "[a]nti-Sinoism in Taiwan has penetrated the state, crystallizing into an ethnic conflict that has escalated to include induced immigration, and pressured emigration" (n.p.).

MAIN FOCUS OF THE CHAPTER

ICTs, Social Media and Social/Civil Disobedience Movement

Despite past studies have generated mixed results on whether social media lead to civic engagement and political participation (Conroy, Feezell, & Guerrero, 2011), information-communication technologies (ICTs) are often claimed to contribute to the rise of "networked communities useful in organizing, coordinating, supporting and maintaining 'real life' activism" (Biddix & Park, 2008, p. 871). The potential use of information and communication technologies (ICTs) in social movements and collective behavior for activism has been explored as early as Myers' paper in 1994. Recent scholarship exploring the relationship between ICTs and political participation begins to discuss the "communication-enabling potentials for facilitating political talk in interpersonal spaces and subsequently, political participation in public domains" (Hsieh & Li, 2014, p. 26). The same position is adopted by Gainous and Wagner (2013) when they claim that Twitter has created "a fundamental shift in the way people interact with each other, obtain and process information, and ultimately use this information to choose who governs" (p. 3). On the basis of the analysis of three social movement cases in India (i.e., *Right to Information Act Movement* in 2005, the *India Against Corruption Movement* in 2011, and the *Net Neutrality Movement* in 2015), Madhavan (2016) examined the role of Internet in fostering deliberative democracy. Zúñiga, Molyneux, and Zheng (2014) used a large national online survey in the U.S. to empirically examine whether political expressions on social media predict users' political participation. Their study found that information use of social media for news has direct effects on political participation offline, while the use of social media for interactions does not have direct effects on users' political engagement (Zúñiga et al., 2014).

The emergence of ICTs and social media has challenged the hegemony of existing media institutions. Participants in politics can easily circumvent traditional media (Gainous & Wagner, 2013). A similar position is taken by Olubumi (2015) who also argues that new ICTs have allowed protestors to stay connected, to circulate news around the world, and to develop strategies. Traditionally, organizers of social/civil disobedience movements often do not have little or no control over "the intensity or what is covered by mainstream media" (Giltin, 1980, cited in Jha, 2008, p. 713). The framing of social movements and protests among the main stream media tends to focus on the violent and disorderly aspects. Given the media environment, governmental control, and professional practices in journalism, Jha (2008) noted that "[c]overage of demonstrations undercounts the crowds, concentrates on when it comes to social protests, moreover, journalists also adhere strongly to the fairness doctrine, going out of their way to carry the views of counter-demonstrators and the establishment every time they cover the views of the protesters (Small, 1994, cited in Jha, 2008, p. 713). Mattoni and Treré (2014) also critically assessed the role of media in facilitating social movements and propose a theoretical framework in which the interactions between media and social movements are examined.

The advent of social media has led to a brand new scenario when social and traditional media interact with each other in terms of political participation and civic engagement. In their discussion of *Occupy Wall Street Movement* in the U.S., Penney and Dadas (2014) observed that this social movement initially attracted little media coverage at the beginning. However, the mainstream media caught up and created "media frenzy" in the fall of 2011. Emerging social media and traditional media, as well as the dynamics created by media synergy have contributed to the success of this movement. Similar synergetic interactions among multiple media platforms can be observed in the Egyptian Revolution (Khamis & Vaughan, 2011), and Hong-Kong's *Umbrella Revolution* and *Occupy Central with Peace and Love* movements (Lee, 2014). Twelve tweets were posted on Twitter every second at the height of *the Occupy Central* movement, when compared with 19 tweets per minute at the beginning of the activity (Lee, 2014). As described in the examples above, Olubumi (2015) therefore concluded that the ambiguous power of social media has made these platform a tool for social movement resistance.

Social media, like other information-communication technologies (ICTs), have been viewed as "enabling technologies" for political mobilization among sexual minorities (Soriano, 2014), the revolution in Egypt (Khamis & Vaughan, 2011), and a tool of resistance for social movements (such as *Burkinabé Uprising*, *Occupy Wall Street*, and *the Arab Spring*) (Olubumi, 2015). Penney and Dadas (2014) concluded the instrumental role of social media platforms to trigger mobilization of the participants on the basis of Khamis and Vaughan's study (2011). In their study of the role of Twitter in the Egyptian Revolution, Khamis and Vaughan (2011) found that social media via mobile devices were used as instruments to allow citizen journalists, activists, and participants to bypass mainstream television media. Activists used social media to document military violence in Tahrir Square in Cairo (Khamis & Vaughan, 2011). Furthermore, activists also set up their *We Are Khaled Said* page on Facebook to allow more than 50,000 participants to coordinate their attendance of the protest event (Khamis & Vaughan, 2011). In conclusion, a review of existing literature has confirmed that the advent of ICTs has been praised for their potential power to transform society (Chen, 2014; Shirky, 2011) and to be used a tool of resistance for social movements (Olubumi, 2015). Communication scholars have used theorists such as Jürgen Habermas' (1962) public sphere concept to describe whether new ICTs and social media can create "space for discussion and agreement among politically engaged citizens, often before the state had fully democratized" (cited in Shirky, 2011, p. 6).

Other theorists have explored the linkage between ICTs and democracy (Madhaven, 2016). For example, Pool (1983) studies the empowering capacity of new ICTs in terms of social, economic, and political aspects. Deriving from Pool's position on the capabilities of new ICTs in fostering and shaping social and political changes, his technology-determinism perspective focuses on what technologies can enable social movements. His prediction of what ICTs can do to society can be observed in the *Sunflower Student Movement* and many other social movements (Olubumi, 2015), all of which have demonstrated what social media can do to contest the state power by ordinary citizens. Some scholars have gone further to say that these ICTs can become a "liberation technology" (Diamond & Plattner, 2012, cited in Bondes & Schucher, 2014, p. 46) and encourage public engagement with political activities.

Another line of research focuses whether new ICTs can foster a "deliberative democratic public sphere" (Madhaven, 2016, n.p.). The capability of social media to encourage citizens' political participation is clearly demonstrated in the resource mobilization, participant congregation, and protest coordination in the *318 Sunflower Student Movement* discussed in this chapter. This chapter will adopt the perspectives developed from Resource Mobilization Theory (henceforth, RMT) (Eltantawy & Wiest, 2011) to examine the resource mobilization roles of various social media platforms as seen in the *318 Sunflower Student Movement* in Taiwan in 2014. Apparently, the success of the *318 Sunflower Student Movement* is contributed to its sophisticated integration of social media into mobilizing Taiwanese society through participant recruitment, domestically and globally, competing with (and replacing) the agenda-setting and framing functions of pro-government or state-controlled mass media, and publicizing their causes to both domestic and international audiences.

Social media have been considered as an emerging public sphere to foster the development of a civil society (Mou, Atkin, & Fu, 2011) and online activism (Choi & Park, 2014). Most studies have explored the functions of social media on individual's psychology to enhance citizens' political participation (see Hsieh & Li, 2014 for review). Taken from users' perspectives, social media create venues to allow users to seek information and interact with others by means of posting and sharing commentaries (Kushin & Yamamoto, 2010). Choi and Park (2014) proposed a concept of "mobilizing structure" that is composed of networks "to facilitate informal gatherings with collective identity, mobilizing others to join their actions, in order to achieve political or social goals" (p. 131).

However, the success of any technology-enabled social/civil disobedience movement is contingent on many factors, ranging from the cultivation of collective identities, the framing of movement agendas, and the mobilization of collective actions (Gamson & Wolfsfeld, 1993; Smith, 2001; Watkins, 2001, cited in Jha, 2008, p. 717). Among these factors, the abilities to mobilize a variety of resources among protestors are very critical to the sustainability of these social movements (Yang & Kang, 2017). This book chapter centers on the mobilization of collective actions through the mobilization of resources in *the 318 Sunflower Student Movement* in Taiwan as described in the English language media through a large scale text-mining analysis.

Resource Mobilization Theory (RMT)

Resource Mobilization Theory (henceforth, RMT) is developed from studies of collective action during the 1960s. The theory has been gaining increasing prominence as a feasible theory to study social movements (Jenkins, 1983) throughout the 1970s and 1980s (Eltantawy & Wiest, 2011) and there has shown a rekindled interest of applying RMT to study technology-enabled social movements (Yang & Kang, 2017). RMT examines the problems that a social movement organization encounters when organizers attempt to coordinate and mobilize resources to form collective action (Löblich, & Wendelin, 2011). RMT is also based on the principles that resources—such as time, money, organizational skills, and certain social or political opportunities—are critical to the success of social movements (Eltantawy & Wiest, 2011). The capabilities to mobilize and manage these resources by "social movement organizations" (SMOs) to pursue their own "strategy of social protests" (a term previously proposed by Gamson (1990), are critical to the success of social movements (Carroll & Hackett, 2006). SMOs such as mass media and civil society organizations are sometimes in conflict with each other due to their contradicting agendas to maximize profits or to disseminate messages (Carroll & Hackett, 2006).

The theoretical components of RMT are composed of forms of activities, organizations, and resources (Löblich, & Wendelin, 2011). According to RMT, the emergence of new ICTs such as the Internet and social media will establish a dense communication infrastructure to enable social movements and protests to be orchestrated through different collective action. The repertoire of collective action includes cultural jamming, demonstrations, media publicity events, and strikes (Carroll & Hackett, 2006). New social media platforms will facilitate a new type of participatory dynamics on the basis of personal networks embedded in the electronic infrastructure (Wellman, Quan-Haase, Boase, & Chen, 2003). Furthermore, collective identity can be built through interpersonal connection with other members in the network (Friedman & McAdam, 1992). A sense of in-group solidarity and distinction between "us" and "them" can also help the formation of collective identity to motivate potential participants to take part in these movements (Friedman & McAdam, 1992). Scholars have claimed that social media will also contribute to the establishment of a social network structure to enable interactive exchange among and between members of the frameworks (byod, 2011). However, to ensure the affordances of social media will be beneficial to a social movement, Enjolras, Steen-Johnsen, and Wollebæk (2012) posited that individuals' economic resources, individual characteristics, motivation, and skills are likely to affect the effectiveness of social media.

Issues, Controversies, Problems/Research Method

In recent years, conventional communication research are often constrained and criticized by its data processing ability to content analyze a large amount of media data (Lin, Hao, & Liao, 2016; Yang & Kang, 2018). Text mining techniques attempt to extract meaningful, repetitive, and useful insights and patterns from unstructured textual data (He, Zha, & Li, 2013) through cluster analysis, categorization, link analysis, and text summarization (Zikopoulos, Parasuraman, Deutsch, Giles, & Corrigan, 2013). This emerging computation research method has been increasingly gaining attention among social science scholars (Diakopoulos et al., 2013; Kang & Yang, 2018; Teso, Olmedilla, Martinez-Torres, & Toral, 2018). These text mining techniques have allowed researchers to identify repetitive keywords, phrases, topics in the corpus and to explore relationships among these recurrent concepts in the large quantity of media data (Teso et al., 2018). This chapter employed *QDA Miner* and its add-on program

Figure 1.

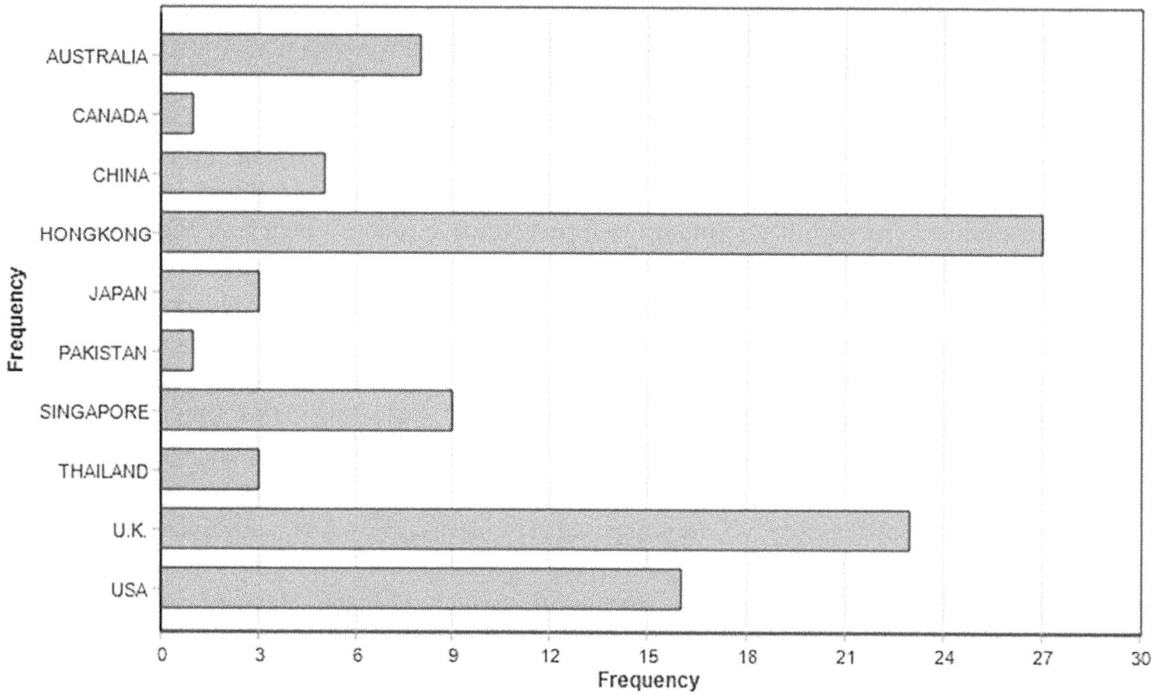

(*Wordstat*) (Silver & Lewins, 2018) to analyze 993 English language media articles in the corpus. *QDA Miner* "offers good coding, memoing, data organisation, retrieval and interrogation functions" (Silver & Lewins, 2018, n.p.). Its add-on *WordStat* program also offers content analysis functions to identify key words, phrases, and topics and to generate graphs such as *WordCloud* or *Link Analysis* to visualize results of the text mining analyses (Silver & Lewins, 2018).

Sampling Method, Sample Characteristics, and the Compilation of Corpus

The authors relied on media articles collected from *Lexis/Nexis Academic* database after using the English keywords, "Sunflower Movement", "Sunflower Student Movement" to identify 993 items to compile the media corpus for later analysis. After carefully reviewing and filter these articles to remove irrelevant and duplicate articles, the media corpus is made up of 90 articles for later analyses. The sampling frame and date range of the article is from March 25, 2014 to October 15, 2015. The types of media articles include *BBC Monitor Asia Pacific* (N=26) from U.K., *China Daily* (N=3) from China, *South China Morning Post* (N=25) from Hong-Kong, *The Strait Times* (N=8) from Singapore, *The New York Times* (N=8), (*Nikkei Asia Review* (N=3) from Japan, and several Australian newspapers (N=8). The corpus includes media texts from major world newspapers, industry and trade presses, web-based publications, newswires and trade press releases—mainly print media. These articles were published in 10 countries such as Australia, Canada, China, Hong-Kong, Japan, Pakistan, Singapore, Thailand, U.K. and U.S.A. The top three countries represented in our media corpus are Hong-Kong (28,1%), U.K. (24.0%) and USA (16.7%) (Refer to Figure 1 below).

Figure 2.

SOLUTIONS AND RECOMMENDATIONS

To answer the second research questions, several text mining techniques (such as *Word Cloud*, *Key Phrase Extraction*, and *Topic Modelling*) were employed to provide empirical data for later analyses. Word Cloud analysis is a popular text mining technique that represents frequency of keywords, phrases, and terms in a graphical manner (Srivastava, 2014). The extraction of keywords, phrases, or terms often depends on their relative importance by examining the frequency statistics, called Term-Frequency (TF) or TF-IDF (Term-Frequency-Inverse document Frequency) (Teso et al., 2018). TF statistics refer to the frequency of words appearing in the document (UC Business Analytics R Programming Guide, n.d.). To reduce the problems of commonly used articles or pronouns, TF-IDF is a statistics to decrease "the weight for commonly used words and increases the weight for words that are not used very much in a collection of documents" (UC Business Analytics R Programming Guide, n.d.).

The second research question aims to identify recurrent keywords and terms that are used by media outlets around the world to frame *the 318 Sunflower Student Movement* to describe the geographic characteristics and protest nature of this student-led movement. As shown in Figure 2 below, it is apparent that *the 318 Sunflower Student Movement* has often been associated with terms such as "Hong-Kong", "China, "Taiwan", "Movement", "Beijing", "Government", etc., suggesting the world media outlets have not fully recognized the resource mobilization strategies of this student-led movement at the level of analyzing words. The dominant representations of the movement are clearly demonstrated in the *Word Cloud* (Refer to Figure 2).

Key Phrase Extraction

QDA Miner and *WordStat* text mining applications provide a self-explanatory instrument to extract key phrases from the unstructured texts from the media corpus by identifying the most prominent phrases in the documents is useful for "document categorization, clustering, indexing, search, and summarization"

Figure 3.

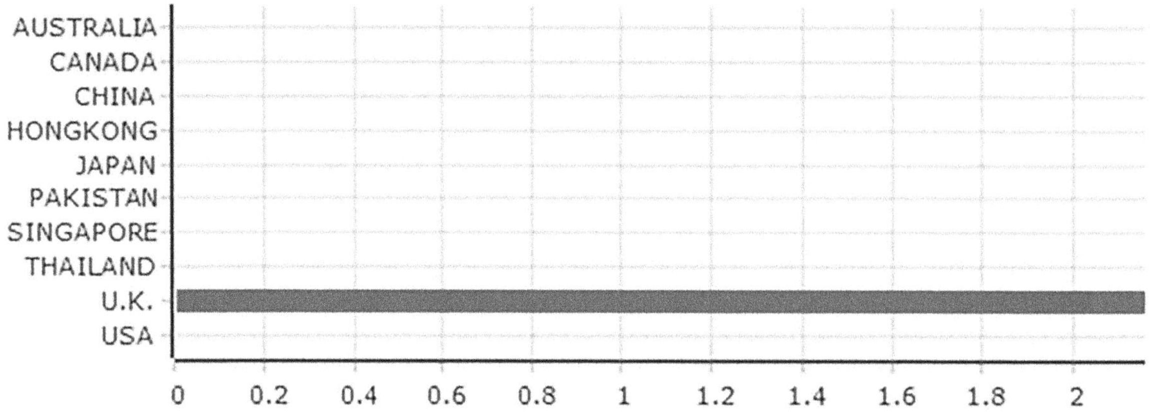

Figure 4.

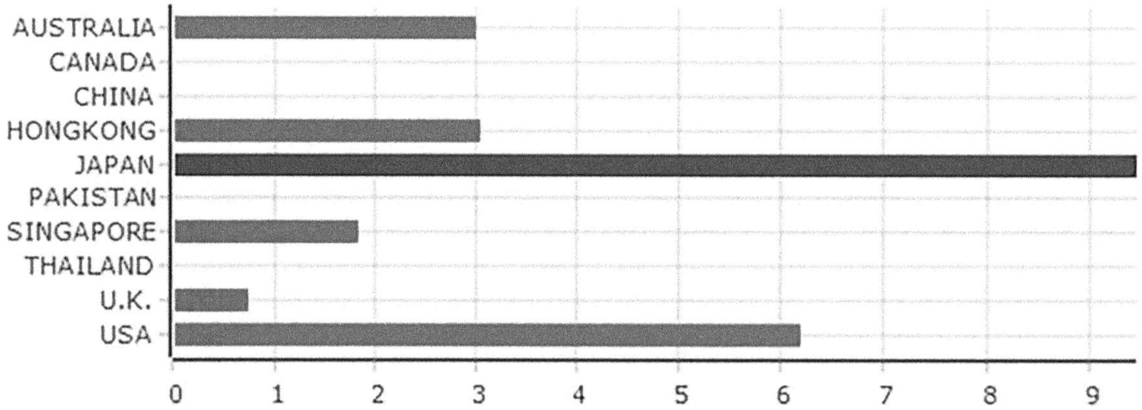

(DeWilde, 2014, n.p.). As seen Table 2 below, the key phrases, "social media" is the most prominent phrase when the print media in these regions talk about *the 318 Sunflower Student Movement*. The term has appeared 119 times (TF-IDF=10.1). Remarkable key phrases in the media corpus that are related resource mobilization strategies is "Political Donation" (TF-IDF=5.9) (Figure 3) to recruit financial resources, . "Partly Motivated by Student Movement" (TF-IDF=4.4) and "Efforts to Persuade Young Students" (TF-IDF=4.4) to recruit human resources to generate public support, "Social Media" (TF-IDF=17.2) and "Grass Roots" (TF-IDF=10.3) to mobilize technological capacities to mobilize the grass roots.

Cross-Country Variations

To answer the third research question in this chapter, data were run to provide cross-country variations in terms of the media representations of *the 318 Sunflower Student Movement* and its resource mobilization strategies. To examine if countries vary in their representations of *the 318 Sunflower Student Movement* in the English language media outlets, the authors employed the following figures to demonstrate these differences (Figure 3 to Figure 6 below).

Figure 5.

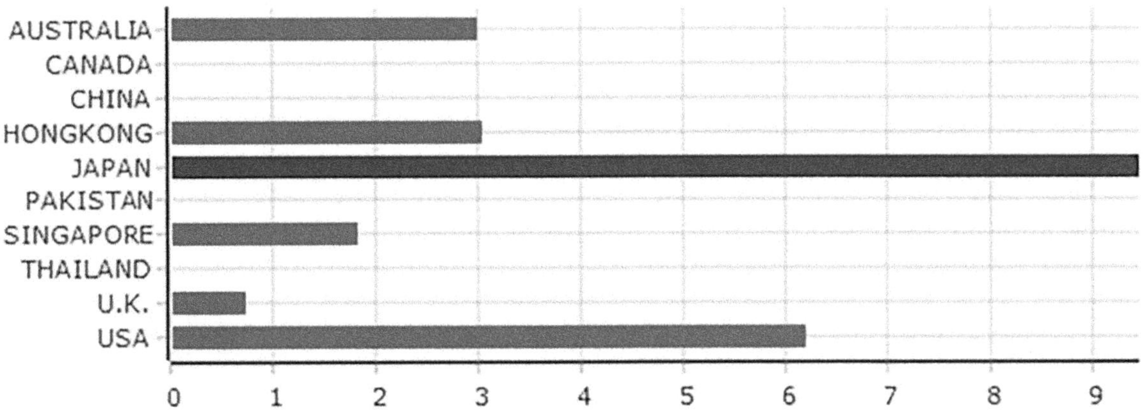

Figure 6.

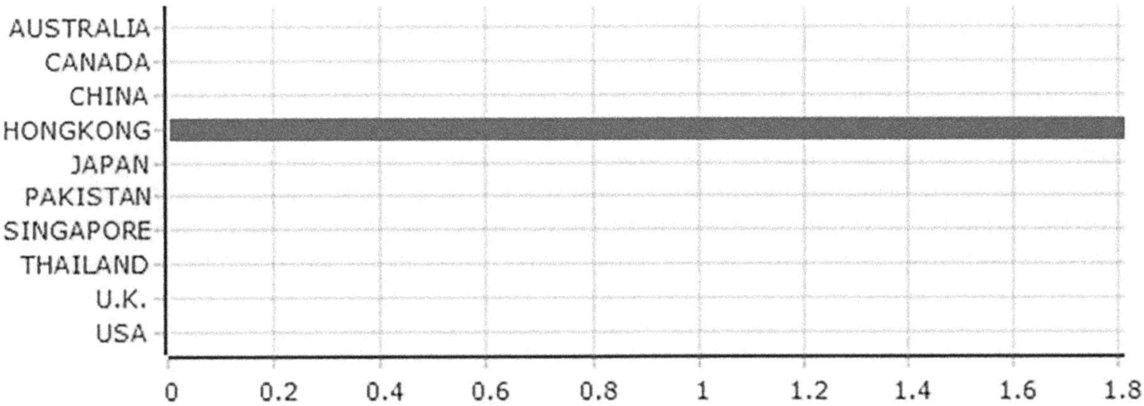

In terms of using social media as a platform to mobilize resources to support *the 318 Sunflower Student Movement*, noticeable variations have been found across countries about the use of this mobilization tool (Refer to Figure 4). For example, Japan and US have focused on this aspect of *Sunflower Student Movement,* while other countries (such as Canada, China, Pakistan, and Thailand) have less reported the use of social media.

The success of *Sunflower Student Movement* depends on activists' abilities to generate grass roots support. Due to close geographical and cultural proximities, Hong-Kong has focused on this aspect of resource mobilization, while other countries have not discussed this (Refer to Figure 5).

Mobilizing human resources are critical to the success of a social movement. To accomplish these, social support can be obtained by motivating the public (Refer to Figure 6), including the persuasion of young students to continue to momentum (Refer to Figure 7). Due to recent events in Hong-Kong, media outlets in this special administration region have widely reported the human resource mobiliza-

Figure 7.

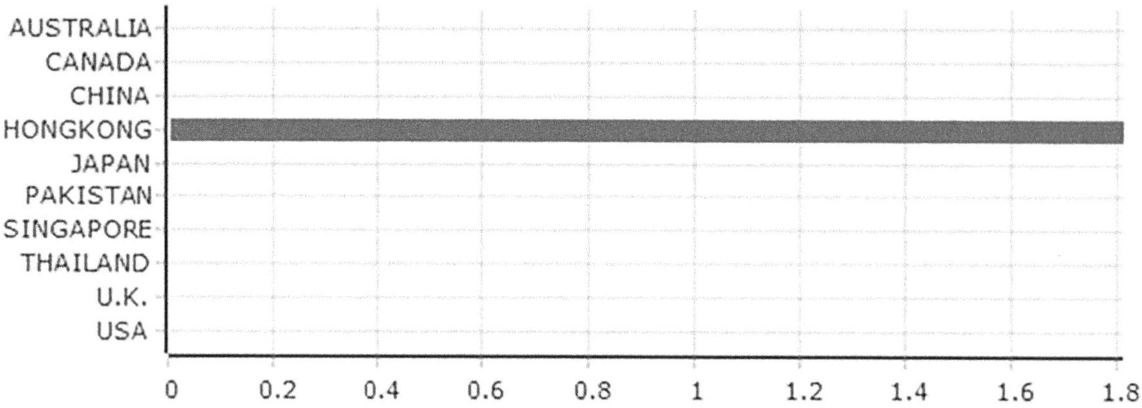

tion strategies as seen in *the 318 Sunflower Student Movement*; other countries have not focused on this aspect of resource mobilization strategies.

The 318 Sunflower Student Movement as a Social Media-Enabled Political Mobilization Movement

One of the most noteworthy characteristics of *the 318 Sunflower Student Movement* is its sophisticated integration of social media into mobilizing Taiwanese society through participant recruitment, domestically and globally, competing with (and replacing) the agenda-setting and framing functions of mass media, and publicizing their causes to both domestic and international audiences. Positioned within a larger context to discuss ICTs' role in political mobilization, civic engagement, and civil disobedience movements in Taiwan, this book chapter attempts to understand the importance of emerging ICTs and their relationships with the practices of using these ICTs to mobilize resources in *the 318 Sunflower Student Movement*. Bondes and Schucher (2014) examined the role of *Weibo* (or *microblogging*) in the radicalization, composition, and transformation, of claims in a mass incident in China. Using a text mining method, the authors further examined *the 318 Sunflower Student Movement* as an example to analyze the interrelations among social media, civil society, and resource mobilization in Taiwan and provide detailed analyses of this significant student-led social disobedience movement in Taiwan.

ICTs such as the Internet, social media, and mobile devices are claimed to affect how activists collaborate, communicate, and demonstrate to accomplish their objectives in a social movement (Garrett, 2006). The same applications of these ICTs have contributed to the success of *the 318 Sunflower Student Movement* (Yang & Kang, 2016). As demonstrated in the text mining analyses in this chapter, world's English language media have also observed the same resource mobilization strategies.

For example, in Yang and Kang's (2016) thematic analysis study, both have identified the roles of ICTs to create new media platforms and apps to challenge existing mainstream media by garnering social and cultural capital. As observed by the reporter from *South China Morning Post* in Hong-Kong, Lawrence Chung (2014a), while Taiwan's local news media actually criticized the forcible and bloody eviction of student protestors from the Executive Yuan, most mainstream media are highly polarized in terms of the framing, portrayal, and assessment of *the 318 Sunflower Student Movement* because of the influence of media's own ideology and ownership. As a resource mobilization tool, four new media innovations have been identified in this movement, ranging from four live broadcast sites (to offer non-censored contents), to hot topics and discussion forums through PTT Bulletin Boards, Facebook, and blogs, to timely updates of the Command Center inside the Legislative Yuan, and to live updates and announcements from all occupation sites (AdvansIdea, 2014; Yang & Kang, 2016). Exposure to these alternative news sources have led to a reexamination of the biases and agendas in the existing mainstream media among consumers.

Yang and Kang (2016) also identified another theme that focuses on the role of social media platforms in mobilizing multi-movement resources. For example, *Flying V* (https://www.flyingv.cc), the largest crow-funding platform in Asia, used social media to mobilize, organize, and manage resources. *Flying* accumulated over 6.39 million NTD in less than 12 hours to allow the organizers of *the 318 Sunflower Student Movement* to buying ads in the popular *Apple Daily* (Taiwan) and *New York Times* to garner social and cultural capital from Taiwan's society (Yang & Kang, 2016). The well-known "Democracy at 4 am" ad was published at the *New York Times* to mobilize international support for this social movement to provide a rationale behind *the 318 Sunflower Student Movement.*

Other social media outlets employed by *the 318 Sunflower Student Movement* include the Facebook-based spin-off crowd-funding *vDemocracy* (https://zh-tw.facebook.com/vdemocracy) to solicit financial resources to support this social movement. Furthermore, a dedicated Facebook (http://www.cool3c.com/article/78108) was used to mobilize potential participants to protests against *the Cross-Strait Service Trade Agreement (CSSTA).* Live updates of vacant spots at various locations were made available to everyone to sign up to recruit human resources.

FUTURE RESEARCH DIRECTIONS

The text mining analyses reported in this book chapter have shown what emerging ICTs can do for social movements to create effective resources for social movement organizations. However, whether the same resource mobilization strategies and applications can be found in other countries remains to demand more cautious consideration. For example, scholars have identified several determinants on the relationships between ICTs and political mobilization to better assess the impacts of ICTs. First, it is still debatable whether lower communication and coordination costs will actually increase political participation and engagement (Garett, 2006). Secondly, the characteristics of civil society organizations are also an important factors because ICTs are believed to favor resource-poor social movement organizations (Löblich & Wendelin, 2011). Thirdly, the employment of social media for social movements is still limited by government's ICT regulations. For example, the newly-implemented real name registration and facial recognition in China is likely to reduce the mobilization functions of social media by imposing the fear of government retaliatory actions (Yang & Kang, 2016). Similarly, Hong Kong's recent civil disobedience movements (such as *Occupy Central with Love and Peace*, *The Umbrella Movement*, and *Anti-Extradition Law Protest* (Chan, 2019) has shown the role of ICTs in mobilizing resources.

CONCLUSION

The 318 Sunflower Student Movement has been praised to continue "a further democratization of Taiwan, with additional safeguards to let the people, not any political party, decide the fate of Taiwan." according to BBC (Sui, 2014). Other Chinese-majority countries or regions (such as Hong-Kong, Macao, China, and Singapore) have also felt the impacts with their own social movements (Chung, 2014b; *The Liberty Times,* 2014). With Xi's oppressive regime luring over many of its neighbors, it would be interesting to see whether these ICTs are able to create a public sphere to facilitate the formation and development of civil society through the mobilization of social, political, and financial capitals domestically and internationally.

LIMITATIONS

There are several limitations that need to be taken into consideration when interpreting these research results. Despite the widespread use rising applications of text mining techniques, scholars of resource mobilizations among civil society activists and organizations need to be cautious in interpreting their findings. Several research limitations need to be taken into consideration. First, the comprehensiveness of sampled data in the media corpus is always a major concern for any type of text mining research (Yang & Kang, 2018, 2019). Secondly, the media corpus that the authors have compiles is based on the *Lexis/Nexis* database that mainly collects English-language media, non-English publications are often excluded and could limit our understanding of how *the 318 Sunflower Student Movement* are represented in these countries where English is not the main language. Thirdly, related to the fundamental methodological limitations, the processing of words, keywords, phrases, and dictionaries in identifying recurrent linguistic patterns and trends to generate findings will be constrained by the corpus itself (Tesoa et al., 2018). For example, the commonly-used words (such as pronouns and articles) are likely to how different extracted keywords and phrases are reported (UC Business Analytics R Programming Guide, n.d.). Furthermore, the reliance on a single word may ignore the diversity of word meanings (i.e., polysemy) (Tesoa et al., 2018). The use of keywords and phrases similarly runs into problems of reducing their importance in different contexts and should be addressed by statistical procedures (Tesoa et al., 2018; Yang & Kang, 2018, 2019).

REFERENCES

AdvansIdea. (2014, March 23). *The 318 Sunflower Movement: A test field for new media innovations.* Retrieved July 5, 2015 from http://advansidea.Tumblr.Com/post/80371944080/318%e5%ad%b8%e9%81%8b%e6%98%af%e6%96%b0%e5%aa%92%e9%ab%94%e5%89%b5%e6%96%b0%e9%81%8b%e7%94%a8%e7%9a%84%e8%a9%a6%e9%a9%97%e5%a0%b4

Albert, E. (2019, June 27). China-Taiwan Relations. *Council on Foreign Relations.* Retrieved August 4, 2019 from https://www.cfr.org/backgrounder/china-taiwan-relations

Associated Press. (2019, August 4). The Latest: HK police tear gas protesters in shopping area. *The Washington Post*. Retrieved August 4, 2019 from https://www.washingtonpost.com/world/asia_pacific/the-latest-ex-hk-leader-offers-bounty-for-info-on-flag/2019/2008/2004/2640ba2000-b2685-2011e2019-acc2018-2011d2847bacca2073_story.html?noredirect=on&utm_term=.bfa2217e22143

Au, A. (2017, April 27). The Sunflower Movement and the Taiwanese National Identity: Building an Anti-Sinoist Civic Nationalism. *Berkeley Journal of Sociology*. Retrieved August 5, 2019 from http://berkeleyjournal.org/2017/2004/the-sunflower-movement-and-the-taiwanese-national-identity-building-an-anti-sinoist-civic-nationalism/

Bardenhagen, K. (2014, December 2). Taiwanese send 'democratic message' to ruling Kuomintang. *DW*. Retrieved July 20, 2014 from http://www.dw.com/en/taiwanese-send-democratic-message-to-ruling-kuomintang/a-18106103

Biddix, J. P., & Park, H. W. (2008). Online networks of student protest: The case of the living wage campaign. *New Media & Society*, *10*(6), 871–891. doi:10.1177/1461444808096249

Bondes, M., & Schucher, G. (2014). Derailed emotions: The transformation of claims and targets during the Wenzhou online incident. *Information Communication and Society*, *17*(1), 45–65. doi:10.1080/1369118X.2013.853819

Bush, R. C. (2016, January 16). *Taiwan's election results, explained*. Washington, DC: Brookings. Retrieved July 4, 2019 from https://www.brookings.edu/blog/order-from-chaos/2016/01/16/taiwans-election-results-explained/

Campbell, C., Meick, E., Hsu, K., & Murra, C. (2013, May 10). *China's "core interests" and the East China Sea*. US-China Economic and Security Review Commission. Retrieved July 5, 2015 from http://www.uscc.gov/sites/default/files/Research/China's%20Core%20Interests%20and%20the%20East%20China%20Sea.pdf

Carroll, W. K., & Hackett, R. A. (2006). Democratic media activism through the lens of social movement theory. *Media, Culture & Society, 28*(1), 83-104. doi:10.1177/0163443706059289

Chan, L. (2019, April 24). Hong Kong's 'Occupy Central' activists handed prison terms. *Al Jazeera News*. Retrieved July 29, 2019 from https://www.aljazeera.com/news/2019/2004/hong-kong-occupy-central-activists-handed-prison-sentences-190424013728788.html

Chen, W.-H. (2014). Taking stock, moving forward: The Internet, social networks and civic engagement in Chinese societies. *Information Communication and Society*, *17*(1), 1–6. doi:10.1080/1369118X.2013.857425

Ching, C. (2014, April 7). Sunflower movement dims cross-strait ties. *The Strait Times*. Retrieved July 11, 2015 from http://www.straitstimes.com/st/print/2246667

Chiou, C. L. (2014, June 17). *The 318 Sunflower Student Movement and its impact on Taiwanese politics and cross-strait relations*. Retrieved July 30, 2015 from https://www.griffith.edu.au/__data/assets/pdf_file/0006/614796/Poster-China-Brief-Prof-Chiou-June-2014.pdf

Choi, S., & Park, H. (2014). An exploratory approach to a Twitter-based community centered on a political goal in South Korea: Who organized it what they shared, and how they acted. *New Media & Society*, *16*(1), 129–148. doi:10.1177/1461444813487956

Chung, L. (2014a, March 29). Premier open to scrutiny of pacts; Jiang Yi-Huah says the government will consider passing law to increase oversight of controversial trade agreements made with the mainland. *South China Morning Post.* Retrieved July 5, 2015 from http://www.scmp.com/news/china/article/1459862/taiwan-premier-jiang-yi-huah-open-formal-review-future-trade-pacts

Chung, L. (2014b, October 1). Civil disobedient movement in Taiwan, HK protests similar, but goals differ. *South China Morning Post.* Retrieved July 5, 2015 from http://www.scmp.com/news/hong-kong/article/1604956/civil-disobedience-movements-taiwan-and-hong-kong-similar-goals

Cole, J. M. (2014, July 1). Was Taiwan's Sunflower Movement successful? Did Taiwan's Sunflower Movement succeed? *The Diplomat.* Retrieved July 4, 2015 from http://thediplomat.com/2014/2007/was-taiwans-sunflower-movement-successful/

Conroy, M., Feezell, J. T., & Guerrero, M. (2012). Facebook and political engagement: A study of online political group membership and offline political engagement. *Computers in Human Behavior*, *28*(5), 1535–1546. doi:10.1016/j.chb.2012.03.012

Eltantawy, N., & Wiest, J. B. (2011). Social media in the Egyptian Revolution: Reconsidering resource mobilization theory. *International Journal of Communication*, *5*, 1207–1224.

Enjolras, B., Steen-Johnsen, K., & Wollebæk, D. (2012). Social media and mobilization to offline demonstrations: Transcending participatory divides? *New Media & Society*, *15*(6), 890–908. doi:10.1177/1461444812462844

Friedman, D., & McAdam, D. (1992). Collective identity and activism. Networks, choices and the life of a social movement. In A. D. Morris & C. M. Mueller (Eds.), *Frontiers in social movement theory* (pp. 156–172). New Haven, CT: Yale University Press.

Gainous, J., & Wagner, K. M. (2013). *Tweeting to power: The social media revolution in American politics.* New York: Oxford University Press. doi:10.1093/acprof:oso/9780199965076.001.0001

Gamson, W. A. (1990). *The strategy of social protest.* Belmont, CA: Wadsworth.

Garrett, R. K. (2006). Protest in an information society: A review of literature on social movements and new ICTs. *Information Communication and Society*, *9*(2), 202–224. doi:10.1080/13691180600630773

Herrington, J., & Lee, K. (2014). The limits of global health diplomacy: Taiwan's observer status at the world health assembly. *Globalization and Health*, *10*(71). Retrieved from http://www.globalizationand-health.com/content/pdf/s12992-12014-10071-y.pdf PMID:25270977

Hioe, B. (2019, March 18). The Sunflower Movement, Five years on. *New Bloom.* Retrieved July 4, 2019 from https://newbloommag.net/2019/2003/2018/sunflower-movement-five-years/

Horton, C. (2019, January 19). Faced with tough words from China, Taiwan rallies around its leader. *The New York Times.* Retrieved August 4, 2019 from https://www.nytimes.com/2019/2001/2019/world/asia/china-taiwan-president.html

Hsieh, Y. P., & Li, M.-H. (2014). Online political participation, civic talk, and media multiplexity: How Taiwanese citizens express political opinions on the web. *Information Communication and Society*, *17*(1), 26–44. doi:10.1080/1369118X.2013.833278

Hsu, C.-M. (2015, April 1). *One year after the 318 student movement: New and old media*. Retrieved July 5, 2015 from http://www.Feja.Org.Tw/modules/news007/article.Php?Storyid=1675

Hsu, S. (2019, June 23). Protesters gather in Taipei, asking 'red media' to leave Taiwan. *Focus Taiwan*. Retrieved August 5, 2019 from http://focustaiwan.tw/news/acs/201906230011.aspx

Jenkins, J. C. (1983, August). Resource Mobilization Theory and the study of social movements. *Annual Review of Sociology*, *9*(1), 527–553. doi:10.1146/annurev.so.09.080183.002523

Jennings, R. (2014, August 11). In Taiwan, students protest reminders of repressive rule. Los Angles Time, p. 2.

Jha, S. (2008). Why they wouldn't cite from sites: A study of journalists' perceptions of social movement web sites and the impact on their coverage of social protest. *Journalism*, *9*(6), 711–732. doi:10.1177/1464884908096242

Kan, S. A., & Morrison, W. M. (2011, August 4). *U.S.-Taiwan relationship: Overview of policy issues*. Congressional Research Service. Retrieved July 2, 2015 from https://www.fas.org/sgp/crs/row/R41952.pdf

Keck, Z. (2014, April 17). China Responds to Taiwan's Sunflower Movement. *The Diplomat*. Retrieved August 5, 2019 from https://thediplomat.com/2014/2004/china-responds-to-taiwans-sunflower-movement/

Khamis, S., & Vaughan, K. (2011). Cyberactivism in the Egyptian revolution. *Arab Media & Society*, *13*, 1–37.

Kuo, L. (2019, May 17). Taiwan becomes first in Asia to legalise same-sex marriage. *The Guardian*. Retrieved July 4, 2019 from https://www.theguardian.com/world/2019/may/2017/taiwan-becomes-first-asian-county-to-legalise-same-sex-marriage

Kushin, M. J., & Yamamoto, M. (2010). Did social media really matter? College students' use of online media and political decision making in the 2008 election. *Mass Communication & Society*, *13*(5), 608–630. doi:10.1080/15205436.2010.516863

Lee, D. (2014, October 30). The role of social media in Occupy protests, on the ground and around the world. *South Morning China Post*. Retrieved July 5, 2015 from http://www.scmp.com/news/hong-kong/article/1628305/role-social-media-occupy-protests-ground-and-around-world

Levine, S. (1997, December 8). Hong Kong's return to China. *Encyclopædia Britannica*. Retrieved July 29, 2019 from https://www.britannica.com/topic/reversion-to-Chinese-sovereignty-1020544

Li, X. (2014, March 24). Students store office of Taiwan premier: About 200 lay siege to the executive yuan building; riot police sent to scene. *The Straits Times*. Retrieved July 11, 2015 from http://www.straitstimes.com/asia

Lin, C.-Y. (2015, March 18). 9 in 1 election. 60% believe that Pan Blue was defeated by people's power. *NewTalk*. Retrieved July 5, 2015 from http://newtalk.tw/news/view/2015-2003-2018/57910

Lind, J. (2018, March/April). Life in China's Asia; What regional hegemony would look like. *Foreign Affairs*. Retrieved on August 4, 2019 from https://www.foreignaffairs.com/articles/china/2018-2002-2013/life-chinas-asia

Liu., F. C.-s. (2014, September 24). Taiwan's Sunflower Movement and Generation Politics. *Asia Dialogue*. Retrieved July 4, 2019 from https://theasiadialogue.com/2014/2009/2024/taiwans-sunflower-movement-and-generation-politics/

Löblich, M., & Wendelin, M. (2011). ICT policy activism on a national level: Ideas, resources and strategies of German civil society in governance processes. *New Media & Society*, *16*(4), 899–915.

Madhavan, E. S. (2016). Internet and Social Media's Social Movements Leading to New Forms of Governance and Policymaking: Cases from India. *Glocalism, 2016*(1). Retrieved August 5, 2019 from http://www.glocalismjournal.net/Issues/NETWORKS-AND-NEW-MEDIA/Articles/Internet-And-Social-MediaS-Social-Movements-Leading-To-New-Forms-Of-Governance-And-Policymaking-Cases-From-India.kl

Morris, J. X. (2018, July 18). Brian Hioe: The Sunflower Movement, 4 years later. *The Diplomat*. Retrieved August 5, 2019 from https://thediplomat.com/2018/2007/brian-hioe-the-sunflower-movement-2014-years-later/

Mou, Y., Fu, H., & Atkin, D. (2011). Predicting political discussion in a censored virtual environment. *Political Communication*, *28*(3), 341–356. doi:10.1080/10584609.2011.572466

Myers, D. J. (1994, July 1). Communication technology and social movements: Contributions of computer networks to activism. *Social Science Computer Review*, *12*(2), 250–260. doi:10.1177/089443939401200209

O'Neill, M. (2017, June 17). 1.5 million Mainland migrants change Hong Kong. *ejinsights on the pulse*. Retrieved July 29, 2019 from http://www.ejinsight.com/20170619-20170611-20170615-million-mainland-migrants-change-hong-kong/

Olubunmi, A. P. (2015). The ambiguous power of social media: Hegemony or resistance? *New Media and Mass Communication, 13*. Retrieved August 5, 2019 from https://www.iiste.org/Journals/index.php/NMMC/article/view/19213

Palmer, J., & Allen-Ebrahimian, B. (2018, April 27). China threatens U.S. airlines over Taiwan References. *Foreign Policy*. Retrieved August 4, 2019 from https://foreignpolicy.com/2018/2004/2027/china-threatens-u-s-airlines-over-taiwan-references-united-american-flight-beijing/

Pao, J. (2019, July 14). Anti-extradition Hong Kong protesters march in Shatin. *Asia Times*. Retrieved July 29, 2019 from https://www.asiatimes.com/2019/2007/article/anti-extradition-hong-kong-protesters-march-in-shatin/

Penney, J., & Dadas, C. (2014). (re)tweeting in the service of protest: Digital composition and circulation in the occupy wall street movement. *New Media & Society*, *6*(1), 74–90. doi:10.1177/1461444813479593

Pesek, W. (2014, April 3). A Taiwan spring? *National Post,* p. FP9.

Schubert, G. (2017, July 19). Pension Reform Made in Taiwan. *Taiwan Insights*. Retrieved July 4, 2019 from https://taiwaninsight.org/2017/2007/2019/pension-reform-made-in-taiwan/?blogsub=confirming#blog_subscription-2015

Shirky, C. (2011, January/February). The political power of social media: Technology, the public sphere, and political change. *Foreign Affairs*, 1–12.

Smith, N. (2017, August 21). Taiwan is suffering from a massive brain drain and the main beneficiary is China. *Time*. Retrieved August 4, 2019 from https://time.com/4906162/taiwan-brain-drain-youth-china-jobs-economy/

Smith, S. (2018, November 7). Who are France's 'Yellow Jacket' protesters and what do they want? *CNBC News*. Retrieved July 4, 2019 from https://www.nbcnews.com/news/world/who-are-france-s-yellow-jacket-protesters-what-do-they-n940016

Soriano, C. R. R. (2014, January). Constructing collectivity in diversity: Online political mobilization of a national LGBT political party. *Media Culture & Society*, *36*(1), 20–36. doi:10.1177/0163443713507812

Spangler, J. (2014, March 27). Taiwan and the future of the Cross-Strait Services Trade Agreement. *The Diplomat*. Retrieved July 5, 2015 from http://thediplomat.com/2014/2003/taiwan-and-the-future-of-the-cross-strait-services-trade-agreement/

Taiwanese Central News Agency (CNA). (2014, May 19). Taiwan student protests form new group to tackle referendum rules. *BBC Monitoring Asia Pacific*.

The History Channel. (2010, February 9). Mohandas Gandhi begins 241-mile civil disobedience march. *The History Channel*. Retrieved July 4, 2019 from https://www.history.com/this-day-in-history/gandhi-leads-civil-disobedience

The Policy Tensor. (2013, August 2). Offensive realism. *Geopolitics*. Retrieved July 4, 2015 from http://policytensor.com/2013/08/02/offensive-realism/

UC Business Analytics R Programming Guide. (n.d.). Text Mining: Term vs. Document Frequency. *UC Business Analytics R Programming Guide*. Retrieved August 8, 2019 from https://uc-r.github.io/tf-idf_analysis

Wellman, B., Quan-Haase, A., Boase, J., Chen, W. H., Hampton, K., Díaz, I., & Miyata, K. (2003, April). The social affordances of the Internet for networked individualism. *Journal of Computer-Mediated Communication*, *8*(3), 0. doi:10.1111/j.1083-6101.2003.tb00216.x

Winkler, S. (2012). *Taiwan's UN dilemma: To be or not to be*. Retrieved July 5, 2015 from http://www.brookings.edu/research/opinions/2012/06/20-taiwan-un-winkler

Wong, A. (2018, May 31). Beijing is upping the pressure on Taiwan: "Expectation of reunification is certainly increasing." *CNBC News*. Retrieved August 4, 2019 from https://www.cnbc.com/2018/2005/2031/mainland-china-and-taiwan-increased-tensions-about-one-china-policy.html

Yang, K. C. C., & Kang, Y. W. (2017). *Representing the Internet and World Wide Web in mass media: A comparative text mining study of mass media in the Greater China Region and the U.S.* Paper Presented at the *24th International Conference of the International Association for Intercultural Communication Studies (IAICS)*, De Paul University, Chicago, IL.

Yang, K. C. C., & Kang, Y. W. (2017). Social media, political mobilization, and citizen engagement: A case study of March 18, 2014 Sunflower Student Movement in Taiwan. In Citizen engagement and public participation in the era of new media (pp. 362-390). Hershey, PA: IGI-Global Publisher.

Zúñiga, H. G., Molyneux, L., & Zheng, P. (2014). Social media, political expression, and political participation: Panel analysis of lagged and concurrent relationships. *Journal of Communication*, *64*(4), 612–634. doi:10.1111/jcom.12103

ADDITIONAL READING

Castells, M. (2007). Communication, power and counter-power in the network society. *International Journal of Communication*, *1*, 238–266.

Castells, M. (2009). *Communication power*. Oxford: Oxford University Press.

Fuchs, C. (2014). Social media and the public sphere. *Triple C (Cognition, Communication, Co-Operation)*, *12*(1), 57-101.

Habermas, J. (1984). Theory of communicative action (Thomas McCarthy, Trans.). Boston, M.A.: Beacon Press.

Habermas, J. (1989). *The structural transformation of the public sphere: An inquiry into a category of bourgeois society*. Cambridge, MA: MIT Press.

Habermas, J. (2006, November 6). Political communication in media society: Does democracy still enjoy an epistemic dimension? The impact of normative theory on empirical research. *Communication Theory*, *16*(4), 411–426. doi:10.1111/j.1468-2885.2006.00280.x

Huyer, S., & Silkoska, T. (2003, April). *Overcoming the gender digital divide: Understanding ICTs and their potential for the empowerment of women*. Retrieved November 18, 2014 from http://www.iiav.nl/epublications/2003/Overcoming.pdf

Jacobs, A., & Ansfield, J. (2011, May 10). Catching scent of revolution, China moves to snip jasmine. *New York Times,* Retrieved September 19, 2014 from http://www.nytimes.com/2011/2005/2011/world/asia/2011jasmine.html?_r=2010

Jude. (2012, October 31). Weibo penetration rate among Chinese netizens. Retrieved March 8, 2014 from http://www.chinainternetwatch.com/1760/chinese-weibo-users-proportion-on-different-platforms/

Khondker, H. H. (2011). Role of the new media in the Arab Spring. *Globalizations*, *8*(5), 675–679. doi:10.1080/14747731.2011.621287

King, G., Pan, J., & Roberts, M. E. (2013). How censorship in China allows government criticism but silences collective expression. *The American Political Science Review*, *107*(2), 326–343. doi:10.1017/S0003055413000014

Liu, Y.-B., & Zhou, Y.-X. (2011, May 31-June 3). *Social media in China: Rising Weibo in government.* Paper presented at the 2011 Proceedings of the 5th IEEE International Conference on Digital Ecosystems and Technologies Conference (DEST). Daejeon, South Korea. 10.1109/DEST.2011.5936628

Lyytinen, K., & Hirschheim, R. (1988). Information systems as rational discourse: An application of Habermas's theory of communicative action. *Scandinavian Journal of Management*, *4*(1-2), 19–30. doi:10.1016/0956-5221(88)90013-9

Mathiason, J. (2013, June 20). *Information and communication technologies and e-participation for the empowerment of people and e-governance.* Paper presented at the Expert Group Meeting on E-Participation: Empowering People through Information Communication Technologies (ICTs), Geneva, The Switzerlands.

McGowan, A. M., & Kaiser, K. S. (2014, May). Discovering civil discourse: Using the online public sphere for authentic assessment. *Communication Teacher*, *28*(3), 170–176. doi:10.1080/17404622.2014.911339

Meng, Q., & Li, M. (2001, September). *New economy and ICT development in China.* Helsinki, Finland: UNU World Institute for Development Economics Research. Retrieved September 15, 2014 from http://www.econstor.eu/bitstream/10419/53080/1/335220010.pdf

Mou, Y., Atkin, D., Fu, H., Lin, C. A., & Lau, T. Y. (2013). The influence of online forum and SNS use on online political discussion in China: Assessing "Spirals of Trust.". *Telematics and Informatics*, *30*(4), 359–369. doi:10.1016/j.tele.2013.04.002

Wallis, C. (2011). New media practices in China: Youth patterns, processes, and politics. *International Journal of Communication*, *5*, 406–436.

Yeung, R. L. K. (2008, April). *Digital democracy: How the American and Hong Kong civil societies use new media to change politics.* Washington, D.C.: The Brookings Institution.

KEY TERMS AND DEFINITIONS

Arab Spring: The term refers to a revolutionary upsurge of demonstrations and protests in the Arab world, spreading from Tunisian Revolution to other countries in the Arab League on December 17, 2010. Leaders in Tunisia, Egypt, Libya, and Yemen have been overthrown by the end of February 2012. Repercussions of this historical event are still felt with the civil war in Syria and the collapse of ISIS regime.

Big Data: A term that describes a large dataset that grows in size over time. It refers to the size of dataset that exceeds the capturing, storage, management, and analysis of traditional databases. The term refers to the dataset that has large, more varied, and multifaceted data structure, accompanies by difficulties of data storage, analysis, and visualization. Big Data are characterized with their high volume, velocity, and variety information assets.

Chinese Jasmine Revolution: This civil society movement is also known as *The 2011 Chinese Pro-democracy Protests*. Chinese Jasmine Revolution was a social movement organized and mobilized through China's popular social media, *Weibo* (or Microblog), to launch protests simultaneously in 13 major cities in China on the date of February 20, 2011. Despite national and international attention, the Chinese Jasmine Revolution did not lead to wide-spread protests in China, due to Chinese Communist Government's preemptive actions. After the mass incident, a large number of dissidents had been arrested and detained by the government.

Civil Disobedience: Proposed by the American transcendentalist, Henry David Thoreau, as a peaceful revolt against undesirable government actions, the term is equivalent to non-violent resistance to avoid enabling the government to make them the cause of injustice (such as the war with Mexico at Thoreau's time). The term is also defined as the active, professed refusal to abide by laws, demands, and commands of any government. Recent applications of this term include Taiwan's 318 Sunflower Movement, Hong-Kong's Umbrella Movement, and China's Jasmine Revolution.

Civil Society: The term, civil society, refers to a range of not-for-profit and non-governmental organizations that enable the expression of the interests and values of the public as well as their members for cultural, ethical, political, philanthropic, scientific, and religious considerations. Civil society organizations refer to charitable organizations, community groups, faith-based organizations, foundations, labor unions, non-governmental organizations (NGOs), labor unions, and professional associations.

Co-Word Analysis: A content analysis technique that is used to map the strength of association between keywords in textual data. This technique measures the co-occurrence of keywords to examine content in the textual data. This research technique has been used in analyzing a large amount of data from social media.

Content Filtering Mechanisms: Used as a computer program to filter or block inappropriate Internet contents before delivered to users' end. The mechanisms function as a safeguard between the Internet and other service providers to block materials deemed objectionable by the authoritarian government.

Electronic Frontier Foundation (EFF): The Electronic Frontier Foundation (EFF) is the leading non-profit organization that specializes in the protection of civil liberties in the digital world. EFF was founded in 1990 and has championed user privacy, and free expression, and issues related to grassroots activism, litigation, policy analysis, and technology development.

Information-Communication Technologies (ICTs): Also abbreviated as ICTs. The term is used as an umbrella to cover all communication devices and applications such as cellular phones, computer, notebook, smartphone, tablet, and social media.

Mobile Social Media: A term to refer to social media Apps such as Facebook, Foursquare, Instagram, Pinterest, Twitter, etc., that are delivered via mobile devices such as smartphone, tablet, or laptop computer.

Online Activism: Also known as Internet activism, digital activism, online organizing, electronic advocacy, cyber-activism, online mobilization, and e-activism. The term is defined as the use of new information-communication technologies (ICTs) to support social and citizen movements.

Occupy Central With Love and Peace Movement: Refer to as a civil disobedience movement in Hong-Kong's financial district. The movement began on September 28, 2014 to respond to whether Beijing and Hong-Kong's government will implement universal suffrage to elect its own chief executive in 2017.

Occupy Wall Street Movement (OWS): The term refers to a protest movement that began on September 17, 2011 in Zuccotti Park, in the Wall Street financial district. The event ushered in many occupy movements around the world to challenge social and economic inequality status-quo and demands a society with more social justice.

Political Mobilization: The term refers to activities that intend to motivate masses of organized or unorganized participants to express themselves and to undertake a particular political action to accomplish political aims.

Public Sphere: Habermas (1962, 1984) defined the concept of public sphere as "a realm of our social life in which something approaching public opinion can be formed" (p. 49). Habermas's (1962, 1984) conceptualization of public sphere stresses the important of access to all citizens to enable them to transform from private individuals into a public body.

Resource Mobilization Theory (RMT): A major sociological theory that focuses on the resource acquisition and management to facilitate and support social movements. RMT aims to analyze the followings: 1) the acquisition of resources; 2) the mobilization of people to achieve the movement's goals.

Social Media: Social media refer to various Internet-based applications to facilitate collaborative projects (such as *Wikipedia*), microblogs and blogs, contents (such as *YouTube*), social networking services (such as *Facebook* and *Instagram*), virtual games, and virtual social life (such as *Second Life*).

Text Mining: Also, known as text analytics, is a computation method of analyzing and exploring a lot of unstructured or structure data by popular text mining software packages (such as QDA Miner, or PolyAnalyst).

Topic Modeling: A popular text mining technique from machine learning and natural language processing research. The term usually refers to a type of statistical model to discover the abstract and latent topics and to identify the hidden semantic structure that occur in media corpus.

Twitter: A social media platform that allows users to send and receive messages about 140 words, called "tweets." This social media platform was created in March 2006 and launched by July 2006. Twitter has attracted a lot of users since its launch, due to its ease of use to deliver messages. President Trump is known for its tweets that offer disclose important policies before they are officially announced.

Umbrella Revolution: A sit-in and civil disobedience protest in Hong-Kong that began in September 2014. Also known as umbrella movement, this movement was prompted when the Standing Committee of the National People's Congress proposed an unsatisfactory and highly restrictive electoral system reform as promised in the Basic Law. According to the reform, only pre-screened candidates in line with China's political agendas can take part in Hong-Kong's election. Areas such as Admiralty, Causeway Bay, and Mong Kok were occupied by the protesters for over 70 days.

***Weibo* (Microblog):** The Chinese micro-blog and social networking website, equivalent to *Twitter* that is banned in China. *Weibo*, meaning microblog in Chinese, is a Chinese version of *Twitter*. *Weibo* services in China include well-known *Weibo* companies include *Sina Weibo* and *Tencent Weibo* to offer retweeting, social sharing, and many social media functions.

Word Cloud Analysis: A popular text mining analytical technique to provide graphical representation of word frequency to highlight relative important words on the basis of their prominence in the media corpus or source texts.

Chapter 15
Social Media and Public Sphere in China:
A Case Study of Political Discussion on Weibo After the Wenzhou High-Speed Rail Derailment Accident

Zhou Shan
University of Alabama, USA

Lu Tang
Texas A&M University, USA

ABSTRACT

This chapter seeks to answer the question of whether a microblog can function as a promising form of public sphere. Utilizing a combined framework of public sphere based on the theories of Mouffe and Dahlgren, it examines the political discussion and interrogation on Sina Weibo, China's leading microblog site, concerning the Wenzhou high-speed train derailment accident in July of 2011 through a critical discourse analysis. Its results suggest that Weibo enables the creation of new social imaginary and genre of discourse as well as the construction of new social identities.

INTRODUCTION

Two high-speed trains clashed and derailed near Wenzhou, China on July 23, 2011, killing 39 and injuring hundreds of passengers. Up to then, the high-speed railway project had been celebrated as the symbol of China's economic success. Not surprisingly, mainstream media were ordered by government to limit their coverage of this incident (Xu, 2016). However, only this time, the tightly controlled traditional media were unable to keep the Chinese public in the dark. Minutes after the accident, messages started to be posted on Weibo, China's microblog sites and immediately drew great public attention. The public started to ask further questions when a little girl was recued from a wrecked train hours after the government

DOI: 10.4018/978-1-7998-1828-1.ch015

announced that they had ended the search and rescue effort because no more survivors could be found. Later, they became outraged when a video was posted to Weibo, showing the Ministry of Railway used bulldozers to bury the wrecked trains only 38 hours after the accident before any in-depth investigation had been conducted. This widely circulated video triggered unprecedented nationwide discussion and political interrogation concerning government accountability. In informing the public and provoking political discussion, Weibo made a notable case for inquiring the potential of social media in creating a public sphere.

The theme of media and public sphere has occupied a critically important place on the research agenda of communication scholars for decades, and the field has witnessed continuing debates on the ambivalent roles played by the media in public life. More recently, Internet-based social media are believed to have the potential to give voices to disadvantaged groups and direct public's attention toward social issues that would otherwise be ignored. Thus it is important to examine whether social media will contribute to a more democratic political sphere, and with what risks and limitations, or they will be more inclined to conform to the existing media environment characterized by government control and surveillance (Cappella & Jamieson, 1997).

The rise of social media has been considered especially important in the context of China. While Chinese mainstream media such as TV and newspapers are tightly controlled and tend to function as the mouth-piece of the Chinese Communist Party, social media are less censored due to the technical difficulties in controlling tens of millions of users as well as an astronomical amount of information. Therefore, social media represent a new opportunity for more freedom of speech and open discussions about social issues (Yang, 2009). One prominent type of social media in China is Weibo or microblogs. Having the features of both Twitter and Facebook, Weibo is one of the two most used social media applications in China. Evidence shows that Weibo is subject to the least amount of governmental or corporate control among all types of social media (Bamman, O'Connor, & Smith, 2012), and is becoming an important instrument in revealing social injustices and promoting discussions on social issues (Harp, Bachmann, & Guo 2012). Despite its potential, the actual role played by Weibo is yet to be examined.

Presented here is a case study of the discussion about the Wenzhou derailment accident on Weibo through a critical discourse analysis (Fairclough, 1995). Utilizing a combined framework of public sphere based on Mouffe (1995)'s theory of agonistic public sphere and Dahlgren (2005)'s theorization about Internet as public sphere, it examines how China's microblogs lead the political deliberation and interrogation related to the derailment scandal, and how political uses of microblogs constitute China's public sphere. What makes this study different from previous studies is its conceptual framework of public sphere adapted to the changing social reality and new media landscape in China. It offers a civic and cultural approach to public sphere and bridges the gap between observable evidences and their theoretical corroboration. Broadly, the analysis will further elucidate the concept of public sphere and its applicability to different ideological and social contexts.

LITERATURE REVIEW

Theories of Public Sphere

The notion of a public sphere centered around the role of communication among citizens in the political process came into being in ancient Greece and evolved during Renaissance in Europe. However, it was after the publication of Habermas' *The Structural Transformation of the Public Sphere* in 1962 that the notion established its central place in political discourse and "transformed media studies into a hard-headed discipline" (Gitlin, 2004). Habermas (1962/1989) states that the normative, abstracted public needs a space that is informed and transparent where critical deliberation and discussion can take place to form consensus and to build democratic polity. According to him, mass media have failed to fulfill all the ambitious demands of the participatory model of public sphere because mass media are biased by economic interests and political preferences.

The Habermasian model of bourgeois public sphere is based on a few problematic assumptions. First, Habermas conceptualizes the public as passive audiences, and, as a result, citizens are relegated to the passive role of receiving and consuming media content. However, the rise of the Internet and online political discussion changes the one-way dialogic character of the public sphere based on traditional media, rendering gate-keeping journalism and mass media institutions less important (Jankowski & van Selm, 2000; Slevin, 2000; van de Donk et al., 2004). The second problematic presumption of the Habermasian bourgeois public sphere is that it relies "on a traditional, limited conception of politics... asserting a polarized theory of power" (Livingstone, 2005, p. 19). Privileging one public sphere over others, Habermas neglects other emancipatory movements besides that of the bourgeois class and ignores the existence of multiple overlapping and contradicting public spheres (Negt & Kluge, 1993). Furthermore, striving for a rational consensus may reinforce the hegemony and dominance of ruling elites and lead to the marginalization of minority positions and rights (Lyotard, 1984).

In addressing the question of how to revitalize citizen engagement and participatory democracy, Chantal Mouffe proposes an agonistic model of public sphere in opposition to the aggregative model by Harbermas. Mouffe (2000) contends that consensus is always "temporary respites in an ongoing confrontation," and the quest for rationalistic consensus denies the true nature of the political, which is featured by inevitable antagonism among different social groups (p. 102). Instead, Mouffe's agonistic pluralism recognizes the claims of unrecognized and marginalized social groups (Glover, 2012). Furthermore, in recognizing multiple conflicting identities, practices and democratic discourses, it shifts the focus to the negotiation of difference and plurality, and the creation of agonistic space in which one's own identity can be constructed. In addition, while the Habermasian model emphasizes reasonableness, agonistic public sphere values the role of passions in politics and argues that reason on its own is not sufficient for meaningful political engagement.

Peter Dahlgren, on the other hand, theorizes about public sphere with a focus on the role of the Internet. He contends that the Internet holds the capacity for "horizontal communication" (Dahlgren, 2005, p. 155) of civic participation, which contributes to the destabilization of political communication system. The Internet occupies a central place in this arena of new politics, where many citizens redirect their political attention from the governmental system to social movements. The interactional dimension of the online public spheres render politics "not only an instrumental activity for achieving specific goals, but also an expressive activity, a way of asserting, within the public sphere, group values, ideals, and belonging" (Dahlgren, 2005, p. 155). Dahlgren (2005) proposes three analytic dimensions of public sphere: social structure, media representation and sociocultural interaction. The latter two will be useful for the critical discourse analysis this paper. Representational dimension is concerned with media content, patterns of conveying the content, modes of discourse, and character of debates and discussion. The dimension of interaction has two aspects: interaction between citizens and the media and the interaction among citizens. Hence in understanding social media's role in the promotion of civic engagement in China, it is necessary to examine not only the content of discussion but also patterns of interaction.

This chapter integrates Mouffe's agonistic model (1995) and Dahlgren's three-dimension model (2005) of public sphere in analyzing the discussion about the Wenzhou derailment accident on China's leading microblog site – Sina Weibo. Plurality of voices, expression of dissensus and passion underlined by Mouffe are objects in discourse examination. In applying Dahlgren's three-dimension model, content, representation patterns, ideology, plural views, discourse modes are the main focus of representation dimension; interaction among micro-bloggers will be the focus of interaction dimension.

Social Media in China

China is known for its "commandist media system" (Pan, 2000, p. 73) and media censorship. Government- operated state media are required to follow strict guidelines created by the Propaganda Department of the Chinese Communist Party in covering politically sensitive topics such as democracy and corruption. Within this context, the rise of the Internet in the past several decades and the popularity of social media in the last few years have been greeted with great optimism that such new media could provide Chinese citizens with an alterative platform for civic and political engagement. Today, researchers generally agreed that the democratizing potential of the Internet has not been fulfilled partly due to China's sophisticated Internet censorship and control (Yang, 2012). However, there is still limited theoretical or empirical understanding of the role of social media in promoting civic engagement (Chen, 2014). Furthermore, because of the Internet control in China, global social media sites such as Facebook, Twitter, and Youtube are not available to Chinese Internet users. This has interestingly allowed China to develop its unique social media landscape that is worth studying.

In recent years, China has witnessed many online public events that are demonstrative of social media's constructive role in the creation of civil society. Yang (2003) systematically examined basic ele- ments, dynamics and political functions of Chinese online cultural sphere and found a strong tendency for public engagement. He argued that online public sphere in China fulfilled three political functions: public expression, civic association and popular protest. Yang and Calhoun (2007) studied public debates about the Nu River hydropower project and found the rise of a "green" public sphere, in contrast to the "red" and authoritarian communicative spaces (p. 211). This green public sphere fostered political debates and pluralistic views concerning a variety of issues and enabled new forms of public engage- ment in contemporary China. The democratizing potential of social media has been supported by a few empirical studies as well. For instance, Mou, Atkin, Fu, Lin, and Lau (2012) surveyed college students in China on their social media usage and found positive relationships between students' social media use and their levels of political efficacy as well as online political discussion. Similarly, Harp et al. (2012) found that compared to their counterparts in Latin America and the United States, activists in China put greater importance on social media in promoting political debate. From the government's perspective, it increasingly considers online communication to the "voice of the public" and use social media as the means to assess public opinion about controversial issues (Gang & Bandurski, 2001, p. 39).

At the same time, researchers have cautioned against an overly utopian view about the social media in China. First, while China's social media are under relatively looser control compared to traditional mass media, they are nevertheless censored, and as a result, users might not be allowed to discuss certain politically sensitive issues. Two primary methods used in controlling the social media are search censorship and message deletion (Bamman, O'Conner, & Smith, 2012). First, certain politically sensitive terms are made unsearchable on social media sites. For instance, Liu Xiaobo, a political dissident in China, is unsearchable on all social media sites. Second, social media companies censor their own contents by blocking posts containing blacklisted words automatically as well as hiring human censors to scan and delete instigative posts by hands (Rauchfleisch & Schafer, 2015). Furthermore, even when people are allowed to post unorthodox opinions and criticize the establishment on social media, whether they are likely to do so is another question. It is possible that the state-controlled mass media have successfully primed people's understanding of social issues and in doing so, made them adopt the sanctioned positions about these issues. Hassid (2012, p. 212) studied the role of blogs in Chinese political life, and concluded that on issues where the mass media had set the agenda, blogs functioned as a "safety valve" by releasing public's anger towards the government. Such discussion was largely tolerated by the government. However, when blogs were setting the agenda for traditional media, they could be considered a "pressure cooker," which might instigate more anger and protest. Such discussions were harshly censored.

The Case of Weibo

Weibo is a Chinese microblog application. Although it is generally compared to Twitter, as both applications have the 140-character limit, Weibo has a set of unique functions such as commenting directly on others' posts without reposting them, attaching video clips, multiple photos and long blogs, and obtaining monthly usage data of one's own accounts (Poell, Kloet, & Zengm 2014). It enables users to form and follow conversational discussions and to build on others' thoughts. Moreover, the 140-character limit allows users to write big chunk of paragraph due to the nature of the Chinese language (Poell et al., 2014). Data published in 2012 indicate that 88% of Internet users over 19 in China are Weibo users (Data Center of China Internet, 2012). More recently, WeChat, another mobile social network application, has taken over as the most dominant social media app in China; however, Weibo still remains an important player in the market. Among all the microblog platform providers in China, Sina Weibo has the largest number of users. By the end of 2014, Sina Weibo had 176 million monthly active users (Millward, 2015).

Since its creation in 2009, Weibo has been the platform for many large-scale online discussions about sensitive topics such as social justice and corruption. Scholars refer to such events as online mass incidents (e.g., Tong & Lei, 2013). However, such online discussions have been dismissed by some scholars as short-lived venting of emotions with no real rational discussion and real offline events (e.g., Leibold, 2012)

Weibo was instrumental in disseminating censored information about the high-speed train derailment accident described at the beginning of the chapter and in creating nation-wide discussion online as well as offline about the reliability of the high-speed railway system and the government's problematic handling of the accident. Bones and Schucher (2014) conducted a content analysis of 4600 Weibo posts about the accident and found that while Weibo allowed users to express their anger, there was no discussion of mobilization. Hence, they concluded, "expectations about a democratizing impact of online debates might be premature" (p. 45). However, the concept of public sphere is based on the assumption that open political discussion alone is the first step in civic engagement because such discussion might alter the power structure in a society by bringing discursive changes. Hence, in this chapter, we propose a study of the Weibo discussion of the derailment accident through a discursive approach and ask the following research question (RQ):

RQ: How does Sina Weibo as a social media foster plural views and political engagement of public issues?

METHOD

Sampling

Gunter (2000) contends that sampling in discourse analysis should be theoretically informed: researchers choose those cases that represent the phenomena under study in a particular way. For the purpose of this study, we examined posts and replies about the derailment accident on Sina Weibo. We searched posts containing key words "Wenzhou High-speed Railway accident" and "23, July Wenzhou" on Sina Weibo website published between July 23, 2011 and July 23, 2012 in order to take both the immediate public reaction and cumulative media effect into consideration. However, for data analysis in this study, we focused on 200 posts with the highest numbers of reposts. This practice has been used in previous studies to identify the most influential Weibo posts (e.g., Poell et al., 2014).

Data Analysis

Critical discourse analysis (CDA) was used to analyze the Weibo posts. CDA is a method of discourse analysis that is conducted on three levels: the textual level, the discourse level, and the society level (Fairclough, 1995). This method recognizes the dialectical relationship between social structure and discourse (Fairclough, 1995). Social structures, such as social institutions and behavioral norms, are simultaneously being represented as well as being shaped by discursive practices . This dialectical relationship allows us to consider not only how public participation constructs public opinion and social identity, but also how public participation is shaped by public opinion and social identity.

On the textual level, our analysis focused on how the derailment accident was discussed. We first examined the content of the Weibo posts and the language used. In doing so, we identified several prominent linguistic features. Each feature then was examined in detail. Key words and phrases were translated from Chinese to English by the second author with special attention paid to preserving the semiotic equivalence. The second author is a Chinese native who currently resides in the United States, and has been using English as her primary working language for 19 years. On the discursive level, we focused on the genres used in the online discussion of the accident. Finally, on the societal level, we explored how such online discussion reflected and contributed to the creation of new social identities.

RESULTS

In the result section, we will first describe the prominent linguistic features of the Weibo posts about the derailment accident, as such linguistic choices are indicative of underlying discourses and social relations. Notice these linguistic features are not mutually exclusive and bloggers often use more than one of them in a single post.

Textual Level

On the textual level, the discussion about the derailment accident on Sina Weibo was characterized by a number of linguistic features, including the opposition between they and we, the use of questions to express skepticism and anger, word play, irony, the language of comparison, among others.

The Language of "They" vs. "We"

There was a consistent, pronominal contrast between different social groups manifested by the personal pronouns "we"— the Chinese public, and "they"— government and special interest groups, especially the Ministry of Railway. For example, one Weibo post stated,

If we just let the Ministry of Railway dally with us, the only outcome would be the consolidation of this interest group (which has been in existence for too long). We would allow them to hijack the national economy.

The blogger constructed two social groups by distinguishing self and other. "We" referred to himself and the potential audiences, and "they" referred to special interest groups who were only concerned with political achievements and economic benefit instead of the wellbeing of the state and its citizens. The use of pronouns articulated in- and out-group status, negotiated social distance (Wilson, 1990; Halmari, 1993), and enabled readers to claim membership of the public.

The Use of Questions

A large portion of the Weibo posts about the derailment accident asked questions. Bloggers frequently asked questions about the real facts about the accident. For instance, many bloggers asked the questions, "What is the real death toll of this accident," or "Is the death roll really 39," as there were widespread speculations about the number of people killed ranging from somewhere in the thirties to more than 200. Such questions reflected bloggers' distrust of the government and traditional media. Sometimes, bloggers asked questions about the cause of this tragic accident. One post asked, "Whose responsibility is it? Is it Ministry of Railway alone? ... How could the search and rescue team decide that there was no sign of life in wrecked trains?"

Other times, bloggers asked rhetorical questions, i.e. they asked a question in order to express an opinion rather than obtaining an answer. In one post, the blogger criticized the irresponsible behaviors of the special interest group (in this case, officials in Ministry of Railway) and asked, "When the establishment only cares about pumping the GDP, and making millions for themselves, who will bother to innovate and to improve the lives of ordinary people?" Another blogger directly spoke up against Sina

Corporation for deleting posts, "China, what are you afraid of? So many videos about Weizhou were deleted. You could delete videos, posts, pictures, and audios, but can you delete your ugliness? China, what is wrong with you? What are you afraid of? What are you trying to hide?"

The Use of Comparison

Sometimes, bloggers tried to make sense of the derailment accident by comparing it to catastrophic accidents in other countries. Past research in risk perception showed that individuals tend to use comparison to assess the level of risk associated with a disaster, since a familiar risk is more acceptable than an unfamiliar one (Slovic, 1987). For instance, one Weibo post said, "The catastrophic nuclear disaster of Chernobyl and the nuclear melt-down at Fukushima in Japan both revealed the fault and oversight of the national administration system." Some bloggers compared the Weizhou derailment accident to other serious railway or highway accidents in China to show that this accident and the government's problematic handling of the accident was not an isolated incident. For instance, one blogger posted, "On May 23 of last year, a K859 train derailed in a remote part of Jiangxi Province. The accident happened at 2 am; however, everything was cleaned up at 6 pm on the same day so that the train service could be restored. They dug a hole in the ground and buried the train together with the limbs of some victims still inside. Two weeks later, when nobody was paying attention anymore, they dug out the train, cleared it out, and hauled it off." In other instances, bloggers compared how Chinese and foreign governments handled such mass accidents differently to express their anger and dissatisfaction. For instance, quite a few posts compared the Chinese government's handling of the Wenzhou derailment accident with the 1998 derailment of an ICE train in Germany. A blogger who identified himself as a college student said, "Look at how the Germans responded to their derailment accident. I am losing confidence in the Chinese society and government."

Poems of Mourning and Condolence

It is a tradition for Chinese people to write poems to express sadness and condolences toward the deceased while expressing anger toward the government. One such poem-writing event on the national scale occured in the spring of 1976 right after the passing of then Premier Zhou Enlai (Kraus, 1991). Tens of thousnds of poems were written and posted in public places not only to express the people's sadness about the loss of a beloved national leader, but also their anger toward the Gang of Four responsible for the Cultural Revolution. The publication of these poems was banned by the government. In response, people would travel to different places to copy these poems by hand and share them with friends and co-workers. This practice was observed on Weibo in the aftermath of the derailment accident. A large number of posts used very emotional and poetic language to express sadness and mourning. For instance, one week after the accident, a blogger posted a message with the headline "We are all passengers:"

On an endless railway, we are all passengers. That day, you stepped onto a train, not knowing, it would not arrive at its destination. That night, I looked for you among a sea of faces, but you remained hidden in the darkness. Today, I come to visit you, but couldn't find your tombstone. May we no longer live in a miracle. The truth is behind us.

Notice that while this poem was written mainly to mourn the loss of a friend, it also subtly expressed its dissatisfaction with the government by saying, "May we no longer live in a miracle." Another widely shared Weibo post contained the following poem that directly criticized the Chinese government and society:

China, please slow down your flying pace, wait for your people, wait for your soul, wait for your morality, wait for your conscience! Don't let the train run out off track, don't let the bridges collapse, don't let the roads become traps, don't let houses become ruins. Walk slowly, allowing every life to have freedom and dignity. No one should be left behind by our era.

Writing poems allow Chinese people to express their criticism of the government publicly, which would be otherwise forbidden.

Irony

Irony was another prominent linguistic feature in the discussion about the derailment accident on Weibo. Irony can be defined as implying the opposite of what is said (Dynel, 2014). In order to perform an irony successfully, bloggers relied on the shared context and on the hearers' willingness to search for the intended meaning. For instance, one blogger asked, "which temporary worker is responsible for this accident?" In the years before the derailment accident, temporary workers were often used as scapegoats in accidents and scandals. So in making this ironic remark, the blogger was expressing his worry that the government would find a scapegoat instead of holding the real culprit responsible. In another instance, a blogger posted a picture of the Minister of Railway being interviewed in an air-conditioned bus and commented, "With so many dead and injured, our esteemed Minister of Railway appeared in person to supervise the rescue effort in an air-conditioned bus. What kind of spirit it is! Let's share this post and let the public get to know this great Minister of Railway." By calling him "a great Minister" yet portraying him as unconcerned with the victims, the blogger expressed his criticism of this governmental official indirectly.

Word Play

Word play referred to appropriating the words of governmental officials and appropriate in different contexts to express sarcasm. In the Weibo discussion about the derailment accident, bloggers played with the word miracle to express their disappointment and indignation. Weiyi, a three-year old girl, was found alive in a wrecked train hours after the Ministry of Railway had announced that there was no one alive in the train and stopped the search and recue effort. In response to journalists' inquiry, the spokesperson of the Ministry of Railway could not offer any explanation for the Ministry's dangerous decision to end rescue effort prematurely and simply said, "it is a miracle." Since then, bloggers started to play with the word miracle to express their distrust of the government and their anger. In a post, the blogger criticized the undertraining of high-speed train drivers in China by saying,

While it took German engine drivers three months to learn how to drive a high-speed train, it only took Chinese drivers ten days. It is a miracle that learning to drive a high-speed rail engine is easier than learning to drive a car.

In the second half of this post, the blogger ridiculed the Chinese government's use of life detectors in searching for survivors and its covering up of the cause of the accident by burying the trains shortly after the accident,

Life detectors made in China failed to detect living people, a miracle of Chinese independent innovation. When you are alive, you cannot afford to buy an apartment. When you are dead, you cannot afford to buy a grave plot. But if you take the high-speed rail, both of the two problems can be solved. This is truly the buy-one-get-one free with Chinese characteristics.

In this post of less than 140 characters, the blogger used the word miracle twice to ridicule the things that did not make sense: the very short training of high-speed engine drivers, the life detectors that did not detect survivors, and the hurried burial of wrecked trains. Furthermore, the blogger made fun of the skyrocketing housing price in China and provided an ironic solution to this problem: getting into a railway accident.

The Language of Celebration

Although definitely belonging to the minority position, some Weibo posts adopted the typical positive approach used by traditional media in disaster coverage by celebrating the dedication of the search and rescue team and goodness of ordinary people. This linguistic feature has been prominent in the media coverage of previous disasters such as the Sichuan Earthquake in 2008. In the case of the derailment accident, many Weibo posts shared pictures of rescue teams and volunteers to praise their selfless work. One blogger said, "Let's pray for all the victims and solute the rescue team. Let's stay united to face the disaster!" Another blogger praised the rescue workers and volunteers and called them "The real spine of China." Very interestingly, a post that celebrated the nouveau riche of Wenzhou was also widely reposted:

These are the new money of Wenzhou. When the accident happened, residents waded through mud to rescue the injured. When TV stations cannot access the accident scene, they flew their own helicopters to take pictures. When the blood bank has no more blood left, they drove their own luxury cars to donate blood. When injured passengers were sent to the local hospital, the director said saving life was more important than money. China could use more new money like them.

INTERACTION AND DISCUSSION

Interaction among users is an important criterion of Dahlgren's model of online public sphere, which attached great significance to the efficiency of communicative process and deliberation in daily life. Because Weibo allows substantive comments to be posted, it has the potential to enable real discussion and interaction.

In the following post, heated discussion occurred between the blogger (B1) and his friends (B2, B3, B4, B5).

B1: *Our country has done nothing to guarantee our safety: the expensive high-speed rail is plagued with frequent accidents. Dangerous coalmines often injure and even kill workers. Bridges collapsed into pieces. The problem is that there are no investigations after such accidents. What can we believe in?*
B2: *The Accountability system is totally useless!*
B1: *Yes, if you asks for an explanation from the government, all you can get is "I don't care if you are convinced or not, because I firmly believe in it.*
B3: *Is it that China's social problems are out of control?*
B1: *In a country that is so shadowy, don't even dream about personal safety, information transparency and so forth.*
B3: *Orwell's Animal Farm is an accurate depiction of our country.*
B4: *Cheer up, these are just accidents. Usually, there is some kind of guarantee.*
B1: *For example?*
B5: *I agree. Media are keeping an eye on the government, and change is taking place.*
B1: *Media coverage does get public attention for a while, but that's only temporary. All the government has to is to wait until the discussion cools down, and then they don't need to apologize to the public before they repeat their misconducts all over again.*

Here B1, B2 and B3 added to each other's negative view of Chinese political system. B4 and B5 mildly challenged the argument of B1, and B1 asked B4 for supporting evidence of his argument. There were not only confirming words or phrases such as "yes" and "I agree" indicating agreement, but also concessional phrases "does...but" to mildly contend one's own view. In this way, both consensus and dissensus in respect of ideological positions can be achieved.

Discourse Level

The meso level of critical discourse analysis requires an observation of the employed genres and an examination of the discourses and assumptions. On this level, we identified three main genres of in terms of the style and content of the posts: tirade, satire, and eulogy.

The Genre of Tirade

We use the term tirade to refer to an emotionally charged accusatory speech. It is natural that when a tragic accident like this happened, bloggers wanted to find out the causes of the accident and make sure those responsible are duly punished. The genre of tirade expresses the emotions of anger and sadness directly using an accusatory tone. Several linguistic features, such as comparisons and questions, were frequently associated with this genre. Poems that expressed condolence and anger also belonged to this genre because of their primary appeal was the pathos. However, our analysis also indicated that in using the genre of tirade, expression of emotion was given priority over rational discussion about the causes of the accident and potential solutions to prevent similar accidents from happening again in the future.

The Genre of Satire

While tirade was used in a significant portion of the Weibo posts about the derailment accident, another prominent genre was that of satire. Humor and satire have been found to be an important part of the Chinese Internet culture (Yang & Jiang 2015). Satire involved the use of humor such as irony and word play to express one's anger, frustration, and sadness. This is consistent with the finding of several existing studies. For instance, Li (2010) argued that Internet users in China use parody (*egao*) to mock Chinese authorizes and in doing so, reverse the established power structure of the Chinese society. Yang and Jing (2015) examined different practices of online political satire in China and concluded that the sharing of political satires online is "not only critiques of power, but popular mobilizations against power" (p. 216).

The Genre of Eulogy

We use to word eulogy in a broad sense to mean good words, which is the original Greek word eulogia means (Pepe, 2007). Eulogy was written for the victims of the accidents. However, more often good words were said about those people participating in the rescuing efforts: search and rescue team, local volunteers, etc. The language of mourning and condolence was often associated with the former while the language of celebration was most used in the latter. This genre has been customarily adopted in the mainstream media coverage of disasters in China and has been very much criticized by Internet users. Despite that, we still see this genre employed from time to time on Weibo, which could be a demonstration of how online discussion can sometimes be framed by traditional mass media.

Societal Level

The highest level of critical discourse analysis involves the identification of groups, ideas, and social identities. An analysis of the discussion about the Wenzhou derailment accident shows that the identity of the public (*gongzhong*) is gradually replacing the identity of the people (*renmin*).

To start, the concept of people (*renmin*) has been central to the identity of the Chinese people since 1949. The communist idea of people or *renmin* is a class concept. It refers to the proletarian class. The opposite of people are enemies: capitalist class. Since people were the ruling class of the Communist China, people and the government shared the same interest. As a result, people were supposed to have complete faith in the government and their good intentions instead of challenging the government. More recently, the privatization of the Chinese economy has changed the meaning of people. According to Communist Party's new theory of socialism with Chinese characteristics, people refers to all workers in socialist China, all patriots who support socialism, and all patriots who support China's unity (Constitution of the People's Republic of China, 1982). The new definition differs from the Maoist definition by including the capitalist and bourgeois classes as part of the Chinese people. Both the old and new definitions assume complete support of the Chinese government. In the Weibo discussion, this identity was manifested when bloggers called on others to give Chinese government the benefit of doubt and when they adopted the traditional genre of eulogy in describing how government and volunteers responded to the derailment accident. However, the identity of people is gradually giving way to the identity of public, at least within the online community in China.

Compared to the identity of people, the identity of public (*gongzhong*) is a relatively new idea. While people is a political concept, public can be considered a communication concept (Livingston, 2005). Here, public refers to savvy media consumers and Internet users who share similar concerns and who could seek out and critically evaluate the information and make evaluations and judgments. There could be potentially multiple publics (Livingston, 2005). Different from people, the public scrutinizes the government in a mediated fashion and demands accountability and transparency in the conducts of the government. Because of this new identity, Internet users in China hold themselves as someone who deserve to be informed and respected and someone capable of independent thinking. As a result, the public is often distrustful toward the government. Furthermore, the public is often wary and critical of government-controlled mass media and regards them as government's accomplice in covering up scandals. The existence of Weibo allows the Internet users in China to form a public and allow them to question the government collectively.

DISCUSSION

Social media are becoming integrated with the established system of political communication, yet they are also being used to challenge established power structures. This chapter does not ask whether Weibo as social media can be counted as public sphere or not, but examines complications of public sphere in Chinese social media, its political functions and its limits through a critical discourse analysis.

Guided by Mouffe's (1995) theory of agonistic public sphere, and Dahlgren's theorization about public sphere on the Internet, we analyze the discussion of the derailment accident on Sina Weibo on three levels: textual, discourse and societal. Our analysis shows that Weibo allows Internet users to express their anger and disappointment at the government collectively. More importantly, it enables them to question the legitimacy of the government in public through tirade and satire, an act that was unthinkable in the past. Furthermore, as indicated in the posts that celebrate the new money in Wenzhou, the haves and have-nots can be considered two different publics that are united in this particular instance. While traditionally there is deep divide and antagonism between the rich and the poor in China, in facing the disaster, these two groups are able to come together in making sense of the accident and demand more accountability from the government. This is consistent with idea of multiple publics and agonistic public sphere proposed by Mouffe (2000). At the same time, we also notice that there is very little rational discussion on Weibo, as most of the posts highly emotional. While the original Habermasian idea of public sphere emphasizes rationality, Mouffe (2000)'s agonistic public sphere values the role of passion in political discussion, arguing that reason itself is not sufficient for civic engagement. Next, we also notice that there is certain overlap in the coverage of the accident on Weibo and traditional media, indicating that as a public sphere, social media are still influenced by the ideology propagated by the traditional media. Hence the progressive and subversive role of the social media should not be overestimated (Kalathil & Boas, 2003).

One major limitation of the current study is the sampling method. All Weibo posts analyzed were downloaded retrospectively well after the incident. It can be assumed that a significant number of posts had been deleted either by Sina censors or bloggers themselves at the time of data collection. As a result, we might have missed some truly significant discussion on Weibo right after the accident. Future research should collect data from Weibo as major events are unfolding to capture the true depth and breadth of discussion. Finally, the conclusion drawn from this study is based on the case study of a single event in a single country. More empirical research is needed before we can make more general claims about the political potential of the social media in different kinds of political contexts.

REFERENCES

Bamman, D., O'Conner, B., & Smith, N. A. (2012). Censorship and deletion practices in Chinese social media. *First Monday, 17*(3), 152–173. doi:10.5210/fm.v17i3.3943

Bondes, M., & Schucher, G. (2014). Derailed emotions: The transformation of claims and targets during the Wenzhou online incident. *Information Communication and Society, 17*(1), 45–65. doi:69118X.2013.853819 doi:10.1080/13

Cappella, J., & Jamieson, K. H. (1997). *Spiral of cynicism: The press and the public good*. New York: Oxford University Press.

Ceron, A. (2015). Internet, news, and political trust: The difference between social media and online media outlets. *Journal of Computer-Mediated Communication*. Retrieved from http://onlinelibrary.wiley.com/doi/10.1111/jcc4.12129/abstract

Chen, W. (2014). Taking stock, moving forward: The Internet, social networks and civic engagement in Chinese societies. *Information Communication and Society, 17*(1), 1–6. doi:8X.2013.857425 doi:10.1080/136911

Constitution of the People's Republic of China. (1982). Retrieved from: http://www.hkhrm.org.hk/english/law/const01.html

Crosbie, V. (2002). *What is social media?* New York: Oxford University Press.

Dahlgren, P. (2005). *Television and the public Sphere: Citizenship, democracy and the media*. London: Sage.

Data Center of China Internet. (2012). *2012 bluebook of China microblog*. Author.

Dynel, M. (2014). Isn't it ironic? Defining of the scope of humorous irony. *Humor: International Journal of Humor Research, 27*(4), 619–639. doi:10.1515/humor-2014-0096

Fairclough, N. (1993). Critical discourse analysis and the marketization of public discourse: The universities. *Discourse & Society, 4*(2), 133–168. doi:10.1177/0957926593004002002

Fairclough, N. (1995). *Critical discourse analysis: The critical study of language*. London: Longman.

Flew, T. (2008). *Social media: An Introduction*. New York: Oxford University Press.

Fraser, N. (1990). Rethinking the public sphere: A contribution to the critique of actually existing democracy. In *Habermas and the public sphere* (pp. 56–80). Cambridge, MA: MIT Press. doi:10.2307/466240

Gang, Q., & Bandurski, D. (2011). China's emerging public sphere. In S. Shirk (Ed.), *Changing media, changing China* (pp. 38–76). Oxford, UK: Oxford University Press.

Gitlin, T. (2004). Jurgen Habermas: The sage of reason. *Time Magazine*. Retrieved from http://content.time.com/time/magazine/article/0,9171,994032,00.html

Glover, R. W. (2012). Games without frontiers? Democratic engagement, agonistic pluralism and the question of exclusion. *Philosophy and Social Criticism*, *38*(1), 81–104. doi:10.1177/0191453711421605

Gunter, B. (2000). *Media research methods: Measuring audiences, reactions and impact*. London: Sage; doi:10.4135/9780857028983

Habermas, J. (1989). *The structural transformation of the public sphere: An inquiry into a category of bourgeois society* (T. Burger, Trans.). Cambridge, MA: The MIT Press. (Original work published 1962)

Harp, D., Bachmann, I., & Guo, L. (2012). The whole online world is watching: Profiling social networking sites and activists in China, Latin America, and the United States. *International Journal of Communication*, *6*, 298–321.

Hassid, J. (2012). Safety valve or pressure cooker? Blogs in Chinese political life. *Journal of Communication*, *62*(2), 212–230. doi:10.1111/j.1460-2466.2012.01634.x

Jankowski, N. W., & van Selm, M. (2000). The promise and practice of public debate. In K. L. Hacker & J. van Dijk (Eds.), *Digital democracy: Issues of theory and practice* (pp. 149–165). London: Sage. doi:10.4135/9781446218891.n9

Kohn, M. (2000). Language, power, and persuasion: Towards a critique of deliberative democracy. *Constellations (Oxford, England)*, *7*(3), 408–429. doi:10.1111/1467-8675.00197

Kraus, R. C. (1991). *Brushes with power: Modern politics and the Chinese art of calligraphy*. Berkeley, CA: University of California Press.

Leibold, J. (2012). Blogging alone: China, the Internet, and the democratic illusion? *The Journal of Asian Studies*, *70*(4), 1023–1041. doi:10.1017/S0021911811001550

Li, H. (2011). Parody and resistance on the Chinese Internet. In D. Herold & P. W. Marolt (Eds.), *Online society in China: Creating, celebrating, and instrumentalising the online carnival* (pp. 71–88). New York: Routledge.

Livingstone, S. (2005). On the relation between audience and publics. In S. Livingston (Ed.), *Audiences and publics: When cultural engagement matters for the public sphere* (pp. 17–41). Bristol: Intellect Books.

Lyotard, J. F. (1984). *The postmodern condition: A report on knowledge*. Minneapolis, MN: University of Minnesota Press.

Millward, S. (2015, March 11). *Weibo ends 2014 with slow but steady growth, now has 176 million monthly active users*. Retrieved from: https://www.techinasia.com/weibo-2014-176-million-monthly-active-users/

Mou, Y., Atkin, D. J., Fu, H., Lin, C. A., & Lau, T. (2012). *The influence of social media on online political discussion in China*. Paper presented at the annual meeting of the International Communication Association, Phoenix, AZ.

Mouffe, C. (1999). Deliberative democracy or agonistic pluralism? *Social Research*, *66*(3), 745–753.

Mouffe, C. (2000). *The democratic paradox*. London: Verso.

Mouffe, C. (2005). *On the political*. London: Routledge.

Negt, O., & Kluge, A. (1993). *Public sphere and experience: Toward an analysis of the bourgeois and proletarian public sphere*. Minneapolis, MN: University of Minnesota Press.

Pan, Z. (2000). Improvising reform activities: The changing reality of journalistic practice in China. In C. C. Lee (Ed.), *Power, money, and media: Communication patterns and bureaucratic control in cultural China* (pp. 68–111). Evanston, IL: Northwestern University Press.

Pepe, C. (2007). Civic eulogy in the epitaphios of Pericles and the citywide prayer service of Rudolph Giuliani. *Advances in the History of Rhetoric*, *10*(1), 131–144. doi:10.1080/15362426.2007.10557278

Poell, T., Kloet, J. D., & Zeng, G. (2014). Will the real Weibo please stand up? Chinese online contention and actor-network theory. *Chinese Journal of Communication, 7*(1), 1–18. doi:.2013.816753 doi:10.1080/17544750

Rauchfleisch, A., & Schafer, M. S. (2015). Multiple public spheres of Weibo: A typology of forms and potentials of online public spheres in China. *Information Communication and Society*, *18*(2), 139–155. doi:10.1080/1369118X.2014.940364

Slevin, J. (2000). *The Internet and society*. Polity Press.

Slovic, P. (1987). Perception of risk. *Science*, *236*(4799), 280–285. doi:10.1126cience.3563507 PMID:3563507

Tong, Y., & Lei, S. (2013). War of position and microblogging in China. *Journal of Contemporary China*, *32*(80), 292–311. doi:10.1080/10670564.2012.734084

Van de Donk, W., Loader, B. D., Nixon, P. G., & Rucht, D. (Eds.). (2004). *Cyberprotest: Social media*. Blackwell.

Xu, J. (2016). *Media events in web 2.0 China: Interventions of online activism*. Eastbourne, UK: Sussex Academic Press.

Yang, G. (2003). The Internet and the rise of a transnational Chinese cultural sphere. *Media Culture & Society*, *25*(4), 469–490. doi:10.1177/01634437030254003

Yang, G. (2012). A Chinese Internet? History, practice, and globalization. *Chinese Journal of Communication*, *5*(1), 49–54. doi:10.1080/17544750.2011.647744

Yang, G., & Calhoun, C. (2007). Media, civil Society, and the rise of a green public sphere in China. *China Information*, *21*(2), 211–236. doi:10.1177/0920203X07079644

Yang, G., & Jiang, M. (2015). The networked practice of online political satire in China: Between ritual and resistance. *The International Communication Gazette*, *77*(3), 215–231. doi:10.1177/1748048514568757

Compilation of References

Abers, R. (2000). *Inventing Local Democracy: Grassroots Politics in Brazil*. Boulder, CO: Lynne Rienner Publishers.

Adamic, L. A., & Adar, E. (2003). Friends and neighbors on the web. *Social Networks*, *25*(3), 211–230. doi:10.1016/S0378-8733(03)00009-1

AdvansIdea. (2014, March 23). *The 318 Sunflower Movement: A test field for new media innovations*. Retrieved July 5, 2015 from http://advansidea.Tumblr.Com/post/80371944080/318%e5%ad%b8%e9%81%8b%e6%98%af%e6%96%b0%e5%aa%92%e9%ab%94%e5%89%b5%e6%96%b0%e9%81%8b%e7%94%a8%e7%9a%84%e8%a9%a6%e9%a9%97%e5%a0%b4

Aggio, C., & Sampaio, R. (2013). Democracia digital e participação: os modelos de consulta e os desafios do Gabinete Digital. Gabinete digital: análise de uma experiência. Porto Alegre: Companhia Rio-Grandense de Artes Gráficas (CORAG), 19-38.

Ahem, R. K., Stomer-Galley, J., & Neuman, W. R. (2000). *When voters can interact and compare candidates online: Experimentally investigating political web effects*. Paper presented at the meeting of the International Communications Associations Annual Conference, Acapulco, Mexico.

Albert, E. (2019, June 27). China-Taiwan Relations. *Council on Foreign Relations*. Retrieved August 4, 2019 from https://www.cfr.org/backgrounder/china-taiwan-relations

Alhames, R. (2013, May 22). *14-year-old Citizen Journalist Killed Covering Clashes in Syria*. Retrieved from http://globalvoicesonline.org/2013/05/22/teen-citizen-journalist-killed-in-syria/

Ali, S. R., & Fahmy, S. (2013). Gatekeeping and citizen journalism: The use of social media during the recent uprisings in Iran, Egypt, and Libya. *Media War Conflict*, *6*(1950), 55–69. doi:10.1177/1750635212469906

Alicea, S., Pardo, G., Conover, K., Gopalan, G., & McKay, M. (2012). Step-up: Promoting youth mental health and development in inner-city high schools. *Clinical Social Work Journal*, *40*(2), 175–186. doi:10.100710615-011-0344-3 PMID:23564983

Allegretti, G. (2013). Os orçamentos participativos sabem escutar? Reflexões para reforçar a sustentabilidade dos orçamentos participativos. In Orçamento Participativo olhares e perpesctivas. Livraria Paulo Freire Ed.

Allegretti, G. (2014). Paying attention to the participants perceptions in order to trigger a virtuous circle. In Hope For Democracy. 25 Years Of Participatory Budgeting Worldwide. S. Brás de Alportel: In Loco.

Allegretti, G. (2005). *Porto Alegre:una biografia territoriale. Ricercando la qualità urbana a partire dal patrimonio sociale*. Florence: University Press. doi:10.26530/OAPEN_347516

Allegretti, G. (2012). From Skepticism to Mutual Support: Towards a Structural Change in the Relations between Participatory Budgeting and the Information and Communication Technologies? In *Legitimacy_2.0. E-Democracy and Public Opinion in the Digital Age*. Frankfurt am Main: Goethe University Press.

Allegretti, G. (2017). When Citizen Participation Unexpectedly Grows in Quality and Quantity. In *Crisis, Austerity, and Transformation. How Disciplinary Neoliberalism is Changing Portugal* (pp. 157–178). London: Lexington Books.

Allegretti, G., & Copello, K. (2018). Winding around money issues. What's new in Participatory Budgeting and which windows of opportunity are being opened? In *Hope for Democracy - 30 Years of Participatory Budgeting Worldwide* (pp. 35–54). Faro, Cuba: Oficina/Epopeia.

Anderson, M., & Caumont, A. (2014). How social media is reshaping news. *Pew Research Center*. Retrieved on June 1, 2015, from http://www.pewresearch.org/fact-tank/2014/09/24/how-social-media-is-reshaping-news/

Anderson, R., Baxter, L. A., & Cissna, K. N. (Eds.). (2004b). *Dialogue. Theorizing Difference in Communication Studies*. Thousand Oaks, CA: Sage Publications. doi:10.4135/9781483328683

Anderson, R., & Cissna, K. N. (2008). Fresh perspectives in dialogue theory. *Communication Theory, 18*(1), 1–4. doi:10.1111/j.1468-2885.2007.00310.x

Andersson, E., Burall, S., & Fennell, E. (2010). *Talking for a Change: a distributed dialogue approach to complex issues*. London: Involve. Available online at: http://www.involve.org.uk/wp-content/uploads/2011/03/Involve2010TalkingforaChange2.pdf

Anduiza, E., Gallego, A., & Cantijoch, M. (2010). Online Political Participation in Spain: The Impact of Traditional and Internet Resources. *Journal of Information Technology & Politics, 7*(4), 356–368. doi:10.1080/19331681003791891

Aquino, F., Donzelli, G., De Franco, E., Privitera, G., Lopalco, P. L., & Carducci, A. (2017). The web and public confidence in MMR vaccination in Italy. *Vaccine, 35*(35), 4494–4498. doi:10.1016/j.vaccine.2017.07.029 PMID:28736200

Armoogum, N. (2013). *Can Citizen Journalists produce Professional Journalism?* Center for International Media Ethics. Retrieved from http://www.cimethics.org/home/newsletter/jun2013/Nanda%20Armoogum_EDITED.pdf

Arnold, D. (2012, June 30). *Syrian-Armenians Seek A New Life Far From Fighting*. Retrieved from http://www.rferl.org/content/syria-war-reported-by-citizen-journalists-social-media/24630841.html

Arnup, K. (1992). Victims of vaccination? Opposition to Compulsory immunization in Ontario, 1900-90. *Canadian Bulletin of Medical History, 9*(1), 159–176. doi:10.3138/cbmh.9.2.159 PMID:11616229

Asakura, K., & Craig, S. L. (2014). "It Gets Better" … but How? Exploring Resilience Development in the Accounts of LGBTQ Adults. *Journal of Human Behavior in the Social Environment, 24*(3), 253–266. doi:10.1080/10911359.2013.808971

Associated Press. (2019, August 4). The Latest: HK police tear gas protesters in shopping area. *The Washington Post*. Retrieved August 4, 2019 from https://www.washingtonpost.com/world/asia_pacific/the-latest-ex-hk-leader-offers-bounty-for-info-on-flag/2019/2008/2004/2640ba2000-b2685-2011e2019-acc2018-2011d2847bacca2073_story.html?noredirect=on&utm_term=.bfa2217e22143

Au, A. (2017, April 27). The Sunflower Movement and the Taiwanese National Identity: Building an Anti-Sinoist Civic Nationalism. *Berkeley Journal of Sociology*. Retrieved August 5, 2019 from http://berkeleyjournal.org/2017/2004/the-sunflower-movement-and-the-taiwanese-national-identity-building-an-anti-sinoist-civic-nationalism/

Avritzer, L., & Navarro, Z. (2003). A inovação democrática no Brasil: o Orçamento Participativo. Ed. Cortez.

Ayala, V., & Patriau, E. (2017). Equipos en campaña. In F. Tuesta (Ed.), Perú Elecciones 2016: un país dividido y un resultado inesperado (pp. 155-177). Lima: PUCP.

Baase, S. (2008). *A Gift of Fire* (3rd ed.). Lebanon: Prentice Hall.

Bachrach, P., & Baratz, M. S. (1970). *Power and Poverty: Theory and Practice*. New York: Oxford University Press.

Baierle, S. G. (2007). *Urban Struggles in Porto Alegre: Between Political Revolution and Transformism*. Document prepared for the Project MAPAS Active Monitoring of Public Policies under Lula's Government (2004-2005), coordinated by the Brazilian NGO IBASE. Available for download at www.ongcidade.org

Baiocchi, G. (2005). *Militants and citizens: the politics of participatory democracy in Porto Alegre*. Stanford, CA: Stanford University Press.

Baiocchi, G., & Ganuza, E. (2014). Participatory budgeting as if emancipation mattered. *Politics & Society*, *42*(1), 29–50. doi:10.1177/0032329213512978

Baker, J. P. (2003). The pertussis vaccine controversy in Great Britain, 1974–1986. *Vaccine*, *21*(25), 4003–4010. doi:10.1016/S0264-410X(03)00302-5 PMID:12922137

Baker, J. P. (2008). Mercury, vaccines, and autism: One controversy, three histories. *American Journal of Public Health*, *98*(2), 244–253. doi:10.2105/AJPH.2007.113159 PMID:18172138

Bamman, D., O'Conner, B., & Smith, N. A. (2012). Censorship and deletion practices in Chinese social media. *First Monday*, *17*(3), 152–173. doi:10.5210/fm.v17i3.3943

Barabas, C., Narula, N., & Zuckerman, E. (2017, Sept. 8). Decentralized social networks sound great. Too bad they'll never work. Wired. Retrieved from https://www.wired.com/story/decentralized-social-networks-sound-great-too-bad-theyll-never-work/

Bardenhagen, K. (2014, December 2). Taiwanese send 'democratic message' to ruling Kuomintang. *DW*. Retrieved July 20, 2014 from http://www.dw.com/en/taiwanese-send-democratic-message-to-ruling-kuomintang/a-18106103

Barge, J. K. (2002). Enlarging the meaning of group deliberation. In L. R. Frey (Ed.), *New directions in group communication* (pp. 159–177). Thousand Oaks, CA: Sage Publications.

Barge, J. K., & Little, M. (2002). Dialogical Wisdom, Communicative Practice, and Organizational Life. *Communication Theory*, *12*(4), 375–397. doi:10.1111/j.1468-2885.2002.tb00275.x

Barker, C., & Martin, B. (2011). Participation: The Happiness Connection. *Journal of Public Deliberation*, *7*(1), 9.

Barney, D. (2007). Radical Citizenship in the Republic of Technology: A Sketch. In L. Dahlberg & E. Siapera (Eds.), *Radical Democracy and the Internet*. New York, NY: Palgrave Macmillan. doi:10.1057/9780230592469_3

Barrett, B. (2018, March 19). Facebook owes you more than this. Wired. Retrieved from https://www.wired.com/story/facebook-privacy-transparency-cambridge-analytica/

Barzilai-Nahon, K. (2008). Toward a Theory of Network Gatekeeping: A Framework for Exploring Information Control. *Journal of the American Society for Information Science and Technology*, *59*(9), 1493–1512. doi:10.1002/asi.20857

Bastos, M. T., Raimundo, R. L. G., & Travitzki, R. (2013). Gatekeeping Twitter: Message diffusion in political hashtags. *Media Culture & Society*, *35*(2), 260–270. doi:10.1177/0163443712467594

Batty, D. (2011, December 29). Arab Spring Leads Surge in Events Captured on Cameraphones. *The Guardian*. Retrieved from http://www.theguardian.com/world/2011/dec/29/arab-spring-captured-on-cameraphones

Baumgartner, J. C., & Morris, J. S. (2010). MyFaceTube politics: Social networking websites and political engagement of young adults. *Social Science Computer Review*, *28*(1), 24–44. doi:10.1177/0894439309334325

Baxter, D. (2014). Opposition to vaccination and immunisation: The UK experience - from Smallpox to MMR. *Journal of Vaccines & Vaccination*, *5*(6). doi:10.4172/2157-7560.1000254

Baym, N. K., Zhang, Y. B., & Lin, M.-C. (2004). Social interactions across media interpersonal communication on the internet, telephone and face-to-face. *New Media & Society*, *6*(3), 299–318. doi:10.1177/1461444804041438

Beauvais, E., & Warren, M. (2015). *Can Citizens' Assemblies Deepen Urban Democracy?* Paper presented at the American Political Science Association conference.

Becker, L. B., & Dunwoody, S. (1982). Media use, public affairs knowledge and voting in a local election. *The Journalism Quarterly*, *59*(2), 212–218. doi:10.1177/107769908205900203

Beiner, R. (1983). *Political Judgment*. Chicago, IL: University of Chicago Press.

Bekafigo, M. A., & Pingley, A. (2014). *Tweeting negative: Determinants of negative campaigning in the 2011 gubernatorial elections*. Presented at the Annual Meeting of the Midwest Political Science Association, Chicago, IL.

Benner, K. (2017). Inside the Hotel Industry's Plan to Combat Airbnb. *The New York Times*. Retrieved from https://www.nytimes.com/2017/04/16/technology/inside-the-hotel-industrys-plan-to-combat-airbnb.html

Bennett, W. L. (2012). *News: The Politics of Illusion* (9th ed.). Chicago, IL: University of Chicago Press.

Bennett, W. L., & Pfetsch, B. (2018). Rethinking political communication in a time of disrupted public spheres. *Journal of Communication*, *68*(2), 243–253. doi:10.1093/joc/jqx017

Bennett, W. L., & Segerberg, A. (2012). The logic of connective action: Digital media and the personalization of contentious politics. *Information Communication and Society*, *15*(5), 739–768. doi:10.1080/1369118X.2012.670661

Bentivegna, S. (2006). Rethinking politics in the world of ICTs. *European Journal of Communication*, *21*(3), 331–343. doi:10.1177/0267323106066638

Bentley, C. H. (2004). *Wanted: Your Ideas, Your Prose, Your Photos*. Retrieved from http://groups.yahoo.com/group/freecycleColumbiaMO/

Bentley, C. H. (2008, June 20-21). *Citizen Journalism: Back to the Future*. Discussion paper presented at the Carnegie Knight Conference on the Future of Journalism, Cambridge, MA. Retrieved from http://blogimg.ohmynews.com/attach/752/1098233647.pdf

Bentley, C. H., Hamman, B., Littau, J., Meyer, H., Watson, H., & Welsh, B. (2005). *The Citizen Journalism Movement: MyMissourian as a Case Study*. Presented at AEJMC Annual Convention San Antonio, Texas. Retrieved from http://citizenjournalism.missouri.edu/researchpapers/casestudy.doc

Besson, S., Marti, J. L., & Seiler, V. (2006). *Deliberative Democracy and Its Discontents*. Ashgate Publishing Company.

Best, N. J., Ribeiro, M. M., Matheus, R., & Vaz, J. C. (2010). Internet e a participação cidadã nas experiências de orçamento participativo digital no Brasil. Cadernos PPG-AU/UFBA, 9.

Betsch, C., Brewer, N. T., Brocard, P., Davies, P., Gaissmaier, W., Haase, N., & Stryk, M. (2012). Oppor- tunities and challenges of Web 2.0 for vaccination decisions. *Vaccine*, *30*(25), 3727–3733. doi:.vaccine.2012.02.025 doi:10.1016/j

Betsch, C., Bohm, R., & Chapman, G. B. (2015). Using behavioral insights to increase vaccina- tion policy effectiveness. *Policy Insights from the Behavioral and Brain Sciences*, *2*(1), 61–73. doi:10.1177/2372732215600716

Biddix, J. P., & Park, H. W. (2008). Online networks of student protest: The case of the living wage campaign. *New Media & Society*, *10*(6), 871–891. doi:10.1177/1461444808096249

Bimber, B. (1998). The Internet and political transformation: Populism, community, and accelerated pluralism. *Polity*, *31*(1), 133–160. doi:10.2307/3235370

Bimber, B. (2014). Digital media in the Obama campaigns of 2008 and 2012: Adaptation to the personalized political communication environment. *Journal of Information Technology & Politics*, *11*(2), 130–150. doi:10.1080/19331681.2014.895691

Bimber, B., & Davis, R. (2003). *Campaigning online*. New York: Oxford University Press.

Bimber, B., Flanagin, A., & Stohl, C. (2012). *Collective Action in Organizations: Interaction and Engagement in an Era of Technological Change*. Cambridge, UK: Cambridge University Press. doi:10.1017/CBO9780511978777

Bittle, S., Haller, C., & Kadlec, A. (2009). *Promising Practices in Online Engagement*. Occasional Paper, n. 3, Center for Advancement of Public Engagement.

Bjorkman Nyqvist, M., & Svensson, J. (2007). *Power to the People: Evidence from a Randomized Field Experiment of a Community-Based Monitoring Project in Uganda*. Policy Research Working Paper Series 4268, The World Bank.

Bjur, J., Schrøder, K., & Hasebrink, U. (2014). Cross-media use: Unfolding complexities in contemporary audiencehood. In N. Carpentier, K. C. Schrøder, & L. Hallet (Eds.), *Audience Transformations. Shifting Audience Positions in Late Modernity* (pp. 15–29). London: Routledge.

Blackman, S. (1995). *Youth: Positions and Oppositions—Style, Sexuality and Schooling*. Aldershot, UK: Avebury Press.

Blackman, S. (2014). Subculture theory: An historical and contemporary assessment of the concept for understanding deviance. *Deviant Behavior*, *35*(6), 496–512. doi:10.1080/01639625.2013.859049

Blanchet-Cohen, N., & Salazar, J. (2009). Empowering practices for working with marginalized youth. *Relational Child & Youth Care Practice*, *22*, 5–15.

Blas, A., & Ibarra, P. (2006). La participación: Estado de la cuestión. *Cuadernos Hegoa*, *39*, 5–35.

Bloom, B. R., Marcuse, E., & Mnookin, S. (2014). Addressing vaccine hesitancy. *Science*, *344*(6182), 339–339. doi:10.1126cience.1254834 PMID:24763557

Bochner, E. (2015). *We support Dr. Andrew Wakefield.* Retrieved August 5th, 2015, from http://www. wesupportandy-wakefield.com/

Bohm, D. (2003). *On dialogue, E-library*. Taylor and Francis.

Bokeno, R., & Gantt, V. W. (2000). Dialogic mentoring. Core relationships for organizacional learning. *Management Communication Quarterly*, *14*(2), 237–270. doi:10.1177/0893318900142002

Bolton, K., Memory, K., & McMillan, C. (2015). Herd immunity: Does social media affect adherence to the CDC child-hood vaccination schedule? *The Journal of Undergraduate Research at the University of Tennessee*, *6*(1), 5.

Bondes, M., & Schucher, G. (2014). Derailed emotions: The transformation of claims and targets during the Wenzhou online incident. *Information Communication and Society*, *17*(1), 45–65. doi:69118X.2013.853819 doi:10.1080/13

Bondes, M., & Schucher, G. (2014). Derailed emotions: The transformation of claims and targets during the Wenzhou online incident. *Information Communication and Society*, *17*(1), 45–65. doi:10.1080/1369118X.2013.853819

Bonney, R., Cooper, C. B., & Ballard, H. (2016). The Theory and Practice of Citizen Science: Launching a New Journal. *Citizen Science: Theory and Practice*, *1*(1), 1. doi:10.5334/cstp.65

Bonney, R., Cooper, C. B., Dickinson, J., Kelling, S., Phillips, T., Rosenberg, K. V., & Shirk, J. (2009). Citizen science: A developing tool for expanding science knowledge and scientific literacy. *Bioscience*, *59*(11), 977–984. doi:10.1525/bio.2009.59.11.9

Borra, E., & Rieder, B. (2014). Programmed method: Developing a toolset for capturing and analyzing tweets. *Asian Journal of Information Management*, *66*(3), 262–278. doi:10.1108/AJIM-09-2013-0094

Botan, C. (1992). International public relations critique and reformulation. *Public Relations Review*, *18*(2), 149–159. doi:10.1016/0363-8111(92)90006-K

Botha, A., Vosloo, S., Kuner, J., & van den Berg, M. (2009). Improving cross-cultural awareness and communication through mobile technologies. *International Journal of Mobile and Blended Learning*, *1*(2), 39–53. doi:10.4018/jmbl.2009040103

Bourdieu, P. (1991). *Language and Symbolic Power*. Cambridge, MA: Harvard University Press.

Bowman, S., & Willis, C. (2003). We Media: How Audiences Are Shaping the Future of News and Information. *New Directions for News and the Media Center, American Press Institute*. Retrieved March 21, 2015 from http://www.hypergene.net/wemedia/download/we_media.pdf

Bowman, S., & Willis, C. (2003). *We Media: How Audiences are Shaping the Future of News and Information*. Reston, VA: The Media Center at the American Press Institute. Retrieved from http://www.hypergene.net/wemedia/weblog.php?id=P36#5

Brammler, J. R., Brunet, N. D., Burton, A. C., Cuerrier, A., Danielsen, F., Dewan, K., & … . (2016). The role of digital data entry in participatory environmental monitoring. *Conservation Biology*, *30*(6), 1277–1287. doi:10.1111/cobi.12727 PMID:27032080

Brehm, J. M., Eisenhauer, B. W., & Stedman, R. C. (2013). Environmental Concern: Examining the Role of Place Meaning and Place Attachment. *Society & Natural Resources*, *26*(5), 522–538. doi:10.1080/08941920.2012.715726

Brin, S., & Page, L. (1998). The anatomy of a large-scale hypertextual Web search engine. *Computer Networks and ISDN Systems*, *33*(1-7), 107–117. doi:10.1016/S0169-7552(98)00110-X

Brofeldt, S., Argyriou, D., Turreira-García, N., Meilby, H., Danielsen, F., & Theilade, I. (2018). Community-Based Monitoring of Tropical Forest Crimes and Forest Resources Using Information and Communication Technology – Experiences from Prey Lang, Cambodia. *Citizen Science: Theory and Practice*, *3*(2), 4. doi:10.5334/cstp.129

Bruns, A. (2009, September 9-10). *Citizen Journalism and Everyday Life: A Case Study of Germany's myHeimat.de*. Paper presented at Future of Journalism Conference, Cardiff, UK. Retrieved from http://snurb.info/files/2010/Citizen%20Journalism%20and%20Everyday%20Life.pdf

Buber, M. (1970). *I and Thou* (W. Kaufmann, Trans.). New York: Charles Scribner's Sons.

Bucchi, M. (1996). When scientists turn to the public: Alternative routes in science communication. *Public Understanding of Science (Bristol, England)*, *5*(4), 375–394. doi:10.1088/0963-6625/5/4/005

Bucher, T., & Helmond, A. (2017). The affordances of social media platforms. In J. Burgess, T. Poell, & A. Marwick (Eds.), *The SAGE handbook of social media* (pp. 233–253). London: Sage.

Büscher, B. (2016). Nature 2.0: Exploring and theorizing the links between new media and nature conservation. *New Media & Society*, *18*(5), 726–743. doi:10.1177/1461444814545841

Bush, R. C. (2016, January 16). *Taiwan's election results, explained.* Washington, DC: Brookings. Retrieved July 4, 2019 from https://www.brookings.edu/blog/order-from-chaos/2016/01/16/taiwans-election-results-explained/

Butler, R., & MacDonald, N. E. (2015). Diagnosing the determinants of vaccine hesitancy in specific subgroups: The guide to Tailoring Immunization Programmes (TIP). *Vaccine, 33*(34), 4176–4179. doi:10.1016/j.vaccine.2015.04.038 PMID:25896376

Buttle, F., & Maklan, S. (2008). *Customer Relationship Management* (2nd ed.). Routledge. doi:10.4324/9780080949611

Buytaert, W., Zulkafli, Z., Grainger, S., Acosta, L., Alemie, T. C., Bastiaensen, J., ... Zhumanova, M. (2014). Citizen science in hydrology and water resources: Opportunities for knowledge generation, ecosystem service management, and sustainable development. *Frontiers of Earth Science*, *2*(26), 1–21. doi:10.3389/feart.2014.00026

California Coalition for Vaccine Choice. (2015). *No Shot. No school. California sb277 mandated vac- cination every child every vaccine.* Retrieved July 29, 2015, from http://www.sb277.org/

Cammarota, J. (2011). From Hopelessness to Hope: Social Justice Pedagogy in Urban Education and Youth Development. *Urban Education, 46*(4), 828–844. doi:10.1177/0042085911399931

Campbell, C., Meick, E., Hsu, K., & Murra, C. (2013, May 10). *China's "core interests" and the East China Sea*. US-China Economic and Security Review Commission. Retrieved July 5, 2015 from http://www.uscc.gov/sites/default/files/Research/China's%20Core%20Interests%20and%20the%20East%20China%20Sea.pdf

Campbell, S. W., & Kwak, N. (2011). Political Involvement in 'Mobilized' Society: The Interactive Relationships Among Mobile Communication, Network Characteristics, and Political Participation. *Journal of Communication, 61*(6), 1005–1024. doi:10.1111/j.1460-2466.2011.01601.x

Campbell, S. W., & Park, Y. S. (2008). Social implications of mobile telephony: The rise of personal communication society. *Sociology Compass*, *2*(2), 371–387. doi:10.1111/j.1751-9020.2007.00080.x

Cantrill, J. G. (2016). On Seeing "Places" for What They Are, and Not What We Want Them to Be. *Environmental Communication, 10*(4), 525–538. doi:10.1080/17524032.2015.1048268

Cappella, J., & Jamieson, K. (1997). *Spiral of cynicism.* New York: Oxford University Press.

Cappella, J., & Jamieson, K. H. (1997). *Spiral of cynicism: The press and the public good.* New York: Oxford University Press.

Capurro, D., Cole, K., Echavarría, M. I., Joe, J., Neogi, T., & Turner, A. M. (2014). The use of social networking sites for public health practice and research: A systematic review. *Journal of Medical Internet Research, 16*(3), e79. doi:10.2196/jmir.2679 PMID:24642014

Carey, J. (1995). The press, public opinion, and public discourse. In T. Glasser & C. Salmon (Eds.), *Public Opinion and the Communication of Consent.* Guilford.

Carroll, W. K., & Hackett, R. A. (2006). Democratic media activism through the lens of social movement theory. *Media, Culture & Society, 28*(1), 83-104. doi:10.1177/0163443706059289

Castells, M. (1997). The Information Age: Economy, Society and Culture: Vol. I. *The power of identity.* Oxford, UK: Blackwell.

Castells, M. (2009). *Communication Power.* Oxford, UK: Oxford University Press.

Castilla, O., Castro, J., & Yañez, L. (2016). *Dueños de la Noticia.* Retrieved from https://duenosdelanoticia.ojo-publico.com/articulo/los-duenos-de-la-noticia/

Centers for Disease Control. (2014). *Vaccines and autism: a summary of CDC conducted or sponsored studies*. Retrieved July 29, 2015, from http://www.cdc.gov/vaccinesafety/00_pdf/CDCStudiesonVac- cinesandAutism.pdf

Centers for Disease Control. (2015). *Measles, cases and outbreaks*. Retrieved from http://www.cdc.gov/ measles/cases-outbreaks.html

Centola, D. (2013). Social media and the science of health behavior. *Circulation*, *127*(21), 2135–2144. doi:10.1161/CIRCULATIONAHA.112.101816 PMID:23716382

Ceron, A. (2015). Internet, news, and political trust: The difference between social media and online media outlets. *Journal of Computer-Mediated Communication*. Retrieved from http://onlinelibrary.wiley. com/doi/10.1111/jcc4.12129/abstract

Chadwick, A. (2005). *The Internet, political mobilization and organizational hybridity: 'Deanspace', MoveOn.org and the 2004 US Presidential campaign*. Retrieved on Feb 10, 2016 from http://www.rhul.ac.uk/politics-and-ir/About-Us/Chadwick/pdf/A_Chadwick_Internet_Mobilization_and_Organizational_Hybridity_PSA_2005.pdf

Chadwick, A., & May, C. (2003). Interaction between states and citizens in the age of the Internet: 'e-Government' in the United States, Britain, and the European Union. *Governance: Int. J. Policy Admin. Institutions*, *16*(2), 271–300. doi:10.1111/1468-0491.00216

Chaffee, S. H., & Frank, S. (1996). How Americans get political information: Print versus broadcast news. *The Annals of the American Academy of Political and Social Science*, *546*(1), 48–58. doi:10.1177/0002716296546001005

Chaffee, S. H., Zhao, X., & Leshner, G. (1994). Political knowledge and the campaign media of 1992. *Communication Research*, *21*(3), 305–324. doi:10.1177/009365094021003004

Chan, L. (2019, April 24). Hong Kong's 'Occupy Central' activists handed prison terms. *Al Jazeera News*. Retrieved July 29, 2019 from https://www.aljazeera.com/news/2019/2004/hong-kong-occupy-central-activists-handed-prison-sentences-190424013728788.html

Chan, J. J., & Chan, J. E. (2000). Medicine for the millennium: The challenge of postmodernism. *The Medical Journal of Australia*, *172*(7), 332–334. doi:10.5694/j.1326-5377.2000.tb123981.x PMID:10844921

Chan, M., & Guo, J. (2013). The role of political efficacy on the relationship between Facebook use and participatory behaviors: A comparative study of young American and Chinese adults. *Cyberpsychology, Behavior, and Social Networking*, *16*(6), 460–463. doi:10.1089/cyber.2012.0468 PMID:23505970

Chassy, B. M. (2007). The History and Future of GMOs in Food and Agriculture. *Cereal Foods World*, *52*(4), 169–172.

Chen, A. (2019). *Desperate Venezuelans are making money by training AI for self-driving cars*. Retrieved from https://www.technologyreview.com/s/614194/venezuela-crisis-platform-work-trains-self-driving-car-ai-data/

Chen, W. (2014). Taking stock, moving forward: The Internet, social networks and civic engage- ment in Chinese societies. *Information Communication and Society*, *17*(1), 1–6. doi:8X.2013.857425 doi:10.1080/136911

Chen, W.-H. (2014). Taking stock, moving forward: The Internet, social networks and civic engagement in Chinese societies. *Information Communication and Society*, *17*(1), 1–6. doi:10.1080/1369118X.2013.857425

Chien, O. K., Hoong, P. K., & Ho, C. C. (2014). *A Comparative Study of HITS vs PageRank algorithms for Twitter users analysis*. Presented to *International Conference on Computational Science and Technology*, Kota Kinablu, Malaysia.

Chin-Fook, L., & Simmonds, H. (2011). Redefining Gatekeeping Theory for a Digital Generation. *McMaster Journal of Communication*, *8*, 7–34.

Ching, C. (2014, April 7). Sunflower movement dims cross-strait ties. *The Strait Times*. Retrieved July 11, 2015 from http://www.straitstimes.com/st/print/2246667

Chiou, C. L. (2014, June 17). *The 318 Sunflower Student Movement and its impact on Taiwanese politics and cross-strait relations*. Retrieved July 30, 2015 from https://www.griffith.edu.au/__data/assets/pdf_file/0006/614796/Poster-China-Brief-Prof-Chiou-June-2014.pdf

Choi, S., & Park, H. (2014). An exploratory approach to a Twitter-based community centered on a political goal in South Korea: Who organized it what they shared, and how they acted. *New Media & Society*, *16*(1), 129–148. doi:10.1177/1461444813487956

Chou, W. S., Prestin, A., Lyons, C., & Wen, K. (2013). Web 2.0 for health promotion: Reviewing the current evidence. *American Journal of Public Health*, *103*(1), e9–e18. doi:10.2105/AJPH.2012.301071 PMID:23153164

Chung, L. (2014a, March 29). Premier open to scrutiny of pacts; Jiang Yi-Huah says the government will consider passing law to increase oversight of controversial trade agreements made with the mainland. *South China Morning Post*. Retrieved July 5, 2015 from http://www.scmp.com/news/china/article/1459862/taiwan-premier-jiang-yi-huah-open-formal-review-future-trade-pacts

Chung, L. (2014b, October 1). Civil disobedient movement in Taiwan, HK protests similar, but goals differ. *South China Morning Post*. Retrieved July 5, 2015 from http://www.scmp.com/news/hong-kong/article/1604956/civil-disobedience-movements-taiwan-and-hong-kong-similar-goals

Clark, P. (2012). *Youth Culture in China: From Red Guards to Netizens*. Cambridge, UK: Cambridge University Press. doi:10.1017/CBO9781139061162

Codagnone, C., Biagi, F., & Abadie, F. (2016). *The Passions and the Interests: Unpacking the 'Sharing Economy*. JRC Science for Policy Report.

Codagnone, C., & Martens, B. (2016). *Scoping the Sharing Economy: Origins, Definitions, Impact and Regulatory Issues*. JRC Technical Reports.

Cohen, R. (2011). Facebook and Arab dignity. *New York Times,* Retrieved on Feb 10, 2016 from http://www.nytimes.com/2011/01/25iht-edcohen25.html

Cohn, D. (2007, November 15). *Time Citizen Journalism Pulled Its Acts Together*. Retrieved from http://www.pressgazette.co.uk/node/39443

Cole, J. M. (2014, July 1). Was Taiwan's Sunflower Movement successful? Did Taiwan's Sunflower Movement succeed? *The Diplomat*. Retrieved July 4, 2015 from http://thediplomat.com/2014/2007/was-taiwans-sunflower-movement-successful/

Coleman, S. (2001). The Transformation of Citizenship? In B. Axford & R. Huggins (Eds.), *New Media and Politics* (p. 111). London: SAGE Publications. doi:10.4135/9781446218846.n5

Coleman, S., & Ross, K. (2010). *The media and the public: "them" and "us" in media discourse*. Oxford, UK: Wiley-Blackwell. doi:10.1002/9781444318173

Computer Hope. (n.d.). *Who Invented the Internet?* Retrieved from http://www.computerhope.com/issues/ch001016.htm

Conner, J., & Slattery, A. (2014). New media and the power of youth organizing: Minding the gaps. *Equity & Excellence in Education*, *47*(1), 14–30. doi:10.1080/10665684.2014.866868

Conroy, M., Feezell, J. T., & Guerrero, M. (2012). Facebook and political engagement: A study of online political group membership and offline political engagement. *Computers in Human Behavior, 28*(5), 1535–1546. doi:10.1016/j.chb.2012.03.012

Constitution of the People's Republic of China. (1982). Retrieved from: http://www.hkhrm.org.hk/ english/law/const01.html

Cornfield, M. (2010). Game-changers: New technology and the 2008 presidential elections. In L. J. Sabato (Ed.), *The year of Obama* (pp. 205–230). New York: Longman.

Cornwell, M. L., & Campbell, L. M. (2012). Co-producing conservation and knowledge: Citizen-based sea turtle monitoring in North Carolina, USA. *Social Studies of Science, 42*(1), 101–120. doi:10.1177/0306312711430440

Corrales, J. (2019). *The Expansion of LGBT Rights in Latin America and the Backlash. In The Oxford Handbook of Global LGBT and Sexual Diversity Politics*. doi:10.1093/oxfordhb/9780190673741.013.14

Corthesy, J. (2012). *The Frayed Edges of Citizen Journalism: An Analysis of Al Jazeera's Relationship with Citizen Journalism*. Geneva: Webster University. Retrieved from www.webster.ch/sites/www.webster.ch/files/Cortesy.pdf

Cox, R., & Schwarze, S. (2015). The Media/communication strategies of environmental pressure groups and NGOs. In A. Hansen & R. Cox (Eds.), *The Routledge Handbook of Environment and Communication* (pp. 73–85). London: Routledge.

Coyer, K., Dowmunt, T., & Fountain, A. (2007). *The Alternative Media Handbook*. London: Routledge Taylor and Francis Group.

Craig, S. L., McInroy, L. B., McCready, L. T., Di Cesare, D. M., & Pettaway, L. D. (2014). Connecting without fear: Clinical implications of the consumption of information and communication technologies by sexual minority youth and young adults. *Clinical Social Work Journal, 43*(2), 159–168. doi:10.100710615-014-0505-2

Crall, A. W., Jarnevich, C. S., Young, N. E., Panke, B. J., Renz, M., & Stohlgren, T. J. (2015). Citizen science contributes to our knowledge of invasive plant species distributions. *Biological Invasions, 17*(8), 2415–2427. doi:10.100710530-015-0885-4

Crenshaw, K. (1995). Mapping the margins: Intersectionality, identity politics, and violence against women of color. In K. Crenshaw, N. Gotanda, G. Peller, & K. Thomas (Eds.), *Critical race theory: The key writings that formed the movement* (pp. 357–383). New York, NY: The New Press.

Crosbie, V. (2002). *What is social media?* New York: Oxford University Press.

Crouch, D. (2012, February 21). *Arab Media Make Most of Citizen Journalism.* Retrieved from http://www.ft.com/cms/s/0/6e224b6a-5bb2-11e1-a447-00144feabdc0.html#axzz2az4ozSTE

Cummings, S., & van Zee, A. (2005). Communities of practice and networks: Reviewing two perspectives on social learning. *Knowledge Management for Development, 1*(1), 8–22.

Cunha, E. S., Allegretti, G., & Matias, M. (2011). Participatory Budgeting and the Use of Information and Communication Technologies: A Virtuous Cycle? *Revista Critica de Ciencias Sociais*, 3.

Dahlgren, P. (2001). The public sphere and the net: Structure, space, and communication. *Mediated politics: Communication in the future of democracy*, 33-55.

Dahlgren, P. (2005). *Television and the public Sphere: Citizenship, democracy and the media*. London: Sage.

Dahlgren, P. (2005). The Internet, Public Spheres, and Political Communication: Dispersion and Deliberation. *Political Communication, 22*(2), 147–162. doi:10.1080/10584600590933160

Dahl, R. A. (1961). *Who Governs? Democracy and Power in an American City*. New Haven, CT: Yale University Press.

Dalrymple, K., & Scheufele, D. (2007). Finally informing the electorate? How the Internet got people thinking about presidential politics in 2004. *The Harvard International Journal of Press/Politics, 12*(3), 96–111. doi:10.1177/1081180X07302881

Danielsen, F., Burgess, N. D., & Balmford, A. (2005). Monitoring Matters: Examining the Potential of Locally-based Approaches. *Biodiversity and Conservation, 14*(11), 2507–2542. doi:10.100710531-005-8375-0

Danielsen, F., Enghoff, M., Magnussen, E., Mustonen, T., Degteva, A., Hansen, K. K., & Slettemark, Ø. (2017). Citizen Science Tools for Engaging Local Stakeholders and Promoting Local and Traditional Knowledge in Landscape Stewardship. In C. Bieling & T. Plieninger (Eds.), *The Science and Practice of Landscape Stewardship* (pp. 80–98). Cambridge, UK: Cambridge University Press. doi:10.1017/9781316499016.009

Data Center of China Internet. (2012). *2012 bluebook of China microblog*. Author.

Davidson, J., Wien, S., & Anderson, K. (2010). Creating a Provincial Family Council to Engage Youth and Families in Child & Youth Mental Health Systems. *Journal of the Canadian Academy of Child and Adolescent Psychiatry, 19*(3), 169–175. PMID:20842271

Davis, A. (2007). *The Mediation of Power: A Critical Introduction*. London: Routledge. doi:10.4324/9780203945827

Davis, R. (2009). *Typing politics*. New York: Oxford University Press.

De Cindio, F., Gentile, O., Grew, P., & Redolfi, D. (2003). Community Networks: Rules of Behavior and Social Structure Special Issue: ICTs and Community Networking. *The Information Society, 19*(5), 395–406. doi:10.1080/714044686

De Groen, Maselli, & Fabo. (2016). *The Digital Market for Local Services: A one-night stand for workers? An example from the on-demand economy*. Academic Press.

De Groen, W. P., Kilhoffer, Z., & Lenaerts, K. (2018). Digital Age - Employment and working conditions of selected types of platform work: National context analysis Germany. *Eurofound*. Retrieved from https://www.ceps.eu/publications/digital-age-employment-and-working-conditions-selected-types-platform-work-national

de Haana, M., Leanderb, K., Ünlüsoya, A., & Prinsenc, F. (2014). Challenging ideals of connected learning: The networked configurations for learning of migrant youth in the Netherlands. *Learning, Media and Technology, 39*(4), 507–535. doi:10.1080/17439884.2014.964256

Dearden, A., & Rizvi, S. M. H. (2015). ICT4D and Participatory Design. In R. Mansell & P. H. Ang (Eds.), *The International Encyclopedia of Digital Communication and Society*. John Wiley & Sons; doi:10.1002/9781118767771.wbiedcs131.

Dedman, T. (2011). Agency in UK Hip-Hop and Grime Youth Subcultures—Peripherals and Purists. *Journal of Youth Studies, 14*(5), 507–522. doi:10.1080/13676261.2010.549820

Delgado, M. (2002). *New frontiers for youth development in the twenty-first century: Revitalizing and broadening youth development*. New York, NY: Columbia University Press.

Deloitte. (2015). *The sharing economy: Share and make money. How does Switzerland compare?* Author.

Demicheli, V., Rivetti, A., Debalini, M. G., & Di Pietrantonj, C. (2012). Vaccines for measles, mumps and rubella in children. In The Cochrane Collaboration (Ed.), *Cochrane Database of Systematic Reviews*. Chichester, UK: John Wiley & Sons, Ltd. Retrieved December 21, 2015, from http://doi.wiley. com/10.1002/14651858.CD004407.pub3

Deuze, M., Bruns, A., & Neuberger, C. (2007, September 19). Preparing for an Age of Participatory News. *Journalism Practice, 1*(3), 322–338. doi:10.1080/17512780701504864

Diakopoulos, N., & Zubiaga, A. (2014). Newsworthiness and Network Gatekeeping on Twitter: The Role of Social Deviance. *International Conference on Weblogs and Social Media.*

Dias, M. R. (2002). *Sob o signo da vontade popular: o orçamento participativo e o dilema da Câmara Municipal de Porto Alegre.* Rio de Janeiro: IUPERJ.

Dias, N. (2018). *Hope for Democracy - 30 Years of Participatory Budgeting Worldwide.* Faro, Cuba: Oficina/Epopeia.

Dickinson, J. L., Crain, R. L., Reeve, H. K., & Schuldt, J. P. (2013). Can evolutionary design of social networks make it easier to be "green"? *Trends in Ecology & Evolution, 28*(9), 561–569. doi:10.1016/j.tree.2013.05.011 PMID:23787089

DiMaggio, P., Hargittai, F., Neuman, W. R., & Robinson, J. P. (2001). Social implications of the Internet. *Annual Review of Sociology, 27*(1), 307–336. doi:10.1146/annurev.soc.27.1.307

Dimitrova, D. V., Shehata, A., Stromback, J., & Nord, L. W. (2014). The effects of digital media on political knowledge and participation in election campaigns: Evidence from panel data. *Communication Research, 41*(1), 95–118. doi:10.1177/0093650211426004

Dimitrova, D., Mok, D., & Wellman, B. (2015). Changing Ties in a Far-Flung, Multidisciplinary Research Network The Case of GRAND. *The American Behavioral Scientist, 59*(5), 599–616. doi:10.1177/0002764214556803

Dormitzer, J. (2018). What is ActivityPub, and how will it change the internet? Retrieved from https://jeremydormitzer.com/blog/what-is-activitypub-and-how-will-it-change-the-internet/

Downey, J., & Fenton, N. (2003). New media, counter publicity and the public sphere. *New Media & Society, 5*(2), 185–202. doi:10.1177/1461444803005002003

Downing, J. D. H., & Brooten, L. (2009). ICTs and political movements. In The Oxford handbook of information and communication technologies (pp. 537-544). Oxford University Press. doi:10.1093/oxfordhb/9780199548798.003.0023

Drahokoupil, J., & Fabo, B. (2017). *Outsourcing, offshoring and the deconstruction of employment: New and old challenges in the digital economy.* Retrieved from https://papers.ssrn.com/sol3/papers.cfm?abstract_id=2975363

Dreier, T. (2012, August-September). Al-Jazeera Enables Citizen Journalism With Online Video. *Streaming Media Magazine.* Retrieved from http://www.streamingmedia.com/Articles/Editorial/Featured-Articles/Al-Jazeera-Enables-Citizen-Journalism-With-Online-Video-84268.aspx

Drew, D., & Weaver, D. (2006). Voter learning in the 2004 presidential election: Did the media matter? *Journalism & Mass Communication Quarterly, 83*(1), 25–42. doi:10.1177/107769900608300103

Druckman, J. N. (2005). Media matter: How newspapers and television news cover campaignsand influence voters. *Political Communication, 22*(4), 463–481. doi:10.1080/10584600500311394

Dubé, E., Gagnon, D., & MacDonald, N. E. (2015). Strategiesintendedtoaddressvaccinehesitancy: Review of published reviews. *Vaccine, 33*(34), 4191–4203. doi:10.1016/j.vaccine.2015.04.041 PMID:25896385

Duffy, M., Thorson, E., & Jahng, M. (2010, June 22). *Comparing Legacy News Sites with Citizen News and Blog Sites: Where is the Best Journalism?* Paper presented at the Annual Meeting of the International Communication Association, Suntec Singapore International Convention and Exhibition Centre, Suntec City, Singapore.

Durbach, N. (2004). *Bodily matters: the anti-vaccination movement in England, 1853–1907.* Durham, NC: Duke University Press; doi:10.1215/9780822386506

Dutil, P. A., Howard, C., Langford, J., & Roy, J. (2008). Rethinking government-public relationships in a digital world: Customers, clients, or citizens? *Journal of Information Technology & Politics, 4*(1), 77–90. doi:10.1300/J516v04n01_06

Dynel, M. (2014). Isn't it ironic? Defining of the scope of humorous irony. *Humor: International Journal of Humor Research, 27*(4), 619–639. doi:10.1515/humor-2014-0096

Edmonds, R., Guskin, E., Rosenstiel, T., & Mitchell, A. (2012). Newspapers: Building digital revenues proves painfully slow. *The State of the News Media 2012*. Retrieved on January 1, 2015, from http://www.stateofthemedia.org/2012/newspapers-building-digital-revenues-proves-painfully-slow/

Educause Learning Initiative. (2007, November). *7 Things You Should Know About Citizen Journalism.* Retrieved from http://net.educause.edu/ir/library/pdf/ELI7031.pdf

Eisenstein, M. (2014). Public health: An injection of trust. *Nature, 507*(7490), S17–S19. doi:10.1038/507S17a PMID:24611174

Elbroch, M., Mwampamba, T. H., Santos, M. J., Zylberberg, M., Liebenberg, L., Minye, J., ... Reddy, E. (2011). The Value, Limitations, and Challenges of Employing Local Experts in Conservation Research. *Conservation Biology, 25*(6), 1195–1202. doi:10.1111/j.1523-1739.2011.01740.x PMID:21966985

Ellis, R., & Waterton, C. (2004). Environmental citizenship in the making: The participation of volunteer naturalists in UK biological recording and biodiversity policy. *Science & Public Policy, 31*(2), 95–105. doi:10.3152/147154304781780055

Ellul, J. (1980). *The Technological System* (J. Neugroschel, Trans.). New York, NY: The Continuum Publishing Corporation.

Eltantawy, N., & Wiest, J. B. (2011). Social media in the Egyptian Revolution: Reconsidering resource mobilization theory. *International Journal of Communication, 5*, 1207–1224.

Enjolras, B., Steen-Johnsen, K., & Wollebæk, D. (2012). Social media and mobilization to offline demonstrations: Transcending participatory divides? *New Media & Society, 15*(6), 890–908. doi:10.1177/1461444812462844

Ersing, R. L. (2009). Building the Capacity of Youths through Community Cultural Arts: A Positive Youth Development Perspective. *Best Practices in Mental Health, 5*(1), 26–43.

Esarey, A., & Xiao, Q. (2008). Below the Radar: Political Expression in the Chinese Blogosphere. *Asian Survey, 48*(5), 752–772. doi:10.1525/AS.2008.48.5.752

Esarey, A., & Xiao, X. (2011). Digital communication and political communication in China. *International Journal of Communication, 5*, 298–319.

Eskola, J., Duclos, P., Schuster, M., & MacDonald, N. E. (2015). How to deal with vaccine hesitancy? *Vaccine, 33*(34), 4215–4217. doi:10.1016/j.vaccine.2015.04.043 PMID:25896378

Eveland, W. P., Cortese, E., Park, H., & Dunwoody, S. (2004). How Web site organization influences free recall, factual knowledge, and knowledge structure density. *Human Communication Research, 30*(2), 208–233. doi:10.1111/j.1468-2958.2004.tb00731.x

Eveland, W. P. Jr, & Dunwoody, S. (2000). Examining information processing on the World Wide Web using think aloud protocols. *Media Psychology, 2*(3), 219–244. doi:10.1207/S1532785XMEP0203_2

Eveland, W. P. Jr, & Dunwoody, S. (2001). User control and structural isomorphism or disorientation and cognitive load? Learning from the Web versus print. *Communication Research, 28*(1), 48–78. doi:10.1177/009365001028001002

Eveland, W. P. Jr, & Dunwoody, S. (2002). An investigation of elaboration and selective scanning as mediators of learning from the Web versus print. *Journal of Broadcasting & Electronic Media, 46*(1), 34–53. doi:10.120715506878jobem4601_3

Eveland, W. P. Jr, Marton, K., & Seo, M. (2004). Moving beyond "just the facts": The influence of online news on the content and structure of public affairs knowledge. *Communication Research, 31*(1), 82–108. doi:10.1177/0093650203260203

Eveland, W. P. Jr, & Scheufele, D. A. (2000). Connecting news media use with gaps in knowledge. *Political Communication, 17*(3), 215–237. doi:10.1080/105846000414250

Eveland, W. P. Jr, Seo, M., & Marton, K. (2002). Learning from the news in campaign 2000: An experimental comparison of TV news, newspapers, and online news. *Media Psychology, 4*(4), 355–380. doi:10.1207/S1532785XMEP0404_03

Eysenbach, G. (2008). Medicine 2.0: Social networking, collaboration, participation, apomediation, and openness. *Journal of Medical Internet Research, 10*(3), e22. doi:10.2196/jmir.1030 PMID:18725354

Fairclough, N. (1993). Critical discourse analysis and the marketization of public discourse: The uni- versities. *Discourse & Society, 4*(2), 133–168. doi:10.1177/0957926593004002002

Fairclough, N. (1995). *Critical discourse analysis: The critical study of language*. London: Longman.

Falanga, R. (2018). *Como aumentar a escala dos orçamentos participativos? O Orçamento Participativo Portugal (OPP) e o Orçamento Participativo Jovem Portugal (OPJP)*. ICS-Policy Brief.

Falk, J. H., Storksdieck, M., & Dierking, L. D. (2007). Investigating public science interest and understanding: Evidence for the importance of free-choice learning. *Public Understanding of Science (Bristol, England), 16*(4), 455–469. doi:10.1177/0963662506064240

Farrar, C., Fishkin, J. S., Green, D. P., List, C., Luskin, R. C., & Paluck, E. L. (2010). Disaggregating deliberation's effects: An experiment within a deliberative poll. *British Journal of Political Science, 40*(02), 333–347. doi:10.1017/S0007123409990433

Farrar, C., Green, D. P., Green, J. E., Nickerson, D. W., & Shewfelt, S. (2009). Does discussion group composition affect policy preferences? Results from three randomized experiments. *Political Psychology, 30*(4), 615–647. doi:10.1111/j.1467-9221.2009.00717.x

Fedozzi, L. (2000). *O poder da aldeia: gênese e história do orçamento participativo de Porto Alegre*. Porto Alegre: Tomo Editorial.

Fedozzi, L. (2007). *Observando o Orçamento Participativo de Porto Alegre. Análise histórica de dados: perfil social e associativo, avaliação e expectativas*. Porto Alegre: Tomo Editorial/Prefeitura de Porto Alegre/OBSERVAPOA.

Feenberg, A. (2002). *Transforming Technology: A Critical Theory Revisited* (2nd ed.). Oxford: Oxford University Press.

Fernandes, J., Giurcanu, M., Bowers, K. W., & Neely, J. C. (2010). The writing on the wall: A content analysis of college students' Facebook groups for the 2008 presidential election. *Mass Communication & Society, 13*(5), 653–675. do i:10.1080/15205436.2010.516865

Ferreira, D. E. S. (2010). *Inclusão, Participação, Associativismo e Qualidade da Deliberação Pública no Orçamento Participativo Digitalde Belo Horizonte*. Paper presented IV Congresso Latino Americano de Opinião Pública.

Fiebelkorn, A. P., Redd, S. B., Gallagher, K., Rota, P. A., Rota, J., Bellini, W., & Seward, J. (2010). Measles in the United States during the post elimination era. *The Journal of Infectious Diseases, 202*(10), 1520–1528. doi:10.1086/656914 PMID:20929352

Fiedler, T. (2009). Crisis Alert: Barack Obama Meets a Citizen Journalist. In S. Allan & E. Thorson (Eds.), *Citizen Journalism: Global Perspectives* (p. 211). New York: Peter Lang Publishing.

Finkel, S. (1995). *Causal analysis with panel data*. Thousand Oaks, CA: Sage. doi:10.4135/9781412983594

Fishkin, J. S., & Luskin, R. C. (2005). Experimenting with a democratic ideal: Deliberative polling and public opinion. *Acta Politica, 40*(3), 284–298. doi:10.1057/palgrave.ap.5500121

Flew, T. (2007). *A Citizen Journalism Primer.* Presented to Communications Policy Research Forum, University of Technology, Sydney, Australia. Retrieved from http://eprints.qut.edu.au/10232/1/10232.pdf

Flew, T. (2008). *Social media: An Introduction.* New York: Oxford University Press.

Flinn, J., & Frew, M. (2014). Glastonbury: Managing the mystification of Festivity. *Leisure Studies, 33*(4), 418–433. do i:10.1080/02614367.2012.751121

FloraQuebeca. (2015). Devenir membre ou renouveler votre adhésion. *FloraQuebeca.* Retrieved June 16, 2015, from http://www.floraquebeca.qc.ca/a-propos/devenir-membre/

Floridia, A. (2012). La legge toscana sulla partecipazione: una difficile scommessa. In F. Bortolotti & C. Corsi (Eds.), *La Partecipazione politica e sociale tra crisi e innovazione: il caso della Toscana* (pp. 331–362). Roma: Ediesse.

Foot, K., & Schneider, S. M. (2006). *Web campaigning.* Cambridge, MA: MIT Press. doi:10.7551/mitpress/7186.001.0001

Fournier, P., van der Kolk, H., Kenneth Carty, R., Blais, A., & Rose, J. (2011). *When Citizens Decide: Lessons from the Citizen Assemblies on Electoral Reform.* Oxford, UK: Oxford University Press. doi:10.1093/acprof:oso/9780199567843.001.0001

Fox, R. (2006). *Helen's story: a routine vaccination ruined my daughter's life forever. This is the inspir- ing story of how I took on the government... and won.* London: John Blake Publishing.

Fraser, N. (1990). Rethinking the public sphere: A contribution to the critique of actually existing democ- racy. In *Habermas and the public sphere* (pp. 56–80). Cambridge, MA: MIT Press. doi:10.2307/466240

Frenken, K. (2015). *Smarter regulation for the sharing economy.* Retrieved from https://www.theguardian.com/science/political-science/2015/may/20/smarter-regulation-for-the-sharing-economy

Friedman, D., & McAdam, D. (1992). Collective identity and activism. Networks, choices and the life of a social movement. In A. D. Morris & C. M. Mueller (Eds.), *Frontiers in social movement theory* (pp. 156–172). New Haven, CT: Yale University Press.

Fuller, J. (1996). *News Values: Ideas for an Information Age.* University of Chicago Press.

Fung, A., & Warren, M. (2011). The Participedia project: An introduction. *International Public Management Journal, 14*(3), 341–362. doi:10.1080/10967494.2011.618309

Fung, T. K. F., Vraga, E., & Thorson, K. (2011). When bloggers attack: Examining the effect of negative citizen-initiated campaigning in the 2008 presidential election. In J. A. Hendricks & L. L. Kaid (Eds.), *Techno politics in presidential campaigning* (pp. 83–101). New York: Routledge.

Gainous, J., & Wagner, K. M. (2013). *Tweeting to power: The social media revolution in American politics.* New York: Oxford University Press. doi:10.1093/acprof:oso/9780199965076.001.0001

Galata, L., Karantininis, K., & Hess, S. (2014). Cross-Atlantic Differences in Biotechnology and GMOs: A Media Content Analysis. In *Agricultural Cooperative Management and Policy* (pp. 299–314). doi:10.1007/978-3-319-06635-6_16

Gamson, W. A. (1990). *The strategy of social protest.* Belmont, CA: Wadsworth.

Ganesh, T. K. (2006). *Digital Media: Building the Global Audience.* Delhi: GNOSIS Publishers of Educational Books.

Gangarosa, E. J., Galazka, A. M., Wolfe, C. R., Phillips, L. M., Miller, E., Chen, R. T., & Gangarosa, R. E. (1998). Impact of anti-vaccine movements on pertussis control: The untold story. *Lancet, 351*(9099), 356–361. doi:10.1016/S0140-6736(97)04334-1 PMID:9652634

Gang, Q., & Bandurski, D. (2011). China's emerging public sphere. In S. Shirk (Ed.), *Changing media, changing China* (pp. 38–76). Oxford, UK: Oxford University Press.

Gans, H. (1979). *Deciding What's News*. New York, NY: Pantheon Books.

Ganuza, E., & Frances, F. (2012). *El círculo virtuoso de la democracia: los presupuestos participativos a debate*. Madrid: Colección Monografías CIS.

Garcia, A., Mirra, N., Morrell, E., Martinez, A., & Scorza, D. (2015). The Council of Youth Research: Critical literacy and civic agency in the digital age. *Reading & Writing Quarterly*, *31*(2), 151–167. doi:10.1080/10573569.2014.962203

Garnets, L. D. (2002). Sexual orientations in perspective. *Cultural Diversity & Ethnic Minority Psychology*, *8*(2), 115–129. doi:10.1037/1099-9809.8.2.115 PMID:11987589

Garnham, N. (1993). The mass media, cultural identity, and the public sphere in the modern world. *Public Culture*, *5*(2), 251–265. doi:10.1215/08992363-5-2-251

Garrett, R. K. (2006). Protest in an information society: A review of literature on social movements and new ICTs. *Information Communication and Society*, *9*(2), 202–224. doi:10.1080/13691180600630773

Gastil, J., Richards, R. Jr, Ryan, M., & Smith, G. (2017). Testing assumptions in deliberative democratic design: A preliminary assessment of the efficacy of the Participedia data archive as an analytic tool. *Journal of Public Deliberation*, *13*(2), 1. Available at https://www.publicdeliberation.net/jpd/vol13/iss2/art1

Gehl, R. (2018). Alternative Social Media: From Critique to Code. In SAGE Handbook of Social Media (pp. 330–350). SAGE. doi:10.4135/9781473984066.n19

Gehl, R. W. (2015, July). The Case for Alternative Social Media. Social Media + Society, 1-12. doi:10.1177/2056305115604338

George, E. (2005, November 30). *Guest Writer Liz George of Baristanet Reviews Backfence.com Seven Months After Launch*. Pressthink. Retrieved from http://archive.pressthink.org/2005/11/30/lz_bcfc.html

Gerber, A. S., & Green, D. P. (2000). The effect of canvassing, direct mail, and telephone contact on turnout: A field experiment. *The American Political Science Review*, *94*, 653–663. doi:10.2307/2585837

Gerlitz, C., & Rieder, B. (2013). Mining one percent of Twitter: Collections, baselines, sampling. *M/C Journal*, *16*(2). Retrieved from http://journal.media-culture.org.au/index.php/mcjournal/article/view/620

Gharabaghi, K., & Anderson-Nathe, B. (2012). In Search of New Ideas. *Child and Youth Services*, *33*(1), 1–4. doi:10.1080/0145935X.2012.665317

Gibson, R., Römmele, A., & Williamson, A. (2014). Chasing the Digital Wave: International Perspectives on the Growth of Online Campaigning. *Journal of Information Technology & Politics*, *11*(2), 123–129. doi:10.1080/19331681.2014.903064

Gillmor, D. (2006). We the Media: Grassroots Journalism by the People, For the People. Beijing: O'Reilly.

Gillmor, D. (2008, July 14). *Where Did "Citizen Journalist" Come From?* Retrieved from http://citmedia.org/blog/2008/07/14/where-did-citizen-journalist-come-from/

Gillmor, D. (2004). *We the Media: Grassroots Journalism by the People, for the People*. Sebastopol, CA: O'Reilly Media. doi:10.1145/1012807.1012808

Ginwright, S., & James, T. (2002). From assets to agents of change: Social justice, organizing, and youth development. *New Directions for Youth Development*, *96*(96), 27–46. doi:10.1002/yd.25 PMID:12630272

Gitlin, T. (2004). Jurgen Habermas: The sage of reason. *Time Magazine*. Retrieved from http://content. time.com/time/magazine/article/0,9171,994032,00.html

Gitlin, T. (1980). *The Whole World Is Watching: Mass Media in the Making & Unmaking of the New Left*. Berkeley, CA: University of California Press.

Gitlin, T. (1980). *The whole world is watching: Mass media in the making & unmaking of the new left*. University of California Press.

Gladwell, M. (2010). *Small Change: Why the revolution will not be tweeted*. Retrieved June 20, 2014, from http://www.newyorker.com/reporting/2010/10/04/101004fa_fact_gladwell?currentPage=all

Glaser, M. (2006, September 27). *Digging Deeper: Your Guide to Citizen Journalism*. Retrieved from http://www.pbs.org/mediashift/2006/09/your-guide-to-citizen-journalism270.html

Glaser, B., & Strauss, A. (1967). *The discovery of grounded theory: Strategies of qualitative research*. Chicago, IL: Aldine.

Global Journalist. (2012, July 26). *Citizen and Professional Journalists Killed While Covering Conflicts in Syria*. Retrieved from http://www.globaljournalist.org/freepresswatch/2012/07/syria/citizen-and-professional-journalists-killed-while-covering-conflicts-in-syria/

Glover, R. W. (2012). Games without frontiers? Democratic engagement, agonistic pluralism and the question of exclusion. *Philosophy and Social Criticism*, *38*(1), 81–104. doi:10.1177/0191453711421605

Goh, R. (2007, April 20). *Mainstream Media Meets Citizen Journalism: In Search of a New Model* (CMS Senior Thesis). Retrieved from http://www.mediagiraffe.org/tufts-thesis/tufts-thesis.pdf

Goldfrank, B. (2012). The world bank and the globalization of participatory budgeting. *Journal of Public Deliberation*, *8*(2).

Goldfrank, B., & Schneider, A. (2006). Competitive Institution Building: The PT and Participatory Budgeting in Rio Grande do Sul. *Latin American Politics and Society*, *48*(3), 1–31. doi:10.1111/j.1548-2456.2006.tb00354.x

Goode, L. (2012). News as conversation citizens as gatekeepers : Where is digital news taking us? *Ethical Space: The International Journal of Communication Ethics*, *9*(1), 32–40.

Gordon, E., & Walter, S. (2016). *Meaningful Inefficiencies: Resisting the Logic of Technological Efficiency in the Design of Civic Systems*. MIT Press.

Gorski, D. (2015, May 21). *The measles vaccine protects against more than just the measles*. Retrieved August 14, 2015, from https://www.sciencebasedmedicine.org/the-measles-vaccine-protects-against- more-than-just-the-measles/

Gow, G., Jayathilake, C., Hambly Odame, H., Dissanayeke, U., McMahon, R., Jayasinghe-Mudalige, U. K., & Waidyanatha, N. (2018). An Introduction to Technology Stewardship for Agricultural Communities of Practice: Course Workbook (2nd ed.). doi:10.7939/R3QV3CK28

Gow, G. (2018). Introducing a Technology Stewardship Model to Encourage ICT Adoption in Agricultural Communities of Practice: Reflections on a Canada/Sri Lanka Partnership Project. In R. Duncombe (Ed.), *Digital Technologies for Agricultural and Rural Development in the Global South* (pp. 43–53). Boston: CABI; doi:10.1079/9781786393364.0043.

Gow, G., Chowdhury, A., Ganpat, W., & Ramjattan, J. (2018). Enhancing ICT adoption and use through change leadership approach: Technology Stewardship Training for Caribbean Agricultural Communities of Practice. *Journal of Learning for Development*, *5*(3).

Graham, M. (2004). Networks of Influence: Internet Activism in Australia and Beyond. In G. Goggin (Ed.), *Virtual Nation: The Internet in Australia* (pp. 76–83). Sydney: University of New South Wales Press.

Graham, M., & Anwar, M. A. (2019). The global gig economy: Towards a planetary labour market? *First Monday*, *24*(4). doi:10.5210/fm.v24i4.9913

Grant, G. (1974). *English-Speaking Justice*. Toronto: Anansi.

Grant, L., Hausman, B. L., Cashion, M., Lucchesi, N., Patel, K., & Roberts, J. (2015). Vaccination per- suasion online: A qualitative study of two provaccine and two vaccine-skeptical websites. *Journal of Medical Internet Research*, *17*(5), e133. doi:10.2196/jmir.4153 PMID:26024907

Gray, J. M. (1999). Postmodern medicine. *Lancet*, *354*(9189), 1550–1553. doi:10.1016/S0140-6736(98)08482-7 PMID:10551517

Groshek, J. (2014). *Twitter Collection and Analysis Toolkit (TCAT) at Boston University*. Retrieved July 14, 2015 from http://www.bu.edu/com/bu-tcat/

Groshek, J. (2015). *Geolocation in Gephi with Twitter Data Tutorial*. Retrieved July 21, 2015 from http://www.jgroshek.org/blog/2015/5/5/geolocation-in-gephi-with-twitter-data-tutorial

Groshek, J., & Tandoc, E. T. (2016). *The Affordance Effect: Gatekeeping and (Non)reciprocal Journalism on Twitter*. Paper presented at the Social Media and Society Conference, London, UK.

Groshek, J., & Al-Rawi, A. (2015). Anti-Austerity in the Euro crisis: Modeling Protest Movements through Online-Mobile-Social Media Use and Content. *International Journal of Communication*, *9*, 3280–3303.

Groshek, J., & Dimitrova, D. (2011). A Cross-section of voter learning, campaign interest and intention to vote in the 2008 American election: Did Web 2.0 matter? *Studies in Communications*, *9*, 355–375.

Groshek, J., & Han, Y. (2011). Negotiated Hegemony and Reconstructed Boundaries in Alternative Media Coverage of Globalization. *International Journal of Communication*, *5*, 1523–1544.

Gross, D. (2012, March 12). *Tweeting Osama's Death: The Accidental Citizen Journalist.* Retrieved from http://edition.cnn.com/2012/03/10/tech/social-media/twitter-osama-death/

Grossardt, T., Bailey, K., & Brum, J. (2003). Structured public involvement: Problems and prospects for improvement. *Transportation Research Record: Journal of the Transportation Research Board*, (1858): 95–102.

Grubisich, T. (2005, October 5). Grassroots Journalism: Actual Content Vs. Shining Ideal. *Online Journalism Review*. Retrieved from http://www.ojr.org/p051006/

Guardian. (2015, May 24). *Tens of thousands march worldwide against Monsanto and GM crops*. Retrieved July 24, 2015 from http://www.theguardian.com/environment/2015/may/24/tens-of-thousands-march-worldwide-against-monsanto-and-gm-crops

Gunter, A. (2010). *Growing Up Bad.* London, UK: Tufnell Press.

Gunter, B. (2000). *Media research methods: Measuring audiences, reactions and impact*. London: Sage; doi:10.4135/9780857028983

Gupta, J., Bouvier, J., & Gordon, E. (2012). *Exploring New Modalities of Public Engagement. An Evaluation of Digital Gaming Platforms on Civic Capacity and Collective Action in the Boston Public School District*. Engagement Lab Evaluation White Paper.

Gurstein, M. (2005). Sustainability of Community ICTs and its Future. *Journal of Community Informatics*, *1*(2), 2–3.

Habermas, J. (1984). *The Theory of Communicative Action – Reason and the Rationalisation of Society* (Vol. I; T. McCarthy, Trans.). Boston, MA: Beacon Press.

Habermas, J. (1989). *The structural transformation of the public sphere: An inquiry into a category of bourgeois society* (T. Burger, Trans.). Cambridge, MA: The MIT Press. (Original work published 1962)

Hallin, D. C., & Mancini, P. (2004). *Comparing Media Systems: Three Models of Media and Politics*. Cambridge, UK: Cambridge University Press. doi:10.1017/CBO9780511790867

Halverson, E. R. (2010). Film as Identity Exploration: A Multimodal Analysis of Youth-Produced Films. *Teachers College Record, 112*(9), 2352–2378.

Hamdy, N., & Gomaa, E. (2012). Framing the Egyptian uprising in Arabic language newspapers and social media. *Journal of Communication, 62*(2), 195–211. doi:10.1111/j.1460-2466.2012.01637.x

Hampton, K., & Wellman, B. (2002). The not so global village of Netville. In B. Wellman & C. Haythornthwaite (Eds.), *The Internet in everyday life* (pp. 345–371). Oxford, UK: Blackwell. doi:10.1002/9780470774298.ch12

Hanson, C., West, J., Neiger, B., Thackeray, R., Barnes, M., & McIntyre, E. (2011). Use and acceptance of social media among health educators. *American Journal of Health Education, 42*(4), 197–204. doi:10.1080/19325037.2011.10599188

Happy 400th Birthday for Newspapers: Gutenberg Museum Says Birth Certificate of First Newspaper Dated 1605, And Not 1609. (2005, March 3). *The Times of India,* p. 13.

Hargreaves, I. (1999). The Ethical Boundaries of Reporting. In M. Ungersma (Ed.), *Reporters and the Reported* (p. 4). Cardiff, UK: Centre for Journalism Studies.

Haridakis, P., & Hanson, G. (2011). Campaign 2008: Comparing YouTube, social networking, and other media use among younger and older voters. In J. A. Hendricks & L. L. Kaid (Eds.), *Techno-politics in presidential campaigning* (pp. 61-82). New York: Routledge.

Harlow, S., & Salaverría, R. (2016). *Regenerating Journalism.* Digital Journalism. doi:10.1080/21670811.2015.1135752

Harmanci, R. (2008, October 5). Citizen Journalism Carries Unique Pitfalls. *San Francisco Chronicle.* Retrieved from http://www.sfgate.com/cgibin/article.cgi?f=/c/a/2008/10/05/MNIV13B9E4.DTL

Harp, D., Bachmann, I., & Guo, L. (2012). The whole online world is watching: Profiling social net- working sites and activists in China, Latin America, and the United States. *International Journal of Communication, 6*, 298–321.

Harper, J. (2008, March 17). *Journalism Troubled, Not Lost.* Retrieved from http://www.washingtontimes.com/news/2008/mar/17/journalism-troubled-not-lost-reportsuggests/print/

Hasebrink, U., & Hepp, A. (2017). How to research cross-media practices? Investigating media repertoires and media ensembles. *Convergence (London), 23*(4), 362–377. doi:10.1177/1354856517700384

Hassid, J. (2012). Safety valve or pressure cooker? Blogs in Chinese political life. *Journal of Communication, 62*(2), 212–230. doi:10.1111/j.1460-2466.2012.01634.x

Hausman, D. M., & Welch, B. (2010). Debate: To Nudge or Not to Nudge. *Journal of Political Philosophy, 18*(1), 123–136. doi:10.1111/j.1467-9760.2009.00351.x

Haywood, B. K. (2014). A “Sense of Place” in Public Participation in Scientific Research. *Science Education, 98*(1), 64–83. doi:10.1002ce.21087

Haywood, B. K., Parrish, J. K., & Dolliver, J. (2016). Place-based and data-rich citizen science as a precursor for conservation action. *Conservation Biology*, *30*(3), 476–486. doi:10.1111/cobi.12702 PMID:27110934

Heaton, L., Millerand, F., Dias da Silva, P., & Proulx, S. (Eds.). (2018). *La reconfiguration du travail scientifique en biodiversité: pratiques amateurs et technologies numériques*. Montréal: Presses de l'Université de Montréal.

Heaton, L., Millerand, F., Liu, X., & Crespel, É. (2016). Participatory Science: Encouraging public engagement in ONEM. *International Journal of Science Education. Part B*, *6*(1), 1–22. doi:10.1080/21548455.2014.942241

Heaton, L., Millerand, F., & Proulx, S. (2011). *The Role of Collaborative Tools in Making Coordination Sustainable : The Case of TelaBotanica*. Presented at the *International Communication Association Annual Conference*, Boston, MA.

Hefner, R. W. (1999). Civic Pluralism Denied? The New Media and *Jihadi* Violence in Indonesia. In D. F. Eickelman & J. W. Anderson (Eds.), *New Media in the Muslim World: The Emerging Public Sphere*. Bloomington, IN: Indiana University Press.

Hendricks, J., & Denton, R. Jr. (2010). *Communicator-in-Chief: How Barack Obama use new media technology to win the White House*. New York: Lexington Books.

Henig, R. M. (2000). *The Monk in the Garden: The Lost and Found Genius of Gregor Mendel, the Father of Genetics*. New York, NY: Houghton Mifflin.

Herrington, J., & Lee, K. (2014). The limits of global health diplomacy: Taiwan's observer status at the world health assembly. *Globalization and Health*, *10*(71). Retrieved from http://www.globalizationandhealth.com/content/pdf/s12992-12014-10071-y.pdf PMID:25270977

Hines, J. M., Hungerford, H. R., & Tomera, A. N. (1987). Analysis and synthesis of research on responsible environmental behavior: A meta-analysis. *The Journal of Environmental Education*, *18*(2), 1–8. doi:10.1080/00958964.1987.9943482

Hintz, A. (2012). Challenging the Digital Gatekeepers : International policy initiatives for free expression. *Journal of Information Policy*, *2*, 128–150. doi:10.5325/jinfopoli.2.2012.0128

Hioe, B. (2019, March 18). The Sunflower Movement, Five years on. *New Bloom*. Retrieved July 4, 2019 from https://newbloommag.net/2019/2003/2018/sunflower-movement-five-years/

History of Vaccines. (n.d.). *Vaccine Injury Compensation Programs*. Retrieved July 23, 2015 from http:// www.historyofvaccines.org/content/articles/vaccine-injury-compensation-programs

Hodkinson, P., & Lincoln, S. (2008). Online Journals as Virtual Bedrooms? Young People, Identity and Personal Space. *Young*, *16*(1), 27–46. doi:10.1177/110330880701600103

Hofstede, G., Hofstede, G. J., & Minkov, M. (2010). *Cultures and Organizations: Software of the Mind* (3rd ed.). New York: McGraw-Hill.

Holler, M. J. (2015). Paternalism, Gamification, or Art: An Introductory Note. *Homo Oeconomicus*, *32*(2), 275.

Holloway, J. (2018). What on earth is the fediverse and why does it matter? Retrieved from https://newatlas.com/what-is-the-fediverse/56385/

Holmsen, C. A., Palter, R. N., Simon, P. R. & Weberg, P. K. (1998). Retail Banking: Managing Competition among Your Own Channels. *The McKinsey Quarterly*, (1).

Horn, I. (2010). Teaching replays, teaching rehearsals, and re-visions of practice: Learning from colleagues in a mathematics teacher community. *Teachers College Record*, *112*(1), 225–259.

Hornig, M., Briese, T., Buie, T., Bauman, M. L., Lauwers, G., Siemetzki, U., & Lipkin, W. I. (2008). Lack of association between measles virus vaccine and autism with enteropathy: A case-control study. *PLoS One*, *3*(9), e3140. doi:10.1371/journal.pone.0003140 PMID:18769550

Horton, C. (2019, January 19). Faced with tough words from China, Taiwan rallies around its leader. *The New York Times*. Retrieved August 4, 2019 from https://www.nytimes.com/2019/2001/2019/world/asia/china-taiwan-president.html

Horton, G. (2013, September 13). *What Is Citizen Journalism and How Does It Influence News?* Retrieved from http://www.brandwatch.com/2013/09/what-is-citizen-journalism-and-how-does-it-influence-news/

House Committee on Agriculture. (2015, July 23). *House Passes H.R. 1599, the Safe and Accurate Food Labeling Act*. Retrieved July 24, 2015 from http://agriculture.house.gov/press-release/house-passes-hr-1599-safe-and-accurate-food-labeling-act

Howard, P. N., Duffy, A., Freelon, D., Hussain, M., Mari, W., & Mazaid, M. (2011). Opening Closed Regimes: What Was the Role of Social Media During the Arab Spring? *Project on Information Technology & Political Islam*. Retrieved from: http://pitpi.org/wp-content/uploads/2013/02/2011_Howard-Duffy-Freelon-Hussain-Mari-Mazaid_pITPI.pdf

Howard, P. N., & Parks, M. R. (2012). Social Media and Political Change: Capacity, Constraint, and Consequence. *Journal of Communication*, *62*(2), 359–362. doi:10.1111/j.1460-2466.2012.01626.x

Howe, J. (2006). The rise of crowdsourcing. *Wired*. Retrieved from https://www.wired.com/2006/06/crowds/

Hsieh, Y. P., & Li, M.-H. (2014). Online political participation, civic talk, and media multiplexity: How Taiwanese citizens express political opinions on the web. *Information Communication and Society*, *17*(1), 26–44. doi:10.1080/1369118X.2013.833278

Hsu, C.-M. (2015, April 1). *One year after the 318 student movement: New and old media*. Retrieved July 5, 2015 from http://www.Feja.Org.Tw/modules/news007/article.Php?Storyid=1675

Hsu, S. (2019, June 23). Protesters gather in Taipei, asking 'red media' to leave Taiwan. *Focus Taiwan*. Retrieved August 5, 2019 from http://focustaiwan.tw/news/acs/201906230011.aspx

Hughes, W. (2010). *Citizen Journalism: Historical Roots and Contemporary Challenges* (Honors College Capstone Experience/ Thesis Projects. Paper 305, Western Kentucky University, Kentucky, USA). Retrieved from http://digitalcommons.wku.edu/stu_hon_theses/305

Humphreys, M., Masters, W. A., & Sandbu, M. E. (2006). The role of leaders in democratic deliberations: Results from a field experiment in São Tomé and Príncipe. *World Politics*, *58*(04), 583–622. doi:10.1353/wp.2007.0008

Hungerford, H. R. (1996). The Development of Responsible Environmental Citizenship: A Critical Challenge. *Journal of Interpretation Research*, *1*(1), 25–37.

Hunter, W. (2009). *The Transformation of the Workers' Party in Brazil, 1989-2009*. Cambridge University Press.

Hynan, A., Murray, J., & Goldbart, J. (2014). 'Happy and excited': Perceptions of using digital technology and social media by young people who use augmentative and alternative communication. *Child Language Teaching and Therapy*, *30*(2), 175–186. doi:10.1177/0265659013519258

IFEX. (2013, February 6). *Gallery: The Arab Spring Uprisings through the Eyes of Citizen Journalists*. Retrieved from http://www.ifex.org/middle_east_north_africa/2013/02/06/gallery_arab_spring_citizen_journalists/

Iglesias, E., & Cormier, S. (2002). The transformation of girls to women: Finding voice and developing strategies for liberation. *Journal of Multicultural Counseling and Development*, *30*, 259–271. doi:10.1002/j.2161-1912.2002.tb00523.x

Internet Society. (2017). Internet Society Global Internet Report: Paths to Our Digital Future. Retrieved from https://future.internetsociety.org/2017/

Issemberg, S. (2012). *The Victory Lab: The Secret Science of Winning Campaigns*. New York: Crown Publishers.

Iwasaki, Y., MacKay, K., Mactavish, J., Ristock, J., & Bartlett, J. (2006). Voices from the margins: Stress, active living, and leisure as a contributor to coping with stress. *Leisure Sciences: An Interdisciplinary Journal*, *28*(2), 163–180. doi:10.1080/01490400500484065

Jankowski, N. W., & van Selm, M. (2000). The promise and practice of public debate. In K. L. Hacker & J. van Dijk (Eds.), *Digital democracy: Issues of theory and practice* (pp. 149–165). London: Sage. doi:10.4135/9781446218891.n9

Jansen, J., Van Den Bosch, F., & Volberda, H. (2006). Exploratory innovation, exploitative innovation, and performance: Effects of organizational antecedents and environmental moderators. *Management Science*, *52*(11), 1661–1674. doi:10.1287/mnsc.1060.0576

Jarvis, J. (2008, December 1). Mumbai Terror-digital Media. *Guardian*. Retrieved from http://www.guardian.co.uk/media/2008/dec/01/mumbai-terrordigital-media

Jefferson, T., Price, D., Demicheli, V., & Bianco, E. (2003). Unintended events following immunization with MMR: Asystematicreview. *Vaccine*, *21*(25–26), 3954–3960. doi:10.1016/S0264-410X(03)00271-8 PMID:12922131

Jenkins, J. C. (1983, August). Resource Mobilization Theory and the study of social movements. *Annual Review of Sociology*, *9*(1), 527–553. doi:10.1146/annurev.so.09.080183.002523

Jennings, R. (2014, August 11). In Taiwan, students protest reminders of repressive rule. Los Angles Time, p. 2.

Jennings, M. K., & Zeitner, B. (2003). Internet use and civic engagement: A longitudinal analysis. *Public Opinion Quarterly*, *67*(3), 311–334. doi:10.1086/376947

Jha, S. (2008). Why they wouldn't cite from sites: A study of journalists' perceptions of social movement web sites and the impact on their coverage of social protest. *Journalism*, *9*(6), 711–732. doi:10.1177/1464884908096242

Jiang, H. (2014). Thoughts on Standard Orientation of News Gatekeeper in the Context of Modern Media. *Proceedings from the 3rd International Conference on Science and Social Research*, 849–853. 10.2991/icssr-14.2014.186

John, P., Cotterill, S., Moseley, A., Moseley, A., Stoker, G., Wales, C., & Smith, G. (2011). *Nudge, Nudge, Think, Think: Experimenting with Ways to Change Civic Behaviour*. London: Bloomsbury Academic. doi:10.5040/9781849662284

Johnson, T. J., Briama, M. A., & Sothirajah, J. (1999). Doing the traditional media sidestep: Comparing the effects of the Internet and other nontraditional media with traditional media in the 1996 presidential campaign. *Journalism & Mass Communication Quarterly*, *76*(1), 99–123. doi:10.1177/107769909907600108

Johnson, T. J., & Kaye, B. K. (2004). Wag the blog: How reliance on traditional media and the Internet influence perceptions of credibility of weblogs among blog users. *Journalism & Mass Communication Quarterly*, *81*(3), 622–642. doi:10.1177/107769900408100310

Jones, S. G. (1997). The Internet and its social landscape. In S. G. Jones (Eds.), Virtual Culture: Identity and Communication in Cybersociety (pp. 7-35). Thousand Oaks, CA: Sage.

Jung, Y., & Lyytinen, K. (2014). Towards an ecological account of media choice: A case study on pluralistic reasoning while choosing email. *Information Systems Journal*, *24*(3), 271–293. doi:10.1111/isj.12024

Jurgens, D., Finnethy, T., McCorriston, J., Xu, Y. T., & Ruths, D. (2015). Geolocation Prediction in Twitter Using Social Networks: A Critical Analysis and Review of Current Practice. *Association for the Advancement of Artificial Intelligence.* Retrieved July 21, 2015 from http://cs.mcgill.ca/~jurgens/docs/jurgens-et-al_icwsm-2015.pdf

Jürgens, P., Jungherr, A., & Schoen, H. (2011). Small Worlds with a Difference : New Gatekeepers and the Filtering of Political Information on Twitter. *Websci, 11*, 1–5. doi:10.1145/2527031.2527034

Kahn, R., & Kellner, D. M. (2005) Oppositional politics and the Internet: A critical /reconstructive approach. In M.G. Durham & D. M. Kellner (Eds.), Media and cultural studies. Revisited (2nd ed.; pp. 703-725). Malden, MA: Blackwell Publishing Ltd.

Kahne, J., Middaugh, E., Lee, N. J., & Feezell, J. T. (2012). Youth online activity and exposure to diverse perspectives. *New Media & Society, 14*(3), 492–512. doi:10.1177/1461444811420271

Kaid, L. L., McKinney, M. S., & Tedesco, J. C. (2007). Political information efficacy and young voters. *The American Behavioral Scientist, 50*, 1093–1111. doi:10.1177/0002764207300040

Kakar, S. (1996). Leprosy in British India, 1860–1940: Colonial politics and missionary medicine. *Medical History, 40*(02), 215–230. doi:10.1017/S0025727300061019 PMID:8936062

Kalathil, S., & Boas, T. C. (2003). *Open Networks, Closed Regimes.* Carnegie Endowment for International Peace.

Kalsnes, B. (2016). The Social Media Paradox Explained: Comparing Political Parties' Facebook Strategy Versus Practice. *Social Media and Society, 2*(2), 1–11. doi:10.1177/2056305116644616

Kan, S. A., & Morrison, W. M. (2011, August 4). *U.S.-Taiwan relationship: Overview of policy issues.* Congressional Research Service. Retrieved July 2, 2015 from https://www.fas.org/sgp/crs/row/R41952.pdf

Kapin, A., & Ward, A. S. (2013). *Social Change Anytime Everywhere: How to Implement Online Multichannel Strategies to Spark Advocacy, Raise Money, and Engage Your Community.* San Francisco: John Wiley and Sons.

Karpf, D. (2012). *The MoveOn Effect: The Unexpected Transformation of American Political Advocacy.* New York, NY: Oxford University Press. doi:10.1093/acprof:oso/9780199898367.001.0001

Karpowitz, C. F., Mendelberg, T., & Shaker, L. (2012). Gender inequality in deliberative participation. *The American Political Science Review, 106*(03), 533–547. doi:10.1017/S0003055412000329

Kata, A. (2010). A postmodern Pandora's box: Anti-vaccination misinformation on the Internet. *Vaccine, 28*(7), 1709–1716. doi:10.1016/j.vaccine.2009.12.022 PMID:20045099

Katiraee, L. (2015, January 26). 10 studies proving GMOs are harmful? Not if science matters. *Genetic Literacy Project.* Retrieved July 25, 2015 from http://www.geneticliteracyproject.org/2015/01/26/10-studies-proving-gmos-are-harmful-not-if-science-matters/

Katz, S. L., King, K., Varughese, P., Serres, G. D., Tipples, G., & Waters, J. (2004). Measles elimination in Canada. *The Journal of Infectious Diseases, 189*(s1), S236–S242. doi:10.1086/378499 PMID:15106117

Kaufhold, K., Valenzuela, S., & Gil de Zuniga, H. (2010). Citizen journalism and democracy: How user-generated news use relates to political knowledge. *Journalism & Mass Communication Quarterly, 87*(3-4), 515–529. doi:10.1177/107769901008700305

Kawalec & Menz. (2013). Die Verflüssigung von Arbeit | Crowdsourcing als unternehmerische Reorganisationsstrategie – das Beispiel IBM. *Arbeits- und Industriesoziologische Studien, 6*(2), 5–23.

Keck, Z. (2014, April 17). China Responds to Taiwan's Sunflower Movement. *The Diplomat*. Retrieved August 5, 2019 from https://thediplomat.com/2014/2004/china-responds-to-taiwans-sunflower-movement/

Kedzie, C. R. (1997). *Communication and democracy: Coincident revolutions and the emergent dictator's dilemma.* Retrieved on Feb 10, 2016 from http://www.rand.org/pubs/rgs_dissertations/RGSD127.html

Keipi, T., & Oksanen, A. (2014). Self-exploration, anonymity and risks in the online setting: Analysis of narratives by 14–18-year olds. *Journal of Youth Studies*, *17*(8), 1097–1113. doi:10.1080/13676261.2014.881988

Keller, B., Labrique, A., Jain, K. M., Pekosz, A., & Levine, O. (2014). Mind the Gap: Social media en- gagement by public health researchers. *Journal of Medical Internet Research*, *16*(1), 8–15. doi:10.2196/jmir.2982 PMID:24425670

Kellett, T. (2008, March 5). *The Origins of Citizen Journalism.* Retrieved from http://www.helium.com/items/909409-the-origins-of-citizen-journalism

Kellner, D. (2000). Habermas, the public sphere, and democracy: A critical intervention. *Perspectives on Habermas*, 259-288.

Kelly, J. (2009). *Red Kayaks and Hidden Gold: The Rise, Challenges and Value of Citizen Journalism.* Reuters Institute for the Study of Journalism Challenges, University of Oxford. Retrieved from https://reutersinstitute.politics.ox.ac.uk/fileadmin/documents/Publications/Red_Kayaks___Hidden_Gold.pdf

Kennelly, J. (2011). *Citizen youth: Culture, activism, and agency in a neoliberal era.* London, UK: Palgrave Macmillan. doi:10.1057/9780230119611

Kenski, K., & Stroud, N. J. (2006). Connections between Internet use and political efficacy, knowledge, and political participation. *Journal of Broadcasting & Electronic Media*, *50*(2), 173–192. doi:10.120715506878jobem5002_1

Kent, M., & Taylor, M. (1998). Building dialogic relationship through the World Wide Web. *Public Relations Review*, *24*(3), 321–334. doi:10.1016/S0363-8111(99)80143-X

Kent, M., & Taylor, M. (2002). Toward a dialogic theory of public relations. *Public Relations Review*, *28*(1), 21–37. doi:10.1016/S0363-8111(02)00108-X

Khamis, S., & Vaughan, K. (2011). Cyberactivism in the Egyptian revolution. *Arab Media & Society*, *13*, 1–37.

Khisty, C. (1996). Education and training of transportation engineers and planners vis-a-vis public involvement. *Transportation Research Record: Journal of the Transportation Research Board*, *1552*(1), 171–176. doi:10.1177/0361198196155200123

Kilhoffer, Lenaerts, & Beblavý. (2017). *The Platform Economy and Industrial Relations: Applying the old framework to the new reality.* CEPS Research Report 2017/12.

Kilhoffer, Z., Baiocco, S., Beblavý, M., & Cirule, E. (2019). Final Report - The impact of digitalisation on labour market inclusion of people with disabilities. *Bundesministerium für Arbeit, Soziales, Gesundheit und Konsumentenschutz (BMASGK)*. Retrieved from https://www.sozialministerium.at/cms/site/attachments/2/3/1/CH3839/CMS1563200794559/endbericht-en.pdf

King, G., Pan, J., & Robert, M. (2012). How censorship in china allows government criticism but silences collective expression. *The American Political Science Review*, *107*(2), 1–18.

Kiousis, S. (2000). Explicating Media Salience: A Factor Analysis of New York Times Issue Coverage During the 2000 U.S. Presidential Election. *Journal of Communication, 54*(1), 71-87, doi:10.1111/j.1460-2466.2004.tb02614.x

Kleine, D. (2013). *Technologies of Choice? ICTs, Development, and the Capabilities Approach.* Cambridge, MA: MIT Press; doi:10.7551/mitpress/9061.001.0001.

Kluknavska, A. (2014). A Right-wing Extremist or People's Protector?? Media Coverage of Extreme Right Leader Marian Kotleba in 2013 Regional Elections in Slovakia. *Intersections, 1*(1), 147–165. doi:10.17356/ieejsp.vlil.35

Knight, A. (2012, April 26). *The Limits of Citizen Journalism.* Retrieved from http://alanknight.wordpress.com/2012/04/26/the-limits-of-citizen-journalism/

Kohn, M. (2000). Language, power, and persuasion: Towards a critique of deliberative democracy. *Constellations (Oxford, England), 7*(3), 408–429. doi:10.1111/1467-8675.00197

Kosmala, M., Wiggins, A., Swanson, A., & Simmons, B. (2016). Assessing data quality in citizen science. *Frontiers in Ecology and the Environment, 14*(10), 551–560. doi:10.1002/fee.1436

Kotter, J. P. (2007, January). Leading Change: Why Transformation Efforts Fail. *Harvard Business Review*, 96–103.

Kovach, B., & Rosensteil, T. (2001). *The Elements of Journalism: What Newspeople Should Know and The Public Should Expect.* New York: Three Rivers Press.

Kraus, R. C. (1991). *Brushes with power: Modern politics and the Chinese art of calligraphy.* Berkeley, CA: University of California Press.

Kraut, R., Egido, C., & Galegher, J. (1988). Patterns of contact and communication in scientific research collaboration. In *Proceedings of the 1988 ACM conference on Computer-supported cooperative work* (pp. 1–12). New York: ACM. 10.1145/62266.62267

Kreisi, H. (2004). Political context and opportunity. In The Blackwell Companion to Social Movements (pp. 68-90). Blackwell. doi:10.1002/9780470999103.ch4

Kreiss, D. (2012). *Taking our country back: The crafting of networked politics from Howard Dean to Barack Obama.* New York, NY: Oxford University Press. doi:10.1093/acprof:oso/9780199782536.001.0001

Kuo, L. (2019, May 17). Taiwan becomes first in Asia to legalise same-sex marriage. *The Guardian.* Retrieved July 4, 2019 from https://www.theguardian.com/world/2019/may/2017/taiwan-becomes-first-asian-county-to-legalise-same-sex-marriage

Kushin, M. J., & Yamamoto, M. (2010). Did social media really matter? College students' use of online media and political decision making in the 2008 election. *Mass Communication & Society, 13*(5), 608–630. doi:10.1080/15205436.2010.516863

Kwon, K. H., Oh, O., Agrawal, M., & Rao, H. R. (2012). Audience Gatekeeping in the Twitter Service: An investigation of tweets about the 2009 Gaza Conflict. *Transactions on Human-Computer Interaction, 4*(4), 212–229. doi:10.17705/1thci.00047

Lacy, S., Duffy, M., Riffe, D., Thorson, E., & Fleming, K. (2010, Spring). Citizen Journalism Web Sites Complement Newspapers. *Newspaper Research Journal, 31*(2), 34–46. doi:10.1177/073953291003100204

Laidlaw, E. B. (2015). *Regulating Speech in Cyberspace: Gatekeepers, Human Rights and Corporate Responsibility.* Cambridge, UK: Cambridge University Press. doi:10.1017/CBO9781107278721

Lambert, J., Mullen, N., Paull, C., Paulos, E., Soundararajan, T., Spagat, A., & … . (2007). *Digital storytelling cookbook and travelling companion.* Digital Diner Press.

Lam, W. S. E. (2014). Literacy and capital in immigrant youths' online networks across countries. *Learning, Media and Technology, 39*(4), 488–506. doi:10.1080/17439884.2014.942665

Landemore, H. (2013). *Democratic Reason: Politics, Collective Intelligence, and the Rule of the Many*. Princeton, NJ: Princeton University Press.

Lang, K., Lang, G.E. (2009). Mass Society, Mass Culture, and Mass Communication: The Meaning of Mass. *International Journal of Communication, 3*, 998-1024.

Langelier, S. (2011). Que reste-t-il de l'expérience pionnière de Porto Alegre? Le Monde Diplomatique.

Langelier, S. (2015). *Le démantèlement du Budget Participatif de Porto Alegre? Démocratie participative et communauté politique*. l'Harmattan.

Larson, H. J., Eckersberg, E., Smith, D., & Patterson, P. (2014). Understanding vaccine hesitancy around vaccines and vaccination from a global perspective: A systematic review of global literature, 2007-2012. *Vaccine, 32*(19), 2150–2159. doi:10.1016/j.vaccine.2014.01.081 PMID:24598724

Lawrence, E., Sides, J., & Farrell, H. (2010). Self-segregation or deliberation? Blog readership, participation, and polarization in American politics. *PS: Persepctives on Politics, 8*(1), 141–157.

Leander, K., & de Haan, M. (2014). Editorial. *Learning, Media and Technology, 39*(4), 405–408. doi:10.1080/17439884.2014.964257

Lee, D. (2014, October 30). The role of social media in Occupy protests, on the ground and around the world. *South Morning China Post.* Retrieved July 5, 2015 from http://www.scmp.com/news/hong-kong/article/1628305/role-social-media-occupy-protests-ground-and-around-world

Lee, B., Lancendorfer, K., & Lee, J. (2005). Agenda-setting and the Internet: The intermedia influence of Internet bulletin boards on newspaper coverage of the 2000 general election in South Korea. *Asian Journal of Communication, 15*(1), 57–71. doi:10.1080/0129298042000329793

Lee, N. J., Shah, D. V., & McLeod, J. M. (2013). Processes of political socialization: A communication mediation approach to youth civic engagement. *Communication Research, 40*(5), 669–697. doi:10.1177/0093650212436712

Lee, N., & VanDyke, M. (2016). Set it and forget it: The one way communication of social me- dia by government agencies communicating science. *Science Communication, 37*(4), 533–541. doi:10.1177/1075547015588600

Leibold, J. (2012). Blogging alone: China, the Internet, and the democratic illusion? *The Journal of Asian Studies, 70*(4), 1023–1041. doi:10.1017/S0021911811001550

Lerner, J. (2014). *Making Democracy Fun: How Game Design Can Empower Citizens and Transform Politics*. Cambridge, MA: MIT Press. doi:10.7551/mitpress/9785.001.0001

Levine, S. (1997, December 8). Hong Kong's return to China. *Encyclopædia Britannica*. Retrieved July 29, 2019 from https://www.britannica.com/topic/reversion-to-Chinese-sovereignty-1020544

Lewicka, M. (2011). Place attachment: How far have we come in the last 40 years? *Journal of Environmental Psychology, 31*(3), 207–230. doi:10.1016/j.jenvp.2010.10.001

Lewis, S. C., Holton, A. E., & Coddington, M. (2013). Reciprocal journalism: A concept of mutual exchange between journalists and audiences. *Journalism Practice, 8*(2), 229–241. doi:10.1080/17512786.2013.859840

Li, X. (2014, March 24). Students store office of Taiwan premier: About 200 lay siege to the executive yuan building; riot police sent to scene. *The Straits Times*. Retrieved July 11, 2015 from http://www.straitstimes.com/asia

Li, H. (2011). Parody and resistance on the Chinese Internet. In D. Herold & P. W. Marolt (Eds.), *Online society in China: Creating, celebrating, and instrumentalising the online carnival* (pp. 71–88). New York: Routledge.

Lim, M. (2014). Seeing spatially: people, networks and movements in digital and urban spaces. *IDPR*, *36*(1).

Lim, M. (2012). Clicks, cabs, and coffee houses: Social media and oppositional movements in Egypt, 2004-2011. *Journal of Communication*, *62*(2), 363–248. doi:10.1111/j.1460-2466.2012.01628.x

Lin, C.-Y. (2015, March 18). 9 in 1 election. 60% believe that Pan Blue was defeated by people's power. *NewTalk*. Retrieved July 5, 2015 from http://newtalk.tw/news/view/2015-2003-2018/57910

Lind, J. (2018, March/April). Life in China's Asia; What regional hegemony would look like. *Foreign Affairs*. Retrieved on August 4, 2019 from https://www.foreignaffairs.com/articles/china/2018-2002-2013/life-chinas-asia

Lind, C. (2008). Knowledge development with adolescents in a PAR process. *Educational Action Research*, *16*(2), 221–233. doi:10.1080/09650790802011874

Ling, R. (2010). *New tech, new ties: How mobile communication reshapes social cohesion*. Cambridge, MA: The MIT Press.

Liu., F. C.-s. (2014, September 24). Taiwan's Sunflower Movement and Generation Politics. *Asia Dialogue*. Retrieved July 4, 2019 from https://theasiadialogue.com/2014/2009/2024/taiwans-sunflower-movement-and-generation-politics/

Livingstone, S. (2005). On the relation between audience and publics. In S. Livingston (Ed.), *Audiences and publics: When cultural engagement matters for the public sphere* (pp. 17–41). Bristol: Intellect Books.

Livingstone, S. (2009). *Children and the Internet: Great Expectations, Challenging Realities*. Cambridge, UK: Polity Press.

Li, X., & Qin, X. (2001). Who is setting the Chinese agenda? The impact of BBS forums on the agenda of party press in prominent news events. *Journal of Communication*, *3*, 55–62.

Li, X., Qin, X., & Kluver, R. (2003). Who is setting the Chinese agenda? The impact of online chatrooms on Party press. In K. C. Ho, R. Klwer, & C. C. Yang (Eds.), *Asian.Com: Asian encounters the Internet* (pp. 143–158). London, UK: Routledge.

Löblich, M., & Wendelin, M. (2011). ICT policy activism on a national level: Ideas, resources and strategies of German civil society in governance processes. *New Media & Society*, *16*(4), 899–915.

Loiaza, R., & Jauregui, S. (2015). Evolución del Mercado de Telecomunicaciones Móviles en el Perú. Gerencia de Políticas Regulatorias y Competencia Subgerencia de Evaluación y Políticas de Competencia | OSIPTEL, Lima.

Lowden, N. B., Anderson, P. A., Dozier, D. M., & Lauzen, M. M. (1994). Media use in the primary election: A secondary medium model. *Communication Research*, *21*(3), 293–304. doi:10.1177/009365094021003003

Luo, Y. (2014). The Internet and Agenda-setting in China: The Influence of Online Public Opinion on Media Coverage and Government Policy. *International Journal of Communication*, *8*(204), 1289–1312.

Luschen, K., & Bogad, L. (2010). Youth, new media and education: An introduction. *Educational Studies: Journal of the American Educational Studies Association*, *46*(5), 450–456. doi:10.1080/00131946.2010.510402

Lynch, M. (2011). After Egypt: The limits and promise of online challenges to the authoritarian Arab state. *Perspectives on Politics*, *9*(2), 301–310. doi:10.1017/S1537592711000910

Lyotard, J. F. (1984). *The postmodern condition: A report on knowledge*. Minneapolis, MN: University of Minnesota Press.

Madhavan, E. S. (2016). Internet and Social Media's Social Movements Leading to New Forms of Governance and Policymaking: Cases from India. *Glocalism, 2016*(1). Retrieved August 5, 2019 from http://www.glocalismjournal.net/Issues/NETWORKS-AND-NEW-MEDIA/Articles/Internet-And-Social-MediaS-Social-Movements-Leading-To-New-Forms-Of-Governance-And-Policymaking-Cases-From-India.kl

Maher, V. (2005). *Citizen Journalism is Dead. New Media Lab.* School of Journalism and Media Studies, Rhodes University.

Malani, P. (2015). *Vaccination rates for us children remain generally high, but measles outbreaks under- score shortfalls in some regions.* Retrieved June 7, 2015, from http://newsatjama.jama.com/2013/09/16/vaccination-rates-for-us-children-remain-generally-high-but-measles-outbreaks-underscore-shortfalls-in-some-regions

Mannheim, K. (1971). *Ideology and Utopia. An Introduction to the Sociology of Knowledge.* New York: Harcourt Brace and World - Harvard Books.

Mansbridge, J. J., Bohman, J., Chambers, S., Christiano, T., Fung, A., Parkinson, J. R., ... Warren, M. (2012). A systemic approach to deliberative democracy. In J. R. Parkinson & J. J. Mansbridge (Eds.), *Deliberative systems: deliberative democracy at the large scale. Theories of Institutional Design.* Cambridge, UK: Cambridge University Press. doi:10.1017/CBO9781139178914.002

Mansuri, G., & Rao, R. (2013). *Localizing Development: Does Participation Work?* World Bank Policy Research Reports.

Mao, Y., & Adria, M. (2013). Deciding who will decide: Assessing random selection for participants in Edmonton's Citizen Panel on budget priorities. *Canadian Public Administration/Administration publique du Canada, 56*(4), 610-37.

Mariner, W. K., Annas, G. J., & Glantz, L. H. (2005). Jacobson v Massachusetts: It's not your great- great-grandfather's public health law. *American Journal of Public Health, 95*(4), 581–590. doi:10.2105/AJPH.2004.055160 PMID:15798113

Markman, K. D., Proulx, T., & Lindberg, M. J. (Eds.). (2013). *The psychology of meaning.* Washington, DC: American Psychological Association. doi:10.1037/14040-000

Markovitz, I. L. (1999). Constitutions, The Federalist Papers, and the Transition to Democracy. In L. Anderson (Ed.), *Transitions to Democracy.* New York: Columbia University Press. doi:10.7312/ande11590-005

Marks, L. A., Kalaitzandonakes, N., Allison, K., & Zakharova, L. (2003). Media Coverage of Agrobiotechnology: Did the Butterfly Have an Effect? *Journal of Agribusiness, 21*(1), 1–20.

Martins, V. (2015). O Sistema de participação popular e cidadã de Canoas. Redes. Reflexões (in)oportunas, (2), 52-57.

Maselli, Lenaerts, & Beblavý. (2016). *Five things we need to know about the on-demand economy.* CEPS Essay 21.

McChesney, R. (1999). *Rich Media, Poor Democracy: Communication Politics in Dubious Times.* Chicago, IL: University of Illinois Press.

McCombs, M., Einsiedel, E., & Weaver, D. (1991). *Contemporary public opinion.* Hillsdale, NJ: Erlbaum.

McCombs, M., & Shaw, D. (1976). Structuring the "unseen environment.". *Journal of Communication, 2*(2), 18–22. doi:10.1111/j.1460-2466.1976.tb01374.x

McCracken, B. J. (2011, May 11). *Are New Media Credible? A Multidimensional Approach to Measuring News Consumers' Credibility and Bias Perceptions and the Frequency of News Consumption* (Master's thesis). The Rochester Institute of Technology, Department of Communication, College of Liberal Arts. Rochester, NY. Retrieved from https://ritdml.rit.edu/bitstream/handle/1850/13729/BMcCrackenThesis5-11-2011.pdf?sequence=1

McKinley, D. C., Miller-Rushing, A. J., Ballard, H. L., Bonney, R., Brown, H., Cook-Patton, S. C., ... Ryan, S. F. (2017). Citizen science can improve conservation science, natural resource management, and environmental protection. *Biological Conservation, 208*, 15–28. doi:10.1016/j.biocon.2016.05.015

McLuhan, M., Fiore, Q., & Agel, J. (1967). *The medium is the massage*. New York: Bantam Books.

McSweeney, P. J. (2009). *Gephi Network Statistics*. Google Summer of Code 2009 Project Proposal. Retrieved July 15, 2015 from http://web.ecs.syr.edu/~pjmcswee/gephi.pdf

Medaglia, R. (2007). The challenged identity of a field: The state of the art of eParticipation research. *Information Polity, 12*(3), 169–181. doi:10.3233/IP-2007-0114

Mendoza, M. (2015). Gestión de las empresas periodísticas regionales: El Sol, de Cusco; El Tiempo, de Piura e ímpetu, de Ucayali. *Revista de Comunicación, 14*, 70–99.

Mensing, D. (2007, Spring). Online Revenue Business Model Has Changed Little Since 1996. *Newspaper Research Journal, 28*(2), 22–37. doi:10.1177/073953290702800202

Meraz, S. (2009). Is there an elite hold? Traditional media to social media agenda setting influence in blog networks. *Journal of Computer-Mediated Communication, 14*(3), 682–707. doi:10.1111/j.1083-6101.2009.01458.x

Meraz, S., & Papacharissi, Z. (2013). Networked gatekeeping and networked framing on #egypt. *The International Journal of Press/Politics, 18*(2), 138–166. doi:10.1177/1940161212474472

Meyer, E. P. (1995, September). *Public Journalism and the Problem of Objectivity.* Speech Given at Investigative Reporters and Editors Conference on Computer Assisted Reporting in Cleveland. Retrieved from http://www.unc.edu/~pmeyer/ire95pj.htm

Meyrowitz, J. (2005). The Rise of Glocality: New senses of place and identity in the global village. In N. Kristóf (Ed.), *A Sense of Place: The global and the local in mobile communication* (pp. 21–30). Vienna: Passagen Verlag.

Miller, A., & Kurpius, D. (2008, August 6). *A Citizen-Eye View of Television News Source Credibility.* Paper presented at the Annual Meeting of the Association for Education in Journalism and Mass Communication, Marriott Downtown, Chicago, IL.

Millward, S. (2015, March 11). *Weibo ends 2014 with slow but steady growth, now has 176 million monthly active users.* Retrieved from: https://www.techinasia.com/weibo-2014-176-million-monthly-active-users/

Milner, H. (2002). *Civic Literacy. How Informed Citizens Make Democracy Work.* Hanover: University Press of New England.

Miraftab, F. (2004). Invited and invented spaces of participation: Neoliberal citizenship and feminists' expanded notion of politics. *Wagadu, 1*, 1–7.

Mishra, K. D., & Krishnaswami, K. (2015, June). A New Genre of Journalism - Citizen Journalism. *International Journal of English Language, Literature and Humanities, 3*(4), 65. Retrieved from http://ijellh.com/papers/2015/June/06-52-67-June-2015.pdf

Mody, M., & Gomez, M. (2018). Airbnb and the Hotel Industry: The Past, Present, and Future of Sales, Marketing, Branding, and Revenue Management. *Boston Hospitality Review, 6*(3). Retrieved from https://www.bu.edu/bhr/2018/10/31/airbnb-and-the-hotel-industry-the-past-present-and-future-of-sales-marketing-branding-and-revenue-management/

Mohd, A. F. S., Kew, Y., & Moy, F. M. (2017). Vaccine hesitancy among parents in a multi-ethnic country, Malaysia. *Vaccine, 35*(22), 2955–2961. doi:10.1016/j.vaccine.2017.04.010 PMID:28434687

Mok, D., Wellman, B., & Carrasco, J. (2010). Does distance matter in the age of the Internet? *Urban Studies (Edinburgh, Scotland)*, *47*(13), 2747–2783. doi:10.1177/0042098010377363

Molaei, H. (2014). Discursive opportunity structure and the contribution of social media to the success of social movements in Indonesia. *Information Communication and Society*, *18*(1), 94–108. doi:10.1080/1369118X.2014.934388

Mondak, J. (1995). *Nothing to read*. Ann Arbor, MI: University of Michigan Press. doi:10.3998/mpub.10442

Morrell, M. E. (1999). Citizen's evaluations of participatory democratic procedures: Normative theory meets empirical science. *Political Research Quarterly*, *52*(2), 293–322.

Morris, J. X. (2018, July 18). Brian Hioe: The Sunflower Movement, 4 years later. *The Diplomat*. Retrieved August 5, 2019 from https://thediplomat.com/2018/2007/brian-hioe-the-sunflower-movement-2014-years-later/

Motta, R. (2015). Transnational Discursive Opportunities and Social Movement Risk Frames Opposing GMOs. *Social Movement Studies*, *14*(5), 576–595. doi:10.1080/14742837.2014.947253

Mou, Y., Atkin, D. J., Fu, H., Lin, C. A., & Lau, T. (2012). *The influence of social media on online po- litical discussion in China.* Paper presented at the annual meeting of the International Communication Association, Phoenix, AZ.

Mouffe, C. (1999). Deliberative democracy or agonistic pluralism? *Social Research*, *66*(3), 745–753.

Mouffe, C. (1999). Deliberative Democracy or Agonistic Pluralism? *Social Research*, *66*(3).

Mouffe, C. (2000). *The democratic paradox*. London: Verso.

Mouffe, C. (2005). *On the political*. London: Routledge.

Mou, Y., Atkin, D., & Fu, H. (2011). Predicting political discussion in a censored virtual environment. *Political Communication*, *28*(3), 341–356. doi:10.1080/10584609.2011.572466

Moy, P., & Pfau, M. (2000). *With malice toward all?* Westport, CT: Praeger.

Mutere, M., Nyamathi, A., Christiani, A., Sweat, J., Avila, G., & Hobaica, L. Jr. (2014). Homeless Youth Seeking Health and Life-Meaning Through Popular Culture and the Arts. *Child and Youth Services*, *35*(3), 273–287. doi:10.1080/0145935X.2014.950416

Myers, D. J. (1994, July 1). Communication technology and social movements: Contributions of computer networks to activism. *Social Science Computer Review*, *12*(2), 250–260. doi:10.1177/089443939401200209

Nandi, C. (2006). *Print Media and Photojournalism*. New Delhi: Media Offset Press.

Nascimento, S., Pereira, Â., & Ghezzi, A. (2014*). From Citizen Science to Do It Yourself Science. An annotated account of an on-going movement* (No. JRC93942). Luxembourg: Publications Office of the European Union. Retrieved April 7, 2015, from http://publications.jrc.ec.europa.eu/repository/handle/JRC93942

National Digital Stewardship Alliance. (2013, February 15). *Case Study: Citizen Journalism.* Retrieved from http://www.digitalpreservation.gov/ndsa/working_groups/documents/NDSA_CaseStudy_CitizenJournalism.pdf

National Health Service. (2013, November 21). *MMR vaccine does not cause autism - NHS Choices.* Retrieved August 11, 2015, from http://www.nhs.uk/news/2007/January08/Pages/MMRvaccinedoes-notcauseautism.aspx

Negroponte, N. (1995). *Being Digital*. London: Hodder and Stoughton.

Negt, O., & Kluge, A. (1993). *Public sphere and experience: Toward an analysis of the bourgeois and proletarian public sphere*. Minneapolis, MN: University of Minnesota Press.

Nel, F., Ward, M., & Rawlinson, A. (2007). Online Journalism. In P. J. Anderson & G. Ward (Eds.), *The Future of Journalism in the Advanced Democracies* (pp. 121–122). Aldershot, UK: Ashgate.

Neuman, W. R. (1981). Differentiation and integration: Two dimensions of political thinking. *American Journal of Sociology*, *86*(6), 1236–1268. doi:10.1086/227384

Neuman, W. R., Just, M. R., & Crigler, A. N. (1992). *Common knowledge*. Chicago: University of Chicago Press.

Newman, M. E. J. (2006). Modularity and community structure in networks. *Proceedings of the National Academy of Sciences of the United States of America*, *103*(23), 8577–8582. doi:10.1073/pnas.0601602103 PMID:16723398

Nitzsche, P., Pistoia, A., & Elsãber, M. (2012). *Development of an Evaluation Tool for Participative E-Government Services: A Case Study of Electronic Participatory Budgeting Projects in Germany*. Revista de Administratie si Management Public.

Norris, P. (2000). *A virtuous circle*. Cambridge, UK: Cambridge University Press; doi:10.7208/chicago/9780226161174.001.0001.

Norris, P. (2001). *Digital divide: civic engagement, information poverty, and the internet worldwide*. Cambridge, UK: Cambridge University Press. doi:10.1017/CBO9781139164887

O'Neill, M. (2017, June 17). 1.5 million Mainland migrants change Hong Kong. *ejinsights on the pulse*. Retrieved July 29, 2019 from http://www.ejinsight.com/20170619-20170611-20170615-million-mainland-migrants-change-hong-kong/

O'Reilly, T., & Battelle, J. (2009). *Web squared: Web 2.0 five years on*. Retrieved from http://blsciblogs. baruch.cuny.edu/art3057fall2010/files/2010/08/OReilly-Battelle-websquared-whitepaper.pdf

Ober, J. (1996). *The Athenian Revolution: Essays on Ancient Creek Democracy and Political Theory*. Princeton, NJ: Princeton University Press.

Offit, P. A. (2005). *The Cutter incident: how America's first polio vaccine led to the growing vaccine crisis*. New Haven, CT: Yale University Press.

Okuhara, T., Ishikawa, H., Okada, M., Kato, M., & Kiuchi, T. (2017). Readability comparison of pro- and anti-HPV vaccination online messages in Japan. *Patient Education and Counseling*, *100*(10), 1859–1866. doi:10.1016/j.pec.2017.04.013 PMID:28532860

Olubunmi, A. P. (2015). The ambiguous power of social media: Hegemony or resistance? *New Media and Mass Communication, 13*. Retrieved August 5, 2019 from https://www.iiste.org/Journals/index.php/NMMC/article/view/19213

Omer, S. B., Salmon, D. A., Orenstein, W. A., deHart, M. P., & Halsey, N. (2009). Vaccine refusal, mandatory immunization, and the risks of vaccine-preventable diseases. *The New England Journal of Medicine*, *360*(19), 1981–1988. doi:10.1056/NEJMsa0806477 PMID:19420367

ONEM. (2007, December 9). *Un livre sur Saga pedo, pourquoi, quand, comment?* Retrieved June 26, 2015, from http://www.onem-france.org/saga/wakka.php?wiki=LivreArgumentaire

Onwuegbuzie, A., Dickinson, W., Leech, N., & Zoran, A. (2009). A qualitative framework for collecting and analyzing data in focus group research. *International Journal of Qualitative Methods*, *8*(3), 1–21. doi:10.1177/160940690900800301

Osborne, H. (2016). Uber loses right to classify UK drivers as self-employed. *The Guardian*. Retrieved from https://www.theguardian.com/technology/2016/oct/28/uber-uk-tribunal-self-employed-status

Outing, S. (2005, January 6). *Taking Tsunami Coverage into Their Own Hands*. Retrieved from http://www.poynter.org/content/content_view.asp?id=76520

Overdevest, C., Orr, C. H., & Stepenuck, K. (2004). Volunteer stream monitoring and local participation in natural resource issues. *Human Ecology Review*, *11*(2), 177–185.

Palmer, J., & Allen-Ebrahimian, B. (2018, April 27). China threatens U.S. airlines over Taiwan References. *Foreign Policy*. Retrieved August 4, 2019 from https://foreignpolicy.com/2018/2004/2027/china-threatens-u-s-airlines-over-taiwan-references-united-american-flight-beijing/

Paltemaa, L., & Vuori, J. (2009). Regime transition and the Chinese politics of technology: From mass science to the controlled Internet. *Asian Journal of Political Science*, *17*(1), 1–23. doi:10.1080/02185370902767557

Pan, J. W. (2009). *Toward a New Framework for Peaceful Settlement of China's Territorial and Boundary Disputes*. Brill: Nijhoff.

Pan, Z. (2000). Improving reform activities: The changing reality of journalistic practice in China. In C. C. Lee (Ed.), *Power, money, and media: Communication patterns and bureaucratic control in cultural China* (pp. 68–111). Evanston, IL: Northwestern University Press.

Pan, Z. (2000). Improvising reform activities: The changing reality of journalistic practice in China. In C. C. Lee (Ed.), *Power, money, and media: Communication patterns and bureaucratic control in cultural China* (pp. 68–111). Evanston, IL: Northwestern University Press.

Pao, J. (2019, July 14). Anti-extradition Hong Kong protesters march in Shatin. *Asia Times*. Retrieved July 29, 2019 from https://www.asiatimes.com/2019/2007/article/anti-extradition-hong-kong-protesters-march-in-shatin/

Papacharissi, Z. (2002). The virtual space: The Internet as a public sphere. *New Media & Society*, *4*(1), 9–27. doi:10.1177/14614440222226244

Park, C. L. (2010). Making sense of the meaning literature: An integrative review of meaning making and its effects on adjustment to stressful life events. *Psychological Bulletin*, *136*(2), 257–301. doi:10.1037/a0018301 PMID:20192563

Parkinson, J. (2004). Why deliberate? The encounter between deliberation and new public man-agers. *Public Administration*, *82*(2), 377–395. doi:10.1111/j.0033-3298.2004.00399.x

Parmelee, J., & Bichard, S. (2012). *Politics and the Twitter revolution*. Lanham, MD: Lexington Books.

Parmet, W. E., Goodman, R. A., & Farber, A. (2005). Individual rights versus the public's health—100 years after Jacobson v. Massachusetts. *The New England Journal of Medicine*, *352*(7), 652–654. doi:10.1056/NEJMp048209 PMID:15716558

Pasek, J., More, E., & Romer, D. (2009). Realizing the social Internet? Online social networking meets offline social capital. *Journal of Information Technology & Politics*, *6*(3-4), 197–215. doi:10.1080/19331680902996403

Pathak-Shelat, M., & DeShano, C. (2014). Digital youth cultures in small town and rural Gujarat, India. *New Media & Society*, *16*(6), 983–1001. doi:10.1177/1461444813496611

Patterson, T. E. (1993). *Out of order*. New York: Knopf.

Patterson, T. E., & McClure, R. D. (1976). *The unseeing eye*. New York: Putnam.

Paul, H. (2011, March 2). *Why is Citizen Journalism Important?* Retrieved from http://sierrabear.com/home/index.php?option=com_content&task=view&id=133\

Paul. (2010, February 21). *CNN IBN Recognizes Muzaffar Bhat's Work with Citizen Journalist Award*. Retrieved from http://www.jkrtimovement.com/cnn-ibn-recognizes-muzaffar-bhats-work-with-citizen-journalist-award-20-feb-2010/

Pavlik, J. V. (1994). Citizen access, involvement, and freedom of expression in an electronic environment. In F. Williams & J. V. Pavlik (Eds.), *The People's Right to Know: Media, Democracy, and the Information Highway, (pp. 139-62).* Hillsdale, NJ: Erlbaum.

Pearce, E. K., & Kendzior, S. (2012). Networked authoritarianism and social media in Azerbaijan. *Journal of Communication, 62*(2), 283–289. doi:10.1111/j.1460-2466.2012.01633.x

Peleg, I. (2007). *Democratizing the Hegemonic State: Political Transformation in the Age of Identity*. Cambridge, UK: Cambridge University Press. doi:10.1017/CBO9780511611254

Penney, J., & Dadas, C. (2014). (re)tweeting in the service of protest: Digital composition and circulation in the occupy wall street movement. *New Media & Society, 6*(1), 74–90. doi:10.1177/1461444813479593

Pepe, C. (2007). Civic eulogy in the epitaphios of Pericles and the citywide prayer service of Rudolph Giuliani. *Advances in the History of Rhetoric, 10*(1), 131–144. doi:10.1080/15362426.2007.10557278

Peruzzotti, E., Magnelli, M., & Peixoto, T. (2011). *Multichannel Participatory Budgeting*. Available online at: http://www.vitalizing-democracy.org/site/downloads/277_265_Case_Study_La_Plata.pdf

Pesek, W. (2014, April 3). A Taiwan spring? *National Post,* p. FP9.

Peters, J. (2000). *Speaking into the air: A history of the idea of communication*. Chicago: University of Chicago Press.

Pettey, G. R. (1988). The interaction of the individual's social environment, attention and interest, and public affairs media use on political knowledge holding. *Communication Research, 15*(3), 265–281. doi:10.1177/009365088015003003

Pew Center for Civic Journalism. (2002, November 4). *Community Impact, Journalism Shifts Cited in New Civic Journalism Study*. Retrieved from http://www.pewcenter.org/doingcj/spotlight/index.php

Pew Research Center. (2012a). *How the presidential candidates use the web and social media*. Retrieved January 1, 2015, from http://www.journalism.org/files/legacy/DIRECT%20ACCESS%20FINAL.pdf

Pew Research Center. (2012b). *Cable leads the pack as campaign news source*. Retrieved June 1, 2015, from http://www.people-press.org/files/legacy- pdf/2012%20Communicating%20Release.pdf

Pew Research Center. (2014). *Millennials in adulthood: Detached from institutions, networked with friends*. Retrieved January 1, 2015, from http://www.pewsocialtrends.org/files/2014/03/2014-03-07_generations-report-version-for-web.pdf

Pew. (2015, July 14). *The Evolving Role of News on Twitter and Facebook*. Retrieved July 21, 2015 from http://www.journalism.org/2015/07/14/the-evolving-role-of-news-on-twitter-and-facebook/

Pickard, V. W. (2008). Cooptation and cooperation: Institutional exemplars of democratic Internet technology. *New Media & Society, 10*(4), 625–645. doi:10.1177/1461444808093734

Pitts, M., Kenski, K., Smith, S., & Pavlich, C. (2017). Focus group discussions as sites for public deliberation and sensemaking following shared political documentary viewing. *Journal of Public Deliberation, 13*(2), 6. Available at https://www.publicdeliberation.net/jpd/vol13/iss2/art6

Poell, T., Kloet, J. D., & Zeng, G. (2014). Will the real Weibo please stand up? Chinese online conten- tion and actor-network theory. *Chinese Journal of Communication, 7*(1), 1–18. doi:.2013.816753 doi:10.1080/17544750

Poell, T., & Dijck, J. v. (2015). Social Media and Activist Communication. In C. Atton (Ed.), *The Routledge Companion to Alternative and Community Media* (pp. 527–537). London: Routledge.

Poland, G. A., & Jacobson, R. M. (2001). Understanding those who do not understand: A brief review of the anti-vaccine movement. *Vaccine*, *19*(17), 2440–2445. doi:10.1016/S0264-410X(00)00469-2 PMID:11257375

Poland, G. A., & Jacobson, R. M. (2011). The age-old struggle against the antivaccinationists. *The New England Journal of Medicine*, *364*(2), 97–99. doi:10.1056/NEJMp1010594 PMID:21226573

Porter, D., & Porter, R. (1988). The politics of prevention: Anti-vaccinationism and public health in nineteenth-century England. *Medical History*, *32*(03), 231–252. doi:10.1017/S0025727300048225 PMID:3063903

Portus, L. M. (2008). How the urban poor acquire and give meaning to the mobile phone. In J. Katz (Ed.), *Handbook of mobile communication studies* (pp. 105–118). Cambridge, MA: MIT Press. doi:10.7551/mitpress/9780262113120.003.0009

Postmes, T., & Brunsting, S. (2002). Collective Action in the Age of the Internet: Mass Communication and Online Mobilization. *Social Science Computer Review*, *20*(3), 290–301. doi:10.1177/089443930202000306

Price, V., & Zaller, J. (1993). Who gets the news? Alternative measures of new reception and their implications for research. *Public Opinion Quarterly*, *57*(2), 133–164. doi:10.1086/269363

Prior, M. (2005). News vs. entertainment: How increasing media choice widens gaps in political knowledge and turnout. *American Journal of Political Science*, *49*(3), 577–592. doi:10.1111/j.1540-5907.2005.00143.x

Project for Excellence in Journalism. (2008). *The State of The News Media: An Annual Report on American Journalism.* Retrieved from http://stateofthemedia.org/2008/overview/major-trends/

Project for Excellence in Journalism. (2012). *Winning the media campaign 2012.* Retrieved January 1, 2015, from http://www.journalism.org/files/legacy/Winningthemediacampaign2012.pdf

Public Health Agency Canada. (2015). *Measles and Rubella Weekly Monitoring Report - Public Health Agency of Canada.* Retrieved July 29, 2015, from http://www.phac-aspc.gc.ca/mrwr-rhrr/index-eng.php

Qiu, L., & Chan, M. (Eds.). (2011). *New Media Events Research.* Beijing: Renmin University Press.

Quinn, S., & Lamble, S. (2008). *Online Newsgathering: Research and Reporting for Journalism.* Amsterdam: Focal Press. doi:10.1016/B978-0-240-80851-2.50006-0

Radsch, C. C. (2012, May). *Unveiling the Revolutionaries: Cyberactivism and the Role of Women in the Arab Uprisings.* James A. Baker III Institute for Public Policy, Rice University. Retrieved from http://bakerinstitute.org/media/files/news/130a8d9a/ITP-pub-CyberactivismAndWomen-051712.pdf

Radsch, C. C. (2013). *The Revolutions will be Blogged: Cyberactivism and the 4th Estate in Egypt* (Doctoral Dissertation). American University.

Raftery, I. (2012, May 30). *US Student Killed While Filming Violence in Syria.* Retrieved from http://worldnews.nbcnews.com/_news/2012/05/29/11943194-us-student-killed-while-filming-violence-in-syria

Ramkissoon, H., Weiler, B., & Smith, L. D. G. (2012). Place attachment and pro-environmental behaviour in national parks: The development of a conceptual framework. *Journal of Sustainable Tourism*, *20*(2), 257–276. doi:10.1080/09669582.2011.602194

Rauchfleisch, A., & Schafer, M. S. (2015). Multiple public spheres of Weibo: A typology of forms and potentials of online public spheres in China. *Information Communication and Society*, *18*(2), 139–155. doi:10.1080/1369118X.2014.940364

Razack, S. (1998). *Looking White people in the eye.* Toronto, Canada: University of Toronto Press.

Reese, S. D., & Danielian, L. H. (1989). Intermedia influence and the drug issue: converging on co- caine. In P. Shoemaker (Ed.), *Communication campaigns about drugs: Government, media and the public* (pp. 47–66). Hillside, NJ: Lawrence Erlbaum Associates.

Reinke, D., & Malarkey, D. (1996). Implementing integrated transportation planning in metropolitan planning organizations: Procedural and analytical issues. *Transportation Research Record: Journal of the Transportation Research Board, 1552*(1), 71–78. doi:10.1177/0361198196155200110

Repalust, A., Šević, S., Rihtar, S., & Štulhofer, A. (2016). Childhood vaccine refusal and hesitancy intentions in Croatia: Insights from a population-based study. *Psychology Health and Medicine, 0*(0), 1–11. doi:10.1080/13548506.2016.1263756 PMID:27899030

Reporters Without Borders. (2012a, May 18). *Citizen Journalist Sentenced to Death for Al-Jazeera Interview.* Retrieved from http://en.rsf.org/syria-citizen-journalist-sentenced-to-18-05-2012,42641.html

Reporters Without Borders. (2012b, July 12). *Targeted Murders of Citizen Journalists.* Retrieved from http://en.rsf.org/syria-number-of-citizen-journalists-01-06-2012,42715.html

Rettberg, J. L. (2008). *Blogging.* Cambridge, UK: Polity Press.

Rice, R. E. (1993). Media appropriateness: Using social presence theory to compare traditional and new organizational media. *Human Communication Research, 19*(4), 451–484. doi:10.1111/j.1468-2958.1993.tb00309.x

Riso, S. (2019). *Mapping the contours of the platform economy.* Eurofound Working Paper, Eurofound. Retrieved from https://www.eurofound.europa.eu/sites/default/files/wpef19060.pdf

Ristock, J. (2002). Responding to lesbian relationship violence: An ethical challenge. In L. Tutty & C. Goard (Eds.), *Reclaiming self: Issues and resources for women abused by intimate partners* (pp. 98–116). Halifax, Canada: Fernwood Press.

Roberts, M., Wanta, W., & Dzwo, T. (2002). Agenda-setting and issue salience online. *Communication Research, 29*(4), 452–465. doi:10.1177/0093650202029004004

Robinson, J. P., & Levy, M. K. (1986). *The main source.* Beverly Hills, CA: Sage.

Rogers, C. (1994). The necessary and sufficient conditions of therapeutic personality change. In R. Anderson, K. Cissna, & R. Arnett (Eds.), *The Reach of Dialogue: Confirmation, Voice, and Community* (pp. 126–140). Cresskill, NJ: Hampton Press.

Rosen, J. (2006, June 27). The People Formerly Known as the Audience. *PressThink.* Retrieved from http://archive.pressthink.org/2006/06/27/ppl_frmr.html

Rose, N. (2004). *Powers of Freedom: Reframing Political Thought.* Cambridge, UK: Cambridge University Press.

Ross, R., & Cormier, S. C. (2010). Handbook for Citizen Journalists. Denver, CO: National Association of Citizen Journalists (NACJ).

Ross, L. (2011). Sustaining Youth Participation in a Long-term Tobacco Control Initiative: Consideration of a Social Justice Perspective. *Youth & Society, 43*(2), 681–704. doi:10.1177/0044118X10366672

Rousseau, S. (2006). Women's Citizenship and Neopopulism: Peru Under the Fujimori Regime. *Latin American Politics and Society, 48*(1), 117–141. doi:10.1111/j.1548-2456.2006.tb00340.x

Rowe, G., & Frewer, L. (2005). A typology of public engagement mechanisms. *Science, Technology & Human Values, 30*(2), 251–290. doi:10.1177/0162243904271724

Rowley, J., Kupiec-Teahan, B., & Leeming, E. (2013). Customer community and co-creation: A case study. *Marketing Intelligence & Planning*, *25*(2), 136–146. doi:10.1108/02634500710737924

Rutigliano, L. W. (2008, August). *Covering the Unknown City: Citizen Journalism and Marginalized Communities* (Ph.D thesis). Faculty of the Graduate School, The University of Texas, Austin, TX. Retrieved from http://repositories.lib.utexas.edu/bitstream/handle/2152/17904/rutiglianol.pdf?sequence=2

Sackett, D. L., Rosenberg, W. M., Gray, J. A., Haynes, R. B., & Richardson, W. S. (1996). Evidence based medicine: What it is and what it isn't. *British Medical Journal*, *312*(7023), 71–72. doi:10.1136/bmj.312.7023.71 PMID:8555924

Saco, D. (2002). *Cybering democracy: public space and the Internet.* Minneapolis, MN: University of Minnesota Press.

Sacramento Daily Union. (1983, October 31). *An International Congress of Anti-vacinators.* Retrieved on March 23, 2015, from http://cdnc.ucr.edu/cgi-bin/cdnc?a=d&d=SDU18831031.2.16

Salama, V. (2012, October). Covering Syria. *The International Journal of Press/Politics*, *17*(4), 516–517. doi:10.1177/1940161212456774

Saletan, W. (2015, July 15). Unhealthy Fixation: The war against genetically modified organisms is full of fearmongering, errors, and fraud. Labeling them will not make you safer. *Slate.* Retrieved July 22, 2015 from http://www.slate.com/articles/health_and_science/science/2015/07/are_gmos_safe_yes_the_case_against_them_is_full_of_fraud_lies_and_errors.html

Salmon, D. A., Teret, S. P., MacIntyre, C. R., Salisbury, D., Burgess, M. A., & Halsey, N. A. (2006). Compulsoryvaccination and conscientious or philosophicalexemptions: Past, present, and future. *Lancet*, *367*(9508), 436–442. doi:10.1016/S0140-6736(06)68144-0 PMID:16458770

Salter, L. (2003). Democracy, new social movements, and the Internet. *Cyberactivism: Online activism in theory and practice*, 117-144.

Sambrook, R. (2005, Winter). Citizen Journalism and the BBC. *Nieman Reports*, *59*(4), 13-16. Retrieved from http://www.encoreleaders.org/wp-content/uploads/2013/06/Nieman-Reports-_-Citizen-Journalism-and-the-BBC.pdf

Sampaio, R. C., Maia, R. C. M., & Marques, F. P. J. A. (2010). Participação e deliberação na internet: Um estudo de caso do Orçamento Participativo Digital de Belo Horizonte. *Opinião Pública*, *16*(2), 446–477. doi:10.1590/S0104-62762010000200007

Sato, A. P. S. (2018). What is the importance of vaccine hesitancy in the drop of vaccination coverage in Brazil? *Revista de Saude Publica*, 52. PMID:30517523

Schattschneider, E. E. (1960). *The Semi-Sovereign People: A Realist's View of Democracy in America.* New York, NY: Holt, Rhinehart & Winston.

Schein, E. (1993). On dialogue, culture, and organizational learning. *Organizational Dynamics*, *22*.

Scheufele, D. A., & Nisbet, M. C. (2002). Being a citizen online: New opportunities and dead ends. *The Harvard International Journal of Press/Politics*, *7*(3), 55–75.

Schmidt, F. A. (2019). *Crowdsourced Production of AI Training Data: How Human Workers Teach Self-Driving Cars How to See.* Working Paper Forschungsförderung 155, Hans Böckler Stiftung. Retrieved from https://www.boeckler.de/pdf/p_fofoe_WP_155_2019.pdf

Schmidt, F.A. (2017). *Digital Labour Markets in the Platform Economy: Mapping the Political Challenges of Crowd Work and Gig Work.* Retrieved from

Schubert, G. (2017, July 19). Pension Reform Made in Taiwan. *Taiwan Insights*. Retrieved July 4, 2019 from https://taiwaninsight.org/2017/2007/2019/pension-reform-made-in-taiwan/?blogsub=confirming#blog_subscription-2015

Schwartz, S. E. O., Rhodes, J. E., Liang, B., Sánchez, B., Spencer, R., Kremer, S., & Kanchewa, S. (2014). Mentoring in the digital age: Social media use in adult–youth relationships. *Children and Youth Services Review*, *47*, 205–213. doi:10.1016/j.childyouth.2014.09.004

Science Communication Unit, University of West of England. (2013*). Science for Environment Policy In-depth Report: Environmental Citizen Science*. European Commission DG Environment. Retrieved June 16, 2016, from http: //ec.europa.eu/science-environment-policy

Scott, M. (2017). *Uber is a transportation company, Europe's highest court rules.* Retrieved from https://www.politico.eu/article/uber-ecj-ruling/

Shah, D. V., Kwak, N., & Holbert, R. L. (2001). Connecting" and "disconnecting" with civic life: Patterns of Internet use and the production of social capital. *Political Communication*, *18*, 141–162. doi:10.1080/105846001750322952

Shah, D., McLeod, D., & Yoon, S. (2001). Communication, context, and community: An exploration of print, broadcast, and Internet influences. *Communication Research*, *28*(4), 464–506. doi:10.1177/009365001028004005

Shifman, L. (2014). *Memes in Digital Culture*. Cambridge, MA: The MIT Press.

Shirky, C. (2011, January/February). The political power of social media: Technology, the public sphere, and political change. *Foreign Affairs*, 1–12.

Shoemaker, P. J., & Vos, T. P. (2009). *Gatekeeping Theory*. New York, NY: Taylor & Francis. doi:10.4324/9780203931653

Simon, D. (2005). *Wire Creator David Simon Testifies on the Future of Journalism.* Retrieved from http://www.reclaimthemedia.org/journalistic_practice/wire_creator_david_simon_testi0719

Simon, J. (2012). The Next Information Revolution: Abolishing Censorship. In *Committee to Protect Journalists. Attacks on the Press in 2011: A Worldwide Survey by the Committee to Protect Journalists* (p. 3). New York: United Book Press.

Simonovitz, B., Shvets, I., & Hannah, T. (2018). Discrimination in the sharing economy: Evidence from a Hungarian field experiment. *Corvinus Journal of Sociology and Social Policy*, *9*(1), 55–79. doi:10.14267/CJSSP.2018.1.03

Singh, A. A. (2013). Transgender Youth of Color and Resilience: Negotiating Oppression and Finding Support. *Sex Roles*, *68*(11-12), 690–702. doi:10.100711199-012-0149-z

Sintomer, Y. (2010). Saberes dos cidadãos e saber político. Revista Crítica de Ciências Sociais, 91, 135-153. doi:10.4000/rccs.4185

Sintomer, Y., & Blondiaux, L. (2002). L'impératif délibératif. *Revue des sciences sociales du politique*, *57*, 17-35.

Sintomer, Y., Herzberg, C., & Röcke, A. (2008). Participatory Budgeting in Europe: Potentials and Challenges. International Journal of Urban and Regional Research, 32(1).

Sintomer, Y., Herzberg, C., Röcke, A., & Allegretti, G. (2012). *Transnational Models of Citizen*. Academic Press.

Sintomer, Y., & Allegretti, G. (2016). *Os Orçamentos Participativos na Europa. Entre democracia participativa e modernização dos serviços públicos*. Coimbra: Almedina.

Sintomer, Y., Allegretti, G., Herzberg, C., & Röcke, A. (2013). *Learning from the South: Participatory Budgeting Worldwide –an Invitation to Global Cooperation*. Bonn: Service Agency for Communities.

Sjoberg, F. M., Mellon, J., & Peixoto, T. (2015). *The Effect of Government Responsiveness on Future Political Participation.* Available at https://www.mysociety.org/research/government-responsiveness-political-participation/

Skoric, M. M., & Poor, N. (2013). Youth Engagement in Singapore: The Interplay of Social and Traditional Media. *Journal of Broadcasting & Electronic Media, 57*(2), 187–204. doi:10.1080/08838151.2013.787076

Slevin, J. (2000). *The Internet and society*. Polity Press.

Sloam, J. (2014). 'The outraged young': Young Europeans, civic engagement and the new media in a time of crisis. *Information Communication and Society, 17*(2), 217–231. doi:10.1080/1369118X.2013.868019

Slovic, P. (1987). Perception of risk. *Science, 236*(4799), 280–285. doi:10.1126cience.3563507 PMID:3563507

S-MAP. (2019). Social Media Alternatives Project (S-MAP). Retrieved from https://www.socialmediaalternatives.org

Smith, A. (2011). *22% of online Americans used social networking or Twitter for politics in 2010 campaign.* Pew Research Center. Retrieved on June 1, 2015, from, http://www.pewinternet.org/files/old-media//Files/Reports/2011/PIP-Social-Media-and-2010-Election.pdf

Smith, A. (2013). *Civic engagement in the digital age*. Pew Research Center.

Smith, A., & Duggan, M. (2012). *Online political videos and campaign 2012*. Pew Research Center's Internet & American Life Project. Retrieved on January 1, 2015, from http://pewinternet.org/Reports/2012/Election-2012-Video.aspx

Smith, M. A., Rainie, L., Shneiderman, B., & Himelboim, I. (2014). *Mapping Twitter Topic Networks: From Polarized Crowds to Community Clusters*. Retrieved July 5, 2015 from http://www.pewinternet.org/2014/02/20/mapping-twitter-topic-networks-from-polarized-crowds-to-community-clusters/

Smith, N. (2017, August 21). Taiwan is suffering from a massive brain drain and the main beneficiary is China. *Time*. Retrieved August 4, 2019 from https://time.com/4906162/taiwan-brain-drain-youth-china-jobs-economy/

Smith, S. (2018, November 7). Who are France's 'Yellow Jacket' protesters and what do they want? *CNBC News*. Retrieved July 4, 2019 from https://www.nbcnews.com/news/world/who-are-france-s-yellow-jacket-protesters-what-do-they-n940016

Smith, G. (2009). *Democratic Innovations. Designing Institutions for Citizen Participation*. Cambridge, UK: Cambridge University Press. doi:10.1017/CBO9780511609848

Smith, G., & Ryan, M. (2014). Defining Mini-Publics: Making Senseof Existing Conceptions. In K. Grönlund, A. Bächtiger, & M. Setälä (Eds.), *Deliberative Mini-Publics: Involving Citizens in the Democratic Process*. Colchester, UK: ECPR Press.

Soriano, C. R. R. (2014, January). Constructing collectivity in diversity: Online political mobilization of a national LGBT political party. *Media Culture & Society, 36*(1), 20–36. doi:10.1177/0163443713507812

Sorice, M. (2019). *Partecipazione democratica*. Milano: Mondadori.

Soroka, S. N. (2012). The Gatekeeping Function: Distributions of Information in Media and the Real World. *The Journal of Politics, 74*(2), 514–528. doi:10.1017/S002238161100171X

Sotirovic, M., & McLeod, J. (2004). Knowledge as understanding: The information processing approach to political learning. In L. Kaid (Ed.), *Handbook of Political Communication Research* (pp. 357–394). Hillsdale, NJ: Lawrence Erlbaum Associates.

Spada, P. (2012). *Political Competition in Deliberative and Participatory Institutions* (Dissertation). Yale University.

Spada, P. (2014). *Political Competition and the Diffusion of Policy Innovations in Local Government: The Case of Participatory Budgeting in Brazil.* Paper presented at the annual Meeting of the Latin American Studies Association. Available online at: http://www.spadap.com/app/download/8877410668/The%20Diffusion%20of%20Democratic%20Innovations_2015.pdf?t=1434577381

Spada, P., Klein, M., Calabretta, R., Iandoli, L., & Quinto, I. (2015). *A First Step toward Scaling-up Deliberation: Optimizing Large Group E-Deliberation Using Argument Maps*. Paper presented at the annual conference of the American Political Science Association. Available online at: http://www.spadap.com/app/download/8877667268/scalingup_june2015.pdf?t=1434577381

Spada, P., & Vreeland, J. R. (2013). Who Moderates the Moderators? *Journal of Public Deliberation, 9*(2).

Spangler, J. (2014, March 27). Taiwan and the future of the Cross-Strait Services Trade Agreement. *The Diplomat*. Retrieved July 5, 2015 from http://thediplomat.com/2014/2003/taiwan-and-the-future-of-the-cross-strait-services-trade-agreement/

Stagliano, K. (2013). *Parents speak out on behalf of Jenny McCarthy*. Retrieved August 9, 2015, from http://www.ageofautism.com/2013/07/parents-speak-out-on-behalf-of-jenny-mccarthy.html

Steele, C., & Stein, A. (2002). Communications revolutions and international politics. In J. E. Allison (Ed.), *Technology, development, and democracy* (pp. 25–54). Albany, NY: State University of New York Press.

Steele, F. (1981). *The sense of place*. Boston: CBI Publishing.

Steenbergen, M. S., Bächtiger, A., Pedrini, S., & Gautschi, T. (2015). Information, Deliberation, and Direct Democracy. In Y. Peter Lang (Ed.), Deliberation and Democracy: Innovative Processes and Institutions (p. 187). Academic Press.

Stephan, H. R. (2014). *Cultural Politics and the Transatlantic Divide over GMOs*. London, UK: Palgrave Macmillan.

Stephens, M. (2012, May 24). *A New Site for Participatory Democracy?: Journalists' Perceptions of Online Comment Sections.* Paper presented at the Annual Meeting of the International Communication Association, Sheraton Phoenix Downtown, Phoenix, AZ.

Stewart, G. T. (1980). Benefits and risks of pertussis vaccine. *The New England Journal of Medicine, 303*(17), 1004. doi:10.1056/NEJM198010233031718 PMID:7412844

Stewart, G. T., & Wilson, J. (1981). Pertussis vaccine and serious acute neurological illness in children. *British Medical Journal (Clinical Research Ed.), 282*(6280), 1968–1969. doi:10.1136/bmj.282.6280.1968 PMID:6786689

Stone, M., Hobbs, M., & Khaleeli, M. (2002). Multichannel Customer Management: the Benefits and Challenges. *Journal of Database Marketing & Customer Strategy Management, 10*(1).

Stone, D. (2008). Global public policy, transnational policy communities, and their networks. *Policy Studies Journal: the Journal of the Policy Studies Organization, 36*(1), 19–38. doi:10.1111/j.1541-0072.2007.00251.x

Stortone, S., & De Cindio, F. (2015). Hybrid Participatory Budgeting: Local Democratic Practices in the Digital Era. In Citizen's Right to the Digital City (pp. 177-197). Springer Singapore.

Strauss, A., & Corbin, J. (1998). *Basics of qualitative research: Techniques and procedures for developing grounded theory*. Thousand Oaks, CA: Sage.

Stromer-Galley, J. (2013). *Presidential campaigning in the Internet age*. New York, NY: Oxford University Press.

Strom, J. (1960). Is universal vaccination against pertussis always justified? *British Medical Journal, 2*(5207), 1184–1186. doi:10.1136/bmj.2.5207.1184 PMID:20788967

Suleiman, A., Soleimanpour, S., & London, J. (2006). Youth action for health through youth-led research. *Journal of Community Practice*, *14*(1-2), 125–145. doi:10.1300/J125v14n01_08

Sunstein, C. R., & Thaler, R. (2008). Nudge. The politics of libertarian paternalism.

Svensson, E., Kiousis, S., & Stromback, J. (2014). Creating a win-win situation? Relationship cultivation and the use of social media in the 2012 campaigns. In J. A. Hendricks & L. L. Kaid (Eds.), *Presidential Campaigning and Social Media* (pp. 28–43). New York: Oxford University Press.

Taiwanese Central News Agency (CNA). (2014, May 19). Taiwan student protests form new group to tackle referendum rules. *BBC Monitoring Asia Pacific.*

Tanaka, M. (2009). El sistema de partidos 'realmente existente' en el Perú, desafíos de la construcción de una representación política nacional y cómo encumbra la reforma política. *Economía y Sociedad*, 79.

Tandoc, E. (2015, May). *Conventional and Dialogical Uses of Social Media in the Newsroom: How Journalists Use Facebook and Twitter, and Why*. Paper presented at the International Communication Association annual convention, San Juan, Puerto Rico.

Tarrow, S. (1998). Fishnets, Internets, and Catnets: Globalization and transnational collective action. *Challenging authority: The historical study of contentious politics*, 228-244.

Taylor, L. E., Swerdfeger, A. L., & Eslick, G. D. (2014). Vaccines are not associated with autism: An evidence-based meta-analysis of case-control and cohort studies. *Vaccine*, *32*(29), 3623–3629. doi:10.1016/j.vaccine.2014.04.085 PMID:24814559

Taylor, M., Kent, M., & White, W. (2001). How activist organizations are using the Internet to build relationships. *Public Relations Review*, *27*(3), 263–284. doi:10.1016/S0363-8111(01)00086-8

Technology has changed way we work, need multi-skilling: Shobhana Bhartia. (2013, May 30). *The Indian Express.* Retrieved from http://m.indianexpress.com/news/technology-has-changed-way-we-work-need-multiskilling-shobhana-bhartia/1122468/

Tewksbury, D., & Althaus, S. L. (2000). Differences in knowledge acquisition among readers of the paper and online versions of a national newspaper. *Journalism & Mass Communication Quarterly*, *77*(3), 457–479. doi:10.1177/107769900007700301

The Cincinnati Daily Gazette. (1879). *Mr. William Tebb, the englishman, renews his war against vac- cination in New York.* Retrieved from August 5, 2015, from http://www.genealogybank.com/gbnk/ newspapers/?lname=Tebb&sort=_rank_%3AD

The Digital Journalist. (2009, December). *Let's abolish the term 'Citizen Journalists'.* Retrieved from http://digitaljournalist.org/issue0912/lets-abolish-citizen-journalists.html

The History Channel. (2010, February 9). Mohandas Gandhi begins 241-mile civil disobedience march. *The History Channel.* Retrieved July 4, 2019 from https://www.history.com/this-day-in-history/gandhi-leads-civil-disobedience

The Lancet Editorial. (2018). Measles, war, and health-care reforms in Ukraine. *Lancet*, *392*(10149), 711. doi:10.1016/S0140-6736(18)31984-6 PMID:30191812

The Open News Room. (2011). *Citizen Journalism: A Primer on the Definition, Risks and Benefits, and Main Debates in Media Communications Research.* Retrieved from http://www.theopennewsroom.com/documents/Citizen_%20journalism_phenomenon.pdf

The Policy Tensor. (2013, August 2). Offensive realism. *Geopolitics*. Retrieved July 4, 2015 from http://policytensor.com/2013/08/02/offensive-realism/

Thiel, M., Penna-Díaz, M. A., Luna-Jorquera, G., Salas, S., Sellanes, J., & Stotz, W. (2014). Citizen scientists and marine research: volunteer participants, their contributions, and projection for the future. In R. N. Hughes, D. J. Hughes, & I. P. Smith (Eds.), *Oceanography and Marine Biology: An Annual Review* (Vol. 52, pp. 257–314). London: CRC Press. doi:10.1201/b17143-6

Thielman, S. (2016). Facebook news selection is in hands of editors not algorithms, documents show. *The Guardian*. Retrieved May 23, 2016 from https://www.theguardian.com/technology/2016/may/12/facebook-trending-news-leaked-documents-editor-guidelines

Thornton, S. (1995). *Club Culture: Music, Media and Subcultural Capital*. Cambridge, UK: Polity Press.

Tilley, E., & Cokley, J. (2008). Deconstructing the Discourse of Citizens Journalism: Who Says What and Why It Matters. *Pacific Journalism Review, 14*(1). Retrieved from http://www.massey.ac.nz/massey/fms/Colleges/College%20of%20Business/Communication%20and%20Journalism/Staff/Staff%20research%20files/ETilley/Deconstructing%20the%20discourse%20of%20citizens%20journalism_Who%20says%20what%20and%20why%20it%20matters.pdf

Tilly, C., & Tarrow, S. (2007). *Contentious Politics*. Paradigm Publishers.

Tong, Y., & Lei, S. (2013). War of position and microblogging in China. *Journal of Contemporary China, 32*(80), 292–311. doi:10.1080/10670564.2012.734084

Torres, L., Pina, V., & Acerate, B. (2006). E-governance developments in European Union cities: Reshaping government's relationship with citizens. *Governance: Int. J. Policy Admin. Institutions, 19*(2), 277–302. doi:10.1111/j.1468-0491.2006.00315.x

Towner, T. L. (2013). All political participation is socially networked?: New media and the 2012 election. *Social Science Computer Review, 31*(5), 527–541. doi:10.1177/0894439313489656

Towner, T. L. (2016). The influence of Twitter posts on candidate perceptions: The 2014 Michigan midterms. In J. A. Hendricks & D. Schill (Eds.), *Media, message, and mobilization*. New York: Palgrave.

Towner, T. L., & Dulio, D. A. (2011a). The Web 2.0 election: Voter learning in the 2008 presidential campaign. In J. A. Hendricks & L. L. Kaid (Eds.), *Techno-politics in presidential campaigning* (pp. 22–43). New York: Routledge.

Towner, T. L., & Dulio, D. A. (2011b). The Web 2.0 election: Does the online medium matter? *Journal of Political Marketing, 10*(1-2), 165–188. doi:10.1080/15377857.2011.540220

Trechsel, A., Kies, R., Mendez, F., & Schmitter, P. (2003). *Evaluation of the Use of New Technologies in order to Facilitate Democracy in Europe. E-democratizing the Parliaments and Parties of Europe*. Study on behalf of the European Parliament for Scientific Technology Options Assessment.

Trentelman, C. K. (2009). Place Attachment and Community Attachment: A Primer Grounded in the Lived Experience of a Community Sociologist. *Society & Natural Resources, 22*(3), 191–210. doi:10.1080/08941920802191712

Trevino, L. K., Lengel, R. H., & Daft, R. L. (1987). Media symbolism, media richness, and media choice in organizations: A symbolic interactionist perspective. *Communication Research, 14*(5), 553–574. doi:10.1177/009365087014005006

Tuchman, G. (1978). *Making News: A Study in the Construction of Reality*. New York, NY: The Free Press.

Tyler, L. (2005). Towards a postmodern understanding of crisis communication. *Public Relations Review, 31*(4), 566–571. doi:10.1016/j.pubrev.2005.08.017

U.S. Census Bureau. (2013). *U.S. Census Current Population Survey's estimate of the 18-29 citizen population*. Retrieved on January 1, 2015, from http://www.census.gov/

UC Business Analytics R Programming Guide. (n.d.). Text Mining: Term vs. Document Frequency. *UC Business Analytics R Programming Guide*. Retrieved August 8, 2019 from https://uc-r.github.io/tf-idf_analysis

Umemoto, K. N. (1998). *You don't see what I see: multiple publics and public policy in a Los Angeles gang war*. Cambridge, MA: Massachusetts Institute of Technology. Retrieved from http://dspace.mit. edu/handle/1721.1/9639

Underwood, D. (1995). *When MBA's Rule the Newsroom*. New York, NY: Columbia University Press.

UNESCO. (2012, May 15). *Director General Condemns Targeting of Syrian Citizen Journalist Abdul Ghani Kaakeh*. Retrieved from http://www.unesco.org/new/en/media-services/single-view/news/director_general_condemns_targeting_of_syrian_citizen_journalist_abdul_ghani_kaakeh/

Unionmetrics. (2012). *Comparing Tumblr analytics for Mitt Romney and Barack Obama*. Retrieved on January 1, 2015, from http://unionmetrics.tumblr.com/post/34660150228/comparing-tumblr-analytics- for-mitt-romney-and

US Department of Health and Human Services. (n.d.). *Safety*. Retrieved on June 5th, 2015, from www. vaccines.gov

Valkenburg, P., & Peter, J. (2013). The differential susceptibility to media effects model. *Journal of Communication*, *63*(2), 221–243. doi:10.1111/jcom.12024

van de Donk, W., Loader, D. B., Nixon, P., & Rucht, D. (Eds.). (2004). Cyberprotest: New Media, Citizens and Social Movements. New York: Routledge.

Van de Donk, W., Loader, B. D., Nixon, P. G., & Rucht, D. (Eds.). (2004). *Cyber protest: Social media*. Blackwell.

van Kruistum, C., Leseman, P. M., & de Haan, M. (2014). Youth Media Lifestyles. *Human Communication Research*, *40*(4), 508–529. doi:10.1111/hcre.12033

Vegh, S. (2003). Classifying forms of online activism: The case of cyberprotests against the World Bank. In M. McCaughey & M. D. Ayers (Eds.), Cyberactivism: Online Activism in Theory and Practice. New York: Routledge.

Vickery, J. R. (2015). 'I don't have anything to hide, but…': The challenges and negotiations of social and mobile media privacy for non-dominant youth. *Information Communication and Society*, *18*(3), 281–294. doi:10.1080/1369118X.2014.989251

Vissers, S., & Stolle, D. (2014). Spill-Over Effects Between Facebook and On/Offline Political Participation? Evidence from a Two-Wave Panel Study. *Journal of Information Technology & Politics*, *11*(3), 259–275. doi:10.1080/19331681.2014.888383

Vitak, J., Zube, P., Smock, A., Carr, C. T., Ellison, N., & Lampe, C. (2011). It's complicated: Facebook users' political participation in the 2008 election. *Cyberpsychology, Behavior, and Social Networking*, *14*(3), 107–114. doi:10.1089/cyber.2009.0226 PMID:20649449

Vorkinn, M., & Riese, H. (2001). Environmental Concern in a Local Context The Significance of Place Attachment. *Environment and Behavior*, *33*(2), 249–263. doi:10.1177/00139160121972972

Vu, H. T. (2013). The online audience as gatekeeper: The influence of reader metrics on news editorial selection. *Journalism*, *15*(8), 1094–1110. doi:10.1177/1464884913504259

W3C. (2018, 23 January). ActivityPub W3C Recommendations. Retrieved from https://www.w3.org/TR/activitypub/

Wagner, A. L., Boulton, M. L., Sun, X., Huang, Z., Harmsen, I. A., Ren, J., & Zikmund-Fisher, B. J. (2017). Parents' concerns about vaccine scheduling in Shanghai, China. *Vaccine*, *35*(34), 4362–4367. doi:10.1016/j.vaccine.2017.06.077 PMID:28687407

Waite, C. (2013). *The Digital Evolution of an American Identity*. New York, NY: Routledge. doi:10.4324/9780203066409

Wajcman, J., & Rose, E. (2011). Constant connectivity: Rethinking interruptions at work. *Organization Studies, 32*(7), 941–961. doi:10.1177/0170840611410829

Wakefield, A. J., Murch, S. H., Anthony, A., Linnell, J., Casson, D. M., Malik, M., ... Walker-Smith, J. A. (1998). RETRACTED: Ileal-lymphoid-nodular hyperplasia, non-specific colitis, and pervasive developmental disorder in children. *Lancet, 351*(9103), 637–641. doi:10.1016/S0140-6736(97)11096-0 PMID:9500320

Wallsten, K. (2010). "Yes we can": How online viewership, blog discussion, campaign statements, and mainstream media coverage produced a viral video phenomenon. *Journal of Information Technology & Politics, 7*(2), 163–181. doi:10.1080/19331681003749030

Walsham, G. (2017). ICT4D research: Reflections on history and future agenda. *Information Technology for Development, 23*(1), 18–41. doi:10.1080/02681102.2016.1246406

Walther, J. B. (1996). Computer-mediated communication impersonal, interpersonal, and hyperpersonal interaction. *Communication Research, 23*(1), 3–43. doi:10.1177/009365096023001001

Wampler, B. (2007). *Participatory Budgeting in Brazil. Contestation, Cooperation, and Accountability*. Penn State Press.

Wampler, B. (2015). *Activating Democracy in Brazil. Popular Participation, Social Justice, and Interlocking Institutions*. University of Notre Dame Press.

Wampler, B., & Hartz-karp, J. (2012). Participatory Budgeting: Diffusion and Outcomes across the World. *Journal of Public Deliberation, 8*(2), 13. Available online at http://www.publicdeliberation.net/jpd/vol8/iss2/art13

Ward, S. J. A. (2012). *Digital Media Ethics*. Centre for Journalism Ethics, School of Journalism and Mass Communication, University of Wisconsin-Madison. Retrieved from http://ethics.journalism.wisc.edu/resources/digital-media-ethics/

Ward, J. K. (2016). Rethinking the antivaccine movement concept: A case study of public criticism of the swine flu vaccine's safety in France. *Social Science & Medicine, 159*, 48–57. doi:10.1016/j.socscimed.2016.05.003 PMID:27173740

Warren, M. E., & Pearse, H. (2008). *Designing Deliberative Democracy*. The British Columbia Citizens' Assembly, Cambridge University Press. doi:10.1017/CBO9780511491177

Wattenberg, M. (2012). *Is voting for young people?* New York: Pearson Longman.

Weaver, D., & Drew, D. (1993). Voter learning in the 1990 off-year election: Did the media matter? *The Journalism Quarterly, 70*(2), 356–368. doi:10.1177/107769909307000211

Weaver, D., & Drew, D. (2001). Voter learning and interest in the 2000 presidential election: Did the media matter? *Journalism & Mass Communication Quarterly, 78*(4), 787–798. doi:10.1177/107769900107800411

Weber, L. (2017). The End of Employees. *Wall Street Journal*. Retrieved from https://www.wsj.com/articles/the-end-of-employees-1486050443

Webster, G. R. (2011). Guard your revolution": Comments on the" Arab Spring" Essays. *Arab World Geographer, 14*(2), 160–165.

Wei, R., & Ven-hwei, L. (2008). News media use and knowledge about the 2006 U.S. midterm elections: Why exposure matters in voter learning. *International Journal of Public Opinion Research, 20*(3), 347–362. doi:10.1093/ijpor/edn032

Wellman, B., Quan-Haase, A., Boase, J., Chen, W. H., Hampton, K., Díaz, I., & Miyata, K. (2003, April). The social affordances of the Internet for networked individualism. *Journal of Computer-Mediated Communication*, *8*(3), 0. doi:10.1111/j.1083-6101.2003.tb00216.x

Wells, C. (2014). Two eras of civic information and the evolving relationship between civil society organizations and young citizens. *New Media & Society*, *16*(4), 615–636. doi:10.1177/1461444813487962

Wenger, E., Trayner, B., & de Laat, M. (2011). *Promoting and assessing value creation in communities and networks: A conceptual framework*. Rapport 18, Ruud de Moore Centrum, Open University of the Netherlands. Available at: http://wenger-trayner.com/wp-content/uploads/2011/12/1104Wenger_Trayner_DeLaat_Value_creation.pdf

Wenger, E., White, N., & Smith, J. D. (2009). Digital Habitats: Stewarding Technology for Communities. Portland, OR: CPSquare.

Wenger, E. (1998). *Communities of practice: learning, meaning and identity*. New York, NY: Cambridge University Press. doi:10.1017/CBO9780511803932

Wenger, E., McDermott, R., & Snyder, W. (2002). *Cultivating Communities of Practice*. Boston: Harvard Business School Press.

Wexler, L. M., DiFluvio, G., & Burke, T. K. (2009). Resilience and marginalized youth: Making a case for personal and collective meaning-making as part of resilience research in public health. *Social Science & Medicine*, *69*(4), 565–570. doi:10.1016/j.socscimed.2009.06.022 PMID:19596503

Weyland, K. (2000). A Paradox of Success? Determinants of Political Support for President Fujimori. *International Studies Quarterly*, *44*(3), 481–502. doi:10.1111/0020-8833.00168

White, D. M. (1950). The Gate-keeper. A case study in the selection of news. *The Journalism Quarterly*, *27*(4), 383–396. doi:10.1177/107769905002700403

William, R. (2003). *Television: Technology and cultural form* (2nd ed.). London: Routledge Classics. doi:10.4324/9780203450277

Williams, J. P. (2011). *Subcultural Theory*. Cambridge, UK: Polity Press.

Williamson, A. (2010). Inside the digital campaign. In The internet and the 2010 election: Putting the small 'p' back in politics? (pp. 17-26). Londres: Hansard.

Wilson, K. G. (1993). *The Columbia Guide to Standard American English*. Columbia University Press.

Wilson, N., Minkler, M., Dasho, S., Carrillo, R., Wallerstein, N., & Garcia, D. (2006). Training students as facilitators in the Youth Empowerment Strategies (YES!) Project. *Journal of Community Practice*, *14*(1-2), 201–217. doi:10.1300/J125v14n01_12

Winkler, S. (2012). *Taiwan's UN dilemma: To be or not to be*. Retrieved July 5, 2015 from http://www.brookings.edu/research/opinions/2012/06/20-taiwan-un-winkler

Witteman, H. O., & Zikmund-Fisher, B. J. (2012). The defining characteristics of Web 2.0 and their potential influence in the online vaccination debate. *Vaccine*, *30*(25), 3734–3740. doi:10.1016/j.vaccine.2011.12.039 PMID:22178516

Wolfe, R. M., & Sharp, L. K. (2002). Anti-vaccinationists past and present. *British Medical Journal*, *325*(7361), 430–432. doi:10.1136/bmj.325.7361.430 PMID:12193361

Wong, A. (2018, May 31). Beijing is upping the pressure on Taiwan: "Expectation of reunification is certainly increasing." *CNBC News*. Retrieved August 4, 2019 from https://www.cnbc.com/2018/2005/2031/mainland-china-and-taiwan-increased-tensions-about-one-china-policy.html

World Health Organization. (2014). *Measles*. Retrieved July 10, 2015, from http://www.who.int/mediacentre/factsheets/fs286/en/

World Health Organization. (2019a). *Ten threats to global health in 2019*. Retrieved March 28, 2019, from https://www.who.int/emergencies/ten-threats-to-global-health-in-2019

World Health Organization. (2019b). *WHO | New measles surveillance data for 2019*. Retrieved July 8, 2019, from https://www.who.int/immunization/newsroom/measles-data-2019/en/

World Health Organization. (2019c, May 9). *Measles*. Retrieved July 9, 2019, from https://www.who.int/news-room/fact-sheets/detail/measles

Wright, S. (2004). Informing, communicating and ICTs in contemporary anti-capitalist movements. In W., van de Donk, D. B., Loader, P., Nixon, & D, Rucht (Eds.), Cyberprotest: New Media, Citizens and Social Movements (pp. 69-83). New York: Routledge.

Wu, S., Hofman, J. M., Mason, W. A., & Watts, D. J. (2011). Who says what to whom on Twitter? Presented to the *International World Wide Web Conference Committee*, Hyderabad, India. 10.1145/1963405.1963504

Wynne, B. (1992). Misunderstood misunderstanding: Social identities and public uptake of science. *Public Understanding of Science (Bristol, England)*, *1*(3), 281–304. doi:10.1088/0963-6625/1/3/004

Xenos, M., & Moy, P. (2007). Direct and differential effects of the Internet on political and civic engagement. *Journal of Communication*, *57*(4), 704–718. doi:10.1111/j.1460-2466.2007.00364.x

Xenos, M., Vromen, A., & Loader, B. D. (2014). The great equalizer? Patterns of social media use and youth political engagement in three advanced democracies. *Information Communication and Society*, *17*(2), 151–167. doi:10.1080/1369118X.2013.871318

Xu, J. (2016). *Media events in web 2.0 China: Interventions of online activism*. Eastbourne, UK: Sussex Academic Press.

Yang, G. (2011). China's Gradual Revolution. *New York Times*. Retrieved on Feb 10, 2016 from http://www.nytimes.com/2011/03/14/opinion/14Yang.html?_r=0

Yang, K. C. C., & Kang, Y. W. (2017). Social media, political mobilization, and citizen engagement: A case study of March 18, 2014 Sunflower Student Movement in Taiwan. In Citizen engagement and public participation in the era of new media (pp. 362-390). Hershey, PA: IGI-Global Publisher.

Yang, G. (2003). The Internet and the rise of a transnational Chinese cultural sphere. *Media Culture & Society*, *25*(4), 469–490. doi:10.1177/01634437030254003

Yang, G. (2009). *The Power of the Internet in China: Citizen Activism Online*. Columbia University Press.

Yang, G. (2012). A Chinese Internet? History, practice, and globalization. *Chinese Journal of Communication*, *5*(1), 49–54. doi:10.1080/17544750.2011.647744

Yang, G., & Calhoun, C. (2007). Media, civil Society, and the rise of a green public sphere in China. *China Information*, *21*(2), 211–236. doi:10.1177/0920203X07079644

Yang, G., & Jiang, M. (2015). The networked practice of online political satire in China: Between ritual and resistance. *The International Communication Gazette*, *77*(3), 215–231. doi:10.1177/1748048514568757

Yang, K. C. C., & Kang, Y. W. (2017). *Representing the Internet and World Wide Web in mass media: A comparative text mining study of mass media in the Greater China Region and the U.S.* Paper Presented at the *24th International Conference of the International Association for Intercultural Communication Studies (IAICS)*, De Paul University, Chicago, IL.

Yang, Y. T., Delamater, P. L., Leslie, T. F., & Mello, M. M. (2016). Sociodemographic Predictors of Vac- cination Exemptions on the Basis of Personal Belief in California. *American Journal of Public Health, 106*(1), 172–177. doi:10.2105/AJPH.2015.302926 PMID:26562114

Yaqub, O., Castle-Clarke, S., Sevdalis, N., & Chataway, J. (2014). Attitudes to vaccination: A critical review. *Social Science & Medicine, 112*, 1–11. doi:10.1016/j.socscimed.2014.04.018 PMID:24788111

Yildiz, M. (2007). E-government research: Reviewing the literature, limitations and ways forward. *Government Information Quarterly, 24*(3), 646–665. doi:10.1016/j.giq.2007.01.002

Yohalem, N., & Martin, S. (2007). Building the evidence base for youth engagement: Reflections on youth and democracy. *Journal of Community Psychology, 35*(6), 807–810. doi:10.1002/jcop.20180

Yom-Tov, E., & Fernandez-Luque, L. (2014). Information is in the eye of the beholder: Seeking informa- tion on the MMR vaccine through an internet search engine. In *AMIA Annual Symposium Proceedings* (p. 1238). American Medical Informatics Association. Retrieved from http://www.ncbi.nlm.nih.gov/ pmc/articles/PMC4419998/

Young, J. A. (2017). Facebook, Twitter, and Blogs: The Adoption and Utilization of Social Media in Nonprofit Human Service Organizations. *Human Service Organizations, Management, Leadership & Governance, 41*(1), 44–57. doi:10.1080/23303131.2016.1192574

Zarya, V. (2015). Meet the 86%: This is why most Etsy sellers are women. *Fortune.* Retrieved from https://fortune.com/2015/08/02/etsy-sellers-women-2/

Zemmels, D. R. (2012). Youth and new media: Constructing meaning and identity in networked spaces. *Dissertation Abstracts International. A, The Humanities and Social Sciences, 72*(10-A), 3570.

Zervas, G., Proserpio, D., & Byers, J. W. (2014). The rise of the sharing economy: Estimating the impact of Airbnb on the hotel industry. *Journal of Marketing Research.* Retrieved from http://journals.ama.org/doi/abs/10.1509/jmr.15.0204

Zhang, M. (2011, November 29). *CNN Lays Off Photojournalists, Citing the Accessibility of Quality Cameras.* Retrieved from http://petapixel.com/2011/11/29/cnn-lays-off-photojournalists-citing-the-accessibility-of-quality-cameras/

Zhao, X., & Chaffee, S. H. (1995). Campaign advertisements versus television news as sources of political issue information. *Public Opinion Quarterly, 59*(1), 41–65. doi:10.1086/269457

Zhao, Y. Z. (2007). After Mobile Phones, What? Re-embedding the Social in China's "Digital Revolution.". *International Journal of Communication, 1*, 92–120.

Zhou, X., Wellman, B. & Yu, J. (2011, July). Egypt: The first Internet revolt? *Peace Magazine*, 6-10.

Zhou, Y., & Moy, P. (2007). Parsing framing processes: The Interplay between online public opinion and media coverage. *Journal of Communication, 57*, 79–98.

Zhu, T., Phipps, D., Pridgen, A., Crandall, J., & Wallach, D. (2013). *The Velocity of Censorship: High-Fidelity Detection of Microblog Post Deletions.* Retrieved from http://arxiv.org/abs/1303.0597

Zúñiga, H. G., Molyneux, L., & Zheng, P. (2014). Social media, political expression, and political participation: Panel analysis of lagged and concurrent relationships. *Journal of Communication, 64*(4), 612–634. doi:10.1111/jcom.12103

About the Contributors

Marco Adria is Professor Emeritus of Communication at the University of Alberta. He is co-editor of Handbook of research in citizen engagement and public participation in the era of new media (IGI Global, 2016). He has been a visiting professor in the Graduate Program in Public and Corporate Communication, University of Milan, Italy, and in the Department of Business at the Tecnológico de Monterrey, Mexico. His book, Technology and Nationalism (Montreal: McGill-Queen's University Press, 2010) won the Lewis Mumford Award for Outstanding Scholarship in the Ecology of Technics, awarded by the New York based Media Ecology Association.

* * *

Giovanni Allegretti is an architect, planner and senior researcher at the Centre of Social Studies of Coimbra University (Portugal). He is visiting fellow at Witwatersrand University in Johannesburg, and member of the Institute for Democracy and democratization of Communication in Brazil. For the mandate 2014-2019 he has been appointed by the Parliament as co-chair of the Independent Authority for the Guarantee and Promotion of Participation of the Tuscany Region (Italy). In 2012 he got his habilitation as Associate Professor in Italy. At the University of Coimbra he teaches at the School of Economics, being co-director of the interdisciplinary Ph.D. "Democracy in the XXI century" and coordinator of the PEOPLES' Observatory on Participation, Innovation and Local Powers. Since 1997, his main research topics are Participatory Budgets and citizens' participation to urban planning, issues on which he published several articles, essays and books in different languages, being a consultant in projects of the Council of Europe, the World Bank, Un-Habitat and United Cities and Local Governments.

Edrick Andrews is a student in the Community Engagement Graduate Program in the Faculty of Extension at the University of Alberta.

Chelsey Ehresman works as a copyright specialist at the Medicine Hat College. Since graduating with an MA in communication and technology from the University of Alberta she enjoys engaging in academic work focused primarily on information creation, access, and sharing.

Gordon Gow is Professor and Academic Director of the Communications and Technology Graduate Program (MACT) at the University of Alberta.

Jacob Groshek is the Ross Beach Chair of Mass Communication Research at Kansas State University. Topically, his areas of expertise concern online and mobile media technologies as their use may relate to sociopolitical and behavioral health change at the macro (i.e., national) and micro (as in individual) levels. His work also include analyses of media content and user influence in social media. Put briefly, his research uses a blend of interpretive as well as relatively advanced statistical tools for network analysis, forecasting, and explaining where and how the use of media has shaped the course of political and health decision making.

Lorna Heaton is Professor of Communication at the Université de Montréal. Her research interests concern collaboration using digital technologies, community innovation, and relationships between design and use in the design and use of digital technologies.

Yoshitaka (Yoshi) Iwasaki is Professor and Chair of the Department of Health Science and Recreation in the College of Health and Human Sciences at San Jose State University in California, USA with over 20 years of experience in community-engaged research and education, knowledge mobilization, and capacity-building from trans-disciplinary, social justice perspectives.

Yowei Kang (Ph.D.) is Assistant Professor at Bachelor Degree Program in Oceanic Cultural Creative Design Industries, National Taiwan Ocean University, TAIWAN. His research interests focus on new media design, digital game research, visual communication, and experiential rhetoric. Some of his works have been published in International Journal of Strategic Communication, and Journal of Intercultural Communication Studies. He has received government funding to support his research in location-based advertising and consumer privacy management strategies.

Zachary Kilhoffer is a Researcher in the Jobs and Skills unit at CEPS. Previously, he worked for the Organization for Security and Co-operation in Europe (OSCE); the International Anti-Corruption Academy (IACA); Human Trafficking and Migrant Smuggling Section (HTMSS) of the United Nations Office on Drugs and Crime (UNODC), and taught research methods at Webster University Vienna. Zachary's current work in the Jobs & Skills unit concerns European labour markets with particular focus on the platform economy and the future of work. Zachary also supports the Finance Unit on occasion, primarily on European investment banks and retail banking markets. In addition to desk research and qualitative research methods, Zachary enjoys webscraping and data analysis using Python and R. Zachary holds a Bachelor's Degree (cum laude) in International Relations from McKendree University, Lebanon, Illinois (USA), and a Master's Degree (summa cum laude) in International Relations from Webster University, Vienna (Austria). At Webster University, he was awarded the title of valedictorian and the Schön Award for his Master's thesis "Purchasing Peace: the Foreign Aid Terrorism Nexus".

Ikbal Maulana is a researcher of Indonesian Institute of Sciences (LIPI), specializing in philosophy of technology and media studies. He has published papers and book chapters on technological development and the impacts of social media on various aspects of human life, such as personal identity, politics, the protection of human rights and consumerism.

Paul R. Messinger serves as Chair of the Service Science Section of the Institute for Operations Research and the Management Sciences (INFORMS) and was Founding Director of the University of Alberta School of Retailing. Paul is an Associate Professor of Marketing and Marketing Group Ph.D. Coordinator at the University of Alberta School of Business, and Visiting Professor at the University of Northern British Columbia.

Rabia Noor is an academician and an independent journalist. She serves as Assistant Professor in the Department of Journalism and Mass Communication at Islamic University of Science and Technology (IUST). She is also the Editor of IUST's campus newspaper. She has pursued her PhD, M.Phil and Master's degrees in Mass Communication and Journalism from Media Education Research Centre, University of Kashmir. Her specialisation includes News Reporting, News Editing, Print Journalism and Business Reporting. A journalist-turned-journalism mentor, she has over 12 years of combined experience in journalism, teaching and research. She has worked as correspondent with English daily, Greater Kashmir, for six years. She was awarded the prestigious fellowship for female journalists, Sanjoy Ghose Fellowship (2007-'08) by Charkha Development Communication Network. She also bagged the National Foundation for India (NFI) fellowship and National Media Award, 2018, and India Science Media Fellowship, 2019. Dr. Rabia has highlighted diverse issues through her writings since 2005. She has written extensively on business, politics, conflict, human rights, health, education, gender issues and various aspects of the society. She has to her credit many national and international publications. She has authored book titled 'Business Leaders of Kashmir: A Series of Success Stories' besides some monographs.

Zhou Shan is a doctoral student of University of Alabama.

Melodie Yun-Ju Song received a PhD in Health Policy. She was supervised by Professor Julia Abelson at the Department of Health Research Methods, Evidence, and Impact (HEI) at McMaster University. Her thesis explored how social media is perceived by public health policy-makers in the advent of vaccine misinformation in Ontario. She is currently a postdoctoral research fellow at the Social Media Lab, Ryerson University, Ontario, Canada.

Terri L. Towner is a Professor of Political Science at Oakland University in Michigan. Her research focuses mainly on the role of social media in campaigns and elections, with a particular focus on Facebook, Twitter, and Instagram. She recently co-edited the book The Internet and the 2016 Presidential Campaign (Lexington Books 2017). Her research has also been published in several book chapters, most recently in: The Presidency and Social Media: Discourse, Disruption, and Digital Democracy in the 2016 Presidential Election and Communication and Mid-Term Elections: Media, Message, and Mobilization. She has also published in numerous journals including The Social Science Computer Review, The Journal of Political Marketing, The Journal of Women, Politics & Policy, New Media & Society, and The Journal of Political Science Education.

Eduardo Villanueva-Mansilla is is Professor at the Department of Communications, Pontificia Universidad Católica del Perú.

Kenneth C.C. Yang is a Professor at the Department of Communication. His research focuses on new media and advertising, consumer behavior in East Asia, impacts of new media in Asia.

Yuan Yuan's research interests center around Internet use, social movement, and political change. She received her Ph.D. in Communication and Information at Rutgers University.

Index

O

P

R

S

T

U

V

W

www.ingramcontent.com/pod-product-compliance
Ingram Content Group UK Ltd.
Pitfield, Milton Keynes, MK11 3LW, UK
UKHW051510290926
15471UKWH00008B/1541

9 781799 836568